# CONTEMPORARY THOUGHT ON
# NINETEENTH CENTURY SOCIALISM

# CONTEMPORARY THOUGHT ON NINETEENTH CENTURY SOCIALISM

*General Editors*
*Peter Gurney and Kevin Morgan*

Volume IV
**Anglo-Marxists**

*Edited by*
*Kevin Morgan*

LONDON AND NEW YORK

First published 2021
by Routledge
2 Park Square, Milton Park, Abingdon, Oxon OX14 4RN

and by Routledge
52 Vanderbilt Avenue, New York, NY 10017

*Routledge is an imprint of the Taylor & Francis Group, an informa business*

© 2021 selection and editorial matter, Kevin Morgan; individual owners retain copyright in their own material.

The right of Kevin Morgan to be identified as the author of the editorial material, and of the authors for their individual chapters, has been asserted in accordance with sections 77 and 78 of the Copyright, Designs and Patents Act 1988.

All rights reserved. No part of this book may be reprinted or reproduced or utilised in any form or by any electronic, mechanical, or other means, now known or hereafter invented, including photocopying and recording, or in any information storage or retrieval system, without permission in writing from the publishers.

*Trademark notice*: Product or corporate names may be trademarks or registered trademarks, and are used only for identification and explanation without intent to infringe.

*British Library Cataloguing-in-Publication Data*
A catalogue record for this book is available from the British Library

*Library of Congress Cataloging-in-Publication Data*
A catalog record for this book has been requested

ISBN: 978-1-138-49019-2 (set)
eISBN: 978-1-351-03570-5 (set)
ISBN: 978-1-138-32105-2 (volume IV)
eISBN: 978-0-429-45232-1 (volume IV)

Typeset in Times New Roman
by Apex CoVantage, LLC

**Publisher's Note**
References within each chapter are as they appear in the original complete work

# CONTENTS

Introduction: the Anglo-Marxists     1
KEVIN MORGAN

PART 1
**The idea of socialism**     17

1   *Socialism Made Plain. Being the Social and Political Manifesto of the Democratic Federation* (Democratic Federation, 1883)     19

2   "The Manifesto of the *Socialist League*", *Commonweal*, February 1885, 1–2.     24

3   "Anarchism", *Justice*, 8, 22, 29 November and 6 December 1884.     29
CHARLOTTE WILSON

4   "Why Not?", *Justice*, 12 April 1884.     38
WILLIAM MORRIS

5   *The Man with the Red Flag* (London: Twentieth Century Press, 1886), 3–12.     42
JOHN BURNS

6   "How I became a Socialist", *Justice*, 30 June 1894.     51
WALTER CRANE

CONTENTS

7   *Social Democracy or Democratic Socialism* (Social
    Democratic Federation: Salford District Council, 1895),
    3–6, 15–16.                                                    55
    H.W. HOBART

8   "Social-democrat or socialist?", *Social Democrat*,
    August 1897, 228–231.                                          59
    H.M. HYNDMAN

9   *Socialism and Art* (Social Democratic Federation, 1907), 5–16.  65
    JACK C. SQUIRE

PART 2
Concepts of political change                                       75

10  "How the Change Came" from *News from Nowhere*,
    chapter 17, reprinted in *Commonweal*, 17, 24 and 31 May 1890.  77
    WILLIAM MORRIS

11  *An Anti-Statist, Communist Manifesto*, International
    Revolutionary Library, 1887, 2–22.                             86
    JOSEPH LANE

12  *The Co-Partnership Snare* (Twentieth Century Press,
    c. 1913), 1–3, 14–16.                                         101
    HARRY QUELCH

13  "Social-Democrats and the Administration of the Poor
    Law", *Social Democrat*, January 1897, 14–18.                 106
    GEORGE LANSBURY

14  "Long Live Syndicalism!", *The Syndicalist*, May 1912.        112
    EDWARD CARPENTER

PART 3
Political economy                                                 115

15  "The Iron Law of Wages", *Justice*, 15 March 1884, 3.         117
    H.M. HYNDMAN

## CONTENTS

16 *Socialism and Slavery* (1884), Social Democratic Federation (London: Twentieth Century Press, 1899 edn), 3–15.  120
H.M. HYNDMAN

17 *Useful Work Versus Useless Toil* (1885), Hammersmith Socialist Society, 1893 edn, 3–12, 19.  132
WILLIAM MORRIS

18 "The Reward of 'Genius'", *Commonweal*, 25 September 1886, 205–206.  142
WILLIAM MORRIS

19 "The Great Money Trick" from *The Ragged Trousered Philanthropists* (1914), ch. 21.  146
ROBERT TRESSELL

### PART 4
### Work and social conditions  155

20 *What a Compulsory Eight-hour Day Means to the Workers* (London: Modern Press, 1886).  157
TOM MANN

21 *Unemployment: Its Causes and Consequences* (London: Twentieth Century Press, 1906), 5–16.  168
COUNTESS OF WARWICK

22 *Prison Reform from a Social-Democratic Point of View* (London: Twentieth Century Press, 1909), 1–14.  177
DORA B. MONTEFIORE

23 *Social-Democracy and the Housing Problem* (London: Twentieth Century Press, 1900), 3–4, 6–7, 22–24.  189
F.O. PICKARD-CAMBRIDGE

### PART 5
### Ways of organising  197

24 "Organised Labour. The Duty of the Trades Unions in Relation to Socialism", *Commonweal*, 14, 21 and 28 August 1886.  199
THOMAS BINNING

## CONTENTS

25 "Social Democracy and Industrial Organisation", *Social Democrat*, 15 April 1910.  211
HARRY QUELCH

26 "Prepare for Action", *Industrial Syndicalist*, July 1910, 31–54.  216
TOM MANN

27 "Leadermania", *Justice*, 13 November 1897, 2.  229
T. HUNTER

### PART 6
### Democracy and the state  235

28 "The Will of the Majority", in *The Ethics of Socialism* (London: Swan Sonnenschein, 1889), 120–128.  237
ERNEST BELFORT BAX

29 "Workmen's Jubilee Ode", *Social Democrat*, February 1897.  243
HENRY SALT

30 "After the Jubilee", *Justice*, 16 October 1897, 2.  246

31 "The 'Monstrous Regiment' of Womanhood", in *Essays in Socialism New and Old* (London: Grant Richards, 1906), 276–279, 282–294.  248
ERNEST BELFORT BAX

32 "Why I Am Opposed to Female Suffrage", *Social Democrat*, April 1909.  257
DORA MONTEFIORE

### PART 7
### The new religion and the old  263

33 "The Socialist Conception of Ethics", in *A New Catechism of Socialism* (London: Twentieth Century Press, 1902), 22–30.  265
E. BELFORT BAX AND H. QUELCH

| | | |
|---|---|---|
| 34 | "A Christmas Sermon which the Bishop of London has been asked to Preach in Westminster Abbey on Sunday, December 25", *Justice*, 24 December 1887, 4.<br>HERBERT BURROWS | 273 |
| 35 | *Socialism and the Survival of the Fittest* (London: Twentieth Century Press [c. 1891], third edition, 1910), 1–17.<br>J. CONNELL | 277 |
| 36 | *Was Jesus a Socialist?* ([1891], Huddersfield: Worker Office, c. 1908), 1–15.<br>JAMES LEATHAM | 294 |
| 37 | "Simplification of Life", in *England's Ideal* (Swan Sonnenschein, Lowrey & Co, 1887), 79–99.<br>EDWARD CARPENTER | 309 |

## PART 8
### Gender, sexuality, family and personal relations — 323

| | | |
|---|---|---|
| 38 | "The Commercial Hearth", *Commonweal*, 8 May 1886, 42 and 15 May 1886, 50.<br>ERNEST BELFORT BAX | 325 |
| 39 | *Some Words to Socialist Women*, Social Democratic Party Women's Committee (London: Twentieth Century Press, 1908), 5–16.<br>DORA B. MONTEFIORE | 333 |
| 40 | *The Future of Woman* (London: Twentieth Century Press, 1909), 1–14.<br>HERBERT BURROWS | 345 |
| 41 | *Socialism and Eugenics* (London: Twentieth Century Press, 1911), 1–15.<br>GEORGE WHITEHEAD | 359 |

## PART 9
## War, peace and internationalism 375

42  *Manifesto of the Socialist League on the Soudan War*, Socialist League, 1885. 377

43  *The Imperial Kailyard. Being a Biting Satire on English Colonisation* (London: Twentieth Century Press, 1896), 3–15. 381
R.B. CUNNINGHAME GRAHAM

44  *The Approaching Catastrophe in India* (London: Twentieth Century Press, 1897), 3–16. 389
H.M. HYNDMAN

45  "Socialism and Colonial Development", *Social Democrat*, July 1898, 208–211. 406
JOHN R. WIDDUP

46  *Social-Democracy and the Armed Nation* (London: Twentieth Century Press, 1900), 3–14, 16. 412
HARRY QUELCH

47  *Anti-militarism from the workers' point of view: why every working man and woman should be an anti-militarist*, Workers' Anti-Militarist Committee, 1913, 1–7. 424
DORA MONTEFIORE

48  "A Continental Revolution", *Forward*, 15 August 1914, 38–42. 431
JAMES CONNOLLY

## PART 10
## The sense of the past 435

49  "George Julian Harney: A Straggler of 1848", *Social Democrat*, January 1897, 3–8. 437
EDWARD AVELING

50  "Bloody Niggers", *Social Democrat*, April 1897, 104–109. 444
R.B. CUNNINGHAME GRAHAM

51  **"Why is Socialism in England at a Discount?",** *Social Democrat*, **March 1898, 69–74 and April 1898, 112–117.**   451
    THEODORE ROTHSTEIN

52  *The First of May: The International Labour Day* **(1900) (London: Twentieth Century Press, 1904), 3–16.**   464
    H.W. LEE

   *Bibliography*   478

# INTRODUCTION
## The Anglo-Marxists

*Kevin Morgan*

Why was Marxism in Britain at such a discount? This was the question posed in 1898 by Theodore Rothstein, an émigré socialist from the Russian empire very well-connected with the socialist movement internationally. To answer it, Rothstein plunged deep into English history and its traditions of political and civic freedom which he strongly contrasted with those of continental Europe. Rothstein referred to socialism and not specifically to Marxism; but Marxist socialism was the form of socialism predominating on the continent, and this was certainly the absence that he had in mind. His analysis is of considerable interest in its own right and is one of the documents reproduced here (Chapter 51). At the same time, it poses questions regarding the meaning, scope and significance of the movement that the volume as a whole represents. "Whilst in Germany, in France, in Belgium, in Austria, in Italy, in Holland . . . the ideas of Socialism are making headway every day, in England . . . they are scarcely able to gain a hearing, let alone a footing". Already the source of much discussion in Rothstein's day, the question has exercised the minds of historians ever since.

For some of them, the absence of a mass Marxist party has been the main focus of attention. In the final quarter of the nineteeenth century socialism became established as a truly international movement. Its strongest section was in Germany: with its mass electorate, membership and political apparatus, the Social Democratic Party (SPD) was already by 1898 the country's largest party with the support of over a quarter of the electorate. In Britain, to Rothstein's dismay, the socialists did not even put up a challenge to the older parties in a by-election that coincided with a major industrial dispute. It was this anomaly that Ross McKibbin had in mind when in 1984 he posed the question "Why was there no Marxism in Great Britain?". Taking Germany as his main comparative point of reference, McKibbin also asked how it was that in "political Marxism's classical moment" before the First World War Britain alone of the major European states produced no mass Marxist party.[1]

The relative weakness of British Marxism has registered just as strongly in respect of socialist ideas. By the end of Marxism's "classical moment" a mass

Labour Party was belatedly emerging in Britain, and in 1918 it formally adopted a socialist objective. For some historians, including McKibbin, socialist ideas of any type had at best a secondary role in this development. Others would put far greater stress on the Independent Labour Party (ILP) and Fabian socialist traditions documented in the third volume of this collection. What all could nevertheless agree on was the weakness of the Marxist ideas which social democrats like Rothstein believed to be the guiding philosophy of modern socialism. In Leszek Kolakowski's monumental survey of these ideas, not a single British socialist is deemed worthy of notice in the volume on Marxism's "golden age". In Geoffrey Foote's account of the Labour Party's political thought, conversely, the chapter on nineteenth-century forerunners disposes of the "Labour Marxists" as a conduit for the ideas of Marx and Engels bereft of independent voice or interest. Between the "non-Marxist" socialism of the ILP and the "anti-Marxist" reformism of the Fabians, Anthony Wright locates a form of English exceptionalism that was "quite distinct from the perspective of European socialism as a whole".[2]

The documents reproduced here allow us to reflect on why Britain's early Marxists should have been so depreciated and how far this is justified. The central, though not exclusive, focus of the compilation is on the Social Democratic Federation (SDF). This was the organisation which Rothstein joined after settling in Britain, and from its formation in the early 1880s it had been Britain's closest counterpart to the SPD. The comparison was not one to the SDF's advantage. Both its membership and its electoral support, for reasons which will become clear, have tended to be described as more characteristic of a sect than of a genuine political party. More damagingly in the present context, its whole conception of socialism was also held by some to have the characteristics of a sort of arid and pedantic ineffectuality. Living in London, Marx before his death had some contact with the SDF's founder H.M. Hyndman. His judgments were not flattering, while Marx's collaborator Friedrich Engels survived him by a dozen years and in his correspondence with the German-American F.A. Sorge offered damning verdicts on the movement Hyndman led. "Anglo-Saxon sectarianism", he wrote, was rife. Exactly like a sect, the SDF had fastened on Marx's theory of development as a rigid orthodoxy and sought to ram it down workers' throats as an article of faith.[3]

Such was the standing of Marx and Engels, and of the Russian revolution that laid claim to their legacy, that not even Marxists themselves showed much inclination to preserve the memory of their earliest British representatives. As the Labour Party took shape between the wars, both the ILP socialist Keir Hardie and the Fabian Sidney Webb were eulogised as its founders by their respective admirers. Not even the communists, as the SDF's direct organisational successors, sought to celebrate the SDF as a forebear in this way. There were important exceptions, notably William Morris and Tom Mann. But no one believed in Marxism's British golden age; there was only a leaden provincialism to be cast off with the guidance of those whose deeper understanding of Marxism was demonstrated by the revolution they had successfully carried out. In the Durham coalfield in the 1920s there were miners' lodges whose banners depicted Hardie's image alongside those of Lenin and the martyred Irish revolutionary James Connolly. Even the communists of the 1920s were more likely to gather in honour of Hardie or to link his name with Lenin's. Only the SDF itself, by this time a dwindling and little-noticed fragment, maintained a sporadic line in commemoration. It was all that seemingly remained of some of the authors represented here.

A substantial historiography appearing in more recent years has shown how inadequate some of the older stereotypes were. Authors of important contributions, to list them alphabetically, include Logie Barrow and Ian Bullock; Mark Bevir; Martin Crick; Karen Hunt; and Graham Johnson. Should publication dates be added, the impression this would leave is of a remarkable upturn in the SDF's historiographical fortunes in the 1980s.[4] This is not to dismiss the contributions that appeared in the heyday of British labour history from the mid-1950s to the 1970s.[5] Nevertheless, the disentangling of this literature from what itself had certain aspects of an orthodoxy can be located in a specific historic moment both intellectually and politically.

Writing in the late 1970s, the late Eric Hobsbawm observed that histories of Marxism had for the most part been defined by a process of exclusion. The context for such an observation was that of the Cold War on the one hand, and of movements, states and parties upholding a quite specific version of Marxism ("Marxism-Leninism") on the other. Both doctrinaire Marxists and committed anti-Marxists, as Hobsbawm characterised them, had stringently applied these lines of exclusion on both ideological and political grounds.[6] Even the challengers to orthodoxy seemed to recognise the same basic categories, as in the competing claims made by British labour historians to "the origins of British Bolshevism".[7]

Hobsbawm himself was a communist; in a broader political sense he identified both personally and intellectually with the powerful Italian communist party. The larger historical project on Marxism in which he expressed these views was thus itself already symptomatic of a loosening up of boundaries within the left and the crisis of the doctrinaire Marxism to which Hobsbawm himself had at one time fervently subscribed.[8] Nevertheless, it was with the sharpening of this crisis over the course of the 1980s that the battlelines between Marxist and anti-Marxist themselves began to lose some of their immediate political force. Within the left, as "actually existing socialism" passed into history, there was an increasing interest in what were sometimes referred to as suppressed alternatives. It was in these circumstances that more nuanced, enquiring and open-ended histories began to appear that neither overlooked the connections between Marxism and other traditions and ideologies nor regarded them simply as a sign of immaturity or adulteration.

In some cases, the emphasis was on connections over time with diverse radical precursors – including the socialist precursors considered elsewhere in this collection. Given the freedom with which the early socialists had in many cases moved in and out of different movements, other accounts registered the linkages between the Marxists and a gamut of contemporaneous causes and campaigns. These included the rival political socialisms that are assembled here in a separate volume, although in practice even party-minded socialists expressed ideas and formed associations that often cut across this division. Other interactions, ranging from mutual support and attempted synthesis to outright denunciation, included those with movements for women's suffrage, anti-colonialism, vegetarianism and a host of other broadly progressive causes. Going beyond the ecumenicalism of what would later be called the left, there were even some highly contentious associations with movements of a predominantly conservative character. These included the national service agitation of the early twentieth century (Chapter 46); while the SDF's founder H.M. Hyndman aroused deep misgivings through his never quite extinguished affinities with Tory democracy.

But Hyndman, according to the newer scholarship, had always loomed too large. Traditionally, the conception of the SDF as a sect had implied a top-down, autocratic leadership exercising a tight control over the party press and such limited political machinery as it possessed. But this again was an image belied by the broadening out of historians' interests to variations of locality, period and the complexities of the individual activist biography. The ideas and commitments of Britain's ever-shifting cast of Marxists turned out to be far more varied and contested than had previously been appreciated. If anything, however, this was at the further expense of the project's intellectual coherence.

It was not so much a correction of the old view that was required but a change of perspective. From their very different political standpoints, Kolakowksi and Hobsbawm were at least agreed that the British contribution to Marxist thought was negligible. James Connolly might have been an exception; but Connolly of course was primarily active in the Irish and (for a time) the American socialist movements and cannot just be appropriated here.[9] Hobsbawm, though seemingly not Kolakowski, would also have allowed in Morris as "a sort of Marxist", and one who, with Walter Crane (also represented here), provided much of the iconographical vocabulary of international socialism.[10] Strangely enough, it is consequently in the visual history of the Second International that the British contribution comes across most powerfully.[11] Nevertheless, even Morris and Crane have not for the most part counted for anything much in studies of Marxist aesthetics.

A collection like this cannot therefore provide an alternative Marxist canon. Its justification must lie instead in a different approach to the history of ideas. Anglo-Marxism, as Tsuzuki characterised it in his study of Hyndman, is not presented here as equivalent to Austro-Marxism: that is, as a school or something like one which both Hobsbawm and Kolakowski could readily recognise. Britain had no experience yet of the Kathedersozialist: even the Fabians began to penetrate the universities only in the very last phase of our period. Ideas were the intellectual currency of a movement, not of a school, and the documentation here of these ideas will be shaped accordingly.

Traditionally the history of ideas has centred on a canon of classic texts and thinkers. Even alternative approaches, like Quentin Skinner's, uphold the notion of the canon while locating it within a broader historical frame of reference. Marxists in theory might have demystified the cult of the individual as the generator of great ideas and inventions. Marx himself disowned such a notion; documents in the present collection show how deep-seated the instinct was among some of those drawn to socialism. As the SDF weekly *Justice* put it on the first anniversary of Marx's death: "Any renewal of the old Pagan and Catholic forms of canonisation of individuals is contrary to the principles of Socialism as we understand it."[12] Nevertheless, there was also a reverence for revolutionary leaders that was compounded by the belief that Marxism was a science of society whose theoreticians were its acknowledged masters.

It was around great individuals, and occasionally a school, that Kolakowski structured his account of the golden age. One surveys the great projects of individual collected works that communism picked up from the Second International, and in the case of its best-known authorities generated on a truly industrial scale – as we indeed have already cited the fiftieth volume of the Marx and Engels *Collected Works*. One wonders if any other field of intellectual history has been so fixated on the canonical few. On such a premise Kolakowski was certainly justified in viewing the British as having made no significant contribution to Marxist doctrine.[13] But the compilation presented here is based on different principles entirely from the Marxist-Leninist cult of the collected works. Without making any claim to be representative, it is at least illustrative of a range of opinions, themes, authorial voices and genres, including examples of the verse and fiction that deserve much closer attention in their own right. While these are abstracted from their immediate publishing context, in just the manner of so many single-author *Works*, it is hoped that through the introductory notes the act of excision this involves is at least acknowledged.

The scope for a more radical application of these principles is certainly there. With the flurry of SDF histories in the 1990s, the exploration of its intellectual history and the restoration of a sense of place and grassroots agency were to some extent pursued independently of each other.[14] Only in the specific context of the "woman question" was something like a synthesis of the two perspectives successfully achieved.[15] An exercise like the present one can do no more than indicate the possibilities of such a field of research. The validity of the canon lies in the wider circulation, study and paraphrasis of works like those of Marx, which thereby acquired a sort of social force and agency in their own right. Nevertheless, socialists did not just learn by rote the catechisms which the SDF prepared for them. Every socialist had their own ideas, many gave voice to them in public arenas, significant numbers expressed them in the relatively formalised and self-conscious medium of print. There can be no political engagement without ideas, and there can be no reconstruction of larger political movements and ideologies without a more expansive conception of these ideas than the canonical approach to Marxist history can possibly provide.

\*\*

"The Social Democratic Party is the most downright and straightforward of the larger Socialist organisations. It is more outspoken and consistent, less hazy and opportunist, than the Independent Labour Party or the Fabian Society. It derives its inspiration from the Social Democrats of Germany and boldly upholds the ideal of revolutionary Socialism."[16] The characterisation is that of *The Times* newspaper in a series of articles on the British socialist movement appearing in 1909. As Graham Johnson observes, there would have been few objections to such a summary on the part of the party's membership. By 1909 it had a clearly established political identity that was quite distinct from other components of the socialist movement. Nevertheless, one could not have seen that quite so clearly even a decade earlier, and certainly not in the formative years of the 1880s. Moreover, with the challenges now arising from the threat and then the actuality of war, alignments on the left would once more be thrown into question as the social-democratic strand in British socialism returned to the fragmented state in which it had begun.

Ironically, the story begins in London at the same Memorial Hall that later witnessed the formation of the Labour Party, from which the SDF took the fateful step of excluding itself. In June 1881, when the Democratic Federation (DF) was inaugurated there, socialism in Britain was a matter of a few tiny isolated groupings and there was no independent movement of labour such as might have loosened the political grip of the older parties. Hyndman as the Federation's founder had already met Marx and read *Das Kapital* in a French translation. Nevertheless, the DF's initial programme did not go beyond the demands of the political radicals and working-men's clubs that Hyndman believed he could bring together in a single organisation. According to his reminiscences, highly entertaining but not always reliable, Hyndman's object from the start was the formation of a socialist party. Nevertheless, it was only two years later, in September 1883, that the DF adopted a socialist programme, *Socialism Made Plain*, which Hyndman further elaborated in his book *The Historical Basis of Socialism in England*. It was at this point that the last of the organisation's non-socialist radicals took their leave. More than compensating were socialists like Morris and Ernest Belfort Bax, who joined in the winter of 1882–1883 and would prove indefatigable proponents of the socialist cause while interpreting it in highly personal ways. At its annual conference in August 1884 the DF took on the designation of Social Democratic Federation by which it was afterwards best known. This merely confirmed the path that was already embarked upon and met with general assent.

The SDF was therefore the earliest of the socialist organisations that were now established in Britain on a national basis. The Fabians followed close behind. George Bernard Shaw, having gone so far as to attend a meeting of the DF's council, signalled his differences with the class war and labour theory of value. Henceforth he would have a major hand in setting out the distinctive socialist alternative to Marxism which Fabians held to be better adapted to the conditions described by Rothstein. Nevertheless, by Shaw's own account, the differences at this stage were more ones of method and of audience than of principle. Fabian socialists were certainly no more middle-class than Hyndman or Morris, but unlike them they would not have taken to the streets or dingy meeting-rooms to address the workers while investing in them their hopes of the future. "When I myself, on the point of joining the Social-Democratic Federation, changed my mind and joined the Fabian instead, I was guided by no discoverable difference in program or principles, but solely by an instinctive feeling that the Fabian and not the Federation would attract the men of my own bias and intellectual habits . . .".[17] The differences of principle and programme would not be long in emerging. Nevertheless, there were some Fabians, notably Hubert Bland, who would freely acknowledge their debt to the early SDF.

In 1907, the Federation would rename itself the Social Democratic Party (SDP). In 1911, it was the chief initiator and largest component of the newly formed British Socialist Party (BSP) in which it now sunk its identity. In a commentary on the SDF's history, Hobsbawm nevertheless referred to an "inextinguishable light of continuity" across the period from the early 1880s to the formation of the Communist Party in 1920.[18] Like most historians, Hobsbawm refers to the SDF across these various changes of name and structure, and the same convention is followed in this volume. Specific reference is therefore made to the DF, SDP or even BSP only when a particular context requires it.

The proliferation of acronyms was not just an arcane ritual of left-wing history: it reflected a basic strategic dilemma between some or other version of an inclusive socialist unity and the consolidation of its less compromised adherents within an organisation of their own. The SDF's monopoly on socialist organisation was over almost as soon as it began; with the ILP's formation in 1893, the division of the socialists' forces seemed to many of them in both parties a contradiction that needed resolution. Nevertheless, the predicament was only intensified by the formation in 1900 of the Labour Representation Committee (LRC), which six years later became the Labour Party. In bringing together the "labour alliance" of socialist bodies and trade unions, this meant that no conception of socialist unity was henceforth possible that did not also extend to the non-socialists and nominal socialists who were always to find a home in the Labour Party. All could agree on an ideal of unity without ever reaching agreement on unity of whom and how and to what immediate ends.

The result, as Hobsbawm further observed, was that the SDF's history was one of multiple crises and splits but with a countervailing tendency to heal the splits, rebuild political bridges and factor in considerations of political effectiveness. This was not so much a light of continuity as an inescapable field of engagement. Still unresolved in 1920, the same dilemma was the SDF's legacy to the communists as they set off lurching left and right in search of an answer. The only difference now was that, with the split within the socialist movement internationally, the same basic predicament was not peculiar to Britain but addressed by both the Second and Third Internationals as a whole.

The persistence of this basic dilemma helps account for the sense of déjà vu that is so common in the history of the left. It also helps explain why left-wing movements have been so conscious of their own past history, and of the arguments, alignments and conflicting personalities that remained as a point of reference for their own times. Britain's long history of socialist factionalism may be dated from the Socialist League (SL) breakaway from the SDF as early as January 1885. Issues of personality played a part, most of them arising from distrust of Hyndman. Nevertheless, the Socialist League was also committed to a less calculating form of socialist politics, and acted not just as a rival to the SDF but as a sort of political conscience upholding a less compromised sense of its founding ideals. Even issues of personality were also ones of principle. Hyndman was distrusted because of his deep roots in Tory democracy, and the presumption of leadership he made on this basis. Socialism, however, was imagined as a new form of political practice requiring something more than a socialistic Randolph Churchill or Joe Chamberlain or even Charles Stewart Parnell. "We are working *for* equality and brotherhood for all the world and it is only *through* equality and brotherhood that we can make our work effective." Thus ran the League's inaugural manifesto as reproduced here (Chapter 2). Headed by Morris and Bax, the SL was not only among the most intellectually fertile of Britain's socialist groupings, but stood for a form of prefigurative politics with which the Owenites would have instantly felt a sense of fellow-feeling.

With the SL's departure, some Fabians thought the moment opportune to enter the SDF themselves. Among them were Bland himself, Edith Bland, better known as the children's writer Edith Nesbit, and the Fabians' first secretary Frederick Keddell. Nevertheless, like most of those around the socialist movement they felt a shock of revulsion when the SDF in the 1885 general election stood two candidates in London with the help of "Tory gold". The Fabians, like many others, quickly made their exit – except for Keddell, who left the Fabians instead and was subsequently the SDF's treasurer. The Tory gold scandal was the second great setback of the SDF's formative years and along with the Socialist League's departure it set the pattern for the years to come.

This, then, was the fissiparousness of a movement that was never strong enough to impose an idea of unity to which all would at least defer. On the one hand, there were organised defections to the left which each in different ways represented a rejection of what was seen as the dominant SDF leadership's politics of expediency and concession to alien ideas. The clearest example of this was the so-called "impossibilist" revolt which in 1903–1904 gave rise to the Socialist Labour Party, based mainly in Scotland, and the London-centred Socialist Party of Great Britain. Certainly no less significant were those who moved on to more immediately practical forms of activity. These did so mainly as individuals, and with so little a sense of occasion that in many cases not even the date of their leaving is recorded for the historian. Among the best-known examples of a much wider phenomenon, one might mention those of Tom Mann, who became the national secretary of the ILP; of John Burns, who afterwards became a Liberal cabinet minister; and, a little later, of George Lansbury, who is better known now as the founder of the *Daily Herald* and sometime leader of the Labour Party. Even the SDF's so-called "old guard" included some, like Bax and Herbert Burrows, who had at some point left and returned. The SDF was notorious for its high membership turnover, and this has naturally been remarked upon as a source of weakness.

Nevertheless, in its pursuit of a robust socialist politics that steered clear of the pitfalls of impossibilism and self-absorption, the SDF did repeatedly recharge itself through engagement with mass movements or a broader conception of socialist unity. In 1886, it was through its involvement in movements of the London unemployed that it regained some of the kudos it had relinquished through the Tory gold affair (Chapter 5). With the explosion of the "new unionism" at the end of the decade, SDF activists took on leading roles and the earlier ambivalence of many socialists towards trade unions was largely overcome (Chapters 24 and 25). The ILP's formation presented it with a formidable political challenge. As the SDF weekly *Justice* saw it, the new rival party had not only declared itself to be socialist and adopted most of the old SDF programme but chiefly employed the same methods of propaganda.[19] Even this, however, meant not just rivalry but a degree of complementarity between the two organisations. Their main political strongholds were in different parts of the country – the SDF's being in London in particular – and in areas where both were well-grounded, as in Manchester and Salford, there were strong tendencies towards co-operation and mutual support. This even included SDF delegates at the ILP's founding conference.[20]

In 1898 these instincts of socialist unity were confirmed by the members of both parties in a ballot to approve the principle of unification. The principal ILP leaders were doggedly opposed; Hyndman in all probability reciprocated the feeling (Chapter 8) and with the establishment instead of the LRC any such hopes were finally dashed. Nevertheless, there remained some within the ILP who would feel deeply uncomfortable with Labour's alignment with the Liberal government that would lead the country through massive strike and protest movements and into war. The SDF was broadly supportive of the idea of socialist representation committees, and in 1907 it welcomed the by-election victory of Victor Grayson as an unendorsed and openly socialist candidate in Colne Valley. The formation of the BSP in 1911 was intended as the realisation of this larger conception of socialist unity, and Grayson, though no longer an MP, was one of its best-publicised recruits. Nevertheless, with the SDF having entered as a bloc and made over to the new party its headquarters, weekly organ and most prominent leaders, it is not surprising that Hobsbawm should have seen no dimming of the light of continuity. If the BSP was not entirely the SDF writ large, nor was it truly a new departure in British politics. With Grayson among those who speedily withdrew, the SDF's thirty-year wait for a political breakthrough was once more to be frustrated.

One of Britain's later Marxist parties once produced a historical retrospect entitled "The smallest mass party in the world".[21] Since 1881 there have been many British organisations that might have thought they had a better claim to the title. The SDF was not the smallest of them, indeed was considerably larger than the SL, the SLP or the SPGB. Nevertheless, the contrast which so impressed itself on Rothstein remained unmissable in any wider comparative context. What Grayson had achieved in getting into parliament, the SDF throughout its existence failed to do. It came closest in the Lancashire cotton districts, where Hyndman was four times its parliamentary candidate in Burnley. In the cotton towns it also had some strictly limited success in council elections, while in West Ham, where the SDF worked through the local labour movement, the SDFer Will Thorne was in 1906 returned for the West Ham South constituency as a Labour member.

Nevertheless, the main effect of Labour's electoral growth was to underline the feebleness of socialist alternatives. In membership terms, meanwhile, the SDF's ranged between a figure of a few hundred in its formative years to a peak figure of at most a few thousand. Certainly, the 35–40,000 members claimed by the BSP on its formation was a figure some two or three times at least in excess of the reality. The German SPD, if that may serve as a yardstick, had by this time a membership approaching a million and as many local councillors as its British counterpart had members. That socialism in the SDF's sense was at a discount was a truism which any observer could confirm at a glance.

Hobsbawm divided social democracy's golden age into three distinct subperiods: one of sudden irruption and advance in the 1880s and early 1890s; one of divergences, splits and intellectual self-reckoning from the mid-to-late 1890s; and one of reviving mass actions, beginning with the Russian revolution of 1905 and culminating in the labour unrest and political ferment of the immediate pre-1914 period.[22] This wider periodisation can be adapted to a British context, but only through a series of local interactions and contingencies that have no immediate parallel in any other European country. The irruption of the 1880s, as Rothstein would have been the first to point out, had neither superseded nor dislodged either liberalism, utilitarianism or the older forms of plebeian radicalism. It had had a material impact on all of these; but in the testing second period around the turn of the century it was the Fabians and the ILP who adapted most successfully to these conditions and drew the most advantage from them.

In a different field of activity, one might also mention the more politically minded co-operators, as documented in the second volume of this collection. Nevertheless, the period's most conspicuous development was the LRC's formation in 1900 and the electoral breakthrough that followed in 1906. The Labour Party had taken shape, but with the SDF outside; for having occupied a place on the original LRC, it withdrew after barely a year, citing the absence of a commitment to socialism and the class war. Many would say that this was the turning point in its history when history turned against it. Having neither pre-empted the formation of a Labour Party, nor taken the decisive role in establishing one, the SDF was left competing with it as an independent socialist party. In the commemorative history it produced in the 1930s, its claim to vindication was not now the SDF itself, but the effect it had on the Labour Party which was now itself "virtually . . . a Social-Democratic Party" in its own right.[23] It was a form of vindication that some at least of the activists of its heyday would have struggled to recognise.

\*\*

S.G. Hobson's was one of those lives in socialist history that makes a dog's breakfast of the dividing lines within which it tends to be written. His most durable contribution was as the originator of the guild socialist doctrines which were taken up by G.D.H. Cole and enjoyed an immense vogue in the years around the First World War. Hobson, however, had been a Fabian socialist as early as 1891, an ILPer from 1894 and an active contributor to the Labour Church movement. A well-known figure in all these milieux, he was also favourably disposed to the SDF and it was over the issue of socialist unity that he resigned from the Fabian Society executive in 1909. Although he thus brought a critical eye to so many movements, one of the problems with such mercurial commitments is that they tend to be overlooked in histories that take these movements as their organising principle.[24]

In his "memoirs of a revolutionist" published in the 1930s, Hobson offered two reasons for the ILP leaders' preference for associating with the non-socialist body of trade unionists rather than their fellow socialists of the SDF. One, which they would have recognised and acknowledged, was the commitment to labour's political independence as their first objective. The other was that they were afraid of the SDF because they recognised their own intellectual inferiority. None of them, said Hobson, was intellectually the equal of Hyndman or Bax, while even the SDF's Harry Quelch could hold his own with them, "sometimes gaining in humour what he lost in dialectics". The Marxists of the SDF were not only the ILP's intellectual masters but had a logical hardness that according to Hobson grated against their sentimentality.[25]

Readers of these volumes will be able to make their own minds up as to how far these observations were justified. Hobson did see quite clearly that the Fabians, if not the ILP, were the Marxists' equals. He might also have seen, but did not, that Ramsay MacDonald's importance for the ILP was in part in articulating with some plausibility and sophistication a version of socialism that rejected Marxism while drawing on both Fabianism and debates within European social democracy. Leaving all such considerations aside, one can nevertheless agree with Hobson that if there was any field in which the Marxists were not overshadowed by their rivals it was that of ideas rather than elections and political careers. Hobson believed it a criminal blunder for the SDF to have withdrawn from the LRC and thus to have gravely impaired the socialist presence within the early Labour Party. Once it had withdrawn, the SDF set about the clearer delineation of its separate claims as a socalist party, and these would be embodied both in the renaming of 1907 and the launching of the BSP in 1911. Nevertheless, it was not through party-building that the light of SDF history continued to shine most brightly, but through the influence of the socialist ideas that it propounded.

A Fabian might have referred to this as permeation. It is worth remembering that when the LRC was formed in 1900, the ILP affiliated on a membership of 13,000, the SDF on a membership of 9,000, and the Fabians on a membership of just 861. It was not just a mass Marxist party that Britain therefore lacked, nor even specifically a mass socialist party. Rather it was the dominance of party as a vehicle of popular politics as so exemplified by the case of Germany. The Fabians might have developed permeationism as a fine art and political credo.

Nevertheless, their Marxist rivals were just as much permeationists of a militant type, and it was as permeationists that they principally achieved whatever measure of effectiveness they had. Hobson himself illustrates the point perfectly: for the guild socialism that he and Cole developed was a manifestly Fabian offshoot that at the same time could not even be imagined without the counter-permeating influence of the Marxists, and particularly of William Morris.

These at least were the arguments with which Marxists consoled themselves and which encouraged them to turn out such extraordinary quantities of political literature. "In the progress of Socialism in this country, as elsewhere, one must distinguish between the party, properly so called, and the general movement", wrote Belfort Bax in 1892. "Within the last decade or thereabouts the Socialist movement has 'permeated' more or less the whole working-classes of the country, and the ideas of Socialism have won for themselves recognition from the intelligent of even the middle class."[26] Belfort Bax was in some ways the most considerable of the Marxist thinkers collected here and socially speaking indistinguishable from any Fabian. In his memoirs a quarter of a century later Bax returned to the theme. The social-democratic party had not prospered in proportion to its ideas, but while the membership of socialist parties languished "the whole of modern Democratic thought is more or less permeated with Socialist ideas and aspirations".[27]

Edward Carpenter is more difficult even than Hobson to categorise within any single specific strand of the socialist movement. He is best described as an idiosyncratic ethical socialist, but one who would acknowledge a debt to the Marxists that others would furiously deny. With no factional axe to grind, Carpenter's retrospective on the years covered by this volume offers further testimony to the permeationist effect described by Bax:

> It is curious indeed in this matter to see how, of all the innumerable little societies – of the SDF, the [Socialist League], the Fabians, the Christian Socialists, the Anarchists, the Freedom groups, the ILP, the Clarion societies, and local groups of various names – all supporting one side or another of the general Socialist movement – not one of them has grown to any great volume, or to commanding and permanent influence; and how yet, and at the same time, the general teaching and ideals of the movement have permeated society in the most remarkable way, and have deeply infected the views of all classes, as well as general literature and even municipal and imperial politics.[28]

As Sidney Webb from his Fabian perspective had also put it around the same time as Bax, "by far the largest part of English Socialism is unconscious of itself as Socialism, and the avowed exponents of the principle appear, on a mere superficial glance, to be of quite minor importance in English public life".[29]

It is as a disseminator of ideas and as a publishing operation that we can therefore approach this Anglo-Marxist strand within the socialist tradition. Weekly papers like the SDF's *Justice* and the SL's *Commonweal* called forth sustained commitments and sometimes subventions from supporters like Carpenter. Along with monthly reviews like the later *Social Democrat*, they also provide a continuous record of these organisations' activities. Bound in library volumes, or called up on computer screens, there may not seem that much difference between an SDF pamphlet and a Fabian tract except in the ideas of socialism which they generated. Nevertheless, there were also important differences of political practice. Anglo-Marxism was not (yet) just a publishing operation. The SDF's founding slogan was "Educate. Agitate. Organise" (Chapter 1), and it was the link between the three that was the key to the political culture of the Marxist groups. As Rothstein put it, those who were drawn to socialism were not the lowest strata of the workers, sunk in misery, sloth and drink, but the "better paid artisan, the skilled labourer, the earnest trade unionist". There is hardly a socialist across the four volumes of this collection who would have disagreed. Socialist ideas, in Rothstein's words, appealed primarily to those prepared for the "conscious effort and unremittant struggle" that the causes of emancipation and enlightenment would require. It is also this that accounts for the sense of "apartness" that is nowhere better attested than by Robert Tressell's novel *The Ragged Trousered Philanthropists* (Chapter 19).

Through the reading of these texts and through the activism which they inspired the socialist bodies represented here embodied a project of collective self-education that would later be formalised through the Plebs League and the labour colleges. The membership turnover that was seemingly detrimental to party-building may in this respect turn out to have been one of the Marxists' strengths; for with informed estimates suggesting some tens of thousands passed through these organisations, one of the commonest claims made on their behalf is that they provided a sort of political training ground.[30] Lansbury may perhaps serve as an example. With his undogmatic Christian socialism, it has been easy to assume that the ILP was Lansbury's "natural home" and that no socialist could have been more like the "conventional ILPer". Nevertheless, even after he left the SDF, Lansbury continued to describe the SDFers as "far and away the most active" of his supporters, and also the most loyal. With the SDF long behind him, there remained such traces of his Marxist commitments as the Poplarist militancy of the 1920s, the ready association with the communists and Lansbury's two wide-eyed visits to Soviet Russia. Politically, there is no such thing as a natural home, only spaces that one may enter and sometimes leave, and which in the case of parties of the left are often cohabited in tumultuous and discordant ways.[31]

The selection of documents presented here to some extent follows this permeationist logic. In his comments on histories of Marxism Hobsbawm maintained that they had often been written "exclusively as that of the development of and the debates within the body of specifically Marxist theory, and therefore to neglect an important . . . area of Marxist radiation". Such accounts may typically focus on political economy or Marxist philosophy or theories of imperialism or the nation. This is also the club that Anglo-Marxists tend to be denied admission to. A considered and very plausible verdict is that they had "few inhibitions against combining the new theory with ideas and values drawn from their native traditions", and did so at the cost of a "rapid loss of coherence".[32] Another judgment, focusing on Hyndman's thinking, is that its incorporation of native elements that in some aspects were far removed from socialism was too idiosyncratic by far even to be labelled as Marxist.[33] There is some support for these views here. As the documents range from Lady Warwick and the former curate Pickard-Cambridge to Edward Carpenter and the vegetarian Henry Salt, some readers will doubtless be reaching for their Orwell and his diatribes against the socialist duchesses, nancy poets, beards and fruit-juice drinkers of a later age. No strict definition of Marxism has been employed to identify these materials, or exclude them. Marxism has been approached not just as a doctrine but as a movement, with a representation of the ideas to be found within the publications of that movement. No editorial boundaries have been set, in other words, beyond those set by the editors of the sources used themselves.

That at least is true with certain caveats. Chronologically, the range extends from 1883 to 1914. Nevertheless, the coverage across this period is not intended to be comprehensive. Another study of Britain's Anglo-Marxist tradition postulates a break around 1910 between the SDF as a "loosely constructed socialist association" and the development of Marxist parties and of a "firm Marxist political culture" culminating in the formation of the CPGB in 1920.[34] Not everyone would accept these characterisations, and they may not be valid in every context. Nevertheless, one cannot mistake the new movements emerging in this latter period, including those like syndicalism and the labour college movement in which the influence of Marxists was strong. There was also both a generational and a political dimension to the conflicts within the BSP that in 1916 would lead to the younger internationalist left assuming control of the party and driving Hyndman and the old guard into forming the breakaway National Socialist Party. This would soon resume the title of SDF and maintained a desultory inter-war existence until 1939 as an ageing, loyal and unnoticed component of the Labour Party.

Any chronological division is to some extent arbitrary. There were nevertheless some tendencies looking more to the future and some deriving more from the past. In addressing this issue in the present collection, the emphasis here is specifically on those traditions emerging in the 1880s that reached a sort of culminating point in the decade of the First World War. The impossibilists of the 1880s are thus included, if the anarchists can be so described, but not those of the early 1900s who in several cases went on to long careers as leading communists. Syndicalism is represented through Mann and Carpenter, whose first writing here again dates from the mid-1880s, and not by the younger militants who in many cases were at the start of labour movement long careers. The period around the First World War was exceptionally fertile in ideas; Anthony Wright has referred to it as "perhaps . . . the high water mark of optimistic social engineering in a modern context".[35] Even so, another volume is required for such classic examples of socialist argument as *The Miners' Next Step* or the writings of the Guild Socialists. No attempt has been made to provide a merely tokenistic coverage here.

INTRODUCTION

## Notes

1. Ross McKibbin (1984), "Why was there no Marxism in Great Britain?". *English Historical Review* 99: 299–331.
2. Leszek Kolakowski, *Main Currents of Marxism. Its Rise, Growth and Dissolution.* (New York: W.W. Norton & Co, 2005 edn); Geoffrey Foote, *The Labour Party's Political Thought* (London: Routledge, 2007 edn), ch. 2; Anthony Wright, *Socialisms* (London: Routledge, 1996 edn), 9–10.
3. Engels to Sorge, 1 May and November 1894 in Karl Marx and Friedrich Engels, *Collected Works Volume 50: Engels: 1892–95* (London: Lawrence & Wishart, 2004 edn), 301, 356.
4. Logie Barrow and Ian Bullock, *Democratic Ideas and the British Labour Movement 1880–1914* (Cambridge: Cambridge University Press, 1996); Mark Bevir (1991), "H.M. Hyndman: A Rereading and a Reassessment". *History of Political Thought* 12, 1 (1991): 125–146; idem, "The British Social Democratic Federation 1880–1885: From O'Brienism to Marxism". *International Review of Social History* 37 (1992): 207–229; idem, "Ernest Belfort Bax: Marxist, Idealist, and Positivist". *Journal of the History of Ideas* 54, 1 (1993): 119–135; Martin Crick, *The History of the Social Democratic Federation* (Keele: Keele University Press, 1994); Karen Hunt, *Equivocal Feminists: The Social Democratic Federation and the Woman Question, 1894–1911* (Cambridge: Cambridge University Press, 1996); Graham Johnson, *Social-Democratic Politics in Britain 1881–1911* (Lampeter: Edwin Mellen Press, 2002).
5. Notably the writings of Chushichi Tsuzuki (1956), "The 'impossibilist revolt' in Britain". *International Review of Social History* 1: 377–397; *H.M. Hyndman and British Socialism* (Oxford: Oxford University Press, 1961); *The Life of Eleanor Marx 1855–1898: A Socialist Tragedy* (Oxford: Oxford University Press, 1967); see also Henry Collins "The Marxism of the Social Democratic Federation" in Asa Briggs and John Saville (eds), *Essays in Labour History 1886–1923* (London: Macmillan, 1971), 47–69; Eric Hobsbawm, "Hyndman and the SDF" in idem, *Labouring Men. Studies in the History of Labour* (London: Weidenfeld & Nicolson, 1964); Stanley Pierson, *Marxism and the Origins of British Socialism. The Struggle for a New Consciousness* (Ithaca, NY: Cornell University Press, 1973); E.P. Thompson, *William Morris. From Romantic to Revolutionary* (London: Lawrence & Wishart, 1955); Dona Torr, *Tom Mann and His Times. Volume One (1856–1890)* (London: Lawrence & Wishart, 1956).
6. Eric Hobsbawm, *How to Change the World: Marx and Marxism 1840–2011* (London, Little Brown, 2011), 211.
7. Raymond Challinor, *The Origins of British Bolshevism* (London: Croom Helm, 1977). A substantial literature on John Maclean was moved by similar concerns.
8. *Storia del marxismo* (Turin: Einaudi, 3 vols, 1978–1982).
9. His response to the outbreak of the First World War in the Glasgow *Forward* is alone included but the scope and richness of Connolly's thought does not even begin to be represented here.
10. Hobsbawm, *How to Change the World*, 249–251.
11. A good example is André Rossel, *1er mai: 90 ans de lutte populaire dans le monde* (Paris: Editions de la Courtille, 1977), 125, 161, 219.
12. *Justice*, 15 March 1884.
13. Kolakowski, *Main Currents*, 366.
14. Notably by Bevir and Johnson on the one hand and Crick on the other.
15. Hunt, *Equivocal Feminists*.
16. Cited Graham Johnson (2000), "'Making Reform the Instrument of Revolution': British Social Democracy, 1881–1911". *Historical Journal* 43 (4): 980.
17. Shaw, *The Fabian Society: Its Early History* (London: Fabian Society, 1892), 4.
18. Eric Hobsbawm, "Hyndman and the SDF" in idem, *Labouring Men. Studies in the History of Labour* (London: Weidenfeld & Nicolson, 1964), 231.

19 "SDF and ILP Amalgamation", *Justice*, 8 September 1897.
20 Jeffrey Hill (1981), "Manchester and Salford Politics and the Early Development of the Independent Labour Party". *International Review of Social History* 26 (2): 171–201.
21 The title of a historical pamphlet by Ian Birchall published by the Socialist Workers Party in 1981.
22 Hobsbawm, *How to Change the World*, 214–216.
23 H.W. Lee and E. Archbold, *Social Democracy in Britain. Fifty Years of the Socialist Movement* (London: Social Democratic Federation, 1935), ch. 32.
24 For details of Hobson's biography see Kevin Morgan (2007), "British Guild Socialists and the Exemplar of the Panama Canal". *History of Political Thought* 28 (1): 1–38.
25 S.G. Hobson, *Pilgrim to the the Left. Memoirs of a Modern Revolutionist* (London: Edward Arnold, 1938), 68–69.
26 *Justice*, 18 June 1892.
27 E. Belfort Bax, *Reminiscences and Reflexions of a Mid and Late Victorian* (London: Allen & Unwin, 1918), 91–92.
28 Edward Carpenter, *My Days and Dreams: Being Autobiographical Notes* (London: Allen & Unwin, 1916), 126.
29 Sidney Webb, *Socialism in England* (1890; London: Swan Sonnenschein edn, 1908), 56.
30 Hobsbawm, "Hyndman and the SDF", 232.
31 John Shepherd, *George Lansbury. At the Heart of Old Labour* (Oxford: Oxford University Press, 2002), 36; David Howell, *British Workers and the Independent Labour Party 1888–1906* (Manchester: Manchester University Press, 1983), 259; Lansbury to Ramsay MacDonald, 1 November 1907 (John Rylands Library, Manchester, RMD 1/2/69). For a presentation of these aspects of Lansbury's career, see Kevin Morgan, *Labour Legends and Moscow Gold : Bolshevism and the British Left Part 1* (London: Lawrence & Wishart, 2006), ch. 4.
32 Stanley Pierson, *Marxism and the Origins of British Socialism. The Struggle for a New Consciousness* (Ithaca, NY: Cornell University Press, 1973), 59.
33 Rodney Barker, *Political Ideas in Modern Britain* (London: Routledge, 1997 edn), 34–37.
34 Edwin Roberts, *The Anglo-Marxists: A Study in Ideology and Culture* (Lanham, MD: Rowman & Littlefield, 1996), ch. 2.
35 A.W. Wright, *G.D.H. Cole and Socialist Democracy* (Oxford: Oxford University Press, 1979), 51–52.

# Part 1

# THE IDEA OF SOCIALISM

# 1

## *SOCIALISM MADE PLAIN. BEING THE SOCIAL AND POLITICAL MANIFESTO OF THE DEMOCRATIC FEDERATION* (DEMOCRATIC FEDERATION, 1883)

[By 1883 the Democratic Federation had become a focal point for all those drawn by the ideas of socialism that were once more in the air. These ideas were crystallised in the declaration of principles adopted at the Federation's second annual conference in June 1883 and issued as the pamphlet *Socialism Made Plain*. Though it was not until the following year that the Federation was renamed the Social Democratic Federation, the views expressed in the pamphlet marked its formal adoption of a socialist objective and meant a political break with radicals who had come this far with Hyndman but felt unable to endorse such a position.

They would have noticed most its clear exposition of the economic case for socialism. It was certainly this aspect that the arch-individualist Herbert Spencer took issue with in his *Man Versus the State* (1884). Hyndman has much to say about the pernicious role played historically by the landed classes. Nevertheless, he leaves no doubt that the rule of the "active capitalist class" was now a still more serious source of oppression.

Even so, the text shows very clearly how Hyndman sought to marry the economic ideas he had found in Marx with traditions of political radicalism that went back to the Chartists and beyond (Pierson 1973, ch. 4). The manifesto thus takes its stance against all established political groupings, and against the alliance of capitalists and landlords that had been cemented by the first Reform Act of 1832 and left largely unchallenged since the decline of Chartism after 1848. In the language of paid delegates and annual conventions one may certainly see the echo of the old Chartist demands for annual parliaments and payment of members. There is also a commitment to adult suffrage, explicitly including both men and women, which would remain a fixture of the SDF's programme and a source of considerable controversy in the period of the suffragettes. In the form of the "direct reference" of grave matters to the country at large, the pamphlet also envisages recourse to the instrument of the referendum. This continued to enjoy much support among some socialists, but at the same time was emphatically opposed by the Fabians with their strong commitment to ideas of professionalised representation (Barrow and Bullock 1996).

Essentially drafted by Hyndman, the text that follows was arguably the first of the decade's summary expositions of socialist argument. As such, it not only predated but helped to inspire those like the Fabians whose socialism would take them in rather different directions. Later in 1883, Hyndman would also publish a fuller exposition, *The Historical Basis of Socialism in England*, in which his debt to Marx's thought was openly acknowledged. The robustly national framework he adopted was one principal cause of the misgivings Hyndman aroused among some socialists, who included Marx and Engels. Another bone of contention was the specification of so-called palliatives, here referred to as "stepping-stones to a happier period". Hyndman's commitment to more immediate objectives would over time give rise to numerous defections from the SDF. The first of them, barely a year or so later, was that of the Socialist League (Chapter 2, this volume).]

FELLOW CITIZENS,

THE time has come when it is absolutely necessary that the mass of the people should seriously take in hand their own business unless they are content to find themselves in the near future worse off than they have ever yet been. At present, social and political power is monopolised by those who live upon the labour of their fellows; and Tories or Conservatives, Whigs, Liberals or Radicals strive only to keep the workers ignorant of the truths which most nearly concern them. After the Reform Bill of 1832 the capitalists entered into alliance with the landlords except on one question, and from the repeal of the Corn Laws in 1846 to this day the lords of the money-bag and the lords of the soil have together been absolute masters of the millions who labour throughout the United Kingdom. So complete has been their control that since the year 1848 no vigorous attempt has even been made to overthrow it. But what has been the result to the workers of this supremacy of the luxurious classes? During fifty years our labourers have competed against one another for wages which barely suffice to keep them alive. Whilst the realised wealth and the annual income of the country have more than trebled, those who create these riches remain a wage-slave class, overworked and underfed, at the mercy of every crisis and the victims of each succeeding depression. The improved machinery, the extension of railways, the great steam and electric communications—that vast increase of the power of man over nature which has been the main feature of our epoch, has brought luxury for the few, misery and degradation for the many. Even in the past ten years what have we seen? The interests of Great Britain utterly neglected, Ireland shamefully misgoverned, India ruined and South Africa estranged. In 1874 the Liberals were dismissed for incapacity and Conservatives ruled in their stead for six years. Not a single measure did they introduce during that long tenure of office which could in any way lighten the lot of the millions who toil. The Conservatives having been turned out in disgust the Liberals again try their hand, and once more not a single measure is before Parliament, not a single measure is proposed for future legislation, which can benefit the working men and women who are really the source of all our wealth.

Fellow-Citizens the further success of this pitiful trickery depends upon your ignorance and will last as long as your apathy. Landlords and capitalists, who own the House of Lords and fill the House of Commons, wish nothing better than to protect their interests under the pretence of looking after yours. Take up then your own heritage, push aside these wealthy hucksters of both factions who trade upon your labour, and trust for the future in your own strength alone.

Consider the figures below.

| | |
|---|---:|
| Total Production of the United Kingdom | £1,300,000,000 |
| Taken by Landlords, Capitalists and Profitmongers | 1,000,000,000 |
| Left for the Producers | 300,000,000 |

Study these figures all who toil and suffer that others may be lazy and rich; look upon the poverty, the starvation, the prostitution around you ye who labour and return the value of your entire day's wages to your employers in the first two or three hours of your day's work. Ponder on these facts, reflect upon these figures, men and women of England, and then ask yourselves, whether it is worth while for such a result as this to bow down in slavish subjection before your "governing classes," whether you will not rather demand and obtain the full fruits of your labour and become your own governing class yourselves. Submit then no longer to a system of Parliamentary Government which is maintained in the interests of those who rob and oppress you—which has proved itself for generations to be alike a failure and a fraud.

EDUCATE! AGITATE! ORGANISE!

Fellow Citizens, we of the DEMOCRATIC FEDERATION demand complete adult suffrage for every man and woman in these islands, because in this way alone can the whole people give free expression to their will; we are in favor of paid delegates and annual Conventions because by this means alone can the people control their representatives; we stand up for the direct reference of all grave issues to the country at large, and for the punishment as felony of every species of corruption, because thus only can tyranny be checked and bribery uprooted; we call for the abolition of all hereditary authority, because such authority is necessarily independent of the mass of the people. But all these reforms when secured mean only that the men and women of these islands will at length be masters in their own house. Mere political machinery is worthless unless used to produce good social conditions.

All wealth is due to labour; therefore to the labourers all wealth is due.

But we are strangers in our own country. Thirty thousand persons own the land of Great Britain against the 30,000,000 who are suffered to exist therein. A long series of robberies and confiscations has deprived us of the soil which should be ours. The organised brute force of the few has for generations robbed and tyrannised over the unorganised brute force of the many. We now call for

Nationalisation of the Land. We claim that land in country and land in towns, mines, parks, mountains, moors should be owned by the people for the people, to be held, used, built over and cultivated upon such terms as the people themselves see fit to ordain. The handful of marauders who now hold possession have and can have no right save brute force against the tens of millions whom they wrong.

But private ownership of land in our present society is only one and not the worst form of monopoly which enables the wealthy classes to use the means of production against the labourers whom they enslave. Of the £1,000,000,000 taken by the classes who live without labour out of a total yearly production of £1,300,000,000, the landlords who have seized our soil, and shut us out from its enjoyment, absorb little more than £60,000,000 as their direct share. The few thousand persons who own the National Debt, saddled upon the community by a landlord Parliament, exact £28,000,000 yearly from the labour of their countrymen for nothing; the shareholders who have been allowed to lay hands upon our great railway communications take a still larger sum. Above all, the active capitalist class, the loan-mongers, the farmers, the mine-exploiters, the contractors, the middle-men, the factory-lords—these, the modern slave-drivers, these are they who, through their money, machinery, capital, and credit turn every advance in human knowledge, every further improvement in human dexterity, into an engine for accumulating wealth out of other men's labour, and for exacting more and yet more surplus value out of the wage-slaves whom they employ. So long as the means of production, either of raw materials or of manufactured goods are the monopoly of a class, so long must the labourers on the farm, in the mine or in the factory sell themselves for a bare subsistence wage. As land must in future be a national possession, so must the other means of producing and distributing wealth. The creation of wealth is already a social business, where each is forced to co-operate with his neighbour; it is high time that exchange of the produce should be social too, and removed from the control of individual greed and individual profit.

As stepping-stones to a happier period, we urge for immediate adoption:—

The COMPULSORY CONSTRUCTION of healthy artisans' and agricultural labourers' dwellings in proportion to the population, such dwellings to be let at rents to cover the cost of construction and maintenance alone.

FREE COMPULSORY EDUCATION for all classes, together with the provision of at least one wholesome meal a day in each school.

EIGHT HOURS or less to be the normal WORKING DAY in all trades.

CUMULATIVE TAXATION upon all incomes above a fixed minimum not exceeding £300 a year.

STATE APPROPRIATION OF RAILWAYS, with or without compensation.

The establishment of NATIONAL BANKS, which shall absorb all private institutions that derive a profit from operations in money or credit.

RAPID EXTINCTION of the NATIONAL DEBT.

NATIONALISATION OF THE LAND, and organisation of agricultural and industrial armies under State control on co-operative principles.

By these measures a healthy, independent, and thoroughly educated people will steadily grow up around us, ready to abandon that baneful competition for starvation wages which ruins our present workers, ready to organise the labour of each for the benefit of all, determined, too, to take control finally of the entire social and political machinery of a State in which class distinctions and class privileges shall cease to be.

Do any say we attack private property? We deny it. We attack only that private property for a few thousand loiterers and slave-drivers, which renders all property in the fruits of their own labour impossible for millions. We challenge that private property which renders poverty at once a necessity and a crime.

Fellow-Citizens, we appeal to every man and woman among you who is weary of this miserable huckster's society, where poverty and prostitution, fraud and adulteration, swindling and jobbery, luxury and debauchery reign supreme, we appeal to you to work with us in a never-ceasing effort to secure a happier lot for our people and their children, and to hold up a high ideal of national greatness for those who come after. Such an ideal of true greatness and glory, needs but intelligence, enthusiasm, and combination, to make it a reality even in our own day. We, at least, will never falter. We stretch out our hands for help, co-operation, and encouragement, to all creeds and all nationalities, ready ourselves to render assistance in every struggle against class injustice and individual greed. The land of England is no mean heritage; there is enough and to spare for all; with the powers mankind now possess wealth may easily be made as plentiful as water at the expense of trifling toil. But to-day the worn-out wage-slaves of our boasted civilisation look hopelessly at the wealth which they have created to be devoured only by the rich and their hangers-on. To the abject poor patriotism is but a mockery, all talk of happiness, of beauty, of morality, is a sneer. We call, then, upon every lover of freedom to support us in our endeavour to form a real party of the people, which shall secure a noble future for our own and other lands.

The aims and objects of the DEMOCRATIC FEDERATION are before you. Success can only be achieved by organised effort.

> EDUCATE! We shall need all our intelligence.
> AGITATE! We shall need all our enthusiasm.
> ORGANISE! We shall need all our force.

*EDUCATE! AGITATE! ORGANISE!*

# 2

# "THE MANIFESTO OF THE *SOCIALIST LEAGUE*", *COMMONWEAL*, FEBRUARY 1885, 1–2.

[A positive view of the SDF might stress how many socialists passed through its ranks and acquired a political training there. A negative view would see these same socialists as having been driven from the organisation by the autocratic leadership of Hyndman and those closest to him. Whichever view one takes, the SDF's history was one of numerous defections both individual and collective.

The Socialist League breakaway was both the earliest and the most important of these. In part this was clearly an issue of personalities, and a first pronouncement issued by the defectors made a good deal of arbitrary rule and shifty leadership on the one hand and fairness and fraternal openness on the other. Nevertheless, when in February 1885 the League set out its objects in its new monthly paper the *Commonweal*, there were clearly also important issues of principle at stake. The manifesto's rejection of modern bourgeois property-marriage and the cultural blight of commercialism suggests a more expansive view of human wellbeing and oppression, and the contempt for "mere politics" a more vigorous antiparliamentarism than Hyndman was ever likely to countenance. There is also a clear opposition between the claims of co-operation and state socialism, and the partial measures and palliatives which they represented, and the uncompromising revolutionary socialism which the Socialist League itself proclaimed. The manifesto also includes a vigorous profession of socialist internationalism, and it was over this issue that some thirty years later Hyndman would end up leading his own breakaway.

The authors of the manifesto were William Morris and Ernest Belfort Bax. For the rest of their lives they published prolifically on socialist themes, including further collaborations, and were certainly among the most gifted of Britain's fin-de-siècle cohort of socialist intellectuals. The Socialist League they had founded, on the other hand, failed to flourish. By the end of the decade it was drifting in an anarchist direction. Even Morris found this uncongenial, and as he sundered the connection in 1890, Bax meanwhile was driven back into the SDF fold. He resumed where he left off, as one of its most active publicists, and his writings are among those represented in the present collection. Bax's subsequent verdict was that personal differences had played a malign role in the rupture with the SDF, and that there had been no such issues of political or theoretical principle as could have justified such a split. Possibly even Hyndman learnt the lesson. He did not underestimate the scale of the setback, and the SDF henceforth was no more centralised, autocratic or beholden to its inner leadership than many other socialist organisations – least of all excluding the ILP.]

Fellow Citizens,

We come before you as a body advocating the principles of Revolutionary International Socialism; that is, we seek a change in the basis of Society – a change which would destroy the distinctions of classes and nationalities.

As the civilised world is at present constituted, there are two classes of Society – the one possessing wealth and the instruments of its production, the other producing wealth by means of those instruments but only by the leave and for the use of the possessing classes.

These two classes are necessarily in antagonism to one another. The possessing class, or non-producers, can only live as a class on the unpaid labour of the producers – the more unpaid labour they can wring out of them, the richer they will be; therefore the producing class – the workers – are driven to strive to better themselves at the expense of the possessing class, and the conflict between the two is ceaseless. Sometimes it takes the form of open rebellion, sometimes of strikes, sometimes of mere widespread mendicancy and crime; but it is always going on in one form or other, though it may not always be obvious to the thoughtless looker-on.

We have spoken of unpaid labour: it is necessary to explain what that means. The sole possession of the producing class is the power of labour inherent in their bodies; but since, as we have already said, the richer classes possess all the instruments of labour, that is, the land, capital, and machinery, the producers or workers are forced to sell their sole possession, the power of labour, on such terms as the possessing class will grant them.

These terms are, that after they have produced enough to keep them in working order, and enable them to beget children to take their places when they are worn out, the surplus of their products shall belong to the possessors of property, which bargain is based on the fact that every man working in a civilised community can produce more than he needs for his own sustenance.

This relation of the possessing class to the working class is the essential basis of the system of producing for a profit, on which our modern Society is founded. The way in which it works is as follows. The manufacturer produces to sell at a profit to the broker or factor, who in his turn makes a profit out of his dealings with the merchant, who again sells for a profit to the retailer, who must make his profit out of the general public, aided by various degrees of fraud and adulteration and the ignorance of the value and quality of goods to which this system has reduced the consumer.

The profit-grinding system is maintained by competition, or veiled war, not only between the conflicting classes, but also within the classes themselves: there is always war among the workers for bare subsistence, and among their masters, the employers and middle-men, for the share of the profit wrung out of the workers; lastly, there is competition always, and sometimes open war, among the nations of the civilised world for their share of the world-market. For now, indeed, all the rivalries of nations have been reduced to this one – a degraded struggle for their share of the spoils of barbarous countries to be used at home for the purpose of increasing the riches of the rich and the poverty of the poor.

For, owing to the fact that goods are made primarily to sell, and only secondarily for use, labour is wasted on all hands; since the pursuit of profit compels the manufacturer competing with his fellows to force his wares on the markets by means of their cheapness, whether there is any real demand for them or not. In the words of the Communist manifesto of 1847:-

> "Cheap goods are the artillery for battering down Chinese walls and for overcoming the obstinate hatred entertained against foreigners by semi-civilised nations: under penalty of ruin the Bourgeoisie compel by competition the universal adoption of their system of production; they force all nations to accept what is called civilisation – to become Bourgeois – and thus the middle-class shapes the world after its own image."

Moreover, the whole method of distribution under this system is full of waste; for it employs whole armies of clerks, travellers, shopmen, advertisers, and what not, merely for the sake of shifting money from one person's pocket to another's; and this waste in production and waste in distribution, added to the maintenance of the useless lives of the possessing and non-producing class, must all be paid for out of the products of the workers, and is a ceaseless burden on their lives.

Therefore the necessary results of this so-called civilisation are only too obvious in the lives of its slaves, the working-class – in the anxiety and want of leisure amidst which they toil, in the squalor and wretchedness of those parts of our great towns where they dwell; in the degradation of their bodies, their wretched health, and the shortness of their lives; in the terrible brutality so common among them, and which is indeed but the reflection of the cynical selfishness found among the well-to-do classes, a brutality as hideous as the other; and lastly, in the crowd of criminals who are as much manufactures of our commercial system as the cheap and nasty wares which are made at once for the consumption and the enslavement of the poor.

What remedy, then, do we propose for this failure of our civilisation, which is now admitted by almost all thoughtful people?

We have already shown that the workers, although they produce all the wealth of society, have no control over its production or distribution: the *people*, who are the only really organic part of society, are treated as a mere appendage to capital – as a part of its machinery. This must be altered from the foundation: the land, the capital, the machinery, factories, workshops, stores, means of transit, mines, banking, all means of production and distribution of wealth, must be declared and treated as the common property of all. Every man will then receive the full value of his labour, without deduction for the profit of a master, and as all will have to work, and the waste now incurred by the pursuit of profit will be at an end, the amount of labour necessary for every individual to perform in order to carry on the essential work of the world will be reduced to something like two or three hours daily; so that every one will have abundant leisure for following intellectual or other pursuits congenial to his nature.

This change in the method of production and distribution would enable every one to live decently, and free from the sordid anxieties for daily livelihood which at present weigh so heavily on the greatest part of mankind.

But, moreover, men's social and moral relations would be seriously modified by this gain of economical freedom, and by the collapse of the superstitions, moral and other, which necessarily accompany a state of economical slavery: the test of duty would now rest on the fulfilment of clear and well-defined obligations to the community rather than on the moulding of the individual character and actions to some preconceived standard outside social responsibilities.

Our modern bourgeois property-marriage, maintained as it is by its necessary complement, universal venal prostitution, would give place to kindly and human relations between the sexes.

Education freed from the trammels of commercialism on the one hand and superstition on the other, would become a reasonable drawing out of men's varied faculties in order to fit them for a life of social intercourse and happiness; for mere work would no longer be proposed as the end of life, but happiness for each and all.

Only by such fundamental changes in the life of man, only by the transformation of Civilisation into Socialism, can those miseries of the world beforementioned be amended.

As to mere politics, Absolutism, Constitutionalism, Republicanism, have all been tried in our day and under our present social system, and all have alike failed in dealing with the real evils of life.

Nor, on the other hand, will certain incomplete schemes of social reform now before the public solve the question.

Co-operation so-called – that is, competitive co-operation for profit – would merely increase the number of small joint-stock capitalists, under the mask of creating an aristocracy of labour, while it would intensify the severity of labour by its temptations to overwork.

Nationalisation of the land alone, which many earnest and sincere persons are now preaching, would be useless so long as labour was subject to the fleecing of surplus value inevitable under the Capitalist system.

No better solution would be that of State Socialism, by whatever name it may be called, whose aim it would be to make concessions to the working class while leaving the present system of capital and wages still in operation: no number of merely administrative changes, until the workers are in possession of all political power, would make any real approach to Socialism.

The Socialist League therefore aims at the realisation of complete Revolutionary Socialism, and well knows that this can never happen in any one country without the help of the workers of all civilisation. For us neither geographical boundaries, political history, race, nor creed makes rivals or enemies; for us there are no nations, but only varied masses of workers and friends, whose mutual sympathies are checked or perverted by groups of masters and fleecers whose interest it is to stir up rivalries and hatreds between the dwellers in different lands.

It is clear that for all these oppressed and cheated masses of workers and their masters a great change is preparing: the dominant classes are uneasy, anxious, touched in conscience even, as to the condition of those they govern; the markets of the world are being competed for with an eagerness never before known; everything points to the fact that the great commercial system is becoming unmanageable, and is slipping from the grasp of its present rulers.

The one change possible out of all this is Socialism. As chattel-slavery passed into serfdom, and serfdom into the so-called free-labour system, so most surely will this latter pass into social order.

To the realisation of this change the Socialist League addresses itself with all earnestness. As a means thereto it will do all in its power towards the education of the people in the principles of this great cause, and will strive to organise those who will accept this education, so that when the crisis comes, which the march of events is preparing there may be a body of men ready to step into their due places and deal with and direct the irresistible movement.

Close fellowship with each other, and steady purpose for the advancement of the Cause, will naturally bring about the organisation and discipline amongst ourselves absolutely necessary to success; but we shall look to it that there shall be no distinctions of rank or dignity amongst us to give opportunities for the selfish ambition of leadership which has so often injured the cause of the workers. We are working *for* equality and brotherhood for all the world, and it is only *through* equality and brotherhood that we can make our work effective.

Let us all strive, then, towards this end of realising the change towards social order, the only cause worthy the attention of the workers of all that are proffered to them: let us work in that cause patiently, yet hopefully, and not shrink from making sacrifices to it. Industry in learning its principles, industry in teaching them, are most necessary to our progress; but to these we must add, if we wish to avoid speedy failure, frankness and fraternal trust in each other, and single-hearted devotion to the religion of Socialism, the only religion which the Socialist League professes.

# 3

# "ANARCHISM", *JUSTICE*, 8, 22, 29 NOVEMBER AND 6 DECEMBER 1884.

## *Charlotte Wilson*

[When he moved to London in the mid-1890s, the anarcho-syndicalist Rudolf Rocker was struck by the degree of toleration which Britain's different socialist groupings appeared to show each other (Kinna 2000, 93). Rocker noted the contrast with his native Germany, and the relatively porous and pluralistic nature of the British left would impress itself on outside observers for many years to come. Even so, there was no period in which dividing lines counted for so little as in the earliest days of the modern socialist movement. Charlotte Wilson (1854–1944) had arguably a better claim than Joseph Lane (Chapter 11, this volume) to have produced "the first English Anarchist home grown pronouncement" (Quail 1978, ch. 5). If this belongs squarely within the present collection, it is because she published it while moving freely both within and across Britain's emerging socialist networks.

Her name is more familiar in a Fabian Society context than a Marxist one. In December 1884, Wilson was one of five elected members of the society's first full executive committee. She retained her place until 1887 and the previous year had compiled the fourth of the Fabian tracts entitled *What Socialism Is*. This included a summary view of collectivism extracted from the German Marxist Bebel (Friedrich Engels having declined) and one of anarchism which Wilson provided on behalf of unidentified "London Anarchists" (Walter 2002). Nevertheless, in 1884 Wilson had also joined the SDF, and it was in *Justice* that she published her first exposition of anarchist principles deriving from a public lecture.

Using the anonymous by-line "An English anarchist", she made no particular claim to originality. Privately she described the lecture as "simply an attempt to summarise in English dress the views of a party which exists in every country in Europe, and counts many hundreds of thousands of adherents" (Walter 2002, 222). In defining these views there was arguably no such authority to turn to as the Marxist might to Engels or Bebel. Wilson cites the anarchist founding fathers Proudhon and Bakunin. Also mentioned are the Italian republican nationalist Mazzini and the American poet Walt Whitman, both names familiar in socialist circles. If there was among the living anarchists an oracular figure to compare with the Marxists', it was the Russian Peter Kropotkin (1842–1921). Among the defendants at the Lyon trial of anarchists in 1883, it was probably Kropotkin who drafted the "Declaration of the Forty-Seven" from which Wilson adopts her opening definition of anarchism. Following his release from prison in 1886, Kropotkin would settle in Britain and for a time he and Wilson worked in close association.

Like Kropotkin, Wilson is often remembered as an anarchist communist. There are also strands in her presentation that seem far closer to anarcho-liberalism. Like his Fabian contemporaries, Kropotkin was much influenced by the social theories of Herbert Spencer while rejecting the hyper-individualism and market fetishism that Spencer derived from them (Adams 2016). Like Kropotkin, Wilson also invokes the force of socialised production and public opinion. Unlike him, she further invokes a competitive ethos that seems very different from Kropotkin's ideas of mutual aid. It is not only Spencer whom she cites but the economic historian Arnold Toynbee (1852–1883). In his *Lectures on the Industrial Revolution in England* (1884), Toynbee had differentiated between competition in production and distribution, maintaining (as does Wilson) that the former but not the latter was allowable and socially beneficent. Few other contributors to *Justice* (or to the *Fabian News*) would have described their theory as one of "*laissez faire*, modified and extended to meet the needs of the future, and avoid the injustice of the past".

In his *Socialism in England* (1890, 56) Sidney Webb described Wilson and Kropotkin as anarchism's principal exponents in Britain. While included in Webb's survey, anarchism had by this time begun to move in distinct political channels with its own distinct political identity. On the one hand, Wilson, had a large hand in launching the anarchist monthly *Freedom* in October 1886. On the other hand, the Fabian socialist Shaw, a self-appointed scourge of anarchism who had always looked dimly on Wilson, replaced her "fortunately little-known" tract with one of the same title which alone remained in print and an item on Fabian reading lists (Shaw 1892, 3; see Chapter 16, volume 3). Even so, the tolerance observed by Rocker was never fully relinquished, while Wilson herself followed the logic of the co-operative principle rather than *laissez-faire*. Remaining a Fabian society member, after a period of seeming inactivity she resumed a leading role within it as the founder in 1907 of the Fabian Women's Group.]

The word Anarchism is open to such grievous misconstruction from English readers, who associate it with mere confusion, or, still more unfortunately, with acts of personal, violence and revenge, that, in the absence of any more competent co-religionist at liberty for the moment to undertake the task, I would crave your permission to explain what our creed really is and especially its bearing on social reconstruction.

Anarchy, as your readers are aware, means simply "without a ruler" or "chief magistrate." Anarchist, therefore, is the name assumed by a certain school of Socialists, who, in the words of the Declaration of the Forty-Seven at Lyons, believe that "the time has come to teach the people to do without government," as well as for teaching them the advantages of common property. They believe, that in the present stage of progress, social union can only be stable when it is based upon absolute economic equality, and perfect individual freedom. They further believe that the rottenness and injustice of the present constitution of society is reaching a climax, and that a revolution is inevitable, which shall sweep away privilege, monopoly and authority, with the laws and institutions which support them, and set free the constructive energies of the new social ideal, already growing up within the outworn formulas of a past phase of civilisation.

Their conception of the mission of revolution as purely destructive, leads Anarchists to face the query of the unknown future less in the form of—What scheme have we to substitute for the *status quo*? than—After the annihilation of the oppressive institutions of the present, what social forces and social conditions will remain, and how are they likely to be modified and developed?

It is hardly needful to enquire, as some cavillers are fond of doing, what would happen if civilised men ceased to be social animals and existed each for himself alone. We do not live together in societies and mutually yield and accomodate ourselves to one another so as to make a common existence possible, because we are coerced to do so by certain laws and institutions. We are drawn together by our social instincts, and moulded into such harmony as we have at present attained, by the perpetual action and reaction of the influence we exert over each other, and by our inherited and acquired habits, sympathies, and beliefs. The Revolution, in breaking up the stereotyped forms into which some of these social instincts and beliefs have crystallised, can, in no sense, destroy the social instincts themselves.

Since the ordered and systematised society of mediæval Europe was dissolved by Individualism, these social instincts have made themselves most powerfully felt in the growth of two vast and ever increasing forces, *i.e.,* Socialised Production and Public Opinion. Both are the direct outcome of the influence of personal freedom, and the energy of individual initiative upon the action of society. Both are amongst the realities, which Revolution directed against shams and hypocrisy, will leave unscathed.

The present highly socialised system of production on a large scale, with its endless division and sub-division of labour, its machinery, its concentrated masses of human "hands," and its complex industrial relations, has taught men the enormously increased command over the forces of nature, which they may obtain by co-operating for existence. It is, moreover, already practically a system whereby all workers labour for society as a whole, and, in return, supply their needs from the general stock of finished products. When the individual monopoly in land and capital, which prevents the workers, firstly, from directing their own labour and, secondly, from adequately supplying their wants, is destroyed the end of social reconstruction must be to enable them to do both as simply and effectually as possible. Will free co-operation and free contract enable the workers to carry on production on a scale adequate to their needs, if they retain the necessary instruments in their own hands, without any State or Communal organisation and direction to take the place of monopolists, masters and organisers? We believe that they will. For a radical change must have come over opinion as to the nature of property and public duty before the Revolution can succeed. Proudhon's famous dictum, "Property is theft," is the key to the equally famous enigma proposed to Socialists by St. Simon, when he wrote "From each according to his capacity, to each according to his needs." When the workers clearly understand that in taking possession of railways and ships, mines and fields, farm buildings and factories, raw material and machinery, and all else they need for their labour, they are claiming the right to use freely for the benefit of society, what social labour has created, or utilised in the past, and that, in return for their work, they have a just right to take from the finished product whatever they personally require, the difficulty will be solved and obstacles in the shape of necessary changes in the detailed working of the system of production and its relation to consumption, will vanish before the ingenuity of the myriad minds vitally concerned in overcoming them. But until they do realise, that, as long as land and capital are unappropriated, the workers are free, and that, when these have a master, the workers also are slaves, no lasting and effectual improvement can be wrought in their condition. The fatal passion of acquisitiveness has got such hold upon men's minds, that masterless things appear now to many of them as monstrous an anomaly as masterless men did to the country justices of Queen Elizabeth. They devise all sorts of elaborate schemes for putting the common property of the people in trust, and appointing administrators to direct its application—a masterful sort of servants, likely to become worse tyrants than the old ones. We Anarchists, who desire neither to rule nor to serve, prefer to trust to the reason of the workers, enlightened by their bitter experience of past slavery.

Anarchism proposes, therefore,—1. That the usufruct of instruments of production—land included—should be free to all workers, or groups of workers. 2. That the workers should group themselves, and arrange their work as their reason and inclination prompt (including those who manage the means of communication). 3. That the necessary connections between the various industries and branches of trade, should be managed on the same voluntary principle, and that the task of furnishing intelligence as to the relations of production and consumption (by means, for instance, of the public press, special trade journals, offices for information, &c.), should be left to brain workers, whose taste leads them to make industry a special duty. 4. That finished goods should be massed in large stores and markets, and that offices for facilitating the mutual convenience of producers and consumers (as for example, house builders and carpenters, and house seekers) should be opened in convenient centres. 5. That each individual should supply his needs therefrom as his self-knowledge prompts.

This is the theory of *laissez faire,* modified and extended to meet the needs of the future, and avoid the injustice of the past. It implies that the majority of men are capable of acting with some approximation to effectiveness, if left free to do so, and is based on the assumption that the individual is the best judge of his own capabilities, and, further, that self-interest, intelligently followed, tends to promote the general economic well-being of the community. It differs from the old system in placing self-interest on the side of just distribution, by the destruction of private property in the means of production, and thus does much to neutralise the dangers of Society from natures whose selfishness is their strongest sentiment. It also allows free play to those social sympathies, the influence of which in determining conduct it was one of the chief mistakes of the orthodox economists to ignore. It assumes that just and generous economic relations are for the interest of the individual, and that he is capable of being taught so, if not by science and the teaching of the moralist, then by the stern lessons of experience. Has not the process of instruction already begun?

The economic theory of Anarchism puts an end to no competition but that for a share of the produce. It affords facilities for the perpetual change and variation on which progress depends. It leaves untouched the influence of emulation, and puts no check upon individual initiative and individual enterprise, upon the friction of opposing methods and ideas, the stimulating irritation produced by contrasted idiosyncrasies and tastes, and the energy inspired by single-handed struggle with difficulty. It gives free scope to the fresh interest, the exercise of originality, and the artist's delight in producing, which make work a pleasure, when, and when only, it is the result of free, spontaneous impulse. But Anarchism unites with the dignity of self-directed labour, the joy of known and recognised endeavour in a common cause, the thrill of a conscious part in the common life, that social spirit which drudgery has driven out of our wage-slaves, even whilst their actual interdependence has increased.

"The struggle of men to outvie one another in production is beneficial to the community; their struggle over the joint produce is not," says Arnold Toynbee. It is commonly, however, asserted that it is necessary to make men work, unless some authority take its place; and we are accused of imagining that we can secure the advantages of competition without its evils, by destroying the mainspring on which its action depends. If the only motive for work is the desire for material wealth, how can the immense amount of voluntary labour, and the frequent choice of the (personally) less productive kinds of labour which we actually see at the present day, be accounted for? Men work from a variety of motives—a desire for fame or honour, the love of invention, the pleasure of creating, or of merely exercising their faculties of mind and body, and giving vent to their energy, and last, but not least, they work for the gratification of doing something useful to others. These are no exceptional sentiments and desires—some of them, at all events, are visible in all children. When their cultivation becomes of paramount importance to the community it will surely not be neglected. Looking at the question from another point of view, let us ask if it is really necessary for a man of average intelligence actually himself to feel the pangs of hunger before he can realise that his labour is essential to the life of the community, and consequently to his own. We believe not. We believe that the vast majority of men are capable of understanding the necessity of work, and that therefore the pressure of public opinion will bear so heavily as to be unendurable upon the idle members of the future society; consequently a very much smaller number will be idle than now, when privileged idleness is looked upon as no disgrace.

It may be objected, that though most men may be willing to work, it does not necessarily follow that their work will be of social utility. But in the great majority of cases habit and education have prepared workmen for nothing but taking a small and definite share in a huge system of production, whether they be sufficiently intelligent to estimate the advantages of such a system or no. When, after the Revolution, existing wealth is consumed, and the workers find themselves face to face with the imperative necessity of working to supply their needs, the method of working to which they will turn will naturally be that to which they are accustomed. It is equally certain, however, that, when they find themselves their own masters, they will modify the old system to suit their convenience in a variety of ways, *e. g.*, short hours for each, supplemented by a succession of shifts to save cost of production, remodelled workshops, factories, &c., with regard to comfort and safety; discontinuance of the manufacture of useless luxuries; improvement of the quality of articles of universal utility; the application of machinery to saving labour of the disagreeable sort (as this sort of work will probably, at first, be left to the most intelligent of the community, the development of invention in this directiou is likely to be very rapid), and such other changes as common sense is likely to suggest to free men.

One other objection must be glanced at. Co-operation, it may be urged, has not hitherto been eminently successful. Is not that amply accounted for by the extent to which it has been hampered by the conditions and prejudices of existing society with regard to (*a*) capital (*b*) remuneration? The first is obvious; not so the second. Co-operative societies in professing to abandon competition amongst themselves for the fruits of their joint labour, still retain the fallacious belief that in the present system of production it is possible to award to each worker the exact proportional social value of his labour. Amid endless jealousies and heart-burnings they attempt to substitute an arbitrary division according to some fixed rule or theory of utility for competition. This root of bitterness is destroyed by the Anarchist theory of distribution.

Does Anarchism, then, it may be asked, acknowledge no *meum* or *tuum*, no personal property? In a society in which every man is free to take what he requires, it is hardly conceivable that personal necessaries and conveniences will not be appropriated, and difficult to imagine why they should not. Anarchism contemplates no hard and fast line between common and personal belongings, any such individual arrangements and mutual concessions are easily conceivable when there is plenty for all. When property is protected by no legal enactments, backed by armed force, and is unable to buy personal service, its resuscitation on such a scale as to be dangerous to society is little to be dreaded. The amount appropriated by each individual, and the manner of his appropriation, must be left to his own conscience, and the pressure exercised upon him by the moral sense and distinct interests of his neighbours.

I endeavoured in my last letter to explain the Anarchist theory of economic development and its relation to the existing system of production. It remains to consider the social and political aspects of Anarchism and its bearing upon present tendencies and ideas.

It passes as a truism, that public opinion—the expression of the collective moral sense—is the real sovereign of to-day. Its sanction has replaced the old religious sanctions as a moral restraint. Law is supposed but to give voice to its mandates, and deliberative assemblies to be its humble servants. It is admitted, that the voice is muffled and unintelligible, and that the servants are treacherous and remarkably ineffective; but it is supposed that Democracy can change all that by judicious lopping and enlargement. In that supposition we Anarchists do not agree. We believe—not only what all thinkers already admit, that a large proportion of the misery of mankind is attributable to bad Government—but that Government is in itself essentially bad, a clumsy makeshift for the rule of each man by his own reason and conscience, which, in the present stage of civilisation, has served its turn.

The idea of government sprang in barbarous times from the authority of the leader in war, and the patriarchal rule of the head of the family; it grew up in the superstition born of the fears of an ignorant age; and on the brute instincts and childishness, the ignorance and fears of mankind it has prospered ever since, until progress began slowly and surely to cut away the ground under its feet.

Whilst government was viewed as a divinely appointed arbiter in the affairs of the uninspired commonalty, it was naturally deemed its duty to watch over its subjects in all their relations, and provide, not only for their protection from all force or fraud but its own, but for their eternal welfare. But now that government and law are looked on as mere conveniences, forms destitute of sanctity, and possessing no authority but such as the aggregate of the nation are pleased to allow, it may be worth considering, if the collective life of the community cannot find expression in some fashion less costly in time, wealth, and human freedom. The future of Democracy in England, as depicted by the *Pall Mall Gazette* for August 11, is not very re-assuring to any but ambitious politicians. "The time in fact, is already upon us, when there is no vital difference between parties, only an unscrupulous scramble for place." If Liberals, however, strike out in a new direction, and accept the policy of opposition to the powers of Parliament, vindicated by Mr. Herbert Spencer, they can hardly fail to reduce the authority of representative government to so thin a semblance, that true Liberty will be plainly visible behind it, and Liberalism be forced by a logical necessity into Anarchism. For representation—the middle-class panacea for all ills, now on its trial—recognises in theory the right of each individual to govern himself, whilst at the same moment it forces him to delegate that right to a representative, and, in return, bestows the privilege of a practical claim to tyrannise over every one else. The freedom of the collectivity to crush the individual is not, however, true Liberty in the eyes of Anarchists. It is one of those shams, which the Revolution is to destroy.

We believe, opinion to be the real and inevitable expression of collective existence in civilized communities, and that its natural outlets in the public press, in literature and art, in societies, meetings, voluntary combinations of all sorts, and social intercourse are amply sufficient to enable it to act as a binding and corrective force in a society relieved from privileges and private property. Even now it is the strongest deterrent from crime; even now its punishment is the bitterest, its reward the highest, and its rule of conduct the most absolute for the average mortal. Yet, unfortunately, its sense of right and wrong is continually blunted and falsified by the action of the authorised exponent of justice. At the present day law is supposed in the abstract to represent the moral sense of the community as against its immoral members. Practically it cannot do so. Public morality is continually fluctuating and, by changing as fast as its want of dignity will admit, law cannot keep up with it and only succeeds in stereotyping the mistakes from which opinion is just shaking itself free, and fitting old precedents upon new conditions, where naturally they look absurd, and do mischief. Being framed to suit a variety of cases, no two of which are alike, it is actually unjust in every one, moreover, becomes so complicated, that after all the efforts of a specially trained class to expound it, its awards are uncertain and mysterious to all concerned. The modes of punishment are necessarily brutal and degrading, not only to those who suffer, but to those who inflict them, and its attempts to enforce contracts and settle disputes, cause at least as much suffering as they avert. Law stands, and—from what experts say of the difficulties of reform—must ever stand, hopelessly in the way of morality, rendering a higher conception of it impossible to the mass of mankind, and consequently to the public opinion, which represents them.

When the collective moral sense is relieved of the incubus of law, it may still be unjust in many instances, but its injustice will take a less permanent form and one more capable of rectification, whereas its sense of justice may be perpetually widened and increased by the growth of knowledge and human sympathy. Certainly, judging from its present influence, it will be strong enough to serve as a restraint upon those individuals, who refuse to respect the rights of others. But when Society has ceased deliberately to condemn certain of its members to infamy and despair from their birth, there are both physical and moral grounds for the belief that the "criminal classes" will cease to exist Crime will become sufficiently rare to give the mass of the population courage to face the fact that moral depravity, like madness, is a terrible affliction, a disease to be carefully treated and remedied, not punished and augmented by ill-treatment. We know this now, but we are too cowardly or too Pharisaical to admit it.

Prevention, however, is better than cure, and the surest mode of securing virtuous citizens, as well as healthy public opinion, is by a sound system of education. The rough discipline of the Revolution will clear the air of many prejudices, and serve to raise men's minds to a higher conception of justice and of duty, but it is on the training of children that the future of society mainly depends. I wish I could quote the fine passages in which Michael Bakounine outlines the Anarchist theory of education in his "Dieu et l'Etat," but that would be trespassing too far upon your space. Suffice it to say, that Anarchism considers that the one end and aim of education is to fit children for freedom. Therefore it teaches, firstly, that intellectual training should be scientific, cultivating the reason and leading it to understand and recognise the immutability of the laws of nature, and to conform to them in all things, taking knowledge of them for rule and guide in place of the arbitrary enactments of men; and, secondly, that moral training, starting with the necessary absolute authority, should proceed by the gradual removal of restraints, and by the inculcation of personal dignity and responsibility, respect for others, and the worship of truth and justice for their own sake, to form free men and women filled with reverence and love for the freedom of their fellows. This view of the subject is familiar also to readers of Mr. Herbert Spencer.

The creed of Anarchism is the cultus of Liberty, not for itself, but for what it renders possible. Authority, as exercised by men over their fellows, it holds accursed, depraving those who rule and those who submit, and blocking the path of human progress. Liberty indeed is not all, but it is the foundation of all that is good and noble, it is essential to that many-sided advance of man's nature, expanding in numberless and ever-conflicting directions, which Walt Whitman likens to the weather, where "an infinite number of currents and forces, and contributions and temperatures, and cross purposes, whose ceaseless play of counterpart upon counterpart brings constant restoration and vitality." For is not the tendency of all rules and organisations to stiffen into set shapes, destitute of life and meaning, one of the chief causes of social deterioration?

Viewed in relation to the thought waves of our times, the strength of Anarchism seems to us to lie in its full recognition and acceptance of two lines of thought, which, though their respective champions delight to pose them as in hopeless conflict, are uniting to bring about the social revolution, *i.e.,* Individualism and Socialism. It ignores neither the splendid triumphs of Individualism in thought and action, nor the need for brotherly association, which Mazzini considered years ago as the primary necessity of modern Europe; but it holds that the longing for freedom, and the growing sense of the dependence of each on all, the responsibility of all for each, are advancing side by side, and that one cannot be sacrificed to the other without provoking a violent re-action. Therefore do Anarchists oppose all measures which tend to increase the power and influence of governments, even if their immediate result seem to be an improvement in the condition of the people. Anarchism is a new faith, as yet imperfectly formulated, and it has been met in the society of privilege with such bitter persecution, that it has retorted with the violence of despair. Contemned, hunted down, reviled, calumniated even in death, the existence of an Anarchist on the Continent at this moment is scarcely more endurable than that of a Christian in the days of the Roman Empire, victim like himself of the hatred of the world for an enthusiasm of humanity beyond its comprehension. But from other Socialists at least, Anarchists should meet with the fair recognition and justice, which you, Sir, have shown in allowing the publication of these letters.

# 4

# "WHY NOT?", *JUSTICE*, 12 APRIL 1884.

## *William Morris*

[Like Bernard Shaw among the Fabians, William Morris (1834–1896) had a readership and public profile far exceeding that of his peers and rivals within the socialist movement. To a wider public he remains best-known as the poet and designer who so largely inspired the arts-and-crafts movement of the late nineteenth century. Politically, he was claimed by all manner of supposed legatees, from the ethical socialists of the ILP to anarchists, communists and even a strand of British fascism. In their different ways, it was probably the anarchists and communists who had the strongest claims. Reacting against Hyndman's "arbitrary rule", Morris was to lead the breakaway Socialist League which with its monthly paper *Commonweal* would henceforth provide the principal vehicle for his political views. Nevertheless, after joining the Democratic Federation in 1883 Morris had at first worked closely with Hyndman and it was under their joint authorship that it issued *A Summary of the Principles of Socialism* on which the imprint of Morris's medievalism and hatred of ugliness and brutality was strongly marked.

Deeply influenced by Ruskin and Carlyle, Morris's socialism was a wholesale rejection of the prevailing notions of utilitarianism and political economy which he also found echoed in the Fabian Society. The document reproduced is among the earliest of his very many contributions to the socialist press and indicates some of the themes that would continue to preoccupy him as a socialist. Most notably, he signals his abiding concerns with the environment, including the built environment and the workplace, and with the alienation of the human spirit through capitalist forms of production. It was characteristic of Morris to begin by referring to the Commons Preservation Society, and he continued to combine his socialism with a leading role in the Society for the Protection of Ancient Buildings. Equally characteristic, both of Morris and of the movements he helped to launch, is that he closes by invoking the religion of socialism, exactly as the founding manifesto of the Socialist League would do (Chapter 2, this volume).

In the spring and early summer of 1884, Morris was to continue pursuing similar themes in articles on "A factory as it might be". As a communist in 1955,

E.P. Thompson (1955, 760) would cite them in the same breath as Stalin and the achievements of socialist construction in the USSR. Anarchists and ethical socialists certainly had the truer claim to Morris on this score. Nevertheless, Morris's most famous socialist work *News From Nowhere* (1890–1891) combined its vision of an "epoch of rest" with a clear indication of the revolutionary means by which it would have to be attained. Morris left a hugely complex and ambiguous legacy and it is certainly true that no single strand of the socialist tradition could make exclusive claim to it (Bevir 2011, ch. 5).]

At a meeting of the Commons Preservation Society I heard it assumed by a clever speaker that our great cities, London in particular, were bound to go on increasing without any limit, and those present accepted that assumption complacently, as I think people usually do. Now under the present Capitalist system it is difficult to see anything which might stop the growth of these horrible brick encampments; its tendency is undoubtedly to depopulate the country and small towns for the advantage of the great commercial and manufacturing centres; but this evil, and it is a monstrous one, will be no longer a necessary evil when we have got rid of land monopoly, manufacturing for the profit of individuals, and the stupid waste of competitive distribution; and it seems probable that the development of electricity as a motive power will make it easier to undo the evils brought upon us by capitalist tyranny when we regain our senses and determine to live like human beings; but even if it turns out that we must still be dependent on coal and steam for force, much could still be done towards making life pleasant if universal co-operation in manufacture and distribution were to take the place of our present competitive anarchy. At the risk of being considered dreamers therefore it is important for us to try to raise our ideals of the pleasure of life; because one of the dangers which the social revolution runs is that the generation which sees the fall of Capitalism, educated as it will have been to bear the thousand miseries of our present system, will have far too low a standard of refinement and real pleasure. It is natural that men who are now beaten down by the fear of losing even their present pitiful livelihood, should be able to see nothing further ahead than relief from that terror and the grinding toil under which they are oppressed; but surely it will be a different story when the community is in possession of the machinery, factories, mines, and land, and is administering them for the benefit of the community; and when as a necessary consequence men find that the providing of the mere necessaries of life will be so far from being a burdensome task for the people that it will not give due scope to their energies. Surely when this takes place, in other words when they are free, they will refuse to allow themselves to be surrounded by ugliness, squalor and disorder either in their leisure or their working hours.

Let us, therefore, ask and answer a few questions on the conditions of manufacture, so as to put before us one branch of the pleasure of life to be looked forward to by Socialists.

Why are men huddled together in unmanageable crowds in the sweltering hells we call big towns?

For profit's sake; so that a reserve army of labour may always be ready to hand for reduction of wages under the iron law, and to supply the sudden demand of the capitalist gamblers, falsely called "organisers of labour."

Why are these crowds of competitors for subsistence wages housed in wretched shanties which would be a disgrace to the Flat-head Indians?

For profit's sake; no one surely would build such dog-hutches for their own sake: there is no insuperable difficulty in the way of lodging people in airy rooms decently decorated, in providing their lodgings not only with good public cooking and washing rooms, but also with beautiful halls for the common meal and other purposes, as in the Colleges of Oxford and Cambridge, which it would be pleasure merely to sit in.

Why should any house, or group of lodgings, arranged in flats or otherwise, be without a pleasant and ample garden, and a good play-ground?

Because profit and competition rents forbid it. Why should one third of England be so stifled and poisoned with smoke that over the greater part of Yorkshire (for instance) the general idea must be that sheep are naturally black? and why must Yorkshire and Lancashire rivers run mere filth and dye?

Profit will have it so: no one any longer pretends that it would not be easy to prevent such crimes against decent life: but the 'organisers of labour,' who might better be called 'organisers of filth,' know that it wouldn't pay; and as they are for the most part of the year safe in their country seats, or shooting—crofters' lives—in the Highlands, or yachting in the Mediterranean, they rather like the look of the smoke country for a change, as something, it is to be supposed, stimulating to their imaginations concerning—well, we must not get theological.

As to the factories themselves: why should there be scarcely room to turn round in them? Why should they be, as in the case of the weaving sheds of over-sized cotton, hot houses for rheumatism? why should they be such miserable prisons? Profit-grinding compels it, that is all: there is no other reason why there should not be ample room in them, abundant air, a minimum of noise: nay they might be beautiful after their kind, and surrounded by trees and gardens: in many cases the very necessities of manufacture might be made use of for beautifying their surroundings; as for instance in textile printing works, which require large reservoirs of water.

In such factories labour might be made, not only no burden, but even most attractive; young men and women at the time of life when pleasure is most sought after would go to their work as to a pleasure party: it is most certain that labour may be so arranged that no social relations could be more delightful than communion in hopeful work; love, friendship, family affection, might all be quickened by it; joy increased and grief lightened by it.

Where are the material means to come from for bringing this about? Fellow-workers, from the millions of surplus value wrung out of your labour by the 'organisers of filth'; screwed out of you for the use of tools and machines invented by the gathered genius of ages, for the use of your share of earth the Common Mother.

It is worth while thinking about, fellow-workers! For while theologians are disputing about the existence of a hell *elsewhere,* we are on the way to realising it *here:* and if capitalism is to endure, whatever may become of men when they *die,* they will come into hell when they are *born.* Think of that and devote yourselves to the spread of the Religion of Socialism.

# 5

# *THE MAN WITH THE RED FLAG* (LONDON: TWENTIETH CENTURY PRESS, 1886), 3–12.

*John Burns*

[The spectacle of riot in London's West End in February 1886 was possibly the greatest of the demonstrative actions that brought the promise and threat of socialism to the notice of a middle-class public. Just three months earlier, the SDF in its first electoral test had gained pitiful votes in two London constituencies. Already badly damaged by the defection of the Socialist League, its reputation was then still further tarnished by the revelation of its cheerful acceptance of "Tory gold". The unemployed movements of the capital were to allow it at least a partial restoration of credibility. As these movements began to stir, the protectionist Fair Trade League had endeavoured to place itself at their head and had met some success in catching the public eye. When the League advertised a demonstration in Trafalgar Square, the SDF therefore organised a counter-demonstration; and when this then headed off in the direction of Hyde Park, there followed scenes in Pall Mall and Piccadilly that seemed like a foretaste of the coming class war.

The document presented includes an account of these events by one of the most prominent participants. John Burns (1858–1943) was an engineer by trade whose working-class credentials stood out sharply among the early leaders of the SDF. Following the February events, Burns was one of four SDF speakers prosecuted on ill-defined charges of sedition. The others included Hyndman and the volatile H.H. Champion, transmitter of Tory gold, as well as the working-class radical J.E. Williams. Nevertheless, it was Burns who seized the moment. A compelling public speaker, he had been the SDF's one relative success in the recent election in gaining nearly six hundred votes in East Nottingham. In the time-honoured fashion of radical movements, he saw his moment in the dock as the perfect opportunity to publicise the ideals that had moved him, and the published extracts from his speech would reach a wide public.

Burns's contempt for the Fair Trade League as Tory stooges is undisguised. He is as sceptical of the Tory democracy of Randolph Churchill and the radical

Liberalism of Joseph Chamberlain as he is of the returning Liberal premier Gladstone. He points to the hypocrisy of those denouncing sedition while being prepared to use violent means to prevent Irish Home Rule. The pamphlet is of special interest in demonstrating Burns's ambivalence in respect of political violence. In disclaiming responsibility for the window-breaking he maintains that it had no role in effecting a change in the system of society "except perhaps as a warning". Nevertheless, he clearly believes it an effective warning, and in the momentary panic of the privileged that followed the riots this was understandable.

Burns would break with the socialists by the end of the decade and go on to enjoy high office as a Liberal. Cynics regarding his motives – and there were many – might single out the claim he makes here that the socialists were the true guardians of public order in seeking to remove the causes of discontent. In defending himself from the dock, one can certainly believe that Burns slurred over the more combative language that he had actually used (Burgess 1911, 51–56). Nevertheless, the deployment of such language and practices to achieve less-than-revolutionary ends was not just some personal idiosyncrasy. It was with just this note of ambivalence that Hyndman in 1881 had warned of the "dawn of a revolutionary epoch" should justified democratic demands remain unattended to. In brandishing violence far more than they actually used it, socialists in their militant phases thus reproduced some of the ambiguities that had long since featured in the history of radical social movements.]

My Lord, and Gentlemen of the Jury: As an unemployed worker, and a Social-Democrat, I am placed in a somewhat peculiar position in this case. I expected when I was of the age of 16 or 17 that, at some time of my life, I should be brought face to face with the authorities for vindicating the class to which I belong. I have from my earliest infancy been in contact with poverty of the worst possible description. I may tell you, my lord, that I went to work in a factory at the early age of ten years, and toiled there until five months ago, when I left my workshop to stand as Parliamentary Candidate for the Western Division of Nottingham. I have done everything I could, in a peaceful manner, to call the attention of the authorities to the frightful amount of poverty and degradation existing among the working class. I have done my best as an artisan to educate my unskilled fellow-workmen, to point out to them that they should educate themselves and organise themselves in such a manner that by peaceful demands a better state of things should be brought about. Our motives have been aspersed by journalists, who are paid to traduce us. We have been charged with being notoriety-hunters, with being men anxious for our own advancement and self-interest.

That is not the case. Since I was 16 years of age I have done everything in my power to benefit the workers in a straightforward way. I have deprived myself, as many of my class have done, of hundreds of meals on purpose to buy books and papers to see if we could not possibly by peaceful consultation, by deliberate and calm organisation, do that which I am inclined to think the middle and upper classes by their neglect, apathy and indifference, will compel artisans to do otherwise than peacefully. I plead "Not Guilty," my lord, to the charge of sedition, particularly to the charge of seditious conspiracy.

## I PLEAD NOT GUILTY, not to deny the words I used on February 8th,

or any other words I ever used, but simply because the language which I used on that occasion had no guilt or any sedition in it. I expressed the virtuous indignation against misery and injustice of a man who from his earliest infancy up to the present moment has struggled and worked hard to support his wife and an aged mother, both of whom would instantly repudiate me if I were to go back from one single statement that I made on February 8th. But I am here to repudiate statements made by other men. I object to being saddled with speeches such as the "bread and lead" phrase, and the "powder and shot" interjections made by men in the crowd at Hyde Park. I do object to words spoken and actions done—not by myself but by men whom I tried to control.

As there has been much misapprehension in the mind of the public, I would briefly refer to the motives which prompted me to go to Trafalgar Square and to the Holborn Town Hall meeting Misapprehension, not to say misrepresentation, exists in the minds of those gentlemen who have had charge of this prosecution. I heard that there was going to be a meeting of the starving Unemployed of London in Trafalgar Square on February 8th. I heard that this meeting was convened by four of the most infamous scoundrels that ever wore boot-leather in the streets of London—four men whose antecedents were bad, who were prepared to trade on the misery of the poor provided their pockets were filled, who on the night after the meeting were ejected from public-houses in Fleet Street for drunkenness and disorderly conduct. I heard that these men were going to trade upon the poverty of the Unemployed and to advocate an economical fallacy, for puffing which they were paid. I reached the place at 1.30. I was recognised, as I am very well known to the workmen of London, by a large number of people who were then present. They called on me for a speech. I declined to speak, and I told them that when the Fair Traders arrived I would move an amendment, and that if they declined to have the amendment moved, I would hold a meeting of my own. The crowd pushed me towards the lower part of the Square, and hoisted me on to the plinth of the Nelson Monument. I then entered into a consultation with the police, I told them I had no desire to interfere with their authority, that I would use what influence I had over the crowd as a means of securing a peaceful meeting, and see that no property was damaged. Superintendent Dunlap, in the exercise of a wise discretion, allowed me to speak. I got up upon the plinth and spoke to 13,000 or 14,000 men, and I would here call attention to the fact that Superintendent Dunlap and the police frankly confessed that, prior to the balustrade meeting, what influence and control I had over the bonâ fide workmen was used in protecting public property, and not exercised against the police. Superintendent Dunlap admits that

I facilitated his duty on that occasion, and it is admitted by other witnesses that I did everything I could to control the turbulent element in the crowd, and so far from my language having a tendency to incite to riot and assault, it had directly the contrary effect.

What was the result of the first meeting at the Monument? I laid a resolution of the Social-Democratic Federation before the meeting. I pointed out that a remedy could only be found by bringing pressure to bear upon Parliament and the local authorities, as I had tried to do twelve months before, when I had to walk the streets of London for seven weeks for daring to speak as to the condition of the workers. For I was boycotted by the employers, then as I have been since I came back from Nottingham, simply because I was a Social-Democrat. I ask you to remember this. I ask you, can you wonder at a workman's language being strong? I am inclined to think that the day is not far distant when stronger language will have to be used than even that of the "Loyalist" members in the House of Commons.

Our meeting at the Nelson Column was satisfactorily conducted. Quietness and order prevailed. After speaking, I called on several whom I recognised in the crowd, and resolutions were submitted to about 20,000 persons, for by this time the crowd had considerably augmented. No damage was done. There was no conflict with the police—we avoided that, as Superintendent Dunlap admits. When the Fair Traders came, I climbed up the balustrade and acted as Chairman of that second meeting. Why? All know that the Fair Traders, Messrs. Peters, Kelly, Kenny, Lemon, and others, are regarded as arrant impostors by the workmen of London, and I was desirous that there should not be a physical conflict between the unemployed and those honest but misguided men who are the dupes of these bogus representatives. I decided upon giving them something better for their purpose than listening to the exploded nostrums of the Tory Party or of others. The day of these mercenaries, I am pleased to say, is now over. The penalty for betraying the workers, I hope, will be heavy enough to deter any man from selling their cause, as it has many times been sold. We had a remarkably good meeting; in fact, we completely stole the audience of the Fair Traders, much to the delight of the Unemployed who were there. I made a speech which Mr. Burleigh says would make about three columns in length—in fact, I almost reiterated the speech that I made on the plinth of the Nelson Monument. I pointed out the steps that were necessary for a peaceful solution of the difficulties which the industrial classes have to encounter, and which press so hardly upon the lower classes of society—as they are falsely called. I pointed out how the unequal incidence of taxation pressed upon the shopkeepers and others, and how the capitalists and the rich only were able to tide over the difficulties. My speech was substantially what the witnesses have said—that laws should be passed that the Government should provide work for skilled and unskilled labourers; that the principles of Socialism recognised to-day by the State in regard to sewage farms and waterworks, railways, post-offices and telegraphs, should be further extended; and that in so far as they were extended, it would conduce to the well-being of the community, of which the Unemployed in Trafalgar Square are a more important part than the club loungers think they are. Is it revolution to demand that the workers should be allowed to live like men? Was it sedition for a man to ask his brothers to combine? If so, sedition of that kind was going to be very popular in the near future.

The meeting passed off satisfactorily. I found that the crowd were becoming somewhat turbulent in consequence of the Fair Traders' platforms being upset, and I thought it my duty to listen to the suggestion which was made to me from many quarters that we should proceed in procession through the West End to Hyde Park. And I would call the Attorney-General's attention to this significant fact, supported by the whole of the evidence—and that is that no damage was done by the procession from the time we left Trafalgar Square until we reached the Carlton Club. And what *was* the initial cause of the damage being done? Probably you, gentlemen, have not been in so many demonstrations and processions as I have, but if you would consult the working classes who think on political and social subjects, and who have attended large mass meetings in Hyde Park, you would find, on investigation, that there is a class of men who make it a practice, on occasions of political demonstrations, to laugh and jeer, from their club windows, at the poverty of what they term "the great unwashed," to jeer at the misery their own greed has created, and yet at elections these very men crave votes of those who previously had received their sneers. The crowd were not in a temper to stand even mere laughing, and they were not disposed to respond to contemptuous jeers by a smile. And what was the result? Stone-throwing commenced. And that was the result of the stupid, ungentlemanly, criminal conduct of the Carlton Club members. I did my best to repress the stone-throwing, instead of inciting the crowd, believing, as I do, that window breaking, except perhaps as a warning, is useless to effect a change in our system of society based as it is upon the robbery of labour. I did everything, as the evidence proved—as you have heard said—that was in my power to conduct the procession as peacefully as possible to Hyde Park, where it was my intention to call on them to disperse. The stupidity of the members of the Carlton decided otherwise. The stone-throwing continued to Hyde Park, but not consecutively. It ceased between the Carlton and the Thatched House, at the bottom of St. James's Street, and very little damage was done between those places, as by this time I was able to exercise some influence in keeping the men quiet. That part of the route is a proof that we did exercise our influence and control in a proper direction. But at the Thatched House Club the contemptuous jeering was renewed. It was more vehement than at the Carlton; and from the Thatched House right up to St. James's Street and down Piccadilly, riot—if you define "riot" as the breaking of windows—was supreme. I was unable to check it. The fault was not mine.

We proceeded thus up St. James's Street until we reached Piccadilly. Williams and I tried our best to stop the stone-throwing, and to restrain the crowd instead of inciting it. Against this system of society I frankly confess

## I AM A REBEL, because Society has outlawed me.

I have protested against this state of society by which at present one and a half millions of our fellow-countrymen, adult males, are starving—starving because they have not work to do. I had very strong feelings upon this matter of the Unemployed, particularly on the day in question, when we were brought face to face with men who for month after month had trod the street in search of work, with men whom I knew were honest, whose only crime was that they let the idler enjoy that which the producer alone should have—not loafers and thieves—but the real Unemployed of our nation city. Talk about strong language! I contend my language was mild when you consider the usage they have received, and that the patience, under severe provocation, displayed by the workers is almost slavish and cowardly.

We reached Hyde Park. I got on the Achilles statue and called upon the workmen to discontinue the violent outrages which had taken place, as it was not by breaking windows that an intelligent reorganisation of Society could be brought about. The men agreed with me. Some hot-headed ones shouted out and asked that they might be led against the soldiers. Mr. Champion and I directed our replies in response to those suggestions. And what was the result? The crowd at the Achilles statue quietly dispersed. And we have it upon the authority of the police themselves that although some from the meeting did go into South Audley Street, and there was rioting there, it was not due to the speeches, because the damage and rioting took place contemporaneously with our speeches at the Achilles statue. It appears that the prosecution have been strangely in want of a case, or the legal gentlemen who are connected with it have been totally at a loss for one, when they waste the time of the jury in listening to a case that common sense would have dictated the rejection of.

Now what have we done? We have pursued the same course for the last five years. These are remarkable defendants who stand in this box. There must be some unusual agitation to prompt one of the idle classes like Mr. Champion, a skilled artisan like myself, an unskilled labourer like Mr. Williams, and a middle-class man like Mr. Hyndman to stand in this box for one simple cause. There must be something unusual to bring us here. We have gained nothing by this agitation; on the contrary, we have lost what material well-being we had, and we come before you not as paid agitators pecuniarily interested in creating riots, tumults, and disturbances, but men anxious to change the existing system of society to one in which men should receive the full value of their labour, in which society will be regarded as something more than a few titled non-producers who take the whole of the wealth which the useful workers alone produce. We are indicted for seditious conspiracy. If it were not so serious a charge in itself, it would be enough to raise a smile. Seditious conspiracy! Why, if there is one thing that the Whigs, Radicals, and the Tory Party accuse us of it is this—that we have brought these questions—and we are the first who have done it—into the open street! When we are again accused of conspiracy it will be when all open methods of securing redress have been tried and have failed. I can understand why the tenth count has been added to the indictment—because the jury would have to reject the nine counts unless the charge had been bolstered up against us.

It is not my intention to lay before this Court any more reasons for my conduct on this particular occasion; but if you want to remove the cause of seditious speeches you must prevent us from having to hear, as we hear to-day, of hungry, poverty-stricken men who from no fault of theirs are compelled to be out of work, who are fit subjects for revolutionary appeals. If you want to remove a seditious agitation, as it is called, you must remove, not the effect, but the cause of such agitation, by bringing about in this disorganised system of society some change, as you were told by the witness Condon, who is compelled to accept starvation wages, and who cannot in his trade get work for more than five months out of the twelve. We are not responsible for the riots; it is Society that is responsible, and instead of the Attorney-General drawing up indictments against us he should be drawing up indictments against Society, which is responsible for neglecting the means at its command. I have not one single word of regret to utter for the part I have taken in this agitation. Some of the phrases that are attributed to me in the indictment are proved to have been used by other men. And if my language was strong, the occasion demanded strong language. I say we cannot have in England, as we have to-day, five millions living on the verge of pauperism without gross discontent. I am inclined to predict that unless the Government adopt our proposals, the shadow of which they have adopted by a recent circular issued by the Local Government Board, I am inclined to think in the near future if Society does not recognise the claims of the workers to a greater share of the comforts and necessaries of life, these meetings would, by hunger and starvation, be made the rule instead of being the exception. Well-fed men never revolt. Poverty-stricken men have all to gain, and nothing to lose by riot and revolution. There is a time, I take it—and such is the present, a time of exceptional depression—when it is necessary for men, particularly for the working classes, to speak out in strong language as to the demands of their fellows; and I contend it would be immoral, cowardly, and criminal to the worst degree if I, having what little power I possess to interpret the wishes of my fellow-workers, were not to use every public occasion for ventilating the grievances of those who, through no fault of their own, are unable to ventilate them themselves. On February 8th a meeting was convened, and we put before the workers legitimate proposals; and, singular to say, that meeting has had a decided effect upon the Local Government Board. Before the riots they would not admit that there was any exceptional distress, and I am sorry to say that it seems to be characteristic of the Government and the governing classes to be influenced only by fear—at least, Mr. Gladstone, Lord Randolph Churchill and Mr. Chamberlain say that their Governments are not susceptible to reason or appeals unless the Hyde Park railings are pulled down, and the club windows are smashed. It shows at least that the riots had a good effect upon the Local Government Board in the direction we indicated. It is true Mr. Chamberlain denied, prior to the riots, that exceptional distress prevailed; but about a fortnight afterwards he admitted that it was exceptional and severe, and he actually sent round a circular to the Boards of Guardians, who partially adopted our proposals such as having unskilled labour on sewage farms. It also made the landlords and capitalists surrender to the Mansion House Fund some of the proceeds of their past robbery in the shape of charity. Riot it was not; it was nothing more nor less than honest poverty knocking at the door of selfish luxury and comfort, poverty demanding that in the future every man should have the wealth created by his own labour. That meeting of February 8th called the attention of the people of Great Britain to this fact—that below the upper and middle strata of society there were millions of people leading hard, degraded lives—men who are forced to live as they do, but who would, if possible, work and live virtuous lives—men who through the unequal distribution of wealth are consigned to the criminal classes, and women into the enormous army of prostitutes, whom we see in the streets of our large cities. And, as an artisan, I cannot see poor, puny, little babes sucking empty breasts, and honest men walking the streets for four months at a time—I cannot hear of women of the working classes being compelled to resort to prostitution to earn a livelihood—I cannot see these things without being moved not only to strong language, but to strong action, if necessary. My language on this occasion was the language of a man anxious to obtain some system where, by a peaceful change, this poverty could be removed. The Social-Democrats, who advocate these changes, are the true policemen and true "guardians of law and order," by preventing poverty and riot by removing the causes. And when the Attorney-General says we incited to riots, I say that the social system is to blame. It prompts men to thieve, and it prompts women of the working class to resort to dishonest acts, by not giving all a fair start in life, and not giving them an opportunity to get honest work. Society journals demand our imprisonment. Why? Because £11,000 worth of windows have been broken. But how about the sacred human lives that have been, and are, degraded and blighted by the present system of capitalism?

We have been told that our meetings had a seditious character. Well, my lord, I have been unable to hear what sedition is. I frankly confess I am inclined to think if any man is to be indicted for seditious speeches you will have to indict the 650 Members of the House of Commons. We have not done as the "Loyalist" members have done in and out of Ireland. We have not asked the Unemployed to line the ditches with rifles to enforce their demands; we have not suggested to the crowd, as Lord Randolph Churchill has suggested, that civil war would be the only product of giving Ireland Home Rule. On the contrary, we have gone to the Government and calmly and deliberately suggested to them matters of an economical character. We have gone with deputations to the Local Government Board, to Mr. Chamberlain, Mr. G. W. E. Russell, and Mr. Jesse Collings, and we have told them for the last three years unless they move in the direction we indicate, there would be sure to be riot and revolt in the streets of London. My predictions made twelve months ago to a Cabinet Minister have proved true. The responsibility, however, is not with us, but on those who neglect the warnings that have been given to them; and I contend everything that we did on February 8th, and at the Holborn Town Hall was consistent with the conduct of peaceful, law-abiding citizens. I ask you, gentlemen, not to forget that the times are exceptional, that the poverty is excessive; all throughout the country people are suffering through no fault of their own; and I ask the jury to recognise this fact—that what might be seditious on an ordinary occasion, is an honest man's duty when destitution exists. Here we have a disorganised mass brought together in Trafalgar Square—not called together by us, and I did my best to lead a portion of the crowd away, for one thing in order to avoid any conflict with the police. If we had not taken this crowd to Hyde Park the result would have been that the Strand would have been looted from the Grand Hotel to Ludgate Hill. That was the opinion of the police, and that was mine, too. We adopted what we thought the best course. We took the crowd as quickly as possible to Hyde Park. We asked the crowd to disperse, and they did. The Prosecution, instead of indicting those who were responsible for the preservation of law and order, indict those men who at great risk to themselves stopped the thieves who were plying their trade, stopped men who were inciting others to rob men and women, and asked the crowd to protect the public property. Those are the men who are indicted for sedition—inciting to a breach of the peace. It is to be regretted, my lord, that your time has been wasted by the hearing of a case of this description. [. . .]

# 6

# "HOW I BECAME A SOCIALIST", *JUSTICE*, 30 JUNE 1894.

*Walter Crane*

[The idea of the conversion narrative figures prominently in accounts of the early socialist movement. Combining the sense of an intellectual rebirth and transformative moment of personal awakening, such conversion narratives underline the notion of socialism as a break with earlier radical traditions and a shedding of the wider society's dominant value-system. Among the best-known examples of such conversions was William Morris, who in his own words crossed a "river of fire" to become a socialist when he was nearly fifty. Other conversion narratives cited by Stephen Yeo (1977, 10) include several figures represented in these volumes such as Percy Redfern (Vol. 2, Chapters 23 and 29), Katherine Bruce Glasier (Vol. 3, Chapter 29), H.W. Hobart ( Chapter 7, this volume) and Edward Carpenter (Chapters 14 and 37, this volume).

Nevertheless, there were many of their contemporaries whose socialist commitments were clearly located within a longer radical tradition and the "continuity narratives" through which they identified with that tradition as individuals. Walter Crane (1845–1915) was the great visual depictor of the socialist cause who was deeply influenced by Morris both politically and artistically and who became a leading public advocate of the arts-and-crafts movement. Many who do not know his name will recognise the unforgettable images Crane produced on occasions like the first workers' May Day in 1890, with the dignity of labour expressed among the pre-industrial trappings of Morris's *News From Nowhere* (Chapter 10, this volume).

Though Crane here acknowledges the influence of both Morris and Hyndman, he also records his debts to John Ruskin, as did so many socialists of his generation, and to the increasingly socialistic writings on political economy of the Liberal John Stuart Mill. Even among his socialist influences, Crane evinces no narrow party spirit, and though he followed Morris from the SDF into the Socialist League he also cites the Danish-American populariser of state socialism, Lawrence Gronlund. Crane also refers to the seeds that were sown by his apprenticeship to the sometime Chartist engraver William James Linton (1812–1897) at the age of thirteen. David Vincent has written of Victorian working-class

# THE IDEA OF SOCIALISM

autobiographers that they were "aware of variety and change, but the separate elements were bound together partly by the fact that they all represented some form of active response to the world in which they lived and partly by the fact that . . . there did appear to be a single tradition of a struggle for political freedom which had begun with Paine and Hardy in the 1790s" (Vincent 1982, 29). Socialism meant not just political but social and economic freedom, and was conscious of having moved these earlier radical forbears. Nevertheless, Crane and his scepticism of conversion narratives may be located squarely within this longer tradition.]

I imagine that as people can be roughly divided into Socialists and Individualists so can they be sub-divided into conscious Socialists and unconscious Socialists. I believe I really belonged to the latter class long before I knew I belonged to the former.

I do not believe in sudden conversions. We are not usually, like St. Paul, stricken blind by the sudden blaze of truth like the noon-day sun.

Propaganda would probably be much easier otherwise, and more fruitful than it is.

Still, if the seed is scattered it is sure to fall *somewhere,* and conviction breeds conviction.

Looking back on my life I have a strong conviction that the circumstance of my having become an apprentice in the office of William James Linton, the eminent wood engraver, Chartist, and poet, and friend of Mazzini and Kossuth, had some influence, though I was only a boy, in opening my mind to something wider than the ordinary middle-class ideas.

The term "Republican" then implied possession of all kinds of unconventional, advanced, and "dangerous" opinions generally.

Linton was always a staunch lover of freedom, and a man of generous impulses and action, and threw himself with ardour into what he judged to be the cause of justice and humanity, regardless of his personal advantage. He was *really* a Socialist, though I do not remember the term being then used.

At that time, too, I began to read Ruskin and this had a great influence in forming my opinions, and I was led through my studies and thoughts about art to its origin in nature and social life and circumstance.

Later I read Mill and Herbert Spencer and Darwin, who led me further on the same road (though in a different sense and from a different point of view), and well remember the passage in Mill's "Political Economy" in which he examines various Socialistic and Communistic systems—those of Fourier and St. Simon for instance—and then he admits that if the choice lay between the adoption of such systems and the continuance of such a system as the present there could be no question as to the superiority of the Socialistic and Communistic systems.

For some years I remained what would be called an ordinary political Radical, I clung to the belief that with the extension of the franchise everything could be won. I imagined that the mere removal of political disabilities would at once give power and freedom to poor men, and that they would be enabled to gain all that they desired.

Hyde Park railings went down. Household suffrage was passed, and the ballot act, but nothing in particular happened.

Much the same sort of men in the main were returned to Parliament and the political game went on as before. Other men (*not* members of Parliament) continued to be overworked and underpaid. Misery and squalor remained, want of work, want of food. I always had enough of both (though I have known poverty), but I narrowly escaped falling into the slough of pessimism. Here on the one hand were a section of our fellow citizens with everything that modern civilisation could give them, rolled up in layer after layer of superfluous riches, owing to their having—or their progenitors—succeeded in diverting lucrative private streams from the main channel of production.

On the other hand another section—the immense mass of mankind—toiling to produce this surperfluous wealth, without the slightest security that their labour would provide them with a living. Their hold of work itself entirely dependent upon the probability of its yielding a profit to someone else. Great monopolies sitting at the very sources and gates of supply. Under the forms and semblance of political freedom, real economic slavery. A grinding commercial system of inhuman competition, threatening to be a worse tyranny than any the world has ever seen, reducing all things to money value, vulgarising life, and ruthlessly destroying natural beauty. Everywhere gambling and greed. And yet a system which did not make *anyone* happy, rich or poor. Fortunately, I saw the alternative in time. I think that I can honestly say that the immediate helping hand was that of our comrade William Morris (with whom I had a correspondence) and I believe it was his lecture "Art and Socialism" that turned the scale. This was printed at Leek, and on the back of the little book was, I think, an advertisement of JUSTICE, which I immediately sent for, and to which I have been a subscriber ever since. This was in 1884—just ten years ago. I may mention that Gronlund's "Co-operative Commonwealth," and H. M. Hyndman's "Historical Basis of Socialism," among other works, helped me at the time.

Between then and now there have been many changes. I joined the S.D.F., and then the Socialist League, and then the Fabian Society and the Hammersmith Socialist Society. It seemed to me as if the movement was so large and wide that there must be room for men of all arms and arts, and that if our principles were the same, we ought not to fall out about methods. If we were going to fight the existing economic system we had our work cut out. Socialists were in the position of an invading army in a hostile country. We should have need of all our resources—horse and foot, artillery, engineers, sappers, and miners. Some are better at undermining than leading Balaclava charges. But what cause can afford to lose either policy or pluck? It takes all sorts to make a world. As I understand it, Socialism ought to enable us to allow the freest development for individuals.

Collective and common ownership of the means of life, or rather the free acknowlegdment on the part of the community of the fundamental right of each and all its members to the full enjoyment of the fruits of their collective labour—since no human wants can be supplied without collective labour. This, being the gist of Socialism as an economic system, it would, by abolishing overwork, anxiety for livelihood, and other debilitating effects of our present system, and by a large increase of leisure and margin to human life generally, afford the fullest opportunity for individual development in any direction except that of injury to others. For the first time in human history there would be the possibility of actually realising the highest human aspirations in all ways that contribute to the enrichment of life.

While each would take their part in the useful and necessary labours and services necessary to the maintainance of the community in health and comfort, everybody would be free to fill the rest of their time by collective pleasures or individual studies according to their natural view, capacity, or inclination.

This is my general conception of the meaning and tendency of Socialism, which, so far from planing down and limiting human life and human power, would immeasurably amplify the one, and set free the other, and lead ultimately to the development of a more distinct and higher individuality, as well as more variety and beauty of environment in every-day life, which would be good for art, and art is the greatest socialiser going.

# 7

# *SOCIAL DEMOCRACY OR DEMOCRATIC SOCIALISM* (SOCIAL DEMOCRATIC FEDERATION: SALFORD DISTRICT COUNCIL, 1895), 3–6, 15–16.

## *H.W. Hobart*

[Unlike Walter Crane (Chapter 6, this volume), Henry William Hobart was one of those who did describe his attachment to the cause of socialism as the result of a quasi-religious sense of conversion. "I listened in rapt attention to the new gospel . . . and was transformed in astonishment", he wrote, and following a "sharp conscientious struggle" now left behind the old religious prejudices of the mission hall (Pierson 1973, 226–227). Though the language Hobart used was very different from Crane's this should not obscure the continuities of practice and belief that can also be detected in his socialism. An active member of the London Society of Compositors, Hobart was active on the London trades council and in supporting striking workers and for a time contributed notes on labour questions to *Justice*. What is also evident in this document is a strain of social thinking that, exactly as with Morris and with Crane, still owed as much to Ruskin as to Marx.

Its most distinctive feature is the use of the army as a counterweight to orthodox political economy. It might seem reasonable to assume that the attitude of the socialist Left to the army was one of "mingled fear and contempt" (Englander 1991, 25). Nevertheless, there is a long tradition of social thinking that has seen the army as a form of organisation achieving a higher motive and social purpose than either the unassisted individual or the market relations of modern capitalism. Examples of such thinking included the French utopian socialist Fourier and the American Edward Bellamy, whose *Looking Backward* (1888) enjoyed an immense success internationally. Nevertheless, it was to Ruskin most of all that British socialists owed such notions.

Hobart's *Social Democracy or Democratic Socialism* includes an exposition of socialist economic argument that has been excluded here and does not materially differ from those represented in numerous other publications of the period. More distinctive, though by no means wholly exceptional, is the framing of such arguments by the army analogies familiar from Ruskin. The pamphlet was issued by the Salford SDF in the year that Hobart stood as its parliamentary candidate in South Salford. In Manchester and Salford there were particularly fluid boundaries between the SDF and ILP, including a general acceptance of the SDF's prior claims on this constituency (Hill 1981; Morris 1982). Though Hobart as candidate gained only 11% of the poll, this was a figure at that time barely inferior to Hyndman's in Burnley. It far exceeded anything so far gained in London constituencies.

A powerful influence locally was Robert Blatchford, whose weekly *Clarion* newspaper was launched and edited from Manchester until 1895. Urging dual membership of the two socialist bodies, Blatchford had resigned from the ILP over this issue and had close connections with the SDF. With his ex-military background, Blatchford was also to be prominent among those describing the army as a model of a socialist order of society. Little in Hobart's pamphlet could be described as a concession to electoralism. It does, on the other hand, provide testimony to the wider body of socialist ideas that could blur the distinctions of faction and ideology and help explain the strong appeal of socialist unity in areas like this.]

Everyone who is anxious to know anything about Social Democracy, whether for the purpose of endorsing, criticising, or opposing, must, for the time being, forget themselves.

It is just as necessary to forget yourself in trying to fathom Socialism as it is to forget the soldier when listening to and trying to appreciate the description of a campaign.

An old veteran who has fought in the Crimean war may give an occasional colouring to his yarn by the introduction of a personal incident here and there, but his anecdote is of the British Army. He speaks of the army as "we." He speaks of "our" men, and our "guns," and "our" daring. Every utterance is made in the collective sense; everything suggests to you a mass, a number, an association of individuals. You cannot think of an army of *one*.

When you talk of an army, you always think of a number of men, organised for a given purpose. You know it is composed of detachments, companies, regiments; foot, horse, artillery; brigades, batteries; officers, men; but the organised mass of trained men is what you think of when you speak about the army.

Our object in using the army as an analogy of Socialism is not so much to compare all the details of an army with all the details of a Social-Democratic State, but to try to make it clear to our readers that in thinking or speaking of Socialism we refer to a system of society made up of individuals. An army is a system of society in which the individual members composing it sink their individuality for the general well-being and triumph of the whole. Every individual is wanted to perfect the whole, and every individual has his special duty to perform.

If our readers can fully appreciate that position, there will be little difficulty in following our arguments as they are presented.

"Social" and "Society" are words derived from the same source, and always refer to association. When we speak of Socialism we mean Societyism—the ism of association—ism being the doctrines of. Socialists or Societyists are believers in the doctrine of association.

Man, according to all authorities on anthropology—the study of man—is a gregarious animal. He will get together, he will associate. He is always congregating in one way or another. He congregates to work, he congregates to worship, he congregates to play, and he congregates to fight: a purely natural instinct of the animal man.

Socialists are people who believe in taking advantage of this gregarious instinct of man and making it as perfect as it is possible. If it be natural for man to associate, why should they not associate for the purpose of bringing the gifts of nature more and more under the control of man? Then if that be granted, why not associate to distribute, consume, enjoy, and own the products?

To explain Socialism in a comprehensive phrase it means a system of association in which every able-bodied adult shall contribute his share of labour towards the social production of the many and varied things which society needs. In order to do this successfully this association must collectively own and control all land, mines, railways, machinery, factories, mills, and raw material.

It should not be difficult for anyone to understand what Socialism is if they will only follow this line of reasoning.

To revert back to our analogy. In the army the guns, ammunition, horses, &c., belong to the army; they are collectively owned, used, and controlled. Then why should not the industrial army own, use, and control collectively the land, machinery, &c.,—their ammunition and weapons?

The special function of a military force is to conquer an enemy.

The special function of the industrial army is to conquer nature.

The arms and ammunition are collective property for the purpose of collective triumph.

Why should not the industrial arms be collective property for the purpose of supplying social needs?

Anyone can see how idiotic it would be for the colonel or field marshal to be the private owner of the weapons of war. If he liked he could prevent the soldiers from performing that duty which is expected of them. Then is it not equally as idiotic for the means of producing wealth to remain in the hands of private individuals?

If the Duke of Cambridge were the private owner of the guns, swords, bayonets and bullets of the British army and chose to send the men into the field without them, would not everyone be inclined to say he was mad? Or if, now that he has retired, supposing him to be the private owner, he declined to allow them to be used till he had effected a sale, would you not be disposed to take them by force from him? And yet you allow the "captains" of industry, the "merchant-princes," to act in exactly that hare-brained manner with your weapons of industrial warfare.

In your strikes and lock-outs the industrial guns and ammunition, which the industrial soldiers only can use, are locked up and remain useless because they are private property.

Just as everybody recognises that the soldier is the man to do the fighting, and that the army is the proper association to own and control the weapons of war, so the Social Democrat sees that the worker, in his social capacity, is the man to use the machinery, and society as a whole the association to own and control.

We are fully aware that there are certain things done in the army which are not for the best interest of the soldiers who compose it, nay, we are quite prepared to admit that the army, as a fighting agency, should be abolished, but we do not wish for one moment that anyone should think that, because we are using the army as an illustration of the advantages of association, we necessarily endorse its shortcomings. The mere fact of the defects of the army being recognised is the first step towards remedying those defects. Nevertheless the principle of mutual association for mutual advantage can be logically put forward in support of the doctrines of Social Democracy. [. . .]

We, Social Democrats, claim that as you are members of society, engaged in supplying the needs of society, you have a right to enjoy the comforts of society. Not only do we claim this in regard to the bare necessaries of life, but we say in every walk in life you should be free. We speak of your economic freedom, (which, by-the-way, has nothing to do with saving money) because under capitalism you will always be economically enslaved. But beyond and above that, reaching away to the highest ideal man's imagination can climb to, we say that if a perfect association is preferable to an imperfect one, then Social Democracy is the nearest approach thereto we know of. You cannot reach a perfect ethical condition of life by ignoring the teachings of association. Science, art, ingenuity, love, friendship, and progress are inseparable from association; but greed, avarice, jealousy, lying and deception are concomitant parts of individualism.

Strive with us, then, patiently and peacefully if possible, to sweep away the individualist capitalist system, and ring in the dawn of the new SOCIAL DEMOCRACY.

Two things are necessary if the conditions under which the workers live to-day are to be improved. You must have an ideal system to strive for, and you must have practical stepping-stones by which this ideal system may be reached. Both of these are supplied by the Social Democratic Federation. Our stepping-stones are found in our programme, and our ideal state of society is a Co-operative Commonwealth, dominated only by Human Brotherhood.

# 8

# "SOCIAL-DEMOCRAT OR SOCIALIST?", *SOCIAL DEMOCRAT*, AUGUST 1897, 228–231.

*H.M. Hyndman*

[Towards the end of 1897 members of the SDF and ILP were balloted on a possible fusion of the two organisations. This was the outcome of discussions of representatives of the two parties in April and July 1897 and resulted in a large majority for the principle of fusion. For the thwarting of this mandate for "socialist unity", historians agree that the prime responsibility lay with the leadership of the ILP (Howell 1983, 314–316; Crick 1994, ch. 7). Nevertheless, Hyndman's excursion into matters of socialist etymology was clearly not intended to assist the process. The author of numerous works that freely invoked the idea of socialism, he had not hitherto insisted on distinguishing it so precisely from social democracy. In insisting on the latter term, he not only implied that a unified organisation should bear a name deriving from the SDF rather than the ILP. He also lent credence to the claims of those ILP opponents who, like J. Bruce Glasier, regarded the SDF as "dogmatic" and "sectarian". Fusion, if at all, on our terms, was what he seemed to demand. Even the SDF's *Justice* was moved to comment (on 8 September 1897) that it was "not for an individual to prescribe the conditions on which . . . fusion is to be brought about".

Reproduced here without its prefatory section, the document's interest lies not just in the immediate circumstances of its production, but in the wider contexts within which Hyndman made his case for social democracy. Essentially there were two of these. One was the wider European movement that notably included the expressly social-democratic mass parties of Germany and Austria. Theoretically and organisationally, the German SPD in particular was a model party; already it headed the popular poll in Reichstag elections, and Hyndman himself would write of how no British counterpart could bear comparison with it (Hyndman 1912, 258). For as long as disunity persisted, the SDF and ILP would continue to make rival claims to the sanction and moral authority of the International. By elevating social democracy to the status of a defining principle, Hyndman thus made clear his view that the SDF alone had any authentic claim to represent the movement in Britain.

In doing so, Hyndman also sought to differentiate the SDF from the more amorphous conceptions of socialism that Marxian social democracy was expected to supersede. In the spirit of Engels's *Socialism: Utopian and Scientific* (1880), appearing in English translation in 1892, he took his stand with Marx and Engels against earlier "utopian" socialists like Owen and Saint-Simon. Hyndman also referred positively to the pioneering German socialist Ferdinand Lassalle, whose stringent criticisms by Marx in the *Critique of the Gotha Programme* did not become available in English until many years later. The ranks of those whom Hyndman excluded as merely socialists stretched from anarchists to Christian socialists. He was also naturally dismissive of the utopian socialist colonies that had sprung up mainly on the other side of the Atlantic: from the Shakers at Mount Lebanon, dating from as early as 1792, to the Topolobampo community founded in Mexico in 1893.

Despite these exclusions, Hyndman had always understood, as Marx himself complained of him, that "the English don't like to be taught by foreigners" (Tsusuki 1961, 42). The idea of social democracy was therefore preferred to the later formulas of "Marxism" or "Marxist socialism"; and in discountenancing the idea that it was a foreign import Hyndman frequently returned to the radical movements of the 1830s–1840s whose spirit the SDF claimed to revive. From a socialist perspective, Bronterre O'Brien was the most significant of these precursors, though Hyndman here seems to mix up O'Brien's *Poor Man's Guardian* with the later *People's Paper* edited by his fellow Chartist Ernest Jones. In writing of social democracy, Hyndman also made the point that not all forms of socialism were democratic. Here, in warning of "State or Bureaucratic Socialism", he might have had the ILP less in mind than the Fabians, who had also taken part in the initial conference on socialist unity in April 1897. On the other hand, in warning of servility to a vigorous personality he could not have had the Fabians in mind, but much more likely the personal sway which Keir Hardie and others exercised over the ILP (see also Chapter 27, this volume).]

## I.

The general impression is that the terms Social-Democrat and Social-Democracy, like a good many other things nowadays, were imported from Germany into this country. This is a mistake. The composite name Social-Democrat was first used, and made to a certain extent popular, by the famous Chartist leader Bronterre O'Brien, in his *People's Guardian,* nearly sixty years ago—that is to say, some time before Marx, Engels, and Lassalle were heard of. O'Brien was a Catholic and a paper-currency man, but he was in some respects the ablest and most farseeing of the Chartists. He held the opinion, for example, that trade unions, being composed of what he called "the aristocrats of labour," with all sorts of rules for restricting the number of apprentices in the skilled trades, and possessed with a distinct desire to constitute a privileged class among the workers, would inevitably develop into a more or less reactionary force as against the interests of the mass of the labouring population. Can anyone deny that his fears have been to a large extent justified? He also declared vehemently against Free Trade as being any panacea for working-class wrongs, and pointed out clearly that such free trade as was proposed by Fox and Villiers, Cobden and Bright, was distinctly a capitalist measure. No good, or very little, could come of it for the people unless land were nationalised and machinery socialised beforehand. His predictions have been amply fulfilled. In short, O'Brien, with all his drawbacks, was what we should ourselves call a Social-Democrat to-day, and he proclaimed the class war as inevitable with quite as much vigour as any Continental Socialist either before or after him. His religious and economic errors did not affect the main truths which he set forth.

A Social-Democrat, then, according to O'Brien, was a man who regarded social questions as of paramount importance, and desired to solve them by collectivist and democratic action. Democratic action might not by any means necessarily be collectivist; and collectivist action might not by any means necessarily be democratic. For the questions which arose at the beginning of the Queen's reign were not very different from those which press for a solution at the end of it; though the great economic development of the past two generations renders our task easy indeed compared with that of the Chartists who held Socialist views. And, moreover, in the ranks of the advanced party, then as now, were men who wanted to substitute personal dictation from above, for voluntary democratic discipline on the same level; and other men who resented anything like interference on the part of a majority with the somewhat conceited display of what they were pleased to call their own individuality, as a direct attack upon personal freedom. O'Brien took and used the term Social-Democrat to express the views of those who wished to bring about a complete social reconstruction under democratic forms.

Of course, much has happened since O'Brien's day. Social-Democrats and Social-Democracy represent now a series of much more clearly defined opinions and a far greater array of disciplined forces than it was possible that they should in 1839. Yet the ideas which those words represent are not much changed from what they were when they first saw the light. The great and growing Social-Democratic parties of Germany and Austria, the Social-Democratic parties of Denmark and Holland, the increasing numbers who demand the democratic and social Republic for France, as well as the Social-Democratic Federation of Great Britain, all tell the same story and all mean the same thing. The work of Marx and Engels, and in less degree of Lassalle, systematised and formulated the ideas which prevailed at the end of the last and the beginning of the present century throughout Europe, and gave a scientific and historical basis to the teachings of St. Simon, Robert Owen, and the socialistic Chartists. Their theories are now being extended, adapted, modified, and applied by Social-Democrats in every civilised country. But much of the original conception remains, and at this hour a Social-Democrat means a man or a woman:—

1. Who recognises the class war between the proletariat and the possessing class as the inevitable historic outcome of the capitalist system and of the direct economic and social antagonisms which it has engendered and fostered.
2. Who sees that those antagonisms can only be resolved by the complete control over all the great means of production, distribution, and exchange, by

the whole people, thus abolishing the class State and the wages system, and constituting a Co-operative Commonwealth or a Social-Democracy.[1]
3. Who observes that the preliminary changes which must bring about this social revolution are already being made, unconsciously, by the capitalists themselves, and is anxious to use political institutions and forms to educate the people and to prepare, as far as possible, peacefully for the social revolution which must result in national and international Communism.
4. Who holds that the methods of giving legal expression to this great Socialist change should be completely democratic in every respect; such democracy, however, not excluding, but rendering essential, thorough voluntary discipline.
5. Who, lastly, is of opinion that close international understandings and agreements between the various national Social-Democratic parties, in order eventually to weld them into one great whole, are to be carefully fostered.

This, I think, is a fair description of the opinions held by a conscious Social-Democrat at the present time in every country.

## II.

The terms Socialist and Socialism were, I believe, first used by Robert Owen to describe the views of those who, like himself, were in favour of the substitution of universal and ordered co-operation for universal and anarchical competition. At any rate, the names are at least forty years older than that of Social-Democrat, and always have been, as they are to-day, of much wider signification. They embrace practically, now, all those who, being discontented with the present state of society, are anxious to re-organise it on a co-operative or communist basis. Thus we have the Christian Socialists, the Socialists of the Chair and Arm Chair (Professors and Fabians), Municipal Socialists, Radical Socialists, Socialists of the type of those who found the so-called Socialist Colonies of Paraguay, Topolobampo, &c., Shaker Socialists, Free Love Socialists, and so on, and so on. Indeed, I believe many Anarchists now call themselves Socialists; while Social-Democrats also, who are the consistent and steady opponents of Anarchism in all its forms, come under this wide designation of Socialists, too.

The drawback to the term Socialist is, therefore, that it is not sufficiently definite. Nobody could reasonably say that Christian Socialists, as Christians Municipal Socialists, and Free Love Socialists have the same ends in view as, Social-Democrats, or anything at all like them. The differences are manifest without further discussion. But more than this, useful as the word Socialist may be as a rough generic popular name, it does not necessarily carry with it the notion of democrat as well. Far from it. Socialists are, indeed, frequently accused of wishing to impose their arbitrary will on the whole population. This is not true, as I believe, of the great majority of them, whether they are Social-Democrats or not. But nobody can truly say that State or Bureaucratic Socialism is not a danger of the immediate future in more than one country. Nobody, I think, also, can question that the experiment of a Cæsarist Socialism—a perfectly possible temporary solution of the politico-economic difficulty in the transition stage—might meet with acceptance from the mass of the people crushed, as they are to-day, under the monopolist tyranny of a set of unscrupulous capitalists. The general, vague term, Socialist, therefore, charitable and Catholic as it may be, can be used to cover too many schools of thought to constitute a proper appellation for a well-organised, disciplined array of class-conscious revolutionaries, who are confident of victory for their party in the near future.

## III.

Now the obstacles to the constitution of a consolidated party of the people in Great Britain on a Socialist basis seem to be narrowed down to this one point of difference between Social-Democrat and Socialist. The Social-Democratic Federation, which has just held its Seventeenth Annual Congress, and which has had the title "Social-Democratic" since 1884—having in those sixteen or seventeen years beyond all question done the bulk of the work, the uphill, dangerous, depressing work of Socialist propaganda in Great Britain—contends that, whatever be the name of the combined Socialist organisations, the word Social-Democratic must appear in it. As a matter of fact, our main difficulty has been to teach the English workers how to be democratic. Our task has been to show them "democratic" does not mean servility to a vigorous personality on the one hand, or petty endeavours to pull everybody down to a low general level on the other: to prove also by experiment that democracy does not lead to anarchy or go-as-you-please, but that it brings with it thorough voluntary discipline, and the choice of leaders absolutely controlled by the organisation. This the S.D.F. has done, and a more Socialist or a more Democratic body cannot exist. The discipline to-day is enforced by the whole of the members, who sometimes go in this direction beyond what the older men in the organisation would have thought of suggesting.

It is easy to understand, therefore, that a body with such a record and such an organisation does not wish, and indeed cannot, cut itself off wholly from its past by giving up its distinctive appellation of "Social-Democratic" any more than it could abandon the principles which underlie that name. Short of that, I believe our members will be willing to do anything to come to an amalgamation with the members of the I.L.P., as we have already come to a political understanding with them. The word Socialist is too vague. But it can hardly be contended that the term Social Democratic (modified by any prefix or appendage that may be desired) is too exclusive to form a portion of the title of what must eventually be the United Social-Democratic Party of Great Britain. And the hopeless incapacity of the Liberal and Radical factions at the present time, their entire inability to rouse anything like enthusiasm among themselves or the people at large, renders it quite possible that ere many years have passed the whole of the advanced political sections in this island may be found fighting side by side with us in such a party for a complete social transformation on democratic and republican lines.

## Note

1 Kropotkin, with that curious disregard for the truth which all Anarchists show in controversy, has repeatedly stated that Social-Democrats wish to retain the system of paying wages. He knows perfectly well that this is not, and never has been, so, and he has been often told as much. But it suits him to misrepresent us, and of course he never stops to consider whether it is right or fair that he should. This is anarchical morality or individualist ethic, I suppose.

# 9

# *SOCIALISM AND ART* (SOCIAL DEMOCRATIC FEDERATION, 1907), 5–16.

## Jack C. Squire

[It was the Marxists through Morris and Walter Crane who in Britain made the greatest contribution to socialist ideas of art. As Hyndman noted in his autobiography, Morris's contribution was irreplaceable, while Crane's designs were reproduced by socialist movements across the continent of Europe. Nevertheless, it would be wrong to regard these as isolated figures, and following his death in 1895 Morris's influence continued to be reflected in the close links in Britain between socialism and ideas of artistic renewal.

In 1907, the later Sir John Collings Squire (1884–1958) was a history graduate and budding poet just down from Cambridge. Squire made his journey to respectability via the literary pages of the *New Age* and *New Statesman* and a failed Labour parliamentary candidacy in 1918. Most likely there was never much more to his socialism than what Beatrice Webb called his loathing of the profit-motive and sympathy for the underdog (Webb 1984, 287–288). Nevertheless, at the age of twenty-three it was under the auspices of the SDF and with an introduction contributed by Crane (omitted here) that Squire explored the connections between his inchoate collectivism and the socialist view of art.

Squire's identification with Morris is clear. He also takes against the bureaucratism of the Bostonian Edward Bellamy, whose utopian *Looking Backward* (1888) had inspired Morris's pastoralist response *News From Nowhere* (1889). Though so recently a Fabian student socialist, Squire further comments acerbically on the paucity of Fabian thinking on the whole subject of art. Like Morris, he locates his ideal of popular art in the Middle Ages, and glories in the medieval building trades. His disdain for the appearance of the modern public library is ill-concealed.

Squire expresses scepticism as to the vagueness of many socialists' notions of the better art to come. With his easy equation of Beauty and Good, one may feel that he does not himself greatly advance matters. Webb in her 1917 diary entry also wrote that Squire had no interest in political democracy or social administration, and was in fact "a conservative of all that is distinguished because it is old". This was borne out by the event. As founding editor of the *London Mercury*,

Squire's conservatism would become increasingly evident in both his literary and his political judgments. Like other devotees of Morris, such as the guild socialist A.J. Penty, he even showed a certain predilection for Mussolini's fascism. Despite his critical comments on Rudyard Kipling's imperialism, Squire was one of those who recoiled from socialism as it became entangled with the state and artistic modernism, and did so without for a moment recanting his preference for Morris over Bellamy.]

THE matter which we are about to consider is not one about which I feel myself peculiarly competent to speak, but it is at least one which many people regard as of very great, if not of supreme importance, and one to which comparatively little really careful attention has been paid either by the opponents of Socialism or by its advocates. It is true that many upholders of the present capitalistic system talk in a vague sort of way about Socialism being destructive of Art, without ever making any attempt to support the statement by serious argument. It is also true that most Socialists speak (equally vaguely) about the "Wonderful Art of the Coming Age"; but they, too, seem to be somewhat diffident about emerging from the region of bald assertion. Of course a few of them (I rather fancy Bellamy was one of these) make imbecile suggestions in favour of some sort of State bureau for the discovery and encouragement of artists; but apart from these and from one or two men like Morris, who have really shed a great deal of light on the question, the majority of writers confine themselves almost entirely to the consideration of the economic, political and ethical aspects of Socialism. Even the Fabian Society, that Universal Provider of propagandist tracts, has not condescended to emit as much as one meagre little pamphlet on Art. So I shall not be bothered, and you will not be bored by a continual cascade of reference to an avalanche of authorities. Nevertheless it is a great pity, that some qualified person does not devote himself to a full inquiry into the relations between the prosperity of Art and the economic structure of society; as the publication of such an inquiry might be the means of bringing into our movement many men and women who, through an apathy towards what they regard as a purely bread-and-butter issue, have hitherto remained outside.

Perhaps the least unsatisfactory mode in which one may deal with this long matter in this short space will be to take the chief contentions on the subject which are used by our opponents, to analyse them, and, in so doing, to use them as pegs whereon to hang any general observations that one may feel moved to make. The recipe for the making of these objections would appear to be a simple one. It is this:—"Think of any conditions which you may consider (wrongly or rightly) indispensable to the proper development of Art, and, without further ado, blankly deny that these conditions could possibly exist in a Socialist State." It is interesting, too, to observe whence these objections come. One would imagine that if they had anything in them, the artists, as being the people most concerned, would cry them aloud on the housetops. But this is not the case. Of the great artists and literary men now living or recently dead, a large number have come out as avowed Socialists, and the rest have been apparently indifferent to the whole thing. I think that one may safely say that no artist of any repute has ever given it as his opinion that Socialism would be bad for Art. The only people who attack Socialism on artistic grounds are the very people who are least in sympathy with Art. One cannot put the position better than in the words of Emile Vandervelde, the Belgian Socialist leader. "We have seen," he says in his book on Collectivism, "the most idle and inert of the capitalist classes reproach Socialism with weakening individual initiative; we have seen the most tyrannical of the employers oppose it in the name of human liberty; it is therefore quite in keeping that in their turn the most tasteless and unappreciative of the bourgeois should undertake the defence of Art against the 'ignorant masses' and the 'modern barbarians.'"

Now, what do these people say? Roughly, it is this: "In your Socialistic society all work will be regulated by the State; and (putting aside the fact that manual labourers always dislike to see other people apparently doing nothing) we fail to see how you are going to regulate intellectual work or how you are going to reward it." "Do you intend," cries an indignant French publicist, "to give artists an eight hours day; to command Victor Hugo to begin having his poetic inspiration at seven o'clock, and to switch it off at nine?"

We do not! But before we proceed to make a more elaborate answer to these questions it might be useful to see what have been the conditions of the patronage of Art in former times and in our own day.

Let us go back a few years; say, to the Stone Age. From the remotest prehistoric times the creative instinct has come to the surface in man. Our cave-dwelling ancestor used to pick up a large bone after he had finished his lunch, and scratch upon it with a flint two lines to represent a horse. No doubt, like the Deity, on the seventh day, he fondly flattered himself that his work was about as good as it could be. But the point is: Why did he do it; and what did he get for it?

Mr. Kipling, in a poem called, I think, "The Story of Ung," has pictured a palæolithic artist getting maintained by his tribe merely for scratching heads on bones. Now one rather imagines that this notion of a savage making Art his only means of subsistence is historically untrue. One conceives rather that in primitive communities the men who do the tattooing and the painting, do also their share of the hunting and the fishing. It is difficult to believe that a primitive tribe would maintain an artist simply qua artist. But whether this is so or not—and I am no palæologist—does not matter two straws. If these early men maintained the artists altogether, one may be safe in saying that a civilised communistic society would scarcely do less. If, on the other hand, the artists, when Art was in its infancy, took their part in the ordinary work as well as doing their own, we may take it that in a Socialistic State the artists could do a few hours ordinary labour a day, and neither they nor their Art, nor their neighbours would be any the worse for it. In fact, a little thought about the origin of Art will make one realise that all this cantish outcry about "Will Socialism starve the artist?" is nothing but a most preposterous red herring. For under moderately free and natural conditions men make poems, pictures, and the rest, because it is their nature so to do; and the chiefest part of their reward is bound to be the pleasure (akin to religious ecstasy) which they feel in the act of producing and in the contemplation of the finished product.

Art then springs from man's primal instincts. Moreover, these instincts are present in every individual to a greater or lesser extent of development. Our capitalistic system has tended to give people the impression that the instinct for Art is present in the few, and totally absent in the many. One cause of this has been the increased specialisation in the production of works of Art, by which most men can find no good medium for the expression of the yearnings that are within them; and another cause is the fact that the majority of our unfortunate fellows find that it takes them all their time to earn enough hard cash to keep body and soul together, and cannot afford to waste a minute in what has come to be regarded (falsely, I think) as a mere luxury and not a necessity of life.

But every human being has in him the longing to create or to imitate (for they come to the same thing); although the actual technical faculty may vary indefinitely in different individuals. Why does the negro give the missionary a ton of rubber or other such commodity for a handful of coloured beads? Simply because the benighted black heathen has a crude craving for beauty, which is satisfied by the beads, and a certain decorative instinct to which he will give play in hanging the beads around his own or somebody else's neck. Why (en passant) does the missionary part with the beads for the rubber? Because his right and proper instincts have been crushed by a profit-mongering system of society which has led him to cherish the laughable and quite erroneous idea that india-rubber is worth more than coloured beads. I have no sympathy with those who accuse the missionary, in this instance, of swindling the native. He is not. He is swindling himself—selling his soul for a mess of caoutchouc. The black man gets the joy that form and colour can give—the European gets money, which turns to dust and ashes in his hand.

The same universal delight in form and colour, the same desire to design and to construct, that one finds in savages, one finds also in children. A very small child will play with pieces of coloured wool by the hour. In spite of the elaborate and expensive toys that are made nowadays for the offspring of the rich, it is unanimously agreed upon by educationalists that the little ones do not take half the delight in them that they do in those simpler ones, which give them the chance of bringing their artistic ingenuity into play. No girl or boy was ever born who could not amuse herself or himself with some paper and a box of crayons for drawing, or a little pile of bricks for building. And, with regard to a slightly more advanced age, is there a man here who does not remember the worthy and desirable things that he used to do with his first penknife?

It is the same all the world over. The civilised child who draws his headmaster's face, and the New Zealand aborigine who tattoos his own nose, are both giving expression to this one great impulse which they have in common with every member of the race.

Man, therefore, is essentially an imitative and a decorative animal. What effect have political, economic and social conditions with regard to the stimulation or repression of his instincts in these respects? Do we find that every system under which he has lived has encouraged his artistic aspirations to an equal extent? A glance at the designs for the new Carnegie Library at Eatanswill-on-the-Quicksands would in itself supply a sufficient answer to that question. But we can come to Capitalism directly, and for the moment confine ourselves to a consideration of previous social structures. Has there ever been a civilised community in which every member has been able to satisfy his desire for Art?

If one asked this question of the man-on-the-magazine-staff, he would doubtless reply: "Oh, yes. Look at Athens, my dear sir. Every citizen an artist and a critic." But the gentlemen (and ladies) who voice these ecstatic sentiments forget that in Athens there were at least seven slaves to every free man. In order that the free citizen might devote himself to general culture, seven of his fellowmen were turned into "dumb drudges." The same thing was to be seen in Rome—unlimited leisure at the top of the social scale, unlimited toil and hardship at the bottom, whether the labourer was slave or nominally free man. The two great requisites for the free development of the artistic instinct—a not too-crushing burden of mechanical labour, and a fair amount of leisure time—were absent as far as the mass of the people were concerned. Art was the concern of the few, and the few were agreed that this was as it should be. Culture, as in our own day, was deliberate, and not spontaneous; and the Romans, like ourselves, laid far too much stress upon the particular in a man's art and too little on the general. With them, as with us, the vast majority of the population was cheated out of its rightful inheritance.

A very similar state of things may be observed in the other great civilisations of the past. In Egypt, in Mexico, in Assyria, in Babylonia, and in the East there has always been a helpless proletariat ground down by a master-class, and the artistic instincts of the majority have been stunted in infancy and stifled in later life. But there has been one period where these instincts have had, to a great extent, free play; and that period was the Middle Age in Western Europe. The reign of omnipotent capital had not yet come, and the worker was, within limits, his own master. He had certain dues to pay to those above him; but when these dues were paid, he was free to do what he liked with his own time. Trade was almost entirely local, and production was necessarily limited by the demands of the locality. Overproduction would have been utterly purposeless. A man who turned out more articles than were wanted by his neighbours would never be able to get the surplus off his hands. The result was that, finding that he had more time at his disposal than was actually taken up with the manufacture of the required number of articles, he spent his spare hours, not in turning out more and more goods, that nobody could want, but in perfecting and ornamenting those which were already made.

It has been estimated that if a man were free from all extraneous burdens he could earn a bare living for himself and his family by about two hours work a day—one says "bare," because one leaves out of account modern machinery which, of course, in a well-ordered community would raise the general standard of living enormously without extending the hours of labour. In the Middle Ages the demands of kings, lords and what-nots undoubtedly raised this necessary number of hours to, say, five or six. But even then there was a margin of time which could not be employed in actual use-production. The consequence was that your mediæval craftsman exercised his ingenuity upon everything that passed through his hands. In William Morris's phrase: "He decorated everything, from a porridge-pot to a cathedral." His surplus time was of no value to anyone else, so he could afford to spend it in pleasing himself.

Thus it is that the Middle Ages were the only times in which there has been a great Popular Art. Popular literary work did not keep pace with popular handicraft. But that was not because the masses of the people had not the requisite faculties, but because the tools were not to hand. Printing had not yet been invented, and, above all, the knowledge of reading and writing was confined to a few. But where the people had a fair chance they took the fullest advantage of it. Think of the exquisite illuminated manuscripts, for example, that were turned out literally by the thousand from the monasteries—and the monks were almost entirely drawn from the lower orders. Go to any museum and compare one of these manuscripts with one of our machine-made products of the present day—say, the "Daily Mirror"—and, then, in the words of the poetaster:

> "Seek thou the lone, sequestered vale,
> And ponder o'er the gruesome tale."

But, above all, the mediæval workman spent his soul upon stone. The tools required for carving and building were not confined to the monks, but were within the reach of every man. Give Robin or Giles a chisel and a stone, and he starts (other things being equal) on level terms with any other man in any other age. And here our ancestors showed how men, when left to please themselves, can far outstrip any work that is done under cold compulsion, with respect both to variety and to power. People look at a Gothic church and come away sighing and complaining that the race of builders has vanished from the face of the earth. But they forget that the conditions of employment have changed. In these days the architect is hampered by a desire for cheapness, and the subordinate workman's individuality counts for nothing. In those bygone centuries the architect was allowed very much of a free hand, provided he turned out a beautiful structure. Money was a very small consideration, and time no consideration at all. Above all, matters of detail were left to the individual mason. Consequently, in every nook and corner of these buildings, we find odd bits of wonderful work, beautiful or grotesque, each expressive of some idea in some one man's mind. Then there was a rich variety: now there is a meagre uniformity.

Thus much for the Middle Ages and the artistic instincts of the people generally; it remains to be added that the more gifted individuals, the geniuses, were better looked after than ever before or since. There was a certain tradition of art patronage amongst the nobles; but an enormous amount of it was done by the monasteries and the various corporations of the towns, pious and otherwise. Wherever you had any noticeable number of men gathered together, they welcomed and gladly employed any man who showed signs of genius. In fact, the gifted child of working-class parents has never been so carefully helped as he was in that age. It is a striking thing that almost all the great mediæval artists came from the lower classes—a sufficient testimony both to the fact that taste was widespread and that there was a corresponding general eagerness to encourage genius. When all men are economically free, or even partially so, culture is bound to be far more general than it ever can be in a population mainly composed of wage-slaves or chattel-slaves; and when culture is general, genius will never be neglected.

We come to Capitalism. Instead of looking back, we will look around. Once more we will see how Art fares in these two great respects: How far is the general artistic instinct of the people given free play, and how far is the individual genius encouraged to exercise his powers to the fullest? As we said before, the two things are bound to stand or fall together, but we may take them separately, nevertheless.

As far as the ordinary worker is concerned, it is not too much to say that he is altogether debarred from making his products artistic, even where he is allowed to make them useful! Two main causes are at work here. In the first place, the worker is kept working so ruthlessly and at such very high pressure that he cannot possibly take any real pleasure in what he is doing. Moreover, his mind and body are so exhausted as a result of the long day's toil in the interests of the profit-makers that he is scarcely in a suitable frame of mind, after his work is over, to turn his attention to any occupation that requires concentrated effort of any kind. When one considers the long hours, the arduous nature of the work, and the evil conditions under which the manual proletarians have to live, one is struck dumb with wonder; not at the fact that so many working men seek a narcotic or a stimulant in the form of alcohol or a cheap music-hall (as our dear sentimentalists complain), but that so many of them have the astonishing endurance to go through with the day's work and still to take some interest in matters not immediately connected with the daily round. The marvel is, not that some of the workers are a trifle unrefined in their pursuits, but that the whole lot have not been brutalised beyond all hope of redemption. It merely serves to show how impossible it is to eradicate men's higher impulses, and the feeling for Art goes with the rest. Take away long hours, take away slums—take away, in fact, everything we've got, and put its exact opposite in its place, and amongst the things which will come again to the surface of the people's soul will be the old, irrepressible yearning after Art.

If these forces were not sufficient to benumb the workers' artistic instincts, Capitalism would at least make sure that those instincts should not be satisfied. If the flame still burns in the poisonous air, Capitalism pours cold water on it. If every single workman in the land were cultured, refined, an artist to his fingertips, he would be quite unable to put artistry into his work. In the first place, a very great deal of our manufacture is nowadays machinafacture, and a machine can scarcely put much soul, emotion, individuality (call it what you like) into its work. In the second place, where the craftsman actually handles the whole thing, he dare not attempt to strike out a line for himself.

Take a concrete example. Suppose one of those unfortunate men who will be compelled to assist in the building of the Eatanswill-on-the-Quicksands Free Library were to say to himself as he contemplated the growing monument: "Heavens! What an eyesore!" and suppose he were to conclude that he would put a little decorative work in which would at least improve a few square inches of the monstrosity, and acted accordingly. What would, in effect, be said to him?

The architect would say, "Clear out! That wasn't in my design." To a certain extent a justifiable remark in a day when we have a totally false conception of the real nature of architecture. But the essential and fundamental remark would be that of the contractor: "My man, I tendered so much for this job. The main thing for me to do is to get it done as cheaply as possible. I don't pay you to waste your time (and, consequently, my money) on anything that isn't in the contract."

I give this merely as an illustration of what I am trying to convey; of course, to suggest that a square foot of decoration on the building in question would look anything but ridiculous is the last thing I should urge. But the whole attitude of Capital towards the æsthetic aspect of things may be summed up in a few words: "Art be damned, if it isn't in the contract." Under a competitive commercial system, where cheapness is the Holy Grail, almost every single thing you can think of is bound to be a triumph of ugliness. For the beautifying of work means the expenditure of a certain amount of the workman's time, and if one firm tried this the others would undersell it with cheaper though uglier articles; and, with things as they are, few men can afford to reject the cheaper in favour of the dearer if they both equally well serve the primary material purpose for which they have been made.

That is where the masses stand as far as concerns any possibility of getting artistic enjoyment as part and parcel of their daily life. But how does Capitalism treat those rare ones who are born with exceptional gifts? How far is genius allowed to travel untrammelled along its own peculiar lines. And this, perhaps, is the crux of the whole matter, for it is in connection with the fate of the individual artist that the hottest attacks from this quarter are made.

Our opponents lay down three dicta: That the artist must be free from the burden of extraneous work, and that he would not be so under Socialism; that he must be given the necessary means to live a decent life, and that he would not get them under Socialism; that the taste of a whole population is bound to be bad, and that under a Socialistic régime the bad artists would be encouraged and the good ones go all unheeded.

The shortest way in which to combat these assaults would be to say right away to Capitalism: "Pluck the beam out of your own eye before thou pluckest out the mote which is in thy brother's—or, rather, thy son's." If the fulfilment or non-fulfilment of these several conditions is the test of a system's attitude towards Art, Capitalism stands trebly condemned out of its own mouth; for it fulfils none of them.

It may be an open question as to whether an artist should be absolutely free from any employment except his art. But at all events he never has been under Capitalism. If one excepts the painters—and most of those have had a very bad time in early life, while some have died in extreme poverty—one finds that the greater number of geniuses, English and foreign, have been forced not only to work for a living, but to do uncongenial and painful work for a living. Think of Chatterton and Haydon, the suicides; think of Burns, the excise-officer (small wonder that he took to drinking whisky when they put him to tapping it); think of Wordsworth, who might have starved had a friend not left him a small income; think of Goldsmith, doing the meanest literary hack work; of Wagner, writing cornet duets; of scores of others who have had to do any work which offered itself, or else live in absolute poverty.

Capitalism has never allowed the artist to live for his art—at least not until he has become almost too old to enjoy his leisure. The only way by which the gifted writer or painter has been able to secure ease and independence in early life has been by prostituting his gifts to the caprice of his masters. If he can persuade himself to stifle his real aspirations and to adapt himself to the taste of Mr. Moneybags he can make the latter disgorge a little of his superfluous spoils. That is what is happening when we see talented painters wasting their time in painting vast portraits of rich nonentities or their wives for the Academy show. Your magnate hears that X.Y.Z. is a good painter, but he would see him a long way further before he would commission him to paint anything but a portrait of himself. Ostentation and taste can never exist side by side.

As the painter can make money by flattering the Capitalist's vanity through reflecting his ugly features, so the literary man can make money by reflecting his ugly thought—political or otherwise. If Kipling had confined himself to bringing out the best that was in him, he would have got fame—eventually—but he would never have become a plutocrat or a public oracle. He was ingenious enough to lay himself out in flattering the rampant Imperialism that was rife amongst the middle-classes when he appeared upon the scene. I have no doubt that if, at the present time, a man similarly gifted should arise to sing the wrongs of the income-tax payer he could feather his nest well in a few weeks.

It is a commonplace that the true test of Art is the test of time. And what is the test of time but the verdict of the people as a whole. One cannot think of a single great writer whose first work has been received with anything but coldness or abuse from the critics. Time has justified them all. The few have over and over again shown themselves utterly without judgment, but as these works have gradually filtered through to the people they have been acclaimed as masterpieces. That there is an unlimited demand for good work when it is within reach is witnessed by the rush that is made for cheap editions, when copyrights of great writers expire.

The whole way along, Capitalism has stifled Art and tortured the artist. For Art there has been a cramped and narrowed existence; for the artist starvation during his best years, and fame when he was too old to enjoy it. There never was a system which was so noxious to Art as this of Capitalism. All the accusations that it hurls at Socialism will rebound with redoubled vigour against its own lying head. The most inconceivably unrefined Socialistic State could not do worse than degrade Art and starve the artist. What will the ordinary Socialist State of our dreams do?

Firstly, with regard to your geniuses. Well, the bureau idea is a rotten one. We have the rudiments of it now in the various scholarships to Schools of Painting and Schools of Music, although they have not yet tried it in respect to Literature. You may discover and encourage technical talent like this—but the chances are that genius will go unnoticed, if nothing more. In such schemes you are bound to have examiners and selectors of a sort, and anything novel (as all works of genius are bound to appear until you get used to them) may give them the impression that it is only bad or eccentric. Genius takes some little time to be appreciated, and then a whole people is always a safer judge than an individual who is asked to give an immediate opinion. But, frankly, is there any reason why you should thus keep the artists as a breed apart, a sort of Levites? A poet eats, sleeps, and drinks, and (if he is a sensible man) plays billiards. There seems to me to be no valid reason why he should not spend three or four hours a day in some socially necessary labour, mental or physical—always giving him a choice of occupation, of course. Our error at present is not in forcing artists to take up other work in order to earn their living, but in giving them so much of this other work, or such distasteful work, that their energies are sapped and their thought deadened.

And as for the community at large, it seems as clear as daylight to me that better material conditions and a freer life will bring out again all those instincts which in many men are suppressed under Capitalism. Art will give pleasure to work and beauty to the world. And beauty breeds like every other living thing—except the upper classes. The more beautiful the world becomes, the more men's efforts will be centred on making it beautiful. On what lines these efforts will run it were a little rash to attempt to forecast. Men will attempt to abolish ugliness wherever possible; ugliness in social conditions of all sorts, in their dwellings, in their clothes, in their habits, in every single article they use. One can scarcely agree with Ruskin that the destruction of all machinery is desirable. But still, it is highly probable that in a communist society men, as regards certain articles of every-day use, would rather go without machinery, and do a little more work, in order to get the beauty that only handicraft can give. Many ugly things, too, that we see around us to-day would disappear of their own accord, because they are only in existence to satisfy an artificial need created by the capitalists in order to find an investment for a portion of their surplus capital. But, indeed, one cannot draw the line between the man who removes ugliness of any description and the man who is consciously serving Art. If we feed a hungry child, we are in a certain sense helping the cause of Art. If we pull down a filthy cottage and erect something habitable in its place, we are doing so no less. The ancient identities between Beauty and Good, and between Ugliness and Evil are as true now as ever they were. Every man who is working for human happiness is, whether he knows it or not, following in the footsteps of the great artists of the past and clearing the road for the great artists of the future.

# Part 2

# CONCEPTS OF POLITICAL CHANGE

# 10

# "HOW THE CHANGE CAME" FROM *NEWS FROM NOWHERE*, CHAPTER 17, REPRINTED IN *COMMONWEAL*, 17, 24 AND 31 MAY 1890.

*William Morris*

[Of all Britain's revolutionary socialists William Morris was the one whose posthumous legacy was not only a matter of general assent but subjected to the widest range of competing claims. Because of Morris's role as protagonist and inspiration of the arts-and-crafts movement, some of those who claimed him had no political interest in doing so and either downplayed or actively discountenanced his socialism. Among the socialists, authors of widely circulated tributes included James Leatham (see Chapter 36, this volume) and J. Bruce Glasier. A former associate of Morris in the Socialist League, Glasier had afterwards moved on to the ILP, and the object of his influential memoir was to minimise Morris's Marxism and demonstrate his closeneness to the ILP at least in spirit.

His "utopian romance" *News from Nowhere* fits somewhat awkwardly into such presentations. Written in "hurried snatches" and originally appearing in instalments, this was Morris's alternative to the "cockney paradise" that Edward Bellamy's *Looking Backward* (1888) had set in the year 2000 (Glasier 1921, 150–151). Bellamy's future vision was one combining machinery and "State Communism" and Morris rejected it for just the reasons that he rejected Fabian collectivism and any conception of socialism predicated on what he called modern civilisation. His review of Bellamy's book appeared in *Commonweal* on 22 June 1889, and the first instalment of Morris's counter-utopia six months later. The predominant impression it left was of a pastoralist ideal that was avowedly closer in spirit to the Middle Ages and carried the alternative title *An Epoch of Rest*.

As the *Commonweal* carried the third instalment on 25 January 1890, Morris in the same issue published his review of the landmark Fabian text *Fabian Essays in Socialism*. It appealed to him no more than Bellamy had. His sharpest barbs were aimed at Sidney Webb and the "fantastic and unreal" conception of socialism as the inexorable further development of tendencies already at work in modern society. Morris envisaged an epoch of rest, but saw no possibility whatsoever of it being established without convulsive political change. It was four months later, in the nineteenth instalment of *News from Nowhere*, that he introduced the alternative view of socialist transformation that he gave the title "How the change came". In his seventh instalment he had evoked the Bloody Sunday demonstration of 1887 (see Chapter 34, this volume). Now he returned to the theme of an attack upon unarmed demonstrators; again, it was to have taken place in Trafalgar Square, but with the date cast forward to 1952. Following Bloody Sunday, Morris had experienced a sort of deflation regarding the unequal contest between forces of authority and those who rose to challenge them. It must therefore have been as a sort of antidote to these feelings that he now presented this, not as a setback, but as the beginning of the revolutionary process. Unnoticed in accounts like Glasier's, he then depicted this process with a vivid immediacy and level of detail that no previous British socialist had ever given the subject.

The readers of *Commonweal* would have recognised the world of their own direct experience. This included free-speech fights in Trafalgar Square, an echo of the current eight-hours campaign and a gesture to anti-parliamentarism in the conversion of the parliament building into a dung market. He also wrote of socialists, so very like the Fabians, who "by hook or by crook" aimed to get hold of the administration of government and industry. In imagining the course of the revolution, Morris did not confine himself to local precedent. In assembling his Federation of Combined Workmen under a Committee of Public Safety, he evoked the most violent phase of the French Revolution in 1793. In later sections of the chapter, which continued over five instalments, the workers' organisation employs the method of the general strike that looked backwards to the Chartists while looking forwards to syndicalism. Morris envisaged a phase of the revolution that Bolsheviks might have described as one of dual power. He also envisaged the "Friends of Order", a counter-revolutionary body, that anyone might have recognised in the militarist and proto-fascist responses to Britain's labour disturbances of the 1920s.

Britain's communists would make a good deal of this chapter in insisting on Morris's commitment to a violent process of revolution. For socialists of a less combative disposition, *News From Nowhere* was more difficult to account for and Glasier maintained that it was no more than a *jeu d'esprit* and never intended as a serious exposition of his socialism. In the six years that remained to him, Morris himself did not make this clarification, nor did he join the ILP when from 1893 he had the opportunity to do so. Published as a book in 1891, his utopian romance was rapidly translated into other European languages and became the most familiar of his writings to political readers. Readers may still come to their own views as to whether its "whimsicalities" were to be taken seriously or not.]

## CHAP. XVII.—How the Change came.

DICK broke the silence at last, saying: "Guest, forgive us for a little after-dinner dulness. What would you like to do? Shall we have out Greylocks and trot back to

Hammersmith? or will you come with us and hear some Welsh folk sing in a hall close by here? or would you like presently to come with me into the City and see some really fine building? or—what shall it be?"

"Well," said I, "as I am a stranger, I must let you choose for me."

In point of fact, I did not by any means want to be 'amused' just then; and also I rather felt as if the old man, with his knowledge of past times, and even a kind of inverted sympathy for them caused by his active hatred of them, was a kind of blanket for me against the cold of this very new world, where I was, so to say, stripped bare of every habitual thought and way of acting; and I did not want to leave him too soon. He came to my rescue at once, and said—

"Wait a bit, Dick; there is someone else to be consulted besides you and the guest here, and that is I. I am not going to lose the pleasure of his company just now, especially as I know he has something else to ask me. So go to your Welshmen, by all means; but first of all bring us another bottle of wine to this nook, and then be off as soon as you like; and come again and fetch our friend to go westward, but not too soon."

Dick nodded smilingly, and the old man and I were soon alone in the great hall, the afternoon sun gleaming on the red wine in our tall quaint-shaped glasses. Then said Hammond:

"Does anything especially puzzle you about our way of living, now you have heard a good deal and seen a little of it?"

Said I: "I think what puzzles me most is how it all came about."

"It well may," said he, "so great as the change is. It would be difficult indeed to tell you the whole story, perhaps impossible: knowledge, discontent, treachery, disappointment, ruin, misery, despair—those who worked for the change because they could see further than other people went through all these phases of suffering; and doubtless all the time the most of men looked on, not knowing what was doing, thinking it all a matter of course, like the rising and setting of the sun—and indeed it was so."

"Tell me one thing, if you can," said I. "Did the change, the 'revolution' it used to be called, come peacefully?"

"Peacefully?" said he; "what peace was there amongst those poor confused wretches of the nineteenth century? It was war from beginning to end: bitter war, till hope and pleasure put an end to it."

"Do you mean actual fighting with weapons?" said I, "or the strikes and lock-outs and starvation of which we have heard?"

"Both, both," he said. "As a matter of fact, the history of the terrible period of transition from commercial slavery to freedom may thus be summarised. When the hope of realising a communal condition of life for all men arose, quite late in the nineteenth century, the power of the middle classes, the then tyrants of society, was so enormous and crushing that to almost all men, even those who had, you may say despite themselves, despite their reason and judgment, conceived such hopes, it seemed a dream. So much was this the case that some of those more enlightened men who were then called Socialists, although they well knew, and even stated in public, that the only reasonable condition of society was that of pure Communism (such as you now see around you), yet shrunk from what seemed to them the barren task of preaching the realisation of a happy dream. Looking back now, we can see that the great motive-power of the change was a longing for freedom and equality, akin if you please to the unreasonable passion of the lover; a sickness of heart that rejected with loathing the aimless solitary life of the well-to-do educated man of that time: phrases, my dear friend, which have lost their meaning to us of the present day, so far removed we are from the dreadful facts which they represent.

"Well, these men, though conscious of this feeling, had no faith in it. Nor was that wonderful: for looking around them they saw the huge mass of the oppressed classes too much burdened with the misery of their lives, and too much overwhelmed by the selfishness of misery, to be able to form a conception of any escape from it except by the ordinary way prescribed by the system of slavery under which they lived; which was nothing more than a remote chance of climbing out of the oppressed into the oppressing classes.

"Therefore, though they knew that the only reasonable aim for those who would better the world was a condition of equality, in their impatience and despair they managed to convince themselves that if they could by hook or by crook get the machinery of production and the management of property so altered that the 'lower classes' (so the horrible word ran) might have their slavery somewhat ameliorated, they would be ready to fit into this machinery, and would use it for bettering their condition still more and still more, until at last the result would be a practical equality (they were very fond of using the word 'practical'), because 'the rich' would be forced to pay so much for keeping 'the poor' in a tolerable condition that the condition of riches would become no longer valuable and would gradually die out. Do you follow me?"

"Partly," said I. "Go on."

Said old Hammond: "Well, since you follow me, you will see that as a theory this was not altogether unreasonable; but 'practically,' it turned out a failure."

"How so?" said I.

"Well, don't you see," said he, "because it involves the making of a machinery by those who didn't know what they wanted the machines to do. So far as the masses of the oppressed class furthered this scheme of improvement, they did it to get themselves improved slave-rations—as many of them as could. And if those classes had really been incapable of being touched by that instinct which produced the passion for freedom and equality aforesaid, what would have happened, I think, would have been this: that a certain part of the working classes would have been so far improved in condition that they would have approached the condition of the middling rich men; but below them would have been a great class of most miserable slaves, whose slavery would have been far more hopeless than the older class slavery had been."

"What stood in the way of this?" said I.

"Why, of course," said he, "just that instinct for freedom aforesaid. It is true that the slave-class could not conceive the happiness of a free life. Yet they grew to understand (and very speedily too) that they were oppressed by their masters, and they assumed, you see how justly, that they could do without them, though perhaps they scarce knew how; so that it came to this, that though they could not look forward to the happiness or the peace of the freeman, they did at least look forward to the war which should bring that peace about."

"Could you tell me rather more closely what actually took place?" said I; for I thought him rather vague here.

"Yes," he said, "I can. That machinery of life for the use of people who didn't know what they wanted of it, and which was known at the time as State Socialism, was partly put in motion, though in a very piecemeal way. But it did not work smoothly; it was, of course, resisted at every turn by the capitalists; and no wonder, for it tended more and more to upset the commercial system I have told you of, without providing anything really effective in its place. The result was growing confusion, great suffering amongst the working classes, and, as a consequence, great discontent. For a long time matters went on like this. The power of the upper classes had lessened as their command over wealth lessened, and they could not carry things wholly by the high hand as they had been used to in earlier days. On the other hand, the working classes were ill-organised, and growing poorer in reality, in spite of the gains (also real in the long run) which they had forced from the masters. Thus matters hung in the balance; the masters could not reduce their slaves to complete subjection, though they put down some feeble and partial riots easily enough. The workers forced their masters to grant them ameliorations, real or imaginary, of their condition, but could not force freedom from them. At last came a great crash. On some trifling occasion a great meeting was summoned by the workmen leaders to meet in Trafalgar Square (about the right to meet in which place there had for long been bickering). The civic bourgeois guard (called the police) attacked the said meeting with bludgeons, according to their custom; many people were hurt in the *mêlée,* of whom five in all died, either trampled to death on the spot, or from the effects of their cudgelling; the meeting was scattered, and some hundred of prisoners cast into gaol. A similar meeting had been treated in the same way a few days before at a place called Manchester, which has now disappeared. The whole country was thrown into a ferment by this; meetings were held which attempted some rough organisation for the holding of another meeting to retort on the authorities. A huge crowd assembled in Trafalgar Square and the neighbourhood (then a place of crowded streets), and was too big for the bludgeon-armed police to cope with; there was a good deal of dry-blow fighting; three or four of the people were killed, and half a score of policemen were crushed to death in the throng, and the rest got away as they could. The next day all London (remember what it was in those days) was in a state of turmoil. Many of the rich fled into the country; the executive got together soldiery, but did not dare to use them; and the police could not be massed in any one place, because riots or threats of riots were everywhere. But in Manchester, where the people were not so courageous or not so desperate as in London, several of the popular leaders were arrested. In London a convention of leaders was got together, and sat under the old revolutionary name of the Committee of Public Safety; but as they had no organised body of men to direct, they attempted no aggressive measures, but only placarded the walls with somewhat vague appeals to the workmen not to allow themselves to be trampled upon. However, they called a meeting in Trafalgar Square for the day fortnight of the last-mentioned skirmish.

"Meantime the town grew no quieter, and business came pretty much to an end. The newspapers—then, as always hitherto, almost entirely in the hands of the masters—clamoured to the Government for repressive measures; the rich citizens were enrolled as an extra body of police, and armed with bludgeons like them; many of these were strong, well-fed, full-blooded young men, and had plenty of stomach for fighting; but the government did not dare to use them, and contented itself with getting full powers voted to it by the Parliament for suppressing any revolt, and bringing up more and more soldiers to London. Thus passed the week after the great meeting; almost as large a one was held on the Sunday, which went off peaceably on the whole, as no opposition to it was offered. But on the Monday the people woke up to find that they were hungry. During the last few days there had been groups of men parading the streets asking (or, if you please, demanding) money to buy food; and what for goodwill, what for fear, the richer people gave them a good deal. The authorities of the parishes also (I haven't time to explain that phrase at present) gave willy-nilly what provisions they could to wandering people; and the Government, which had by that time established some feeble national workshops, also fed a good number of half-starved folk. But in addition to this, several bakers' shops and other provision stores had been emptied without a great deal of disturbance. So far, so good. But on the Monday in question the Committee of Public Safety, on the one hand afraid of general unorganised pillage, and on the other emboldened by the wavering conduct of the authorities, sent a deputation provided with carts and all necessary gear to clear out two or three big provision stores in the centre of the town, leaving blank papers promising to pay the price of them with the shop managers: and also in the part of the town where they were strongest they took possession of several bakers' shops and set men at work in them for the benefit of the people;—all of which was done with little or no disturbance, the police assisting in keeping order at the sack of the stores as they would have done at a big fire.

"But at this last stroke the reactionaries were so alarmed that they were determined to force the executive into action. The newspapers next day all blazed into the fury of frightened people, and threatened the people, the government, and everybody they could think of, unless 'order were at once restored.' A deputation of leading commercial people waited on the government and told them that if they did not at once arrest the Committee of Public Safety, they themselves would gather a body of men, arm them, and fall on 'the incendiaries,' as they called them.

"They, together with a number of the newspaper editors, had a long interview with the heads of the government and two or three military men, the deftest in their art that the country could furnish. The deputation came away from that interview, says a contemporary eyewitness, smiling and satisfied, and said no more about raising an anti-popular army, but that afternoon left London with their families for their country seats or elsewhere.

"The next morning the Government proclaimed a state of siege in London,—a thing common enough amongst the absolutist governments on the Continent, but unheard-of in England in those days. They appointed the youngest and cleverest of their generals to command the proclaimed district; a man who had won a certain sort of reputation in the disgraceful wars in which the country had long engaged in from time to time. The newspapers were in ecstacies, and all the most fervent of the reactionaries now came to the front; men who in ordinary times were forced to keep their opinions to themselves or their immediate circle, but who now began to look forward to crushing once for all the Socialist, and even democratic tendencies, which, said they, had been treated with such indulgence for the last twenty years.

"But the clever general took no visible action; and yet only a few of the minor newspapers abused him; thoughtful men gathered from this that a plot was hatching. As for the Committee of Public Safety, whatever they thought of their position, they had now gone too far to draw back; and many of them, it seems, thought that the government would not act. They went on quietly organising their food supply, which was a miserable driblet when all is said; and also as a retort to the state of siege, they armed as many men as they could in the quarter where they were strongest, but did not attempt to drill or organise them, thinking, perhaps, that they could not at the best turn them into trained soldiers till they had some breathing space. The clever general, his soldiers, and the police did not meddle with all this in the least in the world; and things were quieter in London that week-end; though there were riots in many places of the provinces, which were quelled by the authorities without much trouble. The most serious of these were at Glasgow and Bristol.

"Well, the Sunday of the meeting came, and great crowds came to Trafalgar Square in procession, the greater part of the Committee amongst them, surrounded by their band of men armed somehow or other. The streets were quite peaceful and quiet, though there were many spectators to see the procession pass. Trafalgar Square had no body of police in it; the people took quiet possession of it, and the meeting began. The armed men stood round the principal platform, and there were a few others armed amidst the general crowd; but by far the greater part were unarmed.

"Most people thought the meeting would go off peaceably; but the members of the Committee had heard from various quarters that something would be attempted against them; but these rumours were vague, and they had no idea of what threatened. They soon found out.

"For before the streets about the Square were filled, a body of soldiers poured into it from the north-west corner and took up their places by the houses that stood on the west side. The people growled at the sight of the red-coats; the armed men of the Committee stood undecided, not knowing what to do; and indeed this new influx so jammed the crowd together that, unorganised as they were, they had little chance of working through it. They had scarcely grasped the fact of their enemies being there, when another column of soldiers, pouring out of the streets which led into the great southern road going down to the Parliament House (still existing, and called the Dung Market), and also from the embankment by the side of the Thames, marched up, pushing the crowd into a denser and denser mass, and formed along the south side of the Square. Then any of those who could see what was going on, could see at once that they were in a trap, and could only wonder what would be done with them.

"The closely-packed crowd would not or could not budge, except under the influence of the height of terror, which was soon to be supplied to them. A few of the armed men struggled to the front, or climbed up to the base of the monument which then stood there, that they might face the wall of hidden fire before them; and to most men (there were many women amongst them) it seemed as if the end of the world had come, and to-day seemed strangely different from yesterday. No sooner were the soldiers drawn up as aforesaid than, says an eye-witness, 'a glittering officer on horseback came prancing out from the ranks on the south, and read something from a paper which he held in his hand; which something very few heard; but I was told afterwards that it was an order for us to disperse, and a warning that he had legal right to fire on the crowd else, and that he would do so. The crowd took it as a challenge of some sort, and hoarse threatening roar went up from them; and after that there was comparative silence for a little, till the officer had got back into the ranks. I was near the edge of the crowd, toward the soldiers,' says this eye-witness, 'and I saw three little machines being wheeled out in front of the ranks, which I knew for mechanical guns. I cried out, "Throw yourselves down! they are going to fire!" But no one scarcely could throw himself down, so tight as the crowd were packed. I heard a sharp order given, and wondered where I should be the next minute; and then—— It was as if the earth had opened, and hell had come up bodily amidst us. It is no use trying to describe the scene that followed. Deep lanes were mowed amidst the thick crowd; the dead and dying covered the ground, and the shrieks and wails and cries of horror filled all the air, till it seemed as if there were nothing else in the world but murder and death. Those of our men who were still unhurt cheered wildly and opened a scattered fire on the soldiers. One or two fell; and I saw the officers going up and down the ranks urging the men to fire again; but they received the orders in sullen silence, and let the butts of their guns fall. Only one sergeant ran to a machine-gun and began to set it going; but a tall young man, an officer too, ran out of the ranks and dragged him back by the collar; and the soldiers stood there motionless while the horror-stricken crowd, nearly wholly unarmed (for most of the armed men had fallen in that first discharge), drifted out of the Square. I was told afterwards that the soldiers on the west side had fired also, and done their part of the slaughter. How I got out of the Square I scarcely know: I went, not feeling the ground under me, what with rage and terror and despair.'

"So says our eye-witness. The number of the slain on the side of the people in that shooting during a minute was prodigious; but it was not easy to come at the truth about it; it was probably between one and two thousand. Of the soldiers, six was killed outright, and a dozen wounded."

I listened, trembling with excitement. The old man's eyes glittered and his face flushed as he spoke, and told the tale of what I had often thought might happen. Yet I wondered that he should have got so elated about a mere massacre, and I said:

"How fearful! And I suppose that this massacre put an end to the whole revolution for that time?"

"No, no," cried old Hammond; "it began it!"

# 11

# *AN ANTI-STATIST, COMMUNIST MANIFESTO*, INTERNATIONAL REVOLUTIONARY LIBRARY, 1887, 2–22.

*Joseph Lane*

[Anarchist thought in Britain requires consideration in its own right and cannot be subsumed within a collection like the present one. Nevertheless, it is a commonplace of the literature on anarchism to distinguish between its "communist" and individualist strands (e.g. Guérin 1971; Miller 1984). Among those espousing a form of communist anarchism, there were many ideals held in common with socialists and on certain issues even shared campaigning objectives. This was particularly the case in the formative years of the 1880s when boundaries between movements and organisations were fluid and provisional in character.

Joseph Lane's profession of anti-statist communism mentions anarchists as if to underline that the author is not to be mistaken for one. Reviewing the pamphlet in the anarchist weekly *Freedom*, Charlotte Wilson expressed bemusement at this and commended Lane's text as "an energetic and earnest exposition of Anarchist Socialism from a worker's viewpoint" (Walter 2007; for Wilson, see Chapter 3, this volume). Born in rural Oxfordshire in 1851, Lane on moving to London is said to have had some involvement in the Land Tenure Reform Association led by J.S. Mill. The traces of a radical liberal inheritance are doubtless discernible in Lane's insistence in this pamphlet on the issue of authority or liberty as the central one confronting all societies. Through the Marylebone Radical Association, he had himself also been involved in bringing pressure to bear on radical Liberals.

Nevertheless, for Lane by 1887 there was no reconciling the principles of liberty and authority. By the early 1880s, he had come into contact with exiled German socialists like Johann Most, the proponent of "propaganda of the deed"; and in 1881 he attended the international revolutionary congress in London, whose forty foreign delegates were, like Most, of a predominantly anarchist outlook. In 1882, Lane was one of the founders of the Labour Emancipation League based in east London. It was thus as one of Britain's socialist pioneers that the following year he joined forces with Hyndman's Democratic Federation as it took up a more definitely socialist stance.

The seeds of division existed from the start. In January 1885 Lane was one of the founders of the breakaway Socialist League (Chapter 2, this volume). Nevertheless, his *Anti-Statist, Communist Manifesto* shows that his differences with Hyndman were more fundamental than those of Morris or Bax. The origins of the document lay in divisions within the Socialist League over the issues of parliamentarism and partial reforms like the eight-hour day. Lane's position on both is clearly outlined here, as is his scepticism regarding trade unionism, co-operation, state socialism, temperance, vegetarianism and the current agitation around the unemployed. The earliest pronouncements of the SDF had appeared with the exhortation "educate, agitate, organise" (Chapter 1, this volume). Paraphrasing this as "educate, educate, educate", Lane implies that only on this basis can an organisation be conceived of committed to the destruction of every manifestation of the principle of authority. A final section expressing the hostility of most strands of socialist thought to Malthusianism is omitted here.

Lane's pamphlet was printed by the secularist W.J. Ramsey, who had earlier served a gaol sentence as publisher of the *Freethinker*. Although it was advertised as the first of an International Revolutionary Library, no other title ever appeared. Lane resigned from the Socialist League in May 1889 and until his death in 1920 his subsequent involvement in radical politics was seemingly intermittent and without any wider effect. Socialists would find that it was almost impossible to build a movement on the basis of such resolute abstention from more immediate objectives. Nevertheless, Lane's importance in the present context is to remind us of a strand of anarchist communism that also had its roots in the 1880s and remained a significant counter-current until overwhelmed by the impact of the Bolshevik revolution.]

## GENERAL PRINCIPLES.

### I.

Human Society can only be organized upon the basis of one or the other of the two principles of authority or of liberty. From these two principles are derived two political systems, equally broad and far reaching, though diametrically opposite in their effects, that of the one being the happiness, and of the other the misery of mankind. Beyond these two there is no political system capable of contending for supremacy in this 19th century of ours. All intermediary systems are powerless in equal degree, and can only occasion transient perturbations.

Such has been our situation for a century past, authority losing prestige on the one hand and freedom gaining on the other, but still scarcely understood. Vain attempts have, indeed, been made to reconcile the two, but being by nature incompatible the admixture has only resulted in a yet more debased blend of the two theories, in a conflict of jarring interests which only rend and damage one another.

Thus either liberty or authority each by itself and at issue with each other, must organize society. Where authority flourishes, we shall find the structure of society based upon a fundamental plan of Absolutism. Entirely ignoring the various stages through which humanity has already passed, authority affirms that the world is immutable in its primordial principles; it proceeds from God in the direct line, God the beginning and the end of all things, who has delegated to his representative on earth, Priest or Monarch (both are kings) a portion of his might and power.

The power of king or priest must not be counterbalanced by any other, he is responsible to God alone, and any attempt against his majestic authority is a direct invasion of the prerogatives of the source of all things. Heedless of the fact that the theological and metaphysical phases are spent and exhausted, authority still boldly takes up tradition and appeals to God, who by his grace directly intervenes in the ordering of things human, God. King and Nationalism, the symbols of the most formidable reaction, such is the cry and motto of authority. It believes in God, without whom it would not exist itself; in the King, who is an emanation from God, and in Nationalism, which is a mere jingo sentiment, belonging to the God idea It has no faith or belief in the people, whose existence alone is a reality, and whose emancipation and enfranchisement it dare not permit on pain of suicide.

In order to its maintenance, the system of authority needs a religion above all Be it what it may, religion teaches the renunciation of earthly possessions, and a love for the heavenly beatitudes. It causes uncertainty to predominate over certainty, fiction over reality, things imaginary over things palpable, falsehood over truth. It proclaims the doctrine that misery is of divine institution; that it ever has existed and ever must continue to exist in Gods' ordinance, who will therefore inevitably punish as a crime, any popular insurrection caused by starvation.

After the Church, the army more directly representative of the monarch's power, the mainstay of law and order, and after it, the centralised State uniting in itself all the reactionary forces required to enable it to govern, such are the natural products of authority. Freedom, with such a system, becomes illusory, since it can only exist by dint of the constant, abrigement of force, and of the progressive annihilation of the powers that be, whereas the whole machinery of the state is devised on the contrary, to render the enfranchisement of the people impossible, and to make the power of the government crushing. War, as a matter of course, becomes an indispensable ailment for this type of Society, with which arms, diplomacy and the tribune—the three phases of war, are—necessary phenomena. It is in the shade of such a political system that financial and capitalistic feudality will flourish, since God has decreed in his infinite wisdom that the rich and the poor shall for ever form two distinct castes, one of which was created to exploit the other. This flagrant inequality borrows from its source a semblance of justice, and a sanction against which it would ill be come us to protest. If the political system of Authority prevails now, the policy of Liberty will henceforth rule the destinies of the world; there is no middle path between these two extremes. To day we must have all or nothing, nothing but freedom and its creations can avail any longer to satisfy us. In the system of Liberty, God is deposed, society is the work of man, who is himself its beginning and its end, and the distribution or division of earthly goods shall proceed according to the will of man, regulated by reason and justice; there shall be no longer a class to rule and dominate over another class; each member of Society working for himself and for all, fulfils his social duties.

All useful forces are necessary to the development of Society, and no one shall be at liberty to deprive it of anyone of these. God, no longer the supreme regulator of human destinies, becomes useless, and misery ceases to be irremedial, for labor and intelligence must of necessity triumph over it. The Church, deriving its power from the Absolute, will disappear with it. It is no longer the State, the Army, the Church or God that will preside over the government of the world; it is labour represented by the people that will organize all things.

Religion annihilated, the people will arise from their degradation, intellectual and moral. Politics being eliminated they will emerge from their state of economical servitude, and with these will disappear the financial industrial proprietorial and capitalistic feudalism. Social science appears teaching us the uselessness and the nuisance of politics and government. The economic equilbrium realised, there will be no need of force to maintain it, war, by its nature, being a huge parasite, could only disturb and not consolidate it. Peace is the necessary resultant, and sublime crowning of all the Social forces directed towards labor. The latter being essentially a peace maker, the people being emancipated by the Revolution, will endeavour to guarantee the fruits of their labour and consequently the fruits of the labour of all; instead of creating as must inevitably occur nowadays new monopolies for the benefit of the few, it will extend on the contrary, these guarantees and confederate from town to town, from country to country, internationally. It makes all working men unite together, and creates what is called the life of relationship in the economical order. Is it conceivable that politics and war could find room, be it ever so small, in a Society so transformed? No, and when the constitution of labour shall have definitely replaced the constitution of the old world, the advent of the working classes will be realised with a character so imperious and fateful that the most severe justice must acknowledge its legitimacy.

## II

The object of Socialism is to constitute a Society founded on labor and science, on liberty, equality and solidarity of all human beings. It is consequently a mortal foe to all oppressors, of whatsoever kind, of all speculators and exploiters, be their name what it may. The first form in which oppression is manifested in organized society is the religious oppression, the divine exploitation. Religion seeks to enslave the human intelligence, the God idea is the generator of all despotisms Man will never be free in any of the manifestations of his activity, so long as he shall not have expelled from his brain the notion of God, the product of ignorance, sustained by the exploiting priests. So long as a mystic vision of a divinity shall darken the world, it will be impossible for men to know that world, and as a consequence to possess it. It is by the aid of this notion of a God governing the world, that all forms of servitude, moral and social, have come into existence and been established religion's despotism, classes, property, and the exploitation of man by man. To enable men, therefore, to attain to freedom and to knowledge, that is to realize the object of the Revolution he must first expel God from the domain of knowledge and consequently from Society itself. We can therefore only consider as true revolutionary Socialists, conscious of the object they pursue, those who, like ourselves, declare themselves Atheists and do whatever in their power lies to destroy this corrupting notion of a God in the minds of the masses. The struggle, therefore, against every kind of religion, and the propagation of Atheism must form a part of every socialistic programme that pretends to give a logical exposition of the ideas, the aspirations and the object of the adepts of the Social Revolution.

### III.

Politics properly so-called, that is the science of government or the art of directing men gathered in social community, is entirely based upon the principle of authority, and, it being so, we oppose with all our might the reactionary notion which consists in the pretence that the revolutionary socialists must seek to seize upon the political machine, and to acquire power for themselves. We decline to recognise a divine absolutism because it can only give rise to the enslavery of reason and intelligence. Why, then, should we recognise a human absolutism, that can only engender the material exploitation of the ruled by the rulers? In this argument we are not specially concerned with any particular form of government, for all without distinction had their rise from the same source: Autocratic, Olegarchic systems, constitutional monarchy, plutocracy, the republic, as governmental forms, are all antagonistic to human freedom, and it is because of this that we are opposed to every form of government. If it be admitted that individual man has no right to govern, we cannot admit that a number of men should have this right, be they a minority or a majority. It is claimed that the theory of government is the outcome of a tacit agreement between all the citizens for the acceptance of some form of government, but this theory is inadmissible, for such tacit agreement cannot exist since men have never been consulted anywhere upon the abdication of their own freedom.

A certain school of socialists, while sharing our ideas upon the majority of forms of government, seeks nevertheless to defend what they call the democratic state, ruling nations by means of a parliamentary system, but we argue just precisely that freedom does not exist any more in this system than in any of the others, and it is for this reason that we oppose it. Act as it will, this popular state will nevertheless require for its maintenance to appeal to the reactionary forces, which are the natural allies of authority,—the army, diplomacy, war, centralisation of all the powers which operate in restraint of freedom, and the initiative of individuals and social groups. Once launched upon this arbitrary career, it is an inevitable necessity to mount up round after round of the ladder, there being no resting place. On the contrary they must be ever trenching more and more upon the freedom and automony of the individual until these undergo a process of complete absorption and annihilation. In opposition therefore to those who desire by means of parliamentaryism to achieve a conquest of political power, we say for ourselves that we wish to forego power and monopoly alike, which means that we seek to bring out from the very bosom of the people, from the depths of labour a factor more potent, that shall deal with capital and the state and subdue them. This powerful factor will be realised by the organisation of Industrial and Agricultural groups, having studied and being enabled to apply the laws of exchange possessing the key and secret of the contradictions and antagonism of the Bourgeois political economy, standing possessed in a word of social science. And what does social science teach to those who consult it? It teaches that political reforms, as a preliminary to social reforms, are a Utopia or a mere trick and an eternal mystification, by which the radicals of every shade, including parliamentary socialists have up till now deceived the workers. Social science protests against these subterfuges and palliatives; it repudiates every alliance with the policy of parliaments. Far from expecting any succour from them, it begins its work of exclusion by eliminating politics and parliamentaryism. We revolutionary socialsts desire to organise ourselves in such a manner as to render politics useless and the powers that be superfluous, *i.e.,* that we aim at the abolition of the State in every form and variety. We are waging a battle of labour against capital *i.e.,* against the State proprietary, financial and industrial. We pursue a warfare of freedom against authority, *i.e.,* against the State, the respecter of religion and the master of all systems of teaching. We champion the cause of the producers as arrayed against that of the non-producers, *i.e.,* we combat the State in its military and civil functionaries. We fight the battle of equality against privilege, *i.e.,* we oppose the State, having all monopolies industrial, bankocratic, agricultural, etc. Now in order to subdue capital, to subjugate the powers that be, and destroy them, we in no way need to win by means of a parliamentary system that political power which as a matter of fact we seek to destroy, we do not wish, by acquiring power, to increase the number of non producers that our socialistic organisation is meant to reduce more and more until none are left, *i.e.,* until the complete annihilation of power, until the abolition of the State whatever be its form, monarchical or democratic.

We need not waste time over those Socialists who while condemning the political action of the proletariate, at the same time wish to avail themselves of parliamentary action as a means of propaganda; such Socialists are wanting in logic. If the participation of Socialists in the policy of governments be condemned as fatal to the interests of the proletariate, then a propaganda in favour of parliamentary action on behalf of the proletariate can be neither good in itself nor serviceable in the development of Socialism. On the other hand, as regards socialistic propaganda in times of election, all the good achieved by a candidate for parliamentary honors would be counterbalanced by the evil which he would otherwise cause, by filling the minds of the workers with notions false and reactionary, thus creating complete confusion among those who are struggling for the emancipation of mankind. The only means in our view of making the most of a period of political excitement, such as may be an electoral contest, would be to take advantage of it, to disseminate among the masses revolutionary papers, pamphlets leaflets, etc., got up specially for the occasion, and showing the people that it is not by Parliamentary means but by social revolution, that their lot will be ameliorated materially, morally and socially. Summing up we may, therefore, say that as far as politics are concerned we are Anti statists, and as such we abstain from taking any part whatsoever in parliamentary action, whatever be the end assigned to such action.

## *IV.*

If we are Atheists in point of philosophy, and Anti statists in point of politics, we are communists as regards the economic development of human society. And whereas in the elaboration of all our conceptions, we always start from the principle of liberty, we are free communists as opposed to the state communists. The society that we assail has for its basis of existence the private property of all raw materials, of the soil, of the wealth below the soil, all tools, and machinery, and all capital speaking generally. Private property in its turn is the direct emanation from the principle of authority, and is based upon the theory of remuneration, or reward for individual efforts. Now it is absolutely certain that there is no isolated individual effort, there can only be efforts, general and collective or common; consequently neither should there be individual remuneration or reward, and we may thus logically be allowed to declare that property is robbery.

Social wealth has a threefold source: the forces of nature, the instruments of labour, and labour itself. An individual does not create the forces of nature, and therefore he can not appropriate them to his own use; at most they are the common property of all men. An individual does not create the plant and machinery of work. He therefore can not appropriate them to his own use. It is the generations of men that from century to century have transformed the raw materials into tools of production, and consequently the theory of plant and machinery being regarded as a stock of property held in common must be the only principle accordant with equity and justice. The individual works it is true, but his personal work his particular endeavour, would, as its were, have no value in the immense field of activity of modern production, did he not constitute an integral portion of the work and of the endeavour collective or common of all men.

It follows therefore that private property cannot be regarded as legitimate from any point of view. Society as under its present constitution, which makes of it a pivot of its organisation, political and economical, thus merely becomes an immense financial industrial, agricultural, and mercantile Feudalism, exploiting mercilessly the countless masses of the proletariate. Everything in the regime of individual property belongs to the bourgeoisie, even including thanks to the iron law of wages, the worker himself. In the proprietary system the majority of men are condemned to work for the sustenance and enjoyment of a handful of masters and parasites.

As the ultimate expression of all other forms of servitude, the Bourgeois domination has at last divested the exploitation of labour of the mystic veil that obscured it; governments, family, law, institutions of the past, as of the present have at last shown themselves in this system of society, reduced to the simple terms of wage slaves and capitalists, as the instruments of oppression by means of which the Bourgeoisie maintains its predominance and holds in check the proletariate. Reserving for itself, in order to increase its wealth, all the surplus of the product of labour, the capitalist leaves for the workman only just the scanty store he needs to keep him from starvation.

Forcibly held down in this hell of capitalist and proprietarial production, it would seem as though the working classes are powerless to break their fetters, but the proletariate has at length become alive to its own condition, it is sensible that within it, exists the elements of a new society, that its deliverance shall be the price of its victory over the Bourgeoise and that this class destroyed, the classes will be abolished altogether, and the object of the revolution attained. We desire to reach this object *i.e.,* the triumph of the revolution without stopping at any middle paths which are mere compromises putting off victory and prolonging slavery.

By destroying individual property the Communist overthrows one after another all the institutions of which property is the pivot. Driven from his property, garrisoned by himself and family as though it were a citadel, the rich man will no longer find an asylum for his selfishness and his privileges. With the annihilation of the classes will disappear all the institutions that cause the oppression of the individual and of the social group, the only reason for which has been the maintenance of these very classes—the subjugation of the working man to his master.

Education open to all and equally placed at the disposal of all will produce that intellectual equality, without which material equality would be without value and without charm. No more wage slaves, victims of misery and wretchedness, of want of solidarity, of competition, but a free association of working men with equal rights. distributing the work among themselves. to procure the greater development of the community, the greater sum of well being for each of its members. For every citizen will find the most extended freedom, the largest expansion of his individuality in the greater expansion of the Community.

It is hardly necessary for us to add that we fight against (on the same principle of the abolition of private property), the institution of the family, such as it exists nowadays. Thoroughly convinced partisans of the free union of the sexes, we repel the thought of marriage which institutes for the benefit of the man a new and exorbitant proprietarial right, namely the right of ownership of the woman, but in order to a possible establishment of the free union of the sexes, it is necessary that both the man and the woman shall enjoy the same right in society as well as have the same duties imposed on them, that is, they must be equal a thing that is impossible, unless private property be done away with.

In the same way it seems to us superfluous to state that recognising neither boundaries or frontiers we are concerned in working out the realization of our aspirations, wherever the lottery of events has placed us, regarding each revolutionary associate, no matter whence he comes, as a brother, and each exploiter of humanity, whatever tongue he may speak, as an enemy. And lastly we do not believe in the advent of the new order for which we are struggling by means of legal and pacific methods, and that is why we are revolutionary socialists. The study of history has taught us that the noblest conquests of man are written on a blood-stained book. To give birth to justice, humanity suffers a thousand tortures. Ours be then the force, so often employed against us, ours the force the heritage of the people which has been wrested from it by a coalition of the clever, and from its own want of energy, ours the force less as a desideratum than a consummation, regretfully sought less as a choice than as a necessity. Ours the force as the only means of breaking asunder the iron chains that bind us!

But at the same time let also prudence and caution guide us, the caution that determines the hour for the employment of force, and the firmness that preserves and directs it, unvanquished through all obstacles. Let us mature our ideas and our aspirations. Away with reckless and useless struggles; but no more hesitation nor armistice on the day of battle, and once having commenced the final struggle, let it be no longer merely with the hope of success, but with the certainty of triumph!

So, comrades, we finish by saying we are Atheists, Anti-Statists and Free Communists or International Revolutionary Socialists.

## POLICY.

Having stated our principles I will now briefly state what should be our policy in accordance with our principles, which can be sumed up shortly as *educate, educate, educate,* that an organisation may spring from the body of the people prepared for action, this action to be the destruction and not reform of Government Authority, and Monopoly, of every description.

## OUR ATTITUDE TOWARDS OTHER BODIES.

To the individualists (anarchists or otherwise) we are opposed. We contend that capital is the result not of any one individual's labour, but of all the workers combined, not only of this but of many past generations. Therefore it would be unjust that it should be held as Individual Property. We are also opposed to the idea of every one receiving according to his deeds. that the strong, the able bodied, those well endowed by nature, are to have all they can procure, while the halt, the lame, and the blind are to be left to their own resources, or at best depend on the charity of those better off. Again, so long as private property exists, there can be no freedom for women, all the advantages of co-operative labour are lost, and an enormous amount of labour wasted in providing for separate homes, farms and what not.

## STATE SOCIALISTS.

These believe that the state should be all powerful, that it should own the land, mines, railways, machinery and means of exchange, in fact own all things and organise labor in all its branches, that their policy should be to gain possession of the state machine and then arrange everything for the people. The bureaucracy and officialism of to-day is not to be compared to what it must be when the state undertakes these manifold duties.

The representative farce would have to be resorted to. These representatives at once become the Authority, the Government, superior to the body of the people, and would have to be prepared with force to defend their authority against any rebellious minority.

The march of progress is against isolation and individualism on one hand, and on the other against centralisation and authority of every description. We, the Anti-Statist Communists are the pioneers of that future state of society towards which all progress tends, namely. the free association of groups of workers (call them Towns, Villages, Communes or what you will) holding the land and capital, in common, working it on true co-operative principles, federated with each other for mutual assistance, every member working according to his ability and receiving according to his needs, man and woman being then equally free, would form connections through love alone. Connections of this description would not require a State or Priest to endorse or enforce it. The bond of love would be sufficient, when it was not it would naturally be dissolved. This would be done without injury to anyone, the children being fed, clothed and cared for by the Community.

## TRADES UNIONS.

Trades Unionism like Socialism, is the outcome of of the greed, tyranny, and oppression of the Capitalist class. The Capitalists at first thought the unions meant fighting, and that they would be successful, they became frightened, fearing that this would mean less profits if not the total extinction of their monopoly and privileges, they roundly abused and denounced Trades Unions, and passed laws against combination; but now that the development of the commercial system and the invention of new machinery has placed the workers in a more dependent position, and the Trades Unions are becoming little better than Benefit Societies, with an ever increasing subscription and decreasing reserve funds, helpless in the meshes of capitalism, they now tolerate and even occassionally say a good word for Trades Unions. But with the practical break-down of Trades Unions Socialism springs forth and says the day for this unequal and losing battle between the bloated Capitalist and the starving workman for a mere increase or to prevent a decrease of wage is past. To day and from henceforth, the battle is by the workers as a whole, for the destruction of monopoly and tyranny of every description, as the only means of emancipating themselves.

As commerce grew and expanded, as fresh markets were found for commodities even faster than they could be manufactured, trade went up by leaps and bounds, when a comparative small amount of machinery was used, a large portion of the working population was employed in tilling the soil, this was the time of the prosperity of Trades Unions. Then, though the workers did not get all they wanted or were entitled to, they did by combination get some improvement in their position. But how do they stand to day with a depopulation of the rural districts, crowding in to the towns, an increase of population? The increased use of machinery, the ever growing force of foreign competition are all adding to the number of the unemployed. With all these forces against Trade Unions, is it possible for them to be otherwise than mere benefit Societies.

Our policy towards the Trades Union then, is to show them how this evolution has gone on in the past and will in the future; that as the commercial system expands and new machinery is invented, wealth can be produced to an unlimited extent, and comparatively independent of manual labour; the capitalists reaping all the benefit, the workers becoming more helpless and enslaved in their economical toils. That as the policy and tactics of the Trade Unions have failed to alter this in the past, so still more will they, in the future, their only hope being by developing their organisation, becoming Socialists and rebeling against a system that enslaves them, using their organisations not for a mere increase or to prevent a decrease of wage, but for the destruction of the capitalist system and the emancipation of the whole of the workers.

## EIGHT HOURS LABOR MOVEMENT.

With reference to this, the most prominent proposal put forward by the Social Democrats. In the first place what all socialists protest against is the exploitation of the laborers by the capitalist, whatever the hours of the working day may be. So long as labor has to pay a tribute to capital and is not free we have not achieved our end, moreover, an eight hours bill or even less would not in the long run absorb the reserve army of laborers even if it was carried. Competition at home and abroad would force on the invention and use of new machinery in order to dispense with human labor; capital and machinery would be removed to other countries where cheap labour could be obtained for the benefit of the capitalists. Labor would also be intensified so that an hour's labor would mean much more wear and tear then than it does now, as it does now more than it did fifty years since. For a large part of the workers, an act of this kind would be inoperative as the Factory Acts are for many women and children to day, in short there would still be an ever growing army of unemployed, and the employed would be in much the same position as now. Seeing this so clearly it is not our business to advocate this palliative measure, but to criticise the action of those who do so.

## THE UNEMPLOYED.

This question of the unemployed is one of great difficulty. Our sympathy is naturally with these starving people. But there is no special unemployed class. It is the workers, some of whom are employed, others unemployed, these constantly changing places, employed to-day, unemployed to-morrow; therefore, it is a question for the whole of the workers. The question is, what can we do for the unemployed portion of the workers. It appears hard to call meetings specially of the unemployed, and tell them that they cannot be permanently benefited until the Revolution, and that they must starve in the meantime. The only alternative is to advocate relief works, which no Revolutionist can do. These relief works must be unproductive or productive. If unproductive, it will be task labor, with just sufficient food for the workers to keep life in their bodies until the capitalist requires their services for fresh exploitation; and even at this no society could keep an ever-increasing army of unproductive workers for any length of time.

If on productive works, they are unemployed because wealth is produced for sale at a profit, and at present no profit can be made on their labor. We have wealth, the results of labor, in abundance, and no market for it; therefore, there is no demand for their labor; and if they are set to work producing other wealth, it will cause a still greater abundance for the world's markets. This will mean a fall in prices and a reduction in wages, and the throwing out of work those at present employed. We hear even now of the unfair competition of prison labor, and this employment of the surplus laborers of our commercial system on productive works would have the same effect, only in a much greater degree. The most likely thing to occur by calling meetings specially of the unemployed is that, having their passions aroused by our denunciations of the thieving class, they will destroy a few windows. The paltry bill will be paid by an insurance company, and we lose some of our best advocates as a result. We Socialists do not want to see the aimless destruction of property, but the destruction of the property holders. In the meantime, let the starving people steal, sack shops, or what not, in preference to starving, if they so choose, it is a sign of discontent and of a determination to die fighting rather than starving. We may regard this as a sure forerunner of Revolution, but we must not let it be supposed that it is Socialism. Meetings specially of the unemployed, therefore, should not be called, but meetings of the workers as a whole should be held on every possible occasion. The principles of Socialism should be put plainly before them, and they must be told that the only remedy for their misery, poverty, and constant unemployment is the destruction of a system that puts it in the power of an idle class to employ and enslave the workers, and at best to dole out a small portion of their stolen wealth as charity to those who have produced it all when starving, and that no permanent good can be done for them by relief works, charity, or, in fact, anything under our competitive commercial system, with all the means of producing wealth monopolised.

## RADICALISM.

The official and recognised Radical party is based on what they are pleased to call liberty and freedom Freedom meaning to them Free Trade, Free Contract, and Free Competition; and Liberty to them is the liberty to fleece the destitute and starving workers to their heart's content by the aid of these three F's. They will not admit that there is a class struggle going on, but contend that with the aid of these three F's all the workers have to do is to be more temperate and thrifty, and that under this splendid arrangement there is a chance for every one to rise, blinding the workers to the fact that only a few can do this, and that they then leave their class and become exploiters in one way or another.

But there is an advanced wing of Radicalism formed by the workmen, who, having found that Toryism and Liberalism were of no use to them, have gone as far as they could see or understand. They have no clearly defined principles, and, after all, only agitate for mere superficial reforms. The election of governors and the extension of the suffrage these have been agitated for about 120 years, and more strongly at the commencement than the finish. In 1770, part of the programme was adult suffrage and annual parliaments, but now it is not the question of a useless vote but food for the stomach. This question will not wait a hundred years for settlement, before this social problem the Radical stands helpless, shouting loudly about the cost of Monarchy and the pension list. This is as far as he can grasp at present, failing to see that this is a drop in the ocean compared to the robbery of the landlord and capitalist class. It is from this wing of the Radical party only that we can expect to make converts. We must, then, lay before them our principles, show them that any mere reform is usless. Urge upon them the necessity of studying this social problem, work with them when possible, but make no alliances that would cause us to sacrifice our principles in the least.

## TEMPERANCE, VEGETARIANISM AND THRIFT.

Many people belong to Temperance Societies, and think they have found the cure for poverty and misery by the mere abstention from drink. No greater delusion could enter the mind of man. As Socialists we admit that if people give way to drink they cannot have a clear head to understand the Social problem, and until a large part at least of the people understand this, we shall have the misery and poverty, but if a man becomes a blue ribbonite and nothing more he has done nothing towards the emancipation of the workers.

Where we Socialists fall foul of the temperance thrift and vegetarian advocates is with the iron law of wages argument. We contend, and all political economists agree with us that under a capitalist system of society, with monopoly and competition, wages are ruled by the standard of comfort, adopted by the people of a country, and always have a tendency to fall to the minimum rate or starvation point, therefore a reduction in the standard of comfort by a majority, or even a large minority, would only result in a reduction of the standard rate of wages, and be of benefit only to the capitalist class, being only of benefit to those who practise it so long as they are a small minority, if it can only affect the individual or small minority for good, and the majority for evil, it is a proof that it is no remedy for the workers as a whole.

As a proof of this argument we have only to refer to Ireland with a potatoe-standard, Russia black-bread, India rice, Germany and Italy with their cheap soups, and wages in all these countries accordingly low. The English workers are now complaining of the competition of other countries, particularly Germany. They are told that they are losing their trade because the German is content to work longer hours for less wages than an Englishman. This means that his standard of living is lower than an Englishman's. Are we, then, to take the advice of the capitalists, vegetarians, and temperance advocates, and reduce our standard of comfort to the level of the Germans? or, rather, should we not tell these people that so long as they advocate their doctrines as a remedy for poverty we shall oppose them? That we are determined not to lower our standard of comfort, but rather to increase it, and at the first opportunity overthrow the system of monopoly as the only cure for poverty and misery.

## SECULARISM.

We are in accord with the Freethought party in their battle against superstition and authority divine. The people must be free both economically and mentally. Tyranny, oppression and pea-soup philanthropy on one side, and cringing poverty and hypocrisy on the other, must be put an end to. This, however, can only be done by the destruction of monopoly and authority of every discription. Priestcraft is, after all, only one of the effective weapons used for keeping the workers in slavery. Freedom of thought is of small avail without freedom for all to live as freely as they think.

## LAND NATIONALISATION.

We are in agreement with the Land Nationalisers so far as they advocate the abolition of private property in land; but we contend that if we had land nationalisation alone it would be the capitalists' class, who would benefit by a reduction in taxation, so long as private property in the means of production, transit, and exchange exist, the iron law of wages comes into force, and the workers will only get a bare subsistence wage. We are entirely opposed to the idea of giving compensation to the present holders, believing that their having robbed and enslaved us and our forefathers in the past does not give them a title to farther enslave our children for generations to come in the form of usury, which compensation would mean. Being opposed to centralisation and authority, we are not in favor of the central state under any name or form holding the land and demanding a rent for it, but believe that it should be in the hands of the local communes or towns, and cultivated on co-operative principles, without payment of any compensation or rent whatsoever.

## CO-OPERATION.

The co-operative movement started with a noble ideal: the overthrow of the commercial system by the co-operative and self-employment of the workers. This has been found impossible, and the co-operators have degenerated into mere joint stock companies or distributive agencies, with agents in all parts of the world buying in the cheapest market, which means beating down the wages of the producer for the benefit of those with capital to spare to invest in these societies and, like Building Societies, are a very good investment for those better off, but for the poverty-stricken proletariate this co-operation is not only useless, but often used for their exploitation. Our duty, then, is, while always advocating co-operative effort to show these people that their movement, so far as it effects the condition of the people as a whole, has been a failure, and must be so as long as they attempt to plant it down in the midst of a competitive commercial system, and that until usury and monopoly of every description is destroyed there can be no real co-operation that shall benefit the workers, and unless they are prepared to do their duty and assist in this destruction, they, in the times coming, will be swept away as part and parcel of the old system of Society.

## IMPERIAL FEDERATION.

To Imperialism and Jingoism of every form we, as international Revolutionary Socialists, are bitterly opposed it being entirely in contradistinction to our idea of the brotherhood of man and of the principles of liberty and freedom. This policy is upheld by the capitalists for the purpose of finding markets for their shoddy wares. They are responsible for the wars in which many people are slaughtered or enslaved which are the outcome of this policy. It is not the Tory, Liberal or Radical, but the Capitalists, the Property and Bond holders who are responsible, as let the Soudan, Afghanistan and Burmah testify.

New markets are a necessity of the Capitalist system of production. They must be got in some way, for as soon as the capitalist system ceases to expand, it begins to fall to pieces. The latest move, Imperial Federation, simply means an attempt on the part of the Capitalists of this country to get a monopoly of the trade with the colonies to the exclusion of other countries and that the resources of these colonies shall be used for the defence of the present markets and gaining of new ones in any and every direction, and not only this but that these united forces of the whole shall be used for keeping the workers in bondage to the Capitalists in every part.

# 12

# *THE CO-PARTNERSHIP SNARE* (TWENTIETH CENTURY PRESS, c. 1913), 1–3, 14–16.

*Harry Quelch*

[By the turn of the twentieth century, ideas of profit-sharing and co-partnership had been in the air for decades. Often they were espoused by social reformers seeking alternatives to both socialism and class conflict, like the Liberal co-operator E.O. Greening (1836–1923) whom Harry Quelch mentions here (see Vol. 2, Chapter 36). Nevertheless, the Fabians Sidney and Beatrice Webb would have spoken for many socialists when, in *The Consumers' Co-operative Movement* (1921), they dismissed all such variants of self-interested producer alliance as "the protégé of political Conservatism and profit-making Capitalism". The Webbs' main objections were grounded in their consumer-based ideas of political economy which also explains their scepticism regarding producers' co-operation and the self-governing workshop. Quelch in this pamphlet is as hostile to co-partnership as the Webbs and saw it as a spurious social panacea meant to head off the claims of the rising socialist movement. Like the Webbs, he also condemns the idea of an industry being run for the benefit of those engaged in it, and in this respect groups co-partnership with the working-class movement of syndicalism. Writing from a Marxist perspective, the main emphasis in this case is nevertheless on the snares of class collaboration.

The extracts presented here provide a summary of his main objections. The context Quelch describes is that of a growing awareness of the social ills to which capitalism inevitably gave rise. In the case of Engels's *Condition of the Working Class in England* (1844), the discovery of the social question was a crucial element in the making of Marxism itself. Works like Thorold Rogers's *Six Centuries of Work and Wages* (1884) or D. de B. Gibbins's *The Industrial History of England* (1890) were also read by many socialists. Nevertheless, neither author was himself a socialist; nor was Charles Booth, the pioneering social investigator whose findings were published as *Life and Labour of the People of London* (1889–1891). In the full text of his pamphlet, Quelch provides a detailed discussion of specific schemes like those of Sir William Lever (1851–1925), a Liberal by political persuasion and the archetypal paternalist employer who founded the famous model industrial village at Port Sunlight.]

Imitation is the sincerest form of flattery, and we are warned by advertisements to "beware of spurious imitations," the appearance of which is due to the commercial success of the goods they imitate. The Socialist movement, therefore, should be flattered by the numerous schemes of spurious "social reform" the persistent advocacy of which can but be regarded as a striking and involuntary tribute to the spread and development of Socialist ideas and doctrine, and to the growth in numbers of conscious, active Socialists.

Time was when Socialist propaganda was met with the assurance that any drastic, radical change in social conditions was uncalled for and unnecessary. If in the present system everything were not precisely for the best in the best of possible worlds, it was rapidly becoming so. There was poverty, want and squalor, and the misery, vice and crime produced by these, it was true; but the dark spots on the bright sun of our prosperity were gradually being reduced in size and density. The world was getting better. Progress was being made—slowly, too slowly, perhaps—but none the less surely. The unquestioned enormous increase in the output of national wealth must mean greater prosperity for everybody. It might be true that the bulk of this increase of wealth went to those who "toil not, neither do they spin," and that nothing like a fair share was yet appropriated by the actual producers. Nevertheless, their share was gradually growing greater. Wages had risen, while the rate of interest had fallen; the number of paupers in proportion to population was smaller; and, taken altogether, there were indisputable evidences that the terrible abyss of poverty was being slowly filled up, and that the awful contrasts of wealth and want were being gradually eliminated or bridged over.

That was the sort of language held, and the kind of argument advanced by our opponents when, some thirty years ago, the revival took place in this country of that Socialist movement and agitation which had died down and almost disappeared as a force in our national life with the decease of the "International" nearly ten years earlier. Our indictment of the existing social order was unwarranted by the facts; our picture of the condition of the mass of the people was painted in much too heavy colours; our description of the prevailing poverty grossly exaggerated. So, among others, said Mr. Charles Booth, who declared the Socialist estimate that twenty-five per cent. of our population were living below subsistence level to be a gross over-statement of the case, and undertook to prove it to be so.

All that is now changed. It is now universally admitted that although wages have risen and the material condition of the working class has improved by comparison with the worst period in its history—the first three or four decades of the last century—there is no improvement whatever if a more distant retrospect is made. Engels's "Condition of the Working Classes in England," Gibbins's "Industrial History," Rogers's "Six Centuries of Work and Wages," all support the conclusion that the end of the eighteenth and the beginning of the nineteenth centuries marked the nadir of the condition of the working class in this country, and that, however much their condition may by comparison with that period have improved thirty years ago, it could then, from the point of view of material comfort and of the purchasing power of wages, hardly compare with that of five hundred years earlier. Mr. Booth's investigations, moreover, proved not that we had overstated, but had understated the case as to the proportion of the population living below the "poverty line," and that not twenty-five, but more than thirty, per cent. of the population of this, the richest country in the world, were living at a level of subsistence which meant steady physical deterioration and premature death.

And in the thirty years which have since elapsed there has been no material change for the better—except in so far as by legislative and trade union effort there have been reductions in the length of the working day and some slight provision made for compensating workmen for injuries in the course of their occupation, for relief work for the unemployed, for saving children from absolute starvation, and a meagre provision for the aged. Such increases in wages as have taken place have been more than counterbalanced by the rise in prices, higher rents, and the general increase in the cost of living. In the meantime, we have been passing through a period of unparalleled material prosperity; of increased and intensified production and productivity unprecedented in the world's history; trade has been "booming," and just now is bounding up and still upward, by leaps and bounds. Yet it has only been by the force of combination and by strikes, or the menace of strikes, that the workmen have been able, not to get a reasonable proportion of the increased wealth, but to raise their real wages approximately to the level of the increased cost of living.

These facts and the consequent soundness of the case for Socialism are now so universally admitted that we have all sorts of more or less spurious remedies put forward as measures for the amelioration of evil conditions which Socialism alone can eradicate. These measures include the vicious system of doles for the poor to be provided by a poll-tax on the poor themselves, as in the Insurance Act; bureaucratic surveillance of the working class and suppression of individual liberty, as in the "temperance" legislation, the "Children's Charter," the Labour Exchanges, the so-called "White Slave Traffic" Act, and similar measures.

Of all the schemes now being advocated, ostensibly to improve the position of the working class, but really to head back revolutionary Socialism, probably the most insidious and dangerous is what is known as profit-sharing or co-partnership.[. . .]

It is very remarkable, and, indeed, indicative of the mischief which profit-sharing may inflict upon the working-class movement, that it is being supported by many leading trade unionists who might have been expected to have a keener appreciation of the sinister character of such schemes. They really seem to imagine that it is honestly proposed to give the workers a share of the profits, instead of the intention being to force more work out of them for less pay! Their error in this connection is due to their ignorance of the elementary economic fact that all profit is due to the robbery of Labour, and that Labour will continue to be robbed until profit-making is superseded by Socialism.

Seeing, therefore, the possibility of its application to practically all large industries, the steady extension of this application, and the amount of support it is receiving from various quarters, I cannot but regard profit-sharing, eespecially in the form of co-partnership, as a most serious danger and menace to the working class in its struggle for emancipation from wage-slavery.

It is none the less, but all the more, dangerous on account of its plausibility and its seeming fairness to the workers as producers. Many well-intentioned people support it, and are taken in by it, because they imagine that it really does mean giving the workers something more than mere wages, and ensuring, so far as they are concerned, a more equitable division of the total product of industry.

As I have shown in these pages, that is an entirely fallacious conclusion. Wherever profit-sharing, in any form, has been adopted with success, it has been proved conclusively that what has been shared is not profits, but wages. The proportion of the total product taken by the workers has not been greater, but less. That, although the actual amount of wages per man may have increased, the aggregate expenditure on labour has generally actually decreased, and even where there has not been an actual reduction in the aggregate there has always been a reduction in the *proportion* taken by labour. By the promise of bigger earnings the workers have been stimulated to greater effort, and, while receiving some addition to their wages, have been actually doing more work for less pay.

The idea underlying the advocacy of profit-sharing by most of those who regard it as a solution of the social problem and a way out of the conflict between Capital and Labour—the idea that it gives the workers something like a fair equivalent for their labour and ensures an equitable division of the product, is seen to be a fraud, a delusion and a snare. It does not increase the return to Labour, nor does it reduce the return to Capital. On the contrary, the present disparity—the source of the terrible contrasts of riches and poverty—is increased rather than diminished.

Nor is this the only objection to profit-sharing, nor even the worst of its mischievous results. For not only does it reduce the aggregate return to Labour and increase the disproportion between the share of the product taken by the worker and that taken by the capitalist, but its tendency is always, as a consequence, to increase the productivity of a given number of workers, and, thereby, to steadily reduce the numbers of those employed, and, correspondingly, to increase unemployment. In this respect, in its tendency to increase the numbers of those for whom no work can be found, it may possibly defeat itself. At any rate it will demonstrate its futility as a remedy for the social ills which are so largely due to the existence of an army of unemployed. At the same time, as these will always be in a minority, the majority, content with getting a share of "profits," may be indifferent to their sufferings.

On the other hand, the tendency to speed-up and intensify labour, due to the stimulus of profit-sharing, cannot fail to be excessively harmful to the physical health and well-being of the great body of the working-class. To hustle, to become more efficient, a more prolific wealth-producing and profit-making machine—not to be a better, a healthier and happier human being—that is the ideal set before the workman by every form of profit-sharing. The production of wealth, and of profit, becomes an end in itself: the aim and object of life, instead of being merely the means by which to realise a full, free, and healthy life. To live to work is the ideal, instead of to work in order to live.

Thus profit-sharing is not only not a modified "practical" form of Socialism, as some of its advocates imagine and teach, but is antisocial, and therefore diametrically opposed to Socialism. Socialism will abolish profits altogether, it will not increase them, because it will abolish the system of exploiting unpaid labour, by which profits are created. It will not secure a "share" of the profits for the workmen—thus aiding and abetting the robbery of labour; it will secure the whole product for the whole community—a community of workers.

For these reasons, therefore, and recognising the plausibility of this profit-sharing nostrum and its menace to the Socialist movement, it is necessary for us Socialists to be on our guard; to expose the hollowness of the "industrial peace" promised by co-partnership, and to point out that true industrial peace will only be secured when the causes of the class war are eliminated by the socialisation of all the great means of production, and the social production of wealth for social use.

# 13

# "SOCIAL-DEMOCRATS AND THE ADMINISTRATION OF THE POOR LAW", *SOCIAL DEMOCRAT*, JANUARY 1897, 14–18.

*George Lansbury*

[Despite its early adoption of so-called "stepping stones" to socialism, there was always a strand in and around the SDF that was scornful of palliatives and the diversion of energies into reforms falling a long way short of socialism. Though particularly marked in the SDF's earliest years, the persistence of such attitudes was to be demonstrated by such groupings as the breakaway Socialist Party of Great Britain, formed in 1904 and still in existence today. It is just such attitudes that George Lansbury has in mind when he begins the article reproduced here by defending the humdrum but indispensable work of here-and-now social reform.

Lansbury is better remembered as the parliamentarian of Christian pacifist convictions who in the early 1930s briefly led the Labour Party and who had earlier founded its newspaper, the *Daily Herald*. Lansbury can certainly be counted among the prominent Labour personalities for whom the SDF served as a "training school". But he also reminds us that there was no single approach to such questions within the SDF and nothing to exclude Lansbury's unabashed prioritisation of immediate effectiveness. Lansbury has no time for the callousness towards the poor of the "Manchester School" of liberal political economy. He writes forcefully of the punitive and inhumane character of workhouse relief in particular; and he takes issue with the disdain for the pauper classes of respectable labour leaders whose attitudes in such matters were not unknown within the socialist movement itself. With the absence of property qualifications under the Local Government Act of 1894, Lansbury also urges the use of the Boards of Guardians as organs of local democracy allowed a wide degree of autonomy by the Local Government Board. As an example, he cites the lockout in Lord Penrhyn's slate quarries which was already into its fourth month and lasted for almost a year. Public relief in these circumstances was thus envisaged as a means of support and solidarity with workers in struggle.

Lansbury left the SDF around 1903–1904. For a time he was associated with the Fabians Sidney and Beatrice Webb in producing the famous minority report on poor law reform in 1905; and by 1911 he was urging his views on the question in public debate with the SDFer Harry Quelch. Nevertheless, Lansbury continued to associate closely with the SDF at local level and it was the SDF as training school that would leave the stronger mark upon him. As mayor of Poplar in East London from 1919, Lansbury would lead the rates rebellion which has ever since remained the symbol of a militant local democracy defying the central state (Shepherd 2002, ch. 11). Until finally succumbing in the late 1920s, he was also one of those most resistant to the exclusiveness of party. As late as 1925, he was conjuring up the evangelical spirit of Morris, Hyndman, Quelch and Hardie, as if no party differences had ever separated them. In just that same spirit, Lansbury also embraced "Communists, ILPers, Trade Unionists, revolutionaries, evolutionists": all, he maintained, with their appointed place in the "army of Labour" (*Lansbury's Labour Weekly*, 2 May and 24 October 1925).]

Among the more ardent spirits of the S.D.F. there are to be found those who continually express their regret that the movement to-day is hum-drum and commonplace, compared to the good old days of fourteen years ago, when to be a Social-Democrat was to be, in very deed, "an enemy of society," and when every day brought some new excitement, either in a police outrage or unemployed march. While it is quite true that the work is hum-drum and commonplace, compared with the days just mentioned, there can be no doubt that the movement to-day is more solid and enduring, and although it was necessary to start at the bottom it would never do to revert to the old tactics of mere angry propaganda against the existing order of things, and society has a right to ask us what we have to say to the needs of the present and what policy we have to offer in place of those we denounce as worn-out and useless.

After Parliament the most important question is that of administration, especially in regard to the Poor Law. No one would deny the work done by many excellent men and women on municipalities, school boards, and other local bodies, but the fact remains that no administrative authority comes so close to the people as do the Guardians of the Poor, and no local body in the country has so large powers either for good or evil as they. At the present moment, when Lord Penrhyn is engaged in the pleasant task of starving-out his slaves, the local Board of Guardians could turn his flank by paying out-door relief to the discharged workmen, to such an amount as would make up the wages which are stopped, and, as his lordship is one of the biggest ratepayers, he would soon find it convenient to re-open his works. I only mention this in passing, as it is sometimes urged that time is wasted on such local bodies. It may be to some extent true, but in the main it is just that kind of work which, in times of stress, would most readily help workers.

But this is not all. Say what our Manchester politicians may to the contrary, it is a startling fact that pauperism, especially amongst the aged, is ever increasing, and that, although so-called charitable agencies are treble what they were a few years ago; and not only is pauperism increasing among the aged, but despite prison-like casual wards, where the tasks imposed are harder and the food given is even worse than in prison, tramps and casuals multiply year by year, until it is an acknowledged fact that there are thousands of men and women in England to-day who have never lived other than on the rates. Some of our labour leaders have lately been loud in their denunciation of such as these, but except for frothy denunciation of the individuals their talk leads nowhere. Then there are the children of widows and single women. It is admitted that the factory system has tended to shorten men's lives and consequently to leave widows and orphans for society to care for, and the revelations of the House of Commons Committee prove how much need there is for reform in the treatment of these children. I propose to say a few words on each of the above sections and try to show what policy is the correct one for Social-Democrats to follow.

First, then, as to the aged. These at present are treated either in the workhouse or by out-door relief. For my part I do not know which is the worse, to be treated as a semi-criminal, with all my actions regulated by a set of officials, or to be starved on a miserable pittance called out-relief which is only just enough to keep life going. Both policies are bad, and the sooner we of the S.D.F. couple adequate maintenance in old age with free maintenance in youth the better for all concerned. Both should be a charge on the National Funds, the present ridiculous arrangement, by which each parish is made to bear the cost of the poor within its borders, is one which should be swept away, as its only effect is to press upon the shoulders of the poor the entire burden of supporting the worn-out worker, and in the place of out-door relief as now given, and the workhouse, Boards of Guardians should build cottage homes in country districts for their old people. I say should do so, because they have the power to do this if they will; there is no law to say where the people should be maintained, neither is there any law to say how much relief should be given. Although the Local Government Board is a big bugbear to some, there is no gainsaying the fact that where a Board of Guardians is in real earnest, they generally get their way. Cottage homes need be in no respect like a workhouse, either inside or outside, and instead of leave being regulated it should be free at any time, and if to each cottage were attached a little garden, many an old man and woman would be only too glad to while away the time by cultivating flowers, &c. It is often urged, and with some truth, that the old people get drunk when they go out. This is, I think, accounted for by the fact that they never taste beer or spirits from one leave day to the other, and therefore ever so little knocks them over. I would advocate a small allowance day by day, so as to obviate this, and we all know that at least the majority of men and women only want enough for their needs. As to those who are not able to live by themselves, but must be cared for in institutions of one kind or another, these institutions should *not* be workhouses, but hospitals in the country. These should be made as pleasant as possible, and arrangements should be made for taking the patients out for drives, &c., in fine weather. One objection urged to this is that the old people like to be near their friends, and one well-known labour leader is at the present moment doing his utmost against a scheme such as this for aged married couples at Poplar on the score that the old people would rather be in the workhouse. This is mere rubbish, as in the case of any friend not having the means to go and visit, the Guardians can supply the necessary funds, and everyone knows that for the few almshouses remaining in and around London there are hundreds of applicants if one happens to be vacant.

Now, as to tramps and casuals. I can conceive of no class of men and women so deserving of pity as these. Many of them men of education, and many of them sunk so low that they have no wish to get into better surroundings. It is in vain that tasks and rules are made harder and harder each year, in vain that the ticket system is put into vogue. Driven from one county they flee to another and so in the aggregate ever grow a larger army. That they are, many of them, unfit for useful work no one will deny; that they propagate children to grow up as useless as themselves is equally true; but that prison tasks and the harshest of treatment will remedy the evil I for one entirely deny. Let us imagine all the thousands of tramps honest, decent, well-behaved men. Has society room for them? Are there employers wanting men and women? No; and therefore right behind the fact that these men and women in a commercial sense are valueless, lies the much bigger fact that society has no use for them; that they are pushed out; not because they are unfit, but because no one can make profit by them. What, then, should be our policy? First, we should take charge of the children and rigorously prohibit the carrying of children from one end of the country to the other; this should be done from infancy, and such children should be trained to occupations suited to their capacity. The men and women should be taken care of in settlements in country districts where work of a light character could be engaged in, and where they should be obliged to remain for a stated period not shorter than one year. The cost to the community would be much less than now, for all oakum-picking, stone-breaking, and similar tasks, are simply so much dead loss. Then there are the able-bodied unemployed. Some year or two ago I tried to induce the unemployed in East London to go into the workhouses. A few followed my advice, but the greater portion lacked the courage. Those who did go in, though they themselves benefited very little, so alarmed the Boards of Guardians that thousands of pounds were spent in relief work. It is as well that here, too, it should be clearly understood that Boards of Guardians can pay wages, and that such wages need not be in kind. In Poplar, wages were paid at the rate of 6½d. per hour, and half was paid in money and the other half by a card, which was an order on any tradesman for anything the recipient liked. While they can pay wages, they can also choose the task they will set, and it is to the eternal disgrace of the labour movement in London that long ago Boards of Guardians were not compelled to put men and women to useful work. In this connection it is well to point out that in many workhouses purely skilled work is done by the inmates, who do not receive a penny in wages for their work. In Poplar, the whole of the clothes and boots and shoes, beside innumerable other articles, are made by the inmates, with the aid of four paid men. The argument in favour of this is that these people must be set to work of some sort, and that this is better than oakum-picking and stone-breaking. True as this is, and taking as it proves before a ratepaying audience, it is still also true that such work is sweated work of the vilest description, and Social-Democrats should fight against it with all their might. We must ask that those who do really useful necessary work shall be paid the proper rate of wages. There is nothing illegal in this, as the fact that some are so paid proves. This would, however, only deal with a very few. There are thousands of unskilled men and women for whom no useful work can be found, and among these are many who are as unfit as the tramps and casuals mentioned above. For these we should start farm colonies; and here, again, I say, Guardians have the power to do this, and I can think of no more useful work for Social-Democratic Guardians than that of devising schemes for the co-operative cultivation of land. It may be urged that this would only be a palliative. I agree that it is; and so is everything we do of a like character to-day; but it is a palliative in the right direction, and therefore merits our support.

And now as to the children. This is the biggest problem of all. Everyone has a new scheme, and the very latest is that of the Sheffield Guardians, who have put their pauper children out in all parts of the town in separate houses; but a months trial has proved that this is no solution, and that the stamp of pauperism remains, even though the children never go near the workhouse. Our practical men and women will have to learn that until the whole of the children of the community are treated alike, by being maintained and educated at the cost of the community, all schemes for the regeneration of a section will remain dismal failures. Boarding-out (which has proved to be baby farming on a small scale), cottage homes, and barrack schools have all turned out wrong. In the meantime, though, it may be asked, what are we to do with our power as Guardians? I believe, in spite of the House of Commons Committee, that the barrack school is the best system, if properly carried out. The one school I know intimately is the notorious Forest Gate School, and, without hesitation, I affirm that, with a due regard to the feelings of the children, with proper food and decent recreation, and no half-time, that school could be made an efficient one for the proper training of children. But it is not only the schools that need attention; it is the start in life given the children which demands most consideration. At present domestic service for girls, army, navy and flunkeys for the boys, is the height of the average Guardians' ambition for such children. Social-Democrats should see to it that this is changed, no matter what the child may wish. We should do with these children as we do with our own: choose for them till they are of age. None of us burn our child's fingers in the fire to teach it, we prevent it burning itself till it is of age to know that fire is hot; and those who send boys into the army and navy, because they ask to go, do so to get rid of their responsibility. We must urge that the same code under which the Board and other outside schools work shall be worked in the workhouse school; the same inspectors inspect; that teachers as well qualified as outsiders shall be employed; that in connection with each school shall be technical institutes and workshops for both boys and girls in which their capacities for work could be developed.

This paper has already gone into greater length than it should have done, and therefore, in conclusion, I will only just say that no Social-Democrat must allow the bugbear of the rates to frighten him or her. No doubt rates do press heavily in every poor district; and if we listened to the ratepayers' outcry we should do nothing at all. The right thing is to do our work as Guardians efficiently and well, caring nothing so long as we can show good value for money. To many it may seem not very revolutionary or exciting to go in for the drudgery of Poor Law Administration. All the same, the more of us who do, the better for the movement and for ourselves. For if we can once let men and women understand that our proposals are practical, and in all ways better than those of our opponents, it will not be long before they will give up following party hacks and quack war cries and join with us in working, not to palliate, but to sweep away, commercialism with its workhouses and prisons.

# 14

# "LONG LIVE SYNDICALISM!", *THE SYNDICALIST*, MAY 1912.

*Edward Carpenter*

[The years immediately before the First World War are known to labour historians as those of the Great Unrest. Rising levels of labour militancy reached a peak in 1912, when a first-ever national coal strike followed the transport workers' strikes of the previous year. These were conditions in which the syndicalist alternative to parliamentary socialism could flourish, and since his return to Britain in 1910 Tom Mann had been tireless in propagating its principles of solidarity and direct action (Chapter 26, this volume). In January 1912 he launched the monthly *Syndicalist* under the auspices of the Industrial Syndicalist Education League. Its first issue included an "Open letter to British soldiers" – the famous "Don't shoot" manifesto – which would lead to Mann's arrest in March and his serving a two-month gaol sentence on charges of Incitement to Mutiny. Mann was not just the personification of the syndicalist movement. For an older generation of socialists he was a reminder of the new unionism which some two decades earlier had been its nearest precursor.

Syndicalism was predominantly a movement of younger militants. In many cases, their activist commitments can be traced for many years after the 1914–1918 war. If Edward Carpenter's support for the movement is given preference here, it is because it demonstrates the links there were with earlier socialist traditions and how different themes and arguments would often flourish, fade and reappear in changing forms and circumstances. As David Goodway (2006, 55–56) has noted, Carpenter over the years had steered a course between strands of socialist thought that were variously militant, parliamentarist, co-operative and statist. Despite his early association with both Marxists and anarchists, he had broadly supported the ILP and early Labour Party. Nevertheless, by 1912 the landscape was shifting again, and Carpenter added his voice to the wider reaction against the bureaucratisation of Labour politics that was so evident after 1906.

The article reproduced was one of a number of pronouncements in which he supported the syndicalist agitations in which, by his personal circumstances, he himself could have little direct involvement. His support for the miners' strike and "Don't shoot" propaganda is clearly indicated. He also evokes the older craft guilds whose example had inspired the ideas of guild socialism first propounded in 1906 by A.R. Orage and A.J. Penty. With the stimulus of syndicalism, these were to be more boldly expressed after 1912, first by S.G. Hobson and then by G.D.H. Cole. Over the next few years, these ideas would have an immense appeal for British socialists. Guild socialists like Cole saw William Morris as their direct precursor and inspiration. Though we can only speculate as to how Morris would have reciprocated, the views expressed here by Carpenter show how strong a case there was for their doing so.]

Success to the Syndicalist movement, and hearty congratulations on what has already been done! We are at last beginning to see a way out of the old jungle of commercialism—a light in the distance through the trees. Socialism has certainly taken us a long way in the right direction. It has taught us that the industrial life of the nation must in the future be carried on collectively for the benefit of the mass-peoples, and not for the greedy profits of the few. But we are now beginning to see that its path is in danger of winding through some ugly swamps of bureaucracy, officialism, and over-government (even the Capitalist classes themselves are crying out against Socialism on that score!) and that it may be difficult to get safely through along that line. So the Syndicalists are branching into a new route. They are adopting the entirely sensible scheme of getting the workers in each industry to organise that industry and its conditions of production for themselves.

The splendid thing about the present movement is the rapidity with which the workers themselves are grasping the new idea. The strike of the miners and the way in which the rank and file of them are laying down and deciding on their own conditions of labour is full of promise. And similar movements in the other trades, combined with the success and spread of the "Don't shoot" propaganda among the military, are opening up the way to a new era in our industrial life.

Of course, our opponents say that if each trade is going to organise its industry for its own advantage, and "hold up" its own produce at a monopoly price against the rest of the nation, we shall only have exchanged exploitation on its present scale for exploitation on a much larger scale, and abandoned the petty competition of Capitalists for warfare of a much more serious character among the unions. But such people are only speaking from their own experience and ideals of life. No one who knows the masses of the workers or the present tendencies of the unions could make such a foolish mistake as to suppose that this is really the direction in which they are moving or wishing to move. On the contrary, the immense and growing Federations of the trades and the continual conferences and congresses of sections point most distinctly towards the ultimate harmonising of the various interests in one great scheme.

As I have said, the well-to-do classes have been in terror hitherto at the prospect of possible government by a "cast-iron" bureaucratic Socialism. It only remains for them now to cordially welcome the arrival of an anti-governmental Syndicalism and of a free and voluntary co-operation of workers (all workers, of course, whether manual, clerical, artistic, or what not) in countless guilds, which shall be self-determining as to their own conditions, but federated together in a great whole for the reasonable exchange of their products. For many years now folk have pointed out what a splendid work the old English Craft Guilds did, how they organised the workers of that period and gave them substantial position and comparative affluence in face of the tyranny of the great landholders and barons; how they laid the foundations of England's industrial greatness; what fine and artistic things they produced—what metal-work, wood-work, architecture, and so forth—out of their free and self-determining organisations, and such folk turn with pride to this page in our history. But to-day Syndicalism is going to restore just these very guilds in a form suited to modern conditions, and every one who values what may be called real culture and the restoration of beauty and joy in daily life must surely welcome the movement and lend, as far as he can, a helping hand.

It is true that the movement will ultimately bring to an end the mean and futile social life of the dividend-drawing classes. And a good thing, too! The more one sees of that life the more one sees of its futility and essential wretchedness, and the less one sees that is worth preserving. Even for the sake of these classes themselves one may sincerely say, Long live Syndicalism!

# Part 3

# POLITICAL ECONOMY

# 15

# "THE IRON LAW OF WAGES", *JUSTICE*, 15 MARCH 1884, 3.

## H.M. Hyndman

[The iron law of wages mattered because it seemingly demonstrated the futility of mere trade union activity. Nothing could have illustrated better the preference for dogma over practical engagement which many held to be one of the SDF's defining characteristics. As dogma went, the iron law was less orthodox than it may have appeared. Among socialists, it was most of all associated with the German Ferdinand Lassalle, who believed it offered a crushing indictment of the condition of the worker under capitalism. Marx, on the other hand, had been scathing in his treatment of the notion in his broadside against the Lassalleans in his *Critique of the Gotha Programme* (1875). This, however, did not appear in English translation until after the First World War. Moreover, writings like Marx's *Wage Labour and Capital* (1847), the earliest to be issued via the SDF itself, gave little encouragement to a more positive view of trade union activities. The translator of that text, J.L. Joynes, was also the author of *The Socialist Catechism* (1885) which did explicitly refer to the iron law of wages. Perhaps more surprisingly, the idea is still to be found in the *New Socialist Catechism* of Bax and Quelch (1901), which maintained that the iron law stood "as firmly today as when stated by Lassalle" (Collins 1971, 52–53).

Hyndman at this early stage was much influenced by Lassalle's example of building up a socialist party. Nevertheless, he does not cite him here but invokes the authority of the bourgeois political economists of the nineteenth century, namely Ricardo, Say, Mill and Fawcett. Even Hyndman would not always show such fatalism regarding the prospects for improving working-class conditions through workers' collective action. Other SDFers, like those later involved in the militant "new unionism", were never fatalistic in the least. Nevertheless, Tom Mann later spoke for those of them who believed that Hyndman's lack of perspicacity on such issues had held the SDF back from becoming a far more potent social force. "I venture to believe", Mann would argue in his memoirs, "that had the tactics been different, had it been the recognised and persistent policy to attach what I call proper importance to the co-operative and trade union movements, the growth of the SDF would have been far more rapid, and there would have been no necessity for the corning into existence of the Independent Labour Party" (Mann 1923, 52–53).]

Many a workman who has done more than his share of work during the ten, twenty or thirty years that he has been able to work at all wonders I daresay how it is that he is no nearer to being able to take a holiday than he was when he began. Perhaps too many see sadly that their wages instead of rising are no better than they were, or what with slack times, keener competition, or new machines, or advancing years, are even lower than they earned a few years ago. But few unfortunately stop to think out the matter as forming with their fellow workers part of a great class. Nine out of ten look at the question merely as it touches them individually. A man who gets thirty, five-and-thirty, or forty shillings a week knows that he is a great deal better off than the mass of his fellow-workers; the labourer who toils on for a wage between ten shillings and twenty shillings is too much taken up with making both ends meet, too much troubled about whether he will still get his scanty pay, often too ignorant, to understand his own position. Thus it is that though Trade Unionists are banded together against employers, and unskilled labourers have sometimes an idea that they are not fairly treated, neither combine to change the system which really weighs down both. Certainly very few indeed know that there is no hope for them and their fellows, as a class, until the payment of wages in its present form is put an end to altogether and they have their full share of the product of their own labour.

What however is the law under which artisans and labourers alike work? Plainly stated this:—That in the competition of the labour-market the workers get on the average that sum in weekly wages which enables them to keep themselves and their family in the way to which they have been used in this country, so that the next generation may be as numerous as the present. An English labourer for instance even when paid at his worst gets a much higher money wage than the Indian labourer or even than an Italian or Russian labourer. But the law is that during his life-time he will receive on the average the wages which he earned when he began in the trade which he took up. Circumstances may slightly raise his "standard of life" and therewith his wages; but other circumstances may lower that standard of life, and thus in competition with his fellows lower his wages. To take an instance of this competition and its effects, first on a single man bidding against his fellows, and then on workers who have combined. Here is a man who has always lived in two or three rooms and kept his wife and children decently. His "standard of life" is high for his class. A place is open; he says he wants 30/- a week; times are bad, another man, perhaps a friend, comes along sees the same opening and offers to take 25/-; the master waits until times are still worse and gets an equally good man, forced by sheer necessity, by starvation that is, to sell his weekly labour at 18/-. Now that underselling is constantly going on in all unorganised trades, and the greater part of the workers are unorganised. And in this way the law is brought to bear upon each one of the workers without his being aware of it. He is in the habit from his childhood of selling his labour for what it will fetch, and only grumbles when it doesn't as he thinks fetch enough. But just the same happens with the skilled worker, though combination prevents his fellows from underselling him individually. In bad times such as we see now, what chance have the factory-hands, skilled or unskilled, against the employers who wish to cut down wages. Every day that passes shows that they have little or none. The skilled worker is better paid than the unskilled just as clever slaves in ancient times were often better fed or given finer clothes by their masters; but slaves they remain all the same to furnish riches for the employer while receiving all the time in wages but a small part of the value of what they produce. But this law is universally laid down by the very men who sometimes come forward as the friends of the people—the political economists. They are the men who have found out and registered this iron law of wages which dooms the workers who have no property of their own to toil on as wage-slaves on average subsistence all their lives through. Mere authority goes for very little when men begin to dig down to the bed-rock of political economy, yet when we know that Ricardo, J. B. Say, John Stuart Mill, Henry Fawcett, and many more all teach this law as one not to be disputed, the workers need scarcely look further for proof. To say that wages have risen even relatively during the last fifty years does not alter the fact that wages do tend in this country as in every other towards the cost of subsistence. If a skilled fitter gets a high wage there is always the half-fed agricultural labourer or the worn-out sweater's drudge to pull the balance down, and thousands of able-bodied paupers to take it lower down yet.

Thus, then, the man or woman who begins as a wage-earner in our modern capitalist society in nine hundred and ninety-nine cases out of every thousand ends as a wage-earner. During those long years of work for the profit of others he or she has been without any certainty even of regular work, and on the average can only reckon upon earning just enough to keep body and soul together. So long as we have on the one side a class owning the land, capital, money and machinery, and on the other a class that owns nothing but the power to labour, which power it is obliged to sell in constant competition—so long as this is the case, the workers as a body are wage-slaves working for mere subsistence under the iron law described, and wage slaves they must continue to the end of their lives.

At this moment it is most important that the workers should study and understand this. Wages are falling in every employment. In some employments they are already below the sum needed to buy what is necessary for healthy existence. Yet the men who suffer are absolutely willing not only to bear this pressure themselves, to put up with the "iron law" they could easily break if only they would combine, but they are going to hand on the same miserable lot to their children. There is no way out of it save by revolutionising the whole system.

Workers, study this iron law of wages: ask questions about it, ferret the matter out, then push aside your misleaders, and take control of production and distribution for yourselves.

# 16

## *SOCIALISM AND SLAVERY* (1884), SOCIAL DEMOCRATIC FEDERATION (LONDON: TWENTIETH CENTURY PRESS, 1899 EDN), 3–15.

*H.M. Hyndman*

[The 1880s was not just the moment of the socialist revival. It was also the decade in which the notions of individualism and collectivism entered into the English political lexicon as what seemed the two opposing spirits of the age. Among the most implacable of the individualists was Herbert Spencer (1820–1903), whose *The Man versus the State* (1884) was a sort of counterpart for its times to Friedrich Hayek's *Road to Serfdom* (1944). Like Hayek, Spencer saw the enemies of freedom all around him. Hayek called them "the socialists of all parties", and Spencer too was primarily concerned with the tempering of laissez-faire with the interventionist impulses that would come to be thought of as the new liberalism. His concern with the SDF was therefore as the popular expression of wider "communistic theories" which he believed to be reflected in the continuously encroaching legislation of the state. There were four essays comprising *The Man versus the State*, and in the one he entitled "The coming slavery" Spencer took direct issue with the Federation and its manifesto *Socialism Made Plain* (Chapter 1, this volume).

Hyndman's response takes up specific contentions of Spencer's regarding demands like the nationalisation of railways and the land. He also condemns the punitive character of the New Poor Law of 1834, which Spencer in his article had robustly defended. Also characteristic of the early SDF is Hyndman's delicate allusion to unnamed "German socialists". Just as he explained the iron law of wages without referring to Lassalle (Chapter 15, this volume), Hyndman held that continental theorists had not so much inspired the British as reminded them of the Chartists, Owenites and Spenceans who on British soil had inspired Europe's first great socialist movement. The very designation Social-Democrat was a British coinage of Bronterre O'Brien and only afterwards adopted on the continent.

At the time of Hyndman's response to Spencer, the SDF was the only socialist body that very well could have responded. The Fabian alternative was as yet hardly even embryonic; its earliest proponents such as Hubert Bland looked favourably on the SDF, and Bernard Shaw by his own account was on the verge of joining it. There is little enough in *Socialism and Slavery* that a Fabian need have disavowed. One of the Fabians' founding tenets would be that socialism represented the conscious assertion of principles that were already being adopted unconsciously through the intrinsic logic of large-scale organisation and the well-being of the community. Britain's economic history of the nineteenth century, as Sidney Webb was to put it, had been an "almost continuous record of the progress of Socialism" (Shaw 1889).

Hyndman's response to Spencer shows how far these assumptions were of pre-Fabian origin. In his advocacy of "immediate practical proposals", as already reflected in legislation like the factory and education acts, Hyndman also offers peaceful evolution as the only alternative to violent revolution. State organisation was growing as he wrote; the only question was whether it should be used by the Democracy or by some form of despot. In his opening exposition, Hyndman did admittedly ascribe the advances of the century to popular pressure from below and not just legislative enactment from above. Even so, there was little in his understanding of the underlying course of history from which a Fabian socialist need have demurred. With the defection of the more radical Socialist League at the start of 1885, Fabians like Bland even joined the SDF, until the scandal over Tory gold provoked a more conclusive parting of the ways (Lee and Archbold 1935, 93). Stanley Pierson once observed that "the Fabians carried forward the work in which Hyndman was engaged before his Marxism stiffened into dogmatism" (Pierson 1973, 106). Hyndman, if we knew no better, might by the same token be thought of here as one of Fabianism's unacknowledged forerunners.]

It is now generally admitted that the growth of Socialism in England is one of the features of the time, and this growth has been very surprising to many who have argued from the experience of the last forty years that Socialist ideas could never so much as take root in this country. But the truth is, that the Socialism of to-day is quite as much a revival of an agitation which, owing to various causes, had died down, as a new departure due to the importation of continental theories. We too often forget that the first great Socialist movement in Europe, the first really formidable and organised struggle of labourers against landlords and capitalists, began in England. Englishmen to-day are the direct heirs of the ideas put forward at the beginning of this century by Robert Owen, Thomas Spence, William Cobbett, Thomas Hodgskin, Bray, and others; and carried into the domain of active social and political agitation by the first three, as well as at a later date by such self-sacrificing workers in the cause of the people as Bronterre O'Brien, Ernest Jones, Stephens, Oastler, Frost, Bull, Vincent, O'Connor, and many more whose names are now forgotten save by a few survivors of the movement in the districts where they were specially active. Most of these agitators were quite as bitterly, or more bitterly, opposed to the capitalist class than they were to the landlords, and understood how completely that class had obtained control of economical, social, and political power. Nearly all the legislation in favour of the labouring class which has been carried since the great war may be directly traced to the efforts of these men, who would certainly rank as Socialists if they were now alive. But it can scarcely be said that any of them founded a definite school, and consequently their more radical and revolutionary proposals have, since 1848, been overlooked or attributed to others. None the less, however, the present development of English Socialism is directly connected with the work of the Chartists, Owenites, Spenceans, &c., for the enfranchisement of the wage-earning class.[1]

The elaborate analysis of German Socialists has enabled Englishmen to understand the full historical significance of what was done by their immediate predecessors in the same field, and to grasp effectually the influence which it must have on the present movement. Socialism, in fact, no longer consists in mere Utopian schemes or attempts to stir up general discontent among the suffering classes; it is no longer represented by men who think they can reach at one bound an almost unattainable happiness for mankind, or round up little oases of loving co-operators amid a desert of anarchical competition; it is a distinct, scientific, historical theory, based upon political economy and the evolution of society, taking account of the progress due to class struggles in the past, noting carefully the misery and the inevitable antagonism engendered by our present system of production, and following the movement into the future with a view to handling the ever-increasing power of man over nature for the benefit of the whole community, not to pile up wealth for the capitalist class and their dependents. Such a change can, of course, only be brought about by putting an end both to the existing competition for individual or class gain above, and the competition for mere subsistence wages below. Organised co-operation for existence in place of anarchical competition for existence; equality of conditions in place of class domination; international friendship in place of national rivalry—these are our aims. Thus the class struggle which we see going on under our eyes, the revolution in the methods of production—steam, machinery, electricity, &c.—which is affecting all classes, appears in the thoughts of men as a conflict between the principles of collectivism and individualism, between the system of public and private property. The changes in the economical forces below are, in short, reflected in the philosophy and literature of the time. Just in so far as we understand the facts is it possible to help on the change, and to influence for the better the surroundings of coming generations. True liberty is the accurate appreciation of necessity.

Such being, in brief, the view of Socialists, it is natural that Mr. Herbert Spencer, the principal living champion of individualism, should take the field against us. He sees—no one can help seeing—that, whichever party is in power, the tendency of modern legislation is to interfere with what is so foolishly called "freedom of contract"; that the State, controlled by the middle-class though it has been since 1832, has been forced to step in to thwart the most cherished ideas of that very class, and even in a growing degree to organise and administer complicated branches of production and distribution, chiefly in the interest of the dominant class itself but partly to the advantage of the whole country. In the *Contemporary Review* for April, 1884, therefore, Mr. Herbert Spencer boldly attacked this tendency and showed that it must, if left unchecked, lead straight to the Democratic

Socialism earnestly worked for by the Social-Democratic Federation. Socialism of this character is, according to him, "The Coming Slavery."

It is not a little remarkable however, that although he indulges freely in prophecy as to this hypothethical slavery of the future, Mr. Herbert Spencer declines altogether to recognise the palpable slavery which actually exists to-day, or the still worse slavery which the people suffered from before the enactment of the measures he holds to be so harmful. All that is passed by carefully. But, looking out upon the London streets, Mr. Spencer sees a great number of vagabonds and "corner men," tramps and other useless persons, who, according to his theory, owe their present position to their own idleness, thriftlessness, drunkenness or debauchery; or, if not to these causes, then to the action of the Poor Law which came to an end in 1834. That Society itself may be really responsible for the miserable conditions of life (necessarily leading to drunkenness, debauchery, &c.) in which so many of its poorer members are brought up; that the uncertainty of existence owing to the constant improvement in machinery may make men and women utterly hopeless and despairing; that at such a period of industrial depression as that lately passed through hundreds of thousands of workers are forced into idleness by no fault whatever of their own and loiter about ready to pick up any chance work—ideas like these seem never to have presented themselves to Mr. Herbert Spencer's mind at all. There will be a certain amount of suffering and laziness in any society. No Socialist would deny that. Sloth and lust, like cancer or consumption, would not be cured at once by collectivism, though the sufferings of the victims might be lessened and the diseases themselves gradually uprooted. What we wish to get rid of is avoidable suffering and immorality, directly due to the organisation, or rather disorganisation, of society itself.

Again, Mr. Herbert Spencer remarks that the Christian saying " 'If any would not work neither should he eat' is simply an enunciation of an universal law of nature under which life itself has reached its present height—the law that a creature not energetic enough to maintain itself must die." Why, what is this? There are thousands of creatures in our present society who have never been energetic enough to maintain themselves in any sense whatsoever, yet who have eaten excellently well every day, and will go on so eating from their cradles to their graves. The labour of other creatures has provided them with sustenance, whether the labourers were willing or no, owing to social conventions entered into before they were born. Such idlers as these are surely more harmful to the community at large, and, if ethics are to come in, more open to condemnation, than weary wayfarers who, perhaps, have never had a full meal their life through, however hard they might work. The truth is, our social arrangements breed idlers—wealthy idlers at the top, starving idlers at the bottom.

But the old Poor Law[2] still troubles Mr. Spencer, and the "support of the offspring of the unworthy," the issue of tickets-of-leave to convicts, the foundation of casual wards, and so forth, have done an infinity of mischief. How is it, then, that we find precisely similar phenomena in countries where Poor Laws are unknown, casual wards are not in existence, and the ticket-of-leave system is not in vogue?

There are plenty of tramps, vagabonds and beggars on the continent of Europe, as well as in England. Nay, even in the United States, that paradise of individualism, where Mr. Herbert Spencer himself reigns supreme in the domain of philosophy, and the almighty dollar rules the roast in material affairs, even in wealthy America there were no fewer than 3,000,000 tramps during the last great industrial crisis; and at this moment the number of tramps and unemployed is causing the gravest uneasiness, as well as the enaction of the most brutal laws, in nearly every State of the Union. Surely there must be some general cause at work to bring about this chronic poverty and idleness in the richest countries of the civilised world? Surely something deeper than petty enactments to relieve the wretched, or the provision of sheds to house the wanderer, occasion this universal distress.

Before stating the Socialist view of the matter it may be well to deal with Mr. Spencer's remarks on recent legislation. At page 473 occurs the following passage:—"Meanwhile those who regard the recent course of legislation as disastrous, and see that its future course is likely to be still more disastrous, are being reduced to silence by the belief that it is useless to reason with people in a state of political intoxication." Now I am far from saying that is quite impossible that Mr. Herbert Spencer should be the one sober politician in England and all the rest of us hopelessly drunk together. There have been times when one man alone has withstood legislation or political action which has afterwards proved disastrous to his country. But Mr. Spencer, happily, gives us the opportunity of testing what he means by the word "disastrous"; and it would be interesting to know which one of the measures he thus characterises he would think it beneficial under existing conditions to repeal.

Mr. Herbert Spencer's first disaster, then, was the vote of £20,000 to build schoolrooms in the year 1833. Those who carried this measure, he cries, never thought it would lead to our present School Board policy, "they did not intend to establish the principal that A should be made responsible for educating B's offspring; they did not dream of a compulsion"—this little bit of sentiment is surely rather forced—"which should deprive poor widows of the help of their elder children." Well, no, they did not. But does Mr. Spencer mean that our present education policy is disastrous? Would he have the children of the people grow up in hopeless ignorance rather than see his individualist theories tampered with never so little? It would really seem so. But in that case the "people" need scarcely be in a state of political intoxication if they pay no attention to Mr. Herbert Spencer. His argument that "payment by results" has produced ill effects does not touch the main principle of compulsory education. Such competition and overpressure as sometimes injure the pupils are, at any rate, directly contrary to the first principles of Socialism. Socialists altogether disapprove of encouraging intellectual competition among children. They hold this to be the worst possible form of education, quite apart from the physical injuries produced by overwork.

The next instance of disastrous legislation is more extraordinary still. If there is one set of measures which, by the common consent of the workers, and even of the capitalists, has been beneficial, surely the Factory Acts are so regarded. Mr.

Spencer is of a different opinion, for he says:—"Neither did those who in 1834 passed an Act regulating the labour of women and children in certain factories, imagine that the system they were beginning would end in the restriction and inspection of labour in all kinds of producing establishments, where more than fifty people are employed." I take it therefore that Mr. Spencer is opposed to the Factory Acts. In that case he can never have read the Reports of the Commissioners and the evidence on which the Factory and Workshops Legislation was based. For these measures were proved to be absolutely necessary to save women, children and sickly babes from the most revolting and cruel slavery of which there is any record in history. So beneficial have they been that their further extension is inevitable. Mr. Herbert Spencer is unable to see that the community interfered only to check the frightful tyranny of a profit-making class.

One other example and I leave this part of the subject. Mr. Spencer says that the only result of fixing a maximum load-line for vessels has been that the owners now load up to that line. Say that this is so, would he therefore contend that sailors should go to sea in overladen ships when State regulation could stop it? There is no freedom of contract here. Sailors when they engage to sail in a craft are unable to say whether she is overladen or not. But the loss of able seamen, apart from the infamy of drowning of men for gain, is a direct loss to the country; for it costs a great deal to rear able seamen. Mr. Spencer would seem therefore to be arguing against manifest utility. But it is unnecessary to say more. If legislative interference is "disastrous" in the instances cited, there is, indeed, no more to be said.

Undoubtedly, however, the success which has attended these and similar measures renders their extension certain. Board Schools involve the idea of free compulsory education, and the idea of free compulsory education that of one or more gratuitous meals in those schools. On the other hand interference of the community for the general good naturally develops into organisation *by* the community for the general good. It is manifest that such development is going on to-day. Mr. Herbert Spencer wishes to check it if he can get a hearing.

Why, however, asks Mr. Spencer, is this progressive change described as "The Coming Slavery"? Why indeed? But first let us take Mr. Spencer's definition of a slave. "The essential question is: How much is he compelled to labour for other benefit than his own, and how much can he labour for his own benefit? The degree of slavery varies according to the ratio of that which he is forced to yield up and that which he is allowed to retain; and it matters not whether his master is a single person or a society. If, without option, he has to labour for the society and receive from the general stock such portion as society awards him, he becomes a slave to the society." Certainly. But does Mr. Spencer imagine, then, that no slavery exists to-day? There is not a Socialist living, at any rate, who would not accept his definition as perfectly accurate. But what is the position of the man without property in our present society, without any command of the means of production—land, capital, machinery, raw materials or credit? He must be forced, in order only to live, to labour the greater part of his time for the benefit of others. The wages his class receive on the average are but a fraction of the value of the goods which they produce; certainly not more than one-third. Thus on Mr. Herbert Spencer's own showing the wage-earning producers and distributors of to-day are the slaves of the employers as a class; "and it matters not whether their master is a single person or a society," "the ratio between what the workers yield up and what they are allowed to retain" under this class monopoly of the means of production being, in very truth, the measure of the oppressiveness of such slavery. Labourers may change their master, no doubt, but they are still at the mercy of the employing class and compete against one another for subsistence wages, all that they earn in addition going for nothing into the hands of the possessing classes.

It is almost unnecessary to refer to the victims of the "sweaters" in all our large towns; to the miserable match-box makers and dock-labourers at the East End of London; to the slaves of the machine in close, ill-ventilated factories; to the ill-paid shop girls, exhausted with long hours of toil, driven in many cases te eke out their scanty wages by the earnings of prostitution; to the miners working under the most dangerous and unwholesome conditions just to keep body and soul together; to the overworked serfs of the great railway corporations standing at their points or running their locomotives twelve, fourteen, or sixteen hours a day; to the half-fed agricultural labourers of our English counties—it is needless, I say, to cite such instances of grinding and degrading slavery to show what sort of liberty is that which Mr. Herbert Spencer is so fearful that we shall tamper with, what kind of individuality it is which he is so anxious to maintain.

But Mr. Herbert Spencer admits that the tendency of the time, itself of necessity the reflection of the economical movement is all against him. "Thus," he says, "influences of various kinds conspire to increase corporate action." Now the words "corporate action" here mean State, Municipal, or County action. But, as a matter of fact, the greatest corporations at present are often outside popular control. The Railways, the Gas and Water Companies, the great Shipping Companies, are great corporations worked by Boards of Directors and salaried officials in the interest of shareholders, whose interests are often directly opposed to those of the community at large. When Mr. W. H. Vanderbilt said "the people be damned" he spoke as the head of a great monopolist corporation. It is certainly impossible to contend that the New York Central or the London and North Western Railway, the Cunard or Peninsular and Oriental Steamship Companies are cases of individual enterprise. To argue so is an absurdity. Those corporations and others are really as much organised bureaucracies, with as little volition left to the individual employees, as they would be if managed by the State. In the United States, as is well known, the influence of such corporations, handled as they are with utter unscrupulousness, constitutes a danger to the great Republic—a danger which can only be met by the interference and control of Federal Government for the benefit of the whole country. Mr. Spencer saw this himself when he was on the other side of the Atlantic. The bureaucracies, in short, already exist in every civilised or capitalised country, and the only question is, whether they are to be handled by the community and thus made beneficial to all (much labour being saved thereby as well), or whether the present anarchical conflict of interests and wholesale political corruption, direct and indirect, are to go on.

As Mr. Spencer truly says, "The officials cannot create the needful supplies; they can but distribute among the individuals what the individuals have joined to produce." But, this being so, surely the fewer officials the better; and, what is still more important, the few idlers, or hangers-on of idlers, the better. Socialists, Mr. Spencer should bear in mind, hold that no individuals whatever should be allowed to shuffle off their share of necessary productive labour upon others; so that the "officials" would be as few as possible. Even as it is, the Post Office is managed with less of wasted labour than if two or three large firms were competing, each with a separate staff, for the management and conveyance of mails. What applies to the Post Office would certainly apply in a still greater degree to the Railways. A smaller staff would be needed to do the same amount of work. What is more, it would be done, not for the benefit of the shareholders, but for that of the whole people and as a portion of an organised Democratic system, in which the object of all would be to lessen the hours of labour, whilst maintaining the highest possible standard of general comfort and luxury.

Again, we say that shareholders "have laid hands upon the railways," and Mr. Spencer marks this statement with a note of exclamation. Did the shareholders, then, build the railways? Not at all. They were built by the labour of men now, most of them, dead. Neither the shareholders nor their predecessors organised the labour on the railways; they simply advanced "capital" for their construction. And what was this capital so advanced? Nothing more than the accumulation of the labour of other men, or the assumption of the right to make drafts upon the labour of other men, according to social conventions legalised by the class which holds possession of the entire means of production. Thus, then, the ownership of the railroads of the country, given by the landlord and capitalist Parliament to the middle or capitalist class, means that the shareholders are to have a perpetual right to confiscate the labour of the living, because they or their predecessors confiscated the labour of the dead. Such confiscation, carried on daily by means of a legalised monopoly, we Socialists are striving to put an end to, without compensation if possible—for why should any have a right to dominate their fellows and live without labour?—with compensation, if so it is willed by the majority of the adult population. The economical forces are all ready for the change. The salaried officials who work to-day for the companies would work to-morrow for the Democratic State.

"Already exclusive carrier of letters, exclusive transmitter of telegrams, and on the way to become exclusive carrier of parcels, the State will not only be exclusive carrier of passengers, goods, and minerals, but will add to its present various trades many other trades. Even now, besides erecting its naval and military establishments and building harbours, docks, breakwaters, &c., it does the work of shipbuilder, cannon founder, small arms maker, manufacturer of ammunition, army clothier, and boot maker; and when the railways have been appropriated, 'with or without compensation,' as the Democratic Federationists say, it will have to become locomotive carriage-builder, carriage maker, tarpaulin and grease manufacturer, passenger canal owner, coal miner, stone quarrier, omnibus proprietor, &c. Meanwhile its local lieutenants, the municipal governments, already in many places suppliers of water, gas makers, owners and workers of tramways, and proprietors of baths, will doubtless have undertaken various other businesses."

Just so. Why not? Centralisation and decentralisation will go on together; production for use will gradually supplant adulterated production for profit. Only—and this is the important point—the whole of this vast and far-reaching organisation must be under the control of the people, certainly not carried on for the benefit of a non-producing class. State factories have no interest in making adulterated goods, when there is nothing to be gained and great injury may result; the State will require only the minimum hours of labour, when overwork means exhaustion for the employees and not surplus value for the possessing classes. In a word, State employment, when the State itself is only an organised democracy and class distinctions cease, means not slavery, but freedom; save in so far as every man and woman must ever be a slave to the necessity of providing enough in co-operation with others to give him or her the standard of comfort generally agreed to be sufficient—an amount lessening with every improvement in machinery or knowledge. What capacities of enjoyment and self-improvement would then have free outlet! What a scope for invention and opportunities for art would then open up before millions who now have no leisure for either! When, as is the case to-day, two or three hours' labour out of the twenty-four by all adult males would be enough to give the whole community all the wholesome necessaries and comforts of life, none should be allowed to escape his or her due share of this necessary work. But this would put an end once for all to competition and the sale of men's labour on the market.

Such an overturn of the whole bourgeois system Mr. Spencer evidently cannot bring his mind to contemplate. To him competition alone can mean freedom; the forfeiture by the labourers of the greater part of the labour value of their produce to the employing class and their hangers-on can alone prevent slavery for the workers. For, under Socialism, "each member of the community would be a slave to the community as a whole." Surely the word "slave" is here misused, both in its literal and historical meaning. If it comes to that, all of us are slaves to the forces of nature, and, in a slightly less degree, to the social conditions into which we are born. The very definition which Mr. Spencer himself has already given of slavery excludes the use of the word "slave" under conditions where all co-operate in order that none should be the slave of an individual or of a class. Socialists, at any rate, contend that we now permit the forces of nature, and the social and economical conditions, to master us—that the individual ownership of the means of production and exchange absolutely hampers progress; in the future, by the collective ownership of the means of production and the use of all improvements to enhance that production or lessen toil, mankind will master the forces of nature.

To take a single but very important instance of the way in which our present system works ruin all round. Industrial crises occur more and more frequently in each successive generation. The increasing powers of machinery, the greater facility of transport and communication, do but serve to make matters worse for the mass of the workers in all countries, inasmuch that the uncertainty of employment is greatly increased by these recurring crises, apart from the danger of the workers being driven out on to the streets by the introduction of new labour-saving machines. But these crises arise from the very nature of our capitalist system of production. Thus, when a period of depression comes to an end, orders flow in from home and foreign customers; each manufacturer is anxious to take advantage of the rising tide of prosperity, and produces as much as he can without any consultation with his fellows or any regard for the future; there is a great demand for labourers in the factories, workshops, shipyards, and mines; prices rise all along the line, speculation is rampant; new machines are introduced to economise labour and increase production. All the work is being done by the most thorough social organisation and for manifestly social purposes; the workers are, as it were, dovetailed into one another by that social and mechanical division of labour, as well as by the increasing scale of factory industry. But they have no control whatever over their products when finished. The exchange is carried on solely for the profit of the employing class, who themselves are compelled to compete against one another at high pressure in order to keep their places. Thus a glut follows and then a depression of trade, when millions of men are out of work all over the world, though ready to give their useful labour in return for food; and the capitalists are unable to employ them because the glut which they themselves have created prevents production at a profit. Here, then, is a manifest and growing antagonism between the social system of production and the individual (or profit-making company) control of exchange. Can Mr. Spencer reasonably argue that individual effort will remedy, or that individuals by themselves can influence, this system?

To show how these cycles recur, and the increasing frequency of their recurrence, we have only to take the record of the cotton industry. From 1770 to 1819 there were 41 good and only 5 bad years; from 1822 to 1860 there were 20 good and 19 bad years (this was the period when cotton *was* king); from 1861 to 1884, 9 good years and 15 bad years. The proportions are worth noting. The dangerous increase of bad years accounts fully for the "over-population" in all civilised countries; just as the introduction of new machines and the replacement of the labour of men by the labour of women and children accounts for the growing uncertainty of employment between the periods of crisis. The only means whereby this anarchy can be reduced to order is by removing the fundamental antagonism of proletariat production and capitalist appropriation by giving, that is, to the whole community of workers social control over a manifestly social system of production. As also the crises are international in character, so must eventually be the industrial organisation. England, being the centre of the capitalist system, is the country where the reorganisation must begin.

The immediate practical proposals of the Social-Democratic Federation which Mr. Spencer criticises are being even now accepted as necessary stages in this development. Free schools and free meals in those schools find thousands of advocates to-day where yesterday there were but tens. It is coming to be understood that as the labourers produce all the wealth of the country it is not only unjust to them, but harmful to the community, that their children should be left ignorant and unfed by those who take the greater part of the labour-value they produce in the shape of rent, profit, interest, commissions, &c. Short hours of labour are likewise agitated for in every civilised country. Eight hours as the maximum limit of toil in every industry is now the working-class cry in all lands. Of the construction of artisans' and agricultural labourers' dwellings I need scarcely speak. The manifest failure of our miserable competitive system has absolutely forced both political parties to give up *laissez-faire* in this direction. Good housing, however, can only be got by State or municipal action. Mr. Herbert Spencer points out himself quite clearly how, by the increase of rates, by the competition of better dwellings with the old ramshackle, rack-rented hovels, by the gradual coming into the market of better houses at cheaper prices, owing to the joint action of these two causes, such intervention would break down competition rents, with the accompanying jerry-building, and bring about a proper arrangement of housing and garden ground; eventually putting an end to the harmful separation between country and town.

Nevertheless, so long as mere "supply and demand" rule in the sphere of production and exchange, so long as producers and distributors have no control, either collectively or individually, over the means of production or the methods or exchange, so long, that is, as men and women are obliged to sell their labour-force, or even their mental capacity, to a class in order merely to subsist—so long, I say, as this anarchical system exists, just so long will good education, good feeding, good housing in childhood simply bring up better wage-slaves for capitalists. Even shorter hours of labour will only mean that better and more rapid machinery will be introduced and the glut thus be brought about more rapidly. Here is the blighting curse of our existing competitive system. This is why all so-called reforms, however taking they may seem to superficial, well-meaning philanthropists, are valuable only in so far as they lead up to a complete social revolution. Adulteration, crises, starvation, pauperism will ever go on until that revolution is brought about. The iron law of competition means, and must mean, continued degradation for the workers, even though their physical condition in youth may be improved.

But nationalisation of the land accompanied by "industrial armies" gives our individual philosopher another shock. This surely, he says must be an oversight on the part of the Executive of the Federation. Not at all. Socialism means organisation in place of the existing anarchy; the only difference is that the educated and well-nourished workers of these industrial armies will elect their own leaders and organisers, and, equality of conditions being the rule throughout, there need be no domination, as, certainly, there would be no profit. To lay down laws for a system of society which is being formed under our eyes would, however, be absurd. What all can see clearly is that even bourgeois economists like Mr. Henry Fawcett, who oppose all State management, are forced by necessity to prove as administrators their own utter foolishness as theorists. State organisation grows as we are talking. The only question is whether it shall be used by the Democracy to break down wage-slavery and competition for bare subsistence, or whether some despot shall step in to secure physical welfare for the people at the cost of their freedom. The reign of the middle class with their ideas of mock liberty and real slavery for the producers is coming to an end. Profit-mongering and adulteration are pretty well played out as the objects of human existence.

All this of course is far away from Mr. Herbert Spencer and his individualist philosophy. Evidently he felt so secure of his own position that he has never read a line of any writer on scientific Socialism in his life, while the slight importance which he attaches to political economy unfits him from being the critic of a school of thought which considers the forms of production and distribution of wealth as the real bases of human society at all periods of history. Nevertheless, Mr. Spencer's attack on the Social-Democratic Federation has been of great service to the Socialist cause. His criticisms have at any rate induced many to study the question and assuredly have not weakened the intellectual convictions of a single Socialist,[3] while his admission that somehow, in spite of all his objections, the evolution of society is carrying us necessarily farther and farther into State or Municipal management, led a considerable number of those who have been taught the doctrine of evolution by Mr. Spencer himself to accept Socialism as the only logical outcome of his own earlier theories. Thus Socialists are perfectly satisfied with the exposition of middle-class philosophy by its principal champion.

There are few really unprejudiced thinkers who do not now admit that capitalists and the middle-class generally are quite incapable of handling the growing powers of man over nature for the benefit of the race. That fact comes out more clearly as each year passes by. Socialism therefore—the organised co-operation of men and women educated from early childhood to their share in light, varied and pleasurable labour—must come in to control and develop those forces which individuals did not invent and which individuals cannot turn to the advantage of mankind. This evolution, I say, is inevitable, it is going on all round us at this hour. Shall we help its peaceful development by thoroughly understanding its growth and clearing away obstacles, or shall we render violent revolution inevitable by sheer determination not to see? In either case such harmonious association of workers, such adaptation of surroundings and application of the increasing powers of science to the highest physical, mental, and moral development of man—such Socialism, in a word, as we champion, means for all future generations not Slavery but full and never-ending FREEDOM.

## Notes

1  I may here say that the name Social-Democrat, which so many still think we have derived from Germany, was first used by Bronterre O'Brien early in the thirties, more than fifty years ago, and long before anything was heard of the title outside Great Britain.
2  I have dealt so fully with the Old Poor Law and the circumstances attending its modification in 1834 in my "Historical Basis of Socialism in England" (Kegan Paul, Trench and Co.), that I need say no more on this point here.
3  Since this pamphlet was written Mr. Spencer has published some further criticisms of the "Sins of Legislators." With these I have nothing to do. Socialists have no hope that the middle-class can carry out Socialist legislation effectively. Robbery and jobbery are their only ideas of management when left uncontrolled by pressure from without.

# 17

# *USEFUL WORK VERSUS USELESS TOIL* (1885), HAMMERSMITH SOCIALIST SOCIETY, 1893 EDN, 3–12, 19.

*William Morris*

[William Morris's comments on his reading of Marx's *Das Kapital* were to become well-known. Having joined the Democratic Federation, Morris wrote, he endeavoured to learn the "economical side of Socialism" but "whereas I thoroughly enjoyed the historical part of 'Capital', I suffered agonies of confusion of the brain over reading the pure economics" (*Justice*, June 1894). This professed inability to come to terms with Marxian economics would also feature strongly in Bruce Glasier's much-cited memoir of Morris. "To speak quite frankly, I do not know what Marx's theory of value is, and I'm damned if I want to know", Glasier remembered Morris holding forth. "It is enough political economy for me to know that the idle class is rich and the working class is poor, and that the rich are rich because they rob the poor" (Glasier 1921, 32).

The lecture reproduced here exemplifies Morris's ideas of political economy. Its language, theme and basic premise certainly owe more to Ruskin than to Marx. It was Ruskin whom Morris acknowledged as his "master" in social theory. Like Ruskin, his most basic preoccupation was with the quality of work as a source of human worth and well-being. Like Ruskin too, he rejected the political economist's conception of wealth, and shared the scorn for mere productivism and noisome consumption which Ruskin described as illth. The usefulness of useful work did not depend on a narrow utilitarian calculus let alone a financial one. Freed from "mere toiling to live", Morris conceived of useful work as a sphere of pleasure and creativity that he believed fundamental to any meaningful vision of human fulfilment.

Ruskin's influence alone was not enough to make a socialist. What Morris owed to socialism and to Marx was the idea of a class society that he registered first of all in its different relations to the world of work. A system of Capital and Wages was one in which some did no work, many did no useful work, and the great majority toiled for the "robbery and waste" of a minority. Morris's vision was of a world in which none should live on the labour of others, but in which work itself would not be driven by compulsion but by the free exercise of one's faculties. As Ruskin had taught in *The Crown of Wild Olive* (1866), work was what distinguished humankind from sucking fish and gnats.

If Morris is to be regarded as a Marxist, it is not therefore in respect of Marx's economic theories, but in respect of his sociology and commitment to the idea of class struggle (Bevir 2011, ch. 5). It was because of this, not in spite of it, that Morris's legacy was so valued by later British Marxists who had barely a word to spare for Bax or Hyndman. Among syndicalists like Tom Mann, who had also cut his teeth on Ruskin, the same class-struggle reading of Marxism largely prevailed. Even a communist like the young E.P. Thompson, whose first book was a massive study of Morris, attended far more to Marx's sociology than to his political economy. Interpretations of Morris have been far too often distorted by seeking to claim him for one particular strand for socialism (Bevir 2011, 87). Equally, we can better appreciate the pluralism and knottedness of socialism's different strands by registering the extraordinary attraction that Morris had for so many of them.

*Useful Work Versus Useless Toil* was a lecture which Morris delivered several times after joining the Democratic Federation and published as a pamphlet in 1885. For reasons of space, the latter sections are omitted here: except for the concluding paragraphs, which are included as a reminder that Morris, whatever else he was, was at this point what one admirer called a "barricades" socialist (Leatham 2016b, 12). Whether he afterwards ceased to be one may be judged by consulting his later utopia *News From Nowhere* (Chapter 10, this volume).]

The above title may strike some of my readers as strange. It is assumed by most people now-a-days that all work is useful, and by most *well-to-do* people that all work is desirable. Most people, well-to-do or not, believe that, even when a man[1] is doing work which appears to be useless, he is earning his livelihood by it—he is "employed," as the phrase goes; and most of those who are well-to-do cheer on the happy worker with congratulations and praises, if he is only "industrious" enough and deprives himself of all pleasure and holidays in the sacred cause of labour. In short it has become an article of the creed of modern morality that all labour is good in itself—a convenient belief to those who live on the labour of others. But as to those on whom they live, I recommend them not to take it on trust, but to look into the matter a little deeper.

Let us grant, first, that the race of man must either labour or perish. Nature gives us absolutely nothing gratis; we must win it by toil of some sort or degree. Let us see, then, if she does not give us some compensation for this compulsion to labour, since certainly in other matters she takes care to make the acts necessary to the continuance of life in the individual and the race not only endurable, but even pleasurable.

Yet, first, we must say in the teeth of the hypocritical praise of all labour, whatsoever it may be, of which I have made mention, that there is some labour which is so far from being a blessing that it is a curse; that it would be better for the community and for the worker if the latter were to fold his hands and refuse to work, and either die or let us pack him off to the workhouse or prison—which you will.

Here, you see, are two kinds of work—one good, the other bad: one not far removed from a blessing, a lightening of life; the other a mere curse, a burden to life.

What is the difference between them, then? This: the one has hope in it, the other has not. It is manly to do the one kind of work, and manly also to refuse to do the other.

What is the nature of the hope which, when it is present in work, makes it worth doing?

It is threefold, I think—hope of rest, hope of product, hope of pleasure in the work itself; and hope of these also in some abundance and of good quality; rest enough and good enough to be worth having; product worth having by one who is neither a fool nor an ascetic; pleasure enough for all for us to be conscious of it while we are at work; not a mere habit, the loss of which we shall feel as a fidgetty man feels the loss of the bit of string he fidgets with.

I have put the hope of rest first because it is the simplest and most natural part of our hope. Whatever pleasure there is in some work, there is certainly some pain in all work, the beast-like pain of stirring up our slumbering energies to action, the beast-like dread of change when things are pretty well with us; and the compensation for this animal pain is animal rest. We must feel while we are working that the time will come when we shall not have to work. Also the rest, when it comes, must be long enough to allow us to enjoy it; it must be longer than is merely necessary for us to recover the strength we have expended in working, and it must be animal rest also in this, that it must not be disturbed by anxiety, else we shall not be able to enjoy it. If we have this amount and kind of rest we shall, so far, be no worse off than the beasts.

As to the hope of product, I have said that nature compels us to work for that. It remains for *us* to look to it that we *do* really produce something, and not nothing, or at least nothing that we want or are allowed to use. If we look to this and use our wills we shall, so far, be better than machines.

The hope of pleasure in the work itself: how strange that hope must seem to some of my readers—to most of them! Yet I think that to all living things there is a pleasure in the exercise of their energies, and that even beasts rejoice at being lithe and swift and strong. But a man at work making something which he feels will exist because he is working at it and wills it, is exercising the energies of his mind and soul as well as of his body. Memory and imagination help him as he works. Not only his own thoughts, but the thoughts of the men of past ages guide his hands; and, as a part of the human race, he creates. If we work thus we shall be men, and our days will be happy and eventful.

Thus worthy work carries with it the hope of pleasure in rest, the hope of the pleasure in our using what it makes, and the hope of pleasure in our daily creative skill.

All other work but this is worthless; it is slaves' work—mere toiling to live, that we may live to toil.

Therefore, since we have, as it were, a pair of scales in which weigh the work now done in the world, let us use them. Let us estimate the worthiness of the work we do, after so many thousand years of toil, so many promises of hope deferred, such boundless exultation over the progress of civilisation and the gain of liberty.

Now, the first thing as to the work done in civilisation and the easiest to notice is that it is portioned out very unequally amongst the different classes of society. First, there are people—not a few—who do no work, and make no pretence to doing any. Next, there are people, and very many of them, who work fairly hard, though with abundant easements and holidays, claimed and allowed; and lastly, there are people who work so hard that they may be said to do nothing else than work, and are accordingly called the "working classes," as distinguished from the middle classes and the rich, or aristocracy, whom I have mentioned above.

It is clear that this inequality presses heavily upon the "working" class, and must visibly tend to destroy their hope of rest at least, and so, in that particular, make them worse off than mere beasts of the field; but that is not the sum and end of our folly of turning useful work into useless toil, but only the beginning of it.

For first, as to the class of rich people doing no work, we all know that they consume a great deal while they produce nothing. Therefore, clearly, they have to be kept at the expense of those who do work, just as paupers have, and are a mere burden on the community. In these days there are many who have learned to see this, though they can see no further into the evils of our present system, and have formed no idea of any scheme for getting rid of this burden; though perhaps they have a vague hope that changes in the system of voting for members of the House of Commons may, as if by magic, tend in that direction. With such hopes or superstitions we need not trouble ourselves. Moreover, this class, once thought most necessary to the State, is scant of numbers, and has now no power of its own, but depends on the support of the class next below it—the middle class. In fact, it is really composed either of the most successful men of that class, or of their immediate descendants.

As to the middle class, including the trading, manufacturing and professional people of our society, they do, as a rule, seem to work quite hard enough, and so at first sight might be thought to help the community, and not burden it. But by far the greater part of them, though they work, do not produce, and even when they do produce, as in the case of those engaged (wastefully indeed) in the distribution of goods, or doctors, or (genuine) artists and literary men, they consume out of all proportion to their due share. The commercial and manufacturing part of them, the most powerful part, spend their lives and energies in fighting amongst themselves for their respective shares of the wealth which they *force* the genuine workers to provide for them; the others are almost wholly the hangers-on of these: they are the parasites of property, sometimes, as in the case of lawyers, undisguisedly so; sometimes, as the doctors and others above-mentioned, professing to be useful, but too often of no use save as supporters of the system of folly, fraud, and tyranny of which they form a part. And all these we must remember, have, as a rule, one aim in view: not the production of utilities, but the gaining of a position either for themselves or their children in which they will not have to work at all. It is their ambition and the end of their whole lives to gain, if not for themselves yet at least for their children, the proud position of being obvious burdens on the community. For their work itself, in spite of the sham dignity with which they surround it, they care nothing: save a few enthusiasts, men of science, art or letters, who, if they are not the salt of the earth, are at least (and O, the pity of it!) the salt of the miserable system of which they are the slaves, which hinders and thwarts them at every turn and even sometimes corrupts them.

Here then is another class, this time very numerous and all-powerful, which produces very little and consumes enormously, and is therefore supported, as paupers are, by the real producers. The class that remains to be considered produces all that is produced, and supports both itself and the other classes, though it is placed in a position of inferiority to them; real inferiority, mind you, involving a degradation both in mind and body. But it is a necessary consequence of this tyranny and folly that again many of these workers are not producers. A vast number of them once more are merely parasites of property, some of them openly so, as the soldiers by land and sea who are kept on foot for the perpetuating of national rivalries and enmities, and for the purposes of the national struggle for the share of the product of unpaid labour. But besides this obvious burden on the producers and the scarcely less obvious one of domestic servants, there is first the army of clerks, shop-assistants and so forth who are engaged in the service of the private war for wealth, which as above said, is the real occupation of the well-to-do middle class. This is a larger body of workers than might be supposed, for it includes amongst others all those engaged in what I should call competitive salesmanship, or, to use a less dignified word, the puffery of wares, which has now got to such a pitch that there are many things which cost far more to sell than they do to make. Next there is the mass of people employed in making all those articles of folly and luxury, the demand for which is the outcome of the existence of the rich non-producing classes; things which people leading a manly and uncorrupted life would not ask for or dream of. These things, whoever may gainsay me, I will for ever refuse to call wealth, they are not wealth, but waste. Wealth is what nature gives us and what a reasonable man can make out of the gifts of nature for his reasonable use. The sunlight, the fresh air, the unspoiled face of the earth, food, raiment and housing, necessary and decent; the storing up of knowledge of all kinds, and the power of disseminating it; means of free communication between man and man; works of art, the beauty which man creates when he is most a man, most aspiring and thoughtful—all things which serve the pleasure of people, free, manly and uncorrupted. This is wealth. Nor can I think of anything worth having which does not come under one or other of these heads. But think, I beseech you, of the product of England, the workshop of the world, and will you not be bewildered, as I am, at the thought of the mass of things which no sane man could desire, but which our useless toil makes—and sells?

Now, further, there is even a sadder industry yet forced on many, very many, of our workers—the making of wares which are necessary to them and their brethren, *because they are an inferior class*. For if many men live without producing, nay, must live lives so empty and foolish that they *force* a great part of the workers to produce wares which no one needs, not even the rich, it follows that most men must be poor; and, living as they do on wages from those whom they support, cannot get for their use the *goods* which men naturally desire, but must put up with miserable make-shifts for them, with coarse food that does not nourish, with rotten raiment that does not shelter, with wretched houses which may well make a town-dweller in civilisation look back with regret to the tent of the nomad tribe, or the cave of the pre-historic savage. Nay, the workers must even lend a hand to the great industrial invention of the age—adulteration, and by its help produce for their own use shams and mockeries of the luxury of the rich; for the wage-earners must always live as the wage-payers bid them, and their very habits of life are *forced* on them by their masters.

But it is waste of time to try to express in words due contempt of the productions of the much-praised cheapness of our epoch. It must be enough to say that this cheapness is necessary to the system of exploiting on which modern manufacture rests. In other words, our society includes a great mass of slaves, who must be fed, clothed, housed and amused as slaves, and that their daily necessity compels them to make the slave-wares whose use is the perpetuation of their slavery.

To sum up, then, concerning the manner of work in civilised states, these states are composed of three classes—a class which does not even pretend to work, a class which pretends to work but which produces nothing, and a class which works, but is compelled by the other two classes to do work which is often unproductive.

Civilisation therefore wastes its own resources, and will do so as long as the present system lasts. These are cold words with which to describe the tyranny under which we suffer; try then to consider what they mean.

There is a certain amount of natural material and of natural forces in the world and a certain amount of labour-power inherent in the persons of the men that inhabit it. Men urged by their necessities and desires have laboured for many thousands of years at the task of subjugating the forces of nature and of making the natural material useful to them. To our eyes, since we cannot see into the future, that struggle with nature seems nearly over, and the victory of the human race over her nearly complete. And, looking backwards to the time when history first began, we note that the progress of that victory has been far swifter and more startling within the last two hundred years than ever before. Surely, therefore, we moderns ought to be in all ways vastly better off than any who have gone before us. Surely we ought, one and all of us, to be wealthy, to be well furnished with the good things which our victory over nature has won for us.

But what is the real fact? Who will dare to deny that the great mass of civilised men are poor? So poor are they, that it is mere childishness troubling ourselves to discuss whether perhaps they are in some ways a little better off than their forefathers. They are poor; nor can their poverty be measured by the poverty of a resourceless savage, for he knows of nothing else than his poverty; that he should be cold, hungry, houseless, dirty, ignorant, all that is to him as natural as that he should have a skin. But for us, for the most of us, civilisation has bred desires which she forbids us to satisfy, and so is not merely a niggard but a torturer also.

Thus then have the fruits of our victory over nature been stolen from us, thus has compulsion by nature to labour in hope of rest, gain, and pleasure been turned into compulsion by man to labour in hope—of living to labour!

What shall we do then, can we mend it?

Well, remember once more that it is not our remote ancestors who achieved the victory over nature, but our fathers, nay our very selves. For us to sit hopeless and helpless then would be a strange folly indeed: be sure that we can amend it. What, then, is the first thing to be done?

We have seen that modern society is divided into two classes, one of which is *privileged* to be kept by the labour of the other—that is, it forces the other to work for it and takes from this inferior class everything that it *can* take from it, and uses the wealth so taken to keep its own members in a superior position, to make them beings of a higher order than the others: longer lived, more beautiful, more honoured, more refined than those of the other class. I do not say that it troubles itself about its members being *positively* long lived, beautiful or refined, but merely insists that they shall be so *relatively* to the inferior class. As also it cannot use the labour-power of the inferior class fairly in producing real wealth, it wastes it wholesale in the production of rubbish.

It is this robbery and waste on the part of the minority which keeps the majority poor; if it could be shown that it is necessary for the preservation of society that this should be submitted to, little more could be said on the matter, save that the despair of the oppressed majority would probably at some time or other destroy society. But it has been shown, on the contrary, even by such incomplete experiments, for instance, as co-operation (so-called) that the existence of a privileged class is by no means necessary for the production of wealth, but rather for the "government" of the producers of wealth, or, in other words, for the upholding of privilege.

The first step to be taken then is to abolish a class of men privileged to shirk their duties as men, thus forcing others to do the work which they refuse to do. All must work according to their ability, and so produce what they consume—that is, each man should work as well as he can for his own livelihood, and his livelihood should be assured to him; that is to say, all the advantages which society would provide for each and all of its members.

Thus, at last, would true society be founded. It would rest on equality of condition. No man would be tormented for the benefit of another—nay, no one man would be tormented for the benefit of society. Nor, indeed, can that order be called society which is not upheld for the benefit of every one of its members.

But since men live now, badly as they live, when so many people do not produce at all, and when so much work is wasted, it is clear that, under conditions where all produced and no work was wasted, not only would everyone work with the certain hope of gaining a due share of wealth by his work, but also he could not miss his due share of rest. Here, then, are two out of the three kinds of hope mentioned above as an essential part of worthy work assured to the worker. When class robbery is abolished, every man will reap the fruits of his labour, every man will have due rest—leisure, that is. Some Socialists might say we need not go any further than this; it is enough that the worker should get the full produce of his work, and that his rest should be abundant. But though the compulsion of man's tyranny is thus abolished, I yet demand compensation for the compulsion of nature's necessity. As long as the work is repulsive, it will still be a burden which must be taken up daily, and even so would mar our life, though it be not of long daily duration. What we want to do is to add to our wealth without diminishing our pleasure. Nature will not be finally conquered till our work becomes a part of the pleasure of our lives.

That first step of freeing people from the compulsion to labour needlessly will at least put us on the way towards this happy end; for we shall then have time and opportunities for bringing it about. As things are now, between the waste of labour-power in mere idleness, and its waste in unproductive work, it is clear that the world of civilisation is supported by a small part of its people; when *all* were working *usefully* for its support, the share of work which each would have to do would be but small, if our standard of life were about on the footing of what well-to-do and refined people now think desirable. We shall have labour-power to spare, and shall, in short, be as wealthy as we please. It will be easy to live. If we were to wake up some morning now, under our present system, and find it "easy to live," that system would force us to set to work at once and make it hard to live; we should call that "developing our resources," or some such fine name. The multiplication of labour has become a necessity for us, and as long as that goes on no ingenuity in the invention of machines will be of any real use to us. Each new machine will cause a certain amount of misery among the workers whose special industry it may disturb; so many of them will be reduced from skilled to unskilled workmen, and then gradually matters will slip into their due grooves, and all will work apparently smoothly again; and if it were not that all this is preparing revolution, things would be, for the greater part of men, just as they were before the new wonderful invention.

But when revolution has made it "easy to live," when all are working harmoniously together and there is no one to rob the worker of his time, that is to say his life; in those coming days there will be no compulsion on us to go on producing things we do not want, no compulsion on us to labour for nothing, we shall be able calmly and thoughtfully to consider what we shall do with our wealth of labour-power. Now, for my part, I think the first use we ought to make of that wealth, of that freedom, should be to make all our labour, even the commonest and most necessary, pleasant to everybody; for thinking over the matter carefully, I can see that the one course which will certainly make life happy in the face of all accidents and troubles is to take a pleasurable interest in all the details of life. And lest perchance you think that an assertion too universally accepted to be worth making, let me remind you how entirely modern civilisation forbids it; with what sordid, and even terrible, details it surrounds the life of the poor, what a mechanical and empty life she forces on the rich; and how rare a holiday it is for any of us to feel ourselves a part of nature, and unhurriedly, thoughtfully, and happily to note the course of our lives amidst all the little links of events which connect them with the lives of others, and build up the great whole of humanity.

But such a holiday our whole lives might be, if we were resolute to make all our labour reasonable and pleasant. But we must be resolute indeed; for no half measures will help us here. It has been said already that our present joyless labour, and our lives scared and anxious as the life of a hunted beast, are forced upon us by the present system of producing for the profit of the privileged classes. It is necessary to state what this means. Under the present system of wages and capital the "manufacturer" (most absurdly so-called, since a manufacturer means a person who makes with his hands), having a monopoly of the means whereby the power to labour inherent in every man's body can be used for production, is the master of those who are not so privileged; he, and he alone, is able to make use of this labour power, which, on the other hand, is the only commodity by means of which his "capital," that is to say, the accumulated product of past labour, can be made productive. He therefore buys the labour-power of those who are bare of capital and can only live by selling it to him; his purpose in this transaction is to increase his capital, to make it breed. It is clear that if he paid those with whom he makes his bargain the full value of their labour, that is to say all that they produced, he would fail in his purpose. But since he is the monopolist of the means of productive labour, he can *compel* them to make a bargain better for him and worse for them than that; which bargain is that after they have earned their livelihood, estimated according to a standard high enough to ensure their peaceable submission to his mastership, the rest (and by far the larger part as a matter of fact) of what they produce shall belong to him, shall be his *property* to do as he likes with, to use or abuse at his pleasure; which property is, as we all know, jealously guarded by army and navy, police and prison; in short, by that huge mass of physical force which superstition, habit, fear of death by starvation—IGNORANCE, in one word, among the propertyless masses enables the propertied classes to use for the subjection of—their slaves.

Now, at other times, other evils resulting from this system may be put forward. What I want to point out now is the impossibility of our attaining to attractive labour under this system, and to repeat that it is this robbery (there is no other word for it) which wastes the available labour-power of the civilised world, forcing many men to do nothing, and many, very many more to do nothing useful; and forcing those who carry on really useful labour to most burdensome overwork. For understand once for all that the "manufacturer" aims primarily at producing, by means of the labour he has stolen from others, not goods but profits, that is, the "wealth" that is produced over and above the livelihood of his workmen. Whether that "wealth" is real or sham matters nothing to him. If it sells and yields him a "profit" it is all right. I have said that, owing to there being rich people who have more money than they can spend reasonably, and who therefore buy sham wealth, there is waste on that side; and also that, owing to there being poor people who cannot afford to buy things which are worth making, there is waste on that side. So that the "demand" which the capitalist "supplies" is a false demand. The market in which he sells is "rigged" by the miserable inequalities produced by the robbery of the system of Capital and Wages. [. . .]

It is Peace, therefore, which we need in order that we may live and work in hope and with pleasure. Peace so much desired, if we may trust men's words, but which has been so continually and steadily rejected by them in deeds. But for us, let use set our hearts on it at whatever cost.

What the cost may be, who can tell? Will it be possible to win peace peaceably? Alas, how can it be? We are so hemmed in by wrong and folly, that in one way or other we must always be fighting against them: our own lives may see no end to the struggle, perhaps no obvious hope of the end. It may be that the best we can hope to see is that struggle getting sharper and bitterer day by day, until it breaks out openly at last into the slaughter of men by actual warfare instead of by the slower and crueller methods of "peaceful" commerce. If we live to see that, we shall live to see much; for it will mean the rich classes grown conscious of their own wrong and robbery, and consciously defending them by open violence; and then the end will be near.

But in any case, and whatever the nature of our strife for peace may be, if we only aim at it steadily and with singleness of heart, and ever keep it in view, a reflection from that peace of the future will illumine the turmoil and trouble of our lives, whether the trouble be seemingly petty, or obviously tragic; and we shall, in our hopes at least, live the lives of men: nor can the present times give us any reward greater than that.

## Note

1  When the word "man" or "men" is used in the following pages it is intended to include both sexes, unless otherwise stated.

# 18

# "THE REWARD OF 'GENIUS'", *COMMONWEAL*, 25 SEPTEMBER 1886, 205–206.

*William Morris*

[One of the most common objections to socialism was that it did not recognise the uneven distribution of innate ability. Because of its ideas of social equality, it was therefore held by its opponents that socialism failed to incentivise those with special gifts or capacities to exercise them for the wider social good. These ideas were particularly identified with W.H. Mallock (1849–1929), who over the period covered by this volume was the most systematic, persistent and intellectually coherent of socialism's conservative critics within Britain. The whole debate was reignited in 1908 by the publication of Mallock's definitive exposition of this view, *A Critical Examination of Socialism*. Nevertheless, the issues raised by Mallock had already exercised many within the socialist tradition. These included the Fabian Bernard Shaw, whose *Socialism and Superior Brains* (1909) was based on an article originally published in 1894, and Robert Blatchford, who included a chapter on the "brain-worker" in his *Britain for the British* (1902). One of the earliest examples of such rebuttals was John Burns's article "Inventors and inventions" published in *Justice* on 27 December 1884.

An engineer by trade, Burns was much concerned with patents and the contributions of the Faradays, Newtons and Jacquards. Mallock in his *Critical Examination* was not so concerned with inventors as with industrial power and what he referred to as "directive ability". In the document that follows here, it was just as characteristic of William Morris that he should see the problem as one of "genius". He also had more fundamental objections to ideas like Mallock's than had Fabian socialists like Shaw. The latter were at one with Mallock regarding the specialisation of function, whether in the economic, the social or the political sphere. They differed with him only as regards the incentive powers of remuneration. Like any socialist, Morris also looked to higher motive forces than mere material gain. Nevertheless, he was also concerned with the labour process itself (see Chapter 17, this volume) and resisted the division of labour by which "brains" or "genius" were identified with particular individuals.

It was as a "diagnostician of alienation" (E.P. Thompson) that later generations of socialists would remember him. In the fifteenth chapter of his most famous socialist work *News From Nowhere* (1891) Morris returned to the question of incentive in a communist society. In place of the world-market and cheapening of production he evoked a socialist world of the future in which incentives to work were life, creation and pleasure, "either because of the hope of gain in honour and wealth with which the work is done . . . or else because it has grown into a pleasurable *habit*". These were the most consistent themes in Morris's socialism: the transformation of the quality of both work and worker was the most important of the changes which socialism was to bring about and the one that made possible all the others.]

It is a very common incident at a debate on Socialism for an opponent or doubter to take up the cudgels on behalf of "brain-work" as opposed to hand-work. Even before you avow yourself a Communist (as I have to do), such a questioner is anxious about the future of brain-work in the transitional stages of Socialism. Though this subject has been ably treated before in these columns, I will nevertheless venture on a few plain words in addition to what has been said; which I hesitate to do the less because I have had some small experience of hand-work, though not of the most laborious kind, and abundance of experience of "brain-work," so-called.

Our objectors dwell upon diverse aspects of their anxiety for the future of the brain-workers. Some, for instance, seem most exercised on the question of what is to become of the men of genius when Socialism is realised; but I must beg them not to let this anxiety destroy their appetites or keep them awake at night, for it is founded on a perhaps popular, but certainly erroneous, conception of that queer animal the man of genius, who is generally endowed with his full share of the predatory instincts of the human being, and can take remarkably good care of himself. Indeed, I can't help thinking that even under a Socialistic condition of things he will pull such long faces if he doesn't get everything that he wants, and will make matters so uncomfortable for those that he lives amongst if he falls short of his ideal of existence, that good-natured and quiet people will be weak enough to make up a purse (or its equivalent) for him from time to time to keep him in good temper and shut his mouth a little. I must further say, though, that they *will* be exceedingly weak if they do so, because they will be able to get out of him all the special work he can do without these extra treats. For the only claim he has to the title of a "man of genius" is that his capacities are irrepressible; he finds the exercise of them so exceedingly pleasant to him that it will only be by main force that you will prevent him from exercising them. Of course, under the present competitive system, having been paid once for his work by getting his livelihood by it, and again by the pleasure of doing it, he wants to be further paid in various ways a great many times more. Neither under the circumstances can I blame him much for this, since he sees so many people for doing nothing paid so much more than he is, except in the matter of pleasure in their work. But also of course, he won't venture to claim all that in a Socialist society, but will have at the worst to nibble at the shares of those who are weak enough to stand it. So I will in turn dismiss *my* anxiety, with the hope that they will not be so weak as to coddle him up at their own expense, since they will have learned that so-called self-sacrifice to the exactions of those who are strong in their inordinate craving and unmanliness does but breed tyrants and pretenders.

But furthermore, I do not see, and never could see, why a man of genius must needs be a man of genius every minute of his life. Cannot he work as well as ordinary folk in some directions, besides working better than they in others? Speaking broadly, all men can learn some useful craft, and learn to practice it with ease. I know there may be exceptions; just as there are cultivated people who cannot be taught to write (the late Dean Stanley was one, for instance); but they must be considered as diseased persons, and the disease would die out in a generation or two under reasonable conditions of life. In short, the "man of genius" ought to be able to earn his livelihood in an ordinary way independently of his speciality, and he will in that case be much happier himself and much less of a bore to his friends, let alone his extra usefulness to the community.

As to the comparative wear and tear of "brain-work"—the work of the man, for instance, who is occupied in the literary matters—the theory of our objectors, apart from their strange ideas of the usefulness of this craft, is that he works hard—harder, they will often say, than the hand-worker. Well, if he works under bad sanitary conditions, doesn't get fresh air or exercise enough, no doubt that does exhaust him, as also if he works too long or is harassed in his work by hurry and anxiety. But all these drawbacks are not special to his craft; all who are working otherwise than in the open air work under the first of these disadvantages, and all wage-earners work under the last of them. There is any amount of humbug talked about the hard work of the intellectual workers, which I think is mostly based on the fact that they are in the habit of taking regular and, so to say, socially-legalised holidays, which are supposed to be necessary to their health, and we may admit are so, but which the "non-intellectual" workers have to forego, whether they are necessary to *them* or not. Let us test the wear and tear of this intellectual work very simply. If I have been working at literary work for, say, eight hours at a stretch, I may well feel weary of it, although I have not felt it a mere burden all along, as probably I should have done if I had been carrying a hod of bricks up and down a ladder; but when I have knocked off, I can find relaxation in strong physical exercise—can, for example, take a boat and row for a couple of hours or more. Now let me ask is the hodman after *his* eight hours' work fit for a couple of hours of mental work as a relaxation? We very well know he is not so fitted, but rather for beer and sleep. He is exhausted, and I am on the look out for amusement. To speak plainly, I am only changing my amusement, for I have been amusing myself all along, unless I have added disadvantages to my work which are not essential to it.

And again, has not the hodman's work dealt in some way with his brain? Indeed it has. I have been using my brain, but not exhausting it; but though he has not been using his, he has been exhausting it by his hand-work done at a strain, or else he ought to be able to take the mental relaxation corresponding to my bodily relaxation. In truth, whereas at present the hours of the intellectual worker are really always shorter than those of the hand-worker, the very reverse ought to be the case, or in other words the wear and tear of the hand-labour is far greater.

But our objectors have not as a rule got so far as to consider this matter from the wear and tear side of it. They think that the superior workman should have extra reward because he is superior, and that the inferior must put up with being worn and torn in the service of this divine right. That is their superstition of divine right in this business; but also from the economical point of view they consider that it is necessary to bribe the superior man, for fear that you should lose his talent. What I have said of the man of genius being compelled to work by his genius applies to all superior workmen in greater or less degree, and disposes of the *need* of a bribe. You need not bribe the superior workman to be superior, for he has to work in any case (we must take that for granted), and his superior work is pleasanter, and indeed easier, to him than the inferior work would be: he will do it if you allow him to. But also if you had the need you would not have the power to bribe, except under a system which admitted of slavery—*i.e.,* tormenting some people for the pleasure of others. Can you bribe him to work by giving him immunity from work? or by giving him goods that he cannot use? But in what other way can you bribe him when labour is free and ordinary people will not stand being compelled to accept degradation for his benefit? No, you will have to depend on his aptitude for his special work forcing him into doing it; nor will you be disappointed in this. Whatever difficulties you may have in organising work in the earlier days of Socialism will not be with the specialists, but with those who do the more ordinary work; though as regards these, setting aside the common machine-work, the truth of the matter is that you can draw no hard and fast line between the special workman and the ordinary one. Every workman who is in his right place—that is, doing his work because he is fit for it—has some share in that "genius" so absurdly worshipped in these latter days. The "genius" is simply the man who has a stronger speciality and is allowed to develop it; or, if you please, has it so strongly that it is able to break through the repressing circumstances of his life, which crush out those who are less abundantly gifted into "a dull level of mediocrity." It is a matter of degree chiefly.

I am afraid, therefore, that our anti-Socialist objectors will have in the future—I mean under a social arrangement—to put up with the misery of not having more than they need forced on them in return for their occupying themselves in the way which pleases them most, and with the further misery of seeing those who are not so intellectual as themselves doing their work happily and contentedly, and not being deprived of their due food and comforts because their work is less pleasing and exciting than that of their luckier fellows. No doubt this will be hard for the geniuses to bear (though harder still, I suspect, for the prigs or sham geniuses); but if there be any truth in the old proverb that "other peoples' troubles hang by a hair," the rest of the world—*i.e.,* all except a very few—will bear it with equanimity. Indeed they well might, if they consider in those happier days what enormous loss the world has suffered through the crushing out of so much original talent under the present system; for who can doubt that it is only the toughest and strongest (perhaps the highest, perhaps not) of the geniuses that have not been crushed out. The greater part of genius, shared in various proportions by so many millions of men, has been just wasted through greed and folly.

# 19

# "THE GREAT MONEY TRICK" FROM *THE RAGGED TROUSERED PHILANTHROPISTS* (1914), CH. 21.

*Robert Tressell*

[It was enough political economy for William Morris to know that the idle rich were rich and idle because they robbed the poor (see Chapter 17, this volume). If that were the case, the only political economy he would have needed was the Great Money Trick from *The Ragged Trousered Philanthropists*. Its author, Robert Noonan (1870–1911), was a painter and decorator born in Dublin who for several years lived in South Africa before spending the final decade of his life in Sussex. It was here that Noonan joined the flourishing Hastings branch of the SDF and wrote his marvellous novel of working-class life under the pseudonym Robert Tressell. Noonan did not find a publisher during his lifetime and his novel appeared in a severely abridged and politically truncated version only in 1914. Its reputation as a socialist classic was thus secured only posthumously, and by the time an unabridged edition appeared in 1955 *The Ragged Trousered Philanthropists* had been translated into several languages and sold in numbers running into hundreds of thousands. Of its very nature, it had no influence whatsoever on the socialist movement before 1914. Embroidered as it may have been, it does however remind us of the myriad workplace exchanges and street-corner harangues in which socialist ideas were expounded without leaving any documentary trace.

Its setting was a large house ("The Cave") being renovated by a firm of painters and decorators in the fictional town of Mugsborough, clearly based on Hastings. Sweater was the town's mayor and the owner of the building, and Rushton the owner of the firm charged with carrying out the work. The novel's central character, Frank Owen, stands apart from his workmates as the socialist who alone among them sees the crushing realities of their situation, and gives voice to his views with such fluency that they nickname him the Professor. The gulf between them is relentless conveyed by the fact that Owen alone is allowed to speak in standard English. Describing the novel as a "deeply pessimistic work", Raphael Samuel (1988) noted how well it conveyed the sense that many socialists had of being an embattled minority with a commitment and understanding that set them apart from their fellows.

That is clearly attested by the episode of the Great Money Trick. It was nevertheless as a lesson in political economy and the theory of surplus value that it would come to be so widely known among generations of socialists. The influence of Morris is apparent throughout the novel in Tressell's concern with the frustration of the skilled craft worker who daily experienced the meanness and the shoddiness of capitalist production. The communist leader Harry Pollitt would link its idealisation of craft with the predominance of skilled workers in the working-class movement and the vision of a future society in which values of "labour and craftmanship" would be reflected in the lives of all working people. But embedded in the larger narrative was the simplest of socialist arguments, abstracted with incomparable lucidity. For many other socialists than Morris it was the one that at bottom mattered most of all.]

It was a pathetic and wonderful and at the same time a despicable spectacle. Pathetic that human beings should be condemned to spend the greater part of their lives amid such surroundings, because it must be remembered that most of their time was spent on some job or other. When 'The Cave' was finished they would go to some similar 'job', if they were lucky enough to find one. Wonderful, because although they knew that they did more than their fair share of the great work of producing the necessaries and comforts of life, they did not think they were entitled to a fair share of the good things they helped to create! And despicable, because although they saw their children condemned to the same life of degradation, hard labour and privation, yet they refused to help to bring about a better state of affairs. Most of them thought that what had been good enough for themselves was good enough for their children.

It seemed as if they regarded their own children with a kind of contempt, as being only fit to grow up to be the servants of the children of such people as Rushton and Sweater. But it must be remembered that they had been taught self-contempt when they were children. In the so-called 'Christian' schools they attended then they were taught to 'order themselves lowly and reverently towards their betters', and they were now actually sending their own children to learn the same degrading lessons in their turn! They had a vast amount of consideration for their betters, and for the children of their betters, but very little for their own children, for each other, or for themselves.

That was why they sat there in their rags and ate their coarse food, and cracked their coarser jokes, and drank the dreadful tea, and were content! So long as they had Plenty of Work and plenty of—Something—to eat, and somebody else's cast-off clothes to wear, they were content! And they were proud of it. They gloried in it. They agreed and assured each other that the good things of life were not intended for the 'Likes of them', or their children.

'Wot's become of the Professor?' asked the gentleman who sat on the upturned pail in the corner, referring to Owen, who had not yet come down from his work.

'P'raps 'e's preparing 'is sermon,' remarked Harlow with a laugh.

'We ain't 'ad no lectures from 'im lately, since 'e's been on that room,' observed Easton. ''Ave we?'

'Dam good job too!' exclaimed Sawkins. 'It gives me the pip to 'ear 'im, the same old thing over and over again.'

'Poor ole Frank,' remarked Harlow. ''E does upset 'isself about things, don't 'e?'

'More fool 'im!' said Bundy. 'I'll take bloody good care I don't go worryin' myself to death like 'e's doin', about such dam rot as that.'

'I do believe that's wot makes 'im look so bad as 'e does,' observed Harlow. 'Several times this morning I couldn't help noticing the way 'e kept on coughing.'

'I thought 'e seemed to be a bit better lately,' Philpot observed; 'more cheerful and happier like, and more inclined for a bit of fun.'

'He's a funny sort of chap, ain't he?' said Bundy. 'One day quite jolly, singing and cracking jokes and tellin' yarns, and the next you can't hardly get a word out of 'im.'

'Bloody rot, I call it,' chimed in the man on the pail. 'Wot the 'ell's the use of the likes of us troublin' our 'eads about politics?'

'Oh, I don't see that.' replied Harlow. 'We've got votes and we're really the people what control the affairs of the country, so I reckon we ought to take SOME interest in it, but at the same time I can't see no sense in this 'ere Socialist wangle that Owen's always talkin' about.'

'Nor nobody else neither,' said Crass with a jeering laugh.

'Even if all the bloody money in the world WAS divided out equal,' said the man on the pail, profoundly, 'it wouldn't do no good! In six months' time it would be all back in the same 'ands again.'

'Of course,' said everybody.

'But 'e 'ad a cuff the other day about money bein' no good at all!' observed Easton. 'Don't you remember 'e said as money was the principal cause of poverty?'

'So it is the principal cause of poverty,' said Owen, who entered at that moment.

'Hooray!' shouted Philpot, leading off a cheer which the others took up. 'The Professor 'as arrived and will now proceed to say a few remarks.'

A roar of merriment greeted this sally.

'Let's 'ave our bloody dinner first, for Christ's sake,' appealed Harlow, with mock despair.

As Owen, having filled his cup with tea, sat down in his usual place, Philpot rose solemnly to his feet, and, looking round the company, said:

'Genelmen, with your kind permission, as soon as the Professor 'as finished 'is dinner 'e will deliver 'is well-known lecture, entitled, "Money the Principal Cause of being 'ard up", proving as money ain't no good to nobody. At the hend of the lecture a collection will be took up to provide the lecturer with a little encouragement.' Philpot resumed his seat amid cheers.

As soon as they had finished eating, some of the men began to make remarks about the lecture, but Owen only laughed and went on reading the piece of newspaper that his dinner had been wrapped in. Usually most of the men went out for a walk after dinner, but as it happened to be raining that day they were determined, if possible, to make Owen fulfill the engagement made in his name by Philpot.

'Let's 'oot 'im,' said Harlow, and the suggestion was at once acted upon; howls, groans and catcalls filled the air, mingled with cries of 'Fraud!' 'Imposter!' 'Give us our money back!' 'Let's wreck the 'all!' and so on.

'Come on 'ere,' cried Philpot, putting his hand on Owen's shoulder. 'Prove that money is the cause of poverty.'

'It's one thing to say it and another to prove it,' sneered Crass, who was anxious for an opportunity to produce the long-deferred Obscurer cutting.

'Money IS the real cause of poverty,' said Owen.

'Prove it,' repeated Crass.

'Money is the cause of poverty because it is the device by which those who are too lazy to work are enabled to rob the workers of the fruits of their labours.'

'Prove it,' said Crass.

Owen slowly folded up the piece of newspaper he had been reading and put it into his pocket.

'All right,' he replied. 'I'll show you how the Great Money Trick is worked.'

Owen opened his dinner basket and took from it two slices of bread but as these were not sufficient, he requested that anyone who had some bread left would give it to him. They gave him several pieces, which he placed in a heap on a clean piece of paper, and, having borrowed the pocket knives they used to cut and eat their dinners with from Easton, Harlow and Philpot, he addressed them as follows:

'These pieces of bread represent the raw materials which exist naturally in and on the earth for the use of mankind; they were not made by any human being, but were created by the Great Spirit for the benefit and sustenance of all, the same as were the air and the light of the sun.'

'You're about as fair-speakin' a man as I've met for some time,' said Harlow, winking at the others.

'Yes, mate,' said Philpot. 'Anyone would agree to that much! It's as clear as mud.'

'Now,' continued Owen, 'I am a capitalist; or, rather, I represent the landlord and capitalist class. That is to say, all these raw materials belong to me. It does not matter for our present argument how I obtained possession of them, or whether I have any real right to them; the only thing that matters now is the admitted fact that all the raw materials which are necessary for the production of the necessaries of life are now the property of the Landlord and Capitalist class. I am that class: all these raw materials belong to me.'

'Good enough!' agreed Philpot.

'Now you three represent the Working class: you have nothing—and for my part, although I have all these raw materials, they are of no use to me—what I need is—the things that can be made out of these raw materials by Work: but as I am too lazy to work myself, I have invented the Money Trick to make you work FOR me. But first I must explain that I possess something else beside the raw materials. These three knives represent—all the machinery of production; the factories, tools, railways, and so forth, without which the necessaries of life cannot be produced in abundance. And these three coins'—taking three halfpennies from his pocket—'represent my Money Capital.'

'But before we go any further,' said Owen, interrupting himself, 'it is most important that you remember that I am not supposed to be merely "a" capitalist. I represent the whole Capitalist Class. You are not supposed to be just three workers—you represent the whole Working Class.'

'All right, all right,' said Crass, impatiently, 'we all understand that. Git on with it.'

Owen proceeded to cut up one of the slices of bread into a number of little square blocks.

'These represent the things which are produced by labour, aided by machinery, from the raw materials. We will suppose that three of these blocks represent—a week's work. We will suppose that a week's work is worth—one pound: and we will suppose that each of these ha'pennies is a sovereign. We'd be able to do the trick better if we had real sovereigns, but I forgot to bring any with me.'

'I'd lend you some,' said Philpot, regretfully, 'but I left me purse on our grand pianner.'

As by a strange coincidence nobody happened to have any gold with them, it was decided to make shift with the halfpence.

'Now this is the way the trick works—'

'Before you goes on with it,' interrupted Philpot, apprehensively, 'don't you think we'd better 'ave someone to keep watch at the gate in case a Slop comes along? We don't want to get runned in, you know.'

'I don't think there's any need for that,' replied Owen, 'there's only one slop who'd interfere with us for playing this game, and that's Police Constable Socialism.'

'Never mind about Socialism,' said Crass, irritably. 'Get along with the bloody trick.'

Owen now addressed himself to the working classes as represented by Philpot, Harlow and Easton.

'You say that you are all in need of employment, and as I am the kind-hearted capitalist class I am going to invest all my money in various industries, so as to give you Plenty of Work. I shall pay each of you one pound per week, and a week's work is—you must each produce three of these square blocks. For doing this work you will each receive your wages; the money will be your own, to do as you like with, and the things you produce will of course be mine, to do as I like with. You will each take one of these machines and as soon as you have done a week's work, you shall have your money.'

The Working Classes accordingly set to work, and the Capitalist class sat down and watched them. As soon as they had finished, they passed the nine little blocks to Owen, who placed them on a piece of paper by his side and paid the workers their wages.

'These blocks represent the necessaries of life. You can't live without some of these things, but as they belong to me, you will have to buy them from me: my price for these blocks is—one pound each.'

As the working classes were in need of the necessaries of life and as they could not eat, drink or wear the useless money, they were compelled to agree to the kind Capitalist's terms. They each bought back and at once consumed one-third of the produce of their labour. The capitalist class also devoured two of the square blocks, and so the net result of the week's work was that the kind capitalist had consumed two pounds worth of the things produced by the labour of the others, and reckoning the squares at their market value of one pound each, he had more than doubled his capital, for he still possessed the three pounds in money and in addition four pounds worth of goods. As for the working classes, Philpot, Harlow and Easton, having each consumed the pound's worth of necessaries they had bought with their wages, they were again in precisely the same condition as when they started work—they had nothing.

This process was repeated several times: for each week's work the producers were paid their wages. They kept on working and spending all their earnings. The kind-hearted capitalist consumed twice as much as any one of them and his pile of wealth continually increased. In a little while—reckoning the little squares at their market value of one pound each—he was worth about one hundred pounds, and the working classes were still in the same condition as when they began, and were still tearing into their work as if their lives depended upon it.

After a while the rest of the crowd began to laugh, and their merriment increased when the kind-hearted capitalist, just after having sold a pound's worth of necessaries to each of his workers, suddenly took their tools—the Machinery of Production—the knives away from them, and informed them that as owing to Over Production all his store-houses were glutted with the necessaries of life, he had decided to close down the works.

'Well, and wot the bloody 'ell are we to do now?' demanded Philpot.

'That's not my business,' replied the kind-hearted capitalist. 'I've paid you your wages, and provided you with Plenty of Work for a long time past. I have no more work for you to do at present. Come round again in a few months' time and I'll see what I can do for you.'

'But what about the necessaries of life?' demanded Harlow. 'We must have something to cat.'

'Of course you must,' replied the capitalist, affably; 'and I shall be very pleased to sell you some.'

'But we ain't got no bloody money!'

'Well, you can't expect me to give you my goods for nothing! You didn't work for me for nothing, you know. I paid you for your work and you should have saved something: you should have been thrifty like me. Look how I have got on by being thrifty!'

The unemployed looked blankly at each other, but the rest of the crowd only laughed; and then the three unemployed began to abuse the kind-hearted Capitalist, demanding that he should give them some of the necessaries of life that he had piled up in his warehouses, or to be allowed to work and produce some more for their own needs; and even threatened to take some of the things by force if he did not comply with their demands. But the kind-hearted Capitalist told them not to be insolent, and spoke to them about honesty, and said if they were not careful he would have their faces battered in for them by the police, or if necessary he would call out the military and have them shot down like dogs, the same as he had done before at Featherstone and Belfast.

'Of course,' continued the kind-hearted capitalist, 'if it were not for foreign competition I should be able to sell these things that you have made, and then I should be able to give you Plenty of Work again: but until I have sold them to somebody or other, or until I have used them myself, you will have to remain idle.'

'Well, this takes the bloody biskit, don't it?' said Harlow.

'The only thing as I can see for it,' said Philpot mournfully, 'is to 'ave a unemployed procession.'

'That's the idear,' said Harlow, and the three began to march about the room in Indian file, singing:

'We've got no work to do-oo-oo' We've got no work to do-oo-oo! Just because we've been workin' a dam sight too hard, Now we've got no work to do.'

As they marched round, the crowd jeered at them and made offensive remarks. Crass said that anyone could see that they were a lot of lazy, drunken loafers who had never done a fair day's work in their lives and never intended to.

'We shan't never get nothing like this, you know,' said Philpot. 'Let's try the religious dodge.'

'All right,' agreed Harlow. 'What shall we give 'em?'

'I know!' cried Philpot after a moment's deliberation. '"Let my lower lights be burning." That always makes 'em part up.'

The three unemployed accordingly resumed their march round the room, singing mournfully and imitating the usual whine of street-singers:

'Trim your fee-bil lamp me brither-in, Some poor sail-er tempest torst, Strugglin' 'ard to save the 'arb-er, Hin the dark-niss may be lorst, So let try lower lights be burning, Send 'er gleam acrost the wave, Some poor shipwrecked, struggling seaman, You may rescue, you may save.'

'Kind frens,' said Philpot, removing his cap and addressing the crowd, 'we're hall honest British workin' men, but we've been hout of work for the last twenty years on account of foreign competition and over-production. We don't come hout 'ere because we're too lazy to work; it's because we can't get a job. If it wasn't for foreign competition, the kind 'earted Hinglish capitalists would be able to sell their goods and give us Plenty of Work, and if they could, I assure you that we should hall be perfectly willing and contented to go on workin' our bloody guts out for the benefit of our masters for the rest of our lives. We're quite willin' to work: that's hall we arst for—Plenty of Work—but as we can't get it we're forced to come out 'ere and arst you to spare a few coppers towards a crust of bread and a night's lodgin'.'

As Philpot held out his cap for subscriptions, some of them attempted to expectorate into it, but the more charitable put in pieces of cinder or dirt from the floor, and the kind-hearted capitalist was so affected by the sight of their misery that he gave them one of the sovereigns he had in us pocket: but as this was of no use to them they immediately returned it to him in exchange for one of the small squares of the necessaries of life, which they divided and greedily devoured. And when they had finished eating they gathered round the philanthropist and sang, 'For he's a jolly good fellow,' and afterwards Harlow suggested that they should ask him if he would allow them to elect him to Parliament.

# Part 4

# WORK AND SOCIAL CONDITIONS

# 20

# *WHAT A COMPULSORY EIGHT-HOUR DAY MEANS TO THE WORKERS* (LONDON: MODERN PRESS, 1886).

*Tom Mann*

[The earliest SDF programmes included a commitment to the eight-hour day as one of the palliatives or "stepping-stones" that would pave the way to socialism. This was one of the socialists' oldest demands. Its earliest proponents had included Robert Owen and the Grand National Consolidated Trade Union of the early 1830s. The Webbs in their *History of Trade Unionism* (1894) described various examples of its revival in particular periods or by particular groups of workers in the intervening decades. When Tom Mann (1856–1941) took up the demand, he was a young engineer, originally from the English midlands, who had early on felt the benefit of the Engineers' successful nine-hour strike of 1871. "Classes were started", Mann wrote in his memoirs, "and we youngsters had a chance to attend evening classes" (Laurent 1988, 8); as with many other working-class socialists, Mann's political commitments must be seen, as he would have seen them, as a further realisation of this process of self-education. Moving to London, in 1885 Mann had joined the Battersea branch of the SDF when it was founded by another young militant engineering worker, John Burns (Chapter 5, this volume). Without doubt they were the most important and widely noticed of the working-class activists who were drawn to the SDF in its earliest years.

Though Mann was much mythologised by communist historians, John Laurent has expressed the view that his contribution as a socialist writer and intellectual had been underestimated. Of his long list of published writings, Mann's pamphlet on the eight-hour day was the first of any scope. Unemployment was the period's burning social issue and provided the SDF with the opportunity to regain some of the credibility it had squandered through the previous year's Tory gold scandal. According to his memoirs, important influences on Mann at this time included John Ruskin's more political writings as well as the recently published *Six Centuries of Work and Wages* by J.E. Thorold Rogers. Given the immediacy of the issue of mass unemployment, Mann in his pamphlet naturally makes the connection between the numbers of hours worked and workers employed. Nevertheless, in the spirit of Ruskin's writings and his own life experiences, Mann is not only moved by the relief of unemployment but anticipates the fuller life and opportunities for self-education that a shorter working day would open up.

The pamphlet's history offers insight into both the strengths and limitations of the SDF. Some socialists were simply scornful of such palliative measures (Chapters 11 and 22, this volume). Even Mann's Battersea comrades could not regard this as a central plank of their activities, and Mann therefore helped to organise an independent Eight Hours League. The pamphlet itself was published with the support and encouragement of H.H. Champion (1859–1928), a founder of the SDF who at this point was becoming somewhat disillusioned with it. Champion would soon turn to broader, and in his case sometimes politically compromising, forms of association. Mann, meanwhile, had already addressed the Fabian Society on the eight-hour question. His pamphlet invokes the radical MP Joseph Cowen (1829–1900), who had earlier severed ties with the Democratic Federation, and T.R. Threlfall, the Lib-Lab-leaning secretary of the Labour Electoral Committee (later Labour Electoral Association). Mann concludes his exposition with a non-partisan appeal that could almost be described as popular-frontist. At the same, he looks forward to the "true unionist policy of aggression" that such demands could help to rekindle, and it was in the context of Mann the "revolutionary trade unionist" that the pamphlet would be revisited by the communist historian Dona Torr (1956).

It was Mann rather than his critics who saw more clearly the way things were moving. Stimulated by the movements it had inspired in the USA, the demand for the eight-hour day was the international mobilising slogan for the first workers' May Day in 1890 (Chapter 52, this volume). The SDF was swept along by the tide; Cunninghame Graham (Chapters 43 and 50, this volume) devoted his maiden parliamentary speech to the issue; Mann himself published a second pamphlet *The Eight Hours' Movement* in 1889 and would long remain convinced of the mobilising potential of shorter working hours. "Get at it Fellow Workers! Reduce the Hours and secure Leisure and Pleasure for our class." The year by now was 1912, and the movement that of syndicalism. Mann's immediate objective was the same, but through the instrument of militant Direct Action he now described it as hastening the Social Revolution without dependence on mere parliamentary manoeuvrings ("Now For the Fight", *The Syndicalist*, February 1912).]

*Oh Slaves of these laborious years,*
*Oh Freemen of the years to be:*
*Shake off your blind and foolish fears,*
*And hail the Truth that makes you free.*

The appalling amount of distress that exists in every town in Britain must arrest the attention of all duty loving men and women. No one who sees the effects of want and the fear of want can passively behold the dire poverty of a large section of the workers. Rather will he probe and probe until he finds the cause of the disease. Socialists *have* probed and they find the disease of want to be spread by the profit-making system upon which all industry and society itself is based. They know that five or six centuries ago, without machinery, Englishmen obtained for their work sufficient to keep them in vigorous health and that they were not subject to periodical trade depressions; and when they further reflect upon the fact that the working day then consisted of no more than eight hours, no wonder that socialists are discontented with the present state of affairs, and that they resolve to use every means in their power to replace the present discord, misery, and anarchy, with harmony, happiness, and order.

The effect of our so-called labour-saving machinery (used really by its owners to save *wages* and not *labour*) is to cause continual distress amongst the workers by mercilessly throwing them out of employment without any compensation. It may then take a man often months, sometimes years, to find an occupation of any kind and when found it is at a price much below that he was in receipt of before the machine disturbed him. Yet the machine has increased the ease and rapidity of wealth-production. This increase of wealth is of course enriching *someone* – a class of which many perform but little really useful work while the bulk of them serve no function useful in any way to the community. Look, again, at the effect of increased scientific knowledge. By a better knowledge of chemistry and metallurgy tons of metal are now extracted from the ore with the labour of fewer men than must formerly have been employed to produce one hundredweight. What I am concerned about is, that in spite of our advanced methods of producing wealth, the workers as a class get only a subsistence wage, whilst an increasing number of them cannot get the barest necessaries of life.

Optimist politicians are unwilling to admit that this is so. Anxious to make out a good case for the present basis of society, they ignore the plainest of facts, so in confirmation of my contention I will quote from one or two non-socialists. Professor Thorold Rogers, the present MP for Bermondsey, says on pages 185–6 of 'Six Centuries of Work and Wages', written in 1884.

> It may be well the case, and there is every reason to fear it is the case, that there is collected a population in our great towns which equals in extent the whole of those who lived in England and Wales six centuries ago; but whose condition is more destitute, whose homes are more squalid, whose means are more uncertain, whose prospects are more hopeless than those of the poorest serfs of the Middle Ages and the meanest drudges of the mediaeval cities. The arm of the law is strong enough to keep them under, and society has no reason to fear their despair; but I refuse to accept the superficial answer that a man is an admirer of the good old times because he insists that the vaunts of civilisation should be examined along with, and not apart from its failures. It is not possible to give the solution of one problem, the growth of opulence, and to refuse all attention to the other problem, the growth of penury.

Joseph Cowen MP speaking at a Mechanics' Institute at Newcastle, alluded to the labouring section as 'a hybrid class doomed to eat the bread of penury and drink the cup of misery. Precarious labour provided them with subsistence for the day, but the slightest interruption threw them destitute. A week of broken weather brought thousands of these industrial nomads to the brink of starvation. An inscrutable influence seemed to sink them as it elevated those around and above them. Society, ashamed and despairing, swept them, like refuse, into dismal receptacles, where seething in their wretchedness, they constituted at once our weakness and reproach. How to sweeten these receptacles and help their forlorn occupants to help themselves was the problem of the hour. *If society did not settle it, it would in time settle society.*'

To this socialists answer that there is no permanent way of sweetening the lives of the class referred to except by the complete annihilation of the profit-mongers as a class, by forcing them all into the ranks of the *useful* workers. This will be apparent when it is realised that under the present system we are working to supply profits to profit-mongers instead of working to supply the legitimate requirements of the entire community, and when it is borne in mind that shareholders and employers are contented with nothing less than the *highest* possible profits, it will also be seen that on the other hand we (the workers) can have nothing more than the *lowest* possible wages. To establish society on a proper basis is therefore the work of every right-minded man or woman.

Demagogues have been at work – with good intentions perhaps – but they have misled the workers from the true cause of their troubles. Among the blind leaders of the blind may be mentioned the Malthusians, the Teetotallers, the Financial Reformers, and well-intentioned Radicals. The first mentioned have taught that there are too many people in the country, and that the only way of bettering our condition is by curtailing the population, and this in face of the fact that every year wealth in this country is increasing much faster than population. The Temperance advocates hammer away at the blessings of sobriety as though drunkenness was the cause of poverty, when the fact is the other way about. Well nigh as fast as they surround an old toper with influences that prevent his drinking tastes being gratified, another fills up the hole out of which he was lifted. It is a useless expenditure of energy to be continually preaching temperance and thrift. Let all be blest with leisure, food and healthy enjoyments, as they might be if the economic basis of society was as it should be, and then these matters will all right themselves. The only reason people spend time upon these panaceas is because they fail to understand the law of wages, which is that all above a bare subsistence wage shall go to profit-mongers as profit. The only way out is to *destroy the profit-mongers*.

The same argument applies to the financial reformer. All sensible persons are of course agreed that the country should be governed as economically as is consistent with efficiency, as also all are agreed that we should live soberly. But the reformer fails to see that if we curtail taxation to its lowest possible minimum, reduce it if you will 90 per cent, not one farthing of it would be saved to the workers. The Iron Law would still be in force which says, 'So much as will keep life in you *and no more* shall go to you, O ye workers, so long as the profit making system remains.'

These economic questions cannot be understood in a sufficiently clear manner by the mass of the workers while they are absorbed twelve, fourteen, sixteen, and even more hours a day while in work, and when out of work are walking about with the pangs of hunger eating out their vitals, and the blackness of despair staring them in the face at every turn. Now suppose those of us who can see these things in something like their grim reality, decide that come what may, we at least will do our part towards obtaining remunerative employment for all, and at the same time sufficient leisure that all may have a little breathing time after their work, what course can we take? To this I reply, there is one way by which it can be done, viz, by at once concentrating our efforts towards the establishing of an eight hours working day.

Let us examine a few figures in order to see clearly how this would affect us. We have something like 7,000,000 adult workers in the British Isles, working nominally under the nine hours system, leaving overtime out of consideration for the moment. Let us see how many more hands would be put in employment if we struck off one hour per day from those in work. It is roughly estimated that of the above mentioned workers there are about 900,000 now out of work, representing a total population of 3½ or 4 millions of men, women, and children who cannot get the barest necessaries of life. Now strike off one hour per day from the 6,000,000 in work. The result would be an immediate demand for 750,000 additional workers to keep up production at its present rate, and remembering that these 750,000 would immediately begin to buy more food, clothing, and general comforts, this of course would give an impetus to trade, and so add greatly to the comfort of the entire community for a year or two. These advantages, however, would soon be swallowed up by fresh displacements of labour due to more efficient machinery and advancing scientific knowledge; but, during the year or two that it gave relief, see how immensely it would add to the leisure and therefore to the general intelligence of the workers. And increased intelligence means more active discontent with our conditions of life, and in due course a hastening of the overthrow of the present capitalistic domination.

I am fully aware that there are some who claim to have a knowledge of workers who contend that the very success of an Eight Hours Movement would simply mean a perpetuation of the present wretched system, as the people would become more contented if the conditions of life were made more tolerable. This I hold to be the very reverse of truth. As a workman who has worked from early boyhood on the farm, down the mine, and in the engineer's shop, I repudiate such a slanderous statement. What means the continually increasing restlessness of late years of those workmen who are now, *relatively* to their former position, in a passable state of comfort? I contend that it is in large part due to the additional leisure obtained under the nine hours system, though most of its advantages have now been swallowed up by more rapid machinery and the cursed system of overtime we still tolerate. I ask myself what has been my guide in the formation of my opinions on social and political subjects, and, risking being charged with egotism, I reply that I have ever endeavoured to get correct views upon these and other subjects by fashioning my ideas upon the best models I could find, and the more leisure I had the better my opportunity for finding good models. I can understand a middle-class man holding this – to me – absurd theory. I can also understand some workmen reflecting the opinions of these theory-loving, poverty-accentuating blockheads merely because they are middle-class. But I cannot understand a workman who through youth and early manhood has been battling against long hours in order that he might attend the institute, listen to the lectures, and read the works of able men, and by these means has succeeded in having a mind worth owning – I say I cannot understand such a one hindering rather than helping in a shorter hours movement. He practically says by such conduct that the leisure he used so well as to become a man thereby, others will use so ill that they will continue fools. But men generally love what is best for all, and are prepared to do their part towards carrying it out so soon as they understand clearly what course they should take. Let those of us who see (or think we see) further than the average man, do all in our power towards enabling him to see as clearly as we do, and then, unless I am incapable of reading aright the lesson of life, he too will become in his turn an earnest and an energetic worker for the elevation of his class. I must apologise to some readers who may think that none of this reasoning is necessary. I emphasise it because I know there exist philosophers who strain at gnats and swallow camels, who talk of ameliorating human suffering, but hang back instead of assisting a movement the success of which must for a dead certainty largely ameliorate the pangs of the hungry men, women, and children who are now in the throes of despair.

Another section raise the objection that however desirable it may be to curtail the hours of labour, remembering the severe competition of other countries it is simply impossible either to raise wages or shorten hours unless a similar movement takes place on the continent. I will endeavour to answer this first by showing that the English workers produce more per man than any of the continental nations, and second, by showing that with regard to our staple industries foreign competition is a bogie used by the employer to frighten the workers into accepting harder terms in order that their master may make a greater profit. It may be of some service to point out the relative wealth per annum produced by the useful workers of this and other countries. I am assuming that the reader is clear concerning the source of wealth, that there is no other source than useful labour, so that, having sufficient raw material for workers to exercise their ingenuity upon, it will be seen that the more workers, the more the aggregate wealth, as in all ages men have been able to produce by their labour more than they and their families required for ordinary consumption. Quoting from Mulhall's 'Statistics', we find that Britain with a population of 36 millions produces wealth to the amount of £1,247,000,000 per annum; France with 37½ millions of people produces annually £965,000,000 (or with a million and a half more people about three-quarters the amount the English make), Germany, population 45 millions, wealth per annum, £850,000,000; (or two thirds only of our amount); Russia with 80 millions of people, creates per annum only £760,000,000, Austria, 38 millions population, only £602,000,000 per annum; and similarly with the smaller nations. These figures will serve to show that our method of producing wealth is a more effective one than that in vogue on the continent, as although they generally work longer hours per day than the English yet the result of their year's work compares unfavourably with ours. The important lesson to be learnt here is this, that it is not the amount paid as wages that decides whether or not one country can compete successfully with another; or rather, it is not the countries where wages are low that compete most successfully with this country. This will be seen when it is realised that the severest competitor we have to-day is America, a country that pays at least 25 per cent higher wages than are paid in this country.

This of itself should be sufficient to encourage those timorous mortals who are always attributing our exhausting toil to the competition of the long hours of the continent. The time may arrive when, with an equally advanced method of production, low paid labour will produce wealth as effectively as better paid labour, but that time has not yet come. By way of proving this let me here instance the iron shipbuilding industry. Many have been the disputes between employers and employed in this industry during the past two or three years, the employers continually urging that the continental shipbuilders are getting all the trade, or at any rate will do so, unless our workmen submit to reductions in wages and longer hours. This argument was advanced repeatedly during the year 1885, so in order to thoroughly test the matter a delegation of workers was despatched to the continent to bring back precise information upon the subject. They found that Germany was our chief competitor in iron shipbuilding, and that during the year 1885 that country produced 22,326 tons of shipping. But in this country one firm on the Clyde during the same period turned out 40,000 tons. France produced 10,000 tons, and Russia 7,867 tons – total for the two countries 17,867 tons. But the river Tyne alone launched no less than 102,998 tons. The Belgian output was 5,312 tons, that of Holland 2,651 tons, of Denmark 3,515 tons. To sum up, the whole of the continental output was a little over 50,000 tons, while that of the English shipyards was 540,282 tons, or nearly eleven times as great as that of all the yards on the continent put together. With facts like these before us is it not high time we demanded that our hours were curtailed so as to give a chance to those who now walk about in enforced idleness, without waiting for the continent to take simultaneous action. The Americans, who pay their mechanics better wages, have had to concede the demands of their workmen for the eight hour working day – not universally, it is true, because a universal demand was not made. Just as their success stimulates us, so our success will stimulate the continental workers, and we shall find that they are as well prepared as we are to deal vigorously with the exploiting classes.

To trade unionists I desire to make a special appeal. How long, *how long* will you be content with the present half-hearted policy of your unions? I readily grant that good work has been done in the past by the unions, but, in heaven's name, what good purpose are they serving now? All of them have large numbers out of employment even when their particular trade is busy. None of the important societies have any policy other than that of endeavouring to keep wages from falling. The true unionist policy of *aggression* seems entirely lost sight of; in fact the unionist of to-day should be of all men the last to be hopelessly apathetic, or supporting a policy that plays directly into the hands of the capitalist exploiter. Do not think I am a non-unionist myself, and therefore denounce unionists. I take my share of the work in the trade union to which I belong, but I candidly confess that unless it shows more vigour in the future than it is showing at the present time (June, 1886) I shall be compelled to take the view – against my will – that to continue to spend time over the ordinary squabble-investigating, do-nothing policy will be an unjustifiable waste of one's energies. I am quite sure there are thousands of others in my state of mind – eg all those who concurred with T. R. Threlfall, the president of the Trades Union Congress, when, in his presidential address, he told the delegates assembled at Southport that a critical time had arrived in the history of trades unions, and that in the future they must *lead* or *follow,* and that they could not hope to retain advanced men with their present policy. In his magnificent address Mr Threlfall did all a man could do to stir the unionists up to take action in regard to the eight hour working day, but one looks in vain at each and all of our important trade societies to find any action being taken in the matter. It is not enough to say their funds are low. Their funds are not too low to get up an agitation upon this subject. All over the country they have excellent organisations which might be used in the first place as the means for instructing their own members up to the required standard, and then spreading information amongst the non-unionists, skilled and unskilled alike. When the bulk of these understood the pros and cons of the case the combined forces could make a demand for the immediate passing of an Eight Hours Bill, the details of which could be settled by a duly qualified committee.

While this is being done attention should also be made to another important item alluded to by Mr Threlfall, viz, the payment of election expenses out of the local or imperial rates and the support of Members of Parliament in a similar manner. When this is done we shall be able to command the services of those whom we believe in because of their merits, irrespective of what the depth of their pocket may be.

Let me now invite attention to the effects of an Eight Hour Bill upon some of our monopolies. Let us take the railways as a representative concern, using round figures such as will convey a correct idea to the ordinary reader without confusing him. The Blue Books bear out the following statements: At the present time the annual income of the British Railways may be put at £70,000,000, of this vast sum one half goes to the shareholders, who do no useful work whatever; one fourth to keep up rolling stock, permanent way etc; and the remaining fourth to the workers (including managers' and superintendents' salaries).

The man who has not paid attention to railway income and expenditure will denounce this as trash or probably by a stronger term. He will probably say that the figures must be wrong, as railway shareholders get only some 5 per cent on their capital. Exactly, but where nearly all make the mistake is in not making the distinction between percentage on money invested and percentage of income. There are nominally more than £920,000,000 invested in railways in the British Isles, and 5 per cent on this means about five-eighths of the total income, the entire income of 70 millions amounting only to 8 per cent on the investments. Consequently a railway company paying 4½ per cent to shareholders actually pays more than half of the total income to these utterly useless individuals, leaving the remainder to go in about equal proportions to rolling stock and permanent way and as wages and salaries to employees. This gives about 18s per week to the 350,000 persons engaged on railways in the British Isles. When we remember that superintendents and managers get very large salaries, we see that those who do the hard work and have the longest hours get much less than 18s.

Now that we realise the enormous amount the idle shareholders take, let us see how generously they behave to those in their employ. At Nine Elms are situated the cleaning sheds of the South Western Railway. Until recently the 'dirty cleaners' at this yard received £1 0s 6d per week. Instructions have been issued from Waterloo to curtail their wages from 20s 6d to 15s at one stroke. On the same line, at Waterloo terminus, the parcels porters commence work at 5.20 in the morning and keep on till 9.45 in the evening with one Sunday off per fortnight, their wages being from 18s to 22s per week.

Now assuming the average day on railways to be 12 hours, what loss would it inflict on the shareholders if a Bill were passed enforcing an eight hours' working day? We have seen that the employees get about a quarter of the total income or about £17,000,000. To curtail the hours by one third means of course putting one half more men in work than are at present employed. To pay these at a similar rate to those already working would require £8,500,000 or less than one per cent on the nominal value of the shares, so that a company paying 4½ per cent now, would, if one half more men were employed still pay 3½ per cent to the fleecing shareholders. What arrant nonsense then it is to urge that the company cannot afford to curtail hours.

Let us look now at the conditions of our colliers. Here we have men devoting themselves to underground toil from boyhood to old age, the majority never having the opportunity of paying a visit to the capital, or any other large town, practically kennelled in the earth, tied down with capitalistic chains, '*Spending a sunless life in the unwholesome mines*' for the wretched pittance of about 18s per week. Surely an Eight Hours Bill requires no urging from me on behalf of those who work in and about the mines; when we remember that of the value of coal raised annually in this country (about £66,000,000) one third only goes to the colliers who raise it.

An item worth mentioning also was pointed out by Sir Lyon Playfair in his address before the British Association at Aberdeen in 1885, whilst deploring the fact that the exhaustion of the British coalfields made the coal increasingly difficult to get. It was proved that not only has man's ingenuity conquered these obstacles, but owing to the increased power of steam engines and hand-labour-saving appliances, two men now produce as much as three men did twenty years ago. Yet coal is *dearer* now than it was then!

Thirty years ago eight sailors were required for the management of every 100 tons of shipping. Now, owing to improved machinery, less than half that number suffice. In twenty years the consumption of fuel on our ocean-going steamers has been reduced by one half, chiefly owing to the use of compound engines in place of single ones as formerly. Thus on every hand a greater result is being shown with less labour. And it must be so or else there is no meaning in material progress. But 'less labour' means under our existing system, and must mean so as long as industry is controlled by the idle classes, not 'more leisure' or shorter hours all round, but *less wages,* more unemployed, poverty, famine, and physical and moral degradation.

What then can be more rational than to ease the burden of those in work and the starving stomachs of those who are out, by shortening the working day?

See what is going on in the watch-making industry, a fine example of the effects of machinery. Among the exhibits at last year's Inventions Exhibition was that of the Waltham Watch Co. Some machines were there at work making screws for watches, of which it took 250,000 to make up a pound in weight. These machines were so perfectly made, that at the company's factory in Massachusetts, one boy keeps seven of them going. The best wire to make one pound weight of screws costs ten shillings, but after this wire has been converted into screws by passing through this automatic machine, the screws are worth £350, or seven hundred times the cost of the material. Imagine the number of men here thrown out of employment; the watches in large part being made by girls, and the enormous profits going to the owners of the machinery.

Take another case, that of Bryant and May's match factory in East London. Two years ago this firm was formed into a limited liability company. Their work girls are most miserably paid, getting only some 8s per week, and the company refused to increase their pay when they made a demand a short time since. And yet that company, during the first *six* months of its existence, after paying all working expenses, actually paid over £33,000 to shareholders, who had not done a single stroke of work towards producing it. These girls are working ordinary factory hours, 10½ per day. They cannot live in comfort on such a miserable pittance as they are receiving. How many girls are compelled by this sort of thing, to take to the streets?

The above is only typical of what all our large firms are doing. Armstrong, Mitchell and Co, the great engineering firm at Newcastle-on-Tyne, for instance, last year after deducting for working expenses and depreciation of stock, paid to shareholders £162,000.

Whatever improvement may come through more efficient machinery etc, its effect, while owned by, and used for the profit of, the employing class, will be to throw men out of work and swell the already too full pockets of the capitalists. If we do not decide to curtail the hours of labour, what then can we do? Allow things to go from bad to worse? That is what most assuredly will happen, unless we absorb the unemployed into the ranks of the employed by rigidly suppressing overtime, and curtailing the nominal nine hours per day to something less.

The question will be asked by some, 'What about wages if we work an hour a day less, are we to have an hour's less pay?' Most certainly not. Even when the curtailing principle was only partially applied 15 years ago by the trade unionists this did not happen. On the contrary in many instances the workmen were soon able to get a rise in actual wages in addition to the curtailing of hours. The reason we cannot command a better wage now is because the employer can say, 'If you don't like it you may go, others will be glad to take your place,' but, as I think I have shown, if we make eight hours the labour day when the unemployed will be absorbed and the workers will be able in their turn to dictate terms to the employer.

In conclusion I appeal to the workers of Great Britain to join hands over this business and let us make it a success. In a measure of this kind Liberal and Tory, Christian and freethinker, unionist and non-unionist, mechanic and labourer, radical and social-democrat, teetotaller or vegetarian, whatsoever be your creed or sex, unite on common ground and let us fight this battle of the workers with vigour, with energy and determination. Be no longer apathetic. Take pleasure in the performance of your duty as an honest citizen and the result will be a hastening of that glorious time when the domination of a class shall be a matter of history, and when all shall have enough work and none shall have too much.

# 21

# *UNEMPLOYMENT: ITS CAUSES AND CONSEQUENCES* (LONDON: TWENTIETH CENTURY PRESS, 1906), 5–16.

*Countess of Warwick*

[The figure of Lady Warwick confounds many stereotypes. In the opening years of the twentieth century, it was the Fabians, particularly the Webbs, who drew notoriety by the attempted "permeation" of the British establishment with notions of top-down social reform. Few could have been more top-down than Frances Maynard. Born in Mayfair in 1861, at the age of twenty-two she married the future Fourth Earl of Warwick. Dissatisfied with the inanity of her prescribed roles, she then not only embarked upon the characteristic philanthropies of her gender and social class but in 1895 sought out Robert Blatchford (Vol. III, Chapters 6 and 25) to discover what it was about the present social system to which socialists took such exception. When nine years later she joined the socialist movement, it was in the shape of the SDF and through the personal cultivation of Hyndman. In his memoirs, Hyndman described taking his French guests Jean Jaurès and Georges Clemenceau to lunch with her, and Clemenceau afterwards pronouncing that the English working class was *une classe bourgeoise*. It is not difficult to see why (Hyndman 1911, 327.)

Lady Warwick's views on the unemployed question were originally published in the *Daily Mail* on 12–13 February 1906. The official unemployment figures had in 1904 reached their highest level for a decade, and though the 1905 Unemployed Workmen Act introduced provisions for local relief committees, the funding was to come from private sources. In condemning both the methods adopted and the basic misconception of the social character of the problem, the pamphlet strikes a note familiar to any socialist reader but far less so to readers of the *Daily Mail*. More distinctive in an SDF context is the pamphlet's concern with the reorganisation of agriculture. Lady Warwick had taken a practical interest in rural workers' conditions, including a ten-year stint on the Warwick Board of Guardians, and had also played her part in seeing into print the autobiography of the agricultural workers' leader Joseph Arch.

The SDF published its pamphlet version of the articles with a preface by the editor of *Justice* Harry Quelch. There is no mistaking what might nowadays be described as a weakness for celebrity. Not only one of the wealthiest but, according to Hyndman, the most beautiful woman in Britain, the author gazes out from the cover of her pamphlet in a society portrait that *Daily Mail* readers would have found a good deal more familiar. The image is one that sits uncomfortably within the movement's historiography. Remaining a member of the SDF/BSP until the war, Lady Warwick was reputedly one of the five speakers most in demand for speaking engagements, and the only woman among them (Lee and Archbold 1935, 192). Nevertheless, she does not figure in the one major scholarly account of women and the SDF (Hunt 1996).

Hyndman claimed that she stood alone among her class in Europe in having the courage to embrace the cause of social democracy (Hyndman 1912, 82–100). He might have added that possibly only in Britain would the embrace have been so blandly reciprocated. A hugely perceptive German observer was to comment to just this effect on the later popularity in Labour circles of Sir Oswald and Lady Cynthia Mosley: "How strange that ... none appears to resent the furs of this woman, or to feel as a provocation her air of cultivated, easy well-being ..." (Morgan 2006, ch. 5). The comparison, however, is unfair; for unlike the Mosleys, Lady Warwick remained steadfast and manifestly disinterested in her support for Labour causes, though the combination of good intentions and elevated social standing was also a source of many tensions (Owen 2007b, 44–45).]

The Committees established under the Unemployed Workmen Act, 1905, will have collected and collated much useful information, and may have mitigated the hardships of industrial distress in a few individual cases. Beyond this nothing has been done to touch even the fringe of the Unemployed Question. The significant use of the word "temporary" in the Act and L.G.B. Orders is evidence of no intention to handle the problem.

For the most part "Unemployment" has generally been regarded as (*a*) a passing social ailment or symptom of local disorder; (*b*) a natural and inevitable phase of civilisation; (*c*) the result of intemperance, indolence or incapacity in individuals.

As the last-quoted belief is no longer held by any serious students of the subject, one need only point out that "Unemployment" is not an individual state, but an existing social condition—a slough of despond—into which individuals are constantly being pushed. Personal conduct may decide which of two individuals shall be employed, but it does not decide how many shall be *un*employed. If one discharges a neglectful or incompetent workman it is only because there is, among the unemployed, someone better to replace him. A good workman is pulled out of the slough of despond and an inferior man thrown in. The actual number of unemployed has not thereby been altered. The fact is that unemployment is the result of economic conditions over which the individual has no control.

Indolence and vice are found in all ranks, as much, if not more, among the rich than the poor. At least there is more excuse for the latter, who often drift into bad habits as the result of irregular work, low wages and miserable surroundings, which breed in them disgust and despair; embittered further by the sight of the immense wealth and inordinate luxury of an idle and useless class, into whose laps are poured the results of industry.

Many thoughtful persons, including some students of economics, are inclined to accept unemployment as the result of "bad trade," without being quite clear what they mean by the term. It is very little realised how large are the numbers of unemployed, even in times of "good trade." It is quite a common thing for 2 per cent. of the members of a trade union of skilled men to be out of work. Among the unorganised members of the same trade—usually an inferior class of men—the percentage is very much higher. In times even of best trade some 20,000 to 30,000 trade unionists are on the books of their societies, and it must be remembered that as they are receiving out-of-work pay elaborate care has been taken to weed-out shirkers. Every trade society is a great labour registry and exchange. Since the non-unionists number something like six or seven to one, and since their percentage of unemployed is higher, there can seldom be fewer than 150,000 to 200,000 unemployed workers even in times of good trade. This would at once become apparent if it were not largely disguised by the evil system of casual labour. In such industries, for instance, as dock work, one man is employed on one day, another on another. They are all reckoned as being "employed," but really on any given day more than one-half of them would be found unemployed.

In all such calculations no account is taken of the numbers of unemployed clerks, insurance agents, canvassers, warehousemen, and so on. Nor, of course, of confirmed tramps, beggars and criminals, who when reclaimed can only get employment by displacing someone else.

Those who regard unemployment as the result of "bad trade" should study the Board of Trade Returns for the past year.

The recent crisis actually coincided with the record figures of imports and exports. The returns for November, 1905, exceeded the returns for any previous month in the history of British commerce, and the total returns for that year largely exceeded the returns for any previous twelve months. Yet there exists on every side of us such widespread and bitter distress as would make us stand aghast if we were not all so easily disposed to take everything for granted while things go well with ourselves. "We are fed, we are clothed, we are housed—therefore all is for the best in the best possible of worlds," says Society. So long as one can dine at the Carlton Hotel it is difficult to believe that men cannot get work if they want it, especially if one is considerately abstaining from work, so as to give them a fair chance.

"Bad trade," season work, changes of fashion, the disorganisation caused by war, and many such causes may help to aggravate unemployment and so produce alarming symptoms of the disease, but its roots lie deeper than in these things, and even ameliorative measures cannot hope to succeed unless they are devised with some knowledge of how deep the roots do lie.

No one will pretend that members of any one of the building trades need really be unemployed so far as the demand for their labour goes. A large proportion of our people are worse housed than a decent farmer's cattle, therefore real need for such labour is obvious. It is equally monstrous that a single tailor and shoemaker should be unemployed. Dr. Eichholz, of the Home Office, told the Inter-Departmental Committee on Physical Deterioration that there were 122,000 children in London alone going to school in a starving and underfed condition. What sort of shoes and clothing are they likely to have when even bread is wanting?

Obviously then, there is urgent need and demand for the services of all workmen, but the spending power to make that demand effective is lacked by the very classes that could and would use it.

It is clear to the least thoughtful person that all incomes, whether wages, salaries, pensions, rent, dividends, or interest, come from our industries. But what is not always recognised is that an increasing proportion of the nation's income goes to those who, already having more than they can spend, make no effective use of the increase. Out of our national income of £1,800,000,000 little more than a third goes in wages. The growth of trusts and combines, and the economies resulting from the rapid concentration of industry in fewer hands, increase the proportion going to rent and interest. Now, the natural employers of the people are the people themselves. But the people have to see an increasing proportion of the wealth they produce taken from them, not even to be spent on luxuries which other workers might produce, but simply to make further concentrations and economies, and still further reduce the area of employment for themselves and their fellows. The spending power passes away from those who need to those who have long since been in the position to fully satisfy every desire except one—the desire for more financial power. In case this should seem exaggerated, let me point out that with all our enormous increase in the output of cotton spinning the number of operatives remains almost stationary.

If all the ship-building and cotton-spinning of the country could be done by a few thousand automatic machines and a few hundred operators, a group of financiers might corner the patent rights and become recipients of the entire incomes of the two industries. They would not consider in what other way they might employ the army thus thrown out of work. They would use their revenues to conquer yet other industries, irrespective of who, or how many, were thus employed. Why not? If the greater part of the land and capital of the country can be owned by 100,000 people, why not by 100? If 100,000 workers can be denied the right to work in the country which they have enriched by their labour, why should not a million or ten million be so denied—so long as they are willing to submit? The wrong lies not in the number affected, but in the fact that even a single willing worker can be debarred from employment, whilst land, machinery and tools are lying idle, and others are in urgent need of the things he is able to make.

This evil is an absolutely inevitable result of land, railways, canals, docks, machinery and all other means of producing goods being used to enable a few individuals to live at the expense of their fellows, who are only allowed to live at all in so far as they minister to that end.

As these means of life concentrate in fewer hands the problem will grow more acute, and the ranks of the unemployed will be swollen by an increasing number of managers, clerks, agents, ruined merchants and shop-keepers—an already noticeable feature of the trouble in the United States. These men, at any rate, will not be content with measures of "temporary relief." They will have to recognise, then, if they do not sooner, that there is no solution of the Unemployed Problem save in the organisation by the community of its own resources for the common good of its citizens.

The better educated of the workmen quite clearly see this, and see also that an unemployed class is vitally necessary to the capitalist in resisting movements towards better conditions. Even the less thoughtful rank and file begin to recognise that unemployment is but one phase of the whole question of poverty. Hence it is that the direction of the Labour movement has passed into the hands of the Socialists, in whose ideal alone do the workers see hope for the future.

They have not so long endured want, and hardship, and anxiety, and all the sufferings of wives and little children, out of mere weakness, but because they could not see how matters could ever be much otherwise. The men to whom the term "Class War" once seemed mere vapouring, now realise that it may have a practical significance in the shaping of political programmes. They are tired of attempted palliatives, and turn to those who aim at removing the root causes of all such evils as unemployment. The most that can be hoped for under present conditions is that any attempt at amelioration should be with some due understanding of the nature of the problem.

It is well, perhaps, to consider what might, and what should *not,* be done to palliate the evil under existing conditions.

All palliatives are undesirable when offered as a substitute for facing facts and finding remedies, but of all palliative measures the most pernicious are those dependent on the forms of private philanthropy which we mis-call "charity." The out-of-work man is either a shirker, or he is not. If he *is,* then treat him penally, if you like. Why not, indeed, extend the treatment to all shirkers, in all classes? If he is not a shirker, then it is degrading alike to the man and the State that he should be subjected to the indignity of private alms. What must be the feelings of an unskilled labourer, who, after slaving away more than half his working life at starvation wages (say) in an arsenal or dockyard, finds himself at 45 years of age compelled, for the sake of wife and children, to accept the doles of the rich?

This blight of private charity is the one thing above all that serious remedial measures should avoid, yet it is the one thing above all that the Unemployed Act sought to establish. At best it was but a hard, stale crust of reform. With this provision it was poisoned. The ratepayers must continue to contribute for the benefit of a wastrel or malingerer to whom the loss of a vote means nothing, but the bonâ-fide unemployed man is to be handed over to "charity." Professedly this is to save the latter from the loss of citizenship rights, but that might just as easily have been arrived at by an amendment of the Poor Law, and indeed this should long ago have been made. What a muddle to have got into, when we regard it as more honourable for a man to accept alms from individuals on whom he has no immediate claim, than help from the nation which he has served and enriched by his labour!

Particularly offensive is it to any right-thinking person when this charity—I apologise for the misuse of the beautiful word—is associated with the propaganda of a church or sect. Of all philanthropies, philanthropy plus cant is the most nauseating.

All this not only degrades the recipient and the State and encourages Pharisaism of an offensive sort, but also fosters the typical British vice of inefficiency, the love of muddling-through things, the intellectual indolence which shirks analysis of facts and study of causes. We will beat any kind of drum, vociferate any platitudes and catchwords, cling to any formula, make any kind of bustle or fuss rather than use our brains in finding out the right thing to do and proceed to the doing of it.

In the provision of means, then, we should above all avoid private philanthropy. There are more than ample opportunities for the private help that each one of us gives to the individual in loving friendship. But in the carrying out of remedial measures only harm will be done by such as do not actually increase the spending power of the class employed. Setting men to such work as wood-chopping or mat-making at a mere dole-wage, and then selling their products at low prices, only results in the regular workers in those trades being undersold and thrown out of work. Many of the this or that "Army" workshops are but centres of organised "blacklegism." In the end there are just as many out of work, but the spending power of the class has been reduced, the attempted cure only aggravating the evil—a common result of quack remedies.

The Local Government Board Orders, too, insist on the workers under the Distress Committees being paid below the standard wage; which is like reducing the available sources of water supply as a remedy for drought!

The re-arrangement of a Council's ordinary programme of work—so as (say) to do next summer's work this winter—may serve the purpose of keeping numbers of men from rust and demoralisation; and, as privations are hardest to bear in the winter, good is so far achieved. But it is clear that the sum total of Unemployment has not been reduced, any more than a given amount of butter is reduced by spreading it over a slice of bread. The wages drawn and spent this winter cannot also be drawn and spent next summer. The real problem has not been touched. Nor can it be touched except through increase of the number of persons regularly employed, and through increase of the spending power of those already in work by improvements in wages and reductions in the cost of living.

The laying-out of new parks or recreation grounds, making of sea-walls, cultivation of waste land, and such-like work not otherwise undertaken, is on the right lines if the men are paid a standard wage, but these are of necessity temporary measures, and what is so badly needed is permanence. Of course, the capitalist wants nothing save temporary measures, so that he may always have abundance of cheap labour to exploit; but, generally speaking, what is good for the capitalist—or what he thinks is good for him—is bad for the nation.

To organise a permanent army of 5,000 well-paid men in large schemes (say) of re-afforestation and foreshore reclamation, would do more real good than a few days of work here and there, now and again, for 50,000. It would be better for the morale and physique of the men, better for the trades affected by their spending power, better for a nation permanently enriched by the results of such labour.

Then, the slum districts of our towns are a crying evil. Sooner or later they must be demolished, and better accommodation provided. Every day literally adds to the cost at which it will have to be done. The private builder continues to provide new districts which are but material for more slums. There is absolutely nothing—except indifference and stupidity—to prevent the organisation of building and slum-demolishing armies, under central control, to do the work so long neglected by local authorities.

Again, the ranks of casual workers—in other words, of the intermittently unemployed—are steadily recruited from the agricultural districts. A compulsion on County Councils to provide decent rural housing accommodation would not only thus employ a number of artisans and labourers, but would remove one of the principal grievances which drive families into the towns. The growth of urban centres in the rural districts would make libraries, baths, music and other rational recreations possible.

At the same time there are innumerable methods by which agriculture might be stimulated. Quicker and cheaper marketing of produce, and the more extended use of co-operative methods in dairy-farming could be encouraged, or even provided by the Board of Agriculture. The half of what has been done in Denmark and Hungary would not only check migration *to* the towns, but even create a demand for labour *from* the towns.

One result of this would be a steadying of employment and rise in wages in the very class which is now worst paid and least regularly employed. At present we let agriculture go to rack and ruin, and when the labourer has drifted to the town and failed in the struggle, we transport him or his demoralised, untrained sons and daughters to a temporary farm-colony to try and make men and women of them.

In the end we shall have to re-organise agriculture and make it a national industry, as so obviously it ought to be, but in the meantime much might be done to improve and develop this, the greatest source of employment and national security.

Over and above such measures as these all wise social reforms affect the question of unemployment. A reduction in the working hours of tram, omnibus and railroad employees obviously makes for good. Every raising of the school age not only improves the stamina and intelligence of the race, and raises our standard of production, but increases the number of regularly employed adults. Too many old people are struggling on, often at reduced wages, who would long since have retired on honourable pensions had they been driving quills in Pall Mall instead of creating actual wealth. This is bad for them, bad for our industries, bad for the younger men thus kept unemployed. Others, beyond any work, reduce the already scant spending power of the children who support them. The decent pensioning of the veterans of industry would thus materially affect the problem.

All taxes should be removed from actual industry. A wise Government, too, would remove all taxes from tea, coffee, cocoa, etc., and free many millions of pounds to be spent by the people in other directions.

It will be said that even these moderate reforms must cost much money. Of course they must! If they did not involve expenditure they would not go far to solve the problem of unemployment. We have to spend money which is not now spent, and much of what is already spent we have to spend more wisely. Otherwise let us say frankly that we are not prepared to handle the problem. Possibly, then, the unemployed may handle it for themselves.

If one asks, "Where is the money to come from?" I ask in reply, "Where does the annual tribute of more than £1,000,000,000 for rent, profit and interest come from? Where do all taxes come from? What other source is there of all tribute, public or private, save the product of our trades and industries?" It is true that taxes raised for war purposes, or for spasmodic relief of distress, do little good—perhaps much harm—in the spending, but taxation which goes to organise, develop and regularise industry, and to raise the standard of a people's life, increases the very fund from which it is provided. The share taken by those who have earned nothing would certainly be reduced, but so will it have to be reduced either by our present class of Ministers—or by another class which will supersede them.

The Ministry which declares in effect that it cannot or will not do what is best for the nation because the interests of its class—the privileged class—will not allow it, need not be surprised if the one class which after all out-numbers all others should strip such a statement of all sophistical wrappings and retort in similar spirit, "Very well, then, we will first of all take care to reduce your class to a minority in the House of Commons."

The mass of people know so little even of the comforts of life, expect so few of its joys, are so easily satisfied if they can but somehow pay their way, endure the bitterest hardships and privations with so little complaint, that we have come to think they have less feeling and courage than our cattle.

It is in the nature of bureaucracies—under plutocratic government, as well as autocratic—to mistake a people's ignorance for indifference and its forbearance for weakness. Such mistakes have been known to end in rude awakenings. The schoolmaster's work has incalculable results. The most wonderfully pathetic forbearance has its limits. Even those whose only idea of their lot in life is to be thankful for a job and its rations, even these are stirred into mutiny and into thought when they find that they can rely neither on the job nor the rations. The mutiny you may suppress, but the thought you *cannot*.

Once it used to be said: "Society must settle this problem or it will settle Society." Now we simply say: Society must settle this problem.

# 22

# *PRISON REFORM FROM A SOCIAL-DEMOCRATIC POINT OF VIEW* (LONDON: TWENTIETH CENTURY PRESS, 1909), 1–14.

*Dora B. Montefiore*

[At the time she wrote this pamphlet Dora Montefiore (1851–1933) was a member of the SDP's executive and one of the party's most prominent women activists. Embracing socialism in her late forties, Montefiore brought to the movement her extensive experiences of political campaigning and international travel, including periods living in Australia and France. Of privileged social origin, she enjoyed an independent income following her husband's death in 1889 and gave her time freely to a range of political causes. She had long been a campaigner for women's suffrage and as a member of the Women's Social and Political Union spent time in Holloway prison following a demonstration in 1906. With her knowledge of foreign languages, she travelled extensively abroad, researching social questions and attending international socialist congresses. In 1911 she explained her preference for the SDF over the ILP by invoking its "international and revolutionary basis" (Hunt 2001, 32).

All of these experiences have left a mark on the document published here. As one would expect of a social-democratic perspective, Montefiore alludes in passing to the future socialist society in which the causes of "artificial" crime will have disappeared. Nevertheless, her primary concern is with "Social Democratic palliatives". In presenting these she draws on a wide range of authorities including the ultra-individualist Herbert Spencer and the Humanitarian League's Joseph Collinson, writing to Liberal home secretary Herbert Gladstone. Founded in 1891 by Henry Salt (Chapter 29, this volume), the Humanitarian League's supporters also included the socialist Edward Carpenter (Chapters 14 and 37, this volume), whose *Prisons, Police and Punishment* (1905) Montefiore draws upon extensively. Also mentioned in the pamphlet, Charles Reade's *It Is Never too Late to Mend* (1856) and Marcus Clarke's *For the Term of his Natural Life* (1878) were fictional representations of prison life in England and of the deportation of convicts (like the earlier convict chronicler Margaret Catchpole) to Australia.

The cause of prison reform is thus conveyed as one in which socialists stood alongside a much broader swathe of opinion. Montefiore depicts the English prison system as particularly cruel and punitive and it is striking that she cites so many other countries as examples of more enlightened practices. In respect of political prisoners, of which of course she had personal experience, she even cites tsarist Russia – the country which British socialists were on the whole least of all inclined to extenuate. In France, the "good judge", Paul Magnaud (here wrongly given as Magnier) had in 1898 acquitted a single mother who had stolen bread, and by 1909 Magnaud was also a radical socialist deputy. In this spirit of latitudinarianism, Montefiore closes with the anarchist Peter Kropotkin. This does not mean that there were no differences of outlook between them; and while Kropotkin had ended his *Are Prisons Necessary?* (1887) by arguing against any form of isolation or confinement, Montefiore maintained that even under socialism the quarantining of the "physically and mentally weak" would remain necessary. This was a view widely held by socialists and it easily slipped over into socialist eugenics (Chapter 41, this volume).]

"If life be our legitimate aim, if absolute morality means, as it does, conformity to the laws of complete life, then absolute morality warrants the restraint of those who force their fellow-citizens into non-conformity. . . . If it is right for us to live, it is right for us to remove anyone who either breaks these conditions, or constrains us to break them." This is the carefully worded mandate of Herbert Spencer in his article "Prison Ethics," authorising the community to restrain those who prove themselves anti-social, and "in conflict with the laws of complete life." Further on in the same article, he lays down detailed principles as to how the restraint of those offenders against "the laws of complete life" is to be carried out; and before stating our indictment, as Social-Democrats, against the English prison system under capitalism, it may be of interest to note the simple social ethic, which, according to one of the recognised sociologists of the nineteenth century, should guide our conduct towards the anti-social. "We are warranted," writes Herbert Spencer, "in restraining the actions of the offender to the extent of preventing further aggressions. . . . There must, however, be no gratuitous infliction of pain, no vengeful penalties." If we acknowledge the right of each individual to freedom, in order to fulfil "the laws of life," the life of the offender must be taken into account as an item in this sum. . . . It is commonly said that the criminal loses all rights. This may be so according to existing law, but it is not so according to justice. Such portion only of them is just taken away as cannot be left to him without danger to the community." Just as, in his well-known book on education, Herbert Spencer insists upon allowing the natural consequences of an anti-social act on the part of a young child, or of a young person to form the "punishment," so, in the case of adult offenders against the laws of complete life, does he insist on the same natural consequences being allowed full play, and adds that "these, when vigorously enforced, are quite severe enough." Among these natural consequences of anti-social action are, of course, temporary loss of liberty and self-maintenance during the time of detention.

Let us now contrast this ideal prison ethic with what goes on in our prisons in England in the twentieth century of Christendom, and with capitalism still dominating all forms of social and economic relations. For centuries, both before and after the Christian era, men have had the bad habit of throwing their fellowmen into underground dungeons, and feeding them on bread and water. This simple barbaric notion of the rights of the stronger over the weaker still holds good as the basis of English prison discipline. The primitive barbaric dungeon idea can still be studied under the ruins of many an old castle and keep, and its modern manifestations can be found in Holloway and other prison cells. The established religion of our country hails from Judea, whose Jehovah was an irresponsible wrathful personage, punishing to the third and four generation. The traditions of this spasmodic wrathful authority, mingled with a withering blast of Puritanism, are nowadays vested in judges, magistrates, governors and officials of prisons, whose duties lie in carrying out in detail the designs of this implacable deity. The English, as a race, are not philosophic, not given to formulating theories on which to regulate scientifically their conduct. Though they have among them great thinkers and writers on sociology and on ethics, the ordinary Englishman considers himself too practical to trouble his head about the writings and teachings of these philosophers. It is principally therefore in other nations, whose people read and study more than we do, that the teachings of our great writers are respected and applied. It is only in Latin countries, where the Jehovah conception has been to a great extent superseded by the more human conception of "Le Bon Dieu," that a judge like Magnier, known at present in France as "Le Bon Juge," is possible. It is only in countries where the self-righteous blight of Puritanism has never nipped the tender blossom of the study of Humanitarianism that we have paused in the judicial application of the "Divine law of a life for a life." Great Britain is still hanging, and burying in quick-lime, while many other European countries, less sure in their delegated "Divine" authority, are staying their hand, and respecting human life. Holland abolished capital punishment in 1870, Finland in 1824, Italy in 1879, Switzerland in 1874, Belgium in 1863, whilst Portugal and Roumania have more recently followed the same example. Statistics prove that the number of murders in these various countries has decreased rather than increased. The old traditional dungeon was dark and insanitary, with a grated window high up in the wall, admitting only a feeble ray of light. In the modern British prison cell the window is scientifically constructed on medieval dungeon principles, so that discreet twilight may take the place of darkness, and the health-giving rays of the sun, joined with the hygienic influences of the outer air may, by thick corrugated glass and iron bars, be carefully excluded. When it is realised that the window of a Holloway cell is not made to open, that the glass is so opaque one cannot tell whether the sun is shining or not, that the only "fresh" air comes through a little iron ventilator in the brickwork, or from the inner passage on the rare occasions when the door is opened, it will be at once understood that even in the matter of the physical health of the prisoner there is no regard to Herbert Spencer's ethical prohibition of any "gratuitous inflictions of pain" on the offender who has to suffer imprisonment. . . . In the old dungeon days the door was opened twice or thrice a day, and food was thrust in to keep life in the miserable being shut out from the light of day. In the British Prison the same clanging process of pushing in tins of food is still preceded and followed by the clash and jangle of keys, as three times a day the prisoner is left to eat in sorrow his solitary meal. The victim of the old dungeon system never left his torture chamber; the victim of the modern dungeon system walks daily round and round the prison courtyard for half an hour, and, if he chooses, attends, either the Roman Catholic or the Protestant chapel for another half hour. If, however, when his cell door is unlocked at 6 a.m., he asks to see the doctor in the course of the day, he loses his half hour of exercise and his variety turn at the chapel. On admission to Holloway, each prisoner is asked what religion he professes, and unless he replies that he is either a Roman Catholic, a Jew or a Protestant, he is told in an insulting tone of voice that he will be entered as a Protestant. It is on this basis that the statistics of the various religions are compiled, and it is in this fashion that the rights of the individual are respected. When it is remembered that a large number of those who are sent to Holloway and other local prisons are not criminals or convicted prisoners, but are there, either as debtors, for contempt of court because they refuse to be bound over to keep the peace, or because they refuse, or are unable to pay a fine, the personal and moral indignities to which they are subjected, from the moment they leave "Black Maria" to the moment they find themselves once more in the street outside the prison, are more than ever inexcusable, and more than ever an outrage on humanity.

If this is the treatment of short sentenced or remand prisoners, what is the fate of convicts who have to work out long sentences? Here, again, it is evident that whatever revolutionary changes take place in outside social and economic life, scarcely a ripple of the teachings of "Prison Ethics" breaks the black surface of this abyss of human misery. The old traditions of severity and brutality that inspired our blood-red system in Tasmania and Botany Bay still inspire the twentieth century convict-prison system of England. Yet, though such books as "The Term of his Natural Life" (every detail of which is taken from Government Blue Books) record the terrible story, the mass of people are so poor in imagination and in sympathy where what is hidden away from sight is concerned, that they fail to connect these horrors of a bygone day with the horrors of to-day. Much of the otherwise incomprehensibly obtuse stupidity of the present-day prison system in England is only to be understood when we read such books as the one above mentioned, or "Margaret Catchpole," or "It's Never too Late to Mend."

"Justice," of February 8th, 1908, calls attention to "the large amount of flogging which still exists in the local and convict prisons of England and Wales for breaches of discipline; flogging which the Humanitarian League believes to be as unnecessary as it is cruel." In the most recently published Report of the Commissioner of Prisons, the number of floggings with birch and "cat," for the year ending March 31st, 1908, are given as 30, as against 26 in the preceding year; so it is evident no heed has been paid to the remonstrances of "Justice" or of the Humanitarian League. In July, 1907, the daily papers reported without comment the fact that after the recapture of two young convicts, who escaped during a fog from a working gang at Dartmoor, their punishment was "dark cells, a flogging, and working in chains." The same year, also, Sir John Forrest, of Western Australia, was reported to have decided that the only way to hold refractory natives in Australia was to chain them by the neck; adding, "It was the most humane way." In an old volume of "Our Corner," a magazine edited some years ago by Mrs. Besant, will be found an account by a Mr. Ramsay (imprisoned for blasphemy) of prison life in Holloway twenty-two years ago. The actual régime, the state of the cells, the quality of the food is as fossilised now as it was then; but among the moral tortures he endured was that of hearing the cries of the men being flogged for breaches of prison discipline. I may explain that in each cell hangs a card with a list of prison rules; for breach of these prison rules flogging may be administered to men, while women get cells and bread and water. Among these prison rules are orders as to the exact angle and position of the "books of devotion," the tin mug and wooden spoon, which form the ornaments of the corner shelf. It is not difficult for a tyrannical warder or wardress to discover "a breach of prison discipline" in a mattress insufficiently rolled, or in the wooden spoon being placed where the Bible should be. It may be as well to remind the public here that among other "restraints and punishments" for both men and women prisoners, are close confinement in special cells for refractory prisoners, dietary punishment, close confinement in ordinary cells, and IRONS OR HANDCUFFS! The floggings vary from 12 to 24 strokes.

The questions for us Social-Democrats are:—Is not most of the "crime" for which the inmates of our prisons are now suffering prolonged torture "artificial crime"?—that is, crime induced by the present social and economic conditions, under which the majority of people are forced to lead disorganised, haphasard lives, either on the verge of, or below the level of subsistence. Secondly, is the present prison system a scientific method of dealing with the victims of our own social system? And thirdly, what are the Social Democratic palliatives to prevent so much unnecessary suffering and so many wasted lives?

As regards the first question, it is as well to recall the fact, to which Mr. Joseph Collinson of the Humanitarian League gives prominence in an open letter to Mr. Herbert Gladstone, that "11,000 debtors were imprisoned during the year 1905; and that, as there are now no separate prisons for debtors, these debtors were imprisoned along with criminals, and treated as criminals." "The Manchester Guardian," when commenting on this letter, says:—"There can be no manner of doubt that in this matter of imprisonment for debt there is one law for the rich and another for the poor." The "Saturday Review" says: "There are annually eleven or twelve thousand persons kept in prison for civil debts, and the rate payer, or tax payer has to bear the expense of their maintenance. . . . Moreover, Scotland can carry on its trade without these judgment summonses." And a writer in the Lancet says: "Prison is prison, whatever the reason may be which causes the detention; and in the long run, many prisoners connotes many miserable homes, much privation, and much disease. The sequence is a fairly direct one." In spite of these weighty remonstrances, the Home Office Report for the years 1907-8 states: "There are also 17,918 persons imprisoned as debtors, or on civil process, and 1,212 in default of sureties, making a total of 196,233." And though Mr. Gladstone has a Bill before the country for "The Prevention of Crime," he still appears to hold out no hope for more humane and up-to-date legislation for the thousands of "debtor" prisoners and captives, for whom the orthodox pray so regularly on Sundays.

Now let us turn to the cases of the habitual drunkards and offenders (who spend a great portion of their lives behind prison walls), as described in a Government Blue Book on Inebriate Homes, published in 1906. Under the Inebriates Act of 1879-1900, certain licensed institutions were established for the treatment, and (if possible) the cure of habitual drunkards. The writer of the Blue Book report states: "Our early impressions concerning the mental and physical characteristics of 'habitual drunkards,' for instance, have undergone considerable modification as the result of seven or eight years' experience, and it seems to me that we can hardly do better than devote the most of our space to a description of these persons, as we have learnt to know them, and the balance, to some considerations, which, in my opinion, should regulate our treatment of them." On page 9 we read: "Upwards of 62 per cent. are found to be insane or defective in varying degrees." On page 10: "I am satisfied that the majority of our insane inebriates have become alcoholic because of congenital defect or tendency to insanity, not insane as the result of alcoholism, and that the drunkenness which precedes 'alcoholic insanity' was merely the herald—the only obvious sign—of incipient mental disorder." On page 13: "Those who appreciate the disabilities of mental defect, when it exists to the extent described, need no persuasion to acknowledge irresponsibility. In such cases drunkenness, and all the offences resulting therefrom, are merely the natural results of inability to sensibly direct and control wishes and actions." On pages 14 and 15 the Report deals in detail with some of the causes, other than defective mentality, which lead to alcoholism, among such causes being "incipient disease (which, in the case of the poor, is not recognised and medically treated as among the rich), and loss of work among the older members of the community." The writer sums up: "The cancer cases, and those with heart trouble, the soldiers, the consumptives, the women with morbid uterine conditions, and the kidney disease cases, were all treated for years in the same way; bandied like shuttle-cocks between police-courts and prisons because they had become drunkards, punished, in fact, for disease." And, again: "It will be seen in reference to the table of ages that 55 of the persons admitted to reformatories are over sixty years of age. Some of these old inmates are weakened and prematurely aged owing to their drunken habits, but there is every reason to believe that nearly 65 per cent. have, in their early days, lived decent, useful lives, and that their drunkenness of late years has been due to naturally reduced vitality, with its accompanying defect in power of control. The sequence of events is the same in most old age cases. Loss of work from incapacity due to approaching age, consequent idleness, poverty and friendlessness, impaired power of control, drunkenness. . . . These poor old dements have all been subjected to an average of between six and seven years of prison treatment before being sent to reformatories." At the Aylesbury State Reformatory for Females, out of 32 admitted last year, 8, according to the Government Report, were found to be insane.

As regards the bulk of the other sources of crime which fill our prisons, Edward Carpenter, in his book "Prisons, Police and Punishment," throws a flood of light on their primary and secondary causes. "The landless masses of the people, unable, owing to the obsession and pillage of the land by the few, to set themselves to work, are driven into the towns to seek employment at the hands of the capitalist class. There they become divided into two sections—one, of the more skilful, strong, healthy, pushing and crafty, who obtain employment, and the other, the weak, unhealthy, aged, ineffectual, independent-minded and so forth, who fail even in this, and fall into the ruck of the unemployed, and the life of the tramp and the slum-dweller. . . . The weary mass of the unemployed, pinned between the closed doors of the factory on the one side, and the spiked railings of the workhouse on the other, is the great source from which our criminals proceed." The Governor of Lewes Prison, in his report to the Commissioners of Prisons for the year 1908, remarks: "The present system, under which prisons are regarded as dust-bins, into which, in addition to the men and women found guilty of occasional violation of law, may properly be poured epileptics, weak-minded persons, immature youths, drunkards, tramps and professional criminals, may be regarded as illogical." The Governor of the Lancaster Prison writes in the same Report: "Feeble-minded prisoners, principally men, continue to be received from time to time. They seem to wander about the country, occasionally committing offences, in an aimless fashion. The majority of them are unfit for work, except of the simplest description. They are not fit subjects for prison discipline." And the Governor of Lincoln Prison reports that: "The vagrancy question is a serious one. There have been 2,005 prisoners convicted under the Vagrancy Act during the past year." While the Governor of Reading Prison gives the real clue to this increase in vagrancy when he reports that "Tramps, including the unemployed, who rapidly sink into the condition of tramps, have been largely on the increase."

After thus piecing together the three causes that fill our prisons with debtors, drunkards, and discouraged unemployed, we have only to add the further facts about inebriates contained in the Blue Book of 1906, from which I have already quoted, and we have linked up the whole vicious circle which is responsible for most of the "crime," or anti-social conduct under our present economic and social system. On page 7 of the Blue Book we read: "As a matter of fact, 92 per cent. of the women admitted to reformatories last year were responsible for the birth of 850 children. . . . About 45 per cent. of all children born of these mothers died in infancy or early youth. If a mere handful of 193 women has been responsible for 499 child deaths, what must be the awful total for the thousands of habitually drunken women of the same class?" With the roots of the race steeped in a quagmire of habitual unemployment, alcoholism, slum-dwelling, irregular living, and frequent imprisonment, what can be expected but a spawn of defectives, alcoholics, weak-willed individuals, who sink into unemployment or prostitution, into nervous disease or premature senility? And who help to people those two blots on our so-called twentieth century civilisation—the prison and the workhouse?

Let us now turn to the second part of our proposition: "Is the present prison system a scientific method of dealing with the victims of our own social system?" Chief among the tortures meted out to those whom our existing Governments call "criminals" (but whom a more enlightened age will term "persons suffering from a distressing form of anti-social dementia") is the solitary system. John Daly, an ex-convict, is reported in the "Daily Chronicle" of September 12th, 1906, to have said to an interviewer: "I don't know any language to describe the horrors of penal servitude. You are virtually in a living tomb, cut off from everything; the only human sounds you hear being hard orders and words from the warders. Never a touch of kindness, never a glimpse of humanity, apart from a rare visitor and an occasional letter. . . . The scanty diet, the treatment, the surroundings, the utter desolation, all these gather around you, and you feel as if you were being enveloped by a shroud." Michael Davitt wrote in the same strain: "No prisoner is allowed to do anything except with the permission, and in sight of a warder. He is the object of constant and ceaseless vigilance from sentence to liberation. He is closely watched when at prayer in chapel. He is under the warder's eyes while in his cell, and is never for a second lost sight of while at work. . . . The human will must be left outside of the prison gates where it is to be picked up again five, seven, fifteen years afterwards, and refitted to the mental conditions which penal servitude has created in the animalised machine which is discharged from custody." On leaving Holloway I wrote in an article in the "New International Review": "One had only to watch, as I did, the faces in the prison chapel, the lax facial muscles, the easy flowing tears, the shaking hands; to see the poor hobbling old women being urged round the exercise yard at the same pace as the younger ones; to read the inscriptions scratched by previous tortured occupants on the walls and doors of the cells, to realise that one was shut up and thrust into silent fellowship with the mad and the sad, much more than with the bad. . . . 'Jane Lee, six months for stabbing,' was one glimpse into a remorse-tortured soul, passing on to the next occupant of the cell its stifled cry. And I asked myself over and over again, which is the more guilty, the wealthy brewer and distiller who sets his gin-palace trap at every street corner, and who, on the cursed profits of his flourishing trade, intrigues for 'Birthday Honours,' and a seat among the 'Beerocracy,' or the underpaid, half-starved working man or woman who walks into the warmed and lighted bar because there is nowhere else to go, and who awakes from the temporary relief from hopelessness, which alcohol affords, to the dreary realities of police court proceedings, a nerve-racking journey in 'Black Maria,' and the ordeal of standing for twenty minutes, barefooted, and clad in a single garment, while prison officials go through the usual prison routine of reception?" Dr. Helen Bourchier, another imprisoned suffragist, wrote after a month's imprisonment in Holloway: "I am not a young woman, and a good deal of my life has been spent alone. . . . Yet I found even that short term of imprisonment, in some subtle way affecting my mind. . . . . But the fact which showed me most startlingly the effect produced on my mind by the unnatural conditions of seclusion, silence and monotony, which prevail in Holloway, was the growth of a strange feeling of apprehension, of shrinking from the outside world." The Rev. Dr. Morrison, a prison chaplain, writes: "As far as the criminal part of the population is concerned, force, in the shape of punishment, no matter how severe you make it, will not keep down crime. If the penal laws of the past teach us anything, they teach us that crime cannot be put down by mere severity." Sir Godfrey Lushington wrote in a Government Report: "I regard as unfavourable to reformation the status of a prisoner throughout his whole career; the crushing of self-respect, the starving of all moral instinct he may possess, the absence of all opportunity to do or receive a kindness, the continual association of none but criminals, the forced labour, and the denial of all liberty. I believe the true method of reforming a man, of restoring him to society, is exactly in the opposite direction to all these."

I would like to add here, that the crushing of all self-respect in the prisoner appears to be, from my experience, an integral part of prison discipline, as administered by wardresses.

To suggest that the comb allotted to one has not been sufficiently cleaned since used by the last prisoner is to bring down upon one a shrewish retort to the effect that "You are not in an hotel, and that you will have to use it as it is." If you complain that there are rats in the ground floor cell of the infirmary, into which cell, though ill, you are locked at night, the head wardress will turn to her assistant and remark: "What's this woman in for; has she been drinking?" This, in spite of the fact that, by reading the card on the door, any official can tell at once whether the inmate of the cell is a convicted prisoner, or, as in my case, one who refused to be bound over. The wardresses under capitalism, are, no doubt, drawn from a low strata of society, and are overworked and underpaid (for, let it never be forgotten, there are no worse sweaters than a capitalist Government), and it is also evident that present-day prison discipline could not be carried out by persons of high mental and moral calibre. To quote another witness against the worse than uselessness of the existing prison system, Captain Machonochie states, as a result of observation, that, "a long course of separation so fosters the self-regarding desires, and so weakens the sympathies, as to make even well-disposed men very unfit to bear the little trials of domestic life on their return to their homes. Thus, there is good reason to think that while silence and solitude may cow the spirit or undermine the energies, it cannot produce true reformation." The Inspector under the Inebriates Act, on page 17 of his report (1906), writes: "There remains no available evidence to justify the assumption that a few weeks' imprisonment, spasmodically applied to habitual drunkards, results in either benefit to the individual, deterrence from future offences, or adequate protection to the public. Unless we are prepared to admit that the process is solely one of retaliative vengeance, it is difficult to describe the proceeding as other than useless, and because useless, an absolute waste of public money. If we are prepared to admit the futility of prison treatment, it seems hardly necessary to enlarge upon its inhumanity. . . . . The position becomes worse when we realise that many of them, during the earlier stages, were improvable and educable, but were rendered hopeless by their subsequent treatment." In spite of that official report and recommendation, we find in the last Report of the Commissioners for Prisons, the Governor of Lancaster Prison remarking that, "The frequent recommittal of drunken women for short, and quite useless, terms of imprisonment, is still noticeable. In my opinion they should be committed to Inebriate Reformatories, and not to prison, and earlier in their career." This, in a succinct form is the indictment brought by one observer after another against the present prison system. It is unscientific, brutal, corrupting both to the prisoner and the warder, not merely useless, but directly harmful in its results, and so senselessly vindictive and cruel that it makes the judges, magistrates, and Governors of prisons chargeable with crimes much more horrible than are those of the prisoners whom they condemn. Our existing system of the private ownership of the means of life is admittedly responsible for five-sixths of the crime; and the criminal, once in process of making, comes in contact with such obtuse and continuous official stupidity, that it is not long before the finished article—the habitual criminal, or the habitual drunkard is developed.

From the point of view of the Social-Democrat, whose ideal is the free, self-governing individual in a Collectivist society, what should be our treatment of the anti-social individuals, the inebriates, degenerates, and irresponsibles? In the first place, as some of the more intelligent of our prison governors point out, there must be a sorting process carried on in what they ironically call the "dustbin" of society—the modern prison. Then thorough inquiries must be made into the life-histories of the prisoners; and we must insist that while prisoners are being detained on remand, and while such inquiries are being made, they shall be properly fed and housed, and shall be industrially employed. All the physically and mentally weak must be removed to various grades of farm colonies, and kept there by the community, either for life, or until any of them may be sufficiently recovered to return to society. The results of the lately tried Borstal system on the physique and moral nature of the juvenile-adult prisoners of this country have been most striking and encouraging; and the officials draw particular attention to the beneficial effects of gymnastic exercises on the young and physically undeveloped criminal. The common sense of the matter is, of course, to give the boys these advantages *before* they become criminals; but capitalism, which is stupid as well as unjust, prefers to work on the principle of "cure being better than prevention." Our school curriculum must include education and training for citizenship; both for teaching the wealthy and privileged classes to "render unto the people the things that are the people's," and, for restoring to the children of the people a feeling of social self-respect, and of a *right* to a material share in the wealth and life of the community. We must agitate to put an end to imprisonment for debt, and for the abolition of flogging in our prisons, and of capital punishment. Prisons must be gradually transformed into industrial workshops, where labour is carried on in association, where trades are taught, and wages, over and above the expenses of the prisoner's maintenance, can be earned. Every prisoner must be looked upon as a potential reformed member of society, who may (as did those who in the old days were transported to our Australian Colonies) find in a new environment, and more congenial surroundings that stimulus to right social conduct which helps to make men and women useful members of society. An ordinary model prison that I went over in Budapest had cells far larger and very superior to those of Holloway; the floors were boarded, there were large double French windows, opening inside so as not to interfere with the iron bars outside; the prison utensils were of enamel or china, an advance on the horrible insanitary tin cans and wooden spoons used in England; and the prisoners worked in association in large airy rooms and workshops. In France the prisoners can buy wine and tobacco with the surplus of their earnings.

We must also agitate that persons found guilty of political offences, *whether they be men or women,* should have different treatment from the ordinary criminals. In no country, not even in Russia, are political offenders treated by law so harshly as in England. I have seen in Hungary and in France the rooms inside the prison enclosures, where political prisoners reside. They are well furnished, and the prisoners can pass their time reading, writing, and studying; they can receive friends, and are allowed a reasonable time for exercising by themselves in the prison yard. They wear their own clothes, and their friends supply them with food from outside. A young Russian girl who came to stay with me after suffering three terms of imprisonment on remand, on suspicion of having helped organise Trade Unions on a political basis, described the cells in a St. Petersburg prison as having windows that would open, and as having water laid on to each cell, so that a daily bath was possible. Some of the cells were large, and held two or three prisoners. One of her prison mates was a sculptor, who obtained wax, and occupied her time in modelling. There was a good library of books, constantly replenished by the prisoners, and my friend amused herself by teaching English through the medium of some of the English books she found in the library.

As I have already pointed out, the greater part of our laws have for their object the protection of private property, and the maintenance of the property system; whilst, as Kropotkin says: "A large portion of our criminal laws are for the purpose of keeping the workman subordinate to the employer, so as to ensure to the latter a successful exploitation of the said workman." Any suggestions, therefore, for mitigating the stupidity or cruelty of the existing prison system are merely palliatives, and can never touch the root of the matter. Only a complete sweeping away of the present economic system, and the substitution of a system giving to everyone access to the means of life, can finally empty workhouse, prison, and slum, and help to build up a Co-operative Commonwealth in "England's green and pleasant land." The process of renewed social life will possibly be long and tedious, for the unlearning of the lessons, forced by centuries of industrialism and of competitive trading on a whole population, will take the least evolved among its members many years; but, again, we can point hopefully to Australia, where the grandchildren and great grandchildren of those "who left their country for their country's good," now lead the way as pioneers in social and industrial legislation, and where a sense of social responsibility is growing much more rapidly than it is doing in the old country. To make Socialists who will work for the Social Revolution is our task as Social-Democrats; but during the years that our propaganda is being carried on, we must see to it that the children of the nation are fed and educated, that laws are passed providing work for the unemployed, and that our prison population is as little degraded as may be under a system of capitalism which forces the weak and the helplessly poor into the "criminal" ranks, and which makes one set of laws for the rich and another for the poor.

# 23

## *SOCIAL-DEMOCRACY AND THE HOUSING PROBLEM* (LONDON: TWENTIETH CENTURY PRESS, 1900), 3–4, 6–7, 22–24.

*F.O. Pickard-Cambridge*

[In 1898, the anarchist Peter Kropotkin published his *Fields, Factories and Workshops* which both advocated and documented the growing decentralisation of industry. The same year, Ebenezer Howard published his *Tomorrow*, which under the revised title *Garden Cities of Tomorrow* would capture the imaginations of so many twentieth-century housing reformers. Britain's Marxists made no contributions to the debate of any similar scope or influence. On the other hand, the influence of William Morris made for a receptiveness to such arguments that was not always shared by Fabians and other state collectivists. Written for the SDF and occasioned by the third Housing of the Working Classes Act (1900), the pamphlet from which the following extracts are taken indicates how much common ground there often was on these issues.

The author, Frederick Octavius Pickard-Cambridge (1860–1905), was an Oxford-educated arachnologist and former curate who had become estranged from his comfortable Dorset family because of the political and moral ideas he had taken to expounding. In reality, his pamphlet is as soberly presented as any Fabian tract in its overview of housing conditions, government legislation and schemes for municipal provision and co-partnership. Published during the Anglo-Boer war, the sections reproduced here show how images of Britain's cities as "black holes" and "cesspits" fed the panic over the health and social fitness of their inhabitants that stretched from right to left of the political spectrum. Nevertheless, the pamphlet's final section, "The ultimate goal", calls up the Kropotkin-Howard vision of decentralisation, albeit with the corollary of the strong central authority which is alone held capable of delivering a transformation beyond the scope of the piecemeal muncipal enterprise often identified with the Fabians.]

## WHAT IS THE PROBLEM?

THIS question, which is arousing serious attention at present amongst the more active minds of all parties throughout the nation, may be very briefly and succinctly stated. There is at present raging throughout the length and breadth of Great Britain and Ireland a desperate house famine. There are not sufficient houses to accommodate the multitudes of artisans, day labourers and casual labourers who need them, without an overcrowding, both in the houses and in the separate rooms of houses, which has passed the point of being merely serious, and has now become appalling. This is true, not only of the vast cities and larger towns, but also to a greater or lesser extent of the small towns and country villages as well, whilst the houses themselves both in the towns and country villages are in many cases utterly unfit for human habitation, apart from the fact of their being also overcrowded.

If the problem can be thus simply stated, so, too, can the remedy. There is only one way of meeting a deficiency in house accommodation, and that is to build more houses. At least that is how the matter presents itself to the ordinary man of business. This is the whole case in a nutshell.

But, unfortunately, there are certain difficulties in the way of building houses—first of securing legal powers; next of securing land whereon to build; the bringing of people to and from these abodes to where they happen to be employed; and, not least, the finding of the funds withal to carry out these excellent intentions.

If the machinery for the supply of house accommodation were freed from the trammels of private ownership of land, labour, building materials, the means of transport and the control of wealth which lies in the hands of a hostile class, the demand could easily and automatically be supplied. But these interests of the few vested in the means of satisfying the needs of the many prevent the working of this simple beneficent law recognised by justice and common sense.

We must, however, first of all realise what immense interests, personal and national, are involved in this tremendous problem; a problem, be it remembered, which cries out for solution not only from our centres of industry, but also from every district of rural England as well.

When we have fully realised what are the conditions of existence under which vast numbers of our citizens live and their children are reared, we shall appreciate the nature of the social disease which is undermining the national physique and ruining the national character. We shall perceive the extent of the malady, its deadly nature and the real cause of it, and we shall not fail to foresee what must be the final consequence. Whether we be Big-Englanders or Little-Englanders, Social-Democrats or Jingo-Imperialists, the verdict amongst all men of sound sense will be unanimous. It will be this: that no time must be lost if we are to avert a national disaster.

In making the whole matter clear there is no need for further appeals to sentiment. No one can have read the books and pamphlets published during the last 25 years dealing with the horrors of London slums, without recognising that the present life-conditions of hundreds of thousands of men, women and children are not only a disgrace, but contain also the germs of a terrible national disaster. The devouring tide of the destitute is rising year by year. Little by little, room by room, house by house, street by street, poverty creeps onwards, misery enlarges her borders. The life of thousands of wage-slaves and of those who cannot claim even this poor privilege in the slums of London, north, south, east and west, is one of continual strife and struggle with famine and filth, and the price they have to pay for it. So miserable is the pittance received for work done, and so arduous is the toil itself, that mothers and little ones must all work, and work all day, if they are to earn even then a bare subsistence. That thousands of our tiny brothers and sisters should be wasting and fading, wailing and rotting away, without decent housing, with insufficient clothing, without fresh air; no flowers and waving grass to love, no green fields and lanes to wander in and play—not even a chance to play at all—this can be no longer tolerated on grounds either humanitarian or economic; still less is it to be endured on account of national stupidity, class cowardice, or weak religious cant. [. . .]

## BUT THIS IS NOT ALL.

The terrible extent of the evil of overcrowding and insanitary dwellings will not, however, fully dawn upon us until we can form a mental picture of the evils arising from them in the aggregate. It must be realised, then, that in all towns, and all special districts of those towns, wherever overcrowding occurs, there the mortality is greater. The death-rate increases in direct ratio to the number of persons living in a room or families living in a house. Thirty per thousand, for example, is the death-rate in the slums of Soho, while in the adjacent wealthy district of St. George's, Hanover Square, it is only eighteen per thousand. The infant death-rate is much greater in proportion in the overcrowded districts than even that of the adults; for instance, 115 deaths for a thousand births of infants under one year old in St. George's, Hanover Square, 179 in the Soho district, and 186 for a thousand births in the slums of Southwark. Though many of the rural villages and towns are unhealthy enough, we may note that the average death-rate in the country districts is much lower.

Disease of all kinds is more prevalent and more destructive because the elements, fresh air and sunlight, which would destroy the germs, are absent, while the slums offer a magnificent nidus for the reception and cultivation of the seeds in the body of the slum-dweller enfeebled by this same absence of sun and air. Fresh air and sunlight are the deadly enemies of all disease, but of fresh air, sunlight, pure water and plenty of it, and proper sanitary arrangements, the people are robbed by the slumlords, though compelled to pay highly for the privilege of being housed at all.

The conditions of town life, as they exist under private ownership of land and houses, and of the materials for constructing the latter, constitute a poison zone in which the vitality of the nation is lowered and destroyed. The ranks of all those whose occupations demand health and physical stamina in London are filled year by year with fresh blood from the country. Of the Metropolitan police, out of a total of 13,624 members, no fewer than 10,908 are country born; out of 892 City police, 698 are country born. The same is true to a greater or lesser extent of railway porters, carmen and cab-drivers. Why so? Where are the Londoners, better adapted, one would suppose, through knowledge of their native flag-stones, for policing the London streets? Why, most of them are dead; the rest, who struggle up to a peevish, anæmic, ill-conditioned manhood, are physically unfitted for the work.

For remember that a pure Londoner of the third generation, that is, one whose grandparents as well as his parents, were born in London, is very seldom found; a Londoner of the fourth generation in all probability does not exist.

It is computed that 10,000 country-bred lads betake themselves to London every year. These, too, not of the less capable of the rural population, rather the more intelligent, the more energetic and courageous, the physically and mentally alert. The whole of the *natural increase* of the country population, over and above those who remain to fill up the deficiencies of death, is year by year being engulfed in the maelstrom of city life. We have the witness of the Registrar-General in his report on the Census of 1891: "The combined effect of this constantly higher mortality in the town and of the constant immigration into it of the pick of the rural population must clearly be a deterioration of the whole, in so much as the more energetic and vigorous members of the community are consumed more rapidly than the rest of the population. THE SYSTEM IS ONE WHICH LEADS TO THE SURVIVAL OF THE UNFITTEST."

The best blood of the nation is being vitiated and destroyed, while the slum-owing classes live in luxury and social honour. These are the classes who are betraying the true interests of the nation. These are they who hasten to make England little, decrepit, demoralised, emasculated, unfit to survive amid the coming races of the world. These are the traitors who are hurrying the country to her decline and fall.

Now, if the land or slum-owner takes his stand upon a lawful right to exploit such possessions as he pleases, to do what he likes with his own, then he is personally responsible to the nation for crimes committed under his sanction or in his name. But if he holds it not on personal right, on the sanctity of private property, but simply on sufferance as part of a social system over whose evolution neither he nor his countrymen have hitherto had any control, then must he relinquish that which, once a private right, has now become a hideous national wrong. Then must the nation demand that this right or this sufferance shall cease at once; before her manhood and womanhood have been sapped of health and vigour, her highest interests threatened and her very existence set at stake. This is what the Housing Problem means. [. . .]

## THE ULTIMATE GOAL.

Fortunately, however, there are lines on which societies may be organised where the element of the exploitation of labour does not enter; or else we might indeed despair of this same housing problem amongst many other troubles.

The remedy for the time being lies in the decentralisation not merely of the workers at present engaged in the centres of industry, but in the breaking up and decentralisation of these congested centres of industry themselves. The whole country should be studded with towns built with a view to the health and happiness of the inhabitants, where the social intercourse of the city would be obtainable within easy reach of the charms of country life.

Let us consider briefly this position of decentralisation. We must suppose that a special Board of experts were authorised by the nation to deal with the question and undertake the enterprise. The nation would, of course, have already secured control of the means of transport, and be fully determined to reassume her right to the land, and to deal with it for the advantage of the whole community. The Board would reorganise the country, taking into consideration existing lines of communication, canals, roads, and railways, having regard also to existing towns and cities, deciding which of these should be decentralised, and where others should be organised on suitable sites with a view to the development of home agriculture and trades as well as the extension of international commerce. The reorganisation of industry for public ends lies at the bottom of the whole question—the educational, recreational, and industrial functions of the nation must be all co-ordinated before the life of the community can in any way be considered intelligent or even self-conscious. In the sphere of education this is already beginning to be done, and it must inevitably extend to other spheres as well. The housing problem naturally solves itself during the solution of the others, for they must be all solved together, little by little; neither of them can be settled apart from the others.

But, abstracting the housing question for a moment from the others, we find that it really resolves itself into a question of the number of people to be housed and the space available for their housing.

Omitting for the present the question of transport, what would happen if London were suddenly squandered over the country side, four or five million people in excited groops of 25, each group demanding an acre to live upon, good houses to live in and plenty to eat and drink in return for services rendered?

Would there be any standing room throughout the land?

"Of course not! England cannot possibly support such a multitude; the poor are so improvident; they breed so fast; what should we do if our armies were not murdering the inhabitants of other lands so that our surplus people might take their places?"

Now there are in Great Britain about 40,000,000 folks; let us venture to house them at 25 per acre. It will need 1,600,000 acres for this purpose; not *quite* the whole of Great Britain, for there are 80,000,000 acres, of all sorts, available.

Of these eighty million acres, fifty million (50,000,000) roughly are available for agricultural purposes of all kinds. There will be 30,000,000 left then for housing and recreation purposes. One million six hundred thousand having been withdrawn for planting out the population at 25 to the acre, we have 28,400,000 acres to meditate upon, over and above those absorbed in housing and agriculture.

Houses would naturally not be set, as hundreds of thousands are at present all round our great towns, in the midst of the richest alluvial soils in our great river valleys, so valuable for food production and so detrimental to the health of the inhabitants. Rather would we choose the dry gravelly formations, highly beneficial to health and of no manner of use for cultivation.

The wisdom of competition, individualism and industrial anarchy does the opposite. Why, in Dorset, I know men who have spent fortunes in trying to reclaim land, not worth one stroke of a turnip-hoe—an experiment often quoted to prove that the soil of England does not pay for cultivation, while they cover up thousands of acres of some of the finest soils in the world with slums.

If it be argued that proximity to rivers and streams is necessary in order to get rid of the sewage, we may point out, first, that, if sewage is to be got rid of as a nuisance, perhaps the stupidest way of doing it is to first multiply its volume tenfold by water treatment and then send it forth on its travels. But the one thing we do *not* want to get rid of happens to be the sewage. If it is a crime for a farmer to remove manure from the fields on which it has been raised and deprive them of an essential to fertilisation, what shall we say of a nation which squanders over the bed of the ocean millions of tons of valuable material which ought to go back upon the exhausted arable lands? The earth system of treatment and the sewage-farm system are now so well understood that there is no further excuse for such scandalous waste of wealth.

If it be objected that those whose houses are built on a healthy, gravelly soil must deny themselves the pleasures of a garden, for lack of mould, we may reply that it is perfectly feasible to cart sufficient soil to any locality needing it. They are doing it at the present moment for the thousands of villas building amongst the pine-woods on the heather lands of Bournemouth, for instance. If these things are no obstacle in the way of competitive individualism, why should they stand in the way of the co-operations of Social-Democracy? The fact is, there are no difficulties in the way of any of these undertakings when once the nation has determined to get the thing done.

If we set a map of England before us we shall be able to judge better of the area required to house the whole population compared with that of the whole country. Take the counties of Norfolk and Cambridgeshire; together they represent about 1,856,907 square acres. These two counties then would accommodate the whole 40,000,000 inhabitants at the rate of 25 to an acre. It is not true, of course, that the entire 30 millions of acres of non-cultivatable soil is available for housing purposes. But subtracting, shall we say, 10,000,000 acres of swamp, or mountain districts, forest land or foreshore, we still have 20,000,000 acres at our disposal. How many people shall we be able to house at 25 an acre on this area? Why, a trifle of five hundred million inhabitants, though of course we should sacrifice immense tracts of national park lands in accommodating them. There need, however, be no panic just at present as to the sudden increase of the population from forty to five hundred millions. The twenty million acres of spare land would naturally be reserved for recreational purposes—the Lake Districts in England and Wales, for instance, for health seekers and artists, the Fen and Moorlands, the New Forest, Dartmoor, Exmoor, Savernake, and Sherwood, and hundreds of other wild regions would be held for artists, tourists, and naturalists, and their beauties preserved as permanent national possessions of inestimable value. At present they desire to drain and reclaim the last wild Fenland spot at Wicken, as though forsooth it were the only inch in England which was not highly cultivated, and the people were starving and in need of its instant reclamation.

And now as to the feeding of the present 40,000,000 inhabitants; let us see how far the 50,000,000 acres, which can be tilled, would solve the problem of maintenance. Not, be it understood, that I have any sympathy with that kind of Little Englandism which would deny itself the products of other climes, or shut itself within its own shores and try to believe that England is the only country, or the Englishman the only countryman, worth considering on the planet.

Under the olden system of agriculture, when what was good enough for our grandmothers was held to be good enough for us, it was reckoned that one acre would support five people. Now, in 1898 there were 47,668,183 acres of land under cultivation, and these—50,000,000 shall we call them—would support, at five folks per acre, a population of 250,000,000, a very much larger number than the 40,000,000 at present in existence in these isles.

But experts, like Prince Kropotkin, assert that by intensive cultivation and by a judicious selection of seeds, amongst other operations, we could feed 200 persons from the produce of a square acre—that is to say ($200 \times 50,000,000 = 10,000,000,000$) that England would support ten thousand million inhabitants.

Even if we are not prepared to accept this without some salt, there is not the slightest doubt that our country would support four or five times its present population, and that, on this score of food and standing room, there need be no opening-up of other countries or any starving planet scare.

But this is not the place for any further details. The whole question of a definite scheme would occupy one or more special pamphlets. It must suffice to say that, were the suggested reorganisation of the housing and transport, and the industrial operations of the country, undertaken as a national enterprise, that agriculture would revive under entirely new conditions of industry in which production for use would be the aim in view. The present rush into the towns would thus be automatically regulated, while gradually a national organisation of industries would follow. And when once the elementary threads of correlated industrial enterprise had established themselves on the sound economic basis of use instead of the rotten foundation of profits, with the natural atrophy and dropping off of the parasitic classes as an incidental result, the strengthening and extension of national and international connections would be merely a question of time.

But we must not allow ourselves to be deluded with the idea that municipalism, as we know it, can ever, by itself alone, bring about the desired transformation. Difficulties would arise on every hand, for in the rush for vacant areas, local authorities would soon clash, and there would be no clear or intelligible scheme of transport service set before them. A chaos would result as hopeless, under conflicting municipal interests, as has arisen under those of the individual. All municipal operations must be co-ordinated in the central executive brain, otherwise there must result overlapping, confusion, and a fearful waste of national wealth, for want of intelligent organisation of the resources of the nation. The necessity for political action becomes more and more imperative as municipal action develops.

# Part 5

# WAYS OF ORGANISING

# 24

# "ORGANISED LABOUR. THE DUTY OF THE TRADES UNIONS IN RELATION TO SOCIALISM", *COMMONWEAL*, 14, 21 AND 28 AUGUST 1886.

*Thomas Binning*

[In the wider perception of the SDF's sectarianism an alleged indifference bordering on contempt for trade unionism always figured prominently. In this respect, there was no essential difference between the early SDF and the Socialist League. Thomas Binning was a London compositor whom E.P. Thompson (1955, 442) described as the League's foremost propagandist on trade union questions. In these articles on organised labour, subsequently issued as a pamphlet, Binning is principally concerned to demonstrate the limitations of trade union methods. He does not quite refer, as Hyndman and others did, to an iron law of wages (Chapter 15, this volume). He does, however, largely dismiss the relevance of partial or sectional gains to be achieved by trade-union action. Even the eight-hour day, which would subsequently prove so effective as a mobilising ideal (Chapter 20, this volume), is rejected as having no real bearing on the basic fact of workers' exploitation. Binning does regard the unions as representing all those useful elements of society whose organising and federating nationally and internationally should itself provide the nucleus for the future socialist commonwealth. As the Webbs pointed out in their *History of Trade Unionism* (1894, 395–398), such notions of a general federation of trade unions bore a clear resemblance to the Owenite ideal of general union of the early 1830s (Vol. I, Chapter 32). Binning was later Father of Chapel at Morris's Kelmscott Press, and in 1889–1890 was involved with other Socialist Leaguers in the short-lived "Labour Union". This had a strictly peripheral role in the upsurge of union activity known as the New Unionism. Suggestions of the Marxists' indifference to trade unionism were to be belied by the active commitments of so many of them, as already exemplified by Tom Mann and John Burns. Binning, however, is not known to have played any significant role in these later activities.]

## I.

Fellow-workers,—As a staunch Trades'-unionist for over twenty years, I desire to call your serious attention to the present alarming condition of the unceasing struggle between Capital and Labour. It is useless to cry "Peace, peace," when there is no peace. The hard disagreeable reality forces itself upon us and cannot be evaded, that never has the conflict been fiercer and never has the outlook been more gloomy than now. In the dark days that we have passed through already, there has always been a rift in the clouds to cheer us with the promise of brighter hours, and amidst the din and strife of previous contests the hope of victory brought comfort and encouragement. But the conditions of the warfare are changed. No further successes are possible by the old methods and with the weapons we have hitherto used. Indeed, the utmost care and watchfulness are needed even to retain the positions we have won. For this reason I urge the immediate summoning of a Council of War to deliberate upon the situation and to consider the advisability, nay the imperative necessity of a complete change of tactics in order that the standard of Labour may yet be borne aloft and planted on heights heretofore deemed impossible of access.

Until now we have to a very large extent been struggling aimlessly to attain what is vaguely termed "a fair day's wage for a fair day's work," without the very faintest attempt to logically define what the phrase really means. The consequence is a most unequal and disastrous contest, as far as the workers are concerned, between Capital on the one hand, seeking to obtain the greatest amount of work for the least possible payment of money, and Labour that struggles, or rather tries to struggle, to get the largest amount of pay for the smallest amount of work.

It is true, that other conditions being favourable, combinations amongst the workers to withhold their labour-power from the market have enabled them to secure somewhat higher prices than individual higgling would probably have done. The artificial scarcity thus occasioned would to a certain extent operate in the same way as in the case of corn, or cotton, or other product, held back for a rise, but with this important difference that human labour-power is a very perishable commodity. Owing to the unfortunate fact that a certain amount of food, clothing, etc., things monopolised by a class, is necessary to sustain the life of the worker, it is impossible that labour can be withheld from the market for any considerable length of time and in sufficient quantity to produce any considerable effect. Taking a broad and general survey of the question, it will be seen that the real advantage gained is of the most trifling character, a rise of wages at one period being only too frequently counterbalanced by a depression at another. Even in trades unions where there has been no going back, and where the highest nominal rate of wages obtains, it will be found, as I shall endeavour to show further on, that this results in the benefit of a section only of the members, and is gained, in part at least, by the sacrifice of their weaker comrades. In fact, after all, the workers are simply obliged to sell themselves ("free contract" is the orthodox phrase) to the employers pretty much on the terms that a needy shopkeeper is forced to dispose of his goods, that is at cost-price or a little over it. In other words, wages though constantly oscillating, are to the producers of all created wealth the very smallest share of their productions which will enable them to live and perpetuate their class, while the manipulators of their destinies revel in an excess of riches accumulated as result of the undue proportion of the current wealth creation which the hideously unjust social conditions allow them to appropriate. It must always be borne in mind, too, that any improvement which does occur in the pay and general condition of the workers is always vastly disproportionate to the actual increase in the "national" wealth and resources. Nowadays the average production of the average worker has been many times multiplied by newly-applied elementary forces made available by newly-invented and constantly-improved machinery.

How much longer are we going to stand stolidly and helplessly looking on, feebly protesting, or, worse still, accepting contentedly the scraps from the feast as it were that we have ourselves provided—watching the Capitalist seize upon every development of art and science for his own profit and advancement, regardless of our responsibility in shaping the destinies of ourselves, our families, and our class? It is time that we began seriously to consider for what we are banded together. What is our goal? Whither are we going? For what ought we to strive? The exigencies of the moment doubtless compel a large share of our attention and moreover we are necessarily driven by our daily needs under the present conditions of society, to act very largely on the defensive, to adopt, as it were, a "hand-to-mouth policy." But these petty cares must not be allowed to occupy all our time, or to prevent us from considering matters of greater importance. It is doubtless very advantageous to the enemy to keep us constantly engaged in scattered desultory fighting for the possession of some unimportant outlying positions. But remember that all the while we are doing this our forces are being gradually weakened, our exchequer is becoming exhausted in providing for the care of the wounded (*i.e.,* the sick and unemployed) and so is deferred and rendered more difficult the necessary concentration of attack upon the citadel of Capitalism.

Now, after all, as has been well said, "the end of war is peace." Then what are the terms of the peace which Labour can make with Capital? Is there anything short of absolute and unconditional surrender of the claim of the capitalistic classes to exploit the workers? I say emphatically, No. It is not a question of how much we shall be robbed, but whether we shall permit ourselves to be robbed at all. It may be very well to try and limit the amount of black-mail we are obliged to pay until we are able to resist the obligation altogether; but surely we can never concede as a *right* that which is really taken by *force,* however much it may be veiled under the form of *law.*

I cannot conceive of any sane man justifying the claim of a fellowman, be he idler or organiser, not only to compel him to work for both, but also to take possession of three-fourths of the product of his labour. Yet this is practically the position of the whole of the monopolists to-day in relation to the workers, and it will continue so long as the wage-system lasts, despite the utmost efforts of the trades' unions. This is no mere empty assertion, but is a strictly logical deduction from the facts and figures given in the Reports issued by the various unions; indeed, it is the inevitable outcome of the development of the competitive system of production. These Reports show, I think conclusively that Trades'-unionism has reached its zenith. On its present basis it can do little in the way of ameliorating the lot of the toilers, whilst it is utterly incapable of solving the labour question. So far from there appearing the faintest prospect of any general advance in wages or any material improvement in the condition of the workers, the facts are that the most successful unions are only able to maintain their positions by enormous subsidies to their unemployed; and the stability of some of the strongest provident societies belonging to the people is threatened by the extreme pressure upon their funds due to the chronic distress arising from large numbers of their members being continually out of work. Some of the larger unions, including the Amalgamated Engineers, undoubtedly the most powerful labour organisation of the kind in the world, have been compelled to draw largely on their reserve funds. Thus everything points to the conclusion that the trades' unions, so far from becoming more formidable opponents of capitalism, are really losing ground as a fighting body, and are becoming relatively weaker every year. This may appear to some a startling statement; but if they look into the matter they will find: (1) That the actual number of adult male workers engaged in several of the chief industries is becoming less and less in proportion to the population; and (2) that the increase in the membership of the unions is accompanied by a vastly greater increase in the ratio of unemployed. In my own union (London Society of Compositors), taking three periods of twelve years each from 1848, I find that the amount paid under the head of "Unemployed Allowances" has increased nearly in the ratio of the arithmetical progression—1, 2, 3—rather over than under. That is to say, that nowadays the Society has to spend on an average £3 on merely defensive operations, as against £1 from 1848 to 1859 and £2 from 1860 to 1871. Or to put the matter in another and more striking light, I find that during the earlier years of the Society the amount paid for unemployed averaged only about one-eighth of the total income (in one year, 1854, it reached the extraordinarily low proportion of one-thirtieth), whereas during the last ten years it has never fallen below one-third; in 1879 it amounted to two-thirds of the total income, and during the three succeeding years to more than one-half.

The significance of these figures is vastly increased by the fact that they relate to a Society which has been exceptionally prosperous; which has so far suffered less than most trades from the long-continued and severe depression; and which is peculiarly free from the disturbing influence of machinery, that has worked such havoc amongst the workers in other occupations. If, then, we take the position of the most successful unions to-day, we shall find that we have arrived at the high-water mark of Trades'-unionism; and I ask my fellow-unionists to try and realise what that means, and then ask themselves if they are content to rest and be thankful, and to accept their present condition as the goal of their ambition.

I by no means wish to disparage the value of Trades'-unionism. On the contrary, I claim that the spirit of solidarity evolved, the administrative capacity developed, and the general educational effect produced by the association of the workers for a common object, is of itself an unmixed blessing. Neither am I concerned to deny that the unions have to some slight extent improved the material condition of the workers, and have been a power of good in regulating trade customs and conduct. But what I most strongly insist on is, that their whole course of action results simply in bolstering up a thoroughly vicious state of society—that they are merely attempting to modify some of the evils that it produces, whilst leaving the source of those evils—the wage-system itself—untouched. It must not be forgotten, too, as I have already observed, that the advantages gained, short as they fall of any rational satisfying of the needs of the labourer, are only shared by a fortunate few. In the earlier years of trade combinations, whilst the commercial system was reaching its highest development, and when it was the proud boast of patriotic Britons that England was the workshop of the world, any successes gained by the unions affected pretty well the whole of the members. But as the years went on, with the constant increase and improvement of machinery, the mad competition in the production of cheap goods as the sole end and aim of civilisation spread to other lands, and thus produced the inevitable glut of the markets, with all the terrible consequences of the constantly recurring trade crises and enormous displacement of labour. Thus, notwithstanding the nine-hour movement and the passing of Factory Acts reducing the hours of labour, there is in every trade a large number constantly unemployed; and whilst of course it is true that the individuals who comprise this surplus-labour population are constantly changing, yet it will be found that there is in operation a law of selection which enables the employers to take their pick of the workers, and thus to a certain extent recoup themselves for the higher prices paid for labour. It is matter of common observation that men passed middle-age have increasing difficulty in getting employment; and the evidence of advancing age, such as the appearance of grey hairs or weakening of the sight, brings anxiety to many lest they may be called upon to make way for younger and more robust competitors. The slightly higher remuneration which a proportion of our number receive during their years of youth and vigour is therefore gained on condition of supporting the worn-out slaves of Capitalism, with the prospect before them of being displaced in their turn to swell the ranks of the unemployed.

Trades'-unionism affords absolutely no remedy for this. Even if every non-unionist were to join our ranks to-morrow, the result would simply be a further sifting of the workers, whereby the young, the strong, and the more competent would receive a shilling or two more per week, while the remainder would become chargeable on the "unemployed fund" of their respective societies.

## II.

Now the lot of the worker, even under the most favourable circumstances of full employment at what are termed "high wages," is not a very enviable one; what, then, must it be to our unfortunate comrades who have to drag out a weary existence of precarious toil and anxious idleness?

An agitation for an Eight Hours' Working Day is mooted as a remedy. It is thought by this means that the unemployed will be absorbed, and that the increased demand for commodities will bring about good times and higher wages. But the reasoning is fallacious. In the first place, the amount of exploitation may be as great in eight hours as in nine. A large employer and commercial philosopher, Mr. C. W. Allen, of the Allen Tobacco Company, Chicago, more astute than most of his class, has, from much observation and experience, reached the following conclusion: "The daily capacity of a man for work is an ascertained quantity. Hours worked in excess of eight are a mere waste of physical energy. Men working eight hours a-day gain in capacity for hourly production to such an extent over those whose hours are longer that their day's work becomes nearly an equivalent for the longer day of their fellow-workmen. For this reason we have adopted the eight-hour day without any diminution of pay; and after two months' trial, we are satisfied that we were right in our estimate."

Certain trades, especially those having little to fear from the competition of machinery, may be able to obtain a reduction of hours without a reduction of pay, but the practical result would be an intensification of labour, which might to a certain extent be beneficial to the employés by adding to their leisure, but otherwise would have little or no effect upon the general question. In the case of most trades, however, it would be found very difficult and, in fact, under present conditions, absolutely impossible to get the hours reduced without the pay being also reduced, which, of course, would be of no advantage to the workers as a whole, though it would benefit those who might be enabled to get work thereby. It is exceedingly doubtful whether, after all, the ranks of the unemployed would be materially thinned even if such lessening of the hours were general. It will not do to calculate as some of the short-sighted over-sanguine advocates of the eight-hour movement are apt to do, that the demand for labour will increase in exact proportion to the number of hours reduced. There are very few industries where the employés are fully occupied during the present nominal working-hours; the effect of a reduction of one hour per day in the first place and in most cases would result therefore simply in concentrating and equalising the work of those already employed, whilst the temptation to work overtime which is so difficult to deal with at present, would certainly be increased. The probabilities are that those who expect such a clearance of the labour-market as would enable them to obtain a speedy rise of wages would find themselves mistaken. In any case they would have to fight for it, for the employers would certainly resist; there would be a difficult and costly struggle, and even if the workers succeeded, their victory would be brief and barren.

It is an established economic fact that an increase in the cost of production is the greatest stimulus to invention. Where labour is cheap, it is sometimes preferable to machinery, especially when the machinery is high-priced. The machine needs the investment of large capital. Human labour-power is not fixed nor is it constant capital, the first cost is nothing, which is important to the "poor" capitalist, who can thus pay a small sum for the proceeds, after the labour has been performed. The effect, therefore, of raising the cost of production is to drive out the small employer, to cause more machinery to be used, with as a necessary consequence a repetition of the same miserable weary round of feverish activity, reaction, discharge of workers, lowering of wages, strikes, etc.

Of course, it is obvious that the workers as a whole can only benefit by obtaining a larger absolute share of the total wealth produced. It is absurd to suppose, as the advocacy of a mere reduction of hours as a settlement of the labour question, seems to imply, that the less there is produced the more there will be to divide. It is true that the fewer hours worked under the capitalist system the less surplus-value is created, and that the workers are thus enabled to retain a larger relative proportion of the products of their labour. But this very fact is surely convincing proof of the horribly unjust state of society. Is it not monstrous that the very industry of the people should prove their destruction? That the greater the amount of wealth created the more abject and hopeless should become the condition of vast numbers of our fellowmen? What a satire upon our boasted civilisation that plenty should bring misery to many, and that people should actually starve because of the very abundance? Yet to-day it would really advantage great numbers of the most useful members of the community if after working hard to produce various commodities, they should immediately destroy the product of their labour, in order that they might still continue to be employed in replacing the wealth so destroyed, and thereby avoid being cast out into the streets to become tramps and paupers.

A very little consideration will show that Trades'-unionism is utterly powerless to raise wages all round. Those unions who get a rise of wages benefit only so long as their position is exceptional. Directly there is a general advance of wages, there is a corresponding rise in the prices of the necessaries of life—food, clothing and shelter—which eventually reduces matters pretty much to the condition they were in before the advance was gained. In fact, the inevitable tendency of all efforts to improve the condition of the workers on the ordinary trades'-union lines is simply to bring about an equalisation of wages—an averaging between the highest and lowest price paid for labour, not only in any one country, but over the whole of Europe and America, and in fact wherever the accursed rule of capital extends. Thus any advance which the workers gain in one country is immediately counteracted by the importation of cheap labour, or the transference of capital to places where the workers can be more easily plundered. Nothing less, therefore, than an international combination of the workers to bring about a simultaneous and universal strike, can accomplish even such a comparatively paltry palliative as the eight hour working-day.

But even supposing (for the sake of the argument) that it were possible for such terms to be made with the monopolists by the trades' unions as would entirely satisfy them. What then? They cannot if they would, and they ought not to, if they could, separate their interests from the rest of the workers. There are large classes of the community whose condition daily grows more and more intolerable. These will soon demand in no uncertain terms to have a voice in any settlement that is to be made. What of the thousands of small traders who are being daily crushed out by the large firms—the small employers vainly endeavouring to compete with the big capitalists? beside the hosts of workers of all kinds who are entirely outside the scope of trades-union effort? By every consideration of humanity, and even of expediency, trades' unionists are bound to take the position of these classes into account. An organisation that does not work for all productive interests cannot expect them to look out for its interests; and if the unions are to look out for their own members only, without regard to the well-being of others outside their ranks, they are simply acting like the monopolist who believes that every one else was born for his use and convenience.

Besides, the classes to which I have referred as being outside the pale of Trades'-unionism are being continually largely recruited from the ranks of the artisans and mechanics; for it must be borne in mind that the demand for handicraftsmen, owing to the causes already referred to—increase in the use of improved machinery, etc., etc.—does not keep pace with the population. Notwithstanding the fact, therefore, that the sons of trades'-unionists drive the fathers wholesale into the ranks of the unemployed, the vacancies are still insufficient to supply all the youths in need of employment; and every parent at least knows that the difficulty of finding any occupation for them promising a decent livelihood becomes greater and greater every day.

Trades'-unionists, then, cannot be indifferent to these things. Their welfare and that of their families is involved in the general well-being of the people; but even supposing that, looking merely to their own selfish interests, and by ignoring every other consideration, it were possible for them to gain any substantial benefit by assisting the bourgeoisie to maintain the present corrupt society, with its frightful social inequality and widespread misery and degradation, they would deserve the execration of Humanity if they consented to do so. Such a course of action, however, would be totally at variance with the spirit and traditions of the trades'-union movement, and I for one have no fear of such an unholy alliance. I have a profound conviction that the trades' unions are destined to play an important part in the Social Revolution, when once they perceive how incompatible is the present economic basis of society with the happiness of the people.

### III.

I therefore urge it upon the unions as their highest duty to humanity that they should without delay come to some understanding with the advocates of Socialism. As a Socialist myself it has always appeared to me that Socialism is but the expression of the ideal of Trades'-unionism. The Socialist aims at the emancipation of Labour, the equality and fraternity of the peoples, and the overthrow of class-domination. This being the very antithesis of the present condition of society, implies the destruction of the existing wage-slavery, by which a privileged class is enabled to live in luxury and idleness upon the labour of others.

The present society is social war. It is a system based on inequality of rights and duties, upheld and maintained by force, in order that a few men may be enabled to exploit their fellow-men,—in short, that the Classes may profit by the misery and degradation of the Masses. As a cure for the strife and wretchedness which increases and spreads wherever the baleful influence of capitalism extends, the Socialist advocates the establishment of Co-operative Commonwealths, or communes, which should own and control all the raw material, instruments of labour, and means of transit. The object of such communes would naturally be, not the wholesale production of shoddy goods and Brummagem ware, but the general diffusion of happiness and contentment. Every member of such communities, in return for moderate and congenial labour performed under the most wholesome conditions and with the best appliances obtainable, would be insured the means for enjoying a rational life with due satisfaction of his or her needs, material, moral, and intellectual. Surely there is nothing in such proposals but what should command the assent and approval of every honest man and woman, to whatever class of society they belong; and least of all should those who live by the sale of their labour oppose them.

Whether this necessary and inevitable social change shall be brought about gradually and safely, and with comparative ease and tranquillity, or shall be delayed till a violent and irresistible wave of popular fury overwhelms the present accursed system, depends largely—I might almost say entirely—on the attitude of the trades' unions. Their action henceforth ought to be solely directed to preparing the way for the new social order; in organising and federating nationally and internationally, with the distinct intention of constituting themselves the nucleus of the Socialist Commonwealth. That this is their true function will be at once apparent if we analyse the present society and briefly examine the elements of which it is composed. We find that there is only a small minority of the population engaged in really useful and necessary work, by far the larger proportion being either idle or uselessly employed. For example, there are all those who minister to the laziness and luxury of the rich; the shopkeepers and assistants, the travellers, clerks, etc.; the hawkers, and itinerants of all kinds; the swarms of officials, lawyers, soldiers, priests, policemen, pawnbrokers, publicans, peers, princes, paupers, etc., etc.—not to mention prostitutes, pickpockets, and the criminal classes generally. All these classes are doomed to disappear with the corrupt society which makes their existence possible. But the unions contain within themselves all the elements essential for the constitution of a rational society; they are therefore pointed out as the natural pioneers of the New Era. By the discipline of their organisation and the solidarity which comes of association and collective action, trades'-unionists have been fitting themselves for the fraternal communal life which Socialists hope and believe is to follow the present fratricidal *régime;* while the administrative capacity developed by the conduct of the unions will be of enormous value in organising and assimilating the heterogenous host of non-producers to which I have referred above.

I call upon the unions frankly to recognise their mission, and to make common cause with all those whose fundamental principle is that the brotherhood of labour should be the basis of society. The emancipation of labour is neither a local nor a national, but a social problem. Labour is of no country. The interests of the workers are everywhere identical. Whatever political party be in power, whether the form of government be republican, constitutional-monarchical, or absolutist,—everywhere the workers have to contend with the same evils. The cause of all social misery is the economical subjection of the labourer to the monopoliser of the means of labour, whereby the masses of the people are compelled to sell themselves by a kind of Dutch auction to the capitalist classes in order to obtain the wherewithal to maintain a bare existence. There is absolutely no hope for the workers but in the utter abolition of wage-slavery and the reconstruction of society on a labour basis. Everything that has been put forward as a panacea and for the purpose of keeping the people in a fools' paradise has been tried and failed, and left them in even a worse condition than they were before. Surely they must be blind indeed who do not perceive that neither free trade nor improvements of machinery, no appliance of science to production, no increased means of communication nor new colonies, emigration, opening of new markets, nor all these things put together, can do away with the miseries of the industrious classes; but that whilst society remains on its present false base, every fresh development of the productive powers of labour can only tend to deepen social contrasts and to embitter and accentuate the class-struggle.

It is useless for the trades'-unions to waste further time, trouble, and money in fighting the "bosses" for some petty concession, which is maintained with difficulty, at best benefits a very few, and is only hindering the cause of the People. The present cowardly attitude of the unions is fast bringing British Trades'-unionism into contempt amongst all earnest, honest champions of progress. The charge has been made, I am afraid with only too much truth, that we have allowed ourselves of late years "to be dominated by a pettifogging set of self-seekers—men with no grit—bowers and scrapers to the middle-class god, Respectability." I earnestly entreat my fellow-unionists to exert themselves to remove this reproach. Let us show that we are capable of better things, that we can look beyond the narrow range of our everyday life and the mere selfish struggle for our own advantage. A mighty movement is in progress throughout the whole of the civilised world. Society is steadily, irresistibly dividing itself into two camps—the People on one side, the Privileged Classes on the other. All the ebullitions taking place in the various countries to-day, whatever may be their immediate origin or object, and by whatever name they may be described, have only one root-cause—the revolt of Labour against Monopoly—and are but the preliminary skirmishes before the great and decisive battle that remains yet to be fought ere the Curse of Capital be utterly overthrown and the cause of Labour won.

The paramount duty of the trades' unions seems to me to be clearly defined. It is to make plain to all men that they have no part nor lot with those who would maintain the existing unjust social arrangements, but that they recognise the absolute identity of their interests with those of the opponents of class privilege and domination. The trades' unions have hitherto kept commendably clear of party politics, but there appears some danger at present that they may be "got at" by the professional politicians, and may be induced to turn aside from their proper work to waste their efforts in Parliamentary pottering. The unions should steadily reject all alliances with any of the present political parties; they should refuse to take part in those disgusting farces termed royal commissions; and above all, they should guard against being cajoled by the blandishments which are being craftily bestowed upon some of the weak-kneed "representatives" of labour. The attention of trades' unionists ought to be solely directed to the social question. Nothing short of an Economic Revolution can emancipate labour, therefore no amount of legislative tinkering is of any use, so long as private property in the sources of life is permitted.

The existence of great organisations like the trades' unions with no definite programme is a strange anomaly in these times of active revolutionary propaganda, and with the social question agitating the minds of the workers throughout the whole of the civilised world. It is time that a joint committee was appointed to draw up a manifesto setting forth clearly and distinctly the aims and objects of organised labour. The monstrous doctrine of the bourgeois political economists, that human labour should be dealt with exactly like machinery or raw material, should be utterly repudiated. The workers should no longer contentedly allow their labour-power to be bought and sold like a commodity to make profit for the possessing classes, but should claim for themselves and for all men equal rights as free citizens to work together and to enjoy the fruits of their labour. The future action of the trades' unions, then, ought to be solely directed to the end of substituting production for use in the interest of the whole of the community, for the present system of production for profit in the interest of landlords, capitalists, usurers, etc.

To accomplish this desirable alteration the principle of solidarity must be much more widely accepted amongst all classes of workers than obtains at present; the spirit of fraternity must extend beyond the narrow bounds of nationality and bring about a common understanding with the peoples in other lands. Our brethren in America are considerably ahead of us in this matter. They have realised the inability of local unions among a comparatively small section of the workers to cope with the international conspiracy of the plundering classes, and are consolidating themselves into a vast organisation, which may be termed the New Society in embryo, which will undoubtedly at no very distant date develope into a Co-operative Commonwealth. Let us emulate their example and rally to the standard of labour all those who are willing to do their duty; all who suffer from the present condition of society and all who sympathise with the sufferers; in a word all those who acknowledge truth, justice and morality as the bases of their conduct towards all men, without regard to colour, creed, nationality, or occupation. Only by so doing will it be possible to close the era of social injustice and class war and to inaugurate a happier state of society for all, in which life shall be a thing to be enjoyed, instead of, as now, for far too many of us, a burden to be endured.

Comrades, I have sought to prove the inability of Trades'-unionism alone to liberate Labour from the grasp of Capital, and I have pointed to Socialism as the next stage in the evolution of society. I earnestly hope my words may lead you to inquire more fully into the subject; and I am sure if you do so, you will acknowledge the wisdom and goodness of the principles of Socialism, and will henceforth subscribe yourselves Socialists as well as Trades'-unionists.

# 25

# "SOCIAL DEMOCRACY AND INDUSTRIAL ORGANISATION", *SOCIAL DEMOCRAT*, 15 APRIL 1910.

*Harry Quelch*

[According to Belfort Bax, Harry Quelch (1858–1913) was even more the personification of what the SDF stood for than Hyndman himself (Bax 1914). With the defection of so many leading personalities to the Socialist League, Quelch emerged in 1884 as arguably the foremost Hyndman loyalist, and between 1892 and his death combined the editing of *Justice* with a prolific written output propounding a social-democratic view of the widest range of questions.

Quelch's view of trade unionism in 1910 offers an instructive comparison with Binning's a quarter of a century earlier (Chapter 24, this volume) and to some extent with Quelch's own earlier pronouncements on the issue (Vol. II, Chapter 18). Notwithstanding his being a Hyndman loyalist, Quelch had also had some role in the New Unionism through the South Side Strike Committee and the South Side Labour Protection League based in Deptford. Though his taking over from Hyndman as editor of *Justice* was consistent with Quelch's prioritisation of political organisation, his editorship can be identified with a marked softening of the paper's scepticism towards trade unions and an insistence on the indispenable if limited role that the unions played. On first impressions, it seems that Quelch's views of such matters may have fluctuated with the ebb and flow of union militancy. With the quickening of activity by 1910, there is certainly none of the hostility to the unions which the unguarded comments of Hyndman and others has sometimes conveyed. Nor is there any suggestion that the trade unions only represented a narrow craft elite. Quelch takes pains to associate the SDF with the role of its activists in the "New Unionism", and was a more important figure than Hyndman in shaping the social-democratic view of such questions.

What nevertheless united Binning and Quelch was the clear priority accorded political organisation for political ends. It is on these grounds that Quelch justifies the SDF's withdrawal from the Labour Representation Committee, which by this time had become the Labour Party, and it was he indeed who had taken the lead on the issue only a year after the LRC's formation. It was with a similar logic that SDFers like Quelch would also be so wary of the syndicalist agitation inspired by Tom Mann on his arrival back in Britain a few weeks subsequent to this article. Like the syndicalists, Quelch upheld the idea of trade union federation and amalgamation as a way of overcoming trade sectionalism. His insistence on the irreplaceable role of political organisation would have been endorsed by any orthodox German social democrat. The difference in Britain was that this meant the SDF insisting on its claims to an independent role that, in marked contrast with Germany, was far beyond its organisational resources.]

The principles of Social-Democracy are fixed and immutable; the means to be adopted to give practical effect to those principles change with time, and place, and circumstances. The object aimed at, the end to be attained, remains ever the same; the policy to be followed to attain that end requires to be frequently revised, and sometimes modified, as circumstances change.

All Socialists are agreed upon their object, that object being social and economic freedom and equality for all, and the realisation of the highest individual development and liberty conceivable for all, through the social ownership and control of all the material means of production and existence. They must all agree upon this in order to be Socialists. We are told sometimes that "we are all Socialists now," but only those who believe in the object as here defined can be properly so described. Those who so believe are Socialists, and those who do not so believe are not Socialists, whatever they may say to the contrary notwithstanding.

General agreement on the object, however, by no means presupposes universal agreement on policy, and it is no reproach to Socialists that in this respect there are wide differences between them. On the other hand, these differences ought not to be carried so far as to induce inaction, or to impede progress. They are, however, matters to discuss, to argue out, to confer about, and, so far as the practical work of the moment goes, to come to an agreement upon.

It is for such purposes that our own party holds its annual conferences. It is much to be regretted that those conferences do not include representatives of all Socialists in the Kingdom; that other Socialist bodies should find themselves precluded, by alliances with non-Socialist organisations, from conferring together and coming to a common agreement as to Socialist policy and action in the present and immediate future. In quite a number of localities this is done in relation to local affairs—without any entangling alliances and with mutual benefit. There is no reason, beyond these alliances, why what is done locally should not be done nationally.

During the past year or two there has been manifested in every European country a tendency in the Socialist movement to revolt against the growing influence and claims of Parliamentarism. Unquestionably this tendency has been justified by the undue importance which has latterly been attached to mere political action since the Socialist parties in the different countries have been able to gain seats in their respective Parliaments. On both sides Parliaments have been taken too seriously. The growing number of anti-Parliamentarians have been disappointed with the meagre results of Parliamentary action; while the Parliamentarians have magnified these and at the same time glorified themselves; as though Parliament, important as it is, were the only means to be used; the economic development and the social revolution were going to quietly keep pace with bourgeois legislation; and the functions of a Socialist Party were simply to elect members to Parliament to act as "statesmen," not as rebels, and to co-operate with bourgeois politicians in carrying small pettifogging measures of reform, through centuries of which, perhaps, Socialism might at last be realised; but the real object of which is to put off that realisation as long as possible.

It is through this assumption of the Parliamentarians, this audacity of the elected persons, that the tendency to revolt referred to has manifested itself. We have dealt with it at some length in previous issues of the "Social-Democrat." It is only referred to now in order to point out how mistaken it all is. All means are justifiable that can be bent to our ends; all means are necessary.

Political action is not to be despised, nor is any other that will help to break down the domination of the master class and hasten the emancipation of the proletariat. It will be time enough to forswear political action when the master class no longer strive to retain their mastery of the political machine; it will be time enough to dissolve our trade unions and declare that "never again" will we strike when the employers cease to combine and no longer resort to the lock-out; it will be time enough to abandon our demand for universal military training when all professional armies are disbanded, swords are beaten into plough-shares and spears into pruning-hooks, and big guns are melted down into statues of Peace.

The tendency referred to, however, takes, at the present moment, the direction of a reversion to the older methods of proletarian warfare, and expresses itself in the suggestion that political organisation should be abandoned for purely industrial organisation, and political action for the general strike. Our answer to that is that as Social-Democrats we are in favour of both. Our primary function, however, is to organise a political party, independent, class-conscious, proletarian and Social-Democratic. The function of industrial organisation lies with the trade unions. These two functions are not absolutely distinct and separate, they are co-ordinate, and to some extent interdependent. Yet they are not identical. The trade unions can help us, we can help them. As a matter of fact, we have helped them far more than they have ever helped us.

We Social-Democrats have been reproached in recent years because we left the Labour Party rather than subordinate our Socialism to mere "Labourism." In that combination we were urged by our fellow Socialists—even more than by the trade unionists themselves—to drop our Socialism for the sake of unity! But in a combination between Socialists and trade unionists for political purposes, it is political Socialism which should lead. It is as unreasonable to suggest that in such a combination the Socialist should be the subordinate partner as it would be to suggest that any Socialist body, in supporting a strike, should claim to dictate the policy of the trade union in conducting the strike, or should expect the union to abandon the immediate objects and demands of the strike simply in order to make Socialist propaganda.

The object of a Social-Democratic Party is the realisation of Socialism; and incidentally to assist in the organisation of the working-class and the amelioration of its conditions in existing society. The object of a trade union is to make the best of existing conditions; to make the best terms for its members in competitive society, and, incidentally, to help on the emancipation of the working-class. The co-relation between the two, as well as the difference of function, is thus clearly established. Yet we Social-Democrats are frequently charged with being hostile to trade unions, because we refuse to subordinate the one function to the other.

So far from being hostile to the trade unions, there is no political party in this country which has done so much as the S.D.P. to support the claims, aid the efforts, and further the development of trade unions.

And we have done this with so much success that we have seen a complete transformation in the character of the trade union movement. Originally a narrow, superior, exclusive "aristocracy of labour," trade unionism has become democratised and is now representative of every section of the working-class. If the trade unions even now only include a minority of the working class within their ranks, that is due to various causes, and is no longer the result of their exclusiveness. As it is, however, the numbers of working people organised in trade unions, in spite of all difficulties, have increased by leaps and bounds. There was a quite phenomenal increase in the years 1889-90-91, owing to the inception of the "New Unionism." But although, with the waning enthusiasm, many of the new unions— "twopenny strike clubs," as an "old" trade unionist contemptuously called them— have ceased to exist, and although in others the numbers enrolled have considerably diminished, the total number of trade unionists has steadily increased. According to the latest return issued by the Labour Department of the Board of Trade, the total membership of trade unions at the end of 1898 was 1,688,531. This had increased by the end of 1907 to 2,406,746, an increase of just on eight hundred thousand, or nearly fifty per cent., in the ten years.

What is not less important than the growth of numbers is the development of the trade unions in the direction of class solidarity as opposed to sectional exclusiveness and antagonism. It would be idle to contend that sectional differences and antagonisms have disappeared. On the contrary, they are still among the worst difficulties with which the active trade unionist has to contend. But they are being narrowed down and subordinated to the greater interests. The growth of federation between all trade unions, as well as between those engaged in a given trade, is a hopeful sign of the times. Another is the growing feeling in favour of complete amalgamation in those unions where no difference in occupation or conditions of labour justify separate organisations. It is true that neither federation nor amalgamation has gone nearly far enough yet. But it will need another article to deal fully with this part of the subject. Suffice it to say here that the trade union movement is on right lines, that we can see in its growth and development the result of some of the work put in more than twenty years ago by comrades of the S.D.F.—by Burrows, Williams, Hobart, Thorne, Pearson, Mann, Tillett and many another—as well as encouragement to persist in that work and that policy as defined by the resolution of our recent Annual Conference, as follows:—

> "That this Conference requests all members of the S.D.P., who are eligible for membership of existing trade unions, to join the unions of their respective callings, and, having joined, to carry on a vigorous campaign on behalf of Socialist principles, and also in favour of the ultimate amalgamation of all unions on the basis of class and not craft."

# 26

# "PREPARE FOR ACTION", *INDUSTRIAL SYNDICALIST*, JULY 1910, 31–54.

## Tom Mann

[Though syndicalism was an international movement, it had little real presence in Britain until the return from Australia in May 1910 of Tom Mann (1856–1941). Originally adhering to the SDF (Chapter 20, this volume), Mann had also been an important figure in the early ILP and on returning to Britain had again joined the SDP. Despite these political attachments, he was better known as a leader of the "New Unionism"' of previously unorganised workers in 1889–1890; and in his eight-and-a-half years in Australia he had discovered both the limitations of the political labour movement and what he believed to be the far greater potential for transformation of its organisation in industry.

The Britain he encountered on his return seemed to Mann to confirm such a view. The hopes of collectivists now centred on a reforming Liberal government supported by a substantial parliamentary Labour Party. Having enacted welfare reforms such as the introduction of old age pensions (1909), the government was now locked in the battle over the budgetary powers of the Lords that during 1910 led to two general elections. Mann, however, had no confidence that the issues of a class society could ever be resolved by such methods. With the stirrings of what would become known as the great industrial unrest, in July 1910 he launched the monthly *Industrial Syndicalist* and four months later organised a "first conference on industrial syndicalism" that gave birth to the Industrial Syndicalist Education League. In May 1911 he took the logical step of leaving the SDP.

Syndicalism was a movement whose predominant forms varied from country to country. In the USA, as Mann describes, the Industrial Workers of the World was organised on the principle of dual unionism and the repudiation of the old craft unions. In France, where the word and to some extent the concept of syndicalism originated, it pursued its aims through seeking to transform the Confédération Générale du Travail rather than supplant it. Visiting Paris shortly after his return to Britain, Mann was strongly impressed by the ferment of ideas around publications like *La Guerre sociale*, edited by the combative and inflammatory Gustave Hervé (1871–1944).

Though he characterises it as a "French policy", Mann's case for working within the existing unions was based on British conditions and institutions. Passing briefly by the Owenite scheme of the Grand National Consolidated Trade Union (1834; Vol. I, Chapter 32), he invokes the longer trade union history that he dates from the abolition of the anti-union Combination Acts in 1825. As well as his own experiences of the "New Unionism", he draws on his knowledge of movements in Australia and South Africa to demonstrate the debilitating effects of trade union sectionalism. Interestingly, he makes no reference to the Trades Union Congress, formed in 1868, but looks instead to the transformation of the General Federation of Trade Unions, formed as a result of the national engineering lockout of 1898.

Mann was an engineer by trade. Nevertheless, in describing the ill-effects of sectionalism he lays greatest stress on the role of the transport workers in deciding the outcome of disputes in which they were not themselves immediately involved. In the years immediately following, he was to play an important role in such episodes as the transport workers' strike in Liverpool in 1912. More broadly, the underlying logic of his position was to be reflected in the so-called Triple Alliance of miners, railwaymen and transport workers that was set up the following year. At the moments of its greatest tests, in the great mining disputes of 1921 and 1926, sectionalism in the end would prevail over solidarity and the cause of the miners once more ended in defeat. Though he always retained something of a syndicalist outlook, Mann by this time had made his peace with political socialism and until his death in 1941 would remain a member of the British communist party.]

## The Great World Movement.

In the twentieth century it is no longer possible for members of any political or religious party whatever to deny that there is, on foot, a great world Movement aiming definitely and determinedly at the economic emancipation of the workers.

Even those, who, for obvious reasons, regard this as the greatest evil, have come to realise the futility of attempting to combat this Movement by burying their heads in the sand and pretending to themselves that its influence is merely local and transitory.

There is no need for us to slur over our real weaknesses—weaknesses which, by the way, our opponents have without exception failed to note.

Chief among our faults is our remarkable gullibility. We have been singularly ready to take the word for the deed—and take it with a degree of gratitude and enthusiasm that has gladdened the hearts of the capitalists. We have frequently allowed ourselves to be hypnotised by the flattering assurance that we are reasonable men (and not Revolutionary fanatics) into a quite unreasonable acceptance of the difficulties suggested by the Masters. Moreover our numbers are considerable, and for that reason we have amongst us all sorts and conditions of men. Faint hearts there are; indolent and selfish members there must be amongst so many. But an honest enemy of the Cause would be compelled to admit that not Cowardice but Courage, not indolence and sloth but well directed energy, based upon the principle of Common action for the Common good, is coming to be the predominant characteristic of the Workers of all nations.

The present situation is unique in the history of the World. Never before has there been so extensive a Movement, which, surmounting the barrier of nationality, is consciously striving forward to the next stage in the Evolution of Mankind, where Competition will have to give way to Co-operation as surely as primitive Society had to give way to civilisation.

It is said that history repeats itself and it is quite true that, from time immemorial, the slave-class, which is our class, has arisen against the master class. Many sops have been thrown to the snarling Demos. The earliest on record were "bread and circuses." The latest are profit-sharing and Old Age Pensions. But never before have the masters been face to face with a literate and coherent democracy.

To attain this state of collective fighting efficiency is our immediate object.

## Our Experiences.

I, myself, have had the privilege of sharing in the efforts to extend working class solidarity, cheerfully abandoning myself to the great work of educative agitation, and assisting others in the stupendous work of industrial and political organisation of the toiling millions who, while called the working class, constitute ninety per cent. of the total population. I have seen and rejoiced in the steady progress we have made and are making towards Socialism. Not the least significant fact is the assemblage (upon such occasion as the Ferrer murder protest) of vast, sincere crowds who are out for Socialism and nothing but Socialism. At the last May-day celebration in London, when it was estimated that no less than 40,000 were gathered together in Hyde Park, the capitalist press was disappointed in being unable to report a single instance of drunkenness or disorderly conduct. The capitalists are more afraid of these silent, earnest multitudes than of the old-time rioters. For they suggest the possibility of organisation—and organisation is the one thing that the capitalist dreads, more even than the Ballot box . . . .

Most of us have all along been ready and willing to take our share of work in any direction making for the advance of our ideal, viz., the Abolition of Poverty by the Abolition of CapitalISM (not, as some of our intelligent critics say, by the Abolition of Capital). And in this spirit we have contributed our quota in building up the Trade Union Movement. We have belonged to, and helped in, the Co-operative Movements. We have assisted in political and municipal campaigns. We have tried unceasingly to influence educational authorities and administrative departments, always aiming to achieve the ideal and raise the standard of life as we proceed.

As a result there have been elected hundreds of members of Parliaments and thousands of municipal councillors more or less imbued with the Socialist spirit who are serving in that capacity. We have indirectly inspired an incalculable number of enthusiastic democrats whose ultimate ideals and present objects are almost identical with our own, but who honestly believe that those objects will be attained most readily by adherence to one or other of the capitalist-opportunist political parties. Liberal-Radicalism in particular can claim a large following of this kind—and it caters for its public by hysterical and utterly spurious denunciation of the House of Lords. But the Whig wire-pullers are playing with fire when they preach the immorality of hereditary Landlordism.

For that very considerable section of their adherents who have taken them seriously will, when they find they have been fooled, gradually perceive that the same arguments can be applied to hereditary Capitalism and allay themselves with the only party whose uncompromising hostility to both abuses cannot be doubted.

Lastly, we have been the means of inducing additional scores of thousands to join the industrial organisations. And we are richer, by far, in experiences than we were twenty years ago.

That I am a common soldier in the People's Army is my only warrant for addressing my comrades in the Cause as to the particular stage of development at which we have now arrived, and as to the nature of activities called for on our part.

Our experiences enable us to draw certain conclusions as to the relative merits of the various methods employed.

## Parliamentarism and Trade-Unionism.

Those who have been in close touch with the Movement know that in recent years dissatisfaction has been expressed in various quarters at the results so far achieved by our Parliamentarians.

Certainly nothing very striking in the way of constructive work could reasonably be expected from the minorities of Socialists and Labour men hitherto elected. But the most moderate and fair minded are compelled to declare that, not in one country but in all, a proportion of those comrades who, prior to being returned, were unquestionably revolutionary, are no longer so after a few years in Parliament. They are revolutionary neither in their attitude towards existing Society nor in respect of present day institutions. Indeed, it is no exaggeration to say that many seem to have constituted themselves apologists for existing Society, showing a degree of studied respect for bourgeois conditions, and a toleration of bourgeois methods, that destroys the probability of their doing any real work of a revolutionary character.

I shall not here attempt to juggle with the quibble of "Revolution or Evolution,"—or to meet the contention of some of those under consideration that it is not Revolution that is wanted. "You cannot change the world and yet not change the world." *Revolution is the means of, not the alternative to, Evolution.* I simply state that a working class Movement that is not revolutionary in character is not of the slightest use to the working class.

The Trade Union Movement has beyond question, been of great service to the workers. With its rejuvenescence in 1825 it became, for the time, the means whereby agitation and education were carried on. Results speedily followed, in particular in the all important matter of reducing working hours. The Class War was waged and for a period the battles were conducted by the Unions with an admirable abandon that brought off many victories. It was in the nature of things that periods of relative flatness and inertia should ensue, during which the fighting spirit disappeared and the encroachments of the capitalist class grew apace. The workers succeeded in obtaining political recognition with the right to vote; but, beyond that, nothing that they actually did, or tried to do through Parliaments or through the Unions, could be said to have constituted any considerable advance.

Now the most notable development of the latter half of the nineteenth century is the prodigious increase in the wealth-producing capacity of the people all of which, above the actual subsistence wage of the workers, was taken, as it is to-day, by the Capitalist Class; and it must be admitted that Trade Unionism, up-to-date, has shown itself unable to reduce the universal exploitation save, in a few exceptional instances, by a very meagre percentage.

## Direct Action.

But spasmodic outbursts of renewed Unionist activity appeared from time to time and gave a measure of hope to the workers. As, for instance, in the year 1889, when the Gas Workers of London resolved to obtain an Eight Hour Day in place of the twelve hours then in vogue. Failing to get any promise of assistance from Parliament, the workers resolved to resort to Direct action. They organised an effective Union, showed great courage, and, in a remarkably short time, achieved their object. That the organisation was sectional in character, and not properly linked up on the basis of Industrial Unionism, is seen in the fact that one of the biggest of the London Gas Companies was able to defy the Union and continues to this day on the twelve hour plan.

On the other hand the fight spread to the provinces, and the working time was reduced by one third and a higher actual wage was obtained for the eight hour day than had previously been paid for the full twelve hours.

A few months later in the same year there took place the Great Dock Strike of London which involved the whole of the Port workers. Much healthy activity was shown at this time and the far reaching effects of the psychylogical wave at that period were very considerable.

## The Curse of Sectional Unionism.

But looking back, as one of those connected with the numerous struggles that arose at that time, it would seem that this system, as it stands, considered as an instrument by which the Class War is to be scientifically conducted, is a very "lame dog" indeed. There are innumerable pettifogging sectional interests and very little that is soul inspiring.

That the numbers are somewhat greater than formerly is true. There are about two and a quarter millions out of an eligible industrial and agricultural population of not less than twelve millions.

But this enormous disparity between organised and unorganised is *not* the cause of the present day impotency of the Movement.

That weakness is to be found simply, if not solely, in the sectional character of the eleven hundred Unions of the United Kingdom—in the complete absence of the true spirit of working class solidarity and, therefore, in the inability of the Unionists to utilise the machinery at their disposal for scientifically conducting the Class War. That is to say for obtaining anything worth getting towards mitigating the poverty of the workers.

The prodigal dissipation of energy is at once the characteristic and the curse of the Movement. From this follows inevitably an increasing lack of confidence—and despair of ever being able to achieve anything substantial.

Thus there is a revulsion towards Parliamentary "action" in the excitement of which we are able, for the moment, to merge our own incompetency, with innumerable other incompetents, in the general hogwash of "Parliamentarianism."

Sectional Unionism is our curse. The ability to act trade by trade, occupation by occupation, each independent of the other, may have been of some service a couple of generations ago. But it is no use now! Let us see!

Miners are organised in a given district. Engine drivers at the hauling engines are organised. Miners have trouble with the Masters. They strike. They ask the Engine drivers to help them by refusing to lower blacklegs into the mines, or to haul any stuff whatever that is detrimental to the Miners' interests. The Engine drivers take a vote of their members. They decide it is not their quarrel—why should they risk good jobs? A big majority against the miners decides the latter's fate.

This actually happened to the Gold Miners on the Rand in the Transvaal. They used all the money they could get, and in a few months were at the mercy of the capitalists. Who had beaten them? Not the blacklegs! Beyond any question, the Engine drivers. A little while afterwards the gratitude of the capitalists to the Engine drivers was expressed by a substantial increase in wages.

Now this case of the Johannesburg Miners is typical of present day Unionism. It would be quite wrong to suppose that it was the intention of the Engine drivers to help the capitalists or to interfere with the well-being of their friends. But they had their own Trade Union.

They "attended to their own affairs and let others look after theirs, etc., etc."

And in this way the capitalists score everywhere and every time—solely by the lack of Unionist solidarity.

It is not wise to name instances too pointedly, as this merely tends to open wounds that are better left to heal. Here is another typical case—also at the Mines, but this time in Australia.

The Miners had good cause for quarrel, as the Masters were forcing a reduction. The latter asked for special police, not because there was the slightest disorder, but because, apparently, they thought it would strengthen their case to have mounted police "patrolling"—which is another name for irritating. These police were carefully conveyed a distance of fourteen hundred miles over the railways of three states by enginemen, guards, linesmen, etc., each of whom belonged to his particular trade union. The supplies for these policemen, with their horses and carbines, swords, revolvers, and baggage, were all handled by Union men. And here is the astounding paradox! These same Union men were subscribing given sums per week to help the Broken Hill miners to carry on the fight *While Actually Engaged in Entrenching and Supplying the Enemy*.

But this is so common an occurrence that there is no need to go to Australia for instances.

### "Scabs to Order."

The Shipping Federation systematically supplies British workmen as "scabs to order" in this or any other country. It is no use objecting that these miserable wretches ought not to be called British Workmen. The facts are too palpable. And these blacklegs, with all their necessary food, liquor, bedding, etc., etc., are shipped and conveyed over hundreds of miles by rail and road, as well as water, by other Union men. The drivers of locomotives, conveying them in batches of a hundred to the port, carry their Union card. The Engineers on the boat belong either to the Marine Engineers' Union or the Amalgamated Engineers. The carman, carrying foodstuffs for the scabs, is a member of his Union. The carpenters who make to order the fittings to house them, are Unionists.

It is these Union men, and not the capitalists, who beat the other Unionists trying to resist reduction or obtain increases. And so it must continue until we can organise by Industries and not merely by Trades. Until we can unify the Industrial Movement into one compact fighting force.

Comrades, we have got to face the fact that Sectional Unionism is played out.

### Industrial Unionism the Necessary Outcome of Capitalist Organisation.

The growth of Capitalist industry has compelled this class to organise perfectly. In the case of the large Trusts a decision given at a Board meeting often affects hundreds of thousands of workmen. The Masters' organisations cover all connected with the Industry. In the case of the Engineering and Shipbuilding Industry the action of the Masters is aimed to cover, and succeeds in covering, the whole of those workers in the establishments owned by them, no matter how many trades there may be. It is the entire Shipbuilding Industry they are after, and so they take care to act concertedly over the whole—and this covers some twenty different trades, organised into some twenty-four different Unions. These twenty-four Unions have never been able to take combined action against the capitalists. Hence this weakness!

The unit of organised efficiency must be the whole of the workers connected with an Industry, no matter how many trades there may be. For fighting purposes the Boiler Makers, Moulders, Fitters, Turners, Coppersmiths, Blacksmiths, Patternmakers, Drillers, Strikers, Machinists, Handymen and Labourers, no matter what the occupation—even the clerical staff and drawing office—must combine, and, for fighting purposes, act as one man.

This is the meaning of Industrial Unionism!

It is not in Britain only that this urgency for Industrial solidarity exists. It is in every country alike.

In 1905 there was held a Convention in Chicago, U.S.A., to consider the faultiness and inefficiency of the Trade Union Movement in that country. The outcome of that convention was the formation of a new organisation known as the "Industrial Workers of the World"—the essence of which is the organisation of all workers on the basis of working class solidarity irrespective of occupation. It declared that the old method of organising to protect the interests of those connected with a particular craft or trade is essentially mischievous, and harmful to working class interests as a whole. It creates and perpetuates divisions, instead of making for the unity of the working class. They therefore held that organisation on the lines of the "American Federation of Labour" was essentially reactionary, maintaining craft and sectional bias amongst the workers. Worse still, that the Unions of the A. F. of L. were not aiming at the overthrow of Capitalism, but were compromising with capitalists and merely seeking, at best, to patch up the increasing holes made by that system. The Conveners stated in a circular that their object was to be able to take united action and present a solid front to the enemy—as was being done in some of the European countries.

## The Worker's Own.

Whether or not the decision to ignore the existing Unions and to build up an entirely new organisation on scientific lines is the best method of procedure for the workers of America—is a matter for the Americans themselves to decide. But whilst entirely endorsing all main principles laid down by the I.W.W. and knowing well the shortcomings of the British Trade Unions, I do not believe that it is the best way for us to achieve industrial solidarity. I have given close attention to the arguments submitted by those who adopt this view, and I consider them insufficient. I know it will be a formidable task to get the existing Unions to unite whole-heartedly and share courageously in the Class War. But I believe that it can be done. And I am confident that the proposed alternative would be even more formidable and less likely to succeed. I hold that such entire reconstruction would result in years of bickering; entailing all the present sectionalism, and probably adding thereto by drawing large bodies into an even more reactionary position than they occupy now. In Australia, where the situation is precisely the same on a smaller scale as that which prevails in Britain, I associated my efforts with those who strongly defended Industrial Unionism—but not with those who attacked the existing Unions, seeking to establish a new force. Moreover I am entirely satisfied that the right course to pursue here in Britain is not to show hostility to the existing Unionist Movement, but rather to make clear what it ought to be—the real class-conscious fighting machinery for the overthrow of Capitalism and the realisation of Socialism. The engines of war to fight the workers' battles to overthrow the Capitalist class, and to raise the general standard of life while so doing—must be of the workers' own making. The Unions are the workers' own; and with a clearer conception of the use to which they should be put, and the determination and ability scientifically to unite and use them, locally, nationally, and Internationally they can and will, speedily become a stupendous power, affording the necessary fulcrum upon which to rest our lever for removing the obstacles that bar our progress.

## French Syndicalism.

I am confirmed in this, having just had the opportunity to visit Paris where I got in touch with the C.G.T. (*i.e.,* Confédération Générale du Travail—the General Confederation of Labour).

For ten years past the French Trade Unionists have been busily occupied in re-organising the Unionist Movement—and they have developed more than those of any other country.

There are 700,000 Unionists in France; and a large majority of these are covered by the C.G.T. They possess the fighting instinct. They are genuinely revolutionary. They, too, seek to secure better conditions en route, always giving attention to the reduction of working hours. And they are bent on an international propaganda for the overthrow of the Capitalist system.

Their plan is to organise first in the syndicates or Unions; then, for each Industry a federation of syndicates is formed; then, over all these Industrial federations is the General Confederation. It is the latter body that issues the Union cards to the Federations of Industry, and these again to the Unions. The subscription card contains spaces for each month's subscriptions to the Trade or Industrial Federation and to the Trades Councils—so that harmonious relations are secured and common methods followed.

They have eliminated the antagonisms and sectional craft interests, and they prove by their behaviour, that they dare fight, and know how to fight. They declare themselves revolutionary. They favour resorting, when advisable, to the General Strike. But while working for the Revolution they do not neglect to do all possible to secure general betterment.

They are, for the most part, anti-patriotic and anti-militarist, *e.g.,* they declare that the workers have no country, and are not prepared to fight in the interests of a bureaucracy; but most distinctly *are* prepared to fight for the overthrow of Capitalism in France and elsewhere. They are "non" not "anti" Parliamentary. They issue a weekly paper called "The Voice of the People," a bi-monthly called "The Life of the Worker" and "La Guerre Sociale," a weekly, edited by Gustave Hervé. This latter voices in all particulars the ideals and methods of the C.G.T.

### A Policy to Adopt.

Now, without urging a close imitation of the French or any other method I strongly believe that, on the average, the French policy is one that will suit us best; for whilst the temperament of the French is undoubtedly different from that of the British, their interests are exactly as ours, and their enemy is also as ours—the Capitalist system.

Of course, in some measure we are working on similar lines in this country. We have a number of Trades Union Federations, and we have the General Federation to which many of these belong. But we have no solidarity. Nor have we at present, the Socialist conception in the Unions to help these on to the right lines. And yet I hold that they are wrong who suppose that we have not genuine, class-conscious proletarians in the Unionist movement. I am quite sure that there are many thousands who understand the Class War, and wish to take their rightful share in the fighting; but as yet they can find no satisfactory outlet. Sooner or later these leading turbulent spirits will find a method—and it would be wise on the part of those occupying responsible positions to endeavour to make it easy for such reorganisations as may be necessary, so that those who are determined to fight may not be compelled to find other agencies.

Personally, I would very much prefer to see the existing machinery made equal to the whole work than be driven to the conclusion that new agencies must be brought into existence.

The only existing organisation in this country, which is, as it were, marked out to undertake this all-important task, is *The General Federation of Trade Unions* of which Mr. Appleton is the able Secretary, and there is no reason why it should not become the responsible, reconstructive agency, and supervise, control, and direct the entire Unionist Movement.

Their badge, which is shown opposite, is the best emblem of solidarity that could be found. It reproduces the spirit of the fable of Æsop. Let the General Federation put the meaning of its badge into practice, let them act upon it, and they will have achieved a task of enormous advantage to the workers.

### What is Called for?

But what will have to be the essential conditions for the success of such a movement?

*That it will be avowedly and clearly Revolutionary in aim and method.*

Revolutionary in aim, because it will be out for the abolition of the wages system and for securing to the workers the full fruits of their labour, thereby seeking to change the system of Society from Capitalist to Socialist.

Revolutionary in method, because it will refuse to enter into any long agreements with the masters, whether with legal or State backing, or merely voluntarily; and because it will seize every chance of fighting for the general betterment—gaining ground and never losing any.

Does this mean that we should become anti-political? Certainly not.

Let the politicians do as much as they can, and the chances are that, once there is an economic fighting force in the country, ready to back them up by action, they will actually be able to do what now would be hopeless for them to attempt to do.

The workers should realise that it is the men who manipulate the tools and machinery who are the possessors of the necessary power to achieve something tangible; and they will succeed just in proportion as they agree to apply concerted action.

The curse of Capitalism consists in this—that a handful of capitalists can compel hundreds of thousands of workers to work in such manner and for such wages as please the capitalists. But this again is solely because of the inability of the workers to agree upon a common plan of action. The hour the workers agree and act they become all-powerful. We can settle the capitalists' strike-breaking power once for all. We shall have no need to plead with Parliamentarians to be good enough to reduce hours—as the workers have been doing for fully twenty years without result. We shall be able to do this ourselves—and there will be no power on earth to stop us so long as we do not fall foul of economic principles. One condition only is essential to this—concerted action on the part of the workers. Police and Cabinet alike become powerless to enforce the dictates of the bureaucracy when the workers are united.

I should like here to offer my hearty congratulations to comrades who have done pioneer work in this country in propagating the principles of Industrial Unionism. As a fact, others long ago were aiming at the same idea. Without dwelling on the Owenite attempt at a Unionist Federation there were thousands of Unionists and Socialists seriously discussing, some dozen years ago, the possibility of uniting, for real fighting purposes, all the Industrial organisations. The best men of that time wished, in essence, all that is now covered by the term "Industrial Unionism." But when their efforts resulted in the present General Federation it was evident that the soul had gone and not much remained. Still, I repeat, the existing Federation has now its chance, if it has the spirit, the will, and the vim, to take the responsibility.

I know that many will at once declare that mere federation will be of little value. I am quite sure that mere federation of the kind we are accustomed to will not be worth bothering about. The unifying of the Unions must be, as regards their industrial and economic functions, equal to a real amalgamation. That is, it must ensure unanimity amongst all in an industry. There must be no loose affiliation, each one running off on its own policy. There must be a pooling of interests.

"Ah," some will say, "that means a pooling of funds—and how can it be expected that Unions having £7 or £8 a member will pool with other Unions having only as many shillings?"

I admit at once that it could not be expected. It certainly would not be required. The Unions with relatively large funds hold them chiefly for Friendly Society Benefits, *e.g.,* the Engineers, providing old age pensions, sick benefit, death provision, etc. These funds are, and must remain, entirely the property of the Unions whose members have subscribed to them.

What is asked now is the pooling of the economic or industrial fighting fund only. Where these are not already separated, an alteration of methods of account keeping will be necessary, so that the quota subscribed purely for economic purposes may be thus used. Then we shall get rid of the unnecessary talk about "threepenny unions." As a fact, most of those who pay high subscriptions pay quite as little in proportion for genuine economic purposes as do those whose subscription is nominally lower.

But before we get details let us be content to deal with main principles.

## "Workers of the World, Unite."

In a sense we have come to the parting of the ways. It will no longer be possible for us to continue as we are today—that is to say, as we were eighty years ago. We must not go out to meet a Maxim with a blunderbuss! We may not use in 1910 the same weapon that we used against the Masters in 1829! Can we think that the Masters have sat still all these years while the membership of the Unions has been growing?

We know that they have not. We know, from the records of recent strikes, that the complexities of modern industry have effectually aided the organisation of the Masters to defeat us. We have fought, and wasted our substance, in the acquisition of trifling concessions that have made comparatively little difference in our lives, and no difference whatever in our complete subjection to the Master class. And while we are hesitating the Trust is growing about us. To-day the small manufacturer is doomed. Every year the big men are getting fewer and bigger. That means that every year the organisation of the Masters is automatically simplified against us.

But Unionism is not played out! Rather is Unionism in its infancy! We are only just beginning to get a glimpse of the meaning of the word! Our present organisations, excellent as they may be in many respects, are but feeble affairs compared to the organisation we could achieve if we set our minds to it.

"Unite" was Marx's advice long ago, but we have never thoroughly acted upon it.

Now is the time to do it, and we will do it right here in England. We will lead them a devil of a dance, and show whether or not there is life and courage in the workers of the British Isles.

Now, Comrades of the General Federation, the Engineers' and Shipbuilders, Federations, and members of every Union throughout the land, it is up to us to adapt ourselves to the changed order of things.

Those who are asleep had better wake up or they'll be kicked out of the way. Those who say it can't be done are hereby invited to stand out of the way and look on while it is being done.

**"Workers of the World Unite.
You have a World to Win.
You have Nothing to Lose but your Chains."**

# 27

# "LEADERMANIA", *JUSTICE*, 13 NOVEMBER 1897, 2.

## *T. Hunter*

[When Robert Michels in 1911 expounded his famous "iron law of oligarchies", he drew mainly on his observations of the socialist movement. Himself a sometime member of the German SPD, Michels used the case of the pioneering German socialist Lassalle to demonstrate what he called the cult of veneration among the masses (Michels 1999, 93–97). The revisionist social democrat Eduard Bernstein, who was based for many years in Britain, also wrote of a Lassalle personality cult in a study translated by Eleanor Marx (Bernstein 1893, 188–189). Marx himself, in a private letter, had disowned the *Personenkultus* around his own figure as early as 1877. This was not, however, a phenomenon confined to German socialism. As Michels was at pains to demonstrate, the tendency of socialists to venerate their leaders was evident across the international labour movement and some German observers thought the British particularly prone to it (Beer in Stewart 1921, 279–280).

The appearance of the concept of "Leadermania" in the SDF weekly *Justice* is easy to place within this context. Its most immediate target is evidently the ILP, whose tendency to defer to its leaders had been implicitly targeted by H.M. Hyndman in steering against a precipitate fusion with it of the SDF (Chapter 8, this volume). The arguments of "Leadermania" are nevertheless set within a broader context. The author's name does not appear in the standard histories of the SDF and his motivations in writing have yet to be established. He would certainly have had sympathy with the scholars who have noted a general turn to the figure of the leader in European culture at this time (Cohen 2013). Hunter is also alert to the role of new communications and the place of the mass-produced photograph in the manufacturing of the leader's charisma (Meisel 2012). The article shows how the hero-worship to which it refers was contested by many socialists as inimical to the democratic values for which they stood. One can only conjecture how far the author might also have had in mind the "magnificent" lifelike portrait of Hyndman that the SDF's Twentieth Century Press was at this time energetically promoting. Problems of "Leadermania" had been a factor in the earlier split with the Socialist League and would again play their part in exacerbating the tensions within the BSP after 1914.

In comparison with writers like Bernstein or Michels, Hunter places heavy emphasis on the vanity and self-importance of the leaders themselves. The social psychology of mass movements is a seemingly secondary factor; organisation theory, or the view of bureaucracy so evident in Michels's work, is not present at all. One could hardly rank this article among the products of the new political sociology of the times. But it is precisely because it is free of such lines of reasoning and extenuation that the principled socialist objection to the notion of leadership stands out so clearly.]

You may search through the lexicons of Johnson, Walker, Webster, or Nuttall, and find no trace of the above word; you may consult any manual of known diseases, physical and mental, and meet only with disappointment. Yet it is one of the diseases afflicting modern society; a disease whose virulence is only equalled by its insidiousness. Unlike the majority of complaints of body and mind to which humanity is heir, it will not yield to ordinary treatment; once contracted it becomes ineradicable. Its chiefest danger lies in its subtle power of concealment. Even when discovered by a physician of keener perspicacity than ordinary, who simply calls it "swelled head," his diagnosis is usually ignored, his advice rejected; even the name and character of the disease is changed by the patient and his friends. It is not indigenous to any particular country or clime, but has existed in ages, in some form or other, only differing in the malignity of its attacks.

Its records are writ large on history's pages. From the time when the Israelites cried: "Give us a king to rule over us," Leadermania has been a curse to all nations. Its symptons often begin in early childhood. An infant prodigy of intellect, who can just discern the difference between toffy and tallow, hears its wisdom talked about by its fond but foolish parent, forthwith develops precocity, and quite naturally evolves from juvenile pertness into adult smartness, and so on by successive stages, until its incipiency, growing by what it feeds on, has finally developed into an insolent and impertinent desire to domineer.

Leadermania has now arrived at that stage when, if it is not to utterly subvert the power of democratic thought and action, its deadly character must be checked through the agency of a drastic antidote.

To the individual it is doubtless a pleasing exercise of the faculties for him to persuade himself that he is a born "leader," that he is destined to achieve greatness by being in the forefront of an important movement.

If the desire were but to *lead,* to *pioneer,* to *serve,* by virtue of superior ability, Leadermania would then become a stimulating endeavour worthy of the fullest emulation. Unfortunately for all movements whose aim is human progress, the term "to lead" too often means to *govern;* this, in fact, is an implied condition of those afflicted with Leadermania. And too often the condition is granted. And, having granted this, what more natural than that our "leader" should do our thinking for us? Imagine one man being a sort of thinking-machine for a thousand other men! What a picture of abject human automata it presents! And can we wonder that such a system should breed and develop pride of place, the insolence of office, and what has been fittingly described as the "never-ending audacity of elected persons!" Ninety-nine per cent. of the "leaders" of to-day are more or less dictators, who owe their position to cunning rather than to natural ability. It is not that they possess exceptional or even average wisdom, but that their sheeplike "followers" display a plentiful lack of it. It seems to be a part and parcel of the system that "leaders," having arrogated to themselves the right to think for their "followers," shall, as far as possible, systematically stifle any attempt of freedom of thought, and to their existence as "leaders" do I attribute that apathetic indifference to intelligent inquiry into important questions which would be likely to result in thinking men and women.

Let it not be supposed that man, as he emerges from his youth, is freed from leading strings. He is beset on all sides by insufferable prigs in various stages of Leadermania, all bent upon "leading" him in such a diversity of ways as to perplex him. "Leaders!" Heavens, what an indescribable variety of the genus are to be found! What a motley array of wise and unwise, clever and stupid, sincere and insincere persons, all clamouring to "lead," all afflicted with Leadermania—political leaders, religious leaders, social leaders, trade union leaders, leaders of thought, leaders of morals, leaders of fashion, leaders of fustian; leading books, leading writers, leading talkers, leading articles! Ye gods! Who can wonder that the people are in a political, religious, and social quandary? Why need we be surprised that, as a result of this phantasmagoria of folly, we find ourselves prone to follow the bell-wether whose tinkle is the loudest. For there is much of the showman characteristic in the successful leader. A flock of geese waddling sedately in lengthy file on to the village common, like a lot of fat bishops at an ordination, generally has at its head the goose who can cackle the loudest. We live in a society where any presumptuous jackanapes can become a leader, any pottery-ware idol or paper-machè hero be looked up to with reverence, if not actual awe. And just in proportion as he is looked up to, so he looks down on his worshippers. We wonder as we read, during the present engineers' dispute, the various "interviews with leading officials," how many of the latter there are, or whether they are all "leading officials"?

Who on earth wants to know the opinion of this or that leader? The Mawdsleys, Holmeses, Pickards, Maddisons, and the whole legion of incapables.

The difficulty in a world of shams is to distinguish between the true leader, whose aim is rather to instruct and guide, and the charlatan, whose object is notoriety. I have known men with just sufficient intelligence to warrant their delegation to a trades council to be afflicted with the most deadly form of Leadermania; men, who believed themselves to be heaven-inspired leaders, who could give points to Hannibal or Cæsar, and beside whose oratory Cicero and Demosthenes would pale their ineffectual eloquence.

We are apt to wonder what becomes of those "leaders" who at various trades congresses and similar functions have flashed meteor-like upon the social horizon?

Have the gods, having first driven them to the madness of Leadermania, afterwards destroyed them? Out of sympathy for those whom they would have afflicted by their madness, let us hope so.

We are told that the great want of the Liberal Party is a "leader," the need, nay the hope, of the people who form that, or indeed any other party, is the cultivation of their own individual powers of thought. This becomes plainly apparent the more we consider the political, social, and industrial fog into which will-o'-the-wisp "leaders" have led the great mass of the people. Thinking men would clip the wings of those "leaders" whose excelsior-like efforts at climbing higher and higher up the pinnacle of fame were likely to cause them to forget those below, whom they were supposed to represent and serve. And what about the Socialist movement? Is that entirely free from the dread disease of Leadermania? Perhaps we ought not to wonder that Socialism, as a political force, shall by virtue of hereditary taint exhibit some of the vices which are inherent in the parent organisations of Liberalism and Toryism. The chief danger to Social-Democracy is, I consider, the hero-worship we bestow upon those who lay claim to the title of "leaders." No Socialist can have anything but the highest regard for those who deservedly rank high in the estimation of the general body. This is a form of "hero-worship" which may be regarded with leniency, if the indispensable labour of first catching our hero has not been rewarded with the acquisition of a pinchbeck counterfeit.

Those who use their eyes must have noticed the very perceptible evidences of a dictator-like growth, which, like the rank weed that it is, might easily stifle the more sensitive plant of democratic control. One of the manifestations of this spirit of rabid Leadermania amongst "leading" Socialists is the blatant advertisement of their "counterfeit presentment" which is plastered upon everything which issues from their hands; papers, pamphlets, envelopes and postcards all bear testimony to this form of the disease.

It is questionable if any other movement has given such a stimulus to photographic art as has Socialism. And, contemptible though the Liberal-Labour leader may be from our standpoint, he has—at least, not to the same extent—not yet fallen a victim to this display of personal vanity and exaggerated self-importance. It will, of course, be understood that these strictures do not apply to the recognised fathers of Socialist thought, whose works are a standing and lasting testimony to the value of their services to humanity, and who, out of deference to the wishes of their admirers, consent to have their portraits taken. It would be easy to name such, but modesty and self-respect rather than a mania for notoriety, would deter these men from reducing the foible to the level of patent medicine advertisement.

Unless one has flattery to offer, it is, I know, exceedingly dangerous to tread on I.L.P. ground, especially in the direction of suggesting the slightest evidence of Leadermania. Yet, who is it but the "leaders" in the I.L.P. who elect to fight a hopeless battle like Barnsley at the cost of probably £350? With every desire to do justice to the sincerity of their opinions and the honesty of their intentions, one can but feel some misgivings as to this kind of "democratic" procedure. In its essence it partakes of the same vicious principle which allows imperial government to declare war upon a foreign country, without first submitting the question in dispute to the people who have to pay the cost. This is quite a natural result of having "leaders," even if it is undemocratic. Socialist administration should be on as broad a basis as possible, without the faintest trace of anything in the nature of hierachy—a system by which a select few can do the thinking of the vast majority, and converts what should be an intelligent self-thinking body into a number of animated ventriloquist's dolls, who are expected to loyally squeak their approval of their manipulators. Much might be said on this phase of the subject, but as I shall possibly be accused of spreading schismatic doctrine, I will not pursue my investigations further than to remark that the criticism I have offered is justified by the circumstances. Leadermania in any form is obnoxious to a lover of free thought, and as such I protest against it, leaving it to those who admit the disease to prescribe the remedy.

# Part 6

# DEMOCRACY AND THE STATE

# 28

# "THE WILL OF THE MAJORITY", IN *THE ETHICS OF SOCIALISM* (LONDON: SWAN SONNENSCHEIN, 1889), 120–128.

*Ernest Belfort Bax*

[Even excluding women – as Bax certainly would have excluded them (Chapter 31, this volume) – the "will of the majority" was not made effective in British elections until the introduction of full male suffrage in 1918. Nevertheless, with the franchise reforms of 1884–1885 there was henceforth a working-class majority of the electorate. Arguably the central strategic question facing the small minority of socialists was how far it should feel constrained by this majority in promoting social goals to which it was as yet either indifferent or positively hostile. Socialists were generally agreed that in future conditions of equality and active citizenship, majority rule would represent what Bax here describes as the highest collective wisdom yet attainable. On the other hand, Bax had no such confidence in majority decisions reached under the present conditions of a capitalist class society.

Unlike some reformers, Bax was not impressed by the device of the referendum which contemporaries most of all identified with democracy in Switzerland. In his distrust of what he calls the "mechanical majority", there is perhaps an echo already of the "compact majority" of Henrik Ibsen's play *An Enemy of the People* (1882). Performed to great success in Germany in 1887, Ibsen's play was then translated into English by Bax's fellow social democrat Eleanor Marx-Aveling; and – despite the conservative nature of Ibsen's own political views – was widely esteemed internationally by both anarchists and social democrats. There were, however, exceptions – H.M. Hyndman was one – and the link between their similar attitudes to the "human cabbage stalks" of villadom and slumdom must remain conjectural.

There is no such uncertainty regarding Bax's endorsement of the harm principle of the Liberal J.S. Mill, allowing no interference with any such action as had no detrimental effect upon others. Bax not only refers directly to Mill's famous exposition of this principle in the fourth chapter of his *On Liberty* (1859) but offers some of the same examples of illegitimate infringement of this principle, such as sabbatarianism. Evoking the "healthy freedom of the individual within its own sphere", Bax describes this liberal ideal as one surviving into a socialist society albeit with such modifications as many liberals themselves would soon come to entertain. The idiosyncratic nature of Bax's exceptions to the harm principle – notably the sale of snails for human consumption in Paris – was typical of his prolific journalistic output.

In the hypothetical circumstances of a war launched on Britain by a future socialist Germany, he unhesitatingly states that the duty of British socialists should be to do everything in their power to assist the invader. From a later perspective; it is an anticipation that seems pregnant with meaning. Socialists of Bax's generation were not for most of their lives ever confronted with this dilemma; but when a socialist state was established in Russia in 1917, those that followed were on several occasions to find themselves wrestling with a variant of the same basic choice.]

We are often admonished by the professional politician and by the man of "common sense" of the sacredness of the will of the majority, or as it is sometimes called, the popular will. The expression of this so-called will of the majority in legislation and social and political institutions, is conceived as authoritatively representing the wishes and convictions of the greater number of persons inhabiting the country or the given area; and it is assumed as an axiom by the persons in question that the will of a majority has an inviolable claim to respect. The latter proposition, I am here concerned to show, is not true at all as applied to modern society, and can in fact only be true in the case of a society of equals; further, that even in this case it has one distinct principle of limitation.

What has been hitherto called the will of the people, or the will of the majority as manifested in the modern constitutional state, does not express any act of will at all, but the absence of will. It is not the *will* but the *apathy* of the majority that is represented. How many of the—not majority, but minority—of persons that vote, *consciously will* a particular line of policy? Or even if we concede that they consciously *will* the broad political issue on which the election turns, how much of the subordinate though perhaps as regards social life even more important action, legislative and executive, of the government they have placed in office do they deliberately approve? To show the utter absurdity of the whole thing we have only to remember that in theory the whole common and statute law of England is supposed to be the expression of the public opinion of the existing people of England. Yet if, as in the case of the Swiss referendum, the people of England were formally polled (even those possessing votes) and the whole issue respecting every law placed before each, how many laws, now undisputed, would not be swept away? It cannot be too emphatically impressed upon the ordinary law-abiding citizen that the greater part of law, as it at present exists, does so by the ignorance of the majority, not by its consent. It is the expression, not of the *suffrage* but of the *sufferance* of the people.

But this is not all. Supposing there were a referendum or poll of all the people of England to-morrow, it would be of little avail on any but the very simplest issue. For so long as there is inequality of education and of natural conditions and the majority are at a disadvantage in respect of these things, they are necessarily incapable of weighing the issue before them. Their very wants are but vaguely present to their minds and in their judgment as to the means of satisfying them they are at the mercy of every passing wind. But given an equality of education and economic circumstances, there is yet another condition requisite before the opinion of the majority can be accepted as anything like the last resort of wisdom, and therefore as worthy of all acceptation. It is this. Public opinion, the verdict of the majority, even in a society of equals, if it is to have any value, presupposes a high sense of public duty—a standard of morality which exacts that every one shall take the *requisite interest* in public questions for forming an independent judgment on them. The man who has not taken the trouble to train himself to think out these things cannot help to form an effective public opinion on any question presenting itself. Given the conditions mentioned, on the other hand, and the judgment of the majority would unquestionably represent the highest collective wisdom up to date. But until these conditions are fulfilled, the opinion of the majority as such can have no *moral claim* on the allegiance of minorities or of individuals, although it may be *convenient* in many or in most cases to recognise it.

The only public opinion, the only will of the majority, which has any sort of claim on the recognition of the Socialist in the present day, is that of the majority of those who have like aspirations with him, who have a definite consciousness of certain aims—in other words, the will of the majority of the European Socialist party. Even the Socialist party, owing to the economic conditions under which its members with the rest of society labour, does not fulfil the conditions above stated as necessary for the formation of a public opinion which should command respect. But such as it is, it represents the nearest approach to an authoritative tribunal which we can find to-day.

As to those persons who prostrate themselves before this idol, the will of the majority (of present society)—of the mere mechanical majority, or count of heads—and swear they would yield anything to the authoritative utterance of "the people" (in this sense), it would be interesting to know how far in the direction of its logical conclusion they would be prepared to carry their principles. There are some among them, we believe, who, while avowedly holding the current theology to be pernicious, yet would nevertheless not oppose its being taught in public schools if the "majority of the nation" were in favour of it. Now it must be admitted that it is exceedingly probable that if the majority of the nation were actively in favour of "religious education" they would get their way. But it is also conceivable that were the majority not very energetic, an energetic minority might carry the day. Yet according to the "majority" *cultus,* it would be wrong to assist in opposing the "will" of the majority. Again, we would like to ask the pious majoritist whether he would complacently see the Holy Inquisition, gladiatorial combats, or bull-fighting established; or on the other hand, witness the abolition of all means of travelling on Sunday, the total prohibition of alcohol and tobacco, the closing of all theatres, and all because an ignorant majority decreed these things? Yet unless a man is prepared to follow a majority (so to say) through a quick set hedge, the principle of bare majority worship falls to the ground. Majorities are then tacitly admitted to be nothing *per se,* but only to be respected in so far as their judgments are themselves reasonable, or at least in so far as it is convenient to respect them.

The only conditions which can ensure a judgment on the part of the majority representing the highest practical reason of which human nature is capable up to date, as we have already indicated, are—(1) perfect economic and educational equality; (2) healthy interest in all questions affecting the commonwealth. In a society wherein these conditions were realised, all persons would be competent—some more, some less, of course, but all more or less—and the verdict of the majority ought clearly to be binding on all, so far as active resistance was concerned (and allowance always being made for the right of verbal protest on the part of the minority). There is one exception to this, however—though perhaps not very likely to occur. It is the principle referred to as limiting the right of all majorities—even though the dissentient minority be only one. I refer to actions which Mill calls self-regarding, or those which in no way directly concern the society or corporate body. Were any majority to enforce a particular line of conduct in such actions, and to forbid another, it is the right and duty of every individual to resist actively such interference. For just as the free motion, development and disintegration of the cellular tissue is essential to the life of the animal body, the cause of death in cases of mineral poisoning being the stoppage of this process, so the healthy freedom of the individual within its own sphere is essential to the true life of the social body—as much so as the subordination of the individual in matters directly affecting society. Civilisation with its destruction of the ancient solidarity of kinship and its inauguration of the reign of the individual as such, brought a new element into human life, which can never again be completely suppressed, however much it may be modified by the new whole into which it enters.

Were a majority, therefore, to seek to directly regulate the details of the private life of individuals in points where it does not directly come in contact with public life, any resistance on the part of individuals would be justified. Those entrusted with the carrying out of the mandates of the majority in such a case should be treated as common enemies, and if necessary destroyed. Even though the private conduct of individuals might have an *indirect* bearing on the commonweal, this would not justify *direct* interference; any temporary inconvenience would be better than the infraction of the principle of the inviolability of the individual from coercive restraint within his own sphere. Let us suppose a case. The habit becomes prevalent in a Socialist community of sitting up late at night. This habit renders some of those addicted to it not so capable as they would otherwise be of performing their share in the labour of the community. Now an other-wise sane majority might here easily lose its head and enact a curfew. In this it would be clearly going beyond its function, inasmuch as the habit in question is primarily a private and purely self-regarding matter. Let the majority if so minded exact more stringent standards of discipline and efficiency in work, and enforce obedience to them—such enactments should be binding on all good citizens. But an enactment compelling the citizens to go to bed at a particular time should clearly be resisted at all costs. Of course the probabilities are that a habit which really tended, although indirectly, to be detrimental to the community, would be voluntarily given up in a society where a social morality prevailed.

Again, the fact of an action being distasteful to the majority may be a valid ground for its not being obtruded on public notice, but is no ground for its being forbidden in itself. For instance, a certain order of Parisian palate devours with great gusto a species of large garden snail called *Escargot*. To the present writer, the notion of eating these snails is extremely disgusting. Now supposing an intelligent but unprincipled majority took the same view, as very likely it might, there would likely enough be proposals carried for prohibiting the consumption of these articles of diet—on the ground that it was bestial and degrading. Here, again, would be a case for resistance to the knife, But take the other side to this *escargot* question. The aforesaid molluscs are in Paris hawked about in the early morning in barrows, around the sides of which they crawl, the sight of them tending to produce "nausea and loss of appetite" (to employ the phraseology of the quack medicine advertisement) in those about to take breakfast. Now it is obvious that if this result obtained with the majority, the majority would have a clear right to prohibit the public exposure of these commodities, even if the would-be consumer were thereby *indirectly* debarred from obtaining them.

The same reasoning applies to sexual matters. Society is directly concerned with the (1) production of offspring, (2) with the care that things sexually offensive to the majority shall not be obtruded on public notice, or obscenity on "young persons." Beyond this all sexual actions (of course excluding criminal violence or fraud) are matters of purely individual concern. When a sexual act from whatever cause is not and cannot be productive of offspring, the feeling of the majority has no *locus standi* in the matter. Not only is it properly outside the sphere of coercion, but it does not concern morality at all. It is a question simply of individual taste. The latter may be good or bad, but this is an æsthetic and not directly a moral or social question.

Once more, the drink question, in so far as the consumer gets what he wants, namely, pure liquor and not adulterated stuff, in a great measure comes under the same category, although not so completely, since the directly injurious effects to society invariably resulting with certain temperaments (irresponsible violence, etc.), from the taking of alcohol, might justify prohibitive treatment as regards those cases. Even this, however, would not excuse any general measure of prohibition.

The above, then, is what I have termed the principle of limitation, of the coercive rights of all majorities, however enlightened. When they overstep these limits, whether at the bidding of whim or foolish panic or what-not, the minority or the individual has the right and the duty of resisting it, the efficacy of the means to this end being the only test of their justifiability. On the other side of this clear and distinct line, on the contrary, in a free society of equals, free, that is, economically as well as politically, the will of the majority must be the ultimate court of appeal, not because it is an ideally perfect one, but because, for reasons before given, it is the best available.

The practical question finally presents itself, What is the duty of the convinced Socialist towards the present mechanical majority—say of the English nation—a majority mainly composed of human cabbage stalks, the growth of the suburban villa and the slum respectively? The answer is, Make use of it wherever possible without loss of principle, but where this is not possible disregard it. The Socialist has a distinct aim in view. If he can carry the initial stages towards its realisation by means of the count-of-heads majority, by all means let him do so. If on the other hand he sees the possibility of carrying a salient portion of his programme by trampling on this majority, by all means let him do this also. Such a case, if improbable, is just barely possible, as for instance, supposing Social Democracy triumphant in Germany before other western countries were ripe for the change of their own initiative. It might then be a matter of life and death for Socialist Germany to forestall a military and economic isolation in the face of a reactionary European coalition by immediate action, especially against the stronghold of modern commercialism. Should such an invasion of the country take place, it would be the duty of every Socialist to do all in his power to assist the invaders to crush the will of the count-of-heads majority of the people of England, knowing that the real welfare of the latter lay therein, little as they might suspect it. The motto of the Socialist should be the shortest way to the goal, be it through the votes of the majority or otherwise. As has been often said before, and said with truth, every successful revolution in history has been at least initiated by an energetic minority acting in opposition to, or at least irrespective of, the inert mass constituting the numerical majority in the state. And it is most probable it will be so again. Be this as it may, the preaching of the *cultus* of the majority in the modern State, is an absurdity which can only for a moment go down with the Parliamentary Radical who is wallowing in the superstitions of exploded Whiggery.

# 29

# "WORKMEN'S JUBILEE ODE", *SOCIAL DEMOCRAT*, FEBRUARY 1897.

*Henry Salt*

[Standing out against the late Victorian cult of royalty there existed a strain of radical anti-monarchism which historians have sometimes underestimated. Hostility to the crown went back a long way in British popular politics, and though it fluctuated with the times it was liable to be stirred to life by the sheer excess and provocation of celebrations like the jubilees of 1887 and 1897. On both occasions there were strong military overtones (Taylor 1999, 132). For many radicals this merely exacerbated the sense of scandal and outrage regarding the Empire with which Victoria's reign was now so identified.

At the forefront of their agitations was the radical *Reynold's News*, a survivor from the Chartist era which voiced support for the Democratic Federation and the early SDF. With his grounding in Tory democracy, Hyndman did not always look so favourably on such campaigns. Indeed, at the Federation's founding conference in 1881, he threatened to vacate the chair rather than sanction a resolution for the monarchy's abolition (Crick 1988, 47). Twenty-one years later the same ambivalence was demonstrated on the coronation of Edward VII when *Justice* published an "Open letter to the King" which raised the hackles of republicans by urging him to act in the public interest (Tsusuki 1956, 389–390). Nevertheless, even Hyndman did also uphold the idea of a "great democratic English republic" (*Justice*, 14 June 1884); it was similarly reaffirmed in the SDF's *New Catechism of Socialism* in 1901. If there was sometimes scepticism, it was because of the bogus prospect of better things held out by a liberal or capitalist republic. But the SDF on the whole was an instinctively republican milieu and such sentiments were robustly expressed in the year of the Diamond Jubilee.

The author of the "Workmen's Jubilee Ode", Henry Salt (1851–1939), had been an early supporter of the SDF and contributor to *Justice*. By 1897, he was better-known as founder of the Humanitarian League and an animal-rights campaigner, vegetarian and anti-vivisectionist. Salt's admirers would include Bernard Shaw and Gandhi; his featuring in the newly launched *Social Democrat* is not only suggestive of continuities with earlier agitations, but showed an openness to wider political currents that was a very striking feature of the journal. Opposition to coercion in Ireland had been a major theme in the Federation's early years; in the mid-1890s it was overshadowed for most socialists by events in the wider Empire, but persists as a central plank in Salt's indictment of the monarchy.

The author of "After the Jubilee" (Chapter 30) has not been identified. It shows that SDFers did not think themselves above the sort of humorous debunking characteristic of Robert Blatchford's *Clarion* newspaper. Pointedly, the authorship of the execrable poet laureate Alfred Austin is denied – Austin being a Tory of the deepest hue whose ludicrous ode on the Jameson raid (for which see Chapter 43, this volume) had been published the previous year. Thomas Alfred Jackson was at this point a young apprentice compositor who converted "in a night" to socialism and by the turn of the century had joined the SDF. As a communist in 1935, Jackson would publish a pamphlet *The Jubilee – and How* whose scorn and invective any SDF member would have relished, showing the persistence of such sentiments in changing contexts which in some respects had hardly changed at all.]

> HAIL, Empress-Queen, since thus thy poets fable;
> Though, sooth, a sorry realm is thine indeed;
> To reign o'er groaning lands and hearts unstable,
> And homes made homeless by commercial greed;
> Empress of strife and misery and privation,
> Queen of despair and hate and envy pale—
> If such domain be cause for jubilation,
> On this thy jubilee we bid thee hail?
>
> Hail, fiftieth year of sanctimonious robbery,
> Imperial brigandage, and licensed crime;
> Religion mealy-mouthed, and polished snobbery,
> And soulless art, and priggishness sublime!
> Hail, great Victorian age of cant and charity,
> When all are free, yet money-bags prevail;
> Huge Juggernaut of civilised barbarity,
> Lo! we, thy victims, bid thee hail, all hail!
>
> Lo! we, thy slaves, in field and town and city,
> Who month by month and year by year must toil,
> Wronged, robbed, exploited, ruined without pity,
> While selfish Mammon heaps his stolen spoil,—
> We curse thy creed of comfortable cheating;
> "Live those that prosper; perish those that fail";
> Yea, ere we die, we send thee bitter greeting,
> A famished people to its Empress, hail!
>
> Empress, indeed—of dearth and desolation!
> Ireland, on this thy jubilee of fame,
> Stabbed, injured, maimed, yet still a deathless nation,
> Brands on thy brow eternity of shame.

"Witness," she cries, "these wrongs beyond redressing!
    Witness thy gifts—the gibbet and the jail!
Shall these foul curses bring thee back a blessing?
    Shall trampled Ireland bid her torturer hail?"

Nay—though thine armies win thee trophies glorious,
    Yet is thy glory but a worthless gaud!
Though o'er the seas thy navies ride victorious,
    Yet is thine empire built on guile and fraud.
Lo! all the lands thou holdest in possession
    Send thee for triumph-song the self-same tale;
Falsehood, corruption, selfishness, oppression—
    These are the satellites that bid thee hail!

Hail, then, by these our tears and bitter anguish
    Hail, by our loss of all that life holds dear!
Hail, by the want wherein thy workmen languish,
    That thy rich lords may boast their bounteous cheer!
Hail, by the iron rule of retribution,
    'Gainst which nor wealth nor sceptre can avail!
Yea, by the kindling fire of revolution,
    Great Empress-Queen, we bid thee hail, all hail!

# 30

# "AFTER THE JUBILEE", *JUSTICE*, 16 OCTOBER 1897, 2.

*(A belated ode, NOT by the Laureate.)*

I've done all I can as a "Britain," sir;
    I've shouted, and yelled, and got "screwed"—
I've "Gord Saved the Queen" till I'm sick o' the sound,
    And all my week's money I've "blewed"—
My old gal's a "naggin'" and "jawin," sir,
    And cussin' the waste and the drink—
Yus! now I'm a "chewin' the bitter cup,"
    And begginnin' to bleedin' well *think*.
It's all blimy fine for the "nobs" and "toffs"
    To go mad on the "Jubilee";
But when there's the "nippers" a cryin' for bread,
    Why it's rough on the likes o' me.
There's somethink I'm dyin' to arst yer, sir—
    Now folks 'as got over the fuss—
We knows wot we've done for Victoryer,
    But wot 'ave she done for us?

We've grubbed her, and kept her, and pampered her,
    Wiv taxes we've cheerfully paid:
She can "put by," they say, a "cool thousand" a day,
    And a nice little "nest egg" she's made.
*She* ought to be thankful, not *us* I should think,
    But I shouldn't begrudge her the "bunce"
If she'd only "come up" wiv *her* share ov the brass,
    And jest get *her* "'and down" for once.
Sixty years at the game is a pretty fair spell,
    And at "reignin'" she's 'ad a good go,
So I'm blowed if I know why she nurses up
    That "fifty million" or so.

We'd like her to open her mouth and say "thanks,"
    An' we'd like her to open her "pus;"
We knows what we've done for Victoryer,
    But wot have she done for us?

In the past there's the struggle for bread and cheese,
    In the futur' the "workhouse" in view,
An' we keeps on a workin' an' starvin' in turns—
    Then why all this hulalabaloo?
They tell us Victoryer's pious and good,
    An' she's allus been "proper an' nice";
Well, if that's all wot's wanted, I'll bet there's a few
    As ud take on her job at the price!
Wiv her coachman in front, an' her footman behind,
    She collars the whole "bag 'o tricks,"
While we, as produces the wealth wot she gets,
    Shout "hooray" 'cos we 'avn't got "nix."
My "ole dutch" can't afford a rag doll for the kids,
    Or a ride in a tuppeny bus!
We knows what we've done for Victoryer,
    But what 'ave she done for us?

"Gord Save the Queen!" Wot a silly idea!
    It's "a blind" jest to rake in the "quids";
It's "Gord save the poor" as is gulled an' is robbed—
    And "*Gord 'elp our wives an' our kids,*"
Wiv "redcoats" a eatin' their 'eds orf for show,
    And "bluecoats" at play on the foam,
A flauntin' their colours like pirates abroad,
    While us workers is starvin' at home!
Bah! Supposin' Victoryer "popped orf the hooks"-
    Jest like any other old dame—
Do yer fink as the world 'ud be any wuss off—
    Or it wouldn't go round jest the same?
There's profits a growin' for them as is rich,
    But wages gets *wusser* and *wuss*;
We knows what we've done for Victoryer,
    But what 'ave she done for us?

# 31

# "THE 'MONSTROUS REGIMENT' OF WOMANHOOD", IN *ESSAYS IN SOCIALISM NEW AND OLD* (LONDON: GRANT RICHARDS, 1906), 276–279, 282–294.

*Ernest Belfort Bax*

[Ernest Belfort Bax was a misogynist. There were other opponents of women's suffrage or the extension of women's rights who used arguments of sexual difference that cannot necessarily be described in this way. It was on these grounds, for example, that Beatrice Webb at first expressed views opposing women's suffrage that she came to regret. Bax, however, was a misogynist pure and simple. The "biting satire" and invective that Cunninghame Graham directed at European colonialism (Chapter 43, this volume), Bax applied to advocacy of women's rights and sometimes to women per se. As Sheila Rowbotham (1973, 95) has observed, he was "not just anti-feminist, but anti-woman as a whole". It was not at first a major theme in his writings, but from *The Legal Subjection of Men* (1896) to *The Fraud of Feminism* (1913) it was arguably the issue of current politics that seemed to concern him most. In his *Essays in Socialism New and Old* (1906), for example, three essays are devoted to the subject, contributing somewhat dubiously to the volume's objects of "yield[ing] useful results to the progress of Socialistic thought and the spread of Socialistic doctrine in this country".

"The 'Monstrous Regiment' of Womanhood" takes its title from John Knox's diatribe against female rulers *The First Blast of the Trumpet Against the Monstrous Regiment of Women*, published as recently as 1558. Even so, it is arguably the most reasoned of the three essays, having originally been published in 1897 (in Bax's *Outspoken Essays*) under the less provocative heading "'The everlasting female'". Originating in an undated public lecture, it makes reference to events of the early 1890s like the Hyde Park resolution against the flogging of Russian women prisoners on which Bax had written in protest to *Justice* on 29 March 1890. The lecture's language is not yet at the pitch of the "ruck of hysterical molluscs, who are imposed upon by the sentimental whines anent their 'mothers and sisters'", which appears here having been used without constraint in the SDF press (also in 1897). Nor is there the gratuitous defence of violence against women (or "what might have been a wantonly provoked thrashing") which had appeared in the same article in the pages of the *Social Democrat*. As an otherwise typical example of Bax's views it is nevertheless sufficient.

Where feminist campaigners took inspiration from the achievement of women's suffrage overseas, Bax deplores such examples as Wyoming (dating from 1869) and the more recent case of New Zealand (1893). He also stakes his distance from such radical supporters of women's rights as the MP and journalist Henry Labouchere (1831–1912), whose weekly paper *Truth* was launched in 1876, and the pre-eminent Liberal thinker J.S. Mill, whose essay on *The Subjection of Women* had appeared in 1869. It is nevertheless the standard Marxist text on these issues of the German social democrat August Bebel that Bax describes as having incited him into taking up the cause of anti-women's rights. Bebel's text had appeared in an English translation in 1885 as *Woman in the Past, Present and Future*, and Bax had also commented critically on successive German editions. When confronted with the unanswerable cogency of his arguments, Bebel, according to Bax, had "sought a way out of the difficulty by loftily waving them off and expressing pain for the welfare of my Social-Democratic soul" (*Justice*, 30 November 1895).

Bax's views were never representative of the SDF as a whole (Rowbotham 1973; Hannam and Hunt 2002). They were however widely known, and at least until 1909 more fully ventilated in the social-democratic press than the obvious counter-arguments. Like every male author of the type, Bax took full advantage of his position while convincing himself that he did so as the voice of a beleaguered minority. Bax was one of the most considerable Marxist thinkers in Britain, and his writings have been prioritised in the valuable work of the Marxists' Internet Archive. This does mean that his sexist polemics continue to be more readily accessible than many other writings of the period. There is also an online edition of his Collected Men's Advocacy Writings emanating from Houston, Texas.]

The way in which public opinion is hocused over the whole question is significant. As already stated, the ear of the average man is open on the one side and deaf on the other, and as a consequence the newspapers are open on the one side only. Hence out of twenty cases, civil or criminal, into which the sex question enters, nineteen of which will probably represent flagrant injustice to men, and flagrant partiality to women, but the twentieth may have the semblance of pressing a little hardly on the woman—out of these twenty cases, while the nineteen will be passed by without remark, the twentieth, the exception, will be seized upon with a hawk-like grip, trumpeted forth in every paper, exaggerated and commented upon in every key of indignation as illustrating the habitual tyranny of vile truculent man towards downtrodden woman and the calculated injustice of the courts to women. That's the way the 'trick' is done, and public opinion artificially and sedulously kept in its present course.

It can hardly have failed to be observed by every one, how vast a difference exists between the energy with which any injustice to men is protested against as compared with a corresponding injustice to women, and a still greater difference in the results of the protest. Injustice towards men is perhaps protested against, but in nine cases out of ten the protest is tame and remains barren, but a protest against any assumed harshness in the case of women, however trifling, is *invariably and immediately* effective. Again, a wrong which touches both sexes, let us say, is protested against. It is remedied as far as women are concerned and the protest dies out, even though men may suffer more than before from it. As an instance of this, take the outcry anent the flogging of women in Russia, and the protest raised by a meeting in Hyde Park, *not against the general ill-treatment of Russian political prisoners,* not against flogging, altogether, but a protest embodied in a resolution taking women out of the category of common humanity, and exclusively denouncing cruelties exercised towards female prisoners, thereby implicitly countenancing such cruelties when perpetrated on men. The 'advanced' women present on the occasion referred to, to their shame be it said, did not insist on making the resolution apply to both sexes. And these are the persons who are so eloquent on the subject of 'equality.' Again, take Mr. Labouchere. Mr. Labouchere made it his business in *Truth* to hunt up every obscure case of girl-flogging in the country, and to trumpet it forth in his journal as though it were a crime compared to which common murder were a venial affair. But now, had Mr. Labouchere one word for the brutal floggings of boys, not by private individuals, but in national institutions, such as reformatories and training ships? Not one. What he expressly denounced was not flogging, but girl-flogging.

Again British public opinion is dissolved with indignation at the notion of the solitary woman being taken liberties with in a railway carriage, and demands the heaviest punishment for the offender. But what has either the law or public opinion to say to the female blackmailer? She for years plied her trade on the Metropolitan Railway unmolested by the police. She is never prosecuted, and the law gives her every facility for bringing false charges, whilst public opinion treats the matter as a joke, or as of no importance. The late judge Baron Huddleston stated that in his opinion men stood in much greater need of protection against women than women against men.[1] [. . .]

Now let us take the other side of this woman question. Let us consider the alleged disabilities of women. I have already disposed of one of the alleged injustices to women in discussing the marriage laws; it is, therefore, not necessary to allude to it here. First and foremost, then, comes the question of the franchise. The Woman's Rights advocate is, of course, ever shrieking over the fact that the female sex has not got the suffrage. On the monstrous iniquity of this, she will expatiate in press or on platform by the column or by the hour. (She ignores the fact that a legally privileged body—the Royal Family for example—commonly does not possess the suffrage and yet is not counted 'oppressed.') Now let it be granted as an abstract proposition that women ought to have the suffrage and that the vote is a necessary condition of equality between the sexes. Conceding this, for argument's sake, I contend that, as far as the rights of women are concerned, (1) the want of the suffrage is altogether unimportant, and (2) the granting of the suffrage *immediately and without conditions* could not possibly accord with the principle of equality between the sexes. As to the first point, when you find that every law relating to sex-questions and specially touching women is constructed with a view to giving women prerogatives as against men, as has been the case with the recent laws respecting marriage, and other matters, and when you find that the administration is even more partial to women than the laws themselves, I think one may fairly say that the case for women having direct control over legislation and administration is, even from the point of view of women's rights, not a pressing one. I think it will be admitted that supposing *per impossible* that parsons and landlords invariably administered the law, not in the interests of their own class but of the agricultural labourer—I say, I think if this were so—the case for appointing working-men justices, though theoretically as strong as before, would at least lose much of the urgency that it has now. Yet so it is with the legislators and administrators of law, as far as women are concerned. In this country, in North America and in the British colonies, at least, men make and administer laws not in favour of their own but of the other sex.

Let us turn to the second point, that the immediate and unconditional granting of the suffrage to women would be incompatible with equality between the sexes and give rise to a sex-tyranny exercised by women upon men, not, it is true, directly, but through and by means of men themselves. Such would be the case for the following reasons. Firstly, there is the question of population. I assume, of course, universal suffrage for both sexes, which is the only principle worth discussing in this connection. The population of women exceeds that of men in these and most other countries—very considerably indeed in Great Britain. Now, the result of this on the basis of Universal Adult Suffrage, if conceded directly and unconditionally, is obvious. We should simply have the complete domination of the female vote. This would be moreover reinforced by, at the very least, a large minority of the male vote. For it is important to bear in mind, that whilst chivalry, gallantry, etc. forbids men to side against women,[2] it is a point of honour amongst female upholders of women's rights that they shall back up their own sex, right or wrong. Universal female suffrage, therefore, under present conditions, might easily come to mean the *despotism of one sex.*

But it is sometimes alleged that the *great bulk* of women would not vote solid with their sex, inasmuch as they are not 'political women.' In reply to this I have only to point to the case of Wyoming and other places in America, where, as I am informed, every public office is filled by a woman, except, mark you, that of police constable, and where a man can perform no legal act without the consent of his wife, as also more recently New Zealand. Again it is alleged that just as men on juries judge women leniently, so women on juries would judge men leniently, more especially, it is said, as the quality of mercy is stronger in women than in men. I can only answer that this also is not confirmed by experience. In the case of Wyoming the verdicts brought by the female juries against male offenders have been often of so vindictive a ferocity as to have amounted to a public scandal.

Once more, it is alleged that with the removal of the so-called disabilities under which women at present labour—*i.e.,* the lack of the franchise, the closing of one or two of the professions, etc.—the prerogatives, the chivalry now accorded to and claimed for women, would disappear, leaving the sexes really equal before the law. I again answer that experience does not lend colour to this forecast. For it would almost seem that, *in exact proportion to the removal of any real grievances that may once have existed, has the number of female privileges increased.* At the present day, women have infinitely more advantages as against men than at the beginning of the nineteenth century, let us say, when they were suffering under one or two genuine disabilities (*e.g.* the laws regarding the earnings of the married woman now long since repealed). Then, before a law-court, a man-party in a suit had at least some chance of fair play against a woman opponent. It is not so now. Then, a female criminal had not, as now, any assurance of practical immunity from the severities of the penal law.

The other chief grievance in addition to the want of the suffrage is that some of the professions are closed to women. I ask, 'What profession?' In the United States no trade or profession whatever, that I am aware of, is closed to women as such. In this country the medical profession, the one most sought after by women, is open, and, as far as I know, the law and the church are the only important callings, at all likely to be adopted by women, that are closed to them. And why is this so? Simply, because there has been no movement on the part of women for opening them. The moment women begin to agitate for admission to the legal profession, there is not the least doubt whatsoever that they will obtain it within a year or two. At all events this terrible hardship sinks down to the fact that one or two callings are legally closed. Moreover, as a set-off even against this, you have the enormous reputation, literary and otherwise, which a woman can acquire with slender means. The ability and industry utterly insufficient to raise a man out of the level of mediocrity is often adequate to furnish a woman with a name and fame equal to an income for life. I do not wish to mention individuals, but some instances will probably occur to many of my readers.

Such is the present state of the woman question—a steady determination on the part of public opinion to believe that women are oppressed—a steady determination on the part of women to pose as victims—in the teeth of facts of every description showing the contrary; a further determination to heap upon them privilege on the top of privilege at the expense of men under the impudent pretence of 'equality between the sexes.' The grievances that women labour under as women resolve themselves into three: the fact (1) that the wife has to prove technical cruelty in addition to adultery on the part of her husband (a very easy thing to do) in order to obtain a divorce; (2) that women have not as yet the parliamentary franchise (although without it they succeed in getting nearly every law framed and administered in their favour), and (3) that one or two callings are closed to them (albeit in most branches of intellectual work it is far easier for them to make a profitable reputation with moderate ability than for men). These are the three main grievances existing in this country at present and usually quoted to show the burdens under which divine Womanhood (with a big W) is groaning. Is it too much to ask my readers for ever to clear their minds of cant on the matter and to honestly say whether these disabilities, such as they are, counterbalance the enormous prerogatives which women otherwise possess on all hands. Defend these prerogatives if you will, but do not deny that they exist and pretend that the possessors of them are oppressed.[3]

The foregoing, then, I repeat, is the present state of the woman question—as it exists in our latter-day class society, based on capitalistic production. The last point that we have to consider is as to the relation of this sex-question to Socialism. Some years ago, on its first appearance, I took up my esteemed friend August Bebel's book *Die Frau* in the hope of gaining some valuable hints or at least some interesting speculations on the probable future of sex-relations under Socialism. I was considerably disgusted, therefore, that for the 'halfpennyworth of bread' in the form of real suggestion I had to wade through a painfully considerable quantity of very old 'sack' in the shape of stale declamation on the intrinsic perfection of woman and the utter vileness of man, on the horrible oppression the divine creature suffered at the hands of her tyrant and ogre—in short, I found two-thirds of the book filled up with a secondhand hash-up of Mill's *Subjection of Women* and with the usual demagogic rant I had been long accustomed to from the ordinary bourgeois woman's-rights advocate. It was the reading of the book in question that induced me to take up this problem, and to make some attempt to prick the bladder of humbug to which I was sorry to see that Bebel had lent his name.

In doing this I of course acquired the reputation of a misogynist. This is the natural fate of any one who attempts to expose that most shamelessly impudent fraud (the so-called woman's-rights movement) which was ever supported by rotten arguments, unblushing misrepresentations, and false analogies. I have given some instances of the former in the course of this chapter. I will give one instance of a transparently false analogy which is common among Socialists and Radicals. It is a favourite device to treat the relation between man and woman as on all fours with the relation between capitalist and workman. But a moment's consideration will show that there is no parallel at all between the two cases. The reason on which we as Socialists base our persistent attack on the class-privileged man or woman—on the capitalist—is because we maintain that as an economical, political, and social entity he or she has no right to exist. We say that the capitalist is a mere parasite, who ought to and who eventually will disappear. If it were not so, if the capitalist were a necessary and permanent factor in society, the attitude often adopted by Socialists (say, over trade disputes) would be as unfair and one-sided as the bourgeois represents it to be. Now, I wish to point out that the first thing for the woman's-rights advocates to do, if they want to make good the analogy, is to declare openly for the abolition of the male sex. For until they do this, there is not one tittle of resemblance between the two cases. It is further forgotten that the distinction between men and women as to intellectual and moral capacity is radically different from that between classes. The one is a difference based on *organic structure*; the other on *economic circumstance,* educational advantage and social convention. That such a flimsy analogy as the above should ever have passed muster shows that the blind infatuation of public opinion on this question extends even to some Socialists.

It will be observed that I have not discussed the question of the intellectual and moral superiority, equality, or inferiority of women to men. I am content to concede this point for the sake of argument and take the plainer issue. What does Socialism, at least, profess to demand and to involve? Relative economic and social equality between the sexes. What does the woman's-rights movement demand? Female privilege, and, when possible, female domination. It asks that women shall have all the rights of men with privileges thrown in (but no disagreeable duties, oh dear, no!), and apparently be subject to no discipline but that of their own arbitrary wills. To exclude women on the ground of incapacity from any honourable, lucrative, or agreeable social function whatever, is a hideous injustice to be fulminated against from platform and in press—to treat them on the same footing as men in the matter of subordination to organised control or discipline is not to be thought of—is ungentlemanly, ungallant, unchivalrous! We had an illustration of this recently. At a meeting held not long since, the chairman declared that all interrupters of speakers should be promptly put out. A man at the back of the hall did interrupt a speaker and was summarily ejected. Subsequently a woman not only interrupted, but grossly insulted another speaker, but the chairman declared that he could not turn a woman out. So it is. A woman is to be allowed, of course, full liberty of being present and of speaking at a public meeting, but is not to be subject to any of the regulations to which men are subject for the maintenance of order. And this is what woman's-rights advocates and apparently some Socialists term equality between the sexes!! Advanced women and their male supporters in demanding all that is lucrative, honourable, and agreeable in the position of men take their stand on the dogma of sex-equality. No sooner, however, is the question one of disagreeable duties than 'equality' goes by the board and they slink behind the old sex-immunity.

This sentiment also plays a part in the franchise controversy. Let women have the franchise by all means, provided two things, first of all: provided you can get rid of their present practical immunity from the operation of the criminal law for all offences committed against men and of the gallantry and shoddy chivalry that now hedges a woman in all relations of life[4]; and secondly, provided you can obviate the unfairness arising from the excess of women over men in the population—an excess attributable not only to the superior constitutional strength of women, but still more, perhaps, to the fact that men are exposed to dangers in their daily work from which women benefit, but from which women are exempt, inasmuch as they are, and claim to be, jealously protected from all perilous and unhealthy occupations. Now, surely it is rather rough to punish men for their services to society by placing them under the thumb of a female majority which exists largely because of these services.

Of course all the economic side of the question which for this very reason I have touched upon more or less lightly falls away under Socialism. Many Socialists, indeed, believe that the sex-question altogether is so entirely bound up with the economic question that it will immediately solve itself on the establishment of a collectivist order of society. I can only say that I do not myself share this belief. It would seem there is something in the sex-question, notably, the love of power and control involved, which is more than merely economic. I hold rather, on the contrary, that the class-struggle to-day overshadows or dwarfs the importance of this sex-question, and that though in some aspects it will undoubtedly disappear, in others it may very possibly become more burning after the class-struggle has passed away than it is now. Speaking personally, I am firmly convinced that it will be the first question that a Socialist society will have to solve, once it has acquired a firm economic basis and the danger of reaction has sensibly diminished or disappeared.

Nowadays any one who protests against injustice to men in the interests of women is either abused as an unfeeling brute or sneered at as a crank. Perhaps in that day of a future society, my protest may be unearthed by some enterprising archæological inquirer, and used as evidence that the question was already burning at the end of the nineteenth century. Now, this would certainly not be quite true, since I am well aware that most are either hostile or indifferent to the views set forth here on this question. In conclusion, I may say that I do not flatter myself that I am going to convert many of my readers from their darling belief in 'woman the victim.' I know their will is in question here, that they have made up their minds to hold one view and one only, through thick and thin, and hence that in the teeth of all the canons of evidence they would employ in other matters, many of them will continue canting on upon the orthodox lines, ferreting out the twentieth case that presents an apparent harshness to woman, and ignoring the nineteen of real injustice to man; misrepresenting the marriage laws as an engine of male, rather than of female, tyranny; and the non-possession of the suffrage by women as an infamy without a parallel, studiously saying nothing as to the more than compensating privileges of women in other directions. Working-women suffer to-day equally with working-men the oppression of the capitalist system, while middle-class women enjoy together with middle-class men the material benefits derived from a position of class-advantage. But in either case, as I have shown, *as women,* they enjoy a privileged position as against men *as men.* Only the will not to recognise the truth on the question can be proof against the evidence adduced.

## Notes

1 In this as in most other cases of this kind, we may observe, the allegation is considered a mere joke, that men are in danger from women, because, forsooth, the courts are administered by men. Just as if this mattered when, though they are administered by men it is true, yet in all cases where the sex-question enters they are 'worked' so exclusively in the interest of the other sex, that no barrister dare suggest that a swindling, blackmailing woman is anything worse than a poor, hysterical creature, on pain of losing his case.

2 So much is this the fact, that, as before pointed out, in the worst blackmailing cases, the defendant's counsel is bound in the interests of his client to pretend that he doesn't wish to imply anything against the female witness except that she was liable to hysterical delusions. In another connection, it is seen in cases of infant-murder, when the indignation of modern public opinion is turned not against the mother, who has committed the murder, but against the putative father who has had nothing to do with it; truly a new and improved conception of justice, though a trifle vicarious, which the new Feminist *cultus* has the merit of having originated.

3 Before leaving this side of the question, I may allude to a quasi-argument, supposed to be crushing, which is sometimes brought forward when it is suggested that, in view of the fact that all women are not angels, they should not be allowed to work their undisputed will with the men they come in contact with. 'Women,' it is pleaded, 'are what men have made them.' My answer to this is, that women are just as much what men have made them as men are what women have made them—nay, if there is a difference it is against women, since in the nursery, during the impressionable period of childhood, boys are entirely under their control.

4 A friend of mine is fond of arguing that the privileges of women are simply the obverse side of laws for the protection of the weaker. On this principle I would observe that any system of tyrannical privilege can be condoned. For example, it might be urged that the power of the Southern-state planter over his slaves was necessary to the protection of the physically and numerically weaker white race against the ferocious negro. A similar argument is, in fact, used to-day to justify the action of negro-lynching mobs. Any system of oppression may be explained away, if one chooses, as being designed for the 'necessary protection' of the oppressor against the oppressed.

# 32

# "WHY I AM OPPOSED TO FEMALE SUFFRAGE", *SOCIAL DEMOCRAT*, APRIL 1909.

*Dora Montefiore*

[Because of the prominence it gave Belfort Bax and his supporters, many concluded that the SDF was at best uncommitted to the cause of women's suffrage. Although the SDF press had ostensibly taken a liberal view of discussions around women's rights, in practice this meant Bax using his privileged position to express highly contentious positions which could nevertheless be taken as the SDF's predominant voice on such matters. Even the policy of adult suffrage, adopted by the Federation at its foundation, could be represented as an evasion of the commitment of most suffrage organisations to enfranchising women on an equal if currently limited basis. Karen Hunt (1996, 40) has described how the prominence accorded Bax forced SDF feminists and their supporters into a reactive position. This is exemplified by the document that follows.

Along with Herbert Burrows (Chapter 40, this volume), Dora Montefiore was the Federation's foremost advocate of women's suffrage. She had been active in suffrage campaigns in Australia and in 1899 had published a pamphlet, *Women Uitlanders*, which used the parallel between disenfranchised women and disenfranchised Britons in the Transvaal to demonstrate the double standards of the government now going to war in South Africa. Joining in the SDF in the early 1900s, she at that time had a column in the *New Age* and soon became a frequent contributor to *Justice*. As such she took the opportunity to distance the SDF from the anti-suffragist sentiments not only of Bax but at one point also of Lady Warwick (*New Age*, 20 April 1905). The document reproduced here is among the most substantial of these repudiations.

As an active supporter of the Adult Suffrage Society, Montefiore naturally took her stand for the equality of the sexes and the enfranchisment of women. She had previously been imprisoned assisting the more militant campaigns of the suffragettes (WSPU) and offers a robust response to Bax's allegations of the privileged treatment received by such prisoners. Tellingly, she also cites the commitment to sexual equality which H.G. Wells had expressed in the third part of his *First and Last Things* (1908). Wells had latterly been heavily involved in stirring up the Fabian Society, securing a commitment to the equal citizenship of men and women in the famous Fabian "Basis" which had never before been amended. Not every Fabian may have approved, but this did further underline the obduracy of the SDF in resisting the adoption of a common line on the rights of women.

At its conference in 1909, the SDP voted for Bax's withdrawal from the Anti-Suffrage League with only one dissenting vote. In moving the resolution, Burrows also protested against the issuing of Bax's *Legal Subjection of Men* by the party's Twentieth Century Press. Clearly Burrows and Montefiore were closer to the SDP's majority view. Even so, Bax was once more given the right to reaffirm his case against the acceptance of "Feminist dogma". According to Hunt (1996, 81), there is no evidence that any stronger action was ever taken against him.]

Under this title Mr. Belfort Bax has an article in the March number of the "Social-Democrat." As my hands are more than full just now with daily active work for the cause of Adult Suffrage, I do not know that, under the circumstances, I should have troubled to read the article in question, but the editor of the "Social-Democrat" was good enough to send it to me in galley proof asking me to write a reply, so I propose to jot down replies to one or two points raised. For the rest, the whole question of the position of women in the Socialist movement, including, of course, their political enfranchisment, is treated in a pamphlet I have just written for the use of the Women's Circles of the S.D.P., in which pamphlet I reply more at length to Mr. Bax's oft-repeated staccato shriek of "women being, *as a sex,* organically inferior to men." He now states in the present article that the reason the majority of men do not join him in this shriek is, "that their conviction is a secret conviction," that many men have "the unconscious desire to avoid stating the real ground of their opposition to female suffrage," and adds: "Some, if hard pressed, will try to shuffle out of admitting it, perhaps even to themselves." Others, according to Mr. Bax, "do not wish to appear rude and arrogant to the ladies." Now, these various classes of men known to Mr. Bax, and who, no doubt, have confided to him their secret hopes and fears, have the sincere sympathy of Socialist women like myself, because they must, at the present time, feel themselves but strangers and pilgrims in a froward and naughty world, which insists on taking for granted, both in scientific works, on the platform, in the pulpit, and in the press, women's human claims to equality with men, irrespective of their sex functions. Mr. Bax does not say if these timid friends of his are Socialists, or whether they belong to the ranks of the titled and distinguished personages in the Anti-Suffrage Organisation, of which he is such a bright and particular star. I take it for granted that they are *not* Socialists; because, as he himself admits, "the feminist dogma," having found much favour with Socialists everywhere, officially the demand for feminine suffrage has been embodied among the planks in the immediate political platform of the Socialist Party. As it is only, therefore, with Socialists that I have to deal, the few remarks that I have to make in my reply to Mr. Bax will be made from the Socialist standpoint, and will be addressed to Socialists alone. What, it appears to me, differentiates the Socialist interpretation of social conditions from that of the two orthodox political parties is that Socialism considers the woman first as a human being, and only secondarily as a creature of sex; that is to say, that as a human being her first natural instinct and function is nutrition, or the obtaining for herself of food, clothing and shelter. Her second instinct and function is reproduction. It is not, therefore, as a "feminist dogma" that the woman question has taken its right place in the Socialist demand, but as a "human dogma," and as part of a great evolutionary demand for the social, economic and political freedom of every human being.

Mr. H. G. Wells, in his book, "First and Last Things," writes: "One of the most important and debatable of these ideas is, whether we are to consider and treat women as citizens and fellows, or as beings differing mentally from men, and grouped in positions of at least material dependence to individual men. Our decision in that direction will affect all our conduct from the large matters down to the smallest points of deportment; it will affect even our manner of address, and determine whether, when we speak to a woman, we shall be as frank and unaffected as with a man, or touched with a faint suggestion of the reserves of a cat, which does not wish to be suspected of waiting to steal the milk." That, it seems to me, expresses the difference of view and conduct between a Socialist, who, because of his Socialist interpretation, looks upon women as first of all human beings, and therefore entitled as such to every opportunity of equality, and of those Anti-Socialists, who, being still obsessed by ideas of personal property, consider women as in the first place creatures of sex, which sex is part of that property. Mr. Belfort Bax gives as his supreme reason why women should not be admitted to political equality with men that, in England at least, "women at present constitute an almost boundlessly privileged section of the community." Would he have thought so, one is tempted to speculate, if he had been in the place of the elderly woman who, having married an Englishman and brought up a family of English children, and then on the death of her husband, having married a man of German nationality, when she applied for her old age pension was told she was not entitled to it, because she was not a British subject? If she applied in Germany, she certainly would fail to get a pension there; but if the case had been reversed, and an English widower had married a German woman, he would certainly have not forfeited his English pension. Yet English women, according to Mr. Bax, are "boundlessly privileged." Then, as regards the law passed a few years ago for the feeding by the Poor Law authorities of necessitous children living "with their father." That being the wording of the law, the children of widows, of deserted wives, of wives whose husbands are in prison, or in hospital, are not entitled to be fed. The feelings of these mothers who often work at 2d. an hour, and for 18 hours out of the 24, cannot perhaps be realised by Mr. Bax, whose eye is filled with the "boundless privileges" of the women of England. Under the Unemployed Workmen Act no married woman whose husband has registered at the Distress Committee can also register; so that, though such a woman is ready and willing to work, she has no means of bringing her claims before the public; again, out of the many thousand women who have registered for work on the Distress Committee, only two or three hundred in London have been given work; yet English women are "boundlessly privileged."

Mr. Bax makes the assertion that "No feminist has the smallest intention of abandoning any one of the existing privileges of women." If, by this, he means privileges before the law, I traverse his assertion; for if by "feminists" he means those Socialists who are working for the social, economic and political equality of men and women I can assure him they ask for no privilege, only strict equality. This, they are quite aware, can never be obtained under the tortuous and overwhelming mass of English common law. Such a patched, bedraggled, mouldy and evil-smelling garment can never be repaired; it must be cast on one side, and its place must be taken by the new and purer texture of social revolution.

Mrs. Lida Parce, of the University of Chicago, writes: "Two things are essential to this revolution: The socialisation of industry, which will give woman a free chance to work in a social capacity, and the ballot, which will enable her to remove those special and artificial disabilities which have been placed upon her by male legislation." A fair field and no favour, that is, in effect, what Socialist women are demanding in every country of the world: and when that is understood, I do not think it will be necessary to carry out Mr. Bax's suggestion to myself and to my "feminist friends," to move that a special note be appended explaining that the terms connoting "equality" in the S.D.P. programme are to be taken as "words of limitation." Such an explanation is not necessary among comrades, though it might be possible among the angel men and the brute women of patriarchal times. One word in conclusion. Misstatements of facts never help to strengthen a case; and, as one of those who went to prison for speaking in the Lobby of the House of Commons, I must protest against the statement in Mr. Bax's article that our imprisonment (for there were ten women suffragists in at the same time as myself) was pampered, "with all sorts of privileges thrown in, such as hot water to wash in, and easy chairs." We underwent the same régime as do the drunkards, thieves and prostitutes, who are swept up daily from the London Police Courts in "Black Maria," without, as far as I know, having enjoyed a single privilege. The furnishing of our cells was a plank bed, 2 ft. wide, a mattress made of cocoa-nut fibre, and two thin blankets; the stool had no back to it, the utensils were made of tin, and the daily work of keeping them bright occupied several hours. At six o'clock in the morning, when the cell door was thrown open, we had to get our supply of cold water for the day. If we were ill during the day, as I was before leaving the prison, we had to lie on the cement floor of the cell, as neither the plank bed nor the mattress were allowed to be taken down during the daytime. Our clothes were the ordinary half-cleansed prison garments of the unfortunate class of women to whom I have already alluded. Our food was exactly the same as theirs; our treatment by the wardresses and officials, accustomed to deal with these derelicts of Society, would, I believe, have thoroughly satisfied Mr. Belfort Bax that in our case at least we were not pampered. When I have since been asked at meetings by men comrades if I do not advise the unemployed and their leaders to follow the tactics of the Suffragists and risk arrest and imprisonment, in order to bring their sufferings before the public, I have always replied to the same effect, "I cannot advise men to follow our example, because there is one phase of imprisonment for men which is more degrading than imprisonment for women. Men, when in prison, may be flogged for a breach of prison discipline, women can only have dark cells and bread and water." As flogging is an outrage to the dignity of humanity, I will never be a party to advising men agitators to risk going to prison. A breach of prison discipline may be something as trivial as not cleaning your utensils to the satisfaction of the warder or wardress, or it may be placing your "books of devotion" on that part of the shelf where your tin mug should stand; it is very easy, therefore, for an ill-disposed prison attendant to get up a case of a breach of prison discipline; and a man who went to prison for an ideal might leave prison tingling with rage and embittered for life by the fact that his dignity as a human being had been outraged. One of the first pieces of work for men and women Socialists, I hold, is to do away with flogging in prison for men, and with imprisonment in dark cells in irons for both men and women.

# Part 7

# THE NEW RELIGION AND THE OLD

# 33

# "THE SOCIALIST CONCEPTION OF ETHICS", IN *A NEW CATECHISM OF SOCIALISM* (LONDON: TWENTIETH CENTURY PRESS, 1902), 22–30.

*E. Belfort Bax and H. Quelch*

[No two documents could illustrate better the SDF's broadening conception of socialism than the *Socialist Catechism* it published in 1884 and its *New Catechism of Socialism* of 1902. The original *Socialist Catechism* was written by James Leigh Joynes (1853–1893): a former Eton schoolmaster who had been among Hyndman's earliest socialist associates. There was nothing narrow about Joynes's world-view and philosophy. He was the brother-in-law of Henry Salt, the founder of the Humanitarian League (Chapter 29, this volume): like Salt he was a vegetarian, and for a time he co-edited the *Christian Socialist* which sought to keep alive the ideas of such eminent exponents of such views as F.D. Maurice (1805–1872) and Charles Kingsley (1819–1875). Nevertheless, in producing his *Socialist Catechism* for the SDF Joynes defined the subject in the narrowest economic terms. Sections of his catechism, which originated as a series of articles in *Justice*, include ones on the division of toil, the capitalist system, surplus value, methods of extraction and theories of profit. Though Joynes's translations from the German included works by Marx, he also upheld the iron law of wages (Chapter 15, this volume) which Marx had vigorously repudiated.

The *New Catechism of Socialism* was altogether more ambitious and intended as "a complete view of modern Socialist theory and practice in all their bearings". Economics (including once again the iron law of wages) was still given precedence. However, there were now also sections on the socialist conceptions of history, ethics and the universe, socialist internationalism, national politics, and the state and municipal enterprise. As with his other co-authored works, like those with Morris, Bax appears to have made the greater contribution to the enterprise. He had always had a more expansive conception of socialism, including socialist ethics, than some other social democrats. This is exemplified by the section on socialist ethics reproduced here, which also includes elements of a socialist anthropology of religion and philosophy of history.

In returning to the catachetical format, the production once again gave the impression of a "body of established truth to be learned" rather than critically examined and extended (Crick 1988, 117). At the same time, the ordering in this fashion of so many fields of theory and practice may be taken as a signal of the coming age of party as a more encompassing form of organisation. It was not for another five years that the SDF would assume the formal designation of the Social Democratic Party. Nevertheless, it was Quelch, the co-author of the *New Catechism*, who the year that it was published took the lead in the SDF's withdrawal from the Labour Representation Committee after only twelve months. Following a period dominated by the idea of socialist unity, the mantle the SDF took upon itself as "the English Socialist Party" or "Socialist Party of Great Britain" was in this pamphlet represented in the form of a complete and self-contained conspectus of socialist doctrine.]

*So far you have only given the industrial or economic side of the historical development of human society. Do you mean to suggest that the intellectual, religious, artistic and ethical aspects are entirely subordinate to this?*

Certainly not. From the very beginnings of human development the mind of man has had a more or less independent influence on its surroundings. For this reason it is impossible to reduce history to a mere mechanical reflex of its industrial development. To enter at any length into the question of these other phases of human evolution would take us beyond the scope we have set ourselves in this work. It is, however, necessary to say a few words on the subject of ethics, in its connection with Socialism as a system of society.

*Is there not a fundamental moral law which is the same in all systems of society?*

To a certain extent, yes; but only in so far as all society implies a union of some sort or other, and hence certain broad rules of conduct which are essential to the continuance of this union, but even those broad rules or principles are modified to an almost indefinite extent by changes in the general conditions of social organisation, while many other rules of conduct come into operation and disappear with the varying phases of human society.

*Do you mean to say, then, that Socialism has a distinct standard of ethics of its own?*

Certainly; and not only Socialism but every other stage of human evolution has its own code of ethics. In early tribal society the ethical object, that is to say the end of conduct, was social; in other words, the highest object of devotion on the part of its members was the group, the tribe or clan, or, in a more advanced stage, the people, or confederacy of tribes. The question of good or evil conduct was determined by whether it served the prosperity, honour or glory of the community, or whether it was inimical to these. As man advanced into civilisation ethical ideas expanded, but at the expense of the narrower social morality of group society. Gradually, as civilisation progressed, the forms of the older group society, becoming obsolete, were superseded by the centralised

State organisation, and the ethical centre became shifted from the group to the individual. Good and evil then assumed an absolute value irrespective of society. Religion, which in group society simply meant the conjuration of the spirits of ancestors and of the personified powers of nature in the interests of the tribe, now assumed quite another character, that of the worship of a spiritual deity, who was at once the source and the object of all moral aspiration, directly revealed to the individual conscience. This deity was the central point of the new morality, in which, consequently, man's duty to his fellow men was a matter of secondary consideration. Thus we have first the tribal ethics, the responsibility to society, and in the second place an entirely contrary conception of ethics, the universal or introspective, in which the direct responsibility was to a divinity, who was the supreme power of the universe, and for whom mankind was but a means of realising himself.

*Can you give an illustration of what you mean by universal or introspective ethics?*

All religions of the world which were not tribal nor, at least primarily, idolatrous—as it is termed—and which were founded and preached by individual prophets or teachers who claimed to have a divine mission. All these religions were in the main based upon the introspective conception above stated. Judaism, Buddhism, and even Mohammedanism, in their purer forms, contained this element very prominently, but Christianity is its great historical expression. The declaration of the Founder of Christianity, "The Kingdom of God is within you," gives, in a single phrase, the complete basis of this code of ethics. The Kingdom of God was certainly not "within" the worshipper of a "totem," or emblem of tribal unity; it was indeed "within" the tribe, but outside of any individual member of the tribe.

*Then do you suggest that these religions, which superseded the tribal religions, were based upon an individualist ethic?*

Most decidedly; inasmuch as the stress of their theory rests in a supposed direct relation of the individual soul with its God, or the soul of the universe, in contradistinction to a direct relation with the social body.

*But surely these religions, notably Christianity, embrace moral precepts which are essentially social in their character?*

That is perfectly true; but in the case of these religions, these social maxims, in so far as they are not merely survivals, are entirely secondary and derivative; you are called upon to love your brother, whom you can see, by way of practice, and as a preparatory exercise to loving God, whom you cannot see, and so forth.

*But is not the word "individualism" used in connection with ethics generally understood to mean something very different from even the Christian view of social obligations; is it not usually intended to convey the idea of the most narrow material selfishness, as expressed in the phrase, "The devil take the hindmost"?*

Yes; with the development of civilisation and the more perfect forms of economic individualism, *i.e.,* capitalism, the older theological ethic—which, though primarily individualistic (from an other-worldly point of view), had yet, as you have remarked, a social side—was superseded in actual practice and in the current theory of life, and became a mere pious opinion, having no practical application.

*When did this development of the purely individualistic ethics take place?*

This conception of ethics only became the dominant theory within the nineteenth century, with the advent of what has been described as the Manchester school of political economy. The basis of the theory of that school was the individual scramble for wealth, the cash nexus in place of social personal relations, and the dethronement of old-world sentiment in all the departments of life. It was this exaltation of purely material relations between men which led to the phrase, "The devil take the hindmost." Some social reformers regard this ultra-individualistic ethic as the antithesis of the Christian ethic, that is to say, they oppose the Christian ethic to this fully developed individualism. But the real antithesis is not the Christian ethic, which is also in its way individualistic, but the ethic of tribal society on the one side, and the ethic of the Socialist society of the future on the other.

*What, then, is the ethical conception proper to the Socialist society of the future? Is it not Christian brotherly love?*

No. Paradox as it may appear, the Socialist conception of ethics is not this brotherly love, in the Christian sense, although it may, superficially, seem to bear some resemblance to it. On the other hand, nothing is more erroneous than to suppose that Socialism ignores all ethical considerations which are not immediately concerned with the present class struggle in its narrower sense. Our corrupt capitalist society tends more and more to base its ethical judgments—save the mark!—on the mere interest or expediency of the possessing classes, either as a whole or in their more important sections. This is its ethical standard. It is one of the chief duties of the Socialist Party to hold aloft the banner of those fundamental ethical principles which, as we before remarked, are common to all the various forms through which human society has passed. In fact, the maintenance of a truly high ethical standard in public life is one of the most important functions of the Socialist Party of to-day; more important, indeed, than the attainment of any immediate success either generally as a party, or in such matters as might be considered to lie more especially within its sphere.

*Can you give an illustration of what you mean by this?*

Yes. Two instances in point, from recent and current events, suggest themselves. During the agitation on behalf of Captain Dreyfus it was quite a common thing to hear the remark, "Oh, this is simply a bourgeois affair. Even if the man has been unjustly condemned it is no business of the Socialist Party, which is only concerned when the rights of a workman are assailed." The Socialists of France, with practical unanimity, thought otherwise. They felt by instinct that it was their duty to throw themselves into the breach on behalf of the common principles of justice, and by their vigorous action succeeded in vindicating these principles. Again, the Boer war affords us another instance in which working-class interests were not obviously or directly affected, but where it was a question of asserting the principles of justice on behalf of a small nation of comparatively well-to-do yeoman farmers. Nevertheless, the English Socialist Party with practical unanimity vigorously protested and agitated against the aggressive action of Great Britain, and in favour of the independence of the Republics. Here again, although, of course, there were very vital issues in the class struggle between Capitalism and Socialism, Bourgeoisie and Proletariat, involved, yet they did not lie on the surface, and it might have seemed politic to have ignored the war as far as possible, with a view of conciliating those among the working classes who had been imposed upon as to the side on which their interests lay by the virulent garbage of the jingo press. The Socialist Party of Great Britain has reason to be proud of its uncompromising attitude on this occasion in defence of international morality against crime.

*Are we to understand, then, that the Socialist ethics of the future are no more those of Christianity than they are those of the Manchester school?*

Certainly, apart from the fact that the so-called altruistic ethics of Christianity are subordinate to the theological relation of the soul to its God. Even in their very altruism these ethics are one-sided, seeing that they postulate, not as an exceptional incident, but as their root principle, the negation of the self of the natural man, not only to his God, but also to his fellow man. This one-sided, abstract view of the ethical relation has no part nor lot in the very concrete and tangible morality of the Socialism of the future.

*But are not the ethics of Socialism essentially altruistic? If that is so, can you have any finer expression of them than is to be found in Christianity, e.g., in the Sermon on the Mount?*

Socialist ethics are neither altruistic nor egoistic; they are intrinsically neither selfish nor unselfish. As with other abstractions characterising the phase of human development generally called civilisation—such as the differentiation into separate and even antagonistic classes of the various social functions, of which the cardinal instance is in the two functions of labour and direction separated and embodied in the two antagonistic classes of master and servant—so in ethics we find a purely factitious antagonism set up between the individual and society. This antagonism is based to a large extent on the economic individualism which separates and antagonises the material interests of the individual with his neighbour and with society at large. Given this antagonism, it naturally becomes a virtue on the part of the individual to sacrifice himself habitually for the benefit of others. Where, however, the condition is changed—and in proportion to the degree of this change—the reason for such sacrifice disappears, and to that extent it ceases to be a virtue. The virtue lies in the service rendered to one's neighbour or to society, not in the amount of injury to one's self: thus it would be meritorious to rescue anyone from a burning building, even at the cost of personal suffering or of life itself, and it is difficult to conceive of any set of circumstances in which the reason for such an act might not obtain—but the good would be in the rescue, not in the suffering or sacrifice entailed. Loss, injury, or suffering, is essentially an evil in itself, even if self-inflicted and for a good object. Socialism presupposes a condition of things in which the good of all will mean the good of each; and a society so constituted that the individual cannot serve himself without serving society, and cannot injure society without injuring himself. Thus there will no longer be altruism and egoism, selfishness and unselfishness, existing as antagonistic abstractions, but selfishness and unselfishness must necessarily be alike social in the general run of conduct.

*Then Socialism does not presuppose a complete change in human nature and the entire elimination of selfishness, as has been so often asserted?*

By no manner of means; on the contrary, Socialism only calls for enlightened selfishness. But the fact that this selfishness *is* enlightened, and recognises that it can serve itself only by serving the common interest, will completely change its character, so that it will cease to be the narrow selfishness of to-day, which so often defeats its own ends. Selfishness passing through the refining fire of economic change ceases to be selfishness and becomes Socialism.

*But if this is so, and if the interests of each individual will, by the force of the new circumstances, be best served by serving the common interests, why do the dominant classes of to-day oppose Socialism?*

Because, in the first place, their whole education and point of view, inherited and acquired, prevent them seeing that they, in common with the rest of society, would be happier under Socialism. Further, with the more enlightened among them the fact that they are in a better position materially than the majority, and the timidity engendered by the knowledge that at any time they may suffer by a change for the worse, makes them fear any change at all, and prefer a known certainty to an uncertainty, on the principle that a bird in the hand is worth two in the bush. The bulk of these classes, however, are absolutely blinded by their class position to the fact itself that they would be happier under Socialism.

*Admitting this to explain the attitude of the dominant well-to-do classes, how is it, then, that the great body of the lower middle and working classes are not, as yet, in favour of Socialism?*

Because up to the present time the great majority of these classes are not class-conscious, and hence do not see the direction in which their real interests lie, or that these interests are in antagonism to those of the dominant classes; still less do they see that they are opposed to the existence of a society founded on classes, altogether.

*You speak of these classes not being class-conscious; what do you mean by that term? Surely if what you call the dominant classes have their own point of view, these others should also have their point of view. Yet we often hear a man declare that although he is not a capitalist, not a bourgeois, but one who has to work for his living, yet he cannot agree with Socialists, but is, on the contrary, an official Liberal, or may be a member of the Primrose League and as much opposed to Socialism as Rothschild, Carnegie, or any other plutocrat. How do you explain this?*

The matter is very simple. The individual who gives this apparently crushing answer that he is not a capitalist and wishes he were, but at the same time cannot agree with the Socialists at all, is still under the domination of the point of view of the ruling classes. Hitherto, throughout history and at the present time, these classes alone are completely conscious of their own CLASS INTERESTS—that is what we mean by class-consciousness. Indirectly in consequence of this, and directly in consequence of their dominant economic position, they have hitherto been able to impose their point of view upon the other classes which are not yet class-conscious, and to make this point of view pass current, not for what it is—a class standpoint—but as standing for absolute morality, commonsense, truth, justice—in a word as representing the welfare of the whole community.

*Give an instance of how a dominant class can succeed in imposing its own moral views upon the community at large.*

To take one among many, it commonly expresses the utmost horror at anything like a forcible revolution; while the very same persons who do this in one breath, will, in the next, complacently discuss the advisability of waging an unprovoked war for the purpose of asserting national supremacy, or for securing fresh commercial outlets. The horror at the human suffering entailed, so eloquently expressed in the first case, evaporates under some phrase such as "necessity" or "inevitability" (which, being interpreted, means desirability from their own class point of view) in the other. They well know that, as possessing classes, they have everything to lose and nothing to gain in a domestic revolution, while in a foreign war they often think they have a great deal to gain, and, as they hope, very little to lose. Once more, on the occasion of the assassination of any potentate or statesman, the public opinion of the possessing class and its organs is lashed up to a white heat of artificial fury and indignation against the perpetrator, while they have nothing but approbation for the functionary—military or civil—who puts to death a fellow-creature in the course of what they are pleased to call his duty; as, for instance, in the execution in cold blood, after the event, of the two Boer prisoners simply for attempting to escape at Pretoria. Evidently force and bloodshed, when contrary to the interests of the possessing class, is a monstrous crime, but when it is in their favour it becomes a duty and a necessity.

*How has the dominant class been thus able to impose its own point of view upon the other classes? Has this been done deliberately on their part—so to say, of malice aforethought?*

In the past, the overpowering influence of the dominant class has been in the main unconscious, it has been due to the position of that class, and has not been deliberately imposed. With the development of capitalism, however, and of the consciousness of class interests as such, the leaders of the dominant or possessing class by means of their control over press, pulpit and platform, deliberately seek to impose as truth, morality and religion the ideas which suit their purpose and best serve their class interests.

*Seeing the importance of this point and the very widespread notion that no man who is not a capitalist can be expected to hold capitalistic views of social relations, will you in a few words recapitulate your position on this matter?*

To begin with, throughout civilisation—that is, that period of human evolution in which class divisions are the special characteristic—the dominant class, necessarily, by reason of being the dominant class, imposes its ideas, principles and views upon the whole of any given society. Such a society must necessarily partake of the character and be moulded by the principles which serve the interests of its master class, or cease to exist as such. This imposition of the will and principles of the dominant class may be done consciously or unconsciously. In the earlier stages of civilisation this class used the speculative and religious beliefs which were held by the general body of the people, and even by itself to a large extent, as a cover and justification for its supremacy as a class; this it did in the main (although not always) unconsciously, and without malice aforethought. Now-a-days, however, there is no illusion in the matter; the dominant classes, working on hereditary feelings, deliberately mislead or "bull-doze" the rest of the people, and this is why the man whose class position should make him a Socialist remains as thoroughly reactionary as any member of the dominant class until he becomes class-conscious, *i.e.,* conscious of his class position and the essential antagonism between the interests of his class and those above him in the economic scale. He then sees through the whole fraud of bourgeois religion, morality and politics. Therefore, although the bulk of the recruits to Socialism will come from the working classes, it makes not the slightest difference intrinsically to a man being a Socialist, whether he be rich or poor, so long as he accepts the principle of the class struggle, and recognises the historical function of the proletariat, as a class, to found a new society. A "horny-handed" son of toil is often an enemy of Socialism and of his class, while a wealthy man may be an ardent and sincere Socialist and champion of the workers, devoting his whole life to the task of their emancipation.

# 34

# "A CHRISTMAS SERMON WHICH THE BISHOP OF LONDON HAS BEEN ASKED TO PREACH IN WESTMINSTER ABBEY ON SUNDAY, DECEMBER 25", *JUSTICE*, 24 DECEMBER 1887, 4.

*Herbert Burrows*

[The programme of the SDF contained no clause attacking organised religion. The socialism it professed was to be a movement of all creeds and nationalities, and Hyndman was among those conscious of the political liabilities attaching to dogmatic atheism and the debunking of Christianity as a form of propaganda. On the other hand, the secularist movement dating from the 1840s was at its peak in the years that the SDF took shape. Formed in 1866, the National Secular Society recorded its highest membership in 1884 (Royle 1980, 134) and secularists were prominent among those who transferred their primary allegiance to socialism itself. As embodied in the figure of the NSS president Charles Bradlaugh, secularism lacked any radical social vision or critique of the existing social order. Socialism provided just such a vision, and as the one movement flourished, the other had already entered its period of decline when it was hit by Bradlaugh's death in 1891. According to a correspondent writing to *Justice* three years later, the doctrine of secularism retained its force but was now known by the name of socialism (Pierson 1973, 72).

Among the active secularists who did subsequently go by the name of socialists, the best-known were Annie Besant, Edward Aveling and Herbert Burrows. Besant's attachment was to the Fabian Society and relatively fleeting; Aveling's successively to the SDF, the Socialist League and eventually the ILP. Burrows could not have been more closely associated with Besant at the time of the match-girls' strike of 1888. Nevertheless, he had been an SDF loyalist from the start, and would remain one for many years to come (see Chapter 40, this volume).

Burrows's imaginary Christmas sermon is faithful to the SDF approach which, as Harry Quelch had argued in *Justice* some weeks earlier, saw clericalism as the enemy rather than Christianity itself (Pierson 1973, 75). Burrows could hardly be said to view Christianity as a friend. He would subsequently maintain that even Turkey, which Christians professed to despise, allowed women a legal status that was preferable to the "pure degradation" of the "orthodox Christian and State idea" (Chapter 40, this volume). Nevertheless, Burrows in his mock recantation seeks to expose the gulf between the religion's ostensible founding principles and their betrayal by the modern Church and a merely "so-called" Christian civilisation.

The historical figure of Christ as social rebel was an ambiguous one to which both secularists and Christian socialists could equally subscribe. On 13 November, a Trafalgar Square demonstration linking the issues of Ireland and the unemployed had been attacked by troops and police and earned the epithet of "Bloody Sunday". The following week, at a demonstration in the square to protest against the violence, a young socialist clerk named Alfred Linnell was knocked down by a police horse. Linnell died within a fortnight, and his funeral on 18 December was the occasion of a solemn public demonstration which concluded with the singing of William Morris's "Death Song":

> They will not learn; they have no ears to hearken.
> They turn their faces from the eyes of fate;
> Their gay-lit halls shut out the skies that darken.
> But, lo! this dead man knocking at the gate.
> Not one, not one, nor thousands must they slay,
> But one and all if they would dusk the day.

The mood of the state and propertied classes had hardened since the surge in subscriptions to the Mansion House Fund following the previous year's West End riots. Burrows's sermon appeared in the same issue of *Justice* as reports of Linnell's funeral. Though less well-known than Morris's "Death Song", its indictment of ruling-class hypocrisy is no less effective.]

## TEXT.

> "Go to now, ye rich men, weep and howl for your miseries that shall come upon you. Behold, the hire of the labourers who have reaped down your fields, which is of you kept back by fraud, crieth; and the cries of them which have reaped are entered into the ears of the Lord of Sabaoth. Ye have lived in pleasure on the earth and been wanton; ye have nourished your hearts, as in a day of slaughter. Ye have condemned and killed the just; and he doth not resist you."
>
> James v., 1, 4, 5, 6.

# A CHRISTMAS SERMON

Fellow Citizens,

The text which I have just read to you, and from which I shall preach the last sermon as a bishop that I shall ever deliver from this pulpit, is one which is probably as unfamiliar to you comfortable, well-to-do people as it is familiar to all those who, since it was originally penned, have toiled and suffered for humanity. Although it is read sometimes in the ordinary course of our church service, yet, judging by your conduct, your ears have been deaf to its terrible denunciations. From the days when I was a humble curate to now, I have had a large and varied experience of cathedrals, churches, preachers and sermons, but I have never yet heard a discourse based on these words, and I cannot learn from any of my brother bishops or priests that they have ever thus used them, or heard them so used. I can see by your uneasy demeanour that you are asking yourselves why, on this Christmas day, when, in accordance with custom, I should be preaching smooth things to you, I should be mad enough to offend your delicate susceptibilities by quoting the sayings of one of the common people—words written eighteen centuries ago—which might have been very well then, but which cannot possibly be applied to you or to your class to-day; you who come here clad in purple and fine linen, who, some of you, live in king's houses, who fare delicately every day, and who consider that you have fulfilled every moral obligation when you have dropped a coin into the collection box, before you step into your carriages to be driven to your luxurious homes. It is because I believe that not only James, but Jesus Christ himself, if he could stand in my place to-day, would hurl these words at you with a force and a passion of which we, in this nineteenth century, have but little conception. Not as a bishop, but as a man I repeat them to you, hardly hoping that they may touch your hearts, but more as a justification for my new and strange position.

For years I have been one of you. My home has been, not where Christ's home was, with the masses, but with the classes. I have an abundance of this world's goods; I have lived with the fashionable and the wealthy, and I have been a dignitary of a Church which is the Church of the rich and not the Church of the poor. Without a protest I have mixed in society with men and women whom Christ would have denounced as bitterly as he denounced the Scribes and Pharisees; in the House of Lords I have silently sat side by side with whoremongers and adulterers, and as silently I have welcomed as my personal friends highborn women, some whom I see before me to-day, with whom no decent workman would allow his wife or daughters to associate. I have seen among you, spreading like a canker, the lust of the flesh and the pride of life, and instead of reproving you as Christ would have done I have taken refuge in specious generalities, and have not dared to denounce your individual sins. And all this time there has been going on around me, in this huge city and throughout the land, the surging, toiling life of humanity—the sorrow, the suffering, the poverty, the disease, the sin and the shame which I realised but dimly as something altogether apart from my own existence, but for which I at last see clearly you and I have, up to the present time, been mostly to blame. We and our class have kept back by fraud the hire of the labourers who have reaped our fields, we have lived in pleasure on the earth and been wanton, we have nourished our own hearts while we have starved the bodies of those to whom we owe the very bread we eat and the clothes we wear, and now we are condemning and killing at our very gates the people whose inarticulate cry is entering into the ears of the Lord of Sabaoth, whose faithful servants we pretend to be.

My Fellow Citizens,—I know not how it may be with you, but for me this careless, selfish life has ended. Little by little I have awakened to the fact that all my days I have almost entirely neglected my real duty to my fellow men, and at last I have come to know that my proper place is not here as a well paid bishop of a Church which, in its present condition, is utterly opposed to everything which Christ taught, but among the poor to whom he declared that the Gospel should be preached, among the labourers whose hire we have kept back by fraud. Too long have I neglected the miserable social facts of our so-called Christian civilisation, too long have I spoken to you smooth things, and cried peace when there was no peace. I have known by repute that there was misery among our people, starvation in our midst and prostitution in our streets; but hitherto I have taken these as something for which you and I were not responsible, but which were really due to the inherent wickedness of human nature. But now I have learned that our pleasures and our wantonness have been built upon these hideous foundations, and having learned this, as you may also learn if you will, I have resolved that from this Christmas day my new life shall begin. To-day I lay down my robes, I give up my bishopric, my palace and my income; I resign my seat in the House of Lords; I give up the pleasures of society and of the world, and at last I take my place as a man among men.

It is, I know, a bold step that I have taken, but I have fully counted the cost. Resolved no longer to live on the labour of others, I shall probably have to join the great army of the unemployed. To-morrow I shall attempt to preach my first sermon to them in Trafalgar Square from the same text that I have used here to-day, and it is likely that I shall pass to-morrow night in a police cell. But, there, I shall be no worse off than Jesus Christ would be if he attempted to enter this Abbey now, for he would be arrested and locked up as a vagabond without visible means of subsistence. To you and to your class he would simply be a labourer whose subsistence you have kept back by fraud. To the abolition of that fraud and of the misery and degradation which result from it I shall henceforth devote my life. It will be no easy task, not nearly so easy as being Bishop of London, but the reward of a good conscience and of noble work well done is better far than a palace and ten thousand a year. In this place I shall probably never speak again, but when Freedom shall have opened out her arms and gathered all men into her wide embrace, and when Justice and Truth shall have taken the place of oppression and of fraud, some man of the people shall stand in this temple of the dead, and, inspired by the best traditions of the past, the noble aspirations of the present, and the ideal hopes of the future, shall send ringing through these lofty aisles that living Christmas message which, till then, can never have its full significance, "Peace on earth and goodwill towards men."

# 35

## *SOCIALISM AND THE SURVIVAL OF THE FITTEST* (LONDON: TWENTIETH CENTURY PRESS [c. 1891], THIRD EDITION, 1910), 1–17.

*J. Connell*

[In the recollections of the ILP socialist Philip Snowden, Jim Connell would lecture frequently on the topic "From protoplasm to man" but never reach the end. "He regarded himself as something of an authority on Evolution … and after two hours' talk he had to stop from sheer exhaustion, with the audience in a state of physical collapse" (Snowden 1934, 72–73). Connell's pamphlet *The Survival of the Fittest* may have something of the same effect on some readers. These are advised to skip to the more immediately contemporary reflections that begin at p. 286 ('The social instinct'). But they are reminded that their forbears had more stamina: this was the third but not the last edition of the pamphlet, and the irreplaceable Working Class Movement Library alone has several, including one issued by the Clapham branch of the Independent Labour Party.

Born near Kells in County Meath in 1852, Connell was not always given to prolixity. He is best known in socialist history as the author of *The Red Flag*. This was first published in *Justice* in December 1889 and later displaced Edward Carpenter's *England Arise* as the anthem of the British labour movement. An inveterate poacher, Connell also gave a lecture on the Game Laws which some doubtless found more immediate and entertaining than the one on evolution. Nevertheless, Connell's exposition is of inestimable value as a document of the socialist movement. It shows just how compelling was the idea of socialism as not only consistent with the teachings of modern science but their necessary corollary in the field of society. It also gives an idea of the breadth and cohesiveness of the socialist world-view, which in the space of a penny pamphlet could stretch from the origins of the species to modern patent law.

Most of all, it is a formidable testimony to the hunger for knowledge of the socialist autodidact. We do not know the details of Connell's education, and it must surely have amounted to more than the "few weeks" which by his own account he spent with itinerant "hedge" schoolmasters (Boyd 2001, 17). Nevertheless, the evidence of self-directed reading lies not only in Connell's text but in the fourth edition which the Twentieth Century Press had issued by 1914. Connell is also a figure to confound all stereotypes. He was anything but dour, and Snowden evokes the image of his enormous moustache, broad-brimmed hat, large red cloak and captivating Irish brogue. A member of the Democratic Federation from its origin, he broke with it in the early 1890s but remained active in the ILP.]

There are people who tell us that Socialism is opposed to the teaching of Science, and that, therefore, it must be unsound. Those people say that the struggle for existence is a physiological law, and that to end it, or even to mitigate its severity, must result in the deterioration of the human species. I desire to say at once that if Socialism were opposed to Science I should immediately reject it. However forcibly it might appeal to the sentimental side of human nature it would not, in that case, be worth supporting. Science is knowledge of the laws of nature. If Socialism were opposed to those laws, even if established, it could not last. Nature, in the long run, always shapes her ends in her own way, and fighting against her is folly, or even crime. But I hold that Socialism is not opposed to the teaching of Science, and I hope to prove in this essay that those who say it is know very little about Science or else very little about Socialism, or perhaps very little about either. I undertake to show not only that Socialism is consistent with the laws of nature, but also that its antagonist, Individualism, as we know it, is utterly inconsistent with those laws. In order to do this it is necessary to explain the natural laws which govern the problem under consideration. A knowledge of the road along which man has travelled in the past will enable us to take an intelligent view of his position in the present, and of the possibilities which are open to him in the future.

## ANTIQUITY OF MAN.

The scientific view is that man is the result of an evolutionary process, and if the reader is to understand this process he must banish from his mind the notion that man was first created about six thousand years ago. There is no desire here of attacking theology, but it is necessary for the purposes of the argument to explain that man lived on this earth not only more than six thousand years ago, but more than sixty thousand, and probably very much more than six hundred thousand years ago. If we were to assume that the world was created only six thousand years ago, as is asserted in certain Jewish documents, then the modern scientific theory of evolution would have to be dropped, as that time would be by no means sufficient to account for the immense changes in structure which, according to the teachings of Science, have taken place in almost all species. It has long seemed to the present writer that the facts, which are obvious to all of us, abundantly disprove the reliability of the so-called Mosaic account of creation. It seems utterly incredible that the different races of men on the earth to-day have differentiated and descended from a common stock in six thousand years. The Negro and the Caucasian, the Patagonian and the Laplander, the timid New Hollander and the innovating Frenchman, the stolid Chinaman and the vivacious Celt, the warlike Red Indian and the philosophical Hindu—can all these have descended from the Adam and Eve of Genesis? Let it be borne in mind, that, according to the book, Adam and Eve were created perfect, and even immortal. Had the apple not been eaten, immersion in the depths of the sea for a week, or blowing to pieces with gunpowder, would not have killed them. To what an appalling extent have we degenerated! Do those who scornfully reject the view that men have evolved from monkeys, or some other of the lower forms, quite realise that, according to the alternative theory with which they provide us, men are fast degenerating into monkeys, and ultimately into something very much lower? Let us leave this part of the subject with just one remark. It is not here contended that God did not make man. The contention is that, if he interfered in the matter at all, God, in making Nature, endowed her with laws and forces capable of producing all the results we see, man included.

Evidences of the antiquity of man are scattered all over the earth. One or two points only can be dealt with here. The proofs furnished by the delta of the Mississippi may be taken first.

The Mississippi delta is a triangular stretch of country beginning at the seashore at either side of the river's mouth, and extending, or rather narrowing, to a point some two hundred miles up the stream. It is formed of alluvial matter deposited in a manner about to be described. The Mississippi, with the Missouri, is the longest river in the world, and is fed by numerous tributary streams. It, in fact, drains an immense area. At some part or other of this area floods are constantly occurring. Everybody knows that floods of even moderate dimensions wash away river banks and bottoms, and carry the solid matter downward towards the sea. Thus is the Mississippi constantly being charged at some point with leaves or grass or earth. As the river and its tributaries take their rise in high altitudes, the water flows rather rapidly and carries the solid matter along. This happens until a point is reached about two hundred miles from the sea. Here a level country is encountered, the river widens, the water flows sluggishly, and the solid matter is gradually but surely deposited on the bottom. It happens that this part of the world is peculiarly adapted for the production of cypress trees. If an area be cleared it will be found to be covered with a cypress forest in a very short time.

We will ask the reader to come back with us in imagination to the time when the conformation of this part of the American continent first became what it is to-day. That which is now the delta of the Mississippi was then a valley, bounded on either side by a row of hills, which the Yankees call bluffs. In flowing towards the sea the river selected as its channel the lowest part of this valley. The solid matter which it brought down was deposited on the bottom, with the result that the river-bed at once began to be elevated. The process was continued until the bed of the river was above the level of the surrounding country. The water, naturally, then sought a lower level, leaving the first bed high and dry. This, in a very few years, was covered with a forest of cypress trees. In the meantime the river began to elevate its second bed, as it had elevated the first. In due course, that also became higher than the surrounding country, was then deserted for a third channel, and soon covered with a cypress forest. It will be sufficient to say that the third and all subsequent channels were treated in the same way as the first two. The river at one time or other flowed over every part of the valley. It could not go outside certain limits because of the bluffs. Every part of the surface was elevated in turn, and in time the first bed, which was deserted because it was the highest part of the valley, had again become the lowest. Then the river returned to it, and found growing there a forest of cypress trees, which it promptly levelled, and soon covered with a layer of the solid matter brought down by the water. In due course this bed was again deserted, and after every other part of the valley had been elevated, was again sought. Enough has now been said to enable the reader to understand the process. The alluvial matter of the valley has been found to be 528 ft. deep, and to contain eleven cypress forests, showing that the river has run over some parts as many as eleven times. The rate at which the matter is being deposited can be measured, and is known. Human remains have been discovered in many parts of the delta, under several of the buried forests, and in one case in a stratum which all geologists are agreed is older than all of them. The minimum time which has elapsed since those remains were deposited where they were found has been ascertained in the following manner. The age of a tree can always be found by counting its rings of annual growth. The geologists took one tree from each of the buried forests, counted its rings, added all together, and got a total of over fifty-seven thousand years. Let it be borne in mind that this is but the minimum age of the remains. Each of the forests may have lived much longer than any one of its trees, longer in fact than a dozen trees, but we know it must have lived as long as one. Besides, in this calculation, no account is taken of the long periods which elapsed between the destruction of one forest and the birth of the next. That enormous mass of alluvial matter probably took hundreds of thousands of years to accumulate. But, taking the minimum named, it follows that fifty-seven thousand years ago men lived in North America. What then must we think of the statement that man was first made less than six thousand years ago?

But one need not go to America to find proofs of man's antiquity. They exist here at home. Near the town of Torquay, in Devonshire, there is a cavern called Kent's Cavern, in a limestone hill, which will probably satisfy the most exacting inquirer. Kent's Cavern is simply a hole in the rock, with a floor of dissolved limestone, commonly called stalagmite. In order that the reader may appreciate the significance of the facts, it is necessary to explain how this substance is formed. Pure water will not dissolve limestone, but a slight admixture of the gas known as carbonic acid will enable it to do so. This exists in the air and in plants. The rain, in falling, acquires a little carbonic acid from the atmosphere through which it descends, and a little more from the plants on which it falls. When it reaches the surface of the hill it percolates through fissures in the rock, dissolving the limestone in its descent, and when the roof of the cavern is reached some of the dissolved matter adheres to it in the form of icicles, whilst the remainder falls to the ground and forms a floor. Where the drip from the roof is great the floor rises like a hillock; where it is slight the floor sinks. It is characteristic of the English people that wherever they go they deface objects of interest with their names, or at least with their initials. The pyramids of Egypt, the catacombs of Rome, and the temples of India are alike disfigured by the names of Smith, Brown and Robinson. It is not surprising that the floor of Kent's Cavern has been treated in a similar manner. Not only names, but dates are to be found carved on the stalagmite with a chisel. Some of the dates are hundreds of years old, and are covered with coatings of stalagmite of various thicknesses. By measuring the thickness of these coatings one can ascertain the rate at which the floor is being formed. One inscription in particular was found at a spot where the drip from the roof was greatest, and where, therefore, the floor was being formed most rapidly. The coating of stalagmite over this inscription, which bore a date, was carefully measured, and the rate of formation thus ascertained. The total thickness of the floor was measured next, and it was then perceived that the latter could not have been formed in less than one million years. Yet underneath this floor, implements made by the hands of man have been discovered. For further information on this subject the reader is referred to the writings of William Pengelly on the Cave Men of Devonshire. Mr. Pengelly superintended excavations in, and paid daily visits to, Kent's Cavern for about twenty years.

It is very clear that if men lived in Devonshire a million years ago, the Mosaic account of man's origin cannot be correct. Reliable information concerning that origin must be sought elsewhere, and we will now proceed to seek it.

## ORIGIN OF LIFE.

For many years, Doctor Otto von Schron, Professor of Pathological Anatomy in the University of Naples, has been making investigations into the propagation and development of bacilli. In the course of his experiments he discovered that living matter, largely albuminous in character, takes the crystalline form, and, while still living and crystalline, obeys so many of the laws, and manifests so many of the properties of inorganic crystallisation, as to leave no doubt whatever of its crystalline character. The conclusion he draws from this is that crystallisation in its terrestrial origin is a manifestation of the force called life force.

There are probably few persons who have not observed what are called frost-ferns on their window-panes in the winter mornings. Many of these objects bear but a slight resemblance to ferns, but if a large number be examined some are sure to be found bearing an astonishing resemblance. The line of research here indicated may be followed up with great profit in the following manner.

Let the reader take a block of ice, say, one cubic foot in extent, and place it on a table. Let him cause a beam of heat to play for some-time on one side of the block. Let him now shut off the heat and apply a beam of light to the same side in such a manner as to cause an image of the melted parts of the ice to fall on a screen. He will find that all parts of the ice have not been melted equally, but that some portions have been singled out for attack and others left comparatively untouched. He will find that the melted parts, as shown on the screen, bear the shape of beautiful flowers, each with six petals. How comes it that crystals contain forms similar to those we find endowed with vegetable life in the gardens and the fields? Ice is simply water solidified. It is water to which nothing has been added, and from which nothing but heat has been taken away. How comes it to contain flower-forms? The explanation is that, in coming together to form a solid, particles of water take their places in obedience to fixed laws. Facts such as this are important, for, in considering the problem of the origin of life they will be found to lie at the very root of its solution. Tyndall told us that he observed those things hundreds of times, and every time was more and more astounded. The observer may begin at the simplest of those crystalline forms and go upward through others more complex. At a certain stage he will encounter characteristics of the vegetable kingdom. The farther he goes above this point the more plentiful will become vegetable characteristics and the more scarce crystalline, until the latter cease altogether, and the observer knows definitely that he is in the region of vegetables. In the same way he can ascend through the vegetable kingdom, passing by easy stages from family to family and from species to species, all closely related. At a certain point he begins to encounter animal characteristics. The farther he goes above this point the more frequently does he meet animal characteristics and the less frequently vegetable, until the latter cease altogether, and he knows that he is in the region of animals. In the same way he can pass through the animal kingdom, from the lowest to the highest, which he will find in his own body. The point to be particularly noted is that between the crystalline kingdom and the vegetable kingdom, and again between the vegetable kingdom and the animal kingdom, there is no dividing line. Tyndall said that the man never lived who could tell where one ends and the other begins. In each case the two kingdoms fit into each other like the cogs of two wheels. We have thus a world of forms showing, from the lowest to the highest, a close and unbroken relation, pointing to a common origin and an evolutionary process. In truth, the life principle is at least co-extensive with the material principle, manifesting itself when the conditions are favourable and disappearing when the conditions are unfavourable.

## THE STRUGGLE FOR EXISTENCE AND THE SURVIVAL OF THE FITTEST.

Other crystals are even richer in forms resembling those described, but, as ice has been mentioned, it may as well be adhered to. Every time a drop of water is frozen such forms are produced. When it is remembered that, every winter, many millions of square miles of water are frozen, some idea may be obtained of the enormous number of those forms which are annually called into existence. If, as we suggest, there be a transition from apparently lifeless crystalline forms to living vegetable and animal forms, then some correspondence in point of numbers must be looked for between the former and the lower species of the latter. This is exactly what we find. As the same laws govern the vegetable and animal kingdoms, there is no need to deal with both in this essay. We will take the latter, as it is the more closely connected with the evolution of man.

Very few persons are aware of the enormous number of simple animal organisms which the earth presents evidence of having produced. The chalk-beds, which cover a huge area, are composed almost entirely of animal remains. Almost all the limestone rock in the world is built up of the same material. In many places the sands of the sea-shore are almost wholly the remains of shell-fish. It will be remembered that in marching across the Egyptian deserts our soldiers were almost blinded by the sand which every breeze drove in clouds. But ordinary sand, which is powdered rock, could not be blow so easily. The sand of the desert, like that of some parts of the sea-shore, is really the remains of shell-fish. All this will help to convey some idea of the prodigious number of simple organisms which this earth has produced. The number, in fact, was, and still is, so great that it is impossible for all to find food. The moment food became scarce, there began among the creatures affected what is known to science as the struggle for existence. Each was endowed with the instinct of self-preservation. Each would live if it could, but all could not live. Each strove against its neighbours, and at this stage the struggle often took the shape of cannibalism. All were not built exactly alike. The differences of structure were minute, but the slightest advantage in strength or activity gave its possessor an advantage in the struggle for existence. The creatures which were least able to cope with the difficulties around them perished, whilst those which were best able to do so survived. This result, common enough to-day, is known to science as the survival of the fittest.

## TRANSMISSION OF PECULIARITIES.

The organisms which survived the struggle for existence were the fittest because of certain peculiarities of structure which gave them an advantage over their competitors. They either possessed organs which the others did not possess, or else they possessed similar organs of superior development. There is in nature a law which may be called the law of the Transmission of Peculiarities which sends such endowments down to posterity. This law is well known to stock-breeders, and bird and dog fanciers. If, for instance, a man wishes to breed a pidgeon to win a prize in a show, he must first ascertain the "points" which are valued by those who act as judges in such matters. If he can find a male and a female bird possessing the coveted peculiarities, he may breed a winner; but if he cannot find such, he stands little or no chance of accomplishing his purpose. The same statement holds good of dogs. The "points" or peculiarities which constitute a dog a prize-winner are frequently transmitted to its offspring, and this causes such animals to be highly valued for stud purposes. One other illustration will suffice. The breed of cattle known as "short-horns" was developed by taking advantage of this law. Stock-breeders noticed that certain animals presenting certain peculiarities possessed certain advantages over their fellows which were valuable for market purposes. They selected male and female animals presenting the coveted peculiarities in the most marked degree procurable, and bred from them. From the progeny of those they again selected animals in which the prized peculiarities were most strongly marked, and bred from them. By repeating the operation sufficiently often a new breed of cattle was obtained, differing unmistakably from any previously known. Let us read the facts of nature in the light of this law.

For the sake of simplicity, let us imagine ourselves back at the first generation of living animal organisms. If the individuals composing it were allowed to breed indiscriminately, the second generation would, in all probability, be an exact reproduction of the first. But they were not allowed so to breed. The weakly, the malformed, the unfit, were killed off by the struggle for existence. The fit only were allowed to survive, and were thus, as it were, selected by nature for breeding purposes. It will now be seen that the second generation was not exactly a reproduction of the first, but, instead, was a reproduction of a selected portion of the first. The peculiarities which constituted fitness in the progenitors were reproduced in the offspring. The second generation was, therefore, an improvement on the first.

## IMMENSE POWERS OF REPRODUCTION.

Among the individuals of the second generation the struggle for existence was as keen as among those of the first. This was the result of the immense powers of reproduction possessed by those creatures. Few persons are aware of the extent of those powers even to-day. The common rabbit, if allowed to breed unchecked, would, in five years, eat up every blade of grass, and, in fact, every green thing in Britain, including the bark of trees. Without inflicting a scratch, it would destroy all other land animals, man included, by starving them out. A single pair of rabbits will easily produce one hundred offspring within a year, and have been known to produce one hundred and sixty within that time. There is no more harmless animal than the sheep, but if allowed to breed unchecked it would in a few years cover the whole land with its progeny. Among animals in a lower stage of evolution the reproductive power sometimes passes all understanding. The female cod will lay 9,000,000 eggs in a season, and experiments made in Trinity Bay, Newfoundland, prove that practically all those may be hatched out successfully. During five years the hatchery men placed in certain bays of that island the almost inconceivable number of 2,500,000,000 young lobsters, all the produce of a small quantity of spawn. The reproductive powers of the salmon are so great that it has been calculated that six couples would readily produce annually as many salmon as are consumed by the whole human race. Other creatures known to science are almost independent of reproductive powers for multiplication. They may be cut up into a great many separate parts, and each part will then become a complete fish. Enough has been said to enable the reader to understand how it happened that what we will call the second generation of animal organisms felt the struggle for existence as keenly as did the first. The result also was similar—the elimination of the weakly and malformed, and the survival of the fittest. The same remarks will hold good of all subsequent generations during the millions of years over which geology shows the earth to have existed. It is a case of perpetual struggle, and perpetual improvement.

If the surface of the globe were all over similar, or if, in other words, it presented only one set of conditions, there would in all probability be only one species of animal. Some one type would prove fitter than its competitors, and destroy them. But the surface of the globe is not uniform. On the contrary, it presents an almost infinite variety of conditions, and sets of conditions. Each set of conditions makes for the evolution of a distinct type. Very frequently the endowments which constitute fitness under one set of conditions would mean unfitness under another. One illustration will prove the truth of this statement. The heron is a bird well known in Britain. It is what we call a wader. Its long legs enable it to walk about with ease in shallow rivers and lakes, and its long neck and beak enables it to catch fish under stones and banks without diving. In short, its structure is such that the bird is admirably adapted for the life it leads. It would live where even a good swimmer and diver like the duck would starve. In a country abounding in shallow ponds every generation would see the type accentuated. Its peculiarities of structure give it an advantage in the struggle for existence. But let us suppose the conditions changed. Let the heron be transported to a country containing little water, where it would be compelled to get its living on dry land. Then it would be found that its long legs and long neck, instead of being an advantage, were an incumbrance, and the previous tendency of natural selection to accentuate those peculiarities would disappear. A different structure would now be found useful in the struggle for existence, and the evolution of a fresh type would begin. Herbert Spencer puts the case very neatly when he says—

> "Any species, when placed under new conditions, immediately begins to undergo changes of structure fitting it for the new conditions."

Again—

> "The degrees of difference thus produced are often, as in dogs, greater than those on which distinctions of species are in other cases founded."

Further he says—

> "This influence would produce in the millions of years, and under the great varieties of conditions which geological records imply, any amount of change."

Material conditions are, however, not the only causes which operate to produce improvement. At an early stage the action of mind becomes a highly-important factor in the process, as we will now proceed to show.

## SEXUAL SELECTION.

It is a fact known to all who have studied the habits of animals that, when they come to pair, the female of most species invariably selects for mate the strongest and most courageous male. This she does, doubtless, for purposes of self-protection; but, whatever the motive, the choice has an important effect on her progeny. Let the reader note that, by the process of natural selection already described, the unfit are eliminated and only the fit allowed to survive for breeding purposes. Now, however, a second weeding-out of the rubbishy element takes place by means of sexual selection. Ultimately, therefore, the progenitors of the species are the fittest of the fit. The selection is not always consciously made by the female. In some species, at certain seasons, the males fight one another. During those battles the females stand apart, timidly awaiting the result. When the fight is over they walk off contentedly with the victor or victors. In both cases the result is the same. The fittest only survive and breed, and in accordance with a law already explained transmit the qualities which constitute fitness to the next generation.

But sexual selection does not affect strength and courage only. At a certain stage the artistic faculty makes its appearance, and the female permits admiration of beauty to modify her choice. The female bird of paradise has such an extraordinary appreciation of beauty that the very slightest advantage in the matter of plumage causes a male to be selected in preference to his rivals. The influence of this habit on the artistic development of the species will be obvious. The plumage of the peacock, the antlers of the stag, and the mane of the lion are all largely attributable to this cause.

## USE AND DISUSE OF ORGANS.

Everybody is aware of the difference in muscular development between, say, the average blacksmith and the average clerk. The difference is greatest in the muscles of the arm. The explanation is simple. The muscles receive nourishment from the blood. The exercise of any organ causes the blood to flow freely to that organ, carrying nourishment, and causing the part to develop. On the other hand, the disuse of any organ impedes the flow of blood there, causing starvation of muscle and decay. An animal of any species will naturally use most, if not exclusively, the organs that are useful to it in the struggle for existence. Food is the first consideration with all animals, man included. Therefore, the organs that are useful in procuring food are developed, those that are not useful in that way decline, and in course of ages become rudimentary. This law helps animals still further to accommodate themselves to new conditions. A statement of it will enable the reader to understand that, in the long run, the conditions determine the type. Rudimentary organs enable the observer to perceive the road along which the species has travelled. They mark the stages of the evolutionary process which has been at work. Occasionally individuals appear having fully or at least fairly-developed organs which are rudimentary in the normal member of the species. These are cases of reversion to an earlier type. Under natural conditions they are rare, but where development is hastened by artificial selection, as in the case of pigeons and dogs, they are very common.

## MAN AND BRUTE.

In a short essay like this it is impossible to enumerate all the facts which have a bearing on the subject under discussion. On that subject books sufficient in point of numbers to form a respectable library have been written. All that is aimed at is the presentation in simple language of a few facts which support the modern scientific theory of evolution. It is hoped, however, that enough has been written to make the broad lines of that theory clear. The contention is that the laws and forces inherent in Nature have in the course of ages evolved all existing species, man included. The reader is asked to note that the explanation of organic existence here given is a natural one, and for that reason alone is infinitely more credible than any theory requiring the supernatural for its support. Miracles and acts of special creation have no place in our philosophy. We do not need them, for we can explain all without them.

The writer feels compelled to point out that the modern scientific theory of evolution is only a small part of the true philosophy of existence. That philosophy will be dealt with in a future essay, when the blanks unavoidable in this will be filled up. The present reasoning is, however, sound as far as it goes.

There is probably no human being alive to-day, whose opinion is of the least value, who will not agree that what are called the lower animals are the result of some such evolutionary process as that described above. But many will insist that man forms a class apart from the others, and that his origin must be sought in some different quarter. Yet the most superficial inspection of the facts will reveal so many resemblances between man and the lower animals that the theories of a different origin, and of accident, are at once perceived to be untenable. Let the reader place side by side a human skeleton and a skeleton of any of the mammalia, and he cannot fail to notice that the two are built on the same general plan. There is not in the human body a single bone, muscle, nerve, or blood-vessel which has not its counterpart in that of the monkey, bat and seal. Every fold in the human brain has its counterpart in that of the orang-outang. The embryo of man, dog, bat, seal, and reptile, are all alike up to a certain point. The human fœtus is hairy. The hairs on man's body are the rudimentary remains of a coat which once covered him. That the ear of man was once pointed is shown by the rudimentary point which is still plainly visible, although turned inward, as in the monkey. Every man possesses a rudimentary tail, and instances are known in which this organ attained a length of several inches. Diseases such as hydrophobia, variola, and glanders are communicated by the lower animals to man, and vice versâ, showing similarity of constitution. Monkeys suffer from consumption, apoplexy, and cataract on the eye, and medicines given them produce the same effect as in man. They like alcoholic liquors, and in their wild state are often captured by means of them. Probably the most striking fact of all is that there are on record cases of human reversion to the ape type. In plain language, apes have been born of human parents.

Let no man feel aggrieved at having these facts set forth. The brute is our younger brother, and should be treated with the consideration due to his relationship and helplessness. Being behind us in the evolutionary journey, he should be treated as we would wish to be treated by those who are before us.

## WHAT IS MEANT BY THE FITTEST.

The reader is warned against concluding that the fittest is necessarily the best. In point of fact is may be the worst. The tape-worm will survive in the human intestines until after the death of the man. Yet nobody would think of saying that the tape-worm was the better of the two. Nature abounds in similar examples: rats, mice, and other vermin will survive a famine which kills off human beings by the million. Therefore, the fittest must be understood to mean the animal or type best suited for the conditions in which it happens to be placed. The fittest means the animal or type best able to conquer the difficulties of its situation. The fittest means the animal or type most in harmony with its environment. If the environment be undesirable the fittest for it will be undesirable also.

## THE SOCIAL INSTINCT.

In the foregoing the writer has almost restricted himself to an exposition of the process of purely physical development. This has been done of set purpose for the reason that it is easier for young students of the subject, for whom this essay is intended, to grasp the evolutionary process if only one aspect of it be presented, and especially if that aspect be the physical one. It is hoped, however, that by this time, the reader perceives that, on the lines indicated, physical development without mental development is inconceivable. The richest physical endowments would be useless to an animal if it lacked the wit to use them. Indeed, it may be said with confidence that, in most situations, an animal physically inferior and mentally robust would easily overcome and survive a rival physically superior, but mentally weak. The same laws operate on the two planes, the physical and the mental. A very little reflection will enable the student to perceive that the struggle for existence improved mind as it improved body. The time has now arrived for stating a further, and, for our present purpose, a more important, outcome of the same struggle.

It is a fact, demonstrated by the trend of modern industry, that, say, ten men working collectively, or co-operatively, will achieve a greater result than the same ten men working individually. What is true of men in this matter is just as true of animals. The tendency to work collectively, even in the most minor degree, gave its possessors an advantage in the struggle for existence. Like all other advantages, physical and mental, this was carefully encouraged and developed by nature. The individuals possessing it survived, and produced offspring after their kind, whilst those lacking it perished. Thus did another aspect of nature, the moral aspect, manifest itself. Bearing in mind that the same laws operate on all the planes of nature, the student will now understand that the struggle for existence which produced physical and mental improvement produced moral improvement as well. Under the influence of this latter product the struggle for existence changed its character in course of time. Low down in the organic scale the struggle for existence operates as between individual and individual; higher up it operates as between group and group. At the bottom of the scale universal cannibalism prevails, but the more clearly defined is any species the stronger is its social instinct. At the bottom of the scale we find pure individualism, whilst near the top, as, for instance, among ants, beavers and bees, we find pure communism prevailing. The intermediate stages are worth noting. Lions and tigers do not rob one another of captured prey. When a young lion or tiger captures, say, an antelope, the older and stronger ones, which could readily take it away from him, will not do so. One does not expect to find much to admire in the ferocious carnivora, but it is worth noting that, whilst they war on all the rest of nature, they spare one another. Enough has been said to indicate that when the individuals comprising a species, or some of them, learn to co-operate they find themselves better able than they had previously been to compete with outside nature, and survive in consequence. Natural selection now acts as between species and species.

Some opponents of Socialism urge that when this stage is reached the weaklings of the co-operating species will have an equal chance of surviving with the strong and healthy, and that, in consequence, progress will be no longer made. Those gentlemen forget that, side by side with physical progress, mental and moral progress are taking place, and that when the stage in question is arrived at the physically unfit will be found strong enough mentally and morally to refuse to transmit their infirmities to posterity by means of procreation. If, as will undoubtedly happen, some are mentally and morally weak as well, then Society may be trusted to control them as it now controls most of its imbeciles. It should not be more difficult for a malformed human being to refrain from transmitting his misfortunes to posterity than it is for a hungry tiger to refrain from robbing his younger brother.

## APPLYING THE TEST.

The foregoing is a simple statement of natural conditions and their results. We will now endeavour to discover which social arrangement conforms most closely to those conditions, and would, therefore, be most likely to be productive of similar beneficent results. The existing arrangement is so well known that it needs little describing. It means individual ownership of land and capital, the materials and implements of production, with its accompaniments of competition, production for profit, and the man-made law of inheritance of property. Socialism, on the other hand, means collective ownership of the materials and implements of production, with co-operation in production and distribution, and provision of employment for all as concomitants. Socialism thus means throwing open to human labour the raw materials of nature, and allowing every man's reward to depend on his exertions. Which of these two conforms most closely to natural conditions? Let us run over the ground hastily. We will take first the struggle for existence. In a state of nature all animals, at starting, enjoy equality of opportunity. It is obvious that under Socialism all men would be similarly situated. No portion of the earth's surface would be the exclusive possession of any man, just as no jungle or forest is the exclusive possession of any tiger or lion. No man would have power to compel other men to work for him, just as no lion can compel other lions to hunt for him. No man would be born into the world to find all his work done for him before he arrived, and the results awaiting him in the shape of his father's accumulations, just as no lion ever inherits anything from his parents except a sound constitution. In short, so far as the struggle for existence is concerned, the conditions under Socialism would be exactly similar to those prevailing in a state of nature. Of course cooperation is not to be found among lions or tigers, but, as has been already pointed out, it is in full swing among such animals as ants, beavers, and bees. It follows from all this, that under Socialism, natural selection would operate as freely among men as among wild animals, resulting in the survival of the fittest, and the improvement of the species. Let us now see how it works under the existing Capitalist arrangement.

To many who are born into the world nowadays, the struggle for existence is unknown. They come to find the table ready spread, and they have nothing to do but sit down and eat, with a silver spoon. Their fathers have earned, or stolen (perhaps we should say "made") more than they will ever require. The struggle for existence does not affect *them*. They will probably survive, whether they are fit or not. They escape the test of fitness which nature imposes elsewhere, and transmit to posterity imperfections which ought to be eliminated. There is no struggle for existence; no survival of the fittest; and, consequently, no improvement of the species taking place among them.

On the other hand, those among us who are born poor are almost as far removed from natural conditions. The children of the poor die off many times more rapidly than do the children of the rich, owing to poor food and insanitary surroundings. They may be among the fittest, but they die nevertheless before they are old enough to take part in the struggle. Those who reach maturity find land and capital, the sources of their food supply, monopolised by others, and production for profit restricts their industry. They are handicapped at starting in the struggle. There is no equality of opportunity here. The test to which they are subjected is not a fair one; and, under the circumstances, failure does not prove them unfit to survive. Whether as affecting the poor or the rich, the conditions are not those which prevail in a state of nature, and in the nature of the case the results must differ as widely as do the two sets of conditions. By means of an artificial social arrangement the process of natural selection is thrown out of operation, and evolution brought to a standstill. We will now deal with sexual selection.

We have already seen that in a state of nature the female selects for mate the strongest and most courageous male. After natural selection has done its work, sexual selection takes up the unfinished task and carries it a step further. The powerful influence of this secondary selection in improving the species is obvious at a glance. The choice of the female is determined by the instinct of self-preservation. It is clear that in a state of Socialism, with conditions similar to those prevailing in a state of nature, sexual selection would operate as it does in a state of nature, and would therefore render valuable assistance in evolving a higher type of humanity. Superior physique, courage, beauty, mental power, and moral worth would all attract the female, and influence her choice, thus assuring to the man of the future an unlimited degree of excellence in these qualities. But how does sexual selection act under Capitalism to-day? The instinct of self-preservation prompts the female to find a mate among the rich, and the latter are not endowed to any exceptional extent with the qualities named. It may be said with safety that a hunchback earl or duke of the poorest mental equipment has to-day a thousand times better chance of begetting children than has the most gifted man who possesses no property. The instinct of self-preservation prompts the female to seek first of all an assured living, and it is not easy to see how this can be found among men of no property, whose own living is precarious. To deal exhaustively with the action of sexual selection under Capitalism would require more space than can possibly be devoted to the point in this essay. Doubtless various reflections will arise in the mind of the reader. For the present it must suffice to point out that, for the rich, the production of children is made artificially easy, and that solely because they *are* rich. If wealth were a mark of superiority, this state of affairs might inspire some hope for the future of the race; but is it? It cannot be argued that it is such in the case of those who are born rich, but we will consider whether those who win their wealth do so because they are superior to their neighbours. Everything in this connection depends on the commercial value of excellence, and excellence may be taken to be of three sorts—physical, mental, and moral. We will deal with them in this order.

What is the commercial value of superior physique to-day? Among manual workers there is no class physically equal to navvies. The work of the navvy is so heavy that nobody but a splendidly-built man can perform it. Very many abandon it after a short trial. Is the navvy better paid than the average labourer? He is; but how much? In the experience of the present writer, the difference in wages in favour of the navvy is about one penny per hour. At first sight that seems an appreciable advantage, but a closer examination will show that it is nothing of the sort. Every owner of horses knows that it costs more to keep a Clydesdale horse than a Welsh pony. The animal is bigger, and requires more food, just as a large steam-engine requires more coal than a small one. The navvy eats more than the average labourer. To perform the hard work which falls to his lot, he must eat good food. If the difference in the food consumed by the two men, both as regards quantity and quality, be taken into account, it will be seen that the navvy, notwithstanding his higher wage, has no advantage whatever over the other. So much for the market value of superior physique.

What is the commercial value of superior mental power? In this connection, the first thought that strikes one is that the majority of men and women of genius, to whom the race owes most, died poor. There is, therefore, to put it moderately, no guarantee that high mental power necessarily leads to what is called "success" in life. Grant Allen says:—

"The man who invents a new stopper for soda-water bottles, a new tyre for bicycle wheels—excellent things in their way—often makes a fortune. So, *oftener still*, does the man who buys the patent from the inventor for next to nothing. But the thinker who discovers some great truth of nature; the worker who invents some valuable surgical appliance, some new anæsthetic, some scientific instrument, some optical improvement, usually makes next to nothing, and sometimes even loses his all in the attempt to perfect and bring out his discovery. In other words, reward is not proportioned to the true worth of the invention or discovery to mankind at large, but merely to its *immediate marketable value*."

The original thinker, the man of genius, the creator, is seldom a match for the wide-awake schemer, ever on the alert to snatch a present advantage. Indeed, the former will generally scornfully refuse to stoop to the artifices of the latter, although well aware that refusal means pecuniary loss or even ruin. The mind of the one man is fixed on pelf, that of the other on things higher and nobler. Each achieves a measure of the success he desires, but that of the vulgar man being, under existing conditions, of more immediate value to him as an individual, he survives and propagates the species, whilst the other often perishes.

What is the commercial value of superior morality? Does not the question sound like a joke? The plain fact is that the moment a man dabbles in commerce he is compelled to discard his morality, or at best reserve it for Sunday use. No man engaged in commerce or finance can afford to speak the truth or act honestly. Those who desire to do so find themselves driven to resort to the tricks and subterfuges of their rivals in order to hold their own in the competitive struggle. One unscrupulous man will drag down every trader in his street, or in his town, to his own low level. There are, indeed, men who loudly assert that their success in business is due to the fact that they always gave full value for the money they received. The assertion is absurd on the face of it. If they had given full value they could never have grown rich. The man who grows rich is the one who succeeds in persuading his customers that he is giving them value for their money, when in reality he is doing nothing of the sort. In short, to succeed in business a man must be utterly heartless and unscrupulous. Shakespeare's Shylock typifies the money-making class. In the competitive struggle as we know it physical excellence counts for nothing, mental excellence counts for little, and moral excellence is simply ruinous. The man who comes to the front is the one with a sleepless greed of gain, a head for figures, and a heart like that of Shylock. This is the type to which we are breeding. Not only are the economic conditions shaping this end, but sexual selection is accelerating the pace in the same direction.

We have already pointed out that the fittest is not necessarily the best. The survival of Shylock to-day only proves that he is the fittest to cope with existing conditions. Let the conditions be altered so as to bring them into harmony with those of nature and Shylock will be the fittest no longer. It will thus be seen that existing economic conditions are the cause of human stagnation, and even retrogression.

It has also been pointed out that in a state of nature the exercise of organs useful in procuring food leads to their development, and that the want of exercise tends to make them decay, and become rudimentary. The rich among us do not need to exercise their organs. The food is already procured. This accounts for the shrivelling process which leads to the frequent extinction of our aristocratic families. Unnatural conditions wipe them out. But if exercise is to be beneficial it must not be excessive. Every athlete knows the danger of over-training. Many among the poor are cruelly overworked. Not only are the hours of work far too many, but the work is too heavy, and is begun at too early an age. The result is degeneracy, physical, mental, and moral, which, if continued long enough, causes all three sides of man's nature to become rudimentary.

The reader will now perceive that the taunt of those who say that Socialism is inconsistent with the laws of nature carries no weight. Not only is it quite consistent with nature's laws, but it is the only social arrangement of which so much can be said. Capitalistic individualism has no prototype in nature, and is therefore unnatural. But some opponent will say, "It is here, and therefore it must be a natural product." The answer is simple. It is here, but it is one of nature's failures. We have seen how, low down in the organic scale, nature makes many failures in order to achieve one success. Sometimes even millions perish in order that one of high type may survive. Nature always accomplishes her purposes in the end. We know that her aim is Communism, for some of the higher species have already reached it, and all are tending towards it. It will come. The reader may stand on the seashore when the tide is rising, and watch the waves as they roll in. He may watch each wave recede apparently to the point from which it started. He may watch a long time without being able to perceive that any advance has been made. But let him wait a little longer, let him wait long enough, and he will see the tide infallibly reach its mark. So does nature work. We know what is coming. To-day Capitalist individualism seems firmly rooted and strongly knit, but the laws of nature are fighting on our side. It may hold its ground for many years yet, but the time is coming when the waves of the evolutionary tide will break and roar far, very far above it.

# 36

# *WAS JESUS A SOCIALIST?* ([1891], HUDDERSFIELD: WORKER OFFICE, c. 1908), 1–15.

*James Leatham*

[It was the Liberal politician Sir William Harcourt who claimed in 1887 that "we are all socialists now". The Fabian socialist William Clarke seized with relish on such an admission of the inexorable momentum of their cause. Even Hyndman seemed to adopt such a position in texts like *Socialism and Slavery* (Chapter 16, this volume). In his pamphlet *Was Jesus a Socialist?* James Leatham has no time for such a blurring of the claims that were distinctive to socialism. More particularly, he has no time for the notion that a socialist ethic was prefigured in the teachings of Christ or of the early Christian church. Leatham's contention is that vaguely socialistic sentiments were the common currency of any number of religions and of none. What gave socialism its distinctive power and meaning was not the sense of discontent and partial redress that Leatham associates with diverse Victorian luminaries ranging from Ruskin and Carlyle to Thomas Huxley. What socialism represented was a social and an economic theory, and one moreover which demonstrated that the moralisation of capital was neither possible nor even desirable.

Like Herbert Burrows (Chapters 34 and 40, this volume), Leatham was a secularist before he became a socialist. It was doubtless as a secularist that he came across the *Life of Jesus* by Ernest Renan (1863) that his pamphlet cites extensively and approvingly. Born in Aberdeen in 1865, Leatham was a printer by trade, and as a militant trade unionist took advantage of his intermittent victimisation to satisfy the hunger for self-education so characteristic of the early socialists (Duncan 2016). At the time that he published *Was Jesus a Socialist?* he was a member of the Aberdeen Socialist Society and formerly one of the Scottish Land and Labour League, which affiliated to the Socialist League. Subsequently he was active in the SDF in Lancashire, and again in the West Riding. In *Was Jesus a Socialist?* he not only rails at the limitations of a Christian credo and morality; he also excoriates its cult of poverty and self-abasement with a scorn of which even Nietzsche might have approved. With the ethical socialism of the ILP still to make its full appearance, it is curiously with the "Anarchist-Communists", who were also such a presence in the Socialist League, that Leatham most identifies this negation of what socialism really signified.

The SDF's overwhelming defect, according to the ILP socialist J. Bruce Glasier, was its "strange disregard of the religious, moral and aesthetic sentiments of the people" (Hunt 1996, 7). Few texts could seemingly have confirmed this point as conclusively as Leatham's. Nevertheless, the force of such stereotypes should once again be treated with caution. Among his prolific output of writings, Leatham would in 1897 contribute a series of articles to *Justice*, published in book form as *Socialism and Character*, specifically addressing socialism's fixation on the social and economic at the expense of the personal and ethical. Like Glasier himself, Leatham both knew and revered the figure of William Morris, and in one of the earliest posthumous tributes extolled Morris's revolt against the moral and aesthetic ugliness of capitalism. The present Morris cult, he wrote on reissuing it in 1903, was a healthy and progressive sign of "gratification in the making of life humane and beautiful for others". Glasier, as it happened, followed a rather similar trajectory; it might similarly be thought that Leatham's pamphlet on Jesus represented a phase of his life that he had by this time left behind him. Nevertheless, the text that is reproduced here is that of the apparently unamended eighth edition issued at Leatham's own instigation when in 1908 he moved to the ILP heartland of Huddersfield as editor-manager of the Worker Press. Leatham would remain a socialist of no particular party attachment until his death in 1945. The Deveron Press which he founded has lately been revived and published a centenary edition of ten volumes of Leatham's writings.]

> So far from contemplating any purely political revolutions, it is quite certain that the early Christians expected everything from the multiplied conversions of individuals, and troubled themselves very little about changes of Government. Whatever reforms were to be effected in society were to be wrought by moral influences, by persuasion, by spiritual regenerations. In the decisive words of their greatest leader, they "wrestled not against flesh and blood, but against principalities, against powers, against the world-makers of this darkness, against the spiritual hosts of wickedness in the heavenly places."
> —W<small>ALTER</small> W<small>ALSH</small>.

That Christianity is clearly Socialistic is an opinion widely held. Church-going folk who take no interest in politics, who are opposed to some of the mildest instalments of social reform, and who are certainly above all suspicion of being themselves Socialists, are quite ready to say that Jesus was the first and greatest Socialist the world has ever seen. When we hear of Christian Socialism and of a Society of Christian Socialists, we accept both the theory and the organization as the most natural thing in the world. To those who believe in the Socialism of

Christianity, or the Christianity of Socialism, it never seems to have occurred to ask themselves: If there be so much Socialism in Christianity, and that Socialism so explicit, why is it that those who most diligently study and expound, and mostly believe, the doctrines of Christianity, should be among the most bitter and unreasonable opponents of Socialism? Why is it that Christianity has not produced as rich a crop of Socialist thought and Collectivist institutions as it has of bigotry and persecution, of cant and Phariseeism, and of the almsgiving misnamed charity? It cannot be pretended that Christianity has not had long enough time to effect any good it was capable of doing. For nineteen hundred years it has had an opportunity of regenerating the world; yet still the Christian world is a place in which every man's hand is against his fellow, in which we still have the sword which the Jewish carpenter promised, in which we still look in vain for the peace which he seemed to suppose would follow the sword, in which, industrially, the son is set more than ever against the father, and the daughter and sometimes the mother more than ever against both father and son, as witness Cradley Heath, Dundee, and the sweating system everywhere.

Of course there are many passages in the Bible that are distinctly favourable to Socialism. Socialism is as wide as it is true; and as there is necessarily an enormous amount of truth in a body of tenets so extensive as Christianity, it cannot help favouring and supporting Socialism at many points. But Christianity does not stand alone among the religions of the world in that respect. In Mahommedanism as in Christianity, in the Koran as well as in the Bible, are statements that are strikingly Socialistic. In the Golden Sayings of Confucius, as well as the Parable of the Vineyard, you will find refreshing enunciations of the natural equality of man. In the religious polity of the North American Indians—simple and limited as it would be—one finds as sound a theory of man's birthright in the soil as is contained in even the Land Laws of Moses; and pagan Plato and heathen Lycurgus had each of them a far more detailed and rational theory of social relationships than the author of the Sermon on the Mount or any of his immediate followers.

Were Socialism a vague gospel of discontent, did it consist merely of denunciations of social abuses or passionate assertions of the brotherhood of man, then Jesus would have some claim to be considered a Socialist. But the grand feature of Socialism is, not that it pillories injustice and asserts the brotherhood of man, but that it propounds a certain scheme of social organisation by means of which injustice will cease to be, as it is now, a *necessity* of our social system, and the brotherhood of man will for the first time have an opportunity of showing itself to be a fact instead of an empty sentiment. At no time has it been difficult to get men to agree that the world's affairs were much out of joint. The difficulty has been rather to get them to agree as to the method of setting the dislocated parts. And now, when we have evolved a great, many-sided, and comprehensive plan, on the essentials of which the Social-Democratic party is agreed the wide-world over, it behoves us to set store by our ideal, and to preserve it from association with either harmless error or dangerous perversion. When men of intelligence suppose that Socialism means the giving "a good price for a good article," mere political

Republicanism, State Insurance, Free Education, or a Graduated Income Tax, when the brazen-faced upholders of the existing order of things come forward and say, "We are all Socialists now," and everybody briskly applauds the statement as if they had known it all along—it is necessary that we should state in no uncertain terms what is and what is not Socialism, and who are and who are not Socialists.

Socialism means the socialising of the means and instruments of production, distribution, and exchange. For the individual capitalist it would substitute, as the director and controller of production and distribution, the community in its organised capacity. The commercial and industrial chaos and waste which are the outcome of monopolistic competition would give place to the orderliness of associated effort; and under Socialism society would for the first time in history behave like an organism. This briefly indicates the social theory of Socialism; but it has also an economic theory. This theory is founded on the dictum of Adam Smith that "Labour creates all wealth; therefore to Labour all wealth is due." But it differs from Political Economy in this important respect; that it does not recognise the capitalist as in any sense a labourer. It admits the theory that capital is stored-up labour; but it denies that this stored-up labour is the labour of the capitalist. Socialism regards the capitalist proper, not as a useful captain of industry, but as a mere shareholding, dividend-drawing parasite upon labour, and the Socialist party presses forward to his elimination from the field of production and exchange. It claims complete equality of rewards for all members of society, not on any theologico-metaphysical ground such as the Christian abstract principle of brotherhood, but because it sees men to have on the whole the same natural endowments and the same natural needs. It looks upon all the phases through which society has passed as natural and inevitable stages in a long evolutionary progress. In its criticism of existing institutions it attacks, not individuals, but systems—regarding the domestic servant as a burden on society as well as his or her idle master or mistress, the compositor who sets catchpenny advertisements as a parasite differing only in degree from the quack who pockets the pennies caught, or from the idle rich person who does not even invent a quack medicine.

If these be the basic truths and methods of Socialism, then certainly Jesus was no Socialist. To be discontented with things as they are, to rail at the rich, to flatter the poor, to declare the brotherhood of man, and to prophesy that it will one day be realised—these things do not constitute a man a Socialist. That which differentiates the Socialist from other men is that, while he describes and denounces the things that are, he has a plan for getting rid of that which he condemns. Socialism has not had to formulate all its own gospel of discontent—its own body of critical and negative doctrine. Spencer, Huxley, and Sir Lyon Playfair condemned our educational system. Mr. Gladstone, in introducing a Budget, laments the fact that, "while there is a decrease in the consuming power of the people and an increase in the privations and distress of the labouring class and operatives, there is, at the same time, a constant accumulation of wealth among the upper classes, and a constant increase of capital." Ruskin thunders at the degrading ugliness of our physical surroundings. He batters at the Moloch Gain, and points to the inequity of a capitalism which no longer captains industry, but merely invests money and draws dividends. Huxley and Mulhall inveigh against the slums, and compare unfavourably the life of the slummite with that of the savage. The Herbert Spencer of sixty years ago showed by irrefragable logic the injustice of private property in land. Carlyle condemns *Laissez-Faire,* Party Governments, and Unworking Aristocracies. But though they are discontented with things as they are, Carlyle, and Ruskin, and Spencer, and Huxley, and Gladstone are not Socialists. Socialism embodies the discontents of all these critics, but Socialism has the advantage in that it lays its finger on the causes and sets forth the cures of the evils it sees, instead of bewailing them with for the most part, hopeless and helpless pessimism. It is the affirmations of the Socialist that make him a Socialist, not his negative criticism. It is his positive creed that distinguishes him from other critics. And Jesus gave no indication of having any knowledge of, or belief in, the constructive creed of Socialism. He could not well have had.

In the recorded sayings of Jesus there is no recognition of the fundamental axiom that wealth is created by labour, and that it ought to belong to those who make it. We meet, instead, with passionate abuse of the rich and empty blessings on the needy. Socialism regards poverty as a curse, blasting men, women, and children with its degrading influence; but Jesus said, "Blessed are ye poor." Socialism recognises that wealth is a good thing, and it exists for the purpose of securing a better share of it for the "blessed" poor. But Jesus thought that the mere necessaries of life were enough for anyone, and himself practised a Spartan simplicity of living. Socialism declares that all ought to work, but Jesus did no manual work after he was thirty years of age, and he encouraged his disciples to leave their occupations, to wander about, and to beg, and this last feature of discipleship has in all ages been well maintained. Socialism would give freely the best education to all: Jesus says nothing of that. Socialism incites the workers of all countries to unite for the prosecution of the class war; but Jesus approved of obedience, contentment, and humility of spirit. Jesus said, "Blessed are the meek, for they shall inherit the earth"; but Socialism says, "So long as the workers are meek, not they, but the arrogant and proud, shall inherit the earth." Socialism would put an end to hunger, destitution, and crime; but Jesus was content to preach the feeding of the hungry, the clothing of the ragged, and the visiting of those in prison. Socialism would make rich men an impossibility: Jesus could only say, "Sell all thou hast and give to the poor"—a superficial proposal, which left the sources of inequality and poverty untouched, and was unworkable besides, as if all should sell, who would buy?

Much capital is made of the equalitarian doctrine conveyed in the Parable of the Vineyard; but to pay the same wage to the man who begins work at the eleventh hour of the day as to the man who begins at the first hour is economically impossible in an individualistic, competitive system of production, which offers the bankruptcy court to him who would give two hours' pay for one hour's work.

It may be said—indeed it has been said—that if a particular social system does not permit of individuals carrying out the law of Christ in it, then that is its condemnation; and it is the duty of Christians to alter it so that the law of Christ *may* be carried out. But what is the good of asking people to practise that which you know and they know to be impossible *until* the alteration of the scheme of society is brought about? If they can only achieve the possible with difficulty, are they likely, on any wide scale, to attempt the impossible? Mere discontent and moral heroics without feasible plans of reform are worse than useless; for they beget in the minds of practical people an aversion to all reformers whatever, whether their plans be feasible or not.

The fact is, the average Christian has no conception, as Jesus probably had no conception, of any other method of reforming society than by reforming the individuals composing it. But individual improvement—important though it be—is not all-sufficient. One can conceive of a society composed of men and women of high altruistic feeling being driven by sheer force of bad social arrangements into the most anti-social practices in trade and public life. Society has a corporate existence which is above and beyond, but which still comprehends and dominates, the life of the various units composing society. As a cathedral is more than a heap of stones and timber, so a commonwealth is infinitely more than all the people composing it. It is not enough to have every individual a law unto himself. The relationship of the citizens to one another must be regulated in many essential matters. The mere jostle and jumble of individual instincts and impulses will not produce a harmoniously working social organism. One policeman at a crowded crossing can accomplish by a wave of the hand what could not be secured by filling all the draymen and cabmen choke-full of the virtues of charity, humanity, and self-sacrifice. Christianity has, or at any rate had, its message to the individual; but it supplies nothing that can by any possibility take the place of those civic "rules of the road" which the system of Social-Democracy provides.

To lecture the capitalist to-day because he does not practise the ethics of the Parable of the Vineyard is to attempt to hold him responsible for a system which he has less power to alter than his workers have, since they are many and he is but one. The Moralisation of Capital was perhaps the only thing Jesus could preach in his day; but Socialism has something to offer which is more to the purpose. The Socialist does not believe in the moralisation of Capital. He believes that the only moralised capitalist is the defunct or the bankrupt one; that the only way in which Capital can cease to be immoral is by ceasing to be Capital. I am using no merely wild and whirling words. I mean what I say in sober earnest. For what is the capitalist's *modus operandi*? In fixing prices, so much is allowed for material, so much for labour, so much for use (or depreciation) of machinery, so much for rent, insurance, and, in short, all the legitimate items in the total cost of production. After everything has been included in the estimate, an additional item is set down. That item is profit; and if the capitalist were asked why he added that, his only truthful answer would be that he did so because everyone else did it. That is to say, all other capitalists rob the community, and he is entitled to rob it also. Socialists do not blame him. It is all in order and part of the system. But they propose that society should take the business of supplying its own wants into its own hands. That is all.

Supposing the average employer, full of a Christlike unselfishness, were to divide up his profits among his employés, accepting the wages of a workman himself, what would be the net economic gain to his "hands"? There are 250 of them, and his profits amount to £2,500 a-year. The partition of this would mean that each worker would get £10 extra a-year—3s. 10d. more a-week! Does anyone suppose that we wish to turn the world upside down to secure 3s. 10d. a-week more to the worker? If anyone does, let him disabuse his mind of the idea. That is the very most that could be effected by the so-called moralisation of capital. But Socialism is more ambitious. It recognises that the worker suffers, not alone by what is taken from him by the capitalist, but by what is taken from him by the landlord and the professional man as well; and it not only proposes to stop all the stealages, but, above all, it proposes to stop the wastes. The waste of having a class of idle rich. The waste of a class of unemployed poor. The waste of having ten men doing one man's work in superfluous bread vans and coal and milk carts. The waste of insurance agents, hawkers, and sturdy beggars. The waste involved in advertising, with its armies of printers, lithographers, artists, papermakers, sandwich-men, bill-deliverers, bill-posters, painters, iron-workers, enamellers, carpenters. The waste of railway labour in superfluous competitive lines. The waste of thousands of commercial travellers. The wastes of tens of thousands of unnecessary shop assistants. The waste of material embodied in unnecessary shops, banks, and warehouses. The waste of overseers, book-keepers, and timekeepers in a hundred scattered establishments whose products, if wanted at all, could be turned out from under one roof, with enormous saving of labour. In a word, all the waste arising from lack of organisation and consolidation in the processes of life. Can anyone fail to see that if this misused wealth and this physical and mental energy were saved by being directed into useful productive channels we should as communities become richer to a degree at present incalculable? And the civic "rule of the road" which Socialism offers will alone effect these great ends.

I elaborate this point as to the necessity of an ordered civic life because a great many people appear to think that it does not much matter whether they take an interest or active part in politics or not. Their opinion would appear to be that politics do not much avail; that personal character, not institutions, is the essential thing. Arnold held this view in England, Emerson held it in America, Sainte-Beuve held it in France, Goethe held it in Germany. Now, while fully alive to the importance, the indispensableness of sound character and right conduct in the individual, I can only say that the view these gentlemen take of public affairs is to my mind contemptibly short-sighted and even selfish, and it has the effect of leaving politics very largely in the hands of the class of men least fit to be trusted with the conduct of great affairs. But short-sighted and selfish as it *now* is, it is evidently the view that Jesus held. As Renan says:

He paid tribute to Cæsar in order to avoid disturbance. Liberty and right were not of this world. Why should he trouble his life with vain anxieties? Despising the earth, and convinced that the present world was not worth caring for, he took refuge in his ideal kingdom; he established the great doctrine of transcendant disdain, the true doctrine of liberty of souls, which alone can give peace. . . . The revolution he wished to effect was always a moral revolution.

And again:

To establish as a principle that we must recognise the legitimacy of a power by the inscription on its coins, to proclaim that the perfect man pays tribute with scorn and without question, was to destroy republicanism in the ancient form, and to favour all tryanny. Christianity in this sense has contributed much to weaken the sense of duty of the citizen and to deliver the world into the absolute power of existing circumstances.

And yet again the great Frenchman says:

That which in fact distinguishes Jesus from the agitators of his time, and from those of all ages, is his perfect idealism. Jesus, in some respects, was an Anarchist; for he had no idea of civil government. That government seemed to him purely and simply an abuse. He spoke of it in vague terms, and as a man of the people who had no idea of politics. Every magistrate appeared to him a natural enemy of the people of God; he prepared his disciples for contests with the civil powers without thinking for a moment that there was anything to be ashamed of.[1] But he never shows any desire to put himself in the place of the rich and powerful. He wishes to annihilate riches and power, but not to appropriate them. He predicts persecution and all kinds of punishment to his disciples; but never once does the thought of armed resistance appear.

Renan is right. If Jesus can be claimed by any social sect to-day he can most fittingly be claimed by the Anarchist-Communists. Unlike the Socialist, Jesus expressed no desire to amend the political institutions of his country. His social ideal involved no alteration of the laws. The small community of kindred souls sharing all things in common was to him the perfect social aggregate. The legislator, the judge, the "officer" would have no place in his scheme of society. There would be no legal compulsion enforcing compliance with its general arrangements. It would be based on voluntary association alone. All these are distinctive features of the ideal of Anarchist-Communism; and Anarchist-Communism and Socialism are as wide as the poles apart.

Living under the empire of the Cæsars, a unit among a subject people possessing no political power, it is not surprising that Jesus should be no politician. But the gradual conquest of political status by the proletariat opens up a field of civil and moral achievement such as Jesus could not hope to compass for Israel in his lifetime. And the commercial and industrial developments of modern times suggest forms and methods of social organisation such as could not have presented themselves to the Galilean peasant, simple as he was, with all his dignity, his serious wit, and his command of graphic illustration.

The injunction, "All things whatsoever ye would that men should do unto you, do you even so unto them, for this is the law and the prophets," has been extolled as the very pith of Socialist ethics. It has been denominated the Golden Rule, and the credit of its authorship has been accorded to Jesus. But the same truth is enunciated in the Rig Vedas, supposed to be the oldest writing, or collection of writings, in existence. In one form or another it is to be found in the writings of Homer, Hesiod, Herodotus, Xenophon, and Isocrates. Confucius distinctly enunciated the so-called Golden Rule. In Dr. Legge's translation of the Confucian Analects we read, page 266: "Tsze-Kung asked, saying, 'Is there one word which may serve as a rule of practice for all one's life?' The master said, 'Is not reciprocity such a word? What you do not want done to yourself do not to others.' " In his article on Confucius, in the *Encyclopædia Britannica,* Prof. Legge—who as a Christian missionary shows little disposition to accord even bare justice to the Chinese sage—admits, "It has been said that he only gave the rule in its negative form, but he understood it also in its positive and most comprehensive force." I am calling attention to these things because I have long believed that the only doctrines peculiar to, and distinctive of, Christianity relate to forms and ceremonies of little value.

But even supposing the Golden Rule were peculiar to Christian ethics, what is its value as bearing upon the organization of society and the conduct of its individual members? It is rendered of little or no effect by its want of concreteness. It can only be of effect as a canon when men have agreed among themselves that a particular action is immoral. The American Indian looks upon the scalping of his vanquished foe as a perfectly righteous deed; and when the fortune of war places him in a similar position he accepts the inevitable with stoical fortitude as a matter of course. He leaves a scalp-lock for the convenience of the victorious brave, and would probably despise the warrior who neglected to take his scalp when the opportunity came. He is bound to feel that scalping is painful and disagreeable; but his normal sense has not yet condemned the practice, or it would be discontinued. In like manner the landlord does not object to the capitalist's profit, nor the capitalist, as a rule, to the landlord's rent: each regards the other as a necessity of the system, each would do as is done by the other were the positions reversed. But the community in general comes more and more to look upon both as parts of a system prejudicial to the best interest of mankind. The Golden Rule remains inoperative *until men agree as to the thing that should not be done by one man to another*. And then the general principle is no longer needed, because the case is covered by a particular rule.

The blessing pronounced upon the poor by Jesus is sometimes interpreted as meaning that he regarded the poor as honest; and his other saying, "It is easier for a camel to pass through the eye of a needle than for a rich man to enter into the kingdom of heaven," is quoted as showing that he believed there was a curse connected with the riches of the rich man because they were based on robbery. But I contend that robbery is a matter of intention, and on that understanding I say the poor are no more honest than the rich; for if the poor are not rich it is only because they can't help it. They are naturally anxious to become rich, and to leave the honesty and its contingent blessings with others. Here and now in the name of Socialism I deny and protest against the idea that the poor are blessed and the rich cursed. To admit that this is true is to take the *raison d'etre* out of Socialism. There are vices, there is degeneration, and there is punishment inseparable from riches and luxury; but there is vice, and pain, and punishment, and degradation associated with poverty in a tenfold degree. Some people may see in the consignment of Dives to hell and Lazarus to heaven *after* death a kind of poetic justice; but the point for us to note is that while the ultimate destinations of both Dives and Lazarus are alike hypothetical, there can be no doubt at all about the fact that the positions are reversed in *this* world—that it is Lazarus and not Dives who is in hell here and now. One of our song-writers says:

> They live in splendid mansions,
> And we in hovels vile,
> Their lives are spent in pleasure,
> And ours in cheerless toil.
> They jaunt about the world, while we
> Are pinned down to one spot,
> But we'll turn things upside down, we will:
> It's time, lads, is it not?

And though we have no great fondness for Christianity, we cannot help answering in the language of its scriptures, "Yea, verily."

We see the rich living in fine houses, wearing fine clothes, and eating and drinking of the best that sea and land afford. We see their women with clear complexions, well-knit figures, sparkling eyes, good teeth, and with an appearance of animation and enjoyment of life which we covet for our own daughters. We see their young men tall, graceful, and athletic in figure; and we see the lords of the earth themselves portly, ruddy, erect, and self-satisfied; and then if we are the kind of person who thinks, we make our comparisons. We see the man of toil with his bowed and twisted body, his round shoulders, his legs bent with much standing and moving about under heavy burdens; we see his enlarged feet and hands, his shot joints, his lack-lustre eyes, his grey, sapless, long-suffering face. We see the mothers of the race of men that is to be come in from the country, and go into the factories with rosy cheeks, tight figures, fairly good teeth, and a tolerably well-conditioned look on the whole. But after they have been there for some months the good colour fades, the skin grows sallow, the appetite is equal only to tea and buns, the teeth decay, the form becomes scraggy, the voice harsh and querulous. And a few years after this woman is married and has become a mother, we see her outside the public-house door, with her youngest born in her arms, waiting for the unhappy being she calls her husband—hoping that at least one half of his wages will be left when closing time comes. And he, poor wretch, has gone there because he is physically and mentally exhausted—used up with the day's work—and because he knows that a false renewal of his vitality can be obtained there. Glass succeeds glass or pint follows pint until he staggers forth to meet the worn, patient creature who dumbly waits his coming without. Maddened by the fiend which has possession of his faculties, and unable to bear the poignant reproach which her presence conveys, he lifts his grimy hand and strikes the brutal blow. All this we see, and by the love we bear our mothers and sisters, our sweethearts and wives and daughters, if these be the blessings of poverty we shall do what in us lies to raise up in our midst the curse of plenty; for of the blessings we have had more than our fill!

Jesus uttered many things that were emotionally favourable to Socialism; but of the grand truth of associated effort, of organisation and combination for the attainment of a given end, he has said nothing. He spoke to men as individuals having personal lives to be ordered, not as members of a society which had a *corporate* life requiring to be ordered. Some of the leading social truths of Christianity are to be found in the Epistles of Paul; and even these have had much more meaning imported into them than Paul intended them to convey. Of such a character is the famous saying, "If any will not work neither let him eat." (I quote from the R.V.) This, however, was addressed only to the Thessalonians, one of the communistic churches and societies of the early Christian days; and it is exceedingly doubtful whether Paul would have had it apply to society in general. It is well enough known that, although the early Christians lived together on the communistic plan, it was not necessarily because they believed that to be the best form of society for all men and for all time, but because they were persecuted when dwelling among other men, and thus found it convenient to unite their means and their numbers, and draw apart from other men. Above all, they lived in daily expectation of the Second Coming and the Crack of Doom, and it mattered not to them what became of their worldly possessions, since they would enjoy them for so short a space of time. The most Socialistic utterance to be met with in the whole mass of Christian writings is the following passage from 1 Corinthians:—

> The body is not one member, but many. If the foot shall say, Because I am not the hand I am not of the body, it is not therefore not of the body. And if the ear shall say, Because I am not the eye I am not of the body, it is not therefore not of the body. If the whole body were an eye where were the hearing? If the whole were hearing, where the smelling, But now hath God set the members each one of them in the body, even as it pleased him. And if they were all one member, where were the body? But now they are many members but one body. And the eye cannot say to

the hand, I have no need of thee; or again the head to the feet, I have no need of you. . . . And whether one member suffereth all the members suffer with it, or one member is honoured, all the members rejoice with it.

These are the words of Paul, and they might have been made the biologico-metaphysical groundwork of much sound Socialistic theorising; for they affirm the complete solidarity and inter-dependence of the various members of the body politic.[2] But their application is confined to the Church alone; and for our statements of sociological truth we had to wait for More and Bacon, for Hobbes and Harrington, for Campanella, and Cabet, and Louis Blanc, and Herbert Spencer, and above all, to the Socialists of our own day and generation.

That Jesus spoke to his hearers as men and women who had souls to save, and not to citizens who had a social ideal to realise, is shown by his command, "Be ye perfect." It is clear that he believed his message to have such potency and power over the minds and the conduct of men that by its influence they could be elevated above their surroundings and made superior to the accident of birth, natural endowments, and conditions of life and labour. He had no plan of social reorganisation apart from the spiritual awakening and reforming of the individual men and women to whom he spoke. We may well forgive the great preacher who moved the multitude at will if he failed to appreciate how largely his hearers were the creatures of circumstances, the products of their environment. But that is no reason why we should give him credit for being possessed of ideas he did not entertain. Indeed, it is not fair to Jesus to say that he was a a Socialist; for had he been so we could never forgive him for neglecting its fundamental concrete truths. General Booth came to the conclusion that it was no use trying to save men's souls until their bellies were filled; and this social lesson he learned, not in the pages of Scripture, but in the slums of London, and from the inexorable facts of his experience there.

To fall back upon Christianity for aid and confirmation to Socialism is like turning to the sonnets of Shakespeare or the roundels of Swinburne for confirmation of the science of mathematics. Socialism is grand enough and strong enough to stand without Christian props. It is about as reasonable to speak of Christian Socialism as it would be to speak of Christian Arithmetic or Christian Geometry.

What help on the emotional side of Socialism we can get from Christianity we are prepared to take; but while we recognise that no popular movement can succeed without sentiment, let us not forget the substantial part of our creed for the sake of its accidents. We admire the Jewish Carpenter, not as a juggler who turned water into wine, raised the dead, or cast out devils; not because he declared himself to be the only-begotten Son of God; not because his language was extravagant, and he himself manifestly lacking in the humility which he enjoined on others; not because he hardly ever delivered a good injunction without giving a wrong reason for it. We admire him because he held a higher ideal of life than to suppose it was given to be employed in mere getting and spending; because he said, "Man lives not by bread alone"; because he could not brook to see the sins of those in high places, but must needs denounce the wrong he saw at whatever risk of loss and suffering to himself; because he discerned that man was intended to be happy here and now; because he loved Nature, and believed that men did well to consider the lilies; because in his own way he proclaimed and he practised equality; because, advising men to take no thought for the morrow, he declared his conviction that in a well ordered society men should not require to live with the fear of want constantly before them, and scorned the miserly economy developed in men by that fear. He was brave, he was a nonconformist, he had an electric personality, a great gift of speech, a steady and unfaltering love for the people. As Socialists we cannot help loving this man; and if we discriminate as to the value of his teaching, it is done with an intention which he himself would probably be the first to commend.

And if we are in some measure doing the work which he might have done had his times been different, and had social evolution brought society nearer the dawn of justice, we may be pardoned for pointing out his own defects and the defects of his teaching. The chief of these is that he spoke so obscurely that misapprehensions were inevitable; and the fruits of this we can see in the church and society of to-day. He enunciated many truths none the less valuable because they were not original; but in his recorded sayings there is much chaff mixed with the good grain. He was unfortunate in respect to those who took up his work after he disappeared from the scene; for they still further contributed to cover the good grain with chaff. And the chaff remains; and Christianity, through the mystical plausibility and absolutism of its founder, has become so distorted that it is like a set of manacles fastened upon the minds of those who believe in it. It is vain for us to look for aid from the church and Christianity until we no longer require it. It might be supposed that a hungry Christian would rebel against his hunger as readily as a hungry Atheist. But it is not the case, and we cannot doubt the facts of general experience. As George William Foote, one of the latter-day victims of Christianity, once wrote to me, "Christianity trains a race of mental slaves."

Personally I feel called upon to attack Christianity as I would any other harmful delusion. I do not believe in the theology of Jesus any more than I do in his sociology. It is no use pretending that Socialism will not profoundly revolutionise religion. The change of the economic basis of society is the more important thing to strive for; but if the triumph of the Socialist ideal does not crush supernatural religion, then we shall still have a gigantic fabric of falsity and convention upon which to wage war. Happily Christianity becomes less and less of a power every day. The Bible has been used to aid and justify so many horribly wicked and so many absurdly foolish things that when the Christian Socialist tries to recommend his Socialism out of the pages of Isaiah or Amos, the Sermon on the Mount or the Epistle of James, men only laugh. So far, indeed, from Christianity being able to support Socialism, it goes hard with Christianity to stand by itself. As a support to Socialism it would surely prove a broken reed.

It is a splendid tribute to the picturesque vitality of the figure of Jesus that he should have been claimed by all reformers, all schools and sects and parties in turn, from Massaniello, the poor, illiterate, revolutionary fisherman of the seventeenth century who, in widely dissimilar circumstances, likened himself to Christ;

from that versatile journalist of the French Revolution, Camille Desmoulins, who acclaimed Jesus as "*le bon sansculotte*" (the good breechless one!), down to the Owenites, Chartists, Land Nationalisers, some of the Anarchists, and many of the Socialists of to-day. But while we own the influence of Jesus as a martyr, as a coiner of moral aphorisms and picturesque parables, let us avoid the futility of reading into his teaching that which is not there and which would be incongruous if it were. Let us make a stand against this persistent hankering after a Christian sanction for a system which carries its own exceeding great recommendation if darkeners of counsel would but hold their peace.

Why this continual harking back to the first century for our intellectual inspiration and our social and manly ideals? Why should men who deny that Jesus was God persist in attributing to him foreknowledge such as is not given to men? Who was this Galilean carpenter from a naked home in a sordid little town that he should recognise social relationships not suggested by the life of the time, relationships which did not occur to men, either before or after his day, who had better opportunities of foreseeing them, and were well equipped by learning and ability to expound them to the world in a classic and enduring form? Rustic as he was, how could he be capable of anticipating great social principles which could only be suggested by a complex social system and to such a system only could apply? Can we produce no wiser, braver, more heroic soul to-day in the vaster and more varied life of our great modern communities? What is there in a Jew to-day to suggest that Israel was the one people of all the earth to produce the perfect man? With our teeming populations, our striking social contrasts, our education, our mechanical progress, with the accumulated lessons of history to show how men and nations failed and succeeded, with all the rich store of experience and all the examples of heroism that lie behind us, prompting to emulation and fortifying to dare, and do, and suffer, can we produce no human type before whose words and works the name and fame of Jesus the son of Mary will dwindle and lose their lustre. The occasion demands such a man, the forces are there to thrust him forward, the democracy looks for him, and would know and welcome him could he but show and approve himself.

Or is it that there are so many Christs, so many noble, quiet, self-sacrificing workers, and so few apostle-scribes to chronicle and magnify their words and works, that they come and go, and the world at large scarce knows that they have been with us. I at least believe so. From all I can gather of the age in which Jesus lived it was an age of such mental and moral barrenness that it was no marvel if wayside preachers like John and Jesus should shine out as bright particular stars in a blank and dreary firmament. It is treason to the western man and to modern civilisation, with all its defects, to think that we cannot better this Oriental type of the first century. You may think: Mazzini's utterances lack the form which is so conspicuous in the Sermon on the Mount; you may remember that Kossuth was not crucified; that Delescluze was a worker and soldier rather than a preacher. You may say: "Your Carlyles and Ruskins, your Liebknechts and Tolstoys and Ibsens are mere comfortable Pharisees, sitting by the fire in slippered feet, and attempting to reform the world from the desk, the platform, and by Act of Parliament; they do not take hold of the imagination as does this Jew of marvellous eloquence and persuasive power, who, with such a following and by such apparently inadequate means, founded a hierarchy which has conquered kings and dominated empires." Granting all that, it is still questionable if the world will not be better for their life and works than for the career and teaching of this zealot, whose fanatic followers turned back the rising tide of science and rationalism in southern Europe, in western Asia, and in northern Africa for more than a thousand years. To-day we have to settle down to our primers and our programmes, our blue books and our social experiments, just as if Jesus had never lived, or perhaps all the more because he lived. We get no assistance from him. His followers are our enemies in every country which owns his influence—and the worst enemies of all because ever professing friendship. But I will not believe that Europe and America, with their brave and wise and intellectually temperate peoples, with their long history linking nation with nation, with their freer women, their more bracing climes, their landscapes, their seacoasts, and their physical magnitude,—I will not believe that they cannot and do not produce men who do more honour to the name of man than this artisan of an exclusive people, a people devoid of humour, full of narrow nationalism, living under foreign tyrants, taking their temperament from bare rocks and deserts, bleak inland seas, and a blinding torrid sun.

Let the painters, sculptors, poets, and musicians do honour to the heroes of humanity, the apostles of science and progress, as they have heretofore lavished their taste and skill and imagination on a conventional Jesus, an ideal Madonna, and imaginary saints and Gospel scenes; let statues rise to Bruno, Vanini, Servetus; let the historian and the biographer recount with loving wealth of detail their struggles, controversies, flights, imprisonments, and martyrdoms; let poets and painters cast the halo of romantic art around Caxton, Galileo, William the Silent, Milton, Harry Vane, and great, masterful Cromwell; let hymns be sung to Copernicus, Newton, Harvey, to Masaniello, Danton, Garibaldi, Delescluze, to Grace Darling, Sister Dora, and Father Damien. Let art in all its forms do as much for modern life as it has done for arid Judaism—Judaism with its mouth full of theoretical morality and its life full of lust and meanness and cruelty—and then let us see if we cannot give East and West, Modern and Ancient, their proper places and proportions. To ask this is to ask the modern world to live its own life, to honour its own heroes, to consider itself, and to remember the past only in so far as it fairly illuminates and helps in the present.

## Notes

1 Matt. x. 17-18; Luke xii., 2.
2 Among the few constructive ideas in Spencer's "Study of Sociology" is the chapter on "Preparation in Biology," which might well have been suggested by this passage from Paul. Of course, these analogies have very little practical value to the reformer, since they can be interpreted in widely different ways.

# 37

# "SIMPLIFICATION OF LIFE", IN *ENGLAND'S IDEAL* (SWAN SONNENSCHEIN, LOWREY & CO, 1887), 79–99.

*Edward Carpenter*

[Edward Carpenter is an archetype of socialism before the age of party and one of those figures impossible to categorise with any particular strand within the socialist movement. Born in 1844, he had been ordained as a minister in 1869 but five years later relinquished his orders and his Cambridge fellowship. Instead he embarked on a lifelong search for social, political and sexual emancipation. It was the first of these that provided the impetus for his embracing socialism when in the early 1880s he came into a legacy and embarked upon the simple life at his smallholding at Millthorpe near Sheffield. Carpenter never actually joined the SDF; the Sheffield Socialist Society he helped establish in 1896 was closer to Morris and the Socialist League. Nevertheless, it was through reading Hyndman's *England for All* that he had discovered socialism in 1883 and it was Carpenter's subventions which helped to get the SDF weekly *Justice* off the ground.

"Simplification of Life" was a paper read before the Fellowship of the New Life in 1886. The Fellowship was a forerunner to the Fabian Society that had carried on independently as a vehicle for an ethical socialism that challenged the whole ethos and motive force of modern commercial civilisation without engaging with the detail of social reform. Carpenter was deeply influenced by the American transcendentalists Walt Whitman and Henry David Thoreau. These influences are more evident here than overtly socialist ones. It is certainly true that Carpenter's advocacy of the rights of "homogenic love" and what he styled the intermediate sex would not be taken up by either Fabians, Marxists or ILPers as a body. To this extent, he represents a strand like Charlotte Wilson's anarchism (Chapter 3, this volume) that became separated from the main course of socialism even including its several tributaries. Nevertheless, Carpenter reminds us of the breadth of campaigning issues that socialists took up. He was a popular speaker at the Labour Church meetings that for a period in the 1890s were almost like the religious wing of the ILP. He was a writer who enjoyed considerable success, reaching many whom Fabian or Marxist economics never could have. In Carpenter's case, Anglo-Marxism is all Anglo and very little Marxism; nevertheless he took from the latter what he needed, namely an "excellent text for an attack upon the existing competitive system" (Carpenter 1916, 114–115) and encapsulated what Morris called the religion of socialism.]

> "As I preferred some things to others, and especially valued my freedom, as I could fare hard and yet succeed well, I did not wish to spend my time in earning rich carpets or other fine furniture, or delicate cookery, or a house in the Grecian or the Gothic style just yet. If there are any to whom it is no interruption to acquire these things, and who know how to use them when acquired, I relinquish to them the pursuit."
> 
> —*Thoreau.*

Certainly, if you do not want to be a vampire and a parasite upon others, the great question of practical life, and which everyone has to face, is how to carry it on with as little labor and effort as may be. No one wants to labor needlessly, and if you have to earn everything you spend, economy becomes a very personal question—not necessarily in the pinching sense, but merely as adaptation of means to the end. When I came some years ago to live with cottagers (earning say £50 to £60 a year) and share their life, I was surprised to find how little both in labor and expense their food cost them, who were doing far more work than I was, or indeed the generality of people among whom I had been living. This led me to see that the rich dinners and expensive mode of living I had been accustomed to were a mere waste, as far as adaptation to any useful end was concerned; and afterwards I decided that they had been a positive hindrance, for when I became habituated to a more simple diet I found that a marked improvement took place in my powers both of mind and body. At a later time when keeping house myself (still on the same scale, though with a little more latitude owing to visitors) and having, during a short time, to buy *every* article of food, I found that the expenses for a family of four persons were well under 8d. a head per diem, not including firing or labor of cooking. And now I am inclined to consider this needlessly large.

The difference, however, arising from having a small piece of garden is very great, and makes one feel how important it is that every cottage should have a plot of ground attached. A rood of land (quarter acre) is sufficient to grow all potatoes and other vegetables and some fruit for the year's use, say for a family of five. Half an acre would be an ample allowance. Such a piece of land may easily be cultivated by anyone in the odd hours of regular work, and the saving is naturally large from not having to go to the shop for everything of this nature that is needed. At the present time—October, 1885—when growing all fruit and vegetables, eggs also, for our own use, I find that our entire expenses for provisions (including flour, meat, milk, butter, groceries, sugar for preserving, etc.) amount to 5d. a head per day. The flour-bill (baking done at home) is about 1d. per day each, and some portion of this—though I am not in a position at present to say exactly how much—is saved when we grow our own wheat. As a matter of practical interest I find that an acre of wheat in a fairly good year (say 10 "bags," or 180 stone) will provide a year's bread for a family of five. Anyone having a horse will of course find it economical to use it with the plough; but I am inclined to think that a cottager with a little more land than he would want for his garden and with a little spare time, would find it worth while to *spade* up half an acre or so (he would get a rare crop in this way) and grow wheat on it. However, not having tried this plan myself, I will not do more than just to suggest it. A small hand-mill in the house serves with little labor to produce the whole-meal flour, but for white flour the corn must be sent to the miller.

While on this question of wheat I may remark that an impression seems to have got abroad that England is not a good wheat-producing country; but surely there is no ground for this. English grain is actually finer than the American grain, and the yield per acre on our farms is larger. As soon as ever we tried our own flour we found (really to our surprise) that the quality of bread was quite superior to what we had been accustomed to from the bought meal, and this in a district—the Derbyshire dales—by no means so well suited for corn growing as most parts of England. This purer taste of the bread may, however, have been partly due to the fact that millers and flour-dealers are in the habit of mixing different sorts and qualities of flour together (even if they do not adulterate with other substances), much as tea-blenders mix tea, and thus our bread of commerce, like everything else commercial, is sophisticated. The only serious drawback to English wheat is that in some rainy seasons the grain is not so dry as it should be—but millers, it must be remembered, have drying-floors. Undoubtedly the production of wheat in England is just now at a discount because of the extraordinary low-pricedness of the American wheat; but then it should be noted that the English farmer is frightfully burdened by our landlord system as well as by heavy rates and taxes. Whatever may be said about rent not entering into cost of production, and though the theory abstractly considered is a pretty one, yet in practice in England I believe it will be found to apply only very partially. The landlord is on the top of the farmer and has the advantage of him in every way. The latter is loth to leave the place on which he, and perhaps his ancestors before him, have lived so long, and to incur the disastrous expenses of a change; "hope springs eternal" and "though the seasons have been bad they may be better in the future;" then the available amount of land in the country is limited, there is always a large portion of the town population ready to try its hand at agriculture, if only as a hobby and in the face of probable loss; building speculations, favorableness of sites for ornamental estates, etc., re-act on agricultural rents; and though it is contended that all these things adjust themselves in *time,* yet it is just there that the difficulty arises. For during the time so required *the actual conditions of the problem change;* the prices, the cost of production, the situation of the "margin of cultivation" fluctuate, and their adjustment to rent in each particular case has to be re-discovered each year. The problem practically never is solved, but is deferred indefinitely; the landlord continues to reap the advantage of his strong and entrenched position, and the successive generations of burdened farmers, losing all their capital, and what is even more, all heart and courage, neglect their land, and widespread impoverishment, as now, ensues. This, being so, seems obviously a matter requiring immediate attention, for it must always be an object of first-class importance to a country to produce the staple articles of its own food; and if we find that our wheat production is hampered even in a small degree by the obstruction of a privileged class, such obstruction ought to be removed as quickly as possible. Personally I am inclined to think, looking at all the details of the case and the indirect as well as direct influences, that this obstruction is not a small matter, and that if it does not account for the entire difficulty which our farmers have in contending with American prices it accounts for a large part of it, and is therefore a subject more serious and worthy of attention from our statesmen than for instance the opening up of new markets by petty foreign wars.

To return to the question of domestic economy. Of course the current mode of life is so greatly wasteful, and we have come to consider so many things as necessaries—whether in food, furniture, clothing, or what not—which really bring us back next to no profit or pleasure compared with the labor spent upon them, that it is really difficult to know where the balance of true economy would stand if, so to speak, left to itself. All we can do is to take the existing mode of life in its simpler forms, somewhat as above, and work from that as a basis. For though the cottager's way of living, say in our rural districts or in the neighborhood of our large towns, is vastly superior to that of the well-to-do, that does not argue that it is not capable of improvement.

About the largest account in most modern households is the butcher's. I find that our bill runs up to £10 a year, and this is less than in the Royal Household, where it reaches £9,472. If our princes and their attendants were to adopt a more frugal diet (say like that of the Caliph Omar, who rode from Medina to Jerusalem with a bag of dates and a bag of corn at his saddle-bow), they would probably be quite as cheerful and healthy as now, and there would be a great saving to the nation!

The causes of the craving for a meat diet seem to be similar to those of the craving for other stimulants. For though flesh is not generally considered a stimulant, a little attention will show that its action is of like nature. It very quickly produces a sense of well-being, liable to be followed by reaction and depression; and this action, though innocuous in its smaller degrees, becomes seriously harmful when flesh is made a staple article of diet. With regard to the healthfulness of stimulants generally I am inclined to think that as long as they are merely used for *pleasure's* sake (sociality and good-fellowship) they are right enough, and in place; but as soon as ever they go so far as to become *necessities,* and the man learns to lean on them for support, or thinks that he cannot do without them, from that moment they are harmful and lowering to the system. The question of meat involves, of course, the additional question of our moral or sentimental relation to the animals. Probably the great craving for all these things goes with our present conditions of civilisation. The hurry, the overwork—or rather *feverish* work—of modern life;

the bad air—as of women all along in the house, or men in a close workshop; the unnatural stimulations, in sexual affairs as in everything else; and above all the hypersensitiveness of our women, who, having abandoned outdoor life and labor, transmit a feebly nervous organism to the race:—all these things produce a craving for artificial supports. The man cannot walk and must have crutches; and the crutches in their turn atrophise the limbs.

On the whole, and for habitual use, I do not know what can be pleasanter or more nourishing than the cereals (rice, wheat, &c.), milk, eggs, cheese, bread, butter, and any fruit or vegetables that come handy; and they seem to me to stand by one for hard work and endurance better than flesh. Less than a pennyworth of oatmeal will make one person a large dish of porridge, and this with an egg, or some cheese and a little fruit, will form a first-class dinner. As to the fearful and wonderful receipts contained in the cookery books, the formula—*Serve up hot and throw out of the window*—might, with advantage, be appended to most of them. I am convinced there is a most abominable and idiotic waste of time in connection with this subject in all our well-to-do establishments. If the pleasure given bore any proportion to the expenditure of time and labor there might be some sense in the matter, but it doesn't. Fancy a small household of five or six persons requiring a *cook*—*i.e.,* a person engaged all day long in preparing food for them. Is it not out of all reason? But the mistress of the house descends as it were from the skies, "orders dinner," and returns again to her celestial abode. Whether it was worth while that the scullery-maid should be sent scouring round the town, that she should return hot and tired, and quarrel with the cook—that saucepans should be soiled, much time consumed in peeling, and some money wasted—all in order that unseasonable shrimps should be made into indigestible sauce and served up with the fish, is a question which does not enter into her (the mistress's) head as she takes an infinitesimal portion of the said sauce upon her plate.

Once I had the honor of staying in a country house for a few days as a guest of one of the servants, and the view which I thus got of our social arrangements—from that side I suppose from which Moses saw the Almighty—was very curious and interesting.

The orthodox dinner, reduced even to its lowest terms, involves say meat, two vegetables, and a pudding—four dishes, all requiring cooking! The labor this represents per annum, and just for one meal a day, is something fearful. And it is not a comfortable meal; let alone the disagreeable smells involved in its preparation—smells which necessitate sitting-rooms being a long way from kitchens, and houses altogether more extensive and cumbrous than they need be—it is a meal having no centre of gravity; you cannot for the life of you tell the proper proportion these dishes bear to each other.

Would it not be better to have just one dish—(like the family bowl seen in Highland cabins and elsewhere)—one dish combining in itself all needful qualities of nutrition and tastiness, with perhaps a few satellite platters around for any adjuncts or off-sets that might seem appropriate? This central dish (the only one requiring immediate cookery) say some golden-orbed substantial omelet, or vast vegetable pie, or savoury and nutritious soup, or solid expanse of macaroni and cheese, or steaming mountain of rice surrounded by stewed fruit, or even plain bowl of fermenty, would represent the sun or central fire of our system, while round it in planetary order would circle such other useful and inexpensive viands as would give the housewife a minimum of trouble to provide—chunks of bread and cheese, figs, raisins, oatmeal cakes, fresh fruit, or what not. Here would no second relay of plates be necessary, and victuals which could not face each other on the table would not be forced into spiteful conflict within the man. Even the knife and fork would almost disappear, washing up would become an affair of a few minutes, and the woman's work before and after dinner be reduced to a trifle compared with what it is now. For it must be remembered that with this whole matter hangs the question of women's work. Woman is a slave, and *must remain so* as long as ever our present domestic system is maintained. I say that our average mode of life, as conceived under the bourgeois ideal of society, cannot be kept up without perpetuating the slavery of woman. It is quite probable that in the mass she will resist the change; but it may have to come nevertheless.

As to the general question of eating, I am inclined to think that, as in other matters, though moderation is the best general rule, this has to be varied by an occasional orgy. For pleasure in the long run, health, economy of force, &c., a certain sparingness is to be recommended; but the orgy should not be omitted. Among other things it restores the moral tone, and prevents—a most important point—all danger of lapse into pharisaism. Probably if people nowadays had to slaughter for their own use the difficulty would be to get them to "kill the fatted calf." On my little farm we have fowls in plenty, but we cannot get one for dinner, simply because no member of the household is sufficiently goaded by hunger to be willing to perform the sacrifice: and so Peggy and Fluffy, though old, are respited from month to month, or taken to market—such is human inconsistency!—to be killed ultimately by some one else.

No doubt immense simplifications of our daily life are possible; but this does not seem to be a matter which has been much studied. Rather hitherto the tendency has been all the other way, and every additional ornament on the mantel-piece has been regarded as an acquisition, and not as a nuisance; though one doesn't see any reason, in the nature of things, why it should be regarded as one more than the other. It cannot be too often remembered that every additional object in a house requires additional dusting, cleaning, repairing, and lucky are you if its requirements stop there. When you abandon a wholesome tile or stone floor for a Turkey carpet, you are setting out on a voyage of which you cannot see the end. The Turkey carpet makes the old furniture look uncomfortable, and calls for stuffed couches and armchairs, the couches and armchairs demand a walnutwood table; the walnutwood table requires polishing, and the polish bottles require shelves; the couches and armchairs have castors and springs—which give way and want mending; they have damask seats which fade and must be covered; the chintz covers require washing, and when washed they call for antimacassars to keep them clean. The antimacassars, require wool, and the wool requires knitting-needles, and the knitting-needless require a box, the box demands a side-table to stand on, and the side-table involves more covers and castors—and so we go on. Meanwhile the carpet wears out and has to be supplemented by bits of drugget, or eked out with oilcloth, and, beside the daily toil required to keep this mass of rubbish in order, we have every week or month, instead of the pleasant cleaning-day of old times, a terrible domestic convulsion and *bouleversement* of the household.

It is said by those who have travelled in Arabia that the reason why there are so many religious enthusiasts in that country, is that in the extreme simplicity of the life and uniformity of the landscape there *heaven*—in the form of the intense blue sky—seems close upon one. One may almost see God. But we moderns guard ourselves effectually against this danger. For beside the smoke pall which covers our towns, we raise in each household such a dust of trivialities that our attention is fairly absorbed, and if this screen subsides for a moment we are sure to have the daily paper held up before our eyes—so that if a chariot of fire were sent to fetch us, ten to one we should not see it.

However, if this multiplying of the complexity of life is really grateful to some people, one cannot quarrel with them for pursuing it; and to many it appears to be so. When a sewing machine is introduced into a household the simple-minded husband thinks that, as it works ten times as quick as the hand, there will now be only a tenth part of the time spent by his wife and daughter in sewing that there was before. But he is ignorant of human nature. To his surprise he finds that there is *no* difference in the time. The difference is in the flounces—they put ten times as many on their dresses.

Thus we see how little *external* reforms avail. If the *desire* for simplicity is not really present no labor-saving appliances will make life simpler.

Talking about floors, it seems a good plan in upper chambers, and rooms where floors are boarded, to stain and varnish them. This is not expensive, but it takes a little time—two or three days altogether for the different washes to dry; first the stain, then a wash of size, *i.e.,* diluted glue, and then the oak varnish. There is a varnish now commonly sold called brush varnish, which dries very quickly, in a few hours, and does not require any size; but it is hardly so good and durable as the other. The advantage of varnished floors is that they do not require scrubbing, which is a very laborious process, but only to be rubbed over with a damp cloth. One or two rugs, or bits of carpet, are all that is needed for a covering, and these can be easily taken up and shaken and the room swept at the weekly cleaning. A carpet over the whole floor not only smells badly, and makes the air of the room permanently stuffy, but, being difficult to remove, it remains down for months at a time, and harbors all sorts of dirt. Varnished floors however will not stand heavy work, as in a living-room or kitchen where thick boots are in and out all day; and here stone or tile floors, with cocoa-nut matting if a covering is wanted, always seems to me the most appropriate.

The rest of the furniture takes its cue very much from the treatment of the floor. As a rule all curtains, hangings, cloths, and covers, which are not absolutely necessary, should be dispensed with. They all create dust and stuffiness, and all entail trouble and recurring expense, and they all tempt the housekeeper to keep out the air and sunlight—two things of the last and most vital importance. I like a room which looks its best when the sun streams into it through wide open windows and doors. If the furnishing of it cannot stand this test—if it looks uncomfortable under the operation—you may be sure there is something unwholesome about it. As to the question of elegance or adornment, that may safely be left to itself. The studied effort to make interiors elegant has only ended—in what we see. After all, if things are *in their place* they will always look well. What, by common consent, is more graceful than a ship—the sails, the spars, the rigging, the lines of the hull? Yet go on board and you will scarcely find one thing placed there for the purpose of adornment. An imperious necessity rules everything; this rope *could* have no other place than it has, nor could be less thick or thicker than it is; and it is, in fact, this necessity which makes the ship beautiful. Everything in it *has relation*—has relation to the winds and waves, or to something else on board, and is there for purposes beyond its own existence. Or again, after you have been the round of æsthetically-furnished mansions, and seen all that taste and wealth can do in this direction, does it not happen to you at last to turn by chance into some old-fashioned cottage by the wayside and find that, for pure grace and beauty, this interior, without the least effort or intention whatever, has beaten all the rest hollow? Yet, with the exception perhaps of a few plants in the window, everything here is for use. The eye rests on nothing but what suggests a train of thought. Here is the axe hanging, there the gun; here over the dresser a row of plates, there the kettle boiling on the fire; and there, behind the door, the straw hat which the rosy-cheeked girl puts on when she runs out to look to the fowls. Everything is alive, and transparent too with cleanly human life. But your modern drawing-room is dead—a stupor comes over the mind as it gazes at the aimless armchairs, and the room seems full of lumber. You cannot *make* your room beautiful by buying an expensive vase and putting it on the mantel-shelf; but if you live an honest life in it, it will *grow* beautiful in proportion as it comes to answer to the wants of such a life.

The treatment of walls is a somewhat vexed question. Some people prefer paper, while others prefer a color-wash or paint. On the whole there always seems to me something incongruous and even trivial in the idea of *papering* stone and plaster. Color-washes are clean and sweet; they are made of whitening with a little size (flour and water) mixed to prevent rubbing off, and coloring matter according to choice. They are of course quite inexpensive and can be renewed every two or three years. Paint has the advantage of being very durable and of being washable, but it has the drawback of being more laborious and costly in operation, and of course renders a room uninhabitable for a week or two till it is thoroughly dry. In fact care should be taken with regard to this last point. On the whole I think papering is the least trouble, color-washing the least expensive in materials, and paint perhaps the most satisfactory in the long run. If, however, a room is really well plastered to begin with (which does not often happen nowadays) one may very well dispense with all three methods, and that is perhaps after all the most obvious thing to do.

With regard to clothing, as with furniture and the other things, it can be much simplified if one only desires it so. Probably, however, most people do not desire it, and of course they are right in keeping to the complications. Who knows but what there is some influence at work for some ulterior purpose which we do not guess, causing us to artificialise our lives to the extraordinary extent we do in modern times? Our ancestors wore woad, and it does not at first sight seem obvious why we should not do the same. Without however entering into the woad question, we may consider some ways in which clothing may be simplified without departing far from the existing standard. It seems to be generally admitted now that wool is the most suitable material as a rule. I find that a good woollen coat, such as ordinarily worn, feels warmer when *unlined* than it does when a layer of silk or cotton is interposed between the woollen surface and the body. It is also lighter, thus in both ways the simplification is a gain. Another advantage is that it washes easier and better, and is at all times cleaner, No one who has had the curiosity once to unpick the lining of a tailor-made coat that has been in wear a little time, will, I think, ever wish to have coats made on the same principle again. The rubbish he will find inside, the frettings and frayings of the cloth collected in little dirt-heaps up and down, the paddings of cotton wool, the odd lots of miscellaneous stuff used as backings, the quantity of canvas stiffening, the tags and paraphernalia connected with the pockets, bits of buckram inserted here and there to make the coat "sit" well—all these things will be a warning to him. What would be shamed by exposure to the light is all covered up by a sham decorous lining, and if the mess looks unwholesome and suggestive of disease in a comparatively new coat made by a well-to-do tailor, what must it be in the case of a coat made up by a cheap and nasty dealer, or one that has been unwashed (and how can one wash such a thing?) for years?

Now if all these tags are done away with, and a coat is made up of *good* cloth without any lining whatever or any stiffening (except a patch here and there where the buttons are sewn on), and with pockets simply made by the addition of another patch of cloth—patch-pockets as they are called—the relief and the sense of added comfort, warmth, lightness, cleanliness are really delightful. The truth is that one might almost as well be in one's coffin as in the stiff layers upon layers of buckram-like clothing commonly worn nowadays. No genial influence from air or sky can pierce this dead hide, no effluence from within escape. A man's clothing we will say generally consists round his trunk of undervest, shirt, waistcoat and coat, to which must sometimes be added an overcoat—each of the three last-mentioned garments consists, at any rate over the front of the body, of *three* thicknesses—cloth, canvas-stiffening, and lining—in all eleven layers. Eleven layers between him and God! No wonder the Arabian has the advantage over us. Who could be inspired under all this weight of tailordom?

And certainly, nowadays, many folk visibly *are* in their coffins. Only the head and the hands out, all the rest of the body clearly sickly with want of light and air, atrophied, stiff in the joints, strait-waistcoated, and partially mummied. Sometimes it seems to me that is the reason why in our modern times the curious intellect is so abnormally developed, the brain and the tongue waggle so, and fingers are so nervous and meddlesome, because these organs alone have a chance, the rest are shut out from God's light and air: the poor human heart grown feeble and weary in its isolation and imprisonment, the sexual parts degenerated and ashamed of themselves, the liver diseased, and the lungs straitened down to mere sighs and conventional disconsolate sounds beneath their cerements.

But a good woollen shirt and coat, and pants of similar material, are really all a man needs for ordinary wear in our climate—three garments, all simply made, easily washable, and often washed. In quite cold weather a waistcoat can be added, which should also be unlined and with the back made out of cloth the same as the front. Thus even when a greatcoat is worn the maximum will be only four thicknesses over the body instead of eleven, while the normal covering will be two layers instead of eight. The warmth will be just as great as before, but the suffocation and mummydom will be less; we shall be nearer the sources of life, and may possibly even hear spoken to *us* the words: "Lazarus, come forth!"

As to the feet which have been condemned to their leathern coffins so long that we are almost ashamed to look at them, there is still surely a resurrection possible for them. There seems to be no reason except mere habit why, for a large part of the year at least, we should not go barefoot, as the Irish do, or at least with sandals. [Democracy which redeems the lowest and most despised of the people, must redeem also the most menial and despised members and organs of the body.] Even now, effeminated as our feet are, it takes but little practice to accustom them to country roads; in our towns with their excellent pavements the custom might in summer time be adopted at once. And who does not know the pleasure of grasping the ground—the bare earth—with his bare feet? If it be objected that it is really impossible to imagine our modern life carried on on such principles—the brokers on the London Stock Exchange hurrying around, or the visitor appearing at a fashionable afternoon tea, in bare feet(!)—this is not a serious argument; because if the two things are really incompatible, it is quite possible that in the long run the Stock Exchange business may turn out to be the less important of the two—less grounded in the ultimate necessity of things than the freedom and emancipation of a single member of the human body; and so the little toe, like the proverbial worm, though nearly crushed, may at last turn and revenge itself on a civilisation whose oppression it has too long endured.

But, as we are talking about economy, what a saving of labor and expense would be effected by dispensing, if only for six months out of the year, with shoes and stockings? The labor involved in merely *darning* the latter is really a serious item in household life. Though scoffed at by the male part of the community, as beneath their notice—this labor is only another of the links in the chain which binds the women folk down. Again, who does not know the time which is spent, in any self-supporting household, in patching and mending the numerous garments worn, putting in fresh linings and renewing pockets?—time which might be largely saved if the number of garments was much reduced, and their construction altogether simplified from the beginning. Thus, all through for men and similarly for women, a simplification of dress might be adopted—even without departing far from present modes—which would involve far less initial expense, and far less labor of maintenance than the present plan. And if these things seem trivial to some well-bred person, who is in the habit of saying, like the Centurion in the Bible, to his servant:—"Do this, and he doeth it"—we must remember as was said at the outset, that in any honest household, faithfully providing for its own wants, such matters *have* to be faced. The husband *has* out of his labor to provide the initial expense, the wife has to do the most part of the work of repair and renewal, and to such people the affair is is not trivial at all. Rather one might say that if educated and wealthy people would set the example of simplifying these things to the utmost in their own persons, they would do more to lighten the burden of life for the mass of the people than they can expect to do by casually plunging their hands into their pockets in aid of some Charity.

There are many other ways in which the details and labor of daily life may be advantageously reduced, which will occur to anyone who turns practical attention to the matter. For myself, I confess to a great pleasure in witnessing the Economies of Life—and how seemingly nothing need be wasted—how the very stones that offend the spade in the garden become invaluable when footpaths have to be laid out or drains to be made. Hats that are past wear get cut up into strips for nailing creepers to the wall, the upper leathers of old shoes are useful for the same purpose. The under garment that is too far gone for mending is used for patching another less decrepit of its kind. Then it is torn up into strips for bandages, or what not; and when it has served its time thus it descends to floor washing, and is scrubbed out of life—useful to the end. When my coat has worn itself into an affectionate intimacy with my body, when it has served for Sunday best, and for weekdays, and got weather-stained out in the fields with sun and rain—then, faithful, it does not part from me, but getting itself cut up into shreds and patches descends to form a hearthrug for my feet. After that, when worn through, it goes into the kennel and keeps my dog warm, and so after lapse of years, retiring to the manure-heaps and passing out on to the land, returns to me in the form of potatos for my dinner; or being pastured by my sheep reappears upon their backs as the material of new clothing. Thus it remains a friend to all time, grateful to me for not having despised and thrown it away when it first got behind the fashions. And seeing we have been faithful to each other, my coat and I, for one round or life-period, I do not see why we should not renew our intimacy—in other metamorphoses—or why we should ever quite lose touch of each other through the aeons.

With regard to the sum total of labor required for the maintenance of a household according to modern notions, I find on my little farm of seven acres (which is by no means conducted on model principles, but in a very ordinary way) that the figures for last financial year (September, '84-'85) run as follows:—Number of persons, rather over four on the average; household expenses (including provisions and utensils, but not clothing or personal expenses), £38; farm expenses, *i.e.,* seeds, tools, manure &c., £15; taxes, £6; close upon £60 in all. I consider that the farm and market garden could easily be worked by a man and his family, say having a son of fifteen to help him, with just occasional outside help. And the question then would be for them to sell stuff sufficient to cover the above outlay and leave a margin for pocket money and *rent* (payable we should hope to the nation and not to any individual landlord). This they ought to do, and probably would do without difficulty in times of average prices. What exact margin might be expected, or what exact extent of land would yield the best results, are questions which I should find it difficult to answer; all such points depend so very much on considerations of soil, locality, kinds of crop grown, whether ordinary or highly specialised, the state of the markets, &c., that it seems rash and indeed impossible to generalise on them. Personally I feel so very strongly that the present conditions of commercial production are rapidly passing away, that I don't think it very much matters whether the peasant occupier (or any other worker or industrial adventurer) is proved to be a commercial success or a commercial failure just now. When the new conditions of society enable the worker to receive something like an equivalent of the value he produces it is evident that the question of success or failure will be a very different one from what it is to-day.

What I feel more interested to show is the actual expense—as in the figures given above—of carrying on a simple, but unstinted, household life. For though some would consider these figures absurdly small, and others needlessly large, yet on the whole they are probably not far from the average experience on the subject; and at any rate I give them because I can vouch for their accuracy. Not long ago a gentleman told me that he was anxious to adopt a very simple mode of life, and to take a cottage with plot of land to it, for himself and family, but was waiting till he had saved money enough—£15,000 *was the sum he mentioned*—for the venture. I thought it was a pity he should wait so long, if he was really so anxious about it as evidently if he could scrape together only £100 a year, from any professional sources or out of dividends, or what not, he would have amply sufficient for all casualties.

In the more or less socialistic state of society towards which we seem to be trending, the normal condition would probably be for a man to have a cottage and sufficient land—say not less than a rood—to grow a good deal of food for his own use, while daily labor at a really adequate rate of wages would be secured to him outside in workshop, design-room, school, warehouse, or wherever it might be. And this always seems to me, if properly managed, the most satisfactory mode of life for the average man. It avoids the uncertainties and anxieties of running a concern of one's own. There is no reason why the wage-work should not be done under pleasant and wholesome conditions, the hours would not be long, and there would be a home and land of one's own on which to expend superfluous energy. Thus, if we take the household expenses at £40, including purchase of a few tools, &c., for the garden, and rent (payable to the State and therefore no taxes) at £10, we see that a family earning £100 a year would have ample margin for clothing, pocket money, and even travelling within reasonable limits—would be, in fact, quite well off. But even under the present wasteful conditions of society, statistics show, as in the note on last page, that the value created by each family of producers is over £270 a year. Allowing something then for the expenses of distribution, organisation, &c., and allowing *nothing* for the improved productiveness of labor under a better system—we still see that the normal wage per annum may be placed at something like £250 per family. This would be, of course, under the supposition that the hours of labor remained the same as they are now. In this respect, however, under any reasonable condition of society, a man would be at liberty to exercise some choice. If he wished to live *very* luxuriously, or had extraordinary expenses to meet, he could continue working his nine or ten hours as now; if however his domestic wants were only about the ordinary range they would easily be covered by the sum (£100) we have mentioned, and then obviously four hours a day would be sufficient; while if single, and of simple habits, he (or she) could do with less.

In the above sketch my object has been not so much to put forward any theory of the conduct of daily life, or to maintain that one method of living is of itself superior to another, as to try and come at the *facts* connected with the subject. In the long run every household *has* to support itself, the benefits and accommodations it receives from Society have to be covered by the labor it expends for Society. This cannot be got over. The present effort of a large number of people to live on interest and dividends, and so in a variety of ways on the labor of *others,* is simply an effort to make water run up hill: it cannot last very long. The balance then between the labor that you consume and the labor that you expend may be struck in many different ways, but it has to be struck; and I have been interested to bring together some materials for an easy solution of the problem.

# Part 8

# GENDER, SEXUALITY, FAMILY AND PERSONAL RELATIONS

# 38

# "THE COMMERCIAL HEARTH", *COMMONWEAL*, 8 MAY 1886, 42 AND 15 MAY 1886, 50.

*Ernest Belfort Bax*

[The commonest allegation against the SDF was that of its sectarianism. Examples were sometimes cited demonstrating the ambivalence or worse of some leading its personalities towards trade unionism. Not infrequently, SDFers expressed disparaging views of Britain's workers as they actually were. An air of "gloomy antagonism to the bone-headed working man" was strongly marked in some socialists, including those of working-class origin like Harry Quelch (Macintyre 1980, 205–208). Among the middle-class Marxists who were so prominent in the leadership, the tendency was equally marked to disparage the foibles and social practices of their own kind. The Fabians were also middle class, but sought to avoid the distraction of issues that might alienate those of their peers who were otherwise sympathetic. According to the widely known formulation they owed to Bernard Shaw, the Fabian Society thus disavowed any distinctive opinion on "the Marriage Question, Religion, Art, abstract Economics, historic Evolution, Currency, or any other subject than its own special business of practical Democracy and Socialism" (Fabian Tract No. 70, 1896). The publicists of the SDF and Socialist League, by comparison, included some at least who were irrepressible contrarians. They sometimes seemed not only to have strong views on almost everything but a compulsion to let you know what they were.

In his study of William Morris, E.P. Thompson singled out the case of Bax. Working-class socialists like Robert Tressell (Chapter 19, this volume) might feel a strong sense of their "apartness" in relation to their fellow workers. For Bax, on the other hand, middle-class philistinism and joylessness had a "peculiar sort of fascination" that Thompson believed seemed to move him more deeply than did the oppressions of the workers themselves. "It is difficult not feel that there is a taste of provocative armchair jeering ... hardly of service to the movement at a time when the Socialists, in the face of a chorus of abuse, were trying to make their viewpoint unmistakably clear" (Thompson 1955, 439–440).

"The Commercial Hearth", later reissued as "The Capitalistic 'Hearth'", was the sort of thing Thompson had in mind. Its meaning is hardly unclear. Nor does the stereotype of a doctrinaire and tunnel-visioned economic socialism stand up to scrutiny. Originally published in *Commonweal*, Bax included his fusillade against middle-class mores in a collection he called *The Religion of Socialism*, followed up later by one entitled *The Ethics of Socialism*. This may also suggest the possibility of a more generous view of Bax's onslaught on middle-class manners. He was a republican, a secularist and an iconoclast, and according to Mark Bevir his idealist metaphysics meant that exposing moral shams and hypocrisies was for Bax a crucial form of political action. Rather than looking to modes of production and the determining force of economic relations, as the caricatures of the Marxists might suggest, Bax found the explanation of historical change in the shifting relationships between individual and society and the changing character of humanity's ethical consciousness (Bevir 1993).

His socialism was certainly no less ethical than that of ILP reformers; his successful collaborations with William Morris may also be understood in this light. Nevertheless, according even to those politically closest to him, Bax's ethic was strongest in its negative and critical aspect (Leatham [1897] 2016a, ch. 2). While Morris, for example, set about the task of "making socialists", Bax seemed almost as interested in keeping them at bay. That is typified at the final swipe aimed here at John Ruskin, the "'old man' of Coniston", and the St George's Guild that he had founded. Morris deferred to none in his contempt for the shoddy, the jerry-built and the pretentious. Nevertheless, when Bax's diatribe appeared in *Commonweal*, he added a disclaimer observing how many socialists Ruskin had made by his revolt against commercialism.

The challenge to social convention made the SDF and its offshoots a much richer and more diverse political environment than is often allowed. Nevertheless, the assertion of apartness was not conducive to building a thriving political movement. Thompson made the connection with Bax's view of the so-called woman question (Chapter 31, this volume) on which he certainly could not be accused of swimming with the stream. Even leaving aside Bax's misogyny and imperviousness to the contradictions of his own position, what is no less remarkable is that in freely venting his views within the socialist press he not only provoked controversy within the SDF but profoundly alienated what for a time was clearly the most dynamic social movement of the day.]

The throne, the altar, and the hearth—the political emblem, the religious emblem, and the social emblem—have long constituted the mystic trinity to which appeal is made when popular class-sentiment is required to be invoked against influences, disintegrative of the *status quo*. In the bourgeois world of to-day the first two terms may be sometimes modified. The middle-class man's respect for the throne *per se* may be more or less diluted; he may even prefer to substitute for it the presidential chair, but in either case it is the "law"—the legal system of a class-society—which is typified; to the altar he might possibly prefer the "Bible", by which he would wish to be understood Protestant dogmas without the inconveniences of direct sacerdotal domination. Such slight modifications of the original formulæ as these, matter little, however, since in any case the old feudal sentiment for the liege temporal and spiritual has been long since dead. The old formula may, therefore, be conveniently adopted as an impression of the three phases of the modern world, which its votaries are so jealous of preserving. Beneath throne, altar, and hearth, in their present form, all Socialists know that there lies the market. They know that the market is the bed-rock on which the throne, the altar, and the hearth of the 19th century rest, and that once this bed-rock be shattered the said throne, altar, and hearth will be doomed.

Respecting the throne and the altar we have not much to say in the present article. It is with the bulwark of social life, the hearth, otherwise expressed as modern family-life, that we are here chiefly concerned. We refer more especially to the family life whose special architectural expression is the suburban villa. This is the ideal of the middle-class family of a "lower," *i.e.,* poorer degree, while in those of a "higher," *i.e.,* richer degree, its characteristics are exaggerated into the rank luxuriance symbolised in the brand-new country mansion. Let us consider briefly the characteristics of the suburban villa in its daily life and surroundings, much as we would that of some ancient people, as thus:—I. Household Ways; early morning (item 1) Prayers. (2) Breakfast. (3) Departure of Paterfamilias and sons to business. Journey beguiled by morning papers and conversation resembling for the most part undigested "leaders" from same. (N.B.—The modern journalist is, as it were, the cook who boils down and seasons up into a presentable *entrée* the "dead cats" of middle-class prejudice). (4) At home the wife and daughters, after a possible feint at domestic duties, prepare for "shopping." (5) "Shopping," the main occupation in the day for the middle-class female, being over, luncheon follows, then calls, then afternoon tea. (6) Return of paterfamilias, more or less wearied with his daily round of laboriously endeavoring to shift money from his neighbour's pocket into his own, wearied, *i.e.,* and degraded, with doing no useful work whatever. (7) Evening taken up with sleep, or conversation on the affairs of the family, together with its relations and connections, varied with the indifferent performance of fashionable music and the perusal of "current" literature. The above, we contend, is a fair picture of the type toward which the daily life of the average English middle-class family gravitates. We have said English, inasmuch as the commercial system has been more potent in its effect on English domestic life than on that of any other European people; but the same tendency to vapidity, inanity, pseudo-culture, which is the worst form of lack of refinement, obtains to a greater or less extent wherever a commercial middle-class exists. A few words now on the art, the literature, the sentiment, moral and religious, of the class in question.

First, as to the house decoration. Not to speak of furniture proper, what do we see on the walls? Art embodied in "furniture," pictures, among them oftentimes the terrible counterfeit presentment of connections of the family, which, were there a vestige of taste left in the household management, would never be exposed to the gaze even of the casual visitor. The superficiality of average middle-class culture is painfully illustrated in the complete ignorance displayed by the bourgeois man or woman as to the ugliness or commonplaceness of his or her relations. We quite admit that the ancestors or "connections" of a family may have a certain historical importance for those interested in its natural history, but save in a very few cases the interest attaching to them is limited to this. Now we contend that this does not justify the obtrusion of what is intrinsically disagreeable. There is, undoubtedly, considerable historical interest in Captain Burton's "Arabian Nights," but, inasmuch as there is that in it which is intrinsically unpleasant, the man of sensibility keeps it reserved under lock and key for private perusal. True "culture" gives a man the power of rising above the standpoint of his immediate interests, and of taking an objective view of things. It may be too much to expect of a man ever to see himself as others see him, but surely he might see his relations as others see them.

Apart from portraits, what other art does our middle-class parlour present? "Reproductions" by processes varying in badness according to the length of the family purse. In some cases these mechanical reproductions may be of the old masters, in which case they are perhaps the best thing procurable in the way of art. But for the artist it is surely a melancholy best when art in the family is represented by such. Again, let us take furniture and household decorations. A visit to any large upholsterer's shop will suffice to show the superficiality of the varnish of "taste" in matters decorative, even where absolute sordidness does not prevail. But the English lower middle-class family-parlour, or the never-entered drawing-room of the next grade! Can the "family" which has produced these things be in any way worth preserving?

If it be thought that its art and furniture are only superficial, local, and temporary accidents of the modern family, it is only necessary to turn to the rest of its products, to be convinced how very constantly everything connected with it hangs together. Its literature may be divided into two classes—the variable and the constant. The first consists in the circulating library three-volume novel, in which one section of middle-class womanhood delights; the second in "books" designed for "family reading" mostly of a moral or religious tendency, got up in bright colors and gilt leaves, and available at every suburban or provincial bookseller's or stationer's shop, in which another section delights. This class of literature, by the production of which many clergymen of insufficient stipend, and spinsters with disordered organic functions, gain a livelihood, was until the last few years the sole kind certain to be available in the typical middle-class "home." Its way of life, it must be admitted, has fallen somewhat into the sere and yellow leaf of late, but it flourishes more or less still, as the publishing firms of Griffith and Farran, Nisbet and Co., the Religious Tract Society, and even Cassell, Petter and Galpin, will testify.

Closely connected with this subject is that of religious practices. Religion in one or other of its forms is a staple ingredient of bourgeois family life in this country. It constitutes the chief amusement of the women of the family, who find in

Sunday-school teaching, district visiting, bazaars, etc., a virtuous mode of relieving themselves of the *ennui* which otherwise could not fail to overtake their empty lives. The singular part of it is that with all the attempts of these respectable unfortunates to enlighten and elevate the "poor," there is an entire absence of all suspicion that they themselves need enlightening and elevating. Of late years, we note, as a sign of the times, that there has been a tendency to modification of the teaching from theology to economy. Evangelicism with its "conversions," its "changes of heart," has fallen decidedly flat of late, even with that half-educated middle-class, which some quarter of a century ago were its most prominent votaries. It is tacitly acknowledged to be out of date. Its catchwords, moreover, now that they have been dragged through the Salvation Army, and had to serve as convenient trade-marks for tea, sugar, and other groceries, and, in fact, make themselves generally useful to the enterprising firm of Booth and Sons, look decidedly the worse for wear. After the appearance in a provincial town (as reported in the newspapers some time ago) of the ingenious advertisement of a Salvation Army meeting, running, "Why give 10d. a pound for mutton when you can get the lamb of God for nothing?" the well-known phrase is perhaps deemed to be somewhat spoiled for the ministrations of the respectable wife or daughter. There is the possible danger of getting "mixed-up" with the "army" and its proceedings. Be this as it may, the fact remains that "thrift," "teetotalism," "industry," and the rest of the economic virtues, are superseding "immediate repentance," "coming to the Saviour," etc., as the subjects for exhortation in the visitation of the poor.

But however unfashionable the old dogmatics may become, there is one institution which will certainly hold its own so long as the bourgeois family lasts, and that is the "place of worship." In contemporary British social life the church or chapel is the rendezvous or general club for both sexes; it is the centre of many minds, round which the melancholy institution of the suburban or provincial evening party circulates. It is the *bureau de mariage* for the enterprising youth who goes to business to qualify for "success in life," and the commercial virgin anxious to be settled, to meet and form connections. Besides all this, it serves the purpose of a fashionable lounge, where the well-dressed may disport themselves and make physiognomical observations if that way inclined. So, all things considered, the "place of worship" may watch unconcernedly the decay of dogma so long as the "great middle-class" maintains its supremacy—in this country at least.

We defy any human being to point to a single reality, good or bad, in the composition of the Bourgeois family. It is indubitably the most perfect specimen of the complete sham that history has presented to the world. There are no holes in the texture through which reality might chance to peer. The Bourgeois hearth dreads honesty as its cat dreads cold water. The literary classics that are reprinted for its behoof it demands shall be vigorously Bowdlerised, even though at the expense of their point. Topics of social importance are tabooed from rational discussion, with the inevitable result that erotic instances of middle-class womanhood are glad of the excuse afforded by "good intentions," "honest fanaticism," and the like things supposed to be associated with "Contagious Diseases Act" and "Criminal

Law amendment" agitations, to surfeit themselves on obscenity. And these are the people who cannot allow unexpurgated editions of Boccaccio or even of Sterne or Fielding to be seen on their drawing-room tables! Then again, the attitude of the family to the word—"damn." Now if there is an honest straightforward word in the English language—a word which the Briton utters in the fulness of his heart—it is this word; and precisely, as it would seem, for this reason it is a word which is supposed never to enter the "family," even newspapers, in order to maintain their right of entrance to the domestic sanctuary, having to print it with a "d" and a dash—the meaning of which euphemism, by a polite fiction, the "wife" or "daughter" is supposed not to understand. But the word is coarse and offensive in itself, the Bourgeois may retort. You have tried to make it so, I reply, by classing it with the filthy and inane phrases, bred of the squalor which modern capitalism creates, but in reality it is good, expressive English. Nay, more, it has "higher claims on your consideration"—to employ one of your own phrases—it bears the impress of Christianity upon it; for is it not to Christianity that we are indebted for the ennobling idea and spiritual significance of the word? The reputed founder of Christianity, if the authenticity of the gospels is to be relied on in this respect, much affected the expression. In fact, in common consistency you ought to reduce the "damns" of your New Testaments to "d——s," to make the work suitable for family reading. You do not do this, and why? Because your real objection to the colloquial "damn" is, as before remarked, that it has a ring of honest sentiment in it against which your sham family sentiment revolts.

Let us take another "fraud" of middle-class family life—the family party. That ever and anon a wide circle of friends should meet together in a spirit of good-fellowship is clearly right and rational; but the principle of the family party is that a body of persons often having nothing whatever in common but ties of kinship extending in remoteness from the definiteness of blood relation to the indefiniteness of connection—that such a motley crew should thus meet together in exclusive conclave, and spend several mortal hours in simulated interest in each other. Now a cousin, let us say, may be an interesting person, but very often he is not. If he is not, why, in the name of average human understanding, should one be expected every 25th of December or other occasion, to make a point of spending one's leisure with a man who is a cousin but not interesting rather than with another man who is interesting but not a cousin? The reason is, of course, that the tradition of the "family" has to be kept up. A "relation," however remote, is, in the eyes of Bourgeois society, more to a man than a friend, however near. So relations, male and female, congregate together on certain occasions to do dreary homage to this "family" sentiment.

On the same principle the symbolical black of mourning is graduated by the tailor and milliner in mathematically accurate ratio, according to the amount, not of affection, but of relationship. The utter and ghastly rottenness of Bourgeois family sentiment is in nothing more clearly evinced than in the mockery of grief and empty ostentation of tailoring and millinery displayed on the death of a near relation. What is the first concern of the middle-class household the instant the life-breath has left one of its members but to "see after the mourning," as the expression is? Now to a person of sensibility, the notion that the moment he enters on his last sleep his or her relations will "see about the mourning" may well impart to death a terror which it had not before, and thus act as an incentive to carefully-concealed suicide. We believe, indeed, the frequency of "mysterious disappearances" in middle-class circles may be largely explained by this, without resorting to far-fetched hypotheses of midnight murders on the Thames embankment, and the like. No, to signify a bereavement to the outer world (if so desired) by a band of crape on the sleeve or hat, or some such simple emblem, is one thing; to eagerly take advantage of the bereavement for the purpose of decking out the person in trousers designed in the newest cut adapted for the display of the male leg, or "bodies" in which the fulness of the female breast is manifested, is quite another—and nothing less than a ghastly travesty of sentiment.

This, then, is the "hearth," this the family life, the family sentiment which certain writers are so jealous of preserving. In vain do enthusiastic young persons band themselves together, under the benediction of the old man of Coniston, into societies of St George, in the hope that the low level of modern social life, with its vulgarity, its inanity, and its ugliness, by some wondrous educational stimulus, emanating from their own enthusiastic and artistic souls, may undergo a process of upheaval. After some years of Ruskinian preaching, what is the net result? A sprinkling of households among specially literary and artistic circles where better things are attempted, and so far as the elements of furniture and decoration are concerned, perhaps with some measure of success. But even here you generally find the counterbalancing evil inevitably attending a hothouse culture out of harmony with general social conditions—viz., affectation and self-consciousness. No healthy living art or culture has ever been the result of conscious effort. When it comes to saying "go to, now, let us be wise," or "let us be artistic," it is quite certain that the wisdom or art resulting will not be worth very much. The distinction between an artificial culture of this sort, which is *cut off* from the life of the society as a whole, and the natural culture which *grows out of* such life, is as the difference between the flower plucked from its root and withering in the hand and the same flower growing in luxuriance on its native soil. For what, after all, has modern art to offer but at best the plucked flowers of the art of the past, which sprang out of the life of the past? Your societies of St George, your æsthetic movements, etc., only touch a fringe of the well-to-do classes: they have no root in the life of the present day; and because they have no root they wither away, and in a few years remain dried up between the pages of history, to mark the place of mistaken enthusiasm and abortive energies. It is surely time that these excellent young people, together with their beloved prophet, descended for a while from their mount of Ruskinian transfiguration, with its rolling masses of vaporous sentiment, to the prosaic ground of economic science, and saw things as they are. They would then recognise the vanity of their efforts, and the reason of this vanity to lie in their disregard of the economic foundation and substructure of all human affairs; they would see the radical impossibility of the growth of any art, culture, or sentiment in the slimy ooze of greed and profit-mongering—in other words, in a society resting on a capitalistic basis. They would see, further, that the end of the world of profit and privilege cannot be attained by enthusiasms, good intentions, or any available form of class culture, but will have to be reached by a very different route—maybe through February riotings, and possibly still rougher things.

The transformation of the current family-form—founded as it is on the economic dependence of women, the maintenance of the young and the aged falling on individuals rather than on the community—into a freer, more real, and therefore a higher form, must inevitably follow the economic revolution which will place the means of production and distribution under the control of all for the good of all. The Bourgeois "hearth," with its jerry-built architecture, its cheap art its shoddy furniture, its false sentiment, its pretentious pseudo-culture will then be as dead as Roman Britain.

# 39

## *SOME WORDS TO SOCIALIST WOMEN*, SOCIAL DEMOCRATIC PARTY WOMEN'S COMMITTEE (LONDON: TWENTIETH CENTURY PRESS, 1908), 5–16.

*Dora B. Montefiore*

[Until 1904 there was no separate women's organisation inside the SDF. It was not until 1907 that the SDF weekly *Justice* published a woman's column. The notion of providing separate spaces for women's activities had been a source of considerable controversy within the socialist movement. Many women activists were resistant to being compartmentalised in what they feared would be restrictive and auxiliary roles contradicting the socialist aspiration to full equality. Others took part in ad hoc local women's groups, providing a focus for a woman-centred politics that recognised the specific challenges of enabling women's political engagement. That the SDF established a national women's committee in 1904 was due in part to the formation of the Women's Social and Political Union (1903) as both a rival for the attachments of working-class women and an example of the political roles they could take on. Dora Montefiore (for whom see Chapter 22) was herself a sometime WSPU member who was at the forefront of these activities within the SDF.

Montefiore acknowledges that the central theme of motherhood which she pushes in this pamphlet might be seen as old-fashioned. Through the ideas of "social motherhood", "collective motherhood" and "scientific motherhood and fatherhood" it is made clear that there is no suggestion of confining women to the home. To many of her readers Montefiore would already be known as an established campaigner for women's rights and this is reflected here in a range of concerns from communal feeding arrangements to discriminatory marriage and divorce laws. Nevertheless, the motherhood theme does also lend support to some of the maternalist political agendas enjoying wide currency in this period. Linkages between motherhood, peace and welfare, or of the "loss to the race" of thousands under present conditions, suggest affinities with contemporary campaigning around the "endowment of motherhood", as for example in H.D. Harben's Fabian tract on the subject published in 1910. Like every SDP member, Montefiore saw no real difference between the outgoing Conservative prime minister A.J. Balfour and the Liberal government that succeeded him. She also expresses her support for the SDP's adult suffrage position which opposed the extension to eligible women of the current restricted franchise. In 1909–1910, Monetfiore went on to produce a weekly column for *Justice*, "Our Women's Circle", in which she addressed the issue of a woman-focused socialism with a strong sense of developments in the international socialist and women's movements (Hunt 2001, 33). This same sense of internationalism would in 1912 be the immediate cause of her break with what was by his time the BSP (Chapter 47).]

The one common appeal that is sure to go straight home to the heart and head of every Socialist woman: whether she has only been a short time, or for many years in the movement; whether she has carefully studied its economic basis, or has only glad intuitions of it; whether she is able to work for Socialism, only in her home and among a few near neighbours, or is standing for it publicly before the callous and hostile world—is the one common appeal of Motherhood. Some Socialist women, when they read this opening sentence, may think this is rather an old-fashioned way to begin a pamphlet which we hope to spread among non-Socialists, in order to let them know what we Socialist women are working for, both now and in the future. But when I have explained that I am using the word Motherhood in its Socialist, and not in its individualist, sense—that is to say, that I mean it to include, not only physical, but intellectual, spiritual and social Motherhood, those who are students of Socialist principles will understand at once that the word, used in this wide and social sense, *does* make the new and true appeal to all women that the evolved Socialist woman desires to make.

Let me extend the thought a little further. Is it not a fact that actual physical motherhood is quite insufficient to rear, train, educate and develop the character of an ideal citizen? Physical motherhood gives life; but the three other phases step in later on, and each fulfil their function towards the growing child. Nay, is it not true that in these later stages many women, who from one cause or another, have not experienced physical motherhood, are able to share in the joys and sorrows of intellectual, spiritual and social motherhood? There is no necessity to dwell on this point; one has only to remember the thousands of women engaged in teaching and in training the moral and spiritual faculties of the young; of those who are bringing up orphan or deserted children; of those who are working in public administration, and are thus exercising Social Motherhood. Under the present system of capitalism, or of private property, belonging to a privileged few, every woman who feels this appeal of motherhood must suffer daily, when she sees the greater number of the children of the race thrust out by material conditions from any share in real home life, from any just share in the food, and the clothing, and the comforts enjoyed by other children, and from any contact with decent social environment. No woman, with the real mother feeling, can be satisfied to see only *her* children enjoying the advantages which *all* children should enjoy. If the sight of the condition of the majority of the children in the various countries where Capitalism enforces present economic and social conditions, does not warn mothers that something is wrong in the body politic, then it shows how morally deteriorating are conventional religion, conventional ethics, and conventional social conditions. We Socialist women appeal, as mothers, to those who still believe that Christianity has power to alter the heart of man, and cause him to do justice to his fellow-man; and, taking the words and actions of the founder of the religion in which the majority of the people of this country believe, we ask them: How many of those in authority and power should have mill-stones tied round their necks, and be cast into the sea, for allowing, nay, for forcing the little children of our slums and alleys and villages to live as they do live? Under Socialism, this daily reproach, this daily suffering thrust at present on every evolved, potential mother, will cease; for *all* children will, from their birth, have equal advantages and opportunities. Motherhood suffers under the present competitive system when the children of the working classes have to begin to earn their own living before they are physically strong enough to do so, and before their education and training, which should fit them for their life-work, is complete. The loss to the race under the present system, which puts on tens of thousands of growing, ill-nourished children the double strain of wage-earning and of intellectual study, is incalculable. Under Socialism, only adults, that is, grown-up people over twenty-one, would be working for the community; and it is only under such conditions that the best brains, and the best muscles, and the best character among the whole youth of the nation will be developed. Motherhood suffers again at the present time, when the boys and girls, being grown up, come in contact with the vice of the streets and of the public-house, as run at present for profits to the brewers. Here, again, the comparatively few "privileged" young people can be, to some extent, protected and saved from the worst and lowest temptations; but for the masses of the young the only "pleasures" that commercialism offers are those whose unholy profits enrich titled brewers, and aristocratic ground landlords. Collective Motherhood has no power to cleanse and purify the streets, as she would cleanse and purify her home. But, under Socialism, when all places of amusement will be run for the real benefit and pleasure of the community, and not for profit-mongers, the pure mother spirit will reach out further than the four walls of the material home, and will follow with love and wisdom the steps of her sons and daughters through some of the most difficult years of their young lives.

Motherhood is, under present conditions, again outraged and stultified, when her sons and daughters grown to manhood and womanhood, fail to find work in the country of their birth, and have to face the alternative of slow starvation and deterioration, or of being shipped off by the emigration agent, who finds his profit in the economic despair of his fellow-creatures. Motherhood under Socialism will be relieved from the pang of knowing that the child she caresses, feeds, and cares for, for whom she would, if necessary, lay down her life, may some day be faced with the alternatives of registering at a Distress Committee, of breaking stones in a Workhouse, or of committing a crime against property, in order to be sent to prison and obtain the food and shelter which society denies at the present time to the out-of-work. Again, is not Motherhood under Capitalism mocked, when it is told to produce fighting men, in order that commercial wars of aggression may be undertaken, and her sons may be taught to kill, in the quarrels of kings and emperors, the sons of other mothers? Socialism is nothing if it is not international; and this international spirit of comradeship will kill out the competitive spirit of commercial and imperial rivalry, and help the nations in the future to live together in peace. Finally, is it not the mother, she whose life has been spent in ministering to others, who best understands the care and tending of the old—of those whose day's work being done, need a tender, helpful hand down the last painful hill? Under Capitalism it is only a few among the old who receive that sheltering, understanding care; the old among the working classes are forced, either to feel themselves burdens on already overburdened sons and daughters, or they starve in garrets and cellars, or are driven by the relieving officer into the dreaded Workhouse. Under Socialism, Collective Motherhood would fix an age when compulsory work for the community should cease, after which the superannuated could, as the privileged superannuated do now, be maintained by the community, either with their families, or in communal life, or in communal life with their contemporaries in age.

This, then, is why I have chosen the guiding thought of Motherhood, as it is, and as it might be, in this exposition of Socialism from the woman's point of view; in order to prove that the better the woman, the more loving and more evolved the mother, the more actively she should be struggling to replace the present chaos of Capitalism by organised Socialism. This Socialism, of which we hear so much nowadays, may be described, not so much as a system, not so much as a dogma (that is, some belief to be taken on faith), but as an interpretation of *facts* from the point of view of the oppressed, but evolving, masses of the population. Now, in order to emphasise and interpret these facts, and to throw light on what Motherhood under Capitalism is compelled to be, I shall begin by reminding you that, taking our whole population of 43 millions, one-third, or 14 millions of that population, at the present time lives below the level of subsistence; that is to say, in plain English that one-third of the people have not enough food for their stomachs, nor enough clothes to their backs! What sort of motherhood do you think is possible among that one-third of the population of wealthy England? What home life is possible where the woman home-maker never knows from one week-end to another what is the scanty sum she will have at her command to lay out on bread, milk and scraps of meat or fried fish? What home life is possible where the thought of Monday, with the fateful rap of the man calling for the rent, shakes the nerve of the woman home-maker, and drives her forth pitilessly (it may be in merciless cold and wet) to take her place at daybreak on Monday morning in the waiting procession outside the pawnbroker's, with some treasured bit of the home under her ragged shawl? How can the home lamp of love be kept burning under conditions such as these? How can the tender ministry of helpful sympathy, which is a mother's due in her hour of pain and need, be realised in the distressful, disorganised lives, which present society, as a strong, successful, unsympathetic whole, force on the weak and unsuccessful in the daily struggle for existence?

Let me quote from my impressions of that memorable march of the women of the unemployed in November, 1905, when Mr. Balfour found courage to reply to the broken words of women, starving in the midst of plenty: "You have my sympathy, but what can I do?" And then let me remind you women that a Liberal Prime Minister now fills the place of Mr. Balfour; but the wives and children of the unemployed and underpaid are still starving in the midst of plenty. "One out of every three or four women," I wrote then, "carried a more or less puny, ill-nourished infant in her arms; and now and then a child would be passed from one to another, so as to give the overstrained mother a rest. Wonderfully patient and uncomplaining were both mothers and babies, for lack of everything is a stern, relentless task-master, which brings, after a time, men, women, and unconscious children to heel, and eats out the heart of honest rebellion. If you would know what it has cost to get these women to muster in the street, and show forth their dire need before an unsympathetic world, you must first reckon how long they have gone short, and starved in silence; how long they have put up in their front windows well-washed bits of white curtains, when the clothing and furniture had gone piece by piece to the pawnbroker's; how long they had fiercely kept up the exteriors of "respectability," as measured by working-class standards; how much it had cost them to appear before parish authorities, and disclose the cruel emptiness of the squalid rooms they still called 'home,' while they begged for a parish dole to save from starvation themselves and their children. When you have undermined and beaten down fortress after fortress of these reserves, then the woman-soul, the mutilated mother-soul, will perhaps stand revealed for those who have eyes to see, and hearts to understand; and you will recognise in these gaunt, starved, bloated, and at times smitten faces, the souls of heroines, who have performed, and are prepared in their inarticulate, unconscious, but faithful constancy, to perform again and again deeds of self-renunciation, of which most well-to-do women are utterly incapable. Mutilated Motherhood! That is the fate, that is the martyrdom to which England condemns masses of her womanhood. And out of that mutilation, out of that martyrdom she seems to expect that she can breed the citizens of a great and free Empire!"

Now, that description of the submerged motherhood of the East End is just as true of the submerged in our other great towns, and just as true of the wives of our agricultural labourers, wearing out their lives in bringing up an underfed race on the fourteen or fifteen shillings a week, which is the agricultural labourer's share of the food-wealth he produces. Out of the 43 million people of Great Britain, about 5 millions receive half the annual income of the country, while 38 millions receive the other half. You will at once understand, therefore, that those 38 millions must be, more or less, the wage-slaves of the 5 millions; and then, if you think and reason more about it, you will say to yourselves: "Those 38 millions must be very foolish if they do not understand that numbers make strength, and that if they all united together, and knew what they wanted, and worked for what they wanted, they could not fail to get it."

Well, what is it the people of England want; what is it that each of you working-class mothers want in order that the millions of workers may get a fair share of wealth, and comfort, and education? You want, first, the land of England, from which you have been turned away; you want, secondly, the machinery, and workshops and factories for your own, so that you may begin at once to grow food, and make clothes, and build houses for the use of the people, instead of for making profits for the 5 millions, who now receive half the national income. Then you want, further, to get hold of all the railways, and steamers, and canals, so that you may be able to use them as freely as you now do the roads; and transport the food, and the clothes, and the building materials to the parts of the country where they are needed. Then you want everything that is grown and produced to be grown and produced for the *use of all,* and not, as at present, *for the profit of a few.* This scheme is the only remedy that will cure unemployment, sweep away the slums, and feed the hungry children! The 5 million rich people know that this is so; and they do all they can to prevent the 14 million under-paid, under-fed workers from learning about it; and they give every winter, what are called by the newspapers in their pay "magnificent voluntary contributions for the relief of distress"; while all the rest of the year they are themselves manufacturing that distress.

Do not be deceived, you women of the people for whom I am writing; do not be deceived about "those magnificent voluntary subscriptions." When one of you, out of your scanty spending-money, gives a penny to someone poorer than yourself; or when some mother among you gives a slice of bread-and-butter to a neighbour's child going starving to school, you are depriving yourselves of much more than does the rich man or woman who sends in a cheque for £10,000 to be distributed on "charity!" *Don't forget, never forget, that the giver of the cheque, and 5 million others, receive half the annual income!!!* Write out these facts in plain figures, and talk them over with your men, and teach them to your children; and when you have thought about them, and talked about them, and taught them to others, when you have been to Socialist meetings, and perhaps asked questions, and received answers that will set you thinking further, you will find that the only remedy for all the troubles under which you working-class mothers suffer, is Socialism; and that the only people, who are trying permanently to help you are the Socialist leaders. *What those leaders are waiting for now is the help of the millions of workers, men and women, who get such a miserable share of England's great wealth.*

But you will be told by some: "Socialists are wicked people, who don't believe in God, and who want to break up family life." Now Socialism, being, as I have told you already, not a system, not a belief, but an interpretation of *facts,* based on the oppression of the working classes, it can have nothing to do with the question of your belief or unbelief in a personal God. Just as in the matter of food, one food may suit one person, and disagree with another, so in the matter of beliefs, one form of belief may suit one person, and may seem absurd to another. But

Socialism can have nothing to dictate as to the nature of your food, or as to the form of your belief. What Socialism will do is to provide the best quality of food, and the best quality of sound scientific teaching for all, so that there may be no physical deterioration caused by adulterated food, and no intellectual ignorance and error caused by superstition and lack of knowledge. Socialism will teach that ignorance is the only sin; that the time to be happy is *now*, and the place to be happy is *here*; and it will point out how that happiness, under a re-organised system of society, may be obtained. Do not be afraid, you women, of the word "science"; it only means the gathered and ordered knowledge of the past and of the present; and it is only right that all of us, who have to live in this world, should have at our disposal, and be carefully taught the best that men know. We Socialists want you women above all things to think for yourselves, and not believe at once, without inquiring into the matter, when people tell you that established religion has always been the best friend of women. Don't forget that Jehovah, the God of the Jews, is reported by one of the "inspired" writers of the Bible as having said to some of the Jews with whom he was angry: "Thus saith the Lord, Behold, I will raise up evil against thee out of thine own house, and will take thy wives, before thy eyes, and give them unto thy neighbour." What sort of opinion do you think that God had of women, when he simply used them to punish men, with whom he was angry? Never seeming to think for a moment of the horrible suffering and degradation to which he was subjecting those Jewish wives.

We want you also to use your reason, and to think out for yourselves this question of the "breaking up of family life," the blame for which is being fastened on the Socialists. It is quite true that family life is not now exactly what it was when I, and perhaps some of you who are reading this, were young. These changes have not only taken place in the families of the workers, but in the families of the upper and middle classes Many things are now made in factories, and many processes are carried on by steam or electricity, outside the home, which used to be carried on in the home by hand. The facilities now for having meals away from home, and in public and cheap restaurants, are enormous, and are increasing every day. Education is compulsory for all children; and, before long, many of the children will have, at least, one meal at the school which they attend; whilst, as we know, the children of the upper and middle classes go to boarding schools, and have *all* their meals away from home. All these causes, together with the fact that the girls, who used to help their mothers in the home work, and received no pay, now work outside in factories, shops, and restaurants, and get paid for their labour—all these facts, I say, take people out of their homes, and tend to make the home-tie *apparently* less close than it used to be. But it does not make home love and affection less, because those affections go deep down into human nature, and no outside economic causes change or alter them. Neither have Socialists anything to do with this gradual and evolutional change in the conditions of family life. The change is produced by economic causes—those very same causes which are forcing to the front the teachings of Socialism. Those of you who have read history will know that society was not always organised as it is organised now, neither were conventional sex relations what they are now. In the times of the Greeks and Romans, the workers were chattel-slaves, and the property of their masters; later on, when it was no longer profitable to keep slaves, this same class of workers were called serfs, who were attached to the soil, which they had to cultivate for their masters; but they could not be bought and sold, as were the chattel-slaves. Then, with industrialism came wage-slavery, when men and women are "free" to work when work is to be had from the capitalist employer, and are "free" to starve when no work is to be obtained. But through all these economic changes the position of the working woman has always been worse than the position of the working man, because she has had to suffer an added slavery: the slavery of sex. *Her sex has never been her own, to deal with as she herself desires.* As a chattel-slave, her master, besides making her work for his profit, used her body as his property. As a serf, even the married woman serf could not escape the degradation of having to submit herself to the "rights" claimed by the feudal lord; and under industrialism, the woman who is forced by economic necessity to work in a factory, too often finds that the tradition of this sex oppression and sex servitude survives in the power exercised by the foreman. Women of all classes have been legislated for, not as individuals, not as responsible human beings, but as the property of some man. If you doubt this, think of the wording of the marriage service, where the woman has to be given by one man to the other man, proving that she never, in the eyes of the Law or of the Church, belongs to herself. Then, again, in cases of divorce, if the co-respondent (or the man with whom the wife has formed a fresh tie) has property, he is called upon by the law to pay damages for having stolen, or damaged the husband's property; proving once again that this old idea of the woman being the sex-property of some man has not yet died out. As the ideas of Socialism spread, so private property in everything (wives included) will cease to exist, and women of all classes will possess themselves. If you will think out this question for yourselves, you will call to mind the various reasons beside love and inclination, for which women now, too often, enter into marriage; and you will then be able to realise how differently the woman of the future, who will be economically free, will approach the subject of a life-union with a man who is also economically free. Many women marry now because they need a home, and they think that if they marry, the man will make them that home, and they will be happier and have easier lives than when working for themselves, or depending on relations. But, under Capitalism, the woman soon finds that it is very difficult for a man to earn enough for himself, and wife and children; and she herself is too often forced to accept any unorganised, ill-paid work that may offer, in order to keep the wolf from the door. Under Socialism, all child-bearing women, who are fulfilling one of the most important functions in the community, in providing it with healthy future citizens, will be maintained by the community, just as everyone else who works for the community will be maintained. Please note that I write, "healthy children," because the Socialist Commonwealth will require that this question of Motherhood shall, like every other question, be studied and treated scientifically; and men and women will be required to make scientific motherhood and fatherhood a special study. In the sex-unions of the future the fact of paramount importance to the community will be the children that are the result of such unions; because the community, being bound to support the children, has a right to demand that they shall be well and healthily born. With unions that do not result in child-bearing, the community will have no cause for interference (beyond registering when they commence and cease), because that will be part of the private life of the people concerned; and with the private life of grown-up people the Commonwealth, or Administration, will have nothing to do. Remember, my women friends and comrades, that the race itself is growing up, is becoming conscious of its destiny; and an important part of that consciousness must be expressed in its Motherhood and Fatherhood. Once we have gained Adult Suffrage (which is very near in this country, if the people are prepared to show they mean to have it), all legislation must be made to tend less and less towards governing, or interfering with the private life of individuals, and more and more towards the *administration of the affairs of the people as a whole*. We, as an evolved conscious race, will direct our own lives; and together we will co-operatively and democratically manage our own affairs. I have already pointed out that what are called "economic questions" (that is, questions that have to do with wage-earning, the supply of labour, and the opportunities people have of working for wages) always affect the conventional, and often the legalised morals of the day; and to illustrate this point I want you working women to note how differently a domestic servant, who bears an illegitimate child, is treated nowadays by her mistress, to what she used to be treated twenty or thirty years ago. In those days the domestic servant unmarried mother was said to "have lost her character"; it was almost impossible for her to get another place, and her mistress and society usually combined to place the girl in a penitentiary, where she worked for years at the wash-tub without wages. Nowadays, good servants, especially good cooks, are much scarcer than they were twenty or thirty years ago, *and they are therefore of more economic value*; if, therefore, a modern mistress discovers that an "excellent servant" is likely to become a mother, she generally sends the girl away till the child is born, and helps her afterwards to place the child under proper care; and the mistress very often takes the servant back into her service. As you see, the economic conditions have modified the middle-class judgment of the offence against conventional morals.

You will begin, perhaps, to see now that it is all these economic changes, these new economic forces, that are almost imperceptibly changing our opinions, our laws, and the conditions of our daily lives. These changes, these forces, are quite outside ourselves; we can only interpret them, and help others to understand with us what is causing these changes. Some women at the present time are interpreting things wrongly; they feel and resent much of the burdensome economic inheritance of the past; and, forgetting that it presses almost as heavily on unprivileged men as it does on unprivileged women, they try to stir up a sex-war instead of preaching a class-war. That this false interpretation of facts is recoiling on themselves is shown by the fact that, at the present time, wherever these anti-man leaders are holding meetings they fail to get a hearing, because they are making the fundamental mistake of stirring up an hysterical form of feminism, instead of setting before the people an understanding and reforming scheme of humanism. The woman of the people has been the first to see through the shallowness of their propaganda, and every day the working-class women are flocking to the banner of Adult Suffrage, or Votes for All Women and All Men.

To give you a concrete case of how motherhood among the working classes is treated now (although capitalist newspapers are fond of writing about "sacred motherhood" and "the beauty of home") and how it would be treated under Socialism, I will tell you about a "home" in the East End of London, where lives a working woman friend of mine; and then you will be able to judge for yourselves whether it is the teaching of Socialism or the forces of Capitalism which are destroying motherhood and home. This working woman friend is bringing up eight beautiful children in a mean brick box (called a "house"), in a mean street in the crowded East End of London, where no rich woman who keeps pet dogs would allow those "pets" to live for one day. For this old, mean, rotten, dilapidated shelter they are forced to call "home," the parents pay a third of their weekly earnings, and have to take in a lodger in order to help them out with the rent. The children, immediately they are of an age when the law "allows" them to become wage-earners, have to sell newspapers, work in laundries till nine o'clock at night, or do some of the other underpaid and despised work of this busy London. The mother has fulfilled every duty of motherhood since the children were born; and, in spite of their miserable surroundings, they are fair and beautiful. But what help does that woman get in her daily struggle, in her daily deadening round of domestic work in a "home" which no earthly power could ever make clean or home-like? Does the community take into consideration the fact that she is bringing up for the future eight healthy, strong citizens? No; the community, under the present system, never helps her in her struggle, never encourages her in the fulfilment of her duties. If she were a bad mother, if she let her children die by feeding them out of dirty bottles, instead of giving them the breast; if she spent her husband's scanty wage at the public-house, instead of making it go as far as she can among the ten hungry mouths, she would be punished by the community; but of help, praise, encouragement, a fair share of the *necessities,* even, of life—there is nothing of that for the working-class mother of to-day! And under Socialism, what would be the position of my friend? Her eight children would have the *same* conditions, the *same* advantages in life as *all* the other children of the nation. The clothing produced would be for the benefit of all; and all the pretty and useful things that are displayed in the shop windows now for the joy and comfort of a few privileged mothers and babies would then be procurable from the communal stores for the benefit of *all* mothers and babies. The schools would be for all the children of the nation, and none would be taken away from school to work for their living before they were strong enough and healthy enough to stand the burden of work. As all the old, horrible slums, and alleys, and dark, noisome courts would have disappeared, my friend and her children would be living in a house, where the little ones could learn from their baby days what the comfort and beauty of home-life mean. The present system of public restaurants will then be organised and improved, and those whose work or taste lead them to have their meals away from home, will know that the food provided outside by communal care is as free from adulteration as scientifically-taught, Social Motherhood can make it. The walls of the communal restaurants will be hung with the best pictures that Art, under the fostering care of Socialism, can produce; and pleasant, soft music will be played while meals are going on, just as it is played now in the expensive restaurants of the West End, where the privileged rich congregate. Can you, who read this, realise how different would be the life of the East End mother of whom I have written? Do you not believe that this is an ideal worth working for, worth suffering for? And does not every one of you working women, who believes, as I do, that her children should have the same chance as other children, desire to work and to struggle for the realisation of this ideal? Some of our first practical aims must be to get votes for all women and all men, and to see that no children go hungry to school. And when you working-class mothers come out into the streets, and demonstrate for these great reforms, and *show the Government that you mean to have them,* then it will not be long before you get them.

Do not think, my women friends, these are fanciful dreams of the future that I have set before you; but remember that most of the intelligent men and women of the day are writing for, and speaking for, Socialism in all countries; and that each country is helping the other in the struggle to 'give the world to the workers."

In conclusion I am going to quote for you the words of a thinker, who has helped me much by his thought during the last twenty years. I rejoice always when I remember that he is one of the professors at the London University and is there influencing day by day the minds of the young men and young women, who may in their day see the realisation of our Socialist ideals:—

"To those who see in these things an ideal of idle dreamers and not a possibility of the future, I can only reply: Measure well the forces which are at work in our age, mark the strength of the men and women who are dissatisfied with the present, weigh carefully the enthusiasm of the teachers of our new morality, socialistic and sexual, then you will not class them as dreamers only. To those who would know their duty at the present, I can but say: The first steps towards our ideal are the spread of Socialism as a morality, and the complete emancipation of our sisters. To those who, like the aged poet, halt and are faint at heart, seeing in the greatness of our time only pettiness and lust, we must bid a sorrowful but resolute farewell—'Father, thou knowest not our needs. Thy task is done; remain and rest, we must onward. Farewell.' We are full of new emotions, new passions, new thoughts; our age is not one of pettiness and lust, but replete with clearer and nobler ideas than the past, ideas that its sons will generate and its daughters bring to birth. Dangers and difficulties there are: misery, pain and wrong-doing over and enough. But we of to-day see beyond them; they do not cause us to despair, but summon us to action. You of the past valued Christianity: aye, and we value free thought; you of the past valued faith: aye, and we value knowledge; you have sought wealth eagerly: we value more the duty and right to labour; you talked of the sanctity of marriage: we find therein love sold in the market, and we strive for a remedy in the freedom of sex. Your symbols are those of the past, symbols to which civilisation owes much, great landmarks in past history, pointing the direction of man's progress: even suggesting the future—our ideal. But as symbols for our action to-day, they are idle; they denote in the present serfdom of thought, and serfdom of labour, and serfdom of sex. We have other ideals more true to the coming ages—freedom of thought, and freedom of labour, and freedom of sex; ideals based on a deeper knowledge of human nature and its history than you, our fathers, could possess. Term them impious, irrational, impure, if you will: 'tis because you have understood neither the time, nor us. We must leave you sorrowfully behind and go forward alone. The age is strong in knowledge, rich in ideas; we hold the future not so distant when our symbols shall be the guides of conduct, and their beauty brought home to humanity by their realisation in a renascent art."

# 40

# *THE FUTURE OF WOMAN* (LONDON: TWENTIETH CENTURY PRESS, 1909), 1–14.

*Herbert Burrows*

[When Harry Hobart was won over to socialism by a lecture that inspired and astonished him (Chapter 7, this volume), the speaker was Herbert Burrows on the "Morality of Revolution". The son of a Chartist and himself a founding member of Hyndman's Democratic Federation, Burrows (1845–1922) offers a further reminder of commitments that cannot be arranged according to the stereotypes of moral and mechanical reformer. A tax officer by profession, Burrows has been described (by Hunt 1996, 206) as the "archetypal 'faddist'" who was teetotal, anti-tobacco, a vegetarian and, from 1889, an active theosophist. Burrows was also a strong supporter of trade union activities and with the Fabian Annie Besant helped to organise the famous match-girls' strike of 1888. As well as acting as treasurer to the newly formed Union of Women Matchmakers, Burrows would be active in the Women's Trade Union League and Women's Industrial Council until stricken with paralysis in 1917.

Burrows's importance in the SDF's history was also as a counterweight to Bax on what contemporaries referred to as the woman question. At the Federation's very foundation in 1881 Burrows, along with Helen Taylor, had prevailed over Hyndman in securing a commitment to adult rather than manhood suffrage (Crick 1988, 35). As he recounts in *The Future of Woman*, he had made his first speech on the subject when he was only fifteen, and by 1909 had long since expressed his objections to pronouncements like Bax's *Legal Subjection of Men* (1897). The mounting pressure of the women's suffrage campaign brought matters to a head. In January 1909, Bax came under fierce criticism for lending his name to a cross-party appeal for a Man's Committee for Opposing Women's Suffrage. Burrows would lead the movement of censure against Bax, and the following year recorded that Bax "hates me almost as much as he hates women, and that is saying a great deal" (Hunt 1996, 266). The basis for their antagonism is clearly spelt out in the case Burrows made for women's "political, social, economic and sexual" freedom in the lecture of February 1909 that is reproduced here.

The lecture was delivered at London's South Place Ethical Society, whose commitment to ethical humanism Burrows had upheld through long association. Indeed, though it was published by the Twentieth Century Press, the text is anything but a statement of party orthodoxy. Its broader frame of reference includes citations from the former poet laureate Tennyson, the Italian nationalist Giuseppe Mazzini and the American abolitionists Henry Ward Beecher and Elizabeth Cady Stanton. Burrows also refers to the American poets James Russell Lowell (1819–1891), and more particularly Charlotte Perkins Gilman (or Stetson, 1860–1935). Gilman's poem "We, as women" was printed at the end of the pamphlet along with an extract from the Anglican marriage service intended to demonstrate the Church's deliberate destruction of the individuality of the married woman. As well as John Oakesmith, author of *The Religion of Plutarch*, Burrows also makes favourable reference to the ILP socialist and suffrage campaigner Ethel Snowden. The one name more immediately familiar in SDF circles was that of the socialist and adult suffragist Charlotte Despard (1844–1939), whose *Woman in the New Era* was published in pamphlet form in 1910.

Burrows took as his text the first published collection of Olive Schreiner (1855–1920). His pamphlet is dedicated to Schreiner "in deep appreciation of her work for woman", and she in turn thought it "splendid in tone" (letter to Betty Molteno, 11 July 1909 at https://www.oliveschreiner.org/). The dedication is symptomatic of Burrows's enduring concern with the idealism which he believed too many socialists sacrificed to a crude conception of material self-interest. Had it not been for his final illness, Burrows had intended writing the history of the SDF, to which he had devoted his political life. Nevertheless, Burrows's heterodox positions had included active support for the International Arbitration and Peace Association, whose secretary was the SDF treasurer J. Frederick Green. When Hyndman in 1911 announced his support for a strong navy and citizens' army, Burrows, along with Green, at last took the step of breaking off, if only temporarily, an association he had held continuously for thirty years (Clayton 1926, 140).]

During the last few weeks two notable lectures on woman have been delivered on Sunday mornings from this platform. In December, Dr. Oakesmith, in his address on "Woman Triumphant," proved, I think conclusively, that in ancient Greek times woman occupied in the State a much higher position than she does in modern Europe, and in so doing buttressed the opinion which for years I have steadily held, that in what we proudly call advancing civilisation, woman, for generations, has, in many respects, retrograded instead of progressed. A fortnight ago Mrs. Ethel Snowden, in her very interesting lecture on "The Strike of a Sex," with lucid moderation, put forward, in her claim for woman suffrage, the inevitable modern rebellion on the part of her sex against this retrogression. These two addresses touched very important parts of the whole woman question. Dr. Oakesmith's answered the stupid objections that women are unfitted for political functions, and Mrs. Snowden's was the necessary argument that they should be given the opportunity to exercise those functions. Both lectures paved the way for my task to-day, a task which I frankly confess I originally entered on with somewhat of a light heart, but which since has taxed me sorely; for I have not to consider past history or refute the ordinary objections to giving women the vote, but in some measure to play the difficult part of prophet, to take for granted that not only what women are asking for to-day will be achieved, but very much more—that not only will certain technicalities of social and political organisation be accomplished facts, but that new principles of human life will have been brought into play, and that because of these the whole all-round life of woman—and therefore of man—will be practically transformed. I am, of course, fully conscious that in attempting to say anything whatever on these lines I can touch but the very fringe of this great question, even if I were to give you twenty lectures instead of one. Most men and most women, even including many strenuous Suffragists, have failed as yet to apprehend the enormously important fact that the woman question, in its true and real aspect, is the question of the whole human race in its evolution on this planet for countless ages to come. I do not know any man or any woman who has really worked this out, and I know of no book in any language which goes much below the surface of this transcendent subject. Countless volumes have, I am aware, been written on the question, but we have not even had one on that exceedingly important branch, the psychology of sex. Lately there has been much advertisement of a book by Forel, but it only scratches the outside of the matter. The fact is that nearly every one, even the most advanced advocates of women, is apt to consider the question as merely a development—far-reaching, it is true—of what are supposed to be the progressive conceptions of to-day. Behind that thought lie constantly sex theories and sex ideas, and the imagining that these are always to dominate the evolution of women and men. I do not believe this, and my non-belief colours, of course, all my thought on the woman question. This is why I am so very strongly opposed to the sex antagonism which is preached to-day by many of the prominent Suffragettes. I admit that considering the sins of man to woman in the past—and in the present—there is a seeming justification for this antagonism; but leaders of a great movement should rise far superior to this superficial view. Olive Schreiner is supremely right. It is the entire human race which is involved in the woman question, and the question cannot be solved either by woman or by man, but by the co-operative comradeship of both. When both women and men fully recognise that great truth, there will be no more talk that progress depends on woman as woman, or on man as man, but of the human being as the one and only factor in the evolution of collective humanity. Well and truly did Mazzini, the apostle of woman's freedom, declare:—

"In the sight of God the Father there is neither man nor woman. There is only the human being, that being in whom, whether the form be of male or female, those characteristics which distinguish humanity from the brute creation are united—namely, the social tendency, and the capacity for education and progress.

"Wheresoever these characteristics exist, the human nature is revealed, and thence perfect equality both of rights and of duties.

"Like two distinct branches springing from the same trunk, man and woman are varieties springing from the common basis—Humanity. There is no inequality between them, but even as is often the case among men, diversity of tendency and of special vocation. Are two notes of the same musical chord unequal or of different nature? Man and woman are the two notes without which the human chord is impossible."[1]

Wise, tender, and pregnant words; and, although they were written primarily for Italy, they are true for all time, both for woman and for man.

Now this idea, which Mazzini so eloquently expresses, cuts at the root of every objection to the political, the economic, the social, the sexual freedom of woman, and opens out before her the vast and illimitable future—the future which will be co-existent and co-extensive with the whole progress of humanity at large. There is a certain school of thought, mainly in this country, led almost by my friend, the anti-feminist Belfort Bax, which attempts to take up a very superior philosophic attitude in its antagonism to women. Its adherents place themselves on a lofty man-made pedestal of their own, and from that altitude look down with supreme contempt on the inferior woman sex who, in their eyes, crawl around its base. Mothers these men must have had; but in listening to them I have always to ask myself whether they ever had sisters, daughters, or wives. As you know, their contention is that, inherently and hopelessly, woman in every respect is inferior to man, and that, therefore, it is right and proper for man to prevent her from gaining her freedom because, if it were gained, it would be used against the real interests of the race. In arguing thus they forget their own philosophy, their own psychology (if ever they possessed it), their own economics, and their own evolutionary science. By their philosophy they are bound to recognise intellect and emotion in the human being, whether man or woman, of course in varying degrees. They dare not say that all intellect is confined to man and all emotion to woman—that would be too glaring; but they attempt to credit man with most of the intellect, and having, as they think, done that, they then exalt intellect as the supreme thing, to the disparagement of emotion. I deny their use of their philosophy, and I deny their psychology. I deny that intellect is the sole moving spring of progress. We in this place are the last persons in the world to ignore the debt we owe to reason and intellect, but we are also the last persons in the world to put emotion at the very bottom of human qualities, and deny its true place as one of the most important factors in the development of humanity. The world would be very grey and cheerless if intellect alone were king. As my old friend James Russell Lowell wrote, in his wonderful little poem on Robert Burns:—

> All thought begins in feeling—wide
>     In the great mass its base is hid,
> And, narrowing up to thought, stands glorified,
>     A moveless pyramid.
>
> All that hath been majestical
>     In life or death, since time began,
> Is native in the simple heart of all,
>     The angel heart of man.

And as Lowell told me, by man he meant humanity, man and woman, woman and man. I swear by the psychology of Lowell rather than by that of Belfort Bax.

But, again, these men forget their economics. They are Socialists—at least, Bax is—and the one great idea of the Socialism of the future, in which women as well as men will share, is the differentiation of function—that is, that all people will not be called upon to do everything, but that each and all will be encouraged to do that for which they are best fitted, for the good of all, and that each and all will be necessary for the well-being of the social organism. Therefore, all will have equal duties, and should have corresponding equal rights, because it is unjust to expect duties while at the same time rights are withheld. So there will be no further question as to whether women shall always make beds and men always bake bread, and whether these things shall for all time be their allotted functions, and no others. If a man shows he can make a bed better than a woman, and a woman shows she can bake bread better than a man, they will be each encouraged to do their best, and thereby the whole community, both men and women, will gain. This old, wretched idea of the Baxites that men and women must ever remain in the same grooves will be utterly exploded as a relic of the stupid past. Once grasp, as we shall grasp in the future, that every function which tends to the true development of the individual and of society is equally useful and equally honourable, and should be performed by those best fitted for it, whether man or woman, and we have the true foundation, in the human co-ordination of function, of a real human life.

And they forget their evolutionary science. If they continue to talk as they do, they should celebrate this Darwin centenary year by throwing all Darwin's works into the fire, and go back 2000 years to St. Paul and to his reactionary views of the proper position of woman—always behind the man! They argue as if women, and women alone, were a fixed quality in the universe, and would stand to all eternity outside the great evolutionary law of progress, development, and growth—an impossibility from their own Darwinian standpoint. They talk as if all women would always move for all time exactly together, and in one solid block—a thing which can never happen even to two physical atoms, let alone half the human race.

I have dwelt a little on this in order to clear the ground, and because when the ordinary objections of the man in the street to woman's freedom are exhausted and beaten, this show of false philosophy sometimes appeals to those who are supposed to think. This consolation we have that when woman in conjunction with man has attained her real future, Belfort Bax and his school, if they are thought of at all—which is open to question—will be remembered on this subject as babes wrapped in the swaddling clothes of false philosophy, false psychology, false economics, and false science.

The opposition of Mr. Bax and his friends is mainly confined to the agitation for women's franchise, but they are hopelessly beaten at the outset. I suppose there is hardly a man or woman in England to-day, even if like Mr. Bax they are violently against votes for women, but who believes that before long the political future of women will be secured by the concession of the principle of sex equality.

More than that, I recently had it on most excellent authority, that it is highly probable that the limited bills will not be argued again, but that Adult Suffrage for all men and all women, married as well as unmarried, for which so many of us have striven, will be the next move. Most devoutly do I hope that ere long England will set the pace to the future of woman by being the first among the elder nations of the earth generally to recognise all women as, politically, human beings.

But this will, of course, be but the first rung of the ladder of the future. Although the possession of the vote is in itself, under present conditions, an enhancement of the dignity of the human being, it is but a symbol. To use the words of the Prayer-Book—giving them my own meaning—it is the outward and visible sign of the inward and spiritual grace. In the last lecture I heard Henry Ward Beecher give, he said, "The real use of a vote is to teach a man how to vote," and that is precisely true, and will be true for women as it should be now for men. The possession of the vote should be the stimulus for the concrete expression of the latent possibilities of the human mind and the human soul, as those two qualities of the human being should work themselves out in social life. The consciousness of this is the first requisite of human freedom, and on the way in which this consciousness is developed will rest the future of woman and of man.

I leave the outward political side of the subject. Our cause is won—if not to-day, then to-morrow.

I turn now to the other two strands of the cord of woman's complete freedom—the economic and social, and the sexual, for on the working out of these depends absolutely the character of the future of woman.

There is a haunting fear in the minds of the opponents of women suffrage, a fear often expressed, that when women get the vote they will no longer be content with the state of life to which, through long ages, it has pleased men to call them. And that is true. If it were not, I should be ashamed of women as a sex. Women will no longer be content with economic inferiority. They will see that their future will be shaped, not by man for them, but by themselves in conjunction with man. And that will be the great fundamental change, a change which will affect every woman industrially, economically, socially, sexually—a change which will touch in every direction every relation of their lives. The change in idea will not come all at once; it will be of slow growth—too slow, perhaps, for some of the more ardent souls—but it is absolutely assured. As Olive Schreiner allegorically points out: from prostration to her knees, from her knees to upright stature, woman will rise, and as she rises will lift her face more and more to the freedom of her future. Does anyone suppose for a moment that the new woman (and I use that phrase in the highest sense) will be content with sweating in the slums or prostitution in the streets? Will she be content to slave for a contractor at 2¾d. an hour, which is the price that is now being fixed by the Post Office that may be paid to women workers by contractors for Post Office uniforms and clothing? (I had the tender issued by the Post Office in my hands last Thursday night.) And this is but a single example of what is more or less going on through the length and breadth of women's labour, of women's economic life. I verily believe that if some of you could sit with me for a month on some of the committees to which I belong, which have specially to do with women's labour, you would become as extreme Socialists as I am myself. When once women begin really to know and understand and move economically, the structure of our present society will begin to tumble like a pack of cards. For here will come into play on the part of woman what Belfort Bax calls her hysterical emotionalism, but which is often that intuitional insight which is much more common to them than to men—what Lowell calls "the swift flash of right or wrong"—an intuition which, it is true, may make mistakes—as men do! but which, with the increasing responsibility of citizenship, will be tempered and balanced by judgment and by reason.

No human being, man or woman, can foretell exactly what the outcome of all this will be—here the prophetic instinct fails—but one thing is certain, that woman will demand, I think first of all, an enormous change in her whole economic life, and this will affect her in every direction—especially as wife, mother, and worker. I want to guard myself here against any idea that in using these terms I am speaking simply of working women. That is not so. There would be no real future for women if we looked on that future as touching simply the workers as we know them now. I would not lift my voice at all for the future of women if I did not thoroughly believe that the new impulses, principles, ideas, which will be set going will, in a more or less degree, affect the lives of all the women of the nation.

Woman in the future will claim the power of earning her own living and shaping her own life, apart from the direction and domination of man. I can quite foresee that in the rush of the march to the future this may at first, unfortunately, enhance the sex antagonism. But that will be only a passing phase, because sex antagonism is only an artificial accident, and not a fundamental principle of the real life either of man or woman. As experienced now, it is really a part of our present social system, and as that system disintegrates, sex antagonism will correspondingly disappear. So that the new economic woman of the future will be like the new economic man, wise enough to see and know that the best results, even of outward material life, are to be obtained, not by antagonism but by co-operation, not by social discord but by social harmony—and this, of course, from the ethical as well as the material side. Hence with the increasing control by humanity over the forces of nature and the harnessing of those forces to the use and good of the whole community, woman's as well as man's economic status and development will be fundamentally changed. With material work becoming as it will then, a rational pleasure, instead of, as it is often now, a degrading toil, woman will possess and hold what as a sex she has never yet possessed—the *joy* of material creation, and that will react on her mental, moral and spiritual development. Men say that women as a sex have never developed the real artistic faculty. That is not true to begin with, and even if it were it would only prove that the evolution of women has lagged behind. But, on the contrary, I affirm that taking, not the few great artists, but women as a sex and men as a sex, the inner life of countless women, much more than that of men, is a dumb, almost pathetic striving for the opportunity to express the beauty which is latent in their souls, of which they themselves are as yet but dimly and haltingly conscious. We see that everywhere, in every department, men, in the main, are responsible for the ugliness of life. Take one thing only, architecture. Surely it was men and not women who were responsible for the hideousness of our Georgian and early Victorian eras, and surely, also, it is men and not women who are also responsible for the hideous factories, the mean streets, and the smug bourgeois villadom of to-day, while it is only a few men here and there, not the sex as a whole, who have at all elevated our private and public taste. Free woman economically, as well as politically, let her set her face toward even the dawn of the future, not as the antagonist but as the comrade and co-partner of man, and soon man will rub his eyes and wonder in sheer amazement from whence sprang this transformed fellow-worker, without whom *his* future would be drab and drear.

But this, of course, is but a general principle. It has its practical side. Again the opponents of woman's freedom say that owing to the very inherent nature of the case woman will be for ever handicapped by her sex obligations, by her duties as wife and mother. Again, I do not believe it. Give woman her freedom, and she will not be content to be thus handicapped in the future as she has been in the past. I know that I am here entering on a very thorny and difficult subject, a subject on which there is much disagreement even among advanced women's advocates, women as well as men, and as yet we have no real data on which to form a decided judgment. Here again, the subject has never been thoroughly worked out. I can only glance at one or two salient points.

Take this general proposition that if woman in the future has the economic control of her own life, meaning by that the opportunity to earn her own comfortable living, apart from man if she will, but, as I would hope, in harmonious co-operation with him, she will no longer consent to be what countless millions of women have been for ages, the household and industrial drudge. I think that proposition admits of no dispute.

As Charlotte Stetson says in one of her poems:—

> Six hours a day the woman spends on food!
> Six mortal hours a day.
> With fire and water toiling, heat and cold.
> Six mortal hours a day to handle food,
> Prepare it, serve it, clean it all away,
> With allied labours of the stove and tub,
> The pan, the dishcloth, and the scrubbing-brush.
> Developing forever in her brain
> The power to do this work in which she lives;
> While the slow finger of Heredity
> Writes on the forehead of each living man,
> Strive as he may, "His mother was a cook!"

I do not believe that the woman of the future will find her chief glory in the pan, the dishcloth, and the scrubbing-brush. We know that women have been told for ages that their one aim in life should be to be good housewives. Never mind her mental improvement or artistic development! Can she darn a stocking, can she sew a button on, above all can she cook? all meaning nothing less than this—can she minister to man's material and sometimes selfish comfort? even if in so doing she lets her own individuality as a human being go to the dogs. The woman of the future is not going to stand that, as for generations her sisters have stood it. In the future, stockings will still be darned, buttons still sewn on, food still cooked, probably by both sexes; but when the women of to-morrow do these things it will be, not because they are thereby fulfilling the "duties" allotted to by them by man, but because they will find a joy in fulfilling some of the functions of mutual social life. Hence the change which is coming will fundamentally affect woman's position as wife and mother.

Here I am heretic, much more heretic than most women. But on the whole woman question I have for years asked much more for women than nine out of ten of them are willing to ask for themselves. I do not believe that the chief end of woman's life is motherhood. Her chief aim should be the complete development of her own individuality as a human being in comradeship with man, and motherhood is only one of the lines which will lead to that. And just so far as motherhood prevents that—and under present social conditions in countless thousands of cases it does so prevent—motherhood is a real hindrance instead of a help. That arises in one way from the complication of our artificial social life; but, above all, it arises from the way in which for ages the true development and progress of woman has been dominated and hindered by man, who has largely made woman his chattel and bond slave. I know what an exaggeration that will probably seem to many of you, especially perhaps to the women, but yet it is so, as will be easily seen by those who really study the question. I am speaking now of the evolution of woman in so-called Christian Europe during the last 1,700 years, from the time of the Fathers of the Church, from the days of that eminent pillar of Christianity, St. Clement of Alexandria, who declared that woman was the gate to hell, improving a little in the way of exaggeration on his forerunner, St. Paul, who, if he were alive now, would be an ardent follower of Belfort Bax.

If you will study, as I have had to do, the Ecclesiastical and Canon law in its connection with civil law and the polity of the State, with the relation of the sexes in the marriage bond, as shown partly in some of the words of the present marriage service of the Church of England,[2] you will find that from Paul's and Clement's time down to to-day, the orthodox Christian and State idea of woman has been one of pure degradation, in that her one duty was declared to be the production of citizens for the good of the community. And this without a word of her own individuality or the development of herself as a human being. I made my first speech when I was a boy of fifteen in favour of complete Adult Suffrage for men and women. Ever since then I have made a close study of the whole woman question, and I declare to you that if this morning I could lay before you the actual law of England with regard to the power of the husband over the wife, you would be disgusted and horrified. I know, of course, that this power is mostly in abeyance, but it is the law of the land, and I am putting it to you thus in order to show what man has done in the past with regard to woman, and to enforce my point that in the future woman will on no account submit to what at any moment she might have to submit to now. I have been in Turkey, and it is the actual literal fact that, much as we despise that country, the position of the Turkish married woman is, in some respects, much better legally than that of the English wife, in spite of the many improvements which have been introduced here of late years.

So the wife of the future will not be the wife of to-day. I do not enter this morning on the difficult subject of what may be the marriage laws or regulations of the future. No one can prophesy that, and it is useless to speculate. But whatever the actual future relation between the sexes, it will certainly be much more harmonious, much more humane, much more co-operative in the best sense, much more mental, much more spiritual, much more monogamous, and in every way much more equal than it is to-day. Marriage no longer a profession which woman must necessarily economically adopt, the woman not merely the helpmate of the man, but the man equally the helpmate of the woman, because both are human beings who will recognise that the development of each is bound up in the development of the other; the woman relieved, as she will be, by invention from most of the household drudgery which is now often the nightmare of her life, she will then be able to take her full part in the general life of the community politically and socially, and at the same time to develop to the full whatever latent possibilities, capabilities and faculties she may possess, while man will find it his highest joy and delight to work side by side with her in every possible way, with mutual respect, mutual reverence, mutual love. To such a future as that woman's life to-day is but as moonlight unto sunlight, as water unto wine.

Admirably does Mrs. Despard portray this woman of the future:—

"There grows up before me," she says, "the picture of the woman of the future.

"Well-developed in mind and body; capable of bearing and rearing a race that will be truly imperial; independent in thought, vigorous in action, free from those pettinesses and affectations which have been built into women's nature through generations of oppression; drinking in her own cup, be it little or large; performing the duties of a citizen, and endowed with the rights of citizenship; having a career open to her, and her livelihood assured, so that marriage will no longer be a necessity, but, when chosen, will be entered upon with a full sense of responsibility to the race; looking out calmly and courageously on the life of which she knows that she forms an integral part, and enjoying freely earth's beauty and sweetness. So I see her—this woman of a later day."[3]

And Mrs. Stetson again:—

A woman—in so far as she beholdeth
   Her one Belovéd's face:
A mother—with a great heart that enfoldeth
   The children of the Race:

A body, free and strong, with that high beauty
    That comes of perfect use, is built thereof:
A mind where Reason ruleth over Duty,
    And Justice reigns with Love:
A self-poised royal soul, brave, wise, and tender,
    No longer blind and dumb:
A Human Being, of an unknown splendour,
    Is she who is to come!

That is the woman, the wife, the mother of the future.

Ah, but say our carping critics—they who see in woman nothing but the brood mare—you talk of the mother, the children—now you have indeed destroyed your case!

Repeating what I said, that motherhood is only one of the ends of woman's life, let us examine this question of the children of the future.

For woman to have control of her own life she must have complete control over her own body, so in the future the question of the child will primarily rest with her.

I believe that although while men and women are on this planet the question of sex will never be eliminated, yet with advancing knowledge, advancing development, advancing wisdom, and, above all, with the advancing respect, reverence and true love of man for woman and woman for man, it will occupy a much smaller place in the real life of the men and women of the future than at present, and that the outcome will be the rearing of a race which in its infancy will bring with it a glorious heredity from the past, with the promise of as glorious a life in its youth, in its manhood, and in its womanhood. And this *can* be. Never yet in the history of the world has mankind generally paid the smallest attention to this all-important subject. We hear talk nowadays of the endowment of motherhood. In the future it will not be the careworn mother who will be endowed by the State, for careworn mothers will be a thing of the past, it will be the regal mother—regal in body, regal in mind, regal in soul—who with those qualities of her own life will herself endow her child. And in that lies the promise of the true future of the race. The mother of the future, relieved from economic necessity and care, mistress of her body, and mistress of herself, developed to the fullest limits of her individuality, will face her motherly responsibilities, not as often now with fear and trembling of added drudgery or possible penury, but with a joy that to her is given the perpetuation of those qualities in her child which physically, mentally, and morally have made her own life one grand sweet song. Then, and then only, will it be possible for the dream of some like myself and others to be carried out, that for the good of the individual and the race, the whole community shall be helpmates in the development of this richer life by seeing to it that in the preparatory stages the coming mother shall be surrounded, not merely with every physical comfort, but with those higher mental and moral environments, beautiful, artistic, which shall react on the unborn child and lay the foundation of its future joyous and beautiful life. Some of the truest words that Elizabeth Cady Stanton ever uttered are on this very subject. In her autobiography she says:—

"In a true relation the chief object is the loving companionship of man and woman, their capacity for mutual help and happiness and for the development of all that is noblest in each other.[4] The second object is the building up a home and family, a place of rest, peace, security, in which child-life can bud and blossom like flowers in the sunshine.

"The first step toward making the ideal the real is to educate our sons and daughters into the most exalted ideas of the sacredness of married life and the responsibilities of parenthood. I would have them give, at least, as much thought to the creation of an immortal being as the artist gives to his landscape or statue. Watch him in his hours of solitude, communing with great Nature for days and weeks in all her changing moods, and when at last his dream of beauty is realised and takes a clearly defined form, behold how patiently he works through long months and years on sky and lake, on tree and flower; and when complete, it represents to him more love and life, more hope and ambition, than the living child at his side, to whose conception and ante-natal development not one soulful thought was ever given. To this impressive period of human life few parents give any thought; yet here we must begin to cultivate virtues that can alone redeem the world."

Here is the place and the work of the mother of the future, for on her mainly depends this redemption of mankind.

But in that redemption man must be prepared to take his full share by standing side by side with woman, here and now, to help both her and himself to lay the foundations of the future.

America has produced great women, and some of them I have had the extreme good fortune to know and count as my personal friends. The voices of some of them have in the past been heard from this platform. I have known Elizabeth Cady Stanton, Susan Anthony, Frances Willard, Julia Ward Howe, Mary Livermore, Kate Field, Jane Addams, and I honour them all. But there were two whom I would have given much to know, Margaret Fuller and Lucretia Mott. When more than sixty years ago the first International Anti-Slavery Convention was held at Exeter Hall, among the American delegates were Lucretia Mott and William Lloyd Garrison. The stupid Belfort Baxes of that time, who had the ruling of the Convention, refused to allow Lucretia Mott to sit as delegate, because she was a woman. Thereupon, Garrison, to his eternal honour, also refused to sit, and withdrew with her into the gallery, where he simply watched the proceedings in silence. That silence was the truest voice which was sounded for woman in the nineteenth century. It struck the note that the future of woman was also the future of man. Prejudice dies hard. A quarter of a century ago I sat by John Bright in the same hall, when an eminent friend tried to stamp down Miss Sturge, who was speaking on behalf of the downtrodden agricultural labourers. But—E pur si muove—the world of thought moves, and it will move still faster as the years roll on. The woman and the man of the future will look back, not in wrath, but in wonder and in pity that ever such things could have been.

Truly, truly did Tennyson foreshadow in the "Princess" the future of woman and of man—co-equal, not in mere strength, but in aspiration, in everything that tends to make the perfect human being:—

> And so these twain, upon the skirts of Time,
> Sit side by side, full-summ'd in all their powers,
> Dispensing harvest, sowing the To-be,
> Self-reverent each and reverencing each,
> Distinct in individualities,
> But like each other ev'n as those who love.
> Then comes the statelier Eden back to men;
> Then reign the world's great bridals, chaste and calm;
> Then springs the crowning race of humankind.

But Tennyson has done more than this.

In his "Guinevere," the most subtle and powerful of all his "Idylls of the King," he rises to higher heights. In Arthur's farewell to Guinevere the poet first touches the deepest depths of the human heart:—

> Lo! I forgive thee, as Eternal God
> Forgives; do thou for thine own soul the rest.
> But how to take last leave of all I loved?
> O golden hair, with which I used to play
> Not knowing! O imperial-moulded form,
> And beauty such as never woman wore—
> Let no man dream but that I love thee still.

That was King Arthur's last despairing cry of the ecstasy of human passion.

And then, with the swift magic of supreme poetic art, Tennyson, in a flash, exalts not only Arthur, but Guinevere also, to the loftiest universal altitudes of the soul:—

> Perchance, and so thou purify thy soul,
> And so thou lean on our fair Father Christ,
> Hereafter in that world where all are pure
> We two may meet before high God, and thou
> Wilt spring to me, and claim me thine, and know
> I am thine husband—not a smaller soul,
> Nor Lancelot, nor another.

Into that I read my own conception of the future of woman and of man. Putting aside Tennyson's theology, broad as it was, I believe that in that last passage he had glimpses of that close and lasting union of the higher selves of man and woman, the selves which are part of the beating universal life in which we all live, move, and have our being.

> I am thine husband—not a smaller soul,
> Nor Lancelot, nor another.

In that union of soul with soul, which is above and beyond all sex, time, circumstance and place, lies the only real guarantee for the true future of woman, and the true future of man.

In the far-off, lonely African desert, Olive Schreiner dreamed her wonderful dreams of the future of woman. Miles behind her, for she is a genius, I, too, in the rush and turmoil of our busy London life, dream my dreams of the future of woman, side by side with the future of man.

I seem to see through the mists of the present the clear, bright radiance of the years which are yet to come. Gone then are the antagonisms of sex and of class—gone are the unmeaning conventionalities which now cramp and hinder the free development of the human soul. In the place of Prejudice, Justice—in the place of Ignorance, Wisdom—in the place of Oppression, Brotherhood and Sisterhood—in the place of Selfishness, unbounded Love. I see woman co-equal with man in all that makes for her true womanhood. I see man co-equal with woman in all that makes for his true manhood. I see these twain walking hand in hand down the paths of Time, their eager faces ever turned to the golden glory of the rising sun. I see round them troops of little children, of youths and maidens, whose lives are one long song of human joy, and that song, its chorus swelling from every people, from every nation, is the grand future anthem of free and emancipated woman, of noble and regenerated man.

## Notes

1 *On the Duties of Man.*
2 "First, It (matrimony) was ordained for the procreation of children." (*Solemnization of Matrimony.*)
3 *Woman in the New Era.*
4 This is far above the Christian idea of placing pro-creation of children *first*.—H.B.

# 41

## *SOCIALISM AND EUGENICS* (LONDON: TWENTIETH CENTURY PRESS, 1911), 1–15.

*George Whitehead*

[Since the years of the Nazi dictatorship in Germany, eugenicist ideas have become so thoroughly discredited that it is easy to overlook how widely accepted such notions were among social reformers of the early twentieth century (Searle 1976; Freeden 1979). This had nothing to do with Marxism and the best-known examples were not Marxists at all. On the contrary, Fabian socialists were far more susceptible to the concerns with national efficiency that fed the turn towards eugenics that was so pervasive in the Edwardian years. Bernard Shaw and (especially) H.G. Wells were among the more outspoken supporters of eugenicist solutions to the problems of the "base", the failing and unfit. There was also Maurice Eden Paul: an ILP socialist and medical practitioner and a former associate of Beatrice Webb. Though less well-known than Shaw and Wells, in 1911 Paul published for the ILP a pamphlet entitled *Socialism and Eugenics* which aimed to demonstrate the "reciprocal necessity" of socialism and eugenics as complementary methods for promoting the welfare of the "community", which Paul also freely described as the "race".

The prevalence of such language in these years is apparent from the contemporaneous pamphlet of George Whitehead. Where Paul's claimed position was that of the scientist, Whitehead adopted the perspective of the economist and welfare reformer. Even so, there is considerable convergence between the views expressed, and Whitehead even employed the same title while Paul's pamphlet was in the press. Whitehead's almost casual use of the language of race culture, race suicide and racial quality may be noted along with the opposition to social policies aimed at support for the unfit, and the use of sources of evidence like the recent Royal Commission on the Care and the Control of the Feeble-Minded (1904–1908), here described as the commission on degeneracy. Like Paul, Whitehead saw socialism and eugenics as working hand in hand, the one dealing with the facts of heredity, the other with those of environment. Whitehead does not just advocate "positive" or "constructive" eugenicist measures aimed at encouraging the bearing of children by those deemed best fitted to do so. He also writes frankly of the "negative" or "restrictive" eugenicist policy of forced sterilisation which he believes will remain necessary for the congenitally unfit even in a fully socialist society.

Although Paul later became a communist, Marxists in Britain could add little on these matters to the views of top-down collectivists and state reformers of other political traditions. Nevertheless, the publication of Whitehead's tract by the Twentieth Century Press shows how deeply compromised was the SDF's own identification with the politics of the "healthy race".]

One of the most appalling tendencies which the serious student of social problems cannot fail to observe is the increase in the number of physical and mental degenerates. Reliable statistics, backed up by our own observations, demonstrate only too forcibly the extent to which these tendencies operate, and the time has arrived for a more careful examination on the part of the public of those proposals which are being suggested by thoughtful men to remedy the evil. The question of Race Culture—which implies obviously the elimination of those influences responsible for degeneracy—*must* be faced if our civilisation is to last, and our children are to enjoy the heritage which centuries of thought and sacrifice have made possible.

To cope with the evils referred to a new science has sprung up which is gaining the adherence of men and women of every school of political thought, and now, when the word "Eugenics" is mentioned, it cannot be dismissed with a contemptuous shrug, as was the case a few years ago.

The Eugenist and the Socialist are both of the opinion that more attention should be devoted to the *causes* of social disorder rather than to the spending of one's time tinkering superficially with its effects, as do the politicians, both red and blue.

I have elsewhere defined the ideal which I think both Eugenist and Socialist would subscribe to as:—

The evolution of a race of beings physically beautiful, morally pure, soaring to an intellectual platform hitherto unconceived, living a full, happy, human life, with liberty to develop to the sublimest heights that which we call soul.

The realisation of that ideal implies a most careful consideration of all phases of contemporary life with a view to the complete eradication of all the factors which hinder our social and individual advancement. And many cherished opinions will have to be abandoned, much selfish complacency will have to be disturbed, before we lay even the foundations of that mighty edifice which a more fortunate future shall behold.

## The Social Debt.

Some selfish cowards there are who in their hearts and on their lips echo the words of Omar Khayyam:—

> Come, fill the cup! what boots it to repeat
> How time is slipping underneath our feet?
>    Unborn to-morrow and dead yesterday:
> Why fret about them if to-day be sweet?

That, I repeat, is a selfish and cowardly (though plausible) doctrine. It is a doctrine which the earnest ones amongst us cannot tolerate. We *must* fret about the future else the present lacks savour. We *must* think about the unborn to-morrow, because on our present thought depends the happiness of the millions to come. And there is the social debt. That obligation must be discharged if we are to retain our self-respect.

And what is the social debt? It is what we owe to our forefathers for the sacrifices they endured: their labours, their inventions, their discoveries, their martyrdoms and tears. We to-day are indebted for all we know or think, for all our civilisation can boast, *for what we are,* to the countless millions whose bones are dust, but whose energies shall influence humanity to the end of time.

These, our benefactors, we cannot repay; they have departed for ever to the Land of Shades. We are forced to the idea that, just as we have benefited by the thought of the past, so must those who come after us benefit by our thought.

Let us believe that our forefathers did the best that their limited opportunities made possible, and if their best was bad, let us, standing on the ruins of their failures, make a better job of it.

We have increased opportunities. We should be dastards if we did not seek to avail ourselves of them.

## Orthodox Legislation Useless.

Most reformers appear to be satisfied that greater facilities for education, side by side with sympathetic legislative enactments, are quite sufficient to cope with the difficulties which our present complex social life conjures up, and many of them ridicule suggestions which are framed with more far-reaching implications.

Yet, from a *racial* standpoint, it is easy to argue that most legislation is suicidal in its effects. And I do not merely include class legislation palpably framed in the interests of the privileged ones amongst us, but also those laws which frankly have for their object the removal of pain and suffering.

The social consciousness is more sensitive to-day probably than at any previous period, and, coupled with the advance in medical and sanitary science, has helped to remove evils which at one time decimated whole populations.

But sanatoria and asylums, erected for consumptives and lunatics, although making the conditions of life easier for the individual sufferer, have had the effect of allowing incapables to survive and multiply who previously would have been wiped out in the struggle.

The more we multiply these institutions, *without attacking the causes which call for their existence,* the more weedy and degenerate will the human race become.

The law of adaptation is always in operation. If the general conditions of life demand a hardy type of individual, the less hardy cannot adapt itself to this environment, and so disappears. But if by an extension of the social consciousness, or by other means, the environment becomes more charitable, then the less capable persons will be able to conform to the easier conditions, and so will survive and give birth to offsprings inheriting their own weaknesses.

This multiplication of physical and mental degenerates is possible whilst society makes provision for their maintenance, and shelters them from the adverse influences which some generations ago would have exterminated them.

Obviously, reforms on orthodox lines are not adequate enough to grapple with the situation.

On the one hand industrial conditions, associated with the private ownership of the means of life, are stirring into activity the seeds of degeneracy, and then tardy efforts are made to cope with the difficulty—efforts which only have the effect of helping to multiply the disease.

Lunacy and physical degeneracy are growing out of all proportion to our increased population, and the experts tell us that among the causes are evils which a rational method of wealth distribution would completely eliminate. I refer to food adulteration, bad housing conditions, underfeeding, child and female labour, long hours of work in badly ventilated rooms, together with all the worry inseparably associated with the industrial life of the worker. These things could be abolished; and the Socialist and Eugenist alike, to be consistent, must support legislation in that direction.

But to allow the causes which encourage degeneracy to remain untouched whilst we spend millions of pounds upon impossible efforts to cure the victims is alike senseless and brutal, and, besides that, these incapables are allowed to reproduce their kind through the misguided tolerance of the public which has to support them.

## Degeneracy Increases

Let us examine the situation in the light of the evidence furnished by the Royal Commission which considered the question of degeneracy some little time ago.

Lunacy is rapidly growing, we are told, for whilst there were on January 1st, 1908, in England and Wales, 126,084 persons certified as insane, on January 1st, 1909, the number had increased to 128,787—an increase of 2,703.

If we take a longer period, the growth is more alarming. In January, 1859, the total number of certified insane was 36,762, which means that in 50 years the number has increased 92,025, which is out of proportion to the increase in the population.

Lunacy has grown 250 per cent., whilst the general population has only increased 81.6 per cent.

Consider the following, written by Dr. Tredgold, in the "Contemporary Review," June, 1910:—

"It is calculated that of all the workhouse population in the country one-fifth to one-fourth are mentally affected, and quite unfitted to be at large. It is estimated that .83 per cent. of the elementary school population of the country are feeble-minded children. This percentage may not seem very large, but it amounts to a total of over 50,000 children in England and Wales. The evidence of prison medical officers of great experience is to the effect that at least 20 per cent. of the criminal population of the country are mentally defective. Careful inquiries as to the mental condition of chronic inebriates admitted to reformatories under the Act of 1898 show that two-thirds are mentally deficient and irreformable. At least 10 per cent. of the tramps promenading the country are feeble-minded. With regard to rescue homes and penitentiaries, it appears probable that, on the whole, about half of these unfortunate girls are mentally deficient, and quite incapable of looking after their interests."

## Both Cruel and Costly.

The above facts make it clear that orthodox reforms cannot keep pace with the complex problems which confront us. We have a decrease amongst the healthy specimens of humanity and an increase amongst the weeds. We must remember that the latter are much more prolific breeders than the former, and, according to Dr. Tredgold, the average number of children in mentally degenerate families was 7.3 as against an average per normal family of 4.63.

Dr. Potts discovered that in one workhouse alone there were 16 feeble-minded women who had produced no less than 116 children, and in one family of fourteen children only four had been able to perform remunerative work.

Dr. Branthwaite, in his Annual Report (for 1905) on Inebriate Homes, states that 92 habitual inebriate women had had 850 babies!

If one viewed the matter from its lowest standpoint—the financial cost to the nation—it would be sufficiently alarming, for 67 per cent. of the feeble-minded are supported more or less by the general public.

"With regard to many of those in workhouses, it has been calculated that the amount expended by the State, from birth to the grave, must be close on £2,000 per head."

There is a higher standpoint which equally condemns the reproduction of the unfit, and that is the humane standpoint. Twenty per cent. of the inmates of our prisons are mentally unfit!

What does this mean?

It means that unfortunate people who should be pitied are being punished for misdeeds which they are not responsible for.

It means that we as a society produce human tigers, and then punish them for biting!

If a man bred puppies from a mad dog, and then tortured them for acting as their parents had done, we should stigmatise him as a thoughtless brute; but in what way different does society act with many of its criminals? Born with a twisted mentality from degenerate parents, who can expect the offspring to grow up into a normal being? Why, then, punish those who act precisely as they *must* act in obedience to their own twisted nature?

A mad dog or a beast of prey which committed ravages upon us we should eliminate at once. Why, then, do we not eliminate those more-to-be-dreaded scourges who commit greater ravages than the most bloodthirsty animal? For an animal is soon destroyed, and the matter ends; but the human brute, after his death, leaves maybe half-a-dozen others to follow his example.

The lethal chamber? Not by any means.

I am concerned more with the roots of the problem than its branches.

## Causes of Degeneracy.

What, then, must we do to prevent the increase of degeneracy? There are two factors, and only two, at work in the growth and development of a human being from the cradle to the grave. These two factors are heredity and environment.

I use the term environment in its broadest sense, and mean to include by it *all* the influences which help to mould the individual after birth. Now, degeneracy is caused by a certain set of circumstances operating upon predispositions within. If there were no predispositions (or bias) in a given direction, no matter what the outside influences were there would be no mature development of a diseased germ. That means that two persons placed in the same unhealthy surroundings would not of necessity be subject to the same disease. Thus worry, underfeeding, overwork, bad ventilation, etc., might result in one case in consumption, whereas in another lunacy would be the result, and again in a third no appreciable disease would be noticed.

What happens is that all of us inherit some combustible psychic material; if appropriate heat is applied there is a conflagration; if not, all is well. Our obvious duty, then, is to remove as many as possible of the environmental sparks so as to minimise the dangers of fire. Most of these sparks can be stamped out if we organise ourselves to that end.

Why is food adulterated? For profit.

Why are women and children employed instead of men? For profit.

Why are thousands of employees sweated in badly ventilated rooms? For profit.

Why have most of the workers to work long hours for low wages? For profit.

All for profit!

Because industry is organised so that a few wax fat and millions starve. Because in the same trade we have overtime and unemployment side by side. In the same trade are employed women and children, whilst men walk about the streets without work.

Factories and warehouses full of boots and clothing and food, and hungry people willing to work in rags gazing at them! We have slums and bad housing conditions, ill-nourished women and children, and most of the other social evils which the doctors tell us are largely responsible for degeneracy, because profit is more sacred than health and happiness!

If millions of children are losing their lives every year through the ignorance and poverty of their parents, we must do our best as a nation to remove the causes of these twin evils.

Ignorance can be dissipated by knowledge. Poverty can be abolished by a just method of distribution of the wealth of which there is an abundance. And degeneracy of all kinds can only be removed when a favourable environment is provided, in which every incentive is applied to bring out healthy characteristics, and none to develop unhealthy ones. One has only to study the statistics to learn how an improved environment affects the individual, whether young or old.

For instance, the standard average of the Anthropometric Committee for a boy of 13 years is 56.9 inches in height, and 77.6 pounds in weight. According to Dr. Tattersall, 2,000 public school boys averaged 58.5 inches and 79 pounds, whilst 169 Dundee half-timers of the same age averaged only 52.6 inches and 68.5 pounds!

This shows a difference of about 6 inches in height and 11½ pounds in weight between children of 13 living in different environments. The statistics show, too, that between 1888 and 1894, out of 100,000 children examined in the London elementary schools, more than a third of them had some sort of a defect, mainly due to the conditions of life, and an examination of 26,287 boys in 1892-4 demonstrated this fact once again:—

|  | No. Seen. | Development Defect Among. | Nerve Signs Among. | Low Nutrition Among. |
|---|---|---|---|---|
| Upper social class | 6,835 | 8.1 p.c. | 10.0 p.c. | 2.2 p.c. |
| Average social class | 8,432 | 8.5 p.c. | 11.1 p.c. | 3.0 p.c. |
| Lower social class | 11,020 | 9.4 p.c. | 11.2 p.c. | 3.1 p.c. |

And now compare children from Aberdeen and Edinburgh, remembering that the Aberdeen children are drawn from a wealthier class than those of Edinburgh:—

(HAY AND MACKENZIE.)

|  | 600 Edinburgh Children. | 600 Aberdeen Children. |
|---|---|---|
| Poor health | 19.17 p.c. | 0.5 p.c. |
| Bad nutrition | 29.83 p.c. | 9.0 p.c. |
| Mental dullness | 12.33 p.c. | 8.8 p.c. |
| Height of boys aged 12-15 | 55.26 in. | 57.3 in. |
| Weight of boys aged 12-15 | 74.02 lb. | 84.5 lb. |
| Diseased glands | 18.5 p.c. | 2.0 p.c. |
| Nose and throat diseases | 52.54 p.c. | 30.0 p.c. |
| Lung disease | 3.0 p.c. | 1.8 p.c. |
| Heart disease | 4.33 p.c. | 1.0 p.c. |
| Diseases of eyes | 15.5 p.c. | 1.2 p.c. |
| Diseases of ears | 42.04 p.c. | 1.4 p.c. |

The growth of lunacy is mainly confined to the working class, for in 1907 only 2.83 per 10,000 were "private" lunatics, whilst 32.37 per 10,000 were "pauper" lunatics.

There is abundant evidence to prove that, if removed early enough from the filthy surroundings and given a fair chance, most of those who constitute the dregs of our population would develop into decent citizens.

For instance, over 3,000 children taken from the worst of our slums to Canada in connection with the Middlemore Children's Emigration Homes turned out so well that only 60 of these could be accounted as failures! Less than 2 per cent. turned out badly.

They were rescued "from the very lowest haunts of misery and vice, picked up forlorn and wretched from the gutters of Birmingham," where they would have grown up and rotted in ignorance, and in turn many of them would have reproduced offsprings similar to themselves.

## Socialism Essential.

A decent environment, then, is essential: one in which ignorance and poverty and industrial anomalies shall be unknown.

Social reforms can do something to bring about this desirable state of affairs; but as the basic cause of poverty is to be found in the unjust distribution of wealth, only a complete revolution in the methods of wealth distribution can abolish the evil.

Production for use so that profits would not be considered except in connection with the increased well-being of humanity must be in operation before degeneracy will disappear. That, of course, would mean Socialism, and Socialism as yet does not commend itself to the people.

With Socialism would come, of necessity, increased leisure for culture, and this again would react on the physique and mentality of the race.

A cultured man or woman would not choose in marriage a mate who had disgusting traits of character, or who was the victim of a loathsome disease. The consequences would be more profoundly considered, so the degenerates would have less chance of procreating their kind because unable to find partners.

And, besides that, Socialism would imply the economic freedom of woman, and that would have far-reaching influences.

To-day, by virtue of industrial arrangements, women, both rich and poor, are many times obliged to literally sell themselves into matrimonial bondage. In the upper classes the highest bidder too often carries off the prize, and a "good match" is determined not by mental or moral endowments but by the possession of so much £ s. d.

Not by *what he is* but by *what he has* is fitness determined. And also in the lower social strata a man's character is not allowed to weigh for much in hundreds of thousands of cases. Can he *keep* a wife? is the very necessary question which a working girl has to ask herself; and very often no other question is put once that is answered satisfactorily. I am not blaming them. Economic conditions are the primary cause of the legal prostitution which a respectable community tolerates without protest. For it *is* prostitution to permit sexual indulgences from a person whom one does not love.

Women marry to find a home, or to escape workshop drudgery, to escape from monotonous occupations where their labour is remunerated at a much less rate than that of their male comrades; and so vile are the conditions, and so despicable are the wages, that it would be a callous fool indeed who would blame them.

But if a home is assured for life, and if the remuneration and conditions of labour and existence generally are made congenial, women will not rush into the arms of the first man who comes along irrespective of his good or bad qualities. No; then a man will have to be worthy of the name before he is chosen in wedlock by an educated woman who can keep herself in comfort without his help.

What we desire to-day, then, to remove some of the causes of degeneracy is appropriate legislation in the direction of State control of industry, with a view to eliminating all those influences which we recognise as harmful to the social and individual well-being; then we need the removal of ignorance by increased education, paving the way to the time when woman shall be a more conscious and independent factor in the production of a healthy race.

All the above may be summed up in the one word environment.

## Inherited Disease.

But there are many thousands in our midst whom the most favourable environment possible could not transform into decent citizens. People with inborn tendencies to cancer, inebriety, epilepsy, lunacy, and kindred diseases, are engaged in giving birth to children who inevitably inherit the vicious traits of their parents. Not even a Socialist environment could prevent these from manifesting characteristics exceedingly harmful to both themselves and society. Education on them is wasted. Medical and surgical science can do nothing to remove the mist from their clouded brains. The taint has been transmitted from generation to generation, until to-day they face us, staring with their hopeless eyes, cursing us from the depths of their stunted souls. And we can only gaze at them in return with pity and despair.

There they are, a burden to themselves and the community. What shall we do with them? That is a question for the experts. What we shall *not* allow them to do with us is a question for the people. And I submit that we should not allow them to reproduce their kind, because that is cruel to the offspring, and vitiating and costly to the race.

Whether the disease of cancer is directly transmissible or not, according to Dr. Martin, "it is generally conceded that the offspring of cancerous parents are more prone to the disease than those without such a history."

To prove the growth of this disease, he quotes figures from "The Medical Annual," of 1901, which show an increase of 3.5 per cent. per annum, for whilst in 1877 there were 486 per million of population, in 1897 there were 787 per million.

Such diseases as inborn deafness are inheritable to a great extent, for, according to Mr. E. A. Fay, 25.9 per cent. of the children of those congenitally deaf have a like affliction.

In the case of a deaf person there is no particular hardship conferred upon the community *immediately,* although by intermarriage the affliction can easily spread. The main misfortune is suffered by the individuals afflicted, and although we have a right to protest in the interests of the unborn, still our interference is not so palpably justifiable as in the case of the feeble-minded and the born criminal.

I have previously quoted the testimony of Dr. Tredgold, which proves that millions of pounds are spent annually in providing for degenerates who are recklessly breeding their kind without much interference.

Dr. Martin says: "Of 122,000 certified idiots and lunatics in England and Wales on January 1st, 1906, 91 per cent. were paupers. The increase per annum was 2,800."

That is what I call senseless waste of money in view of the fact that no steps are taken to prevent their reproduction, and also that the cost could well be utilised in helping to make brighter the lot of the millions who to-day are denied happiness through economic necessity.

The extent to which civilisation fosters the reproduction of an even worse type than the average lunatic is realised when we face such facts as the following, taken from Dr. Lydston's book, "The Diseases of Society":—

"Rev. O. McCulloch has traced the life histories of 1,750 degenerate criminal and pauper descendants of one 'Ben Ishmael,' who lived in Kentucky, in 1790.

"The Rev. Dr. Stocker, of Berlin, traced 834 descendants of two sisters, who lived in 1825. Among them were 76 who had served 116 years in prison, 164 prostitutes, 106 illegitimate children, 17 pimps, 142 beggars, and 64 paupers.

"It has been estimated by Lichart, Director of Prisons in Wurtemburg, that over 25 per cent. of the German prison population comes from a degenerate ancestry. Vergilis claims 32 per cent. for Italian criminals."

## Two Factors to Consider.

I am not arguing that the above examples of criminality, etc., were solely due to hereditary traits. A tainted heredity supplied the ancestral powder and a vicious environment applied the match which resulted in so many human explosions.

I am pleading for an environment which shall minimise, as far as possible, the number of social excitations so that the explosive hereditary material shall have no chance of manifesting itself.

My quarrel with the average Eugenist is that he does not bother overmuch about the *social and economic* encouragements to degeneracy, but confines his attention to the *breed* of the individual, forgetting that heredity is only one part of the subject. The social reformer goes to the other extreme, and only considers the environmental factor, and very often but superficially at that. For whilst millions of pounds are spent in homes and hospitals trying to cure consumption and inebriety, etc., comparatively little attention is devoted to removing some of the basic causes of these diseases.

The worry of unemployment, the monotony of the worker's life, overwork, food adulteration, underfeeding, overcrowding in fœtid and dust-laden atmospheres, are all factors in the spread of consumption and drunkenness, yet not one reformer in a thousand is prepared to advocate measures which will completely abolish them from our social life. For a system in which the wealth producer received *all* he produced would be necessary to remove the above familiar evils. And that, as I have hinted previously, would be Socialism, which, as the politicians continually inform us, would mean race degeneracy. The staggering, physical, mental, and moral perfection of the race at the present time, of course, justifies their pride in the present system of society and their apprehension of the future.

Well, I suggest that all the malign influences associated with modern conditions must be removed by a juster method of wealth distribution: frankly, Socialism.

Then, I suggest the necessity, both now and in the future, of some form of selective breeding which shall make the reproduction of inheritable degeneracy almost an impossibility.

## Growth of Social Instinct.

In more barbarous times it was unnecessary for man to consciously weed out the unfit; Nature remorselessly performed that duty. In primitive times, if a child inherited a weakly frame or blunted senses, he was speedily exterminated by his natural enemies in the struggle for existence. If he could not bear the rigours of the cold or heat, or if by some misfortune he could not hear or see distinctly enough the approach of an enemy, animal or human, he would soon have been wiped out. Either through the direct attack of a rival hunter, or more slowly by his inability to find food for himself, Nature would decide that he was not fit to survive. Primitive man, I suppose, had a hard enough struggle for the necessities of life on his own account without concerning himself providing food and shelter for a useless friend or relation.

When, through various inventions and contrivances, man had gained access to Nature, and could win, by the aid of his improved tools and implements, sufficient for his needs with much less exertion than hitherto, he began to find time to develop the social virtues. He began to take more interest in the welfare of his fellows, and so in the misfortunes of the weaklings. He began to raise barriers between the merciless operations of Nature's laws and his crippled brethren. If Nature withheld normal development of mind or limb, man stepped in and assisted the weaker one, so that instead of being mercilessly left to perish he was helped to reach manhood's estate, when, of course, he was able to assist in the reproduction of children inheriting his own complaint. So, of necessity, degeneracy would spread until a highly civilised community is face to face with a terrible problem.

Now, I am not bewailing the development of this social instinct, bad as some of its effects have demonstrably been. I want a further extension of sociality, for only on these lines can real progress come. That is why I am a Socialist.

But I want the social instinct to have reason as a guide, so that it may not blindly express itself in channels harmful to the race. Not less care of the unfortunate, but more. And I suggest that a multiplication of individuals with distorted minds is not moral or sensible if we can prevent their manufacture. Let us abolish cant and unthinking sentiment in this matter and face the issues with calmness and reason.

## Methods of Birth Prevention Considered.

What, then, are the methods of elimination at present advocated by responsible students of the question?

There are several more or less prominent, of which the best known are the following:—

(1) The lethal chamber.
(2) Regulation of births by legislation.
(3) Sterilisation by surgical operation.

The first suggestion we may dismiss at once, I think, because, whatever may be the opinions of certain experts upon the subject, the nation as a whole would not tolerate such forcible methods of elimination.

The second method, by State restriction of marriages, might somewhat limit the number of weedy infants, but it would not satisfactorily abolish the evil we are considering, because, marriage apart, men and women would exercise those natural instincts in spite of legislative penalties.

The third suggestion brings us nearer the heart of the matter, whilst not being absolutely an ideal remedy.

According to Dr. Martin: "A method is practised in some parts of Africa and amongst the aborigines of Australia of slitting up the membranous portion of the male urethra in those individuals whom the tribe consider unfit to propagate the race, either from some physical defect or moral quality, as cowardice."

Dr. Rentoul tells us that he advocated sterilisation by surgical operation in 1903, and laid his proposals before the Royal Commission on the Case of the Feeble-Minded; but the Commissioners thought that the general feeling of the public would condemn any artificial methods such as surgical operation as a means of preventing the transmission of hereditary defects. Whether they were correct in this interpretation of the feelings of the British public remains to be seen; but other nations have accepted the idea, right or wrong.

The State of Indiana, in America, on February 10th, 1907, passed an Act which runs as follows:—

"An Act entitled an Act to prevent procreation of confirmed criminals, idiots, imbeciles, and rapists—providing that superintendents or boards of managers of institutions where such persons are confined shall have the authority and are empowered to appoint a committee of experts, consisting of two physicians, to examine into the mental condition of such inmates.

"Whereas heredity plays an important part in the transmission of crime, idiocy, and imbecility, therefore, be it enacted by the General Assembly of the State of Indiana, that on and after the passage of this Act it shall be compulsory for each and every institution in the State entrusted with the care of confirmed criminals, idiots, rapists, and imbeciles to appoint upon its staff, in addition to the regular institution physician, two skilled surgeons of recognised ability, whose duty it shall be, in conjunction with the chief physician of the institution, to examine the mental and physical condition of such inmates as are recommended by the institutional physician and board of managers.

"If in the judgment of this committee procreation is inadvisable, and there is no probability of improvement of the mental condition of the inmate, it shall be lawful for the surgeons to perform such operation for the prevention of procreation as shall be decided safest and most effective. But this operation shall not be performed except in cases that have been pronounced unimprovable."

On August 12th, 1909, a somewhat similar Act was passed by the State Legislature of Connecticut, with the added clause that a board appointed should inquire into the history, as far as it could be ascertained, of patients who are thought to be hopelessly incurable.

Also any person save those authorised who shall perform the operations described (vasectomy or oophorectomy) or allow them to be performed, shall be subject to a fine of one thousand dollars, or five years' imprisonment, or both.

The operations mentioned, says Dr. Rentoul, are very simple, practically painless, make no difference at all to the bodily functions, and have no ill effects of any kind. They are the outcome of modern scientific knowledge, and remove nothing but the power to procreate.

## Another Suggestion.

In the near future, it is quite possible that even this almost painless surgical operation may be rendered unnecessary, and a more efficient substitute still be discovered. I refer to the application of radium and the X-Rays for the removal of disease. It seems that already in Paris, according to Dr. E. T. Worrall, chief of the Electro-Therapeutic Department of University College Hospital, the disease of ringworm is rapidly disappearing, owing to the institution of the Lailer Schools, where children who suffer from the disease are treated by the X-Rays. At his own hospital the method was to give three applications of very short duration in one week. The patient is practically cured in three weeks, but as a result of the treatment he has an absolutely bald head, which, however, after certain ointment is applied, begins to resume normality in three months' time. Diseases like lupus are more stubborn, but yield to the same treatment.

And then both Professor Rowntree and Dr. Lazarus Barlow (the latter being director of the Cancer Research Laboratories of the Middlesex Hospital) have told us there is a distinct connection between the X-Rays and cancer. We are told that this knowledge may have an important practical application in connection with our treatment of this terrible disease.

More important still is another discovery with regard to X-Rays and radium, briefly explained by Dr. Martin in a pamphlet reprinted from "Public Health," October, 1907. It seems that experiments upon animals have led to the discovery that the action of X-Rays upon their reproductive organs will render them sterile. And this action is not confined to the brute creation, but acts also in the case of human beings!

"The sterility so induced in males is purely physiological, the physical part of the procreative process being in no way impaired. The action of the X-Rays seems to be upon the spermatozoa, which in those habitually exposed to the rays are either greatly diminished or absent. A brief course of treatment with the X-Rays results in but a transitory condition of sterility."

Further research in the future is expected to lead to results which can confidently be recommended to the nation which need not be concerned about the practicability of the proposals so much as their advisability.

## Objections Considered.

As to the latter, the only objections seem to be embodied in the question as to who would decide between fitness and unfitness, and the statement that sterilisation is an interference with the liberty of the individual.

These two objections are easily answered, for we have long ago admitted the principle of State interference with the liberty of the individual to act as a menace to society. We insist on a child being educated, whatever his parents' wishes in the matter may be; we insist on a man afflicted with a contagious disease like smallpox being isolated until the danger of infection is removed; we rob the criminal of his liberty to menace the social well-being by years of imprisonment, and yet we hear no protest that any injustice is being perpetrated. We impose a standard of physical, mental and moral fitness for the Army, the Navy, police, excise and postal services, and other State institutions, besides in a more private capacity admitting the same principle in our insurance and friendly societies. A small-pox patient, an ignorant child, or a criminal we rightly regard as a social menace, and we restrict their activities, but apparently the multiplication of cancer, epilepsy, and loathsome brutality is not so important a matter.

We restrict many times the breeding of children with a healthy soldier as parent, because we shall have to provide for the little one, but we cheerfully keep the degenerate offspring of an idiot without protest!

We *are* a wise and liberty-loving nation!

A man must not have a mad dog in the back yard under severe penalties, and if he deliberately bred from it we should be inclined to shoot him, but he can help to breed as many mad children as he likes without interference!

It would be robbing him of his glorious liberty!

As for the other objection as to who would decide between the fit and the unfit, I reply again that if we can appoint responsible persons to decide that question to-day, what is to prevent us adopting the same methods when we become even more rational?

Who decides whether a person is fit to be at large in the criminal world? Obviously, men whom we can trust, such as the constituted authorities, judges and jurymen.

Who decides with regard to those afflicted with contagious diseases but the sanitary and medical authorities?

These men decide that such and such members of society are not fit to be at large because their untrammelled freedom is dangerous to the rest of the community. In short, these authorities determine who are the fit and who are the unfit.

Why, then, should not competent men be appointed to decide this same question under somewhat similar circumstances?

In conclusion, I urge once again the necessity of a study of both sets of influences in the production of a healthy race. Eugenics and Socialism must work hand in hand if we are to have a healthy race. Eugenics shall make us conversant with the facts of heredity, and Socialism shall provide a congenial atmosphere in which man's latent nobility shall have a chance to soar to altitudes undreamt of at the present time.

# Part 9

# WAR, PEACE AND INTERNATIONALISM

# 42

# *MANIFESTO OF THE SOCIALIST LEAGUE ON THE SOUDAN WAR*, SOCIALIST LEAGUE, 1885.

[The founding of *Justice* and then of the *Commonweal* have been described as a turning point in popularising a socialist critique of imperialism (Claeys 2010, 147). This indeed was a part of the rationale for the breaking away of the Socialist League and the launching of the *Commonweal*, in repudiation of what it perceived as a "tendency towards National assertion" in Hyndman's SDF (see manifesto in Mann 1923, 45–46). In the early pronouncements of the Socialist League there was certainly no tendency in this direction. For this the principal credit doubtless lies with Belfort Bax, whose several contributions on these themes included the denunciation of the "hideous race monopolies called empires" in the *Commonweal*'s opening issue. Morris, meanwhile, was in close contact with Wilfrid Scawen Blunt (1840–1922), who had become one of Britain's best known critics of empire since supporting the cause of Egyptian nationalists in 1882.

The League's manifesto on the Sudan war is one of the most trenchant statements that it ever issued. It not only attacks the role of the "market-hunters and filibusters" who in Morris's estimation were the key to the whole subject. It also confronts head-on the role played by the new commercial press, especially the *Pall Mall Gazette* then edited by W.T. Stead, both in the driving of government policy and in the stirring up of popular imperialist sentiment. It offers an initial sideswipe at the late Frederick Burnaby (1842–1885), who had enjoyed considerable popularity as a swashbuckling hero of empire. In defiance of official and much public sentiment, it also deals in scathing terms with the cult of the fallen hero General Gordon, for whom a national day of mourning was held which helped inflame the public mood and calls for vengeance.

There were dissenting views even within the Socialist League. On 20 March, the week after the day of mourning, the Glasgow Socialist Leaguer James Mavor wrote a letter of complaint to which Morris replied unrepentantly. Gordon-worship was a stalking horse for mass murder, to attack it was therefore necessary and justified and to make a hero of such a man was an assault on public morality. The Mahdi who had led the Sudanese revolt in "their heroic defence of their liberties" was to be supported exactly as Garibaldi or William Wallace or struggling Scottish crofters were to be supported. "Surely it must be considered an article of faith with us to sympathise with *all* popular revolutionary movements, though we may not agree with all the tenets of the revolutionists: e.g. we are *internationists not nationalists*, yet we sympathise with the Irish revolt against English tyranny…" (Kelvin 1987, 409–410).]

FELLOW CITIZENS,—A wicked and unjust war is now being waged by the ruling and propertied classes of this country, with all the resources of civilisation at their back, against an ill-armed and semi-barbarous people, whose only crime is that they have risen against a foreign oppression which those classes themselves admit to have been infamous. Tens of millions wrung from the labour of the workmen of this country are being squandered on Arab slaughtering; and for what: (1) that Eastern Africa may be "opened up" to the purveyor of "shoddy" wares, bad spirits, venereal disease, cheap Bibles, and missionary; in short, that the English trader and contractor may establish his dominion on the ruins of the old simple and happy life led by the children of the desert; (2) that a fresh supply of sinecure Government posts may be obtained for the occupation of the younger sons of the official classes; (3) as a minor consideration may be added, that a new and happy hunting-ground be provided for military sportsmen, who, like the late lamented Colonel Burnaby, find life boresome at home, and are always ready for a little Arab shooting when occasion arises. All these ends determine the dominant classes, though in different proportions, to the course they are pursuing.

Citizens, you are the dupes of a plot. Be not deceived by the flimsy pretences that have been, and are, alleged as reasons for the cowardly brigandage perpetrated on weak and uncivilised peoples by these classes in the name of the community. Rest assured the above are the sole motives animating them, whatever their professions; in brief, that, in the words of our manifesto, "all the rivalries of nations have been reduced to this one—a degrading struggle for their share of the spoils of barbarous countries to be used at home for the purpose of increasing the riches of the rich and the poverty of the poor."

With the history and causes of the bondholders' war in Egypt you are probably already sufficiently familiar, but we invite your attention for a moment to the leading facts in this latest development of a career of hypocrisy and crime. After the British conquest of Egypt, General Hicks is allowed to attempt the reconquest of the Soudan in the interest of Egyptian usury. This attempt failing, General Baker is authorised to subdue at least the seaboard. A second failure demonstrating the utter futility of Egyptian arms against the desert spearmen, a fluttering in the dovecotes of the military and the Stock Exchange worlds ensues. But there is balm in Gilead yet. Happy thought—the garrisons—yes, they must be rescued! General Gordon, the successful subduer of rebels in China, and ex-Governor-General at Khartoum, is he not the man to deal with Soudanese malcontents? Assuredly, say the *Pall Mall Gazette* and *Times*. Cabinet Ministers, unable to resist the mandates of the classes these powerful organs represent, bow their heads and submit.

Gordon, after duly consulting with his friends, is despatched, bearing in his hand the instructions of the Government, but—as events have proved—in his *pocket* those of the distinguished newspapers in question. Arrived at Khartoum, the "Christian hero," accordingly, with scarce a feint at negociation, and in defiance of his professions of peace, proceeds to fortify himself within the city, and use it as a base for military raids upon the surrounding tribes, whom he had previously cajoled with protestations of friendship. The play after this move was easy. The wicked Mahdi menaces the life of the "hero;" "hero" demands an expedition to help him "smash the Mahdi." The "rebels," otherwise Soudanese, are base enough to take their own town of Berber from the Egyptian garrison. "Christian hero" feels it his bounden duty to announce his intention of recapturing Berber, and putting all its inhabitants to the sword by way of chastisement. (This pious intention, fortunately for the Berberese, remained unrealised.) Meanwhile garrisons are forgotten. The Jingoes know a cry worth two of that. Gordon abandoned! Despatch your expedition! cry *Times, Pall Mall Gazette,* and company. Cabinet Ministers faintly remonstrate, and at length again bow their heads. Who are Ministers, to dispute the orders of influential newspapers, representing important interests?—

> Theirs not to reason why,
> Theirs not to make reply;
> Theirs but to do and—die,

and dying they are, to all appearance, as Cabinet-Ministers—of *Pall Mall Gazette.* That, however, is no concern of ours.

The Expedition is despatched. British cut-throats slaughter a few thousand Arabs amid the jubilation of the Press, when—oh horror!—Khartoum is fallen: and fallen, too, into the hands of the Soudanese themselves. Gordon, no more! In Fleet Street is there a cry heard; lamentation and weeping and great mourning. Never was the dust of hero so watered by the gush of newspaper before. Nowadays, however, we produce emotion like other things—primarily for profit, and only secondarily for use. Time was when men poured forth each his own grief in his own manner when they sorrowed for some great departed. Under the rule of the great industry we have changed all this. Now the factory system and the division of labour supersede individual emotion: it is distilled for us by the journalist, and we buy it ready-made from the great vats in Fleet Street and Printinghouse Square. The result is that the public sometimes have emotion forced upon them when it suits the purveyor, for other reasons than the greatness of the departed. Perhaps it is so in this case. Anyway, from the well-watered dust of Gordon rises up for the *Times, Pall Mall,* and their clients, the fair prospect of British Protectorate at Khartoum, railway from Suakim to Berber, new markets, fresh colonial posts, etc. Cabinet Ministers once more bow before the all-powerful press, and whispering they will ne'er consent,—consent,—to the reconquest of the country in the interest of English commerce—for the permanent railway from Suakim to Berber can mean nothing less than this.

Citizens, if you have any sense of justice, any manliness left in you, join us in our protest against the wicked and infamous act of brigandage now being perpetrated for the interest solely of the "privileged" classes of this country; an act of brigandage led up to through the foulest stream of well-planned hypocrisy and fraud that has ever disgraced the foreign policy even of this commercial age. Mehemet Achmet (the Mahdi), the brave man who in Oriental fashion is undertaking the deliverance of his country, has repeatedly declared through his agents his willingness to release the Bashi-Bazouk garrisons, and give guarantees to refrain from aggression in Egypt. Mr. Wilfrid Seawen Blunt was in a position, even when the "Christian hero" was wantonly waging an offensive war against the Mahdi, to ensure the success of negociations for his release, as well as that of the garrisons, had he been allowed to make them, as he assuredly would, had this been the real object in view. But such an arrangement was not quite good enough for the market-hunters and filibusters for whom the "influential" press writes. "Not this man, but Wolseley," cried they; and Wolseley was sent, avowedly to rescue their nominee—who by that ostentatious pietism which, as they were well aware, gilds everything with a certain section of the British public, had already so well served their turn—but in reality to engage in the conquest of the devoted land upon which from the first their vultures' eyes had been cast.

And finally, we ask you to consider who it is that have to do the fighting on this and similar occasions. Is it the market-hunting classes themselves? Is it they who form the rank and file of the army? No! but the sons and brothers of the working classes at home. They it is who for a miserable pittance are compelled to serve in these commercial wars. They it is who conquer for the wealthy, middle and upper classes, new lands for exploitation, fresh populations for pillage, as these classes require them, and who have as their reward the assurance of their masters that they are "nobly fighting for their queen and country."

# 43

## *THE IMPERIAL KAILYARD. BEING A BITING SATIRE ON ENGLISH COLONISATION* (LONDON: TWENTIETH CENTURY PRESS, 1896), 3-15.

*R.B. Cunninghame Graham*

[When H.M. Hyndman embraced socialism, it was as a convinced supporter of the Empire. Even when Hyndman condemned the notorious Jameson Raid on the Transvaal (1895–1896) and the subsequent South African war (1899–1902), it was within a European frame of reference. Like other socialists, there were many within the SDF who extolled the virtues of the anti-British settlers in a way they would never have done those of native Africans. Nevertheless, there were alternative voices, who often reflected radical liberal traditions rather than the conservative ones which had left their imprint on Hyndman.

R.B. Cunninghame Graham (1852–1936) had been just such a radical liberal MP (North-West Lanarkshire, 1886–1892) who made outspoken socialist contributions in the Commons before ending his parliamentary career as a candidate of Keir Hardie's Scottish Labour Party. A good friend of Hardie's, who like Hardie was active in the Scottish Home Rule Association, Cunninghame Graham moved freely between the different strands of British socialism. In 1889, he was again with Hardie among the delegates to the "Marxist" congress in Paris that gave rise to the Second International. Nevertheless, he had also associated with SDF supporters during the London unemployed demonstrations of 1887, when he was arrested and imprisoned with John Burns (document Chapter 5, this volume). Cunninghame Graham's pungency as a writer and speaker was never better expressed than in his contributions to the social-democratic press regarding the violence with which the British pursued their claims in what are now the states of Zimbabwe and South Africa. The first of these, *The Imperial Kailyard*, was initially published in *Justice* on 5 September 1896.

The context was the Jameson Raid, and the international "howl of hatred" that it occasioned, and the March 1896 rising of the Ndebelele (Matabele) people against the British South Africa Company (BSAC) now known as the Second Matabele War. The pamphlet does not spare such latterday conquistadors as the fourth Earl Grey (1851–1917), with whom the author had been a contemporary at Harrow, and Cecil Rhodes (1853–1902). As politicians, entrepreneurs and military adventurers, these figures epitomised the nakedly mercenary vision of empire that had given rise to the BSAC following the discovery of gold in the Transvaal in the 1880s. Nevertheless, the pamphlet also evokes the mythologised history of European expansionism that served to dignify such enterprises and fed the culture of popular imperialism on which they depended (see also Chapter 50, this volume). While Hyndman would single out the role of particular capitalist interests, usually German or Jewish, Cunninghame Graham saw no fundamental difference between the different European powers and the cults of the colonising hero in which they shared. His concern was with the peoples like the Ndebeleles and with the racialised moral relativism that justified the violence perpetrated against them.

Readers will feel uncomfortable with the pamphlet's use of the taboo word "nigger". It is not difficult to find examples of it being used with the customary offensive connotations in the socialist press. As used by Cunninghame Graham it clearly conveys neither endorsement nor extenuation; the point, instead, is to expose the racial assumptions that lay behind such usages. Against the sentimentalism of the then-popular Kailyard school of Scottish short-story writers, Cunninghame Graham prefers the cynicism of their French contemporary, the lately deceased Guy de Maupassant (1850–1893). There are ample grounds for such cynicism in the episode with which the pamphlet closes: the murder in a place of sanctuary of the unarmed Matabele spiritual leader Mlimo by the American mercenary Frederick Russell Burnham (1861–1947). Burnham was a founder of the scout movement and was awarded the Distinguished Service Order by Edward VII for his role in the South African war.]

In order to prevent misapprehension, I may say at once that I am for Liberty, Property, and Old England; that I believe in virtue, magnanimity, righteousness, British fair play, the rights of man, and other things of that nature.

Believing as I do in the above national articles, and holding as I do that if such things exist they were invented and patented in England, and that it is impossible without infringement of copyright for any foreign nation, or any individual member of a foreign nation, either to use, aspire to, or in any way to become possessed of any of the aforesaid qualities, or virtues, I own that some recent events have caused me to doubt a little as to the hereditary continuity of moral qualities. I do not think that these doubts render me of necessity either a bad citizen or a disloyal subject. Let me say, therefore, in extenuation of my views, that I am neither an Anarchist nor a member of the Church of England. In my childhood I remember being stirred almost to enthusiasm when I was informed that wherever the British flag floated, all were free and equal before the law, irrespective of race, position, or colour.

All free and independent—the poor elector independently blacking boots, and the rich elector as independently running his course as the bridegroom of the scriptures—it pleased my elders to thus instruct me, and though, with the natural scepticism of youth, I received the information with the distrust that all coming from my elders merited, yet, with the diplomacy of the weak, I forebore to question statements, which I might have been compelled to believe by superior force. The sanctity of British soil, the superior virtue and chivalry of my countrymen, their justice, toleration, and fair dealing with all stronger than themselves, and their generous commercial attitude to weaker nations than themselves, grew to be my most serviceable creed.

With this, and a firm belief in the immutability of female virtue, I felt myself fairly equipped to face the world. The many sacrifices of principle and commonsense, that most men have to endure in order to adjust themselves to the exigencies of their belief, I went on making cheerfully and for years, in order to adapt myself to the creed I had been nurtured in, and only the evidence of my senses and the testimony of an occasional newspaper have caused me to reconsider my position upon the two cardinal items of my ethical programme.

Slowly but surely I have been compelled to abandon the second article of my belief, so that to-day, except from a purely legal standpoint, even seduction seems less founded on probability.

In relation to the first, it may be that my mental vision has become distorted, for who am I to set myself against the universal self-approbation of a mighty empire? Nothing of all this need discourage a philosopher. The world was made for us, that is for Englishmen, and if in certain portions of it Norman French law conflicts with Roman Dutch, both are agreed that Hollander, Royneck, and Africander, must rule in Africa. There were, I think, some natives, as Kaffirs, Zulus, Hottentots, Basutos, and still there are some Matabeles, but what of that? None of them ever wore a *hault de chausse* or rode a bicycle. Therefore it is clear that Britons are not bound by the same moral standard in their dealings with them, as if they were Europeans.

Principles, Maupassant has justly said, are by their very nature false and sterile. Are they not ideas reputed fixed and immutable? Fixed and immutable ideas in a world where all is changing, where light is an illusion, where sound is an illusion of our senses. I do not mean to say that Maupassant, is, as a philosopher, likely to replace Tupper in England, but still even from a Frenchman you may sometimes gather wisdom.

Principles, of course, are acted on by isothermal lines. That which is right in London, is inexpedient at Buluwayo. Commerce is founded, as are politics, upon expediency, and Britain is the home of commerce.

It may be now and then in opening up a new found territory that some slight injustice may be done. But what of that? No change can be accomplished without some class, some race, or individual suffering some loss. Surely, then, the death or wounds, captivity, or even the extermination of some few thousand savages, cannot be weighed against the blessings of a telegraphic service, postal communications, free trade in drink, or the retailing of the same after the plan of Gothenburg.

Let us then keep on and spread the light, make ever broader the phylacteries of our empire, open up markets, and make ourselves hating and hateful to all mankind. To ensure a self-supporting and a prompt millennium, all that is wanted is more markets. Therefore, we must grab all we can, and where we can, even if now and them a grabber is forced to herd with criminals, as a first-class misdemeanant. The phrase to "open up the country" stirs one's soul. Visions of Drake, of Hawkins, and of Captain Kidd, of Aaron Burr, of Claude du Val, Jack Sheppard, Xenophon, Sir Walter Raleigh, and other noble spirits, who launched their barques into an unknown sea in hopes to find the Indies, rise and excite our minds. The explorer, hunter, trapper, lumberman, and "mustanger" with their rifles, cap of skins, lean horse, long knife, and their flint and steel; with their large faith, endurance, spirit of adventure, and occasional brutality, rise from the fiction of Mayne Reid, and trouble our imagination.

Hakluyt and Pemberton and Mungo Park, with Burton, Burckhardt and the rest, as Captain Cook and the Valhalla of the Spanish navigators, who first filled maps with names, have drilled us to think well of all adventurers. As boys we followed their adventures, wept at their troubles, fought with them in imagination, sailed with them, and were knighted alongside them by good Queen Bess, or Ferdinand the Catholic on their return. Thus it is in part our minds are moulded to judge favourably of conquerors from youth. Then the odds seem so great. Cortes in Mexico, alone upon the causeway battling for his life, Rhodes or Pizarro charging amongst the thickest of the foe, seem so heroic. Still, if we pause to think, the odds are all the other way. War club, assegai and boomerang, bolas, parang and krise, even if wielded by thousands avail but little against quick-firing guns. In stern reality the "native" is the hero, and the European "conquistador," as Beit, Barney Barnato, Selous, Rhodes and Co., nothing but cowardly interlopers, presuming on superior weapons.

To open up a territory, then, is something glorious in itself, and also adds to the area of the British Empire. Paterfamilias, when he finally gets off his useless son, imagines him in Africa, extending British influence somewhat as follows:

A fine young fellow in his knickerbocker breeches and tan gaiters, with large straw hat and moral tone, riding about the country, giving orders to obsequious natives. A splendid shot and horseman, though a duffer of the duffers ere leaving home. Distance is sure to make a man a marksman and a rider, though in point of fact most colonists seldom discharge a gun, and as for riding, only those born in the country, or who have gone there very young, ever venture upon a horse except it be as quiet as a cow.

In young hopeful's district his father sees him manfully fighting the wilderness and making money, though he does no work; for work degrades a man who does not profit by it. Throughout the district all the farms are owned by gentlemen. In the bush stores no sale of alcohol or gunpowder is permitted to the natives.

Trifling with the native women is prohibited by law. On Sunday, in the log-built church shaded by palm trees, the preacher (a graduate of St. Bees) holds forth on home, on British pluck, and inculcates the elementary virtues. All is quite home-like, except the offertory, which sometimes dwindles owing to the lack of circulating medium.

After some five or even seven years are passed, Hopeful returns with liver and a fortune, quite unstained by toil, a little boastful about our Empire, perhaps a little inclined to drink, sunburned, but still refined and quite a gentleman.

Reality beholds him in a palm tree hat, red shirt, high boots, and redolent of gin and strong tobacco, crammed in a hut with three more graduates of Oxford, a dead, decaying horse before the door; his cook a native woman, who washes for the camp, and serves by turn at night as concubine to all the four. If he elects a country life, he soon becomes a brute, an honest, whisky-drinking brute, but still a brute, treating the natives not unkindly, but in the British way that now and then brings on a mutiny in India or a revolt in Matabeleland.

If he stays in the country he makes no money, sometimes works hard, at intervals lies on his back for weeks, cursing his folly for leaving England. Needless to say, he gathers nothing worth gathering about the land he lives in. Its botany, geology, its flora never appeal to him. Its fauna may be good for sport, but the damned Dutch, the infernal natives, or the cursed prairie fires, for everything has its condemnatory adjective in his vocabulary, render game scarcer day by day.

If, on the other hand, he casts his lot amongst the dwellers in the towns, his fate is often different. At first, of course, he tries some business which a gentleman can enter without contamination. Sets up as a horse-dealer, or in the wine trade, and comes to grief. After a while he goes upon the local stock exchange, buys, sells, cheats, wins, and takes the steamer home—a millionaire—to build his palace in Tyburnia. Take him for all in all, the Briton colonises well, and would do better if he could ever look at anything from any other standard than that of Tooting. Neither in Canada, Australia, Tasmania, nor any portion of the earth, where hitherto we have carried ourselves, our flag, our beer, and our other institutions, have we developed characteristics like those which Africa calls forth. In our dealings with the natives in older colonies, our intolerance has been tempered by lack of ammunition, and a sort of furtive kindness, which lurks in our natures, if the object on which we exercise it is submissive. One sees a carter crack his whip, with a report like thunder, at the horse he cleans and feeds, and loves far better than his wife, and which he never touches with his thundering whip. He likes to crack it, merely to show his power and to remind the horse what is in store for it, if it should rebel. Such was the Briton's attitude in days gone past. He did not generally ill-treat the "niggger"—only despised him in a sort of amicable manner. In Africa the scene has changed, and the "nigger" has no rights at all, except, of course, to clear out to the inferior lands and work for master at the rate that master chooses. We know, of course, that birds of Paradise, with the small heron, the humming bird, the giraffe, zebra, and all living things, which can be made in any way to minister to fashion, must disappear.

In the same way the "nigger" is also bound to go. What business has a man in his own country to hunt and shoot, refuse to till the soil, or till it only by the labour of his wives, buying no ploughs from us? What right has anyone to anything, if he can make no rifles to defend it? It may be we have gone a little fast in Africa. At least, the howl of hatred raised by all Europe and America against us, during the past six months, would seem to prove it. Not that I think the French, the Germans, or the Scandinavians, would have behaved an atom better than ourselves. The fault lies in our mode of life and the facilities for quick communication, even more than in ourselves. In former days, the colonist was planted there for life, he had to learn the native ways by contact with them, and in the end he got to understand them and to treat them more on an equality. To-day a steamer in a fortnight or three weeks takes a man home to England, and so he never rubs his English angles off, and still remains a stranger in the land he lives in. Throughout South Africa, we have had full scope to civilise the natives. We have dressed them in our clothes, and tried to fashion them as much as possible in our own image. We taught them commerce, established schools in which they learned geography, history, and as much arithmetic as was expedient for them. When possible, we took away their wives, and forced them to rely on prostitution in our own way, to satisfy the natural polygamic tendencies which all men have. We found their native beer too weak, and gave them whisky. Even their diseases seemed too childish for our conversing and we brought the small-pox and syphilis under their observation. Lastly, their "gri-gris" and "fetishes" did not seem apt to us, and so we sent our missionaries to spread the true faith, each missionary belonging to a different, and a differing sect, and setting forth the tenets of the faith according to his individual ignorance of its true nature. And we have prospered greatly. Commerce has prospered, fortunes have been made, and towns have risen, where ten years ago, the springbok and the hartebeest roamed o'er the veldt. The natives are in full revolt against our power and all goes well.

How though does all this spreading of the empire, waving of the flag, thundering of cannons and of speeches in our own praise react upon us? Much the same way as slavery reacted on the planters in South Carolina, who were themselves as much degraded by their "institution" as their "niggers." Never before has such a tone of boasting spread over all the nation. Never before have officers and gentlemen entered into such low and base intrigues as the one the world has talked so much about. Seldom before have Englishmen not fought, when fighting came in their way, to the bitter end. Certainly never in the history of our race have there been such determined efforts to defeat justice, or such an outcry when that justice tardily did justice on some electro-plated filibusters.

But more than all, a tone of callousness is spreading over our dealings with the natives in South Africa. Young gentlemen write letters to the *Westminster Gazette* dwelling with pleasure on an execution in Buluwayo. The twitching of his face, the kicking of his legs, "the nigger's cheek," the weather at the time; all is dished up as if it were matter his mother would be glad to hear of. Reporters, as in duty bound, report or else invent the casualties upon the "native" side; chronicling with much fidelity "the killing of some sixty 'natives' by our 'brave fellows.' "

If, on the other hand, a friendly native happens to get killed, he is returned as "slaughtered." On rare occasions when an imperial Englishman is slain, he has a special paragraph all to himself, generally headed in leaded type, "Massacre of Another Englishman." Lord Grey, who I remember, not at all a swaggerer or even very fond of blood at Harrow, is almost always nearly under fire, if not he, then Mr. Cecil Rhodes has heard the firing quite distinctly from his tent. That way "Buncombe" lies. "Buncombe" itself is harmless, even amusing, but when after the description of a fight a sentence closes the article and deplores that owing to the natives falling flat among the bush the machine guns could not play properly upon them, the case is different. Readers will see at once what cowardly brutes the Matabele are. At great expense the Chartered Company had introduced quick firing guns to enable them to cope with the assegais and old trade guns of the Matabele. But not content with that we had endeavoured by our own example to make them understand how white men think and fight, and to enable them to comprehend fairplay and patriotism and our other qualities.

All was as nothing. At the first attack the savage instinct was too strong, and, shame of shames, instead of standing in the usual way to be mowed down, these barbarous wretches threw themselves upon the ground, rendering our tactics useless, putting us to vast expense in ammunition, and showing the world it is impossible to civilise such a degraded people. Our missionaries, I take it, are to blame for not instructing the chief and headmen of the "niggers" that the first duty that a Matabele owes to Queen Victoria is to stand upright like a man and let our gunners have a chance to play their Maxims in a proper way upon him.

Again, we have the episode of the alleged "shooting" of the native god M'Limo. On this occasion two "heroes," an American and a Briton, set out to capture this official in his own house. In an open and heroic fashion they approached him with gifts, and what the writer designates as "offertories," but leaves us in the dark as to what these "offertories" were. "Accosting him, they said they came to beg his blessing." How like a Briton their conduct was. No artifice after the foreign fashion; merely his blessing, which they must have been in need of. "Being decoyed by the M'Limo into his cave, and seeing the treachery of the natives rendered capture imminent, and finding, in the circumstances, it was impossible to capture the prophet alive, Burnham, without further hesitation, shot him in the cave." A most heroic deed, heroically conceived, well carried out, and quite successful but in one respect, and that is that it was a lie, for recent telegrams declare the M'Limo is alive. Such an adventure, if it had occurred, might have been justified by the result. As it appears, it is apocryphal. It seems to show the kind of faith that Europeans keep with the natives of South Africa, even in their moments of imagination. No one doubts that eventually the Matabele will be conquered, and that our flag will wave triumphantly over the remnant of them, in the same way as it waves triumphantly over the workhouse pauper and the sailors' poor whore in the east end of London. Let it wave on over an empire reaching from north to south, from east to west; wave over every island, hitherto ungrabbed, on every sterile desert and fever-haunted swamp as yet unclaimed; over the sealer amid the icebergs, stripping the fur from the live seal, on purpose to oblige a lady; over the abandoned transport camel, perishing of thirst in the Soudan: and still keep waving over Leicester Square, where music halls at night belch out their crowds of stout imperialists.

# 44

# *THE APPROACHING CATASTROPHE IN INDIA* (LONDON: TWENTIETH CENTURY PRESS, 1897), 3–16.

*H.M. Hyndman*

[By his own account, Hyndman had been "brought up in an atmosphere of imperialism as far as India was concerned" (Hyndman 1911, 167). In some accounts, the persistence of this imperialist outlook is heavily emphasised; it is linked with the "patriotism verging on chauvinism" that dominated Hyndman's ethic and with his later relapse into outright nationalism (Bevir 2011, 75; Etherington 1974). Such judgments must nevertheless be reconciled with the fervency of Hyndman's denunciations of British rule in India. A student of Indian affairs since the early 1870s, Hyndman developed a highly negative view of the economic consequences of British rule. Though this was not so different from some of the arguments of Congress nationalists like Dadabhai Naoroji, Hyndman voiced it in more politically combative terms and already in 1886 had warned of a "hideous economical catastrophe", beside which the Irish famine of 1847 would appear as child's play (cited in Davis 2001, 141).

The famine of 1896–1897 came as a sort of confirmation with as many as a million deaths. Hyndman was not only active in the cause of famine relief but in the pamphlet reproduced here places responsibility for the catastrophe squarely on the callousness of the British administration and the draining of wealth from India to the metropolis. The old imperial ideal has not yet disappeared: it remains in the glimpse of the "glorious empire" that there might have been under wiser and more sympathetic direction. Nevertheless, in calling unequivocally for the overthrow of British rule, Hyndman gave voice to a forthright anti-imperialism that more moderate Indian nationalists found politically compromising.

This support for the Indian national cause was one of the most consistent features of Hyndman's career. During the "brief flowering of revolutionary anti-imperialism" in the London of the early 1900s, he was a valued associate of Shyamji Krishnavarma's Indian Home Rule Society; and as guest of honour when its India House was inaugurated in Highgate, he observed that "loyalty to Great Britain means treachery to India" (Shanker and Shanker 2005–2006; Owen 2007a, 62–63).

Hyndman's further publications included *The Ruin of India by British Rule* (1907), *The Emancipation of India* (1911) and *The Awakening of Asia* (1919). According to the Indian nationalist B.G. Tilak, who had visited Britain in the year that it was published, the last of these was the coping stone to the "magnificent edifice" of Hyndman's work in the Indian cause (Shanker and Shanker 2005–2006).]

> We hold ourselves bound to the natives of our Indian territory by the same obligations of duty which bind us to all our other subjects; and those obligations, by the blessing of Almighty God, we shall faithfully and conscientiously fulfil.
>
> And it is our further will that, so far as may be, *our subjects, of whatever race or creed, be freely and impartially admitted to offices in our service,* the duties of which they may be qualified by their education, ability and integrity duly to discharge.
>
> In their prosperity will be our strength, in their contentment our security, and in their gratitude our best reward. And may the God of all power grant to us, and to those in authority under us, strength to carry out these our wishes for the good of the people. *The Queen's Proclamation to the Princes and Peoples of India in 1858* (*the year after the Mutiny*).

Nothing short of a great famine, a terrible pestilence, or a revolt on a large scale, will induce the mass of Englishmen to devote any attention whatever to the affairs of India; although we have in our vast dependency 300,000,000 of people under our control, of whom some 250,000,000 are under our direct government. The House of Commons is, if possible, more indifferent and lethargic than the nation. Even in this year of death and disaster the Indian Budget, far more important in every way than the English Budget, was not brought forward until the last day of the Session; when a dozen or so of limp and weary legislators sprawled on the benches, overcome with heat and boredom, while that third rate Calonne, Lord George Hamilton, twittered out his official commonplaces from page upon page of type-written notes. Government and Opposition, as represented by the Front Benches on both sides of the House, are in full agreement as to everything being for the best in the best of Indian Administrations possible; and independent criticism, though in the case of Sir William Wedderburn, at any rate, thoroughly honest and well-informed, is neither sufficiently vigorous in itself, nor put with enough oratorical force to produce any serious effect. The result is most unfortunate. Matters are indeed far worse now than they were in the days of the old East India Company. Then a review of the whole system of government in India took place at stated intervals by the House of Commons, and there was some chance that the truth would come out and that justice might be done. Now there is no appeal whatever; for the Nonconformist financial solicitor who last did India the honour of being her Secretary of State is as much concerned to prevent the dangerous blunders to which he was a party from being detected, as is the flippant and ignorant aristocrat who at present holds the office, and glibly misrepresents the whole situation in return for his £5,000 a year.

The only hope of bringing about a beneficial reorganisation peacefully is that the English people should awaken to a sense of their responsibilities, and insist upon it that the solemn pledges of the Queen in 1858, and of the same lady as Queen-Empress twenty years later, to our fellow-subjects in India, shall be fulfilled, instead of being deliberately and systematically broken, as they have been ever since they were given. Those two proclamations, had they been even partially given effect to, would long ere this have secured to the natives of India a fair share in the administration of their own country, and would have stanched that fearful drain of produce from our great dependency without return, which is and has been utterly ruining the unfortunate inhabitants. But anything like good faith is unknown in our dealings with the people of India. Queen-Empress and Ministers together break their most solemn engagements with a light heart, and are evidently amazed that anyone, in Great Britain or in Hindostan, should imagine for a moment that this sort of peccadillo is at all reprehensible, seeing that the breach of honour only involves the death by starvation of some tens of millions of Hindoos.

The history of India, as it is now recorded by Anglo-Indians in their writings and evidence, would lead those who had no other and better sources of information to imagine that, for hundreds, if not thousands, of years before the English became dominant in the country, the inhabitants of Hindostan found almost their sole occupation in cutting one another's throats. According to such Anglo-Indian accounts of the perpetual anarchy and slaughter which everywhere prevailed, the wonder is that we should have discovered even a remnant of the population left to lament the disappearance of their fellows; not to say that, on this reading of the past, the magnificent buildings and vast public works, which undoubtedly existed at the time of our conquest and remain to this day, must have been constructed by some strange supernatural agency. Of course, this nonsense is only produced for the benefit of ignorant people at home, and in order to persuade all classes in the United Kingdom that our rule is infinitely better than anything which has gone before or which could possibly follow after.

The truth, however, is that though India suffered greatly at times from foreign invasions and intestine warfare, prior to our appearance on the scene, the various races and nations which people that great peninsula no more existed in a state of perpetual anarchy and universal confusion than did the Greeks of the period of Pericles, or the Italians of the Middle Age republics. The history of India is full of great deeds, in peace as well as in war; and that India was rich when we first began to rifle it of its wealth is conclusively proved by the fact that our money-loving ancestors thought it worth while to settle there and take what they could get, long before we became the paramount power. It is, indeed, impossible honestly to dispute that, alike under their own native Hindoo dynasties and under the control of Mohammedan rulers, India attained to a high level of wealth and prosperity. Even the raids from Central Asia and the internal wars, of which so much is made nowadays, produced little permanent effect. Nor should it be forgotten that the invaders from the north were either speedily swept back whence they came, with their ill-gotten booty, or settled permanently in India and became, as the Normans did with us, a portion of the native population. In both cases there was no continuous draining away of wealth to foreigners; and if a ruler showed himself too grasping and oppressive, the annals of the East give many examples of the ease with which he could be removed. In fact, no man, not wholly devoid of capacity and imagination, can read through the real history of India during the Hindoo and Mohammedan periods without interest and admiration. Great religions, great literature, great jurisprudence, great monarchs, great warriors, great administrators, beautiful arts and magnificent architecture, exquisite crafts and splendid public works—such were the products of those times of chaos and ignorance, which our pensioned competition-wallahs speak of to-day with superb contempt.

Below the surface, the mass of the agricultural population pursued the same tranquil, industrious, but certainly not unhappy, life which their ancestors had led for centuries before. The inhabitants of the Indian village communities were assuredly far better off in all that goes to make up a contented existence than the villeins, or than most of the free peasants, of Europe, who were their contemporaries. Under the great Bahmuny dynasty of the Deccan, or beneath the sway of the Emperor Akber, it may be doubted whether any wholly rural population was ever more prosperous. The restrictions of caste, the grotesque and often terrible religious ceremonies, the superstitious observances, female child immolation and suttee, the passing tyranny and oppression of rajah or nawab, were so completely portions of their existence that they were no more noticed by the mass of the people, and were much less harmful to them, than the action of the Catholic Church, the Nobles, or the Free Companies, a few thousand miles away to the West. Yet no one has as yet suggested that a peaceful Chinese domination of Europe during the Middle Ages, or after, with Chinese officials filling all the higher posts in the State, would have been preferable to the frequent wars and insurrections which led to the development of our present group of powerful and independent nations. In India every government prior to our supremacy made use of native talent in every department. The Hindoos were employed and trusted by the Mohammedan rulers not only as financiers, judges, and administrators, but as warriors. Thus the wealth produced was retained in India, and, as example after example proves, a man of capacity, however humble his birth, might rise to be the highest functionary under a monarch, or even become the head of a considerable empire himself.

It remained for us Englishmen to change this wholesome system altogether. First, under the East India Company, and then, and far more completely under the direct rule of the Crown and the English people, the natives have been shut out from all the principal positions of trust over five-sixths of Hindostan, and have been prevented from gaining any experience in the higher administration, or in military affairs. Wherever it was possible to put in an Englishman to oust a native an Englishman has been put in, and has been paid from four times to twenty times as much for his services as would have sufficed for the salary of an equally capable Hindoo or Mohammedan official. To a such pitch has this policy been carried since the Mutiny—when we suppressed a justifiable rising with at least as great ferocity and cruelty as the Turks have ever exhibited to Bulgarians or Armenians—that at the present time out of 39,000 officials who draw a salary of more than 1,000 rupees a year 28,000 are Englishmen and only 11,000 natives! Moreover, the 11,000 natives receive as salaries only £3,000,000 a year: the 28,000 Englishmen receive £15,000,000 a year!! Out of the 960 important civil offices which really control the civil administration of India 900 are filled with Englishmen and only 60 with natives. Still worse, if possible, the natives of India have no control whatsoever in any shape or way over their own taxation, or any voice at all in the expenditure of their own revenues. Their entire government—I speak, of course, of the 250,000,000 under our direct control—is carried on and administered by foreigners, who not only do not settle in the country but who live lives quite remote from those of the people, and return home at about forty-five or fifty years of age, with large pensions.

As I have often said in public, India is, in fact, now governed by successive relays of English carpet-baggers, who have as little sympathy with the natives as they have any real knowledge of their habits and customs. Yet, if any Indian of ability dares to denounce this monstrous oppression of his countrymen, he is at once howled down by the Government and the English press as a seditious libeller, and he may think himself lucky if he is not condemned, without trial, like the brothers Nathu, of Poona, to imprisonment for life; or transported into penal servitude by a slavish English judge, *after the jury had found him not guilty,* like the unhappy native journalist recently condemned.

What should we Englishmen say if men of another race were thus crushing down the whole national life of a number of civilised peoples and reducing them to the level of mere serfs of the foreigner? Should we not declare with one accord that such a system of government was infamous, and should we not—that is the point to-day—sympathise with the natives in any endeavour which they might make to throw off such an intolerable yoke? There can be but one answer to that question. Those who argue, also, that the Indian peoples could never rise to the level of their opportunities, and that mere chaos would inevitably follow the withdrawal or overthrow of the English power, conveniently overlook the fact that the Japanese, who are certainly in no respect superior to the great mass of the dwellers in Hindostan, have, in a quarter of a century, raised themselves to the position of a first-class power. But, then, the Japanese, luckily for them, have been free from European domination, while they have been at full liberty to acquire European knowledge. I venture to affirm that if, in the forty years which have passed since the Mutiny, we had devoted ourselves to the uplifting, instead of to the repression, of India, that great country to-day would hold a position in the world far, far ahead of Japan. Nay, that, even in the twenty years which have passed since the last great famine, we could have built up an Empire in the East second in wealth, prosperity, and real greatness to none that the world has ever seen.

Have we, then, done no good? Are there no improvements due to English rule? Some good has indeed been done, but it is of little value in comparison with the wholesale mischief we have wrought. We put down the burning alive of widows two or three generations ago; we have stopped the sacrifice of female children; we have maintained even-handed justice between the various races and religions; we administer the laws without open corruption; we allow, except in times of panic, free speech, a free press, and free discussion; we have built railways and irrigation works; we have spent a little money on education; and we have maintained peace within our borders for the past forty years. And this is all that the Anglo-Indian, who is stone blind of one eye and sees very imperfectly with the other in these matters, can recognise as the outcome of our administration. If there were no overwhelming drawbacks inevitably attendant on the whole system, then we might admit that, as a nation, we have nothing to be greatly ashamed of in our recent connection with India.

But even what appear at first sight to be the best points in our rule will scarcely stand closer examination. Thus it may be freely admitted that English officials are not corrupt. They are, however, paid so heavily to preserve them from temptation that the result to the natives is almost, if not quite, as bad as corruption would be. The duties, also, of the District Officer—"the real ruler of India," as Sir William Hunter calls him—are so multifarious that he cannot possibly perform them all himself; and he is consequently dependent on ill-paid native subordinates, who too often more than make up for his highly-paid honesty by disgraceful roguery. Our laws, which are administered strictly enough, are in most important matters wholly unsuited to the people. Thus the effect of our laws regulating contracts has been to throw the ryots over large districts of India entirely into the hands of the native money-lenders, who make use of our courts to enforce fraudulent claims against the unfortunate cultivators, and to exact outrageous rates of interest as well. Such matters of indebtedness are handled with a rough but reasonable justice under the old native laws administered by native authorities.

In the exaction of the land tax, outside the area of Lord Cornwallis's permanent settlement in Bengal, our methods are so strict and rigid, and so entirely unsuited to the people, that the grossest injustice is perpetually done, though I am aware that no such wrong is intended. For example, in native territory the land which is allowed to lie fallow is taxed but one-eighth of the amount paid for land that is actually under cultivation. In British territory both are taxed the same; thus practically enforcing over-cropping to meet the demands of the revenue officer. If a ryot sinks a well in British territory, he is heavily taxed for it. By native usage he gets the benefit of his own improvement, and is not taxed for what is the result of his own labour. In times of famine our allowances in reduced taxation are so small as to amount to actual cruelty. Native custom exonerates the ryots from any payment for some time. The increase of the English land revenue which may be observed over the greater portion of the territory under our control, is due to the enhanced assessments made when the old settlements of the taxation for twenty or thirty years fall in. These increases have been enforced wholly regardless of the fact that, owing to the gradual fall in the value of agricultural products, such increase of itself would be crushing to the cultivator, even if the land were not over large areas steadily deteriorating. Then the compulsory cultivation of opium, the price of which the Government fixes, is another unjust act that presses heavily on the cultivators in particular regions.

Even the railways and irrigation works, upon which so much stress is laid as having been constructed by us for the benefit of the people of India, have been built by foreign capital; and the interest for that foreign capital, whether it has been earned or not, has been steadily paid to the debenture-holders and shareholders who live in England. The railways, therefore, act as huge syphons to drain away the wealth of the people; while the irrigation works of our engineers have in more than one case proved not only not advantageous, but actually injurious to the land, which the water provided by them was supposed to fertilise. Moreover, although we say that the railways and irrigation works have been built with *English* capital, the truth is, as will be clearly shown below, that this capital, so lent to the Government of India at interest for the construction of public works, had been previously abstracted from the people of India under various pretexts; and therefore was only *their* wealth, which we had laid hands upon and called our own, advanced to them again after having been brought over here.

In short, the entire administration of British India, in spite of all its superficial justice and beneficence, is really a most abominably bad system. It is a government of a vast empire by foreigners, for foreigners, through foreigners. If we were as sympathetic and considerate as we are cold and callous—read in a recently published book by a clergyman of the Church of England how that clergyman glories in having himself regularly thrashed his native servants—it would be impossible for us to cope with this overwhelming disadvantage. No such government could be permanently successful in promoting the welfare of a subject people were it managed never so ably. Conducted as we have conducted it, absolute ruin was inevitable, and is now close upon us.

India, as already stated, was a wealthy country under the great Mohammedan emperors. The best authorities put the revenue raised during the fifty years of Akbar's reign at more than £30,000,000 a year; Aurungzib's revenue, levied more harshly over a wider area, reached as much as £80,000,000 annually. These sums, of course, represented a much greater proportional value in those times than they do to-day. But, in spite of this and of the heavy expenditure of the smaller Courts, and even of the petty Rajahs and Nawabs, the mass of the people were well-to-do.

Furthermore, famine was extremely rare. Such widespread famines as those which have devastated British territory frequently during the present century were, indeed, then unknown. Drought and scarcity, of course, came periodically, and their effects are recorded. But the natives had for centuries made provision against these natural calamities by means of storage of grain, alike in the village communities and in the towns; so that, although acute distress at times prevailed, wholesale starvation of millions, such as occurs under our régime, was unheard of. With the establishment of our administration, however, began the deliberate manufacture of famine for a poverty-stricken people on a scale hitherto unprecedented in the history of India or of the human race.

How has this impoverishment been brought about? Why is it that with the best possible intentions on the part of Englishmen at large towards their fellow-subjects their rule in India is by far the most onerous that the inhabitants of Hindostan have ever experienced? Nobody disputes that the taxation of India per head is very light indeed. It is beyond question that the trade has greatly developed, though, as the trade of the Native States is not discriminated from that with British territory, it is difficult to determine how much of the actual imports, which are as a whole much less than the exports, go to the inhabitants under our direct control. The revenue is slowly growing. The population is increasing. No wonder that people at large fail to see what is wrong apart from the root injustice of our foreign rule. No wonder that it takes some study to comprehend the economic blight which curses with impoverishment, continuous deterioration of the soil, and frightful famines one-sixth of the entire population of the planet.

Yet there is no mystery in the matter. The net revenue of India to-day is between £61,000,000 and £62,000,000, reckoned on the old silver basis of ten rupees to the £. Of this amount £25,000,000 in round figures are raised from the taxation of land, and it is admitted by all who are not directly concerned in misrepresenting the truth, that such a revenue from the land to-day means that the ryots are taxed up to the point which they can pay without starving themselves *and more*. In like manner the salt revenue represents a taxation upon an absolute necessary of life for the people and their cattle to the extent of not less than 1,000 per cent. on the value of the salt. The terrible effects of this monstrous impost on both men and beasts, entailing, as it does, privation and disease, have often been enlarged upon by Government officials of the highest rank. That foreign rulers should have to exact such payments in order to obtain even approximately sufficient revenue to carry on their administration, shows plainly both how poor the people of India must be, and how indifferent we are to their well-being. That we have reached the limit of possible taxation there is no doubt whatever. And yet, as I say, the total actual taxation of less than three shillings per head seems light enough, and is, indeed, light as compared with what is easily paid by the inhabitants of the Native States which are surrounded by our territory.

The impoverishment and ruin of India are due then mainly, not to the mere amount of the taxation, nor even to the rigid and cruel fashion in which it is too often levied, but to the manner in which the taxation, when raised, is expended. I purposely avoid giving many figures in this pamphlet, because I know that they are generally skipped by the ordinary reader. But anyone who will study the figures of the exports and imports into India will discover that, taken over a period of years, and reckoned according to the system laid down in my "Bankruptcy of India," the excess of the exports over the imports nowadays amounts to a value of over £30,000,000 *in gold*. More than half of this large amount is due to direct Government drawings. These drawings represent £4,750,000 for military depôts in England, which the Military Member of Council lately declared in his evidence before the Royal Commission on Indian Finance was a wholly useless expenditure so far as India was concerned. Then there are the many millions paid in pensions for retired officials, civil and military—some eleven hundred colonels receive over £1,000,000 a year—and the charges for the home establishments. Over and above these large amounts there is the charge of more than £8,000,000 for interest and dividends on loans, and railway debentures and shares. This, of course, being as complete a deduction from the wealth of India as the other drawings. In all an average of just £16,000,000 in gold, not silver, are thus taken from poor India every year on direct Government account. All this value abstracted, be it observed again, being measured in gold. In addition, there are the private remittances and profits due to the English exploitation of the country, which bring the total drain of produce up to at least the sum of £30,000,000 stated.

Just consider what this means. According to the official Statistical Abstract, the following are the figures of exports and imports for the year 1894-5, the last year given:—

|  | MERCHANDISE. | TREASURE. | TOTAL. |
| --- | --- | --- | --- |
| Exports | 108,814,999 | 8,158,017 | 116,973,016 |
| Imports | 70,167,438 | 9,559,007 | 79,726,445 |
|  |  |  | 37,246,571 |

Here we have an excess of exports over imports of £37,246,571 in silver at 10 rupees to the £. But, as the value of the imports is reckoned at the Indian ports, we must add at least fifteen per cent. to the value of the exports in order to cover profit, freight and insurance, so as to make a fair comparison. This will bring the disparity up in that one year to some £53,000,000 reckoned in silver. But even so we have not reached the full truth; for it is almost certain that the greater part of the treasure remaining on balance goes into the Native States (who any way take *at least* one-fifth of the total imports) where the princes and people can alike afford to hoard.

It is safe, therefore, to say that although the year taken was one in which the import of treasure on balance was exceptionally low, the total drain of produce from British India on the average of years at the present time is not less than the £30,000,000 a year stated. How the fall in the value of silver has increased the gross amount of the commodities which must be exported from India to meet home charges, interest, &c., *payable in gold* in England, I need not insist upon. The appreciation of gold, however, means that India has to pay in produce without return fully seventy-five per cent. more than she had to pay when silver was at five shillings an ounce, and the rupee was worth two shillings, or one shilling and tenpence.

Beside this fearful drain, and its inevitable economic effect, the continuous financial deficits in the Budget; the generally excessive military expenditure; the £50,000,000 in gold wasted on frontier expeditions in twenty years; the deliberate swindle which robbed the natives of the greater part of the Famine Insurance Fund raised from them by extra taxation, under solemn guarantee, to the tune of

£1,500,000 in gold yearly since 1878; nay, even the millions paid to Europeans in India itself to the exclusion of natives from any share in their own government—beside this frightful continuous tribute forced from a subject population, I say, all these minor and incidental wrongs sink into insignificance. No such infamy has ever before been perpetrated at the expense of any people. It is bad enough that India should be deprived of all self-government: it is criminal that her population should thus be systematically bled to death.

For think what it means. It means, once more, that we are deliberately making famine, and then pretending to mitigate the scourge by so-called Relief Works and the hypocritical Charity of the Mansion House Fund. We are yearly taking the top layer off the soil of India, and then marvel that we are coming to the bed rock. We are daily drawing away the life-blood of our patient by the ounce at a time, and then repine because he cannot show greater vigour. The £500,000,000 in gold as represented in produce, which we have abstracted from India since the great famine of 1876-78, brought about of inevitable necessity the terrible famine of 1896-97. Our loans from the wealth thus extorted back again to India at interest payable in gold, while they avert the declaration of bankruptcy for the moment, do but serve to increase the ruinous drain of produce in the long run. Things are getting worse year by year.

The mode of life of the 150,000,000 of people who form the class directly dependent on agriculture in British India is, as a whole, simpler and more penurious than that of any people in the world. The Indian ryots and labourers are industrious, thrifty and peaceable, and if teetotalism were the talisman to ensure economic well-being, they ought indeed to be well off, seeing that they drink nothing stronger than water. Their pleasures are exceedingly few, and almost the only occasion when the ryot spends any money beyond the cost of his bare keep and miserable clothing is when a marriage takes place in his family. In many districts the habitual food of the cultivators is so unwholesome that it brings about chronic disease in the present and hands on enfeeblement to the next generation. In some provinces the people are better off than in others, those in which the country has most recently come under British rule being as a rule the least poverty-stricken. But wherever our domination has long existed, and the land revenue has been subject to periodical reassessment, the condition of the cultivators is deplorable. Whatever differences of race, language, religion there may be, in this matter of poverty all are pretty much on the same level. If a village seems to be a little in advance of its neighbours, and the sweetstuffs which the natives love find a somewhat readier sale there than elsewhere, this is due to some special local circumstances. But nowadays empty hovels, miserable clothing, an absence of gold or silver bangles and anklets, and other evidence of small accumulations, are the rule throughout our territory. The small artisan class and artificers is little better off than the cultivators, and there seems no sign of improvement in their condition.

Nevertheless, whenever there is a sudden gleam of prosperity for the people, as in Bombay during the cotton famine in America, they are ready enough to purchase

Western goods and speedily give evidence that they are, after all, a civilised and intelligent people. If they do not buy good English wares now that is because they are too poor to do so, and the greatest market in the world for our industrial classes is closed to us by the greed and incapacity of our ruling minority.

As to the capacity of native Indians to rise to a high level in every department, conclusive proof of this is afforded every day, and the names of Dr. Bose, Mr. Chatterji, Prince Ranjitsinhji, and others ought to show us that in crushing down and destroying the intelligence and vitality of the population of British India, we are committing a series of outrages on humanity at large.

And now as to the poverty of India. No such misery on such a scale has ever been known on the planet as is to be seen under British rule in Hindostan at this hour. More than five-and-twenty years ago, Lord Lawrence—no pessimist surely—twice said in public in his official capacity:—"The mass of the people of India are so miserably poor that they have barely the means of subsistence. It is as much as a man can do to feed his family or half-feed them, let alone spending money on what you would call luxuries or conveniences." Sir Evelyn Baring, now Lord Cromer, in 1882, speaking of an estimate that the yearly gross income per head of the people might be twenty-seven rupees a year, said that "the tax-paying population is exceedingly poor," and "he thought it was quite sufficient to show the extreme poverty of the mass of the people."

The poverty of Madras is notorious. There are at least 20,000,000 pauper ryots in that province. Mr. W. R. Robertson, Agricultural Reporter to the Government of Madras, says of the ryot:—"His condition is a disgrace to any country calling itself civilised. In the *best seasons* the gross income of himself and his family does not exceed threepence a day throughout the year, and in a bad season their circumstances are most deplorable." In his "England's Work in India," in 1881, Sir William Hunter, the specially retained official apologist of the Government, who writes the articles on India in the *Times*, expressed himself to the effect that in British territory "forty millions go through life on insufficient food." According to Sir William's own statement, there must be close upon eighty millions of people in 1897 in that state of permanent starvation; seeing that the land under cultivation has deteriorated in the meantime, while its extent has little, if at all, increased, and the population to be fed has steadily grown. Mr. Cotton, of the Bengal Civil Service, says, speaking of the cultivators who are ruined by our shortsighted system: "A bare margin for subsistence alone remains, and the result is that indebtedness"—to the rapacious native usurer who uses the English law to crush his victims—"extends year by year, and that famines recur with ever-increasing frequency and severity." Sir Charles Elliott, late Lieutenant-Governor of Bengal, is reported to have declared: "I do not hesitate to say that half our agricultural population never know from year's end to year's end what it is to have their hunger fully satisfied." Whether Sir Charles said it or not, this is less than the truth. And so I might go on, piling up quotations from official authorities as to the awful poverty of India, until I had extended this pamphlet to the size of a thick closely-printed folio volume.

Not even the most ignorant or most corrupt Anglo-Indian pensioner will dare to challenge what is stated on this point.

But from this miserable, poverty-stricken population, let us not forget, we are still extorting, year after year, over £30,000,000 sterling worth of produce, measured in gold, without any commercial return. *Consequently* the soil is steadily becoming less fertile over vast districts of India, and the physical condition of the people is being enfeebled to such an extent that, if our present system continues, a horde of anæmic and worn-out starvelings will alone remain to chant the "blessings of British rule."

As to the continued deterioration of the soil, the gradual but steady decay of the cattle—perhaps the most serious symptom of all in an agricultural country—the hopeless look-out for the future, I could give passage after passage from men of the highest authority, such as Buck, Harwood, Chester Macnaghten, Carpenter, Cunningham, Irwin, and many more.

I will content myself with setting out once again the often-cited testimony of Sir James Caird on this head, published officially after the last great famine. Sir James at the time was recognised as the leading authority on agriculture in the United Kingdom. He was sent to India as Special Famine Commissioner by the Conservative Government in order to report on the causes of famine. Prior to his departure in 1879 he had a short controversy with me in the *Times*—my articles on the "Bankruptcy of India" had appeared in the *Nineteenth Century* just before—as to the condition of the population under our rule, in which he maintained that my views in relation to our administration of the country were incorrect. The day after his return from India Sir James Caird came to my house, then 10, Devonshire Street, Portland Place, and on entering the room where I was, said, without a word of preface: "You are quite right, Mr. Hyndman. We are working up to a terrible catastrophe in India." In his official report, dated October 31st, 1879, he practically repeated this, and told the Government and the country what some of us had been telling them for years before and have been telling them ever since. What did he say? "The available good land in India is nearly all occupied. The produce of the country on an average of years is barely sufficient to maintain the present population and make a saving for occasional famine. Scarcity, deepening into famine, is thus becoming of more frequent occurrence. As rulers, we are thus brought face to face with a growing difficulty. There are more people every year to feed from land which, in many parts of India, is undergoing gradual deterioration. Of this there can be no stronger proof than that the land revenue in some quarters is diminishing"—even where it is not it represents so much food pumped out of the stomachs of the people— "It is unsafe to break up more of the uncultivated low land. *The diminution of pasture thereby already caused is showing its effect in a lessening proportion of working cattle*"—mark that!—"for an increasing area of cultivation." Again:—"The pressure on the means of subsistence is rendered more severe by the moral disorganisation produced by laws affecting property and debts not adapted to the people. Those British officials who see this feel themselves powerless to influence a central authority for removal from them, *subject to no control of public opinion* and overwhelmed with details with which it is incapable of dealing."

Nor is it wonderful that this wholesale blundering should go on, for, as my old friend, the late Chester Macnaghten, himself an Anglo-Indian, and President of the Rajkumar College, Rajkote, Kattiwar, repeatedly assured me, the English officials do not know the natives nearly so well as their predecessors did. Sir James Caird confirmed this:—"Our officers do not know the natives as they used to do when our Government was less centralised, and they are every year becoming more strange to the people." In fact, legislation wholly unsuited to the people, administration ignorant of the needs of the people, come in to complete the ruin wrought by an economic system utterly indifferent to the starvation of the people. The following passage sums up the whole situation:—"The agricultural system, except in the richer irrigated lands, is to eat or sell every saleable article the land produces, to use the manure of the cattle for fuel, and to return nothing to the soil in any proportion to what is taken away. Every increase of population increases the danger. Crop follows crop without intermission, so that Indian agriculture"—don't forget our system of perpetual rack-renting, of equal taxation of fallow and cultivated land, of charging for wells sunk by the ryot himself, of rigid exaction of revenue even in years of scarcity—"Indian agriculture is becoming simply a process of exhaustion. Even in some tracts of canal-irrigated land, where water is lavishly used without manure, crops have ceased to grow. An exhausting agriculture and an increasing population must come to a dead-lock. No reduction of the assessment "can be more than a postponement of the inevitable catastrophe"! That warning was penned eighteen years ago. Nothing whatever has been done to remedy the evils Sir James denounced.[1] On the contrary, matters are worse in every respect than ever they were before. Yet eight millions of people perished of starvation in the famine of 1876-78.

Now, since 1878 we have taken out of India, without return, produce to the value of more than £500,000,000 in gold. Is it not clear that, even assuming that we had left our administration in India in its present rotten state, there would have been no famine in 1896-97 if this huge sum had been devoted to really valuable public improvements in our territory? I do not see how this can be honestly disputed. We have, then, deliberately created this 1896-97 famine, which brought nearly twice as many people on to the Relief Works as the famine of 1876-78, with certainly a proportionate increase of deaths due to starvation in the towns and villages—we have created the famine, I say, by the extortion of our huge yearly tribute from British India, to say nothing of the payment to the European officials, military and civil, on the spot, and the waste of the Famine Insurance Fund on frontier wars.

That this monstrous extortion of tribute must sooner or later ruin India has long been foreseen. Lord Salisbury himself has frequently spoken of our "bleeding" India. But so long ago as 1838 Mr. Montgomery Martin, a man of great Indian experience, wrote:—

"The annual drain of £3,000,000"—it is now £30,000,000!—"on British India has amounted in thirty years at twelve per cent. (the usual Indian rate) compound interest to the enormous sum of £723,900,000 sterling. So constant and accumulating a drain, even in England, would soon impoverish her. How severe, then, must be its effects on India, where the wage of a labourer is from twopence to threepence a day! Were the hundred millions [now about 250,000,000] of British subjects in India converted into a *consuming* population, what a market would be presented for British capital, skill, and industry?"

Not even this consideration of the certainty of greatly increased trade with a prosperous population has any influence to stanch the drain. It has gone on steadily increasing in volume for sixty years since Mr. Montgomery Martin thus argued.

Twenty years after Mr. Martin sounded this note of warning Sir George Wingate, an Anglo-Indian official of the highest standing, expressed himself, in 1859, strongly as follows, the drain being then no more than £5,000,000 or thereabouts:—"Taxes spent in the country from which they are raised are totally different in their effect from taxes raised in one country and spent in another. In the former case the taxes collected from the population are again returned to the industrious classes. But the case is wholly different when the taxes are not spent in the country where they are raised. They constitute an absolute loss and extinction of the whole amount withdrawn from the taxed country, and might as well be thrown into the sea. Such is the nature of the tribute we have so long exacted from India. From this explanation some faint conception may be formed of the cruel crushing effect of the tribute upon India."

In 1866 came the terrible famine in Orissa. My acquaintance, James Geddes, the Positivist, a Bengal Civilian of the highest character, and one of the noblest men who ever served India, was the hero of that famine. He saw its cause, and, to his own official ruin, boldly proclaimed before a Committee of the House of Commons that it was brought about by the constant drain of Indian produce for nothing to England. This view he further developed in his pamphlet on the "Logic of Indian Deficit," published in 1871. Nobody even attempted to refute his arguments. Then, as now, a conspiracy of silence was organised in the press and in the House of Commons. In 1876 the last great famine began, and from that time to this such men as the late Sir Louis Malet, Mr. Dadabhai Naoroji, Sir William Wedderburn, Mr. C. O. Hume, Mr. A. J. Wilson, and others have done their utmost to force upon the consideration of the Government the irremediable mischief that is being wrought. All to no purpose. Not that our leading statesmen are ignorant of the truth. They know it well enough. Lord Salisbury is just as well acquainted with the facts as I am, the Duke of Devonshire, Lord Rosebery, Lord Cranbrook, Lord Kimberley, Lord Lansdowne, Mr. John Morley, Sir John Gorst, are but little less well-informed. Yet they all mutter in chorus, "It will last our time"; and the Tories put up flippant George Hamilton as Secretary of State, to fib for them in the House of Commons and elsewhere, in succession to that portentous old hypocrite, Henry Fowler, chosen for the same office and the like purpose by the Liberals.

What makes the case worse, and the indictment against the Queen-Empress and her Governments the more crushing, is the fact that all the time that this fearful impoverishment, together with almost continuous famine—for there is famine every year in *some* district of India nowadays, though only the famines in which millions perish are noted at home—all the while this steady descent to ruin has been going on in British territory; close to us, under our suzerainty, and surrounded by the country under our direct control, the great Native States have become exceedingly prosperous, and their inhabitants are well-to-do and contented. About this, also, there is no doubt whatever. And Lord Salisbury and the late Lord Iddesleigh knew well what they were doing when they gave back Mysore to native rule in 1867 and 1868. Mysore itself, so handed back to native administration, is in a flourishing condition, though the present pedantic and narrow-minded Resident at the Maharajah's Court, Mr. Lee Warner, is striving to ruin the place by introducing as many Europeans as he possibly can into the administration.

In like manner, Baroda, Indore, Gwalior, Bhownuggar, Travancore, Hyderabad have thriven exceedingly under native rule with light British supervision. The people, though far more heavily taxed in money value than the inhabitants of British territory, really pay a much less onerous proportion of their receipts to the revenue than with us: and *what they do pay remains in India instead of being sent off out of the country for nothing to England.* That is the crucial difference. Hence it comes about that the treasuries of these Native States nearly always boast of a balance on the right side. Thus it is that public works can be and are built by those States chiefly out of revenue. And in this way men like Holkar, the late Maharajah of Indore, and Scindiah, the late Maharajah of Gwalior, can die, each of them leaving several millions of treasure behind him, while their people are in a condition of positive affluence as compared with ours.[2]

No better evidence of this can be afforded than the fact that while in 1896-97 we have had a terrible famine in British India, involving enormous loss of life, the great Native States, under the same conditions of climate and soil, have only suffered from a moderate scarcity, which they have been easily able to cope with without borrowing huge sums at interest, as our Government has been obliged to do.

Here, then, we can see clearly that it is not English influence, or English sovereignty, or even English lack of knowledge and sympathy, that of themselves spell famine and ruin. But that a system of wholesale Europeanisation in India, and absentee capitalism out of India, inevitably destroy whatever good there might otherwise be in our rule. The more shameful is it, alike to our statesmen, and to ourselves as Englishmen, that we should continue to bleed to death the 250,000,000 of human beings for whose welfare we are directly responsible. The poverty of British India is no inevitable thing. The frightful famines of 1866, of

1876, of 1896, not to speak of minor visitations, are not due to natural causes. The poverty and the famines both are created by us; and the crime of murdering this helpless people by the million lies at our door.

For just four-and-twenty years I have done my best, in season and out of season, to bring home to my countrymen the infamous wrong which is being done in their name, and to warn them of the catastrophe looming directly ahead of them. I have hoped against hope that I might, with others, succeed in moving them to action while yet there was time. My work so far has been in vain, and I much fear that it is now too late to save the situation. The whole of the dominant class in the United Kingdom is interested in maintaining the present system of ruinous and criminal extortion. Governorships, military commands, civil and military appointments at high salaries, fat pensions, well-paid home posts, interest and dividends on money lent, outlets for their sons, and investments for their money, close the eyes of the governing classes in England to the economic and political collapse which is now rapidly approaching.

With a few honourable exceptions, the entire English press is controlled on this question by Anglo-Indian pensioners, whose sole object is to defend and maintain the existing misgovernment. It is sad, indeed, to see the inevitable collapse, which must be the outcome of all this fatuity and greed, coming nearer and nearer each day, while Englishmen are deliberately deceived as to the truth.

What a glorious empire India might have been under wise and sympathetic English leadership it requires but little imagination to conceive. But now famine and pestilence, robbery and oppression, are spreading discontent with our Raj throughout the country. The events at Poona, where the assassins of Mr. Rand and Lieut. Ayerst have not yet been caught, though the very heavy reward of 20,000 rupees is offered to anyone who will betray the actual murderers; the riots at Chitpur, where Mohammedans and Hindoos, of the same race, though of a different religion, we must bear in mind, combined once more against the Europeans; the spread of knowledge, not only in the cities but in the country, of the truth that to the English rule is due the great increase of poverty and the frequent recurrence of famine, which knowledge is producing sullen discontent and stifled hatred among the natives, from the Himalayas to Cape Comorin, and from Burmah to Bombay; the systematic risings of the tribes along our North-West frontier, probably backed by the Ameer, simultaneously with the growing unrest of the Mohammedans within our border—all these things prove that economic dangers are not the only dangers which we shall have to face within the next few years.

Gladly would I see our country escape the retribution which it has so justly earned. Gladly, even at this eleventh hour, would I welcome any steps on the part of the Government towards stanching the drain of produce which is destroying the prosperity of India, and in the direction of the adoption of a policy which should restore to the natives by degrees the administration of their own country. But, assuredly, never in the history of the human race was rebellion, never was *any* form of revolt, more justified than it is in India to-day. If, therefore, reforms are not to be immediately introduced, if English carpet-baggers and English profit-mongers and English pensioners are to do yet more millions to death, in order that they may fill their pockets at the expense of a helpless and patient people; then I, as an Englishman, whose ancestors and relatives have had their share in the conquest and reconquest of India, declare plainly that I hope to live to see the day when a well-organised rising of the whole population will sweep aside for ever the greed and iniquity of the British rule in Hindostan.

## Notes

1 It is only fair to say that Sir James Caird attached very much more importance to what he called over-population than I do. I hold most firmly that if India were not systematically drained of her wealth for the benefit of the well-to-do classes in Great Britain there would be no over-population whatever in British territory to-day.
2 The Government of India promptly "borrowed" Scindiah's millions.

# 45

# "SOCIALISM AND COLONIAL DEVELOPMENT", *SOCIAL DEMOCRAT*, JULY 1898, 208–211.

*John R. Widdup*

[When the BSP after 1914 divided sharply over the question of the war, it was said to be its younger, "heterogeneous" elements who took up an anti-war, internationalist stance. The SDF's "old stalwarts", on the other hand, were held to have remained largely loyal to their traditional leaders like Hyndman and Quelch (Lee and Archbold 1935, 222). There was certainly a nationalist strain running deep within the SDF's history and support for the war in 1914 was prefigured in attitudes that some at least had long since expressed. John Widdup, though not a nationally known figure, may be grouped among them. From around 1893 Widdup had been a leading activist in the SDF stronghold of Burnley, which in 1895 had been the focus of Hyndman's parliamentary ambitions. For a time the SDF's local branches had even produced their own weekly newspaper, with Widdup as one of those chiefly responsible.

His contribution to the socialist debate around colonialism has been described as a "sensible effort to sharpen his party's fuzzy thinking on foreign policy" (Etherington 1974, 96). Widdup identifies a basic contradiction between Hyndman's big navy policy and the SDF's denunciations of British imperialism as lately epitomised by Cecil Rhodes's ventures in southern Africa. To resolve this contradiction, the article offers a bleak alternative: that either the English must plunder the peoples of Africa and Asia or some other European power must. Widdup's alluding to the English rather than the British is telling. For some it might have called to mind writings like Hyndman's *England for All*, which already in 1881 anticipated the necessity of taking sides in the "coming struggle between militarism and democracy". In a more immediate sense, it also linked the British with the USA, which since April 1898 had been engaged in the war with Spain which would lead to it superseding Spanish rule in its remaining colonies. Widdup does not specifically express a judgment on the war. Nevertheless, on grounds of the greater liberties enjoyed by the English, whether at home or in the Empire, he comes down firmly for the principle of Anglo-Saxon world mastery and the association of the British Empire and the USA. By contrast with Hyndman's views on India (Chapter 44, this volume), his article gives no indication of any other possible form of rule than that by one of the white European races.

Norman Etherington has commented that the arguments are "strikingly similar" to those presented two years later by Bernard Shaw in his well-known and controversial *Fabianism and the Empire*. Nevertheless, in the context of the Anglo-Boer war, the SDF experienced no such divisions as the Fabians did. It not only united against the war, but afterwards was largely free of the tendencies towards imperial expansion which Widdup had still entertained. Widdup in any case had now moved on. In the year that he published the article, he emigrated to Canada and appears to have had no further involvement in the British socialist movement. It is easy to imagine that Hyndman's pro-war positions after 1914 would nevertheless have had his wholehearted support.]

The relations of Great Britain, and the leading European powers, during the past five or six months, have been of such a character as to suggest to the Socialist the duty of deciding what the policy of our country should be in periods such as this, when considered solely from the standpoint of Socialist principle and action. It is on occasions such as these that we are compelled to ask ourselves how far we are called upon to support the policy of the capitalist Government in power, and in what respect that policy should be vigorously combatted and condemned. In attempting to give an answer to this question, it is safe to say that more differences are bound to arise than could possibly arise from a consideration of any other phase of Socialist politics. In dealing with this question, we are compelled to furnish an answer, not simply from the point of view of what is best, and what should be done for the exploited masses of the country alone, but from the standpoint of what it is necessary to do in order to defend our country as a whole from the attempts made by other powers to stultify our national greatness, and check our imperial growth.

The view generally adopted by responsible Social-Democrats is more or less an inconsistent one. In some respects the attitude of the antagonistic powers is condoned and supported; in others, the policy of our own Governments is emphasised and applauded. Socialist meetings have been held to protest against all illegitimate extension of colonial activity, the tone and feeling of which made it quite clear that even *legitimate* action in this direction was by no means looked upon with favour. This feeling undoubtedly arises from the belief that, when the capitalist Governments of our country are no longer able to annex and command favourable territories as suitable markets for our surplus produce, it will be more difficult for them to keep together, in something like workable order, the existing antagonistic elements of which the present method of production is composed. Holding such a view as this, it is therefore quite natural that Socialists should feel no pride in the conquests of their country, but that they should desire, on the other hand, the failure of every expedition designed expressly for the purpose of smoothing the bearings of the economic machinery controlled by, and kept in motion for, the express benefit of the ruling classes of our time.

But, in opposition to this view of colonial development, we find ourselves committed, by the statements of responsible and leading members of our party, to the support of a huge navy for the purpose of maintaining our colonial possessions, adding to their number and extent, and in a general way protecting and defending the commerce of our Empire. True, it is claimed that our support of the policy of keeping up the strength of the navy, so that no possible combination shall be able to over match us, is not given with a view to the navy being used for the commercial purposes just alluded to, but in order that we may defend our country from foreign aggression, and thus preserve and develop the degree of political, social, and personal freedom which our worthy sires have won for us. But it must be remembered that if we never built and armed another ship for many years to come, we have already sufficient naval strength to keep any enemy from our shores, and to keep open the waterways along which our food supply is transmitted. The fact is, that by supporting the huge annual naval expenditure of our Governments we are in reality committing ourselves, either consciously or unconsciously, to a policy of territorial plunder and annexation, since such expenditure is primarily intended for this purpose. Between denouncing the Imperialism of Cecil Rhodes, and his subjugation and robbery of the native races of South and Middle Africa, and upholding lavish expenditure on our naval fleets for the purpose of keeping other powers at bay while we, in this or any other way, thus add new territories to our Empire—which, in reality, our fleets are again called upon to protect and defend, no matter whether such territories have a seaboard or not—between these two policies there lies, somewhere, a glaring inconsistency; and it is the duty of every Social-Democrat to try to get rid of this, in order that our position as a political party may be simplified, and strengthened thereby.

In endeavouring to rid ourselves of this inconsistency, it becomes at once apparent that the commercial policy of the governing classes admits of no half-hearted support; it either must be approved in its entirety or denounced in its entirety. In other words, we must either say that we will no longer acquire fresh territory, no matter what other nations may be doing or would do in this respect; or, while we live under a system of open robbery and wholesale murder of defenceless peoples, we will carry on the game as it is played, and come out victorious if possible. For this is the position into which the whole matter is resolved. We must either plunder and slaughter the Matabele, the Mashonas, the Soudanese, and perhaps the Chinese, in the near future, or stand by idle while this is done by some other country equally desirous of adding to her dominions, and extending her commerce. Taking the present situation of the African question as an illustration, we are to ask ourselves if we, in future, are to dominate that continent; or if it is to be left entirely to France, Germany, Portugal, and Italy, to be divided out among themselves, by methods not one whit more righteous and humane than the methods of our own imperial freebooters. I repeat again that between these two policies there is no half-way halting-house. We cannot leave the people of these available territories alone, which has been often suggested, in the hope that English capitalism would thus receive another nail into its coffin. Commercialism cannot break down by its own sheer rottenness and incapacity until economic development has made this an international possibility. Nations may change places in the struggle for commercial supremacy, as they have often done already, but if the destruction of commercialism is to be brought about by the development of evolutionary processes alone, the crash when it does come must be an international one to be effective.

What, then, is our duty in regard to this question? Shall we strike for Anglo-Saxon domination with, as we have seen, all the utterly inhuman and fiendish operations which the carrying out of this policy implies; or shall we become Social-Democratic "Little Englanders"? We are called upon to give a straight answer, not merely, as we have shown, to be consistent, but because the gravity and exceeding importance of the question demand a straight answer. The future may probably bring difficulties so complicated in character, and so pregnant with the possibility of our national existence becoming imperilled, that every other phase of Socialist demand may have to be left out of sight until a common understanding among Socialists of all countries has been arrived at on this momentous matter. It therefore behoves every Socialist to give the fullest attention to this question; and to speak out his honest opinion concerning it, regardless of the favour or disfavour with which his decision may be accepted.

There can be no doubt whatever of the fact that the proletariat under British rule enjoys a greater measure of public liberty and public safety than any other people on the face of the earth. But it is not, here, claimed that this wider field of public action has been conceded to the British working man because of a greater love which his rulers have for him, than the dominant class of other countries have for their subjected millions. It has been found the safest and the most expedient method of conciliating public demand in England to, in a measure, concede such demand. In Italy the ruling class have shown quite recently that, in their opinion, the best way to propitiate the evils of the existing commercial and social system is to shoot down helpless men, women, and children in the streets for daring to break a few panes of glass. The method, it will be seen at once, is widely different; but the intention is the same in both countries. England treats her propertyless mob with some show of respect, because she dare not do otherwise. On the Continent that mob is ruthlessly murdered, because, as yet, it is considered safe to murder it. No credit can, therefore, be given to the ruling class of that country which adopts, apparently, the most humane form of government, since they are merely seeking to achieve the same result by methods which, although more humane in themselves, are not at bottom dictated by more humane or more righteous motives.

The truth is, that the best blood of past generations has been shed for the cause of human liberty in England, and it is as a consequence of the struggles of the pioneers of freedom that the English proletarian enjoys a greater degree of freedom than his Continental brethren. The same struggles and the same martyrdom have taken place in Continental countries to an extent quite as great as and even greater in some countries than that which obtained here at home. But the feature of the fight for personal and political liberty in England which distinguishes it from all such movements abroad is that the English have been to a certain extent successful.

Now, all this has an important bearing on that phase of Socialist politics which deals with foreign and imperial questions. Wherever a people are brought under the flag of our country they are allowed the utmost limit of public freedom consistent with the maintenance of the newly-acquired territories as an integral part of the Empire. Stated in another way, the people of those possessions—and they are made up of settlers of every European nationality, many of whom have made their homes in the new country in order to escape the greater tyrannies of their own land—these people come at a bound to that degree of development in our social and political life that we enjoy at home. Those bright spirits who sacrificed themselves in the past for our liberties were, at the same time, although they knew it not, fighting for the liberties of countries and peoples whom they never once thought of.

Our duty as Socialists seems to be quite clear. We English Socialists hate the word nation as much as our Continental comrades do. But if we are to extirpate national differences in a world-wide commonwealth, surely it will be easier and better to do this by going on with our Imperial development rather than by waiting to see the unappropriated portions of the world fall under the control of Governments who are not compelled to accord to their subjects that degree of freedom which the English governing class are *compelled* to give to their peoples the world over. And when the international collapse of the present order of things is achieved—and it can be achieved sooner by Anglo-Saxon domination—Britain's sons will be the first to drop the thought of any superior racial characteristics, and meet the world on those terms of absolute equality which Socialists of all countries are striving hard to realise. It appears that, out of the hurly-burly of blind unconscious forces by which the development of nations and Empires is ever swept with irresistible power along their separate paths, there do arise, at the same time, systematic, ever-prevailing forces which carry some nations to a height of wealth and power, by the aid of which every obstacle is surmounted which comes in their way. What is the lesson of history but a repetition of this simple fact? And, at the present time, it is clear that the Anglo-Saxon is fast approaching to that condition of world-wide mastery. For this reason we should welcome every attempt to bind the United States and ourselves by one inseparable tie. We may be strengthening the commercial interests of the two nations by such an alliance, but we are, at the same time, binding still firmer the interests of the great mass of proletariat workers of the two countries, and incidentally of the civilised world, an undertaking which is of greater moment to us, as we know that, eventually, that great mass is bound to seize and control the reins of power by which their countries are governed. We must never forget that every single feature of capitalism possesses in itself some germ of future Socialist life. Let us on, then, with the greatest haste, so that we may sooner become healthy by getting, as fast as possible, through the necessary stages of our national disease. Let us extend to the people of those portions of the earth, which must eventually fall under the sway of some form of capitalist government, that form of government which is the least odious, and which contains within itself, to a far greater extent than any other method of government, the elements which are operating to work out its own destruction. By so doing we are planting the *roots* of the tree of liberty in new soil, in the hope and with the intention that the tree may one day blossom forth the wide-world over with a loveliness and a grandeur that all the blasts of a disarmed tyranny shall never be able to destroy.

# 46

## *SOCIAL-DEMOCRACY AND THE ARMED NATION* (LONDON: TWENTIETH CENTURY PRESS, 1900), 3-14, 16.

### Harry Quelch

[On some issues, the positions of the SDF were less clearly differentiated from those of ILP socialists than is sometimes suggested. The question of military service, however, was not one of these issues. It is true that the Fabians, unlike the ILP, were at one with the SDF in supporting the idea of citizens' militia and universal military training. Nevertheless, none of the Fabians' prolific output of tracts was ever devoted to the issue, leaving the SDF as by far the most energetic socialist proponent of such views. Quelch, the editor of *Justice*, was their most prominent advocate and the pamphlet he published in 1900 was widely cited in contemporary debates.

In all his pronouncements on the issue, Quelch took pains to point out that the policy of the armed nation was one upheld by the major social-democratic parties of the continent and represented "the formulated opinions of the International Socialist Party". On the other hand, his positions were closely aligned with those of the National Service League (NSL), formed under largely Conservative auspices in 1901 and aptly characterised as the "military wing of the Tory party". Quelch was not only cited approvingly in the *National Service Journal* but himself sometimes spoke from NSL platforms. He rejected the idea of conscription and here invokes the examples of republican Switzerland, the Italian Risorgimento and the French and the American revolutionary wars. Nevertheless, these positions were also common currency within the NSL; indeed, in 1906 the League even renamed its journal *The Nation in Arms*.

Quelch's pamphlet originally appeared at the time of the South African war, to which its early sections make reference. A revised edition appeared in 1907, and was followed by a Citizen Army Bill presented by the SDF-sponsored MP Will Thorne. Across most sections of the Labour movement, there was widespread suspicion of such proposals, hardly allayed by warnings simultaneously given out regarding the German war threat. As well as the Fabians, similar positions to the SDF's were adopted by socialists close to publications like the *New Age* and Robert Blatchford's *Clarion*. Nevertheless, at conferences of the ILP, the Labour Party and the Trades Union Congress the policies of the citizens' army or armed nation were overwhelmingly rejected (see Vol. III, Chapter 32).

As reproduced here, the pamphlet omits a small section on the organisation of a future citizens' army. It also omits the epigraph which, remarkably, was taken from a speech delivered by the Conservative prime minister Lord Salisbury in May 1900: "It is for you to urge upon all the necessity of placing yourselves in a position of an armed nation – a nation such as the Swiss, whose strength lies not in its numbers or in its military organisation, but in the spirit of those who love their country and are prepared to die for it."]

Recent events have attracted special attention to the question of Militarism, of armaments, and of military organisation. In continental countries Social-Democrats carry on an unceasing agitation against Militarism; the burden of the huge military camps of Europe crushes her peoples beneath its ever-increasing weight, and in France the evils of the present military system have in recent years manifested themselves in so acute a form as to produce the gravest national dangers. So enormously have Militarism and military armaments grown that the great Powers of Europe last year held a conference to consider the possibility of reducing, or at least limiting, the forces of war. But the year which saw the so-called Peace Conference at the Hague saw also an increase in the armaments of all these Christian Powers, and before its close found Great Britain engaged in the most unjustifiable and most costly war that she has entered upon for half a century; and now, so far from considering the possibility, or even the desirability, of universal disarmament, we are engaged in devising schemes of military reorganisation which will still further increase the already bloated armaments of the world. Never has the irony of events, the stern logic of facts, more ruthlessly demonstrated the utter worthlessness of mere pious aspirations and high-flown sentiment.

Social-Democrats are opposed to Militarism of every kind, to war in all its forms; Social-Democracy stands for international co-operation and universal peace. But Social-Democracy deals with actualities; it is not utopian, it is based upon the solid reality of hard fact; and so, while never losing sight of its end, it also never overlooks the conditions which confront it, the circumstances by which it is surrounded, and it seeks to modify those conditions and to bend those circumstances to its end. Militarism is an evil against which we have to fight with all the means in our power, but we have to consider the best means by which we can combat the monster, and to talk of universal disarmament at the present stage is, as we have recently seen, mere utopianism, a crying of peace where there is no peace, and where existing antagonisms make peace impossible. The question of the position to be taken up by Social-Democrats in this connection has not failed to receive due consideration, and the conclusion arrived at is that instead of advocating universal disarmament, they should persistently agitate for universal armament. Thus in the very earliest programme of the S.D.F. is set out the demand of Social-Democrats for the abolition of all standing armies and the establishment of a national citizen force. The latter portion of the proposal is perhaps better expressed by the phrase: The armed nation. For that is what we mean; every citizen armed, and trained to the use of arms. Not only do we regard universal disarmament, under present circumstances, as mere utopianism, a counsel of perfection; but we do not believe it would be the right course to adopt now, even if it could be carried out. We have to first eradicate the causes of conflict, the class antagonisms, and the material, economic bases of those antagonisms, before we can with advantage remove the effects, the results, the mere methods, developed by those causes. To-day the unarmed nation offers itself as a temptation and a prey to some mighty brigand power. Or, if she be too insignificant to attract the attention or excite the envy of a great military power she lies at the mercy of any gang of adventurers who may choose to arm against her. Who can doubt that it was the comparatively defenceless state of the Transvaal, relying upon the good faith of Great Britain and her Conventions, which tempted Jameson and his fellow-conspirators to that criminal raid, which has since been fruitful of such disastrous consequences? Even where there is no foreign enemy to fear, an unarmed people is necessarily at the mercy of a usurping clique, an oligarchy, or an autocrat. War is the last argument of kings, and all governments rest on force. So long as that is the case, it is only the people which is armed that can maintain its freedom, or can indeed, lay claim to be a free people. The first efforts of despots are directed to disarming the people. An armed nation may submit to despotism and suffer many abuses, but it at least has the means of resisting tyranny and asserting its freedom. An unarmed nation may be trampled under foot by a despot with the aid of a handful of mercenaries. The despot need not be either king or kaiser. We have already seen millionaire capitalists and capitalist corporations arm bodies of troops to shoot down rebellious blacks, and to dragoon their revolted white wage-slaves into subjection. We shall, doubtless, see more of this in future, as capitalism becomes more concentrated and capitalist combinations become more compact and formidable. A people without arms, trained only to tend machines, as mere factory "hands," will be absolutely at the mercy of organised, combined capital, with its bands of retainers, its police, and its "Pinkertons." Thus an unarmed nation cannot be free. A standing army, on the other hand, whether maintained under autocracy or under capitalism, for a reigning dynasty or a dominant class, is an instrument of tyranny and suppression, of aggression and spoliation. An armed nation, on the contrary, is a guarantee of individual liberty, of social freedom, and of national independence. So well, indeed, has this been understood in the past that the British propertied classes, while the monarch ruled by "right divine," were strenuously opposed to a standing army. The Tory landlords in the House of Commons, as the history of the seventeenth and eighteenth centuries shows, strongly opposed this institution. Now, however, that the bourgeoisie is the dominant class it is forgotten that a standing army is contrary to the British constitution.

But it is claimed that here in England there is no need of conscription or of any form of compulsory service; a reorganisation of our voluntary system is all that is necessary to give us all the forces we require for national defence or for any other military purpose, and, moreover, the experience of compulsory service in continental countries is such that all friends of popular freedom should oppose, not advocate, anything of the kind. As to the first objection, we are entirely opposed to the present so-called voluntary system, which provides our masters with bands of willing, if frequently involuntary, armed retainers. As a matter of fact, the more voluntary they are, the more dangerous are they. The present war in South Africa has shown us, among other things, that it is not difficult for the exploiting class to raise bands of voluntary mercenaries, ready and willing to sell themselves for their daily bread, to go and crush a people rightly struggling to be free. Those who would volunteer to crush liberty in the Transvaal would volunteer to perform the same vile task here at home. That is the danger of the so-called voluntary system, where the great majority of the people are unarmed and defenceless. With the whole nation armed there might be numbers willing to volunteer for foreign service, even for unjust wars of aggression, but they would not be a direct menace to the liberty of the people at home. As to the second point, we do not advocate the continental system of conscription. Our comrades in all countries where conscription obtains are engaged in vigorously fighting this evil, yet they are all at one with us in our advocacy of the armed nation. Some of our peace friends in this country are at pains to point out to us that in Germany, with its mighty army, its universal military service, we have a military despotism, not a free nation: and that, moreover, there is no more likelihood of an armed revolt, no more hope of the soldiers of the Kaiser refusing to act against the people in Germany than there is in this country. With regard to the latter point, however, that is by no means so certain. It is at any rate clear that a conscript army would not be more willing to act against the people than an army of volunteers. On the other hand, the universality of service would make the whole people better able to resist any act of militarist agression, and where the whole of the men of a nation are trained to the use of arms, even under a system of conscription, a military despotism cannot exist except by the consent of the majority. If, therefore, we are to have militarism, it had better be the compulsory system of conscription than the voluntary system, which brings together, arms, and trains, only those who are perfectly willing, for sheer love of fighting, or for any other reason, to be the tools of our masters. As against the voluntary system then, we should even prefer conscription. But we are far from advocating conscription or compulsory military service. We are opposed to conscription and to all forms of permanent military service. What we advocate is not compulsory military service, but a compulsory and universal military training. That is a totally different matter. Conscription, compulsory military service of any kind, is an evil. It involves the withdrawal of men from civil life, keeping them herded together in barracks, establishing them as a caste apart, as "soldiers," as distinct from civilians or citizens. Conscription, or any form of military service, means a standing army of men decivilised, removed from citizenship, in antagonism to the great body of the people, the citizens. The compulsory military training which we advocate carries with it the avoidance of all these evils.

It means that every citizen shall be trained to act as a soldier at need, but that no one shall become merely a soldier or cease to be a citizen. It means that the flower of the nation shall not be withdrawn from civil life and made to waste some of the best years of its existence in the useless routine and pernicious atmosphere of a barracks. It means that no more of a man's lifetime shall be taken up by military duties than is absolutely necessary for the national defence, as it is only for that purpose that military service should be required. Thus by training every man to the use of arms, from his youth up, we should have, without the waste, the expense, the vice and demoralisation of the barracks—the armed nation, the real "army of a democracy."

It is not necessary that men should be divorced from civil life in order to make them capable of bearing arms and using them effectively against an enemy. In Switzerland, where we have the nearest approach to an armed democracy that is to be found, the recruits in the army service corps serve for 38 days in their first year, those in the ordnance corps 42 days, those in the infantry 45 days, those in the hospital corps 46 days, those in the engineers 50 days, those in the artillery 55 days, and those in the cavalry 80 days. In the aggregate, the terms of service, or training, amount for the infantryman, from his 20th to his 32nd year, to 119 days; a sergeant does 222 days, a lieutenant 440 days, an artillery captain serves till his 38th year and does 530 days altogether. This time is devoted to the actual work of military training and is not wasted in useless drill or idle showy parades which only serve to give a false importance and splendour to militarism, and to stimulate a spirit of jingoism and vainglory, but do nothing to actually equip men for the stern work of war, whose grim realities they but serve to disguise.

It is generally pretended by the supporters of militarism that a citizen force is of little use in actual warfare; that for its successful prosecution the mechanical, the automatic soldier, the product of incessant drill and years of barrack life, is essential. To these it is nothing that over and over again in history we find that raw levies of badly-armed and half-trained civilians have defeated armies of professional soldiers. That the revolutionary armies of France, which beat back the overwhelming military forces of monarchical Europe, the men who won the War of Independence in America, the Garibaldians, even the larger proportion of the armies of the first Napoleon, had never had the training they deem essential to a soldier is of no importance to the upholders of a military caste. The events of history are of the past, circumstances are different to-day. It is urged that in the past almost everyone possessed an arm of some kind, and little skill was required to learn the art of manipulating the weapons, rude and simple compared with the highly developed arms of precision of modern times. The very development of mechanical invention, which has led to specialisation in so many departments of industrial life, makes it necessary that the military art also should be specialised and that the soldier should be withdrawn from civil life and be practically excluded from its duties and its privileges, in order to devote himself wholly and solely to his calling. The advantage of such a military caste to the dominant class is, as we have seen, very clear, but it has not less clearly been demonstrated that for purely military purposes it is entirely unnecessary. If there is one fact which this war in South Africa has more strongly emphasised than any other it is that a well-armed citizen force, capably led, and accustomed to the use of the rifle, can, acting on the offensive-defensive, hold its own against an almost infinitely larger number of the finest troops in the world. If this war has taught us anything it is the soundness, even from a military—as distinct from a militarist—point of view, of the Socialist proposal of a national citizen force instead of a standing army. Of the Swiss system and of its efficiency as a fighting machine continental military experts have spoken in the highest terms of praise. General Brunet—a French officer of deservedly high reputation—said, after witnessing the Swiss manœuvres of 1896: "Alone among European nations Switzerland has solved the problem we have all attempted in vain—to arm all its citizens and to make of each citizen a soldier, though not one single citizen is taken from his country." The Swiss have never been called upon to demonstrate the efficiency of their system in actual warfare, and the only opportunity there has been of judging it has been that presented by the various mobilisations and manœuvres. On the other hand, it is very doubtful if the Boers would receive or even merit such high praise from military experts as have the Swiss; yet they have demonstrated in actual warfare that, with their possibly inferior organisation, they are a formidable fighting force, which no military power in the world could afford to despise. So far as can be judged, the Swiss would certainly not do worse than the Boers under similar circumstances. Every Swiss at 20 years of age, who is capable of the service, is then a recruit, and has to go up for training; and each succeeding year this training is repeated. In the meantime he has his rifle and kit always in his own possession; the result is that the mobilisation of any number of troops can be more speedily, more easily, and more cheaply effected in Switzerland than in any other country in Europe. G. Moch, in the articles already referred to, says: "In Switzerland every year half the *élite* (or active army) and a quarter of the landwehr (territorial) is mobilised; in France it has only happened once since 1871 that there was a 'trial' of mobilisation of two army corps (the tenth of the whole), and it was considered marvellous." In England we have seen in the past twelve months some of the difficulties, delays, and waste of time and money, involved in mobilising a comparatively small body of troops under our costly and cumbrous system. When the reserves were called out, for instance, it was no unusual thing for a man living at Glasgow, or even further south, to have to travel, say, to Aberdeen, there to join a detachment which would then be despatched to Southampton. If the man had had his arms and equipment there was no reason why he should not have travelled direct to Southampton, or at any rate have joined his contingent at some point on the route. As to the capabilities of the Swiss, as shown in these annual manœuvres, there seems to be no reason to doubt that they are quite as good as any troops in Europe. G. Moch says that their work will compare favourably with that done by other armies; he gives an instance where the men marched for twelve days and manœuvred five. This was done by two mountain batteries in mid-winter. They went up to 1,446 metres (more than 4,338 ft.), the snow being about 5 ft. deep, and the cold 20 deg. below freezing point. "In this dreadful weather the batteries marched 340 kilometres under perfect discipline; the horses were all in good condition. No battery in France or Germany could do better, and few could do so well. And none of these men were permanent soldiers, not one, from the major to the gunners; *all, the day before, were citizens, and on their first day they marched 42 kilometres.*"

It may be said that not only is any system of universal military training unnecessary in this country, seeing that we can easily raise sufficient voluntary soldiers for all necessary purposes, but that the Swiss system is not adapted to the conditions which exist here. The men of a nation which is mainly pastoral, like the Swiss, or one which is almost wholly agricultural, like the Boers, may be capable of being turned into fairly good soldiers with comparatively little training, and without being withdrawn from the ordinary avocations of their lives for any considerable period. But the circumstances are entirely different in the case of a nation which consists mainly of town-dwellers, like the English. It may be true that it is possible to raise by the voluntary system all the troops which this country may require for military purposes, although the uneasy rumours which are constantly being circulated as to the imminence of conscription, the frantic efforts which have been made in the present crisis to induce the time-expired men to rejoin, and the wild enthusiasm with which the volunteering of a few thousand men from Australia and Canada has been hailed seem to point to the contrary. But we do not advocate the establishment of a national citizen force simply as an alternative to conscription, or as a means of meeting any difficulty which may have arisen in finding sufficient men for the defence of the Empire. We advocate, as we always have advocated, the establishment of a national citizen force—the nation armed—as the only means of abolishing all standing armies, voluntary or conscript. That universal military training would come harder to a nation of town-dwellers than to a nation of shepherds or of agriculturists is certain. But that only shows the artificial and physically mischievous nature of modern town life; and a regular and compulsory military training, which would have the result of taking the young men of our towns more frequently out into the country and away from the vitiated atmosphere of town life, would be good for the health and manhood of the nation. It may be, too, that the Swiss system is not in every detail adaptable to the conditions existing in this country. We are not concerned with the Swiss system except in so far as it demonstrates the feasibility of maintaining a thoroughly adequate means of national defence without the cost, the waste, the danger, and the demoralisation of a standing army. So far the Swiss have shown the way by which the greatest degree of efficiency may be secured with the least danger and at the lowest cost. Even if in every detail that system may not be suited to the requirements of this country we should be able to adopt some modification of it which would secure the same result. At present the Swiss are able to put a larger proportion of their male population into the field, and with more expedition, than any other nation in Europe. Her equipment is as good as her men. Nevertheless, Switzerland spends infinitely less on armaments per head of her population than any other Power. While France spends 20.80 francs per head of population on her fighting services, England 19.25, Germany 12.45, Russia 10.25, Italy 8.00, and Austria 7.05, Switzerland maintains her national citizen force at a cost of 4.00 francs per head of her population. On the other hand, Switzerland spends nearly twice as much on education as she does on armaments and has the finest educational system in Europe, while enlightened England only spends a seventh as much on education as she spends on armaments, France a sixth, Germany a fifth, Austria and Italy a fourth, and Russia a fortieth.

Artillery and cavalry are the two arms of military service which are supposed to present the greatest difficulties for a citizen force. But the Swiss, according to M. Moch, have not found these difficulties insuperable. In reference to the two batteries whose performance we have cited above, he says: "There is no reason to suppose that the Swiss more than anybody else is a born artilleryman. Any other citizen could do the same. These two batteries belonged to the Canton de Vaud, in French Switzerland, and, as an ex-artillery officer, I may say that I could form excellent gunners in eight or ten weeks if I had to deal with healthy men, and if I were allowed to teach them properly." As to cavalry, the Swiss, who are certainly less a nation of horsemen than the English, secure the maintenance of a sufficient cavalry force by the following means: "When the young cavalry soldier goes home after his time he takes his horse with him, after paying the State half the price. For £10 he has an excellent trained horse, four or five years old; he can use him in his business, but he must keep the animal in good condition. This is assured by inspection, and also every time the man is called he must bring his horse. After his first training a cavalry soldier must attend drills ten days a year for ten years. Each year he gets back a tenth of the price he paid for the horse, and at the end he has the horse for nothing. So that, after paying down half the price once, which he gets back, he has, in addition the horse. He is allowed to borrow the money, so that poor men can enter the cavalry. Thus a farmer may buy a horse for his coachman or for one of his labourers."

Recent experience has shown that so far from modern weapons having made cavalry obsolete, that arm has, by reason of its mobility, become more important than ever. But the use of cavalry has almost entirely changed, and it is mainly as a means of locomotion rather than of battle action that horses are needed. For this, on the good roads we have in this country, bicycles might be largely used instead of horses. The use of bicycles would ensure a much larger number of what would be practically mounted infantry than could otherwise be obtained, as a bicycle would not be so great a difficulty for the citizen-soldier in times of peace as a horse, and bicyclists have too the advantage over horsemen, that they would only need to carry their own food; they would need none for their steeds, and along roads they would move more swiftly and untiringly than if they rode horses.

With a national citizen force as with a standing army, there has to be a permanent staff. But this is maintained for service and not for show; all the posts would be filled by promotion from the ranks, and all officers would gain their posts as the result of competitive examination and by the selection of the general body of their command. Besides the General Staff, whose duties would be those of the General Staff of a permanent standing army, but who would be selected in the most democratic manner, and in accordance with their fitness for those duties, and not because they belong to a ruling or privileged class, there would be also a permanent staff of workmen employed in the arsenals and forts to maintain the arms and material in a state of readiness and efficiency. All these would necessarily have received the training of soldiers, but in no sense would they form a permanent standing army. The whole organisation would be democratic, the army would be the people, and the whole people would control the army, instead of the army being an instrument of despotism in the hands of a privileged few.

Many friends of peace and opponents of militarism strongly condemn all kinds of military training. They are loud in their protests against drilling in the public elementary schools, as they fear that this is calculated to foster a love of fighting, of militarism, and to inculcate a spirit of jingoism. But these mischievous consequences are not necessary results of a military training, and they would be best counteracted if such training were universal and compulsory, and if it were accompanied by a proper education in the rights and duties of citizenship, and by the inculcation of the principles of true patriotism and of international co-operation and inter-dependence. It is not, as a rule, the men who are "commandeered" to fight, but those who volunteer, who are jingoes. It is one thing to train men to the use of arms at the same time that they are educated to regard war as a terrible calamity, never to be resorted to except as a dire necessity in self-defence. It is another and totally different thing to deliberately cultivate the jingo spirit and a love of militarism in order to induce men to volunteer for aggressive warlike enterprises. Except in France (even if France should be excepted) in no country in which military service is compulsory is the jingo spirit so rampant as it is in this country, where we have a voluntary system. Your rabid jingo is, as a rule, not the man who has to fight, willy-nilly, but the creature who is sure of getting his fighting done for him. It was not in the Transvaal, where every man was trained to fight and would be called upon to do so, that angry mobs howled for war, and any man who pleaded for peace did so at the risk of his life. That was in England, where those who howled the loudest scarcely knew the butt end of a rifle from the muzzle, and would have fainted with fright at the discharge of a piece of artillery. All reports go to show that up to the last the Boers hoped, and prayed, and wrought for peace, and when war was forced upon them they left their farms and marched to the front soberly, quietly, regretfully. No howling crowds cheered their departure in a frenzy of jingoist inebriety, with ribald, bombastic songs of braggart imbecility. No, mere military training will not create jingoes; it is much more likely to reduce their number. It is safe to say that there is an infinitely stronger peace party in every country in which military service is compulsory, than there is in this country, with its voluntary system. Even here the best consequence of the war from the point of view of future peace is the fact that so many men have been drawn from industrial pursuits to be sent to the front. Many people regret this, and its consequent dislocation of social, industrial, and family life; but really the more the evil consequences of war are brought home to the people in their everyday life the more will they desire that it should be avoided. The people of this country have had no practical experience of the horrors of war, therefore they are incapable of appreciating the blessings of peace. This war, however, will in some way or other bring mourning into almost every home in England, and that is much more likely to have a sobering effect on the present jingo madness than if the men who were doing the fighting were absolutely and entirely a class apart. It will be found in the long run that the short service system has done more for the cause of peace in this country than all the preachments of peace societies. And the substitution of a system of universal compulsory military training, incumbent on all classes, with no immunity by paying a fine, would do infinitely more. With a professional soldiery, a standing army, as a class apart, separate, cut off from the rest of the community, with no civil ties, rights, or duties, the bulk of the nation finds only a pleasing diversion in a foreign war. Certainly it has to pay, but then it gets all the glory without any of the risk, and, as it would have to pay the soldiers anyhow, it feels that they might as well be earning their money. With a standing army, therefore, especially a voluntary mercenary army of professional soldiers, war becomes almost a necessity; with the armed nation, on the other hand, trained for and capable of military service, but busy with its industrial, social, and domestic interests, war would be a bugbear and a nuisance. Every man would be liable, and, although there would doubtless be a number of fiery adventurous spirits even in such a community, the majority would certainly be in favour of peace and against war. This is not mere theory; we have the experience of past and but recent events to guide us, and that experience fully and conclusively proves the soundness of the Socialist position on this matter. We have seen that those citizens who, in the event of war, would have to bear the battle's brunt, have been the least eager for war, but have also borne themselves bravely when the duty of taking up arms has been thrust upon them. As in industrial life we frequently find the men who are most eager to strike are also the first to give way, so it has been shown by recent events that those who have shouted loudest for war have not been the best fighters.

It may be asked in what this system of universal compulsory military training differs from conscription. It differs in the most essential features. Under conscription, generally speaking, the service is not universal; it does not fall on all classes alike. A certain number of conscripts are drawn each year and any well-to-do youth who may happen to be drawn can escape service by paying for a substitute. Moreover, the officers are almost entirely drawn from the "superior" classes. With the armed nation no one, unless he were physically incapacitated, would be exempt from the compulsory training, and a man would not be an officer simply because he had wealthy or influential friends, but because he had qualified himself by special studies and training for his duties. Above all there is this vital difference, that with the armed nation there would be compulsory military training but no military *service* except in time of war, when all would be liable to be called on in proportion to their age, training, &c. This system would not mean, as conscription means, the maintenance of huge bodies of men, divorced from civil life, in comparative idleness, at the expense of the industrial community. Every citizen would be a soldier, but every soldier would be a citizen. In primitive stages of human society, there is little doubt that to a greater or less degree every man did everything. The energies of each individual would not be confined to one narrow groove. The tendency of social development, however, has been to differentiate, to specialise. One man is a tailor, and nothing but a tailor, another is a carpenter, another a weaver, and so on. So also one man becomes a soldier and nothing but a soldier. So far has this specialisation gone that now one man is no longer master of a particular craft or trade, he is only master of some infinitesimal, some unimportant, detail of his craft or trade. This result has been too often regarded as a triumph of civilisation, but, although its consequence may be to increase the mass of material wealth by making man a more dexterous machine, there can be no question that it also has the effect of stunting and cramping the man as a human being. It may be good that a man should know one thing well, but that is no reason why he should be entirely ignorant of all other things, or should pass the whole of his life in performing some simple mechanical operation. So, too, while it may be necessary, under present circumstances, for a certain number of men to become experts in the art of war, there is no reason why every man should not be sufficiently acquainted with the use of arms to make a standing army of professional soldiers as useless and unnecessary as it is dangerous.

It may be, and is, indeed, objected that no compulsory system would be tolerated in this country, or could be enforced for the defence of an empire such as ours, where the greater part of the service of the soldier has to be performed in foreign climes. But we are concerned with the democratic organisation of our national defence, not with the maintenance of empire. Governments have no right to exist except with the consent of the governed, and the British have no more right to dominate other peoples than other peoples have to dominate us. A national citizen force is hardly likely to serve the schemes or ambitions of a dominant class, but that is only an additional argument in its favour. We certainly do not suggest that there should be any compulsory foreign service. What we can only hold by maintaining an alien garrison had better be given up. The people of these islands would not be the losers but the gainers by such a course. Egypt should have been evacuated long ago, and indeed never ought to have been occupied; in India the organisation of native administration, so well begun, should be carried on until neither difficulty nor danger would attend the withdrawal of the British garrison. As to the British colonies, it would be for them to organise their own military defence on the same lines as this would be organised at home. In cases where they were too weak for self-defence against foreign or neighbouring enemies it would not be difficult to organise bodies of volunteers from the mother country to act as defensive garrisons. That would be a very different matter from maintaining a standing army for foreign service, or for acting as repressive garrisons in any part of the world. Provision might even be made for service in countries outside these islands in case of emergency or when the national defence required it. [. . .]

This, then, the demand for the armed nation, is the cry we have to raise in opposition to the champions of a more extensive militarisation of the people, to the alarmist advocates of conscription, and to the upholders of Rhodesian companies, with their organised bands of lawless freebooters. To the champions of a corrupt militarism, and to the advocates of the noble, if at present impracticable, policy of universal disarmament alike then we reply: Peace the ruling classes at present make impossible. Let us, therefore, all be armed, let us all be soldiers, but let us also all be citizens. Let us all be free men.

# 47

## *ANTI-MILITARISM FROM THE WORKERS' POINT OF VIEW: WHY EVERY WORKING MAN AND WOMAN SHOULD BE AN ANTI-MILITARIST*, WORKERS' ANTI-MILITARIST COMMITTEE, 1913, 1–7.

*Dora Montefiore*

[Among the reconfigurations of the left consequent on the outbreak of war in 1914, one was Hyndman's final break with what was now the BSP. The immediacy of the war made it impossible to contain within a single organisation the different conceptions its members had of nationhood, internationalism and the legitimacy or otherwise of armed service as an exercise in citizenship. These were the principal grounds on which Hyndman and those closest to him broke away in 1916 to form the unhappily designated National Socialist Party.

Dora Montefiore's pamphlet on militarism and anti-militarism shows how the roots of these differences were already clearly exposed before the war. Though Montefiore was not one of the SDF old guard, she had played a leading role within it during the first decade of the century. Like so many of the SDF's founders, she was a person of independent means and in 1910 had embarked upon a period of two years abroad in the USA, Australia and South Africa. Travel had always played a key role in the making of Monetfiore's politics (Hunt 2011). Now, it was on her Australian experience that she drew most directly in repudiating the conception of the armed nation upheld by Hyndman, Quelch and Thorne (Chapter 46, this volume).

In Australia, measures of compulsory military training had already been introduced in 1909. These enjoyed the support of leading figures in the Australian Labour Party and this was prominently advertised by the national service lobby in Britain (e.g. *Nation in Arms*, May 1907, 116–117). Montefiore, however, had aligned herself with the socialist opposition to such measures, contributing to and briefly editing the *International Socialist* of the Socialist Federation of Australasia. In particular, she urged mothers not to allow their sons to be swallowed up in what she called "The baby army" (Hunt 2001, 39). Among the other authorities cited here, C.W. Saleeby stands out as possibly the foremost propagandist for eugenicist ideas at this time. Montefiore also makes reference to the use of troops attacking protestors and striking workers, including the British cases of Peterloo (1819) and Featherstone (1893). Francesco Ferro (1859–1909) was a Catalan anarchist and radical educationalist whose death by firing squad had given rise to an international movement of protest.

Returning to Britain, Montefiore resigned from the BSP over the issue of war and peace, having represented it at the anti-war congress of the International held in Basle in November 1912. The revolutionary socialist parties of the colonies, she wrote, "refuse[d] to be dragged at the tail of any revisionary or reformist party", and if necessary the "Red Internationalists" upholding such views would conduct their own separate revolutionary international. There was also an echo of the themes of social motherhood (Chapter 39, this volume) as she described the famous speech of Clara Zetkin expressing women's concern in the issues of war and peace (Hunt 2007, 337; Partington 2020, 44). It was in this spirit that she published the pamphlet presented here independently in the early part of 1913. Two cartoons, including the cover image, were provided by the *Daily Herald* cartoonist Will Dyson. These underline Montefiore's connection with the *Herald*, which had been founded by George Lansbury the previous year and was for a time the liveliest and least party-minded expression of the radical movements of the day.

In taking this stance she was nothing if not consistent. Montefiore's resolute anti-militarism would become the BSP's predominant position once Hyndman and his supporters were defeated. Montefiore rejoined the party in 1916 and at the famous Leeds Soviet Convention the following June seconded the motion greeting the first Russian revolution. A foundation member of the British communist party, she would be the first woman to sit on the party's executive.]

I want in this little pamphlet to make it very clear to the workers why we anti-militarists take up quite a different attitude towards militarism from that of the Peace Societies and other middle class and sectarian organisations. Many sincere and humanitarian folk are opposed to war, but believe that the best way to maintain peace is for each nation to be armed to the teeth, and ready for every attack. Others, who believe in the protestations of such rulers as the Czar of Russia, or of Kaiser Wilhelm, as expressed in the Hague Conference, and similar jugglings of the ruling classes, cling to some form of pacifism, to some small reduction of armaments, or to some so-called humanitarian device, such as the prohibition of the use in war of dum-dum bullets. These people must know full well, if they think out the question at all, that under our present system of capitalism and of intense competition in the industrial field, to make any appreciable difference in the manufacture and output of armaments, uniforms, munition and commissariat provisions of war, would so dislocate the labour market, and would cause such millions of men and women to be thrown out of employment, that the coming social revolution (so dreaded by the privileged classes) would be by many years precipitated.

The workers, on the contrary, oppose militarism, and every form of compulsory service and conscription from the industrial and international standpoint from which it affects the workers all over the world; and the workers, as a class, suffering, as they do at present under the system of wage-slavery, declare that they refuse any longer to bear children, or to fight and die in the interests of the exploiting class.

The workers now recognise that it is this exploiting class—those who, owning the land, machinery and tools of production, and who only allow the workers access to these means of life in return for their underpaid labour—who decide when and where wars shall be made.

They further recognise that it is they, the workers, who pay in money, in blood, in suffering, for every war that is waged.

Again, they recognise, when their thoughts turn towards the economic conditions under which they live, that there IS a war being constantly waged between the exploiters of, and parasites on, Labour, on the one hand—striving to keep in their own hands the wealth which the workers create—and the workers on the other hand, striving (through bitter sufferings and sacrifice) to get for themselves and their children a fairer share of that wealth. This war is known as the Industrial or Class Struggle; and this is the only war in which the worker, who has nothing but his labour power of brain and hand to sell, should engage.

The capitalists and exploiters used to ignore this class struggle, and say it did not exist. Nowadays, they are forced to give, in the columns of their newspapers, some account of it; and they do so under the heading of "Labour Unrest."

In proportion as Labour becomes more and more "unrestful"—that is, more and more conscious that the capitalist is getting the meat, and Labour the bone—so the financiers and exploiters throughout the world become more and more anxious to divert the attention of Labour from its own pressing interests, and to persuade it to sacrifice itself, as it has always done in the past, in the interests of its masters. The task for the capitalists and exploiters is unfortunately comparatively easy, as they control both the capitalist State, and the education of the workers; and education, which should bring knowledge and light on social and international questions, is the key to the situation.

With this purpose therefore of misleading from their childhood the workers, history is falsified, and is written exclusively from the point of view of the exploiters. The class-rooms, where the children of the workers are educated, instead of being hung with pictures telling of the glorious victories in the past and present of knowledge and of science, are hung with crude pictures of kings charging in battle at the head of their armies, while the workers of one land exterminate the workers of another land, with whom they had no quarrel. Instead of the children of the people being taught how their few precious liberties have been, one by one, wrested with blood and suffering from the privileged classes, they are taught by similar crude pictures how territory has been wrested from one country by the kings and rulers of another country, who have used as pawns in the game of their personal ambitions, the sons and fathers of the "common people." False values, false standards have been cunningly given to the children of the workers, who have been led to believe from childhood that it is an honour to wear the uniform of a king or queen; whereas, if the worker were really conscious of his dignity—as being the source of all wealth, and therefore of all civilisation, he would spurn the shoddy uniform of the traditional representative of the class which exploits him and keeps him from a place in the sun. That shoddy uniform is made by the sweated labour of the wives and daughters of the workers, and is decorated with the cheap Brummagen brass ornaments and buttons, which mark the soldier out as the man who has sold his conscience, his will and his human dignity to another man, who calls himself king, emperor or ruler.

The worker who has donned this uniform, and who has been marched and countermarched, and drilled and bullied till he moves like an animated automaton, is also required to take an oath of allegiance to the ruler whose uniform he wears; and under the terms of this oath he may be, and constantly is, called upon to shoot down his fellow-workers, or other men and women, who, in times of peace, may be objectionable to the exploiters.

Let the workers remember that Francesco Ferrer, the noble Spaniard who strove for real education for the Spanish workers, was shot down by workers in the uniform of a capitalist State, who had taken the military oath to obey whatever commands their "superior" officers imposed on them.

Let the workers remember that it was workers, dressed in the uniforms of a capitalist State, and obeying the orders imposed on them by their military oath, who shot down working men and women at Peterloo, at Featherstone, at Belfast; and most recently of all, on the Johannesburg Rand, when under the orders of Lord Gladstone, British troops were used to shoot down British miners on strike. Let the workers remember that the Swiss army (which is a so-called "Citizen-Army") has, according to the Reformers' Year Book of 1906, "shot down more strikers than any other army." That Bebel, speaking at the 1904 Amsterdam Congress, said "In Switzerland, in this short summer only, the citizen army has been called out six times against the workers, who were making use of their right to combine and associate—even in many small strikes."

Let the workers remember that in every country, where the class, or capitalist State is supreme, there the same struggle is going on between the workers on the one hand, and the exploiters (entrenched within the capitalist State) on the other hand. The kings and rulers to whom this military oath is taken, are the figure-heads of these capitalist States; and it was with this class-struggle in his mind that the German Emperor said to his conscripts a few years ago: "I may call upon you to shoot down or bayonet your own relatives—father and mother, sisters and brothers. My orders in that respect must be executed cheerfully and without grumbling. You must do your duty, no matter what your heart's dictates may be."

The same class struggle is going on in all our colonies; and in Australia, where the so-called "Labour" Party has been captured by the exploiting class (who out there have invested much capital in lands and in industrial undertakings, which they fear may be resumed and socialised by the workers), the same anxiety is being shown by capitalists to manufacture a false and jingoist patriotism, which will appear to divide the interests of the Australian workers from those of the workers in other parts of the world. The capitalists sent Kitchener on a world tour a few years ago, and at the same time spread through their subsidised Press, absurd and ignorant rumours about the danger of a Japanese or of a German invasion of Australia or of New Zealand. The agitation against the Japanese and the Germans was so persistently carried on, and the working men and women of the Australian colonies were so ignorant of the class struggle on which present capitalist society rests, that, although they possess the vote and the right of free speech, they allowed the Defence Acts to be foisted on them, and sold their young sons, from 12 years old upwards, into capitalist military slavery.

The Australian and New Zealand lads have now before them the choice of becoming conscripts or convicts. If they elect to be conscripts, they may have, in obedience to military orders, to shoot down their friends or relatives in times of industrial trouble; or they may be ordered to fight in the quarrels of Great Britain, and to "legally murder" continental and other workers, whose industrial interests are allied to the industrial interests of the Australian and New Zealand workers. If the lads refuse this capitalist proposition of compulsory military service, they will be fined, imprisoned, and branded as convicts. Many thousands of lads have already suffered in this way in our colonies, in order to prove their allegiance to the cause of the workers. Over 6,000 lads have been either fined or imprisoned for refusing compulsory drill and service in the capitalist army.

Among these lads who have suffered for conscience sake are the two sons of Mr. J. Sellar, who was three years ago a farmer in England, and who then emigrated with his wife and four sons to New Zealand. Needless to say the emigration agents did not tell him about the compulsory military service, which compels every lad over 12 years of age to drill and train to be a soldier. Mr. Sellar's two sons have been imprisoned in Wanganui jail, because they refused this conscription and the taking of the military oath. And when they chose, rather than be conscripts, to be convicts, they were told by the magistrate who sentenced them that they had better leave the country, for New Zealand did not want young men of their type.

I repeat, the reason these tyrannous and degrading Defence Acts were initiated and passed was, because the capitalists, being first in the field, they desired to protect their property, the land (which they took before they invited the workers to come out), the Banks, the Stores, the Machinery, the Nationalised railways, and other wealth,—not only from the capitalists of other lands, who might be casting covetous glances at them,—but FROM THE WORKERS THEMSELVES, who are beginning to understand that those who make the wealth should own the wealth. As sops to the awakening workers, the capitalists have nationalised the railways, a mine or two here and there, and some brickworks; but the workers are learning by bitter experience that industries and departments (such as the Post Office or the Railways) nationalized under a Capitalist State, are no cure for wage-slavery, because they are still carried on for profit; and nothing but the SOCIALISATION OF THE MEANS OF LIFE under a free Co-operative Commonwealth will abolish the present system, and give the wealth of the world to the workers of the world.

Do not think, you workers of Great Britain, that this training of, and drilling of, the youth of our colonies does not affect you and your sons; but read what Lord Roberts wrote to Colonel Allan Bell, who was one of the officers taking a prominent part in the enlistment and enslavement of the youth of Australasia. "I hope," wrote Lord Roberts, "your efforts to gain universal training will be ultimately successful; for if you fail there, it will mean we shall not get it here, and, as regards the British Empire, universal training will be put back on the clock of time at least fifty or sixty years."

I would ask the workers, what have their representatives in the capitalist Parliaments of Australasia or of Great Britain done towards putting back the clock of time for universal training?

Have any Labour Members at Westminster asked questions about the jailing and fining of British subjects, who have been persuaded to emigrate to New Zealand without being told of the militarist trap which awaited them? Where are the forty accredited representatives of Labour in the British Parliament, and what are they doing actively and militantly against militarism?

What is the record of the Commonwealth Labour Party in Australia?

I take the answer from the pamphlet "The Curse of Conscription," written by our comrade, Harry Holland. "One of the principal achievements of 'Labour as Lawmaker'—that is the Labour Party as Lawmaker—in 1910, almost immediately after its great victory at the polls, was the extension of the tentacles of the military octopus. The term of compulsory service was lifted from two to seven years! The boy of from 12 to 14 was dragged in, and called a Junior Cadet, and was required to drill for 120 hours in a year—nearly three weeks. The boy of from 14 to 18 became a Senior Cadet, and was required to put in four whole days, 12 half-days, and 24 night drills. Young men from 18 to 25 became members of the Citizen Forces, with a liability of 16 whole days' drill, eight of which must be in camps of continuous training . . . . The Labour Party's Defence Act gives the officers power to inflict fines and other penalties on the boys, WITHOUT ANY FORM OF TRIAL WHATEVER."

I ask the workers, is it worth while their troubling to send to the House of Pretence, either in this country or in the Colonies, "Labour" representatives who thus neglect and flout the interests of the workers and of their children?

Again, the workers are constantly told by their exploiters that military drill is so excellent for the health and stamina of the cadet and growing lad. Let working class mothers and fathers read what has been written on this subject by Dr. Saleeby, in his book, "Parenthood and Race Culture." "But it is in the barrack yard that the pitiable confusion between the survival value of mind and muscle respectively in man is most ludicrously and disastrously exemplified. . . . Every year hundreds of young soldiers, originally healthy, have their hearts and lungs and other vital organs permanently injured by the inbecile attitude of chest—that of abnormal expansion—which they are required to adopt during hard work."

We are threatened in Great Britain with compulsory military service; and it is time the workers of Great Britain made up their minds whether they are going to accept or refuse this added capitalist yoke. If they accept it, as they have accepted the Insurance Act, which marks them down as the servile, and therefore State insured, class of this country, then they will put back for many years the moment of their industrial and social freedom. If they refuse it, they will be manifesting a degree of class-consciousness which will more mightily disturb the calculations of their exploiters than any other act of the modern proletariat has hitherto done. And they will further be showing a spirit of solidarity with their fellow workers and comrades throughout the world, which will go far towards removing misunderstandings, and towards destroying out of date and blatant expressions of patriotism.

In the manifesto to the conscript lads of Australia, which was published in the Socialist paper I was editing in Sydney in 1911, I wrote, in the name of the International comrades who were backing the paper: "The army you lads should enlist in is the Industrial Army. The only enemy you have to fight is Capitalism; and the only State of the future under which you working lads will not be robbed of the greater part of the wealth your labour creates, will be the Socialist State. Workers of the world, instead of taking payment from the capitalists to fight each other, should unite to fight the capitalists, and take over for themselves the land, workshops, mines and factories; and should produce the wealth they are creating for their own uses, instead of for the few who now exploit and govern them; and who, in the organizing of this compulsary military service and training, are only preparing an army of legalised murderers to defend their stolen wealth."

The only scientific way to fight militarism is to fight capitalism. When things are no longer produced for profit, but for the use of those who make them, then there will no longer be any necessity for a capitalist army.

When millions of workers are set free from making munitions and provisions of warfare, then they will be able to turn their attention to building themselves better houses, producing more and better food and clothing for their families, and they will enjoy the leisure, the comfort, the culture and the education which are now the privileges of the exploiters.

DOWN WITH THE GREAT MILITARY CONSPIRACY FOR THE FURTHER ENSLAVEMENT OF THE WORKERS OF GREAT BRITAIN!

# 48

# "A CONTINENTAL REVOLUTION", *FORWARD*, 15 AUGUST 1914, 38–42.

*James Connolly*

[The outbreak of war in August 1914 was a pivotal moment in the history of Marxism. Despite commitments to resisting war reaffirmed as recently as the Basle congress of 1912, the parties of European social democracy mostly lined up with their governments in the prosecution of war. The Bolsheviks in Russia were the most important exception, and in November 1917 led the revolution that took Russia out of the war and set about the construction of a socialist state. With the launching two years later of the Communist International, the divisions of the old International were formalised. In Britain, the BSP took the line of the anti-war "internationalists" like Theodore Rothstein and Zelda Kahan, many of whom then found their way into the Communist Party. The SDF old guard, including Hyndman, Lee and Bax, adopted a pro-war and subsequently an anti-Bolshevik position. What remained of the SDF tradition was afterwards quietly absorbed into the labour movement mainstream.

These developments are beyond the scope of the present volume. Nevertheless, the article that follows is included both for the cogency of the anti-war views expressed and in recognition of one of the great figures contributing to British Marxism who nevertheless cannot simply be classified under this heading. Born in Edinburgh in 1868, James Connolly had joined the SDF there in 1889 and was later the first national organiser of the Socialist Labour Party. Of Irish extraction, Connolly nevertheless spent the greater part of his political career in Ireland and the USA, and it was through the Irish socialist press and organisations like the Irish Socialist Republican Party that his considerable political energies were channelled. Deeply committed to the Irish national cause, Connolly opposed the war in 1914 on both national and internationalist grounds. A Scottish associate described his speeches as a "model of simplicity, conciseness and burning class invective" (Bell 1941, 47) and just the same qualities were equally evident in his political journalism. In April 1916 Connolly was one of the leaders of the Easter Rising. Shot by orders of the British government, he passed into the "great Valhalla of revolutionary pioneers and martyrs" (Bell 1941, 52).]

The outbreak of war on the continent of Europe makes it impossible this week to write to *Forward* upon any other question. I have no doubt that to most of my readers Ireland has ere now ceased to be, in colloquial phraseology, the most important place on the map, and that their thoughts are turning gravely to a consideration of the position of the European socialist movement in the face of this crisis.

Judging by developments up to the time of writing, such considerations must fall far short of affording satisfying reflections to the socialist thinker. For, what is the position of the socialist movement in Europe to-day? Summed up briefly it is as follows:

For a generation at least the socialist movement in all the countries now involved has progressed by leaps and bounds, and more satisfactory still, by steady and continuous increase and development.

The number of votes recorded for socialist candidates has increased at a phenomenally rapid rate, the number of socialist representatives in all legislative chambers has become more and more of a disturbing factor in the calculations of governments. Newspapers, magazines, pamphlets and literature of all kinds teaching socialist ideas have been and are daily distributed by the million amongst the masses; every army and navy in Europe has seen a constantly increasing proportion of socialists amongst its soldiers and sailors, and the industrial organisations of the working class have more and more perfected their grasp over the economic machinery of society, and more and more moved responsive to the socialist conception of their duties. Along with this, hatred of militarism has spread through every rank of society, making everywhere its recruits, and raising an aversion to war even amongst those who in other things accepted the capitalist order of things. Anti-militarist societies and anti-militarist campaigns of socialist societies and parties, and anti-militarist resolutions of socialist and international trade union conferences have become part of the order of the day and are no longer phenomena to be wondered at. The whole working class movement stands committed to war upon war—stands so committed at the very height of its strength and influence.

And now, like the proverbial bolt from the blue, war is upon us, and war between the most important, because the most socialist, nations of the earth. And we are helpless!!

What then becomes of all our resolutions; all our protests of fraternisation; all our threats of general strikes; all our carefully-built machinery of internationalism; all our hopes for the future? Were they all as sound and fury, signifying nothing? When the German artilleryman, a socialist serving in the German army of invasion, sends a shell into the ranks of the French army, blowing off their heads; tearing out their bowels, and mangling the limbs of dozens of socialist comrades in that force, will the fact that he, before leaving for the front, "demonstrated" against the war be of any value to the widows and orphans made by the shell he sent upon its mission of murder? Or, when the French rifleman pours his murderous rifle fire into the ranks of the German line of attack, will he be able to derive any comfort from the probability that his bullets are murdering or maiming comrades who last year joined in thundering "hochs" and cheers of greeting to the eloquent Jaurês, when in Berlin he pleaded for international solidarity? When the socialist pressed into the army of the Austrian Kaiser, sticks a long, cruel bayonet-knife into the stomach of the socialist conscript in the army of the Russian Czar, and gives it a twist so that when pulled out it will pull the entrails out along with it, will the terrible act lose any of its fiendish cruelty by the fact of their common theoretical adhesion to an anti-war propaganda in times of peace? When the socialist soldier from the Baltic provinces of Russia is sent forward into Prussian Poland to bombard towns and villages until a red trail of blood and fire covers the homes of the unwilling Polish subjects of Prussia, as he gazes upon the corpses of those he has slaughtered and the homes he has destroyed, will he in his turn be comforted by the thought that the Czar whom he serves sent other soldiers a few years ago to carry the same devastation and murder into his own home by the Baltic Sea?

But why go on? Is is not as clear as the fact of life itself that no insurrection of the working class; no general strike; no general uprising of the forces of Labour in Europe, could possibly carry with it, or entail a greater slaughter of socialists, than will their participation as soldiers in the campaigns of the armies of their respective countries? Every shell which explodes in the midst of a German battalion will slaughter some socialists; every Austrian cavalry charge will leave the gashed and hacked bodies of Serbian or Russian socialists squirming and twisting in agony upon the ground; every Russian, Austrian, or German ship sent to the bottom or blown sky-high will mean sorrow and mourning in the homes of some socialist comrades of ours. If these men must die, would it not be better to die in their own country fighting for freedom for their class, and for the abolition of war, than to go forth to strange countries and die slaughtering and slaughtered by their brothers that tyrants and profiteers might live?

Civilisation is being destroyed before our eyes; the results of generations of propaganda and patient heroic plodding and self-sacrifice are being blown into annihilation from a hundred cannon mouths; thousands of comrades with whose souls we have lived in fraternal communion are about to be done to death; they whose one hope it was to be spared to co-operate in building the perfect society of the future are being driven to fratricidal slaughter in shambles where that hope will be buried under a sea of blood.

I am not writing in captious criticism of my continental comrades. We know too little about what is happening on the continent, and events have moved too quickly for any of us to be in a position to criticise at all. But believing as I do that any action would be justified which would put a stop to this colossal crime now being perpetrated, I feel compelled to express the hope that ere long we may read of the paralysing of the internal transport service on the continent, even should the act of paralysing necessitate the erection of socialist barricades and acts of rioting by socialist soldiers and sailors, as happened in Russia in 1905. Even an unsuccessful attempt at social revolution by force of arms, following the paralysis of the economic life of militarism, would be less disastrous to the socialist cause than the act of socialists allowing themselves to be used in the slaughter of their brothers in the cause.

A great continental uprising of the working class would stop the war; a universal protest at public meetings will not save a single life from being wantonly slaughtered.

I make no war upon patriotism; never have done. But against the patriotism of capitalism—the patriotism which makes the interest of the capitalist class the supreme test of duty and right—I place the patriotism of the working class, the patriotism which judges every public act by its effect upon the fortunes of those who toil. That which is good for the working class I esteem patriotic, but that party or movement is the most perfect embodiment of patriotism which most successfully works for the conquest by the working class of the control of the destinies of the land wherein they labour.

To me, therefore, the socialist of another country is a fellow-patriot, as the capitalist of my own country is a natural enemy. I regard each nation as the possessor of a definite contribution to the common stock of civilisation, and I regard the capitalist class of each nation as being the logical and natural enemy of the national culture which constitutes that definite contribution.

Therefore, the stronger I am in my affection for national tradition, literature, language, and sympathies, the more firmly rooted I am in my opposition to that capitalist class which in its soulless lust for power and gold would bray the nations as in a mortar.

Reasoning from such premises, therefore, this war appears to me as the most fearful crime of the centuries. In it the working class are to be sacrificed that a small clique of rulers and armament makers may sate their lust for power and their greed for wealth. Nations are to be obliterated, progress stopped, and international hatreds erected into deities to be worshipped.

# Part 10

# THE SENSE OF THE PAST

# 49

# "GEORGE JULIAN HARNEY: A STRAGGLER OF 1848", *SOCIAL DEMOCRAT*, JANUARY 1897, 3–8.

*Edward Aveling*

[The *Social Democrat* was launched to meet the need for a "Social-Democratic Magazine" in January 1897. Styling itself a "monthly socialist review", it was the first such publication since the folding of *Today*, which from 1884–1889 had carried the subtitle "Monthly Magazine of Scientific Socialism". Though the *Social Democrat* had no named editor, Edward and Eleanor Marx-Aveling were among those most active in the new initiative. Since the early 1880s they had passed through the SDF, the Socialist League, an otherwise inconsequential Bloomsbury Socialist Society and the ILP, returning to the SDF fold in 1896. In each successive phase, Aveling had had the gift of arousing deep misgivings on account of his personal conduct. The story would end tragically with Eleanor Marx's suicide in 1898.

Aveling introduced readers to the "old warrior" Harney (1817–1897) in the magazine's very first article, which appears here with a prefatory paragraph omitted. Aveling's object was clearly both to honour and to make a claim upon the founding generations from which the socialist movement had grown. In particular, having lately broken with the ILP, he was signalling how socialism in its Marxist form was deeply rooted in Britain's native traditions of struggle. Like Hyndman in his earliest historical flourishes, Aveling reaches back well beyond the origins of socialism to the seventeenth-century Leveller John Lilburne and the anti-enclosure rebellion led by Robert Kett in 1549. Across the course of the nineteenth century he then traced a more continuous line of development, and as himself a former active freethinker included militant secularism as the link between the movements of the Owenites, Unstamped press and Chartists and the emergence of modern socialism. Some, like Harney's fellow Chartist Thomas Cooper, had succumbed to the respectability of the mid-Victorian decades. But like Tom Mann in his later years, when the communists would make much of him as a symbol of continuity, Harney was employed by Aveling as a personification of steadfastness in the cause.

Most of all, Harney provided a direct link with Marx and Engels and a reminder of their involvement with the British working-class movement over some half a century. It was in Harney's paper *The Red Republican* that the first English translation of *The Communist Manifesto* (by Helen MacFarlane) had appeared in 1850. Relations for a time had been somewhat strained, and Marx and Engels had not shared Harney's enthusiasm for such radical personalities as the French writer Victor Hugo, who remained in exile in the Channel Islands throughout the period of the Second Empire (1852–1870). One of the striking features of Aveling's profile is the veneration for such literary figures that was so characteristic of radical autodidacts. This is rather passed over in Schoyen's otherwise excellent biography of Harney, but like the writings of Hyndman and Morris and Aveling's own pamphlet on *Shelley's Socialism* (1888), it underlines the importance of a sense of the past in legitimising even those socialist traditions that were ostensibly most future-orientated.]

I was reminded of the little play, of Irving's beautiful impersonation when, the other day, I went down to Richmond to see George Julian Harney. Here is a straggler—a straggler of 1848. Here is a man that carried intellectual gunpowder to the Lifeguards of the Chartist movement. As he sits there in his lonely room, crippled by rheumatism, and nearly eighty years of age, it would be difficult to realise that this is the man of whom Ernest Jones said, "He was the boldest of the champions of the Chartist cause," if you did not look at his face.

When you try to get from Harney some reminiscences of that old time, you find the task not too easy. He tells you at the outset "One may live too long;" and indeed from the neglect by the English workers of this fighter in the van, he might not unnaturally conclude that he had worn out his welcome amongst them.

Harney was born on February 17, 1817, in Kent. That is as near as he will let you get to his birthplace. His schools were the inevitable Dame School of that time, and one or two private schools which he says were of no account. His university, from the age of eleven to fourteen, was the Royal Naval School, Greenwich. After all, his university, like that of the Shakespeare of his adoration, was the big world of thought and action. According to himself, he did not learn much at school, and was very often in poor health. He never had any trade, except that of seafaring, and afterwards drifting generally into and along with the advanced movement of his time, until he reached the crest of the oncoming wave, and was at once leader and driven. For six months he was at sea, going to Lisbon and Brazil. After his return, just as some of us have a great fancy to be a railway guard or a circus master, Harney had a great desire to be a printer. But the fates were adverse, although, after all, he was to do more for printing than perhaps any compositor that ever lived.

From the age of sixteen to that of nineteen he was in the thick of the Unstamped Fight. Those were the years of stamped newspapers. The tax upon knowledge took the official form of a fourpenny stamp upon every newspaper; so the energetic spirits of the time declared roundly for unstamped newspapers. The movement was led by Hetherington, Watson, Collet, Moore, and others, and the fight centred especially around the *Poor Man's Guardian*. Under an Act of Queen

Anne, Harney was clapped into prison twice for short terms in London, and then, as there was a vacancy in Derby, he went there in place of some unknown fighter, imprisoned. At Derby he sold the unstamped *Political Register*—not on any account to be confused with Cobbett's paper of the same name. At Derby he got six months, at the very revolutionary age of nineteen. But his imprisonment was a triumph; for whilst it was still going on, the Government gave way, and the fourpenny newspaper stamp was abolished. The victory for education had been won, even if one of the victors was laid by the heels in Derby Gaol. The three prisons that were honoured by the temporary residence of Harney were Coldbath Fields, the Borough Compter, and Derby Gaol. They have all gone the way of all bricks and mortar, been transformed or else vanished, as completely as the church at Luddington, two miles from Stratford-on-Avon, at which William Shakespeare and Ann Hathaway were married.

The Unstamped men of 1836 became the Chartists of succeeding years. It is an interesting study in evolution—the Unstamped movement, the Chartist movement, the Freethought movement, which afforded, after the apparent downfall of Chartism, the only outlet for the energies of the advanced working men, until the next stage in evolution came, and the Socialist movement grew, more or less directly, out of those just named. It is very interesting to see in England how, at your Socialist meetings, you have especially the old and the young rather than the middle-aged. Some stragglers from the Chartist movement are still with us, and they are the youngest of us all. Their grandchildren, rather than their children, form the ever-increasing mass of the class-conscious workers. On the other hand, in many cases, but not in quite all, the children of the Chartists and the fathers of the present race of young workers are, as the inevitable result of their surroundings a few years back, often hide-bound in a hard-and-fast Radicalism diluted with Freethought. None of us will forget, although I have no time to work it out here, the stages of intellectual and political development precedent to the Unstamped movement—the Utopian Socialism of Robert Owen, and from him back through the centuries to the Lilburnes and the Kets.

Harney was a delegate to the first National Convention of the Chartists. Its full name was the General Convention of the Industrial Classes. In his room there hangs, upon walls full of interesting pictures, a picture of that Convention as it met on Monday, February 4, 1839, at the British Coffee House in Cockspur Street. The British Coffee House has vanished, or undergone such transformation as to have practically vanished. After the second or third day, the Convention removed to the Doctor Johnson Hotel, Bolt Court, Fleet Street—which is now, says Harney, with a half-cynical humour so characteristic of him, "a sporting den."

He was delegate to the Convention from Newcastle, and the *Newcastle Weekly Chronicle,* owned by his faithful friend Joseph Cowen, still retains his services as a writer. Between the Derby prison time and the meeting of the Convention he had been, to use his own language, "padding the hoof, preaching the gospel of discontent."

The year 1839 was memorable to him not only for the Convention. At the latter end of July in that year he was arrested again at Bedlington, about eleven miles from Newcastle. It will be observed how faithful he was to Newcastle. This arrest was for a speech made early in the same month at Birmingham. It took place at two o'clock in the morning, and he had to be got across country to Birmingham, handcuffed to a constable of that inspiring town, and hemmed in with Newcastle police. The journey was in a hackney coach to Newcastle; in a ferry across the Tyne to Gateshead; from Gateshead by rail to Carlisle; by stage coach right across Shap Fell, that highest point among the Westmoreland mountains, up to which the London and North Western engines so slowly climb; finally by rail from Preston, at that time the extreme north of the North Western Railway, to Birmingham.

As one heard of the handcuff business, one's eyes involuntarily strayed to the poor rheumatic and yet vigorous hands of nearly fifty-seven years after. At Birmingham there was a commital and a letting out on bail. "I never knew," said the veteran, with a laugh, "how rich I was until then. I was worth one surety in £1,000 and two in £500. The trial did not come off in Warwick in April 1840. The Grand Jury, of which for the first time I began to understand the function, and for which for the first time I began to have some respect, declined to find a true bill.

"The next taking event was my arrest at Sheffield. I was one of fifty or sixty, all of whom were arrested, in 1842, all over England, for taking part in a Convention at Manchester. The real fact was that this convention was connected in point of time, but in no other way whatever, with a big trade union strike in Lancashire, with which were mixed up plug-drawing and other wicked devices of the workmen. We were to be tried at Liverpool before Lord Abinger, alias James Scarlett. He was Scarlett by name and scarlet by nature, and we know that he, like certain judges of to-day—at least so they tell me—had made up his mind to the verdict before a word of evidence was given. It was necessary to play the lawyers with their own cards, and so we "traversed," that is, we contended for a beautiful legal fiction; that as forty days had not elapsed since the time of the arrest, we had not had enough time for the defence. So away to Lancaster—to the Castle, I think—and the Monster Trial at March, 1843. The Judge was Rolfe, and the indictment was riddled through and through by the lawyers on our side. Some of our fellows were represented by Counsel. For those not represented, I "led." Fergus O'Connor brought up the rear of the self defenders, and everybody knows that the big actor always likes to have the stage at the end of the play." The chief Counsel for the prosecution was the Attorney-General, Sir Frederick Pollock, of whom Harney speaks with the greatest respect. "He was a prosecutor, not a persecutor." Ultimately Harney and O'Connor were found guilty on one of the innumerable counts, and the others upon two. Goodness only knows now, and nobody whatever cares, what the counts were, as there was an arrest of judgment—which was turning the tables by the arrested with a vengeance—and a quashing of the whole business in the Court of Queen's Bench, as far as Harney and the rest were concerned, on the ground that the indictment was bad.

"Tom" Cooper, as Harney calls him, was not so lucky. I have a dim memory of Cooper, when I was a very small youth, lecturing to me and a lot of other people, and more or less converting us from the error of our orthodox ways. Cooper had two years in Stafford Gaol, and took them out of humanity in general by writing "The Purgatory of Suicides." He became converted in his later days to Christianity and general respectability.

In the summer of 1841 Harney went in for his first political contest. It was against Lord Morpeth, and the arena was the West Riding of Yorkshire. To get rid of the political contests once for all, there was another opened on July 30, 1847, against that arch-friend of Russia, Lord Palmerston. The Palmerston constituency was Tiverton, and Harney swears that for his fame (Harney's not Palmerston's) he "should have died thereafter." When he went out to America later, even such a man as Horace Greeley knew him chiefly on the ground that he opposed Palmerston. Of course these more or less abortive runnings of candidates were chiefly with the intention of making propaganda by speech. For example, the opposition to Morpeth gave Harney the opportunity of speaking at such towns as Leeds, Huddersfield, Bradford, Dewsbury, Wakefield. There was never any serious intention of going to the poll.

The rest of this life of struggle and event is chiefly journalistic. Thus, in 1843, he joined the *Northern Star* at Leeds, and was first sub-editor and afterwards editor. This connection was ended by disagreement with Fergus O'Connor. The grounds of the diagreement were, according to Harney, that he made too much of the foreign refugees, whilst O'Connor made too much of the old political ideas, and was too much of a King, Lords and Commons man. One epigrammatic summary of O'Connor by Harney is worth preserving. "He was like William Cobbett, without his particular form of genius."

The *Democratic Review,* 1849, the *Red Republican* and *Friend of the People* (June 1850 to July 1851) were his next journalistic and pugilistic ventures. From 1855 to 1862 he was in Jersey, looking after the *Jersey Independent*. He seems to have been attracted to the Channel Islands chiefly because Victor Hugo (whom he knew and loved well afterwards) had been expelled from Jersey to Guernsey. "The first week I was in Jersey," says Harney, "I heard the Bailiff reading the Proclamation of Peace with Russia."

Since the Jersey time, there are the little interludes in such a life as this of a journey to and a sojourn in America, and a return to this country.

I do not think I can give any better idea of the intellectual, moral, and political characteristics of Harney than by telling the reader of the portraits and the like that crowd his walls. I take them just as I saw them, working round his room. Fergus O'Connor; Frost; Joseph Cowen; Oastler, the Factory King; "Knife and Fork" Stephens, the physical force man, who spent eighteen months in Chester Castle; W. J. Linton, engraver and Chartist; Harney himself (he is even now a delightful bit of a beau in his way, as scrupulously dressed and groomed as ever), as a Yankee, with a moustache only, instead of the present venerable beard; Lovett, who drew up the People's Charter; Frederick Engels and Karl Marx, very fitly side by side (Harney had the high honour of their friendship); "Ironsides" Adams, of the *Newcastle Chronicle*. All these are on the walls by his bed and the fireplace that runs to the window, looking south. Over the mantle-piece is a group that reminds some of us younger workers in the workers' movement that perhaps we hardly pay as much attention to pure literature as our political forefathers did—Byron, Scott, Burns, Shelley, Moore, Pope, Dryden, the grave of Fielding, and, high over all, Shakespeare. Between the windows looking south are Miss Eleanor Cobbett, now ninety-one years of age, a letter from Cobbett himself, and the People's Charter. Between the windows and the door, Magna Charta, Darwin, Ruskin, Sidney, Chaucer, Raleigh, De Stael, Mary Wollstonecroft, together with a bust of Shakespeare again. And, by the door, there is a picture of Uncle Toby and the Widow Wadman.

The words of Harney about Engels and Marx (I put them in the order in which he began to know them) will be of interest. "I knew Engels, he was my friend and occasional correspondent over half a century. It was in 1843 that he came over from Bradford to Leeds and enquired for me at the *Northern Star* office. A tall, handsome young man, with a countenance of almost boyish youthfulness, whose English, in spite of his German birth and education, was even then remarkable for its accuracy. He told me he was a constant reader of the *Northern Star* and took a keen interest in the Chartist movement. Thus began our friendship over fifty years ago. In later years he was the Nestor of International Socialism. Not more natural was it for Titus to succeed Vespasian than for Frederick Engels to take the place of his revered friend when Karl Marx had passed away. He was the trusted counsellor whose advice none dared to gainsay. Probably the private history of German Socialism could tell how much the party is indebted to his wise counsels in smoothing acerbities, preventing friction, mildly chastening ill-regulated ambition, and promoting the union of all for each and each for all. The author of 'Das Kapital' was supremely fortunate in having so devoted a friend. The friendship of Marx and Engels was something far from the common. If not positively unique we must go back to ancient legends to find a parallel. Either would have emulated Pythias' offered sacrifice for Damon. In their public work as champions of their ideas they were like the 'Great Twin Brethren who fought so well for Rome.' Engels' like, I believe, most short-sighted people, wrote a very 'small hand;' but his caligraphy was very neat and clear. His letters were marvels of information, and he wrote an immense number in spite of his long hours of original composition or translation. He attended most of the large Eight Hours Demonstrations in Hyde Park [all, except that of 1895, the year of his death, and was always on the International platform, of which I had the great honour to be chairman; E. A.]—but I doubt if sixteen hours covered his average day's work when he was at his best. With all his knowledge and all his influence, there was nothing of the 'stuck up' or 'stand-offishness' about him. He was just as modest and ready for self-effacement at the age of seventy-two as at the age of twenty-two when he called at the *Northern Star* office. Not only his intimate friends, but dependents, servants, children, all loved him. Although Karl Marx was his great friend his heart was large enough for other friendships and his kindness was unfailing. He was largely given to hospitality, but the principal charm at his hospitable board was his own 'table talk,' the 'good Rhine wine' of his felicitous conversation and genial wit. He was himself laughter-loving, and his laughter was contagious. A joy-inspirer, he made all around him share his happy mood of mind."

A letter from Harney to Marx just found by us among the papers of the latter is of great historical interest (look at the dates and names), and is here published for the first time.

"DEAR MARX,—I have been and am very unwell, so can only say that the propositions for holding a Democratic Congress in Brussels in September next have been unanimously adopted by the monthly meeting of the Fraternal Democrats, the German Workingmen's Association, the Metropolitan Chartist Committee, and the Chartist Executive.

"I will write again in the course of the first week of 1848.

"London, Dec. 18, 1847.

"G. J. H."

Turning back from this beautiful retrospect upon one of his own kin by Harney, calling to mind the many happy days when I met him at Engels' house, I am conscious that the two men, Engels and Harney, were cast in the same mould, soldiers in the same regiment.

And as I look in this darkening room at Richmond at this old warrior with his carefully brushed hair and beard, his strongly marked face, his clear eyes—as I listen to the clear voice that expresses his clear thought—my mind goes back to years before he was born, and forward to years after both he and I will be dead, and I see in this old man an unbreakable link between the years and the years. I know that long after the rest of us are forgotten the name of George Julian Harney will be remembered with thankfulness and with tears. A straggler of 1848. But a straggler who cried then, and who will cry with his latest breath that which shall be the motto helping us to remember him, "The people want powder, and by God they shall have it."

# 50

# "BLOODY NIGGERS", *SOCIAL DEMOCRAT*, APRIL 1897, 104–109.

*R.B. Cunninghame Graham*

[Raphael Samuel once observed that in their view of the past the early British Marxists maintained virtually intact the liberal-radical "people's history" of earlier writers like J.R. Green (Samuel 1980, 38–40). Despite their revolutionary colouring, the historical sections of Hyndman's *Historical Basis of Socialism* (1883) and Morris and Bax's *Socialism: its Growth and Outcome* (1893) could certainly be described in this way. The "people" represented were usually the English people; a strain of English self-regard was never too far distant, and the medievalism of Morris's *Dream of John Ball* (1888) and *News of Nowhere* (1890) was also of a distinctively English quality. In some contributions, notably those of Bax, the focus was extended to the other European nations seen as having made the modern world. In socialist views of the contemporary world, with Bax again to the fore, the impact of colonialism registered strongly. Historically speaking, on the other hand, the past was not a foreign country but as familiar as the hedges, fields and spires of Morris's southern English dream-world.

It is within this context that one may imagine the unsettling effect that Cunninghame Graham's contributions must have had upon many readers of the *Social Democrat*. Readers now will notice more the article's shocking title and use of language (for which see Chapter 43) but the author was anything but a racist. Graham's writings had already offered a clear enough alternative to the various socialist apologias for colonialism (Chapter 43, this volume). With the catastrophic famine in India, Hyndman himself struck a radical note in debunking British rule (Chapter 44, this volume). Just the previous month, in March 1897, the missionary and advocate of native peoples' rights Harriette E. Colenso had taken to the pages of the *Social Democrat* to repeat her warnings of famine in Matabeleland. Nevertheless, nothing else in the journal compares with Graham's searing indictment of the racism, cruelty and self-regard of the Celto-Saxon race that laid claim to world dominion. From the mysteries of creation he proceeds to the origins of civilisation and the ascendancy of the self-serving bourgeois Romans who so resembled modern Britons. The latter are traced from Victorian cult figures like the romanticised Alfred the Great to the modern tweed-clad imperialist and the brute realities of

Cecil Rhodes and the British South Africa Company (Chapter 43, this volume). Fraudesia is Graham's epithet for Rhodesia, and the article concludes by returning to the "anthropomorphous fool" whom white Christians enshrined as their god.

One appreciative reader was Joseph Conrad, who read the article in May 1898. Although he demurred from Graham's prolixity, Conrad described it in a letter to the author as "very good, very telling" and the friendship they struck up would last until Conrad's death. Despite their friendly relations, Conrad was never attracted by socialism and Cunninghame Graham could not induce him to take part in an international rally of the SDF the following year (Kopkowski 2011). Nevertheless, Graham's tour de force of anti-colonialism is regarded by Conrad scholars as one of the sources feeding into writings like *The Heart of Darkness* (1899), with its ironic comparisons between the conquests of the Romans and those of modern Europeans (Watts 1977). Conrad's *Lord Jim* (1900) is another novel bearing the traces of Graham's influence, while the character of Charles Gould in *Nostromo* (1904) bears striking resemblances to Graham himself.]

That the all-wise and omnipresent God, to whom good people address their prayers, and for whose benefit, as set forth in the sustentation of his clergy, they hoard their threepenny bits all through the week, is really but a poor, anthropomorphous animal, is day by day becoming plainer and more manifest. He (Jahvé) created all things, especially the world in which we live, and which is really the centre of the universe, in the same way as England is the centre of the planet, and as the Stock Exchange is the real centre of all England, despite the dreams of the astronomers and the economists. He set the heavens in their place, bridled the sea, disposed the tides, the phases of the moon, made summer, winter, and the seasons in their due rotation, showed us the constant resurrection of the day after the death of night, sent showers, hail, frost, snow, thunder and lightning, and the other outward manifestations of his power to serve, to scourge, or to affright us, according to his will.

Under the surface of our world he set the minerals, metals, the coal, and quicksilver, with platinum, gold, and copper, and let his diamonds and rubies, with sapphires, emeralds, and the rest, as topazes, jacinths, peridots, sardonyx, tourmalines, or chrysoberyls, take shape and colour, and slowly carbonise during the ages.

Upon the upper crust of the great planet he caused the plants to grow, the trees, bushes of every kind, from the hard, cruciform-leaved carmamel to the pink-flowering Siberian willow. Palm trees and oaks, ash, plane, and sycamore, with churchyard yew, and rowan, holly, jacaranda, greenheart and pines, larch, willow, and all kinds of trees that flourish, rot, and die unknown in tropic forests, unplagued by botanists, with their pestilent Pinus Smithii or Cupressus Higginbottomiana, rustled their leaves, swayed up and down their branches, and were content, fearing no axe. Canebrakes and mangrove swamps; the immeasurable extension of the Steppes, Pampas, and Prairies, and the frozen Tundras of the north; stretches of ling and heather, with bees buzzing from flower to flower, larks soaring into heaven above them; acres of red verbena in the Pampa; lilies and irises in Africa, and the green-bluish sage brush desert of the middle prairies of

America; cactus and tacuaras, with istlé and maguey, flax, hemp, esparto, and the infinite variety of the compositæ, all praised his name.

Again, in the Sahara, in the Kalahari desert, in the Libyan sands, and Iceland, he denied almost all vegetation, and yet his work seemed good to those his creatures—Arabs, Bosjemen, reindeer, and Arctic foxes, with camels, ostriches and eider ducks who peopled his waste spaces. He breathed his breath into the nostrils of the animals, giving them understanding, feeling, power of love and hatred, speech after their fashion, love of offspring (if logic and anatomy hold good), souls and intelligence, whether he made their bodies biped or quadruped, after his phantasy. Giraffes and tigers, with jerboas, grey soft chinchillas, elephants, armadillos and sloths, ant eaters, marmots, antelopes, and the fast-disappearing bison of America, gnus, springboks and hartbeest, ocelot and kangaroo, bears (grisly and cinnamon), tapirs and wapiti, he made for man to shoot, to torture, to abuse, to profit by, and to demonstrate by his conduct how inferior in his conception of how to use his life, he is to them.

All this he did and rested, being glad that he had done so much, and called a world into existence that seemed likely to be happy. But even he, having begun to work, was seized with a sort of "cacoethes operandi," and casting about to make more perfect what, in fact, needed no finishing touch, he took his dust, and, breathing on it, called up man. This done he needed rest again, and having set the sun and moon just in the right position to give light by day and night to England, he recollected that a week had passed. That is to say, he thought of time, and thinking, made and measured it, not knowing, or perhaps not caring, that it was greater than himself; for, had he chanced to think about the matter, perchance, he had never chosen to create it, and then our lives had been immeasurable, and our capacity for suffering even more infinite than at present, that is, if "infinite" admits comparison. However, time being once created and man imagined (but not yet perfected), and, therefore, life the heavy burden being opposed on him, the Lord, out of his great compassion, gave us death, the compensating boon which makes life tolerable.

But to return to man. How, when, why, wherefore, whether in derision of himself, through misconception, inadvertence, or sheer malignity, he created man, is still unknown. With the true instinct of a tyrant (or creator, for both are one), he gave us reason to a certain power, disclosed his acts up to a certain point, but left the motives wrapped in mystery. Philosophers and theologians, theosophists, positivists, clairvoyants, necromancers, cabalists, with Rosicrucians and alchemists, and all the rabble rout of wise and reverend reasoners from Thaies of Miletus down to Nietzsche, have reasoned, raved, equivocated, and contradicted one another, framed their cosmogonies, arcana, written their Gospels and Korans; printed their Tarot packs, been martyred, martyred others (fire the greatest syllogist on earth), and we no wiser.

Still man exists, black, white, red, yellow, and the Pintos of the State of Vera Cruz. A rare invention, wise conception, and the quintessence of creative power rendered complete by practice, for we must think that even an all-wise, all-powerful God (like ours) improves by practice.

An animal erect upon its feet, its eyes well placed, its teeth constructed to masticate all kinds of food, its brain seemingly capable of some development, its hearing quick, endowed with soul, and with its gastric juices so contained as to digest fish, flesh, grain, fruit, and stand the inroads of all schools of cookery, was a creative masterpiece. So all was ready and the playground delivered over beautiful to man, for men to make it hideous and miserable.

Alps, Himalayas, Andes, La Plata, and Vistula, Amazon, with Mississippi, Yangtsekiang and Ganges, Volga, Rhine, Elbe and Don; Hecla and Stromboli, Pichincha, and Cotopaxi, with the Istacihuatl and Lantern of Maracaibo; seas, White and Yellow, with Oceans, Pacific and Atlantic; great inland lakes as Titicaca, Ladoga, all the creeks, inlets, gulfs and bays, the plains, the deserts, the geysers, hot springs on the Yellowstone, Pitch Lake of Trinidad, and, to be brief, the myriad wonders of the world were all awaiting newly-created man, waiting his coming forth from out the bridal chamber between the Tigris and Euphrates, like a mad bridegroom to run his frenzied course. Then came the (apparent) lapsus in the creator's scheme. That the first man in the fair garden by the Euphrates was white, I think, we take for granted. True that we have no information on the subject, but in this matter of creation we have entered, so to speak, into a tacit compact with the creator, and it behoves us to concur with him and help him when a difficulty looms.

Briefly I leave the time when man contended with the mastodon, hunted the mammoth, or was hunted in his turn by plesiosaurus or by pterodactyl. Scanty indeed are the records which survive of the Stone Age, the Bronze, or of the dwellers in the wattled wigwams on the lakes. Suffice it, that the strong preyed on the weak as they still do to-day in Happy England, and that early dwellers upon earth seem to have thought as much as we do, how to invent appliances with which to kill their fellows.

The Hebrew Scriptures and the record of crimes, of violence, and bad faith committed by the Jews on other races, need not detain us, as they resemble so entirely our own exploits amongst the "niggers" of to-day. I take it that Jahvé was little taken up with any of his creatures, except the people who inhabited the countries from which the Aryans came. Assyrians, Babylonians, Egyptians, Persians and the rest were no doubt useful and built pyramids, invented hanging garders, erected towers, observed the stars, spoke truth (if their historians lie not), drew a good bow, and rode like centaurs or like Gauchos. What did it matter when all is said and done? They were all "niggers," and whilst they fought and conquered, or were conquered, bit by bit the race which God had thought of from the first slowly developed.

Again a doubt creeps in. Was the creator omniscient in this case or did our race compel him, force his hand, containing in itself those elements of empire which he may have overlooked? 'Twere hard to say, but sometimes philosophers have whispered that the Great Power was careless, working, as he did, without the healthy stimulus of competition. I leave this speculation as more fit for thimbleriggers, for casuists, for statisticians, metaphysicians, or the idealistic merchant, than for serious men.

Somehow or other the Aryans spread through Europe, multiplied, prospered, and possessed the land. Europe was theirs, for Finns and Basques are not worth counting, being, as it were, a sort of European "niggers," destined to disappear. Little by little out of the mist of barbarism Greece emerged. Homer and Socrates with Xenophon, Euripides, Pindar and Heraclitus, Bion, Anaximander, Praxiteles, with Plato, Pericles and all the rest of the poets and thinkers, statesmen and philosophers, who in that little state carried the triumphs of the human intellect, at least as far as any who came after them, flourished and died. Material and bourgeois Rome, wolf-suckled, on its seven hills waxed and became the greatest power, conquering the world by phrases as its paltry "Civis Romanus," and by its "Pax Romana," and with the spade, and by the sheer dead weight of commonplace, filling the office in the old world that now is occupied so worthily by God's own Englishmen. Then came the waning of the Imperial City, its decay illumined but by the genius of Apuleius and Petronius Arbiter. Whether the new religion which the pipe-clayed soldier Constantine adopted out of policy, first gave the blow, or whether, as said Pliny, that the Latifundia were the ruin of all Italy, or if the effeminacy which luxury brings with it made the Roman youths resemble the undersized, hermaphroditic beings who swarm in Paris and in London, no one knows.

Popes and Republics, Lombards, French and Burgundians, with Visigoths and Huns, and the phantasmagoria of hardly to be comprehended beings who struggled in the darker ages like microbes in a piece of flesh, or like the Christian paupers in an English manufacturing town, all paved the way for the development of the race, perhaps, intended, from the beginning, to rule mankind. From when King Alfred toasted his cakes and made his candles marked in rings[1] (like those weird bottles full of sand from Alum Bay) to measure time, down to the period when our present Sovereign wrote her "Diary in the Highlands" is but a moment in the history of mankind. Still, in the interval, our race has had full leisure to mature. Saxon stolidity and Celtic guile, Teutonic dullness, Norman pride, all tempered with east wind, baptised with mist, narrowed by insularity, swollen with good fortune, and rendered overbearing with much wealth, have worked together to produce the type. A bold, beef eating, generous, narrow-minded type, kindly yet arrogant; the men fine specimens of well fed animals, red in the blood and face; the women cleanly, "upstanding" creatures, most divinely tall; both sexes slow of comprehension, but not wanting sense; great feeders, lovers of strong drinks, and given to brutal sports as were their prototypes the men of ancient Rome; dogged as bull-dogs, quick to compassion for the sufferers from the injustice of their neighbours; thinking that they themselves can do no wrong, athletic yet luxurious, impatient of all hardships yet enduring them when business shows a profit or when honour calls; moralists, if such exist, and yet, like cats, not quite averse to fish when the turn serves; clear-headed in affairs, but yet idealists and, in the main, wrong-headed in their views of life; priding themselves most chiefly on their faults, and resolute to carry all those virtues which they lack at home to other lands.

Thus, through the mist of time, the Celto-Saxon race emerged from heathendom and woad and, in the fulness of the creator's pleasure, became the tweed-clad Englishman. Much of the earth was his, and in the skies he had his mansion ready, well aired, with every appliance known to modern sanitary science waiting for him with a large bible on the chest of drawers in every room. Australia, New Zealand, Canada, India, and countless islands, useful as coaling stations and depôts where to stack his bibles for diffusion amongst the heathen, all owned his sway. Races, as different from his own as is a rabbit from an elephant, were ruled by tweed-clad satraps expedited from the public schools, the universities, or were administered by the dried fruits culled from the Imperial Bar. But whilst God's favoured nation thus had run its course, the French, the Germans, Austrians, Spaniards, Dutch, Greeks, Italians, and all the futile remnant of mankind outside "our flag" had struggled to equal them. True that in most particulars they were inferior. Their beer was weak, their shoddy not so artfully diffused right through their cloth, their cottons less well "sized," the Constitution of their realm less nebulous, or the Orders of their Churches better authenticated, than were our own. No individual of their various nationalities, by a whole life of grace was ever half so moral, as the worst of us is born. And so I leave them, weltering in their attempts to copy us, and turn to those of whom I wished to write when I sat down, but the exordium, which of course I had to write, has stood so long between us that I fear my readers, if I happen to attain to such distinction, are wondering where the applicability of the title may be described.

I wished to show, as Moses told us, that God made the earth and made it round, planted his trees, his men and beasts upon it, and let it simmer slowly till his Englishman stood forth. It seemed to me his state was become almost anthropomorphous, and I doubted, if, after all, he was so wise as some folks say. In other portions of the earth as Africa, America, Australia, and in the myriad islands of the South Seas people called "niggers" live.

What is a "nigger?" Now this needs some words in order to explain his just position. Hindus, as Brahmins, Bengalis, dwellers in Bombay, the Cingalese, Sikhs and Pathans, Rajpoots, Parsis, Afghans, Kashmiris, Beluchis, Burmese, with all the dwellers from the Caspian Sea to Timur Laut, are thus described. Arabs are "niggers."

So are Malays, the Malagasy, Japanese, Chinese, Red Indians, as Sioux, Comanches, Návajos, Apaches with Zapatecas, Esquimaux, and in the south Ranqueles, Lengwas, Pampas, Pehuelches, Tobás, and Araucanos, all these are "niggers" though their hair is straight. Turks, Persians, Levantines, Egyptians, Moors, and generally all those of almost any race whose skins are darker than our own, and whose ideas of faith, of matrimony, banking, and therapeutics differ from those held by the dwellers of the meridian of Primrose Hill, cannot escape. Men of the Latin races, though not born free, can purchase freedom with a price, that is, if they conform to our ideas, are rich and wash, ride bicycles, and gamble on the Stock Exchange. If they are poor, then woe betide them, let them paint their faces white with all the ceruse which ever Venice furnished, to the black favour shall they come. A plague of pigments, blackness is in the heart, not in the face, and poverty, no matter how it washes, still is black.

In the consideration of the "nigger" races which God sent into the world for whites (and chiefly Englishmen) to rule, "niggers" of Africa occupy first place. I take it Africa was brought about in sheer ill-humour. No one can think it possible that an all-wise God (had he been in his sober senses) would create a land and fill it full of people destined to be replaced by other races from across the seas. Better, by far, to have made the "niggers" white and let them by degrees all become Englishmen, than put us to the trouble of exterminating whole tribes of them, to carry out his plan. At times a thinking man knows scarcely what to think, and sometimes doubts whether he is the God we took him for and if he is a fitting Deity for us to worship, and if we had not better, once for all, get us a God of our own race and fitted for our ways. "Niggers" who have no cannons, and cannot construct a reasonable torpedo, have no rights. "Niggers" whose lot is placed outside our flag, whose lives are given over to a band of money-grubbing miscreants (chartered or not) have neither rights nor wrongs. Their land is ours, their cattle, fields, their houses, their poor utensils, arms, all that they have; their women, too, are ours to use as concubines, to beat, exchange, to barter for gunpowder or gin, or any of the circulating media that we employ with "niggers"; ours to infect with syphillis, leave with child, outrage, torment, and make by consort with the vilest of our vile, more vile than beasts. Cretans, Armenians, Cubans, Macedonians, we commiserate, subscribe, and feel for, our tender hearts are wrung when "Outlanders" cannot get votes. Bishops and Cardinals and statesmen, with philanthropists and pious ladies, all go wild about the Turks. Meetings are held and resolutions passed, articles written, lectures delivered, and the great heart of Britain stirred as if stocks were down. But "niggers," "bloody niggers," have no friends. Witness "Fraudesia," where Selous cants and Colenbrander hangs, whilst Rhodes plays "bonnet," and Lord Grey and Co. add empires to our sway, duly baptised in blood.

So many rapes and robberies, hangings and murders, blowings up in caves, pounding to jelly with our Maxim guns, such sympathy for Crete, such coyness to express opinion on our doings in Matabeleland; our clergy all dumb dogs, our politicians dazed about Armenia; "land better liked than niggers," "stern justice meted out"—can England be a vast and seething mushroom bed of base hypocrisy, and our own God, Jahvé Sabbaoth, an anthropomorphous fool?

## Note

1 Staple industry of the Isle of Wight.

# 51

# "WHY IS SOCIALISM IN ENGLAND AT A DISCOUNT?", *SOCIAL DEMOCRAT*, MARCH 1898, 69–74 AND APRIL 1898, 112–117.

*Theodore Rothstein*

[When Theodore Rothstein wrote these articles in 1898, the grander hopes on which the SDF had been founded were indeed at a discount. Since the ILP's founding five years earlier, the SDF could no longer presume on its pre-eminence in representing the socialist case. With the ebbing of the new unionism, ILPers provided the principal socialist voice in the unions. Both John Burns and Tom Mann, once the SDF's foremost industrial activists, had transferred their allegiances elsewhere. As secretary of the ILP, Mann had leant towards a form of socialist unity but was forced from his position at the start of 1898 (Tsuzuki 1994, 99–105). There was now no socialist in parliament, Keir Hardie having lost his seat in 1895, and in January 1898 a six-month engineering lockout had been settled largely on the employers' terms. Rothstein also refers to a recent by-election in York in which no socialist challenged the older parties and a narrow Conservative victory was secured with the ILP's backing because of the Liberal candidate's support for the Engineering Employers (Howell 1983, 91, 365). These were the gloomy circumstances in which Rothstein turned to the question that so many would later seek to address: that of why the world's first industrial proletariat should lag so far behind in the development of a class-conscious socialist movement.

Rothstein's argument was a distinctive one. At first glance it seems a paean to the English middle classes and the bourgeois revolution which Rothstein traced from the brilliant and momentous battles of the seventeenth century. If in Britain the struggle for political and social freedom had been crowned with success, this according to Rothstein was entirely due to the self-sacrificing efforts of the bourgeoisie. One wonders how far Rothstein was swayed by how a sympathetic liberal public had been mobilised in support of collective bargaining rights following the engineering lockout. He even described the repeal of the anti-trade union Combination Acts in 1825 as an achievement of the middle class. This could hardly have differed more from the Hyndmanite view of English history as a sequence of popular agitations from below. "Nearly all the legislation in favour of the labouring class which has been carried on since the great [Napoleonic] war may be directly traced to the efforts of ... men, who would certainly rank as socialists if they were now alive". That was Hyndman in *Socialism and Slavery* (Chapter 16, this volume) and an emphasis almost diametrically opposed to Rothstein's. Though rejecting certain well-worn exceptionalist tropes, such as the innate conservatism of the British, Rothstein did stress the specificity of the British case, and described how in Germany and France in 1848 and even in the great French Revolution it was the people at large who had challenged the old order and the middle classes who invariably betrayed it. Everywhere in Europe, with Britain almost alone excepted, all those committed to liberty and progress had virtually no alternative but to be drawn towards socialism.

There is much in common here with Lenin's conception of the democratic revolution as expressed in his *What the "Friends of the People Are" and How They Fight the Social-Democrats* (1894) which circulated widely among exiled Russian social democrats. Born in Kovno, Lithuania in 1871, Rothstein had arrived in Britain in 1891 and joined the SDF in 1895. As an accomplished linguist and translator, his awareness of debates within the wider socialist movement was matched by few indeed in Britain and Hyndman came to regard him as a political thorn in the side. Rothstein would afterwards play an important role in the establishment of the British communist party, and on returning to Russia in the early 1920s remained there until his death in 1953. When as a communist in the mid-1920s he assembled his writings on British working-class history, he did not include the present selection among them. Nevertheless, he did in one of the newly added chapters return to the great engineering lockout, and described in detail how the astutely collaborationist instincts of a broader liberal public had undermined the appeals of socialism, so that not the workers but only "a small group of intellectuals disappointed in Liberalism" had at that stage truly supported them (Rothstein 1929, 271–274).]

At the present juncture, when the failure of the engineers' strike, coupled with the disgusting incidents of the York election, have produced a certain feeling of discouragement throughout the rank and file of the Socialist movement in this country, an old question naturally forces itself on our mind—a question that has often been raised, but has never yet, to my knowledge, been satisfactorily answered: How is it that Socialism has made up till now so very little progress in these islands? Seeing that it is essentially a recognition on the part of the proletariat of the antagonisms which exist between it and the property owning class, one might have supposed that the country where the early and unimpeded growth of capitalism has brought out those antagonisms to their fullest, would have proved a far more favourable ground for its rise and progress than others of a less developed industrial structure. Instead of this, as we all know, the case is quite the reverse. Whilst in Germany, in France, in Belgium, in Austria, in Italy, in Holland—in countries where capitalism, being of a posterior date, has not been successful, even so far as to drive away forms of property and methods of production belonging properly to the Middle Ages, and the proletariat accordingly still carries about in many cases the egg shell of its small bourgeois origin in the shape of peasant ideals and sympathies—whilst, I say, in those countries the ideas of Socialism are making headway every day, in England, the home of modern industry, the classic land of capitalist production, where there is scarcely a vestige left, either in the field of economic life or in the minds of the people, of former industrial stages, they are scarcely able to obtain a hearing, let alone a footing. The phenomenon is certainly striking, and, on account of its import, both theoretical and as a guidance in practical politics, it has been, and still is, the subject of ample discussion on the part of students and Socialists. It is manifest, however, that the theories usually advanced by way of explaining it, such as, for instance, the comparative well-being of the English working classes or the "inherent" conservatism of the Anglo-Saxon race, are utterly inadequate. For, as regards the first, experience has taught us by now that, far from presenting the best possible soil for assimilation of Socialist ideas, it is exactly the lower strata of the working classes—the men sunk in sloth, misery and drink, who through want of skill and employment, have lost every sense of their human dignity—that are the least accessible to noble appeals, the least capable to grasp a new idea, the least prepared for a conscious effort and unremittent struggle. Poverty and hunger have stunted their intellect, blunted their moral sense, and emaciated their physique, and, tossed to and fro by their unarticulated instincts, they join popular movements only to plunder, to rape, and to kill. It is the better paid artisan, the skilled labourer, the earnest trade unionist, who is decently clad and fed, who enjoys a home and a friendly circle, who knows how to respect himself and be respected by others, who constitutes the really progressive element in every community; conscious of his rights and duties, used to organised life and action, possessing a mind cultivated by reading and social intercourse, he is the chief actor on the stage of politics and revolutions—the easiest convert to new doctrines and parties. And what is true of different sections of one community is true of whole countries, for it is not the impoverished Italian who leads the Socialist movement, but the comparatively well-off German; not the down-trodden Spaniard, but the highly-skilled and educated Frenchman; not the poor Austrian, but the well-paid Belgian. To say, therefore, that it is the high standard of living which insures the British working men against the Socialist virus is incorrect; whatever the causes of England's backwardness in Socialism may be, *this* certainly is not one amongst them. Nor is another the conservatism of the Anglo-Saxon race. That the English people throughout their career have shown a curious attachment to antiquated traditions and ways, a certain well-pronounced predilection for old and even obsolete forms of life and thought, no one will dispute. The whole course of their history is strewn with fossil remains of institutions, laws, and customs, which have some time served their purpose, but afterwards are long retained and cherished with an exemplary tenderness and veneration. But to assume, on the strength of this, that the English have at any time recoiled from striking out a new line of policy and action, from giving expression to, or assimilating a new idea and doctrine from moulding the old in conformity with new needs, or dismissing it altogether, would evidently be to go too far; it would leave unexplained the elementary fact of the enormous progress made by the nation during the centuries of its existence, as well as its present high position as a "culture-bearer," to use a German phrase, among the communities of Europe. Least of all can it be said that these conservative proclivities have produced in the English people a spirit of tameness and submissiveness. The men who, to mention but a few instances, sent to the scaffold one of their kings, and chased another from the country, who were the first in modern times to make an experiment in republican self-government on a large scale, and gave to the world popular movements, such as the Owenite and the Chartist, and revolutionary methods and organisations such as trade unionism, can scarcely be accused of a lack of courage and independence in the domain of politics and political thought. Conservatism with the English has never spelt reaction, and, consequently, cannot be made responsible for the failure of Socialism in their country. The real cause must be looked for elsewhere, and to this we will now turn.

It has been the singular good fortune of England to have possessed, almost from the very beginning of her national existence, a middle class sufficiently strong and organised to become a serious factor in the political life of the country. The unique geographical position of these islands, eminently calculated to promote a spirit of commerce and maritime enterprise, in conjunction with the absence of any such tendency for centralisation as had been left by Rome to the rest of her late provinces, were instrumental in bringing forth a rich burgherdom that was enabled, not only to preserve the rudiments of self-government handed over from previous ages, but also to develop them further by means of charters obtained from their lords and kings. At the time of the Norman Conquest there were already several burghs, towns, and cities in existence which enjoyed a sort of autonomy in fiscal and juridical matters, having bought, on payment of fixed dues, the right of self-assessment of taxes and exemption from the manor and other courts. It was a very shrewd and business-like set of folk—these early precursors of the modern bourgeoisie—always mindful of their property, always jealous of their privileges, they were never tired of defending them against the arbitrariness of their temporal and spiritual lords, or, as was far more frequently the case, the greed and rapaciousness of the kings. They understood their interests with a clearness that would reflect credit even on the modern British working man, and early made a common cause with the barons in the struggle for civic, personal, and property rights. We know that the very foundation of English liberties—the Magna Charta—was laid only after burgherdom had lent its helping hand; it was the revolt of the Londoners which turned the scale in favour of the aristocracy, and compelled the unlucky John, now bereft of his last hope, to sign the famous articles. And so the fight went on during the rest of this and the whole of the following century. Everywhere, it is true, we find at the head of the movement the barons; it was their landed interests that were primarily at stake; but we seldom, if ever, miss the important element of burgherdom backing up with all its might the demands for the privileges of self-taxation, of trial by one's peers, &c. This co-operation was so conspicuous and valuable that the aristocracy were soon obliged to acknowledge it, and the Earl of Montfort thought it prudent to invite to his Parliament along with two knights from each shire, also two citizens from each city, and two burgesses from each burgh. It would be too long and tedious to trace here the struggle against monarchy step by step; those who have studied their Stubbs or Hallam know what a tremendous amount of energy, patience, tenacity courage, and shrewdness were needed to accustom the kings of England to respect their subjects' rights, to have them taught the elementary lessons in constitutional law and procedure. Every now and then the Edwards and the Henrys were ready to trample upon the charters they had themselves granted; every now and then they broke out in arbitrary demands for tolls, dues, and levies; but each time, after an obstinate fight, they were obliged to issue confirmations of the charters, to grant additional privileges, and make declarations, like the famous *de tallagio non concedendo* of 1279. And at every turning of this arduous, uphill struggle, we find by the side of the gallant baron and knight the sturdy merchant and member of the guild defending their woollen and silken wares with one hand and laying the other on the prerogatives of the crown. But the really momentous and brilliant activity of the middle clases begins with the seventeenth century. As is well known, the period between the fourteenth and the end of the fifteenth century was one continuous process of reaction in the direction of absolutism: through the Black Death, which largely deprived the fields of their tillers, as well as through the Wars of the Roses, which decimated the ranks of the feudal lords, landed property greatly fell in value—and with it the social and political importance and power of the aristocracy. The back of the constitutional opposition was thus broken, and the English kings, especially the Tudors, were enabled to gather up the loosened strings of monarchy and to retrieve their well-nigh lost position. A series of vigorous efforts were now made to assert the prerogatives of the Crown as against the rights of Parliament, and a process kindred to that started in France by Louis XI. and accomplished by Louis XIV., might now be observed in England. But all through these dark times, in the stillness of the counting-houses and warehouses as much as in the bustle of the workshops and merchant ships, grew steadily the class of burgherdom, now the rising masters of the world's commerce. A whole chain of events, each more or less connected with the other, contributed to this effect: the discovery of America, the fall of the Italian republics, the influx of precious metals, the immigration from France and the low countries, the break-down of the sea power and colonial might of Spain, &c.—till about the reign of Elizabeth the middle classes became strong enough to take the place of the former aristocracy—now itself merging more and more into the bourgeoisie—as the leaders in the struggle for political freedom. They did not commence hostilities just at that time; old Bess was more than a match for them, besides being to some extent their benefactress; but as soon as she passed away the fire that lay smouldering for two centuries broke out into a blaze. The new king, James I., was a staunch believer in monarchy by the grace of God, ready to do anything to uphold his views, whilst the Parliament, which he convened early in 1603, showed by the unusually large attendance, which marked its sittings from the beginning, that it, too, was in a fighting mood, not likely to give way before the enemy. A conflict thus became inevitable. In the address to the king the Parliament gently reminded him of the existence in the land of constitutional law, and a little later issued a remarkable vindication of its various prerogatives "to be delivered to His Majesty in a form of apology and satisfaction." This was the beginning of a fight which raged for twenty-two years with unabated force; either side showed an equal stubborness—the king in dissolving his Parliament, in imprisoning its members, in levying arbitrary taxes and duties, and the representatives of the nation, or rather of the middle class, in asserting their legislative and fiscal rights, and in protesting against the infringement of personal liberty. James's death put for a time a stop to the struggle, but the accession of Charles I. rekindled it again. Driven to despair, the Parliament now assumed a thoroughly revolutionary attitude. Not content with merely verbal declarations of its rights, it refused to vote the civil list for more than one year, demanded the impeachment of Buckingham and his friends, and insisted upon the immediate release of two of its members arbitrarily thrown into the Tower. Close upon this, in 1628, the Parliament issued the remarkable Petition of Rights—a complete statement of principles of English citizenship—and the king, being in need of money, was obliged to sign it. In 1629, however, the Parliament came to an abrupt end, but the whole of the subsequent eleven years' personal rule, with its Star Chamber, Writ of Ship-money, and the rest, was powerless to subdue the opposition of the middle classes. On the contrary, it rose and gathered strength at every step, till in April, 1640, when the Short Parliament met, it broke forth in a point blank refusal to grant any money till some glaring abuses were redressed. Again it was dissolved, but only to be convened in a few months—this time to exist for thirty nine years. That was the famous Long Parliament, which broke the back of English monarchy for ever, and lived to see the rise and fall of the Commonwealth. Under the leadership of Pym and Hampden—two of the greatest men the middle classes of England have ever had—it resumed the great fight as soon as assembled, and in the short space of one year overturned the whole fabric of despotism so carefully reared up by the Tudors and Stuarts. It impeached and executed the Earl of Strafford, threw into prison Archbishop Laud, with several others of the king's party, abolished the Star Chamber and the Ship-money, deprived the clergy of temporal jurisdiction, and passed a Bill to the effect that the Parliament cannot be dissolved without its own consent, and must be convened at least every third year. In 1641 it published the Grand Remonstrance—that audacious Act of which Cromwell said that, were it not passed, he, together with many others, would have left England on the following day. It proclaimed liberty of conscience, and declared the Ministers of the Crown to be responsible to Parliament. This was, perhaps, by far the most daring attempt ever made since the days of the Great Charter at the prerogatives of monarchy, and Charles replied to it by impeaching Pym, Hampden, and other leaders of the House, and by appearing there with a military force. That was the beginning of the final act in the great drama, and what followed needs no narrating. King Charles was executed, the House of Lords abolished, the Commonwealth proclaimed, and the country ruled first by the "Rump House," conjointly with a Council of State, and then by Oliver Cromwell. That was the dictatorship of the Radical Left of the bourgeoisie, somewhat similar to the Reign of Terror in France in 1793-1794. It had, just like the other, a very short life, the moderate sections gaining ascendancy and restoring the monarchy. But what a monarchy! It was a mere shadow of the former, leaving practically the whole business of ruling in the hands of the Parliament. In 1665 was passed the Appropriation Act; in 1679, the Habeas Corpus Act, the second of the great Charters of English liberties; and in the same year the long Parliament dispersed, having brilliantly accomplished its task. From that time the course of political and civil liberty in this country has stood firm, weathering every storm and steadily gaining ground. James II. made attempts to resist the tide, but was deposed and expelled, and in his stead was invited the Orange dynasty, in the persons of William and Mary. The first act of the new monarchy—the bourgeois monarchy—was the famous Bill of Rights of 1689. This was the third of the great Charters which crowned the superb edifice of the English Constitution, and the numerous subsequent Statutes and Bills passed by Parliament were nothing but so many improvements on and particularisations of its clauses. In 1695 were abolished the Licensing Laws, which weighed so heavily on the freedom of speech and press; in 1716 were constituted septennial Parliaments, in the reign of George III. fell the royal veto, in 1816 passed the second Habeas Corpus Act, in 1829 was proclaimed the Emancipation of the Catholics, and in 1832 was passed the great Reform Bill. The long struggle for liberty has ended and the nation attained complete rights in all domains—citizenship.

Such is the great drama of which England has been the stage. It may now well be asked, what was the purpose in writing all the above? The SOCIAL-DEMOCRAT, not being an historical review, and the present writer being the last person in the world to pretend to a profound knowledge of English history, it may look as if the foregoing pages were out of place in an article headed as above. But there is a method even in madness, as Hamlet says, and the lesson in history propounded here, has its object, too. It is none other than to remind the English and other Socialists of one important fact which they too often seem to lose sight of, namely, that political and civil freedom, the greatest treasure England possesses as compared with other nations, has been won entirely by the boundless efforts and self-sacrifice of the governing classes of the country. Long before the present social antagonisms had been evolved out of the womb of Time, long before the ever active process of history had worked out the modern proletariat and raised on the horizon of material and spiritual life new forms and ideals, the bourgeoisie of England, first in co-operation with the aristocracy, and then by itself, succeeded in smashing into fragments the stronghold of despotism, and in gaining for the people the rights of self-government, of free speech and conscience, of complete security of person and chattels. It was men like De Montfort, Pym, Hampden, Knox, Cromwell, and, for aught we know, Francis Place, who built up the English democracy of to-day, and the echo of their deeds is still vibrating through the air with a force unknown from the very days of ancient Greece and Rome.

## II.

To grasp the significance of this fact to the full it is necessary to turn for a while to other countries Taking as one instance France, we find the middle classes there acting for generations as the most faithful allies of the Monarchy, and, when at last driven by economic necessity to espouse the cause of political freedom, assuming towards it an attitude full of reserve, hesitation, and uncertainty. In spite of the thunders of Mirabeau, and the glowing eloquence of the Girondists, they were ever ready to compromise and bargain with the king and aristocracy, not unwilling to renounce some of their most important demands for the sake of peace and friendliness. Were it not for the populace of Paris, which took the destinies of France into its own hands, the Bourbon Monarchy would never have been overthrown, the power of feudalism never swept away, and the sovereign rights of the people never proclaimed. It was the people at large, the street mob, the man in the blouse and the fisherwoman, who saved France from the storm-cloud of despotic Europe—not the middle classes; it was the *sans culottes,* with their bloody days of September and the Reign of Terror, who stamped out with red-hot iron, as it were, the aristocratic gangrene in the land—not the *bourgeoisie*. It was, on the other hand, the latter which, as soon as it had gained the upper hand, abolished universal suffrage and instituted the Directory—that infamous Government which for ever remains an indelible blot on the annals of modern Europe. It was the latter which, seeking refuge from the dangers of the awakening of the proletariat, threw itself into the arms of the little corporal and restored the Monarchy, renewed the aristocracy, and finally recalled the Bourbons. It is a disgusting picture—the events of 1795-1815—but still more so is the nightmare of 1848. The bourgeoisie dreamt least of all of overthrowing the Throne and establishing a Republic; aiming only at certain concessions, it did not go further than speech-making and pamphlet-writing, and those it stopped at the first wink of Guizot. It was, again, the people of Paris—this time the genuine proletariat—which threw up barricades, fought in the streets, and drove the Monarchy bag and baggage out of the land, whilst the patriotic middle-class politicians, with Odillon Barrau, Thiers, and other criers, were hiding themselves in their houses, and even in the provinces. Only after the revolution had been accomplished, and the leaders of the proletariat were in possession of the field, did the gallant champions of freedom return to Paris and declare themselves—God knows by what authority and moral right—as the provisional Government. Everything from that moment went on with a view to betraying the people's cause; forced to take into the Government Louis Blanc and Albert, to give employment to the workers of Paris, and to proclaim a Republic with universal suffrage, the bourgeoisie soon contrived to elect a National Assembly of their own, to exclude from it every dangerous element, and to close the mock national workshops which it previously established. The proletariat rose—and a terrible answer was given to its demands in the shape of a ruthless slaughter and torrents of blood during the ever memorable days of June. The middle classes triumphed, and within four years abolished universal suffrage and sold the Republic to the first adventurer. Since then it has had the Republic forced upon it once more, but everyone knows what a distorted shape civil freedom has received at the hands of the French bourgeoisie.

Still worse, perhaps, was the case in Germany. Those whose memories are fresh from reading Marx's trenchant little book, "Revolution and Counter-Revolution," might remember what a pitiful spectacle the German middle classes presented during the struggle of 1848. Here, too, the initiative of the movement belonged to the proletariat of Vienna, Berlin, and other big towns, where, too, the bourgeoisie revealed itself as a set of contemptible cowards, recoiling by all available means from the task thrust upon them. Drunkards and liars, incapacitated in mind and in body, they assembled in Frankfort to draw up a scheme of a Constitution, and spent a whole year in miserable squabbles till they were ignominiously dismissed by the Prussian king. The whole brunt of the fight was borne by the working classes; it was they who expelled Metternich, who shed their blood in Berlin, Baden, and elsewhere, who forced Frederick William IV. to promise a federal government, who extorted the Constitution of '66, and wrung from Bismarck universal suffrage.

It would greatly exceed the limits of this article were we to attempt to pass under review the history of every European country; suffice it to say that whenever on the Continent we find those civil and personal rights in existence which go by the collective name of Constitutional Liberty we are sure to find at the same time the part played by the middle-classes in gaining them to have been not only of a far less important nature than was the case in England, but even reduced sometimes to zero, if not actually to a minus. This is not due to mere chance, or, as some Britishers might be inclined to imagine, to the inferior stuff of which the Continental middle-classes have been made, but is the direct result of the peculiar historical conditions under which those classes were placed during the process of their growth and development. For not enjoying the same natural opportunities for trade and industry as their brethren of this country, they have had, over and above it, to surmount enormous difficulties in the shape of endless wars and other commotions which prevented the necessary accumulations of capital, &c., and never were, in consequence of it, so strong and numerous as not to need the protection which the Monarchy, appreciating their value as fiscal elements and allies in the struggle against the arrogant feudal aristocracy, readily afforded them. In fact, it was only through this help that the middle-classes in most of the European countries reached manhood at all, and small wonder if, when demanding political freedom, they have been neither able to put, nor perhaps justified in putting, their interests in the same direct and uncompromising opposition to those of the Monarchy as the middle classes of England did. Hence the half-hearted and very often weak-kneed stand they made against absolutism at the moment of struggle, and the spirit of compromise they so frequently revealed.

To the same end yet another factor of a kindred nature was contributed. Being, as we have just seen, of an impeded and weakly growth, the middle-classes, unlike those of this country, have attained their class-consciousness at a very late date in history, so that their agitation for political rights in a majority of cases coincided with, if not followed, the moment when the economic forces were already producing a cleavage in the social body and the antagonisms between the property-owning and wage-earning classes began already to tell with a more or less marked distinction. Naturally, when compelled at last to enter the field of battle, the Continental bourgeoisie has had to face a dilemma of which the English in their time had no idea, namely, either to do without the co-operation of the proletariat and be sure to lose, or to associate it in the work, but then to allow it an equal share in the spoil. Either prospect was unpleasant, and the bourgeoisie, in its endeavours to reconcile irreconcilables, landed at once in a policy of half-measures, hypocrisy and treachery, such as we have seen in France and in Germany. It is this cardinal difference between the parts played in history by the middle classes of England and of the Continent respectively that accounts for the failure of Socialism in the former and for its success on the latter. For one need not be possessed of a great penetration of mind to understand what a tremendous object-lesson in class-consciousness the working classes must have been taught in those countries where the bourgeoisie not only showed itself devoid of ability and willingness to win for the nation its civil freedom, leaving the task of accomplishing it to the proletariat, but was at every step demonstrating its antagonism to the latter by the care it invariably took of shutting it out from participation in the political rights of the community, and the readiness it often revealed of selling its very liberty in order to achieve this end. The working classes of the Continent were thus enabled early to discern the gulf which separates them from their masters, and to perceive on the field of politics those incompatibilities of their mutual interests which the social forces have not as yet brought out with sufficient clearness on the field of economics. From this there was but a short step to the growth in their midst of a kind of *esprit de corps,* and then of a sense of class solidarity, on which a few decades later Socialism was easily able to engraft itself.

How very different stands the case with England! The middle classes there having fulfilled their great political mission long before the appearance of the modern proletariat, the latter has never had the opportunity of coming with them into a conflict on that ground on which the inner antagonisms between the two classes receive their first and most palpable expression. It has thus missed a lesson in social practice and theory which enriched so much the experience of the Continental workers, and has been the more unable to understand the real state of things, as the English Constitution, having been worked out at a moment when the middle classes could not have as yet anything to fear from below, contained no trace of class legislation which would open the proletarian's eyes as to the position of his masters in the social and economic world. Besides, being brought up in a spirit of unqualified reverence and esteem which the historical work of the English bourgeoisie could not but command, the proletariat of this country was naturally inclined rather to associate itself with it than to *dis*sociate, and so the gospel of Socialism, preaching class-war, fell upon an entirely unprepared ground, and failed in consequence to strike root.

The causes which have operated in the past are still, to a great extent, operating at the present moment. Whilst in England the progress which Democracy undoubtedly makes every day is mainly due to the initiative and leadership of the middle classes, so that even such distinctly working class legislation as the Factory Acts, the abolition of the combination laws, and the legalisation of the status of the trade unions has been secured by *their* efforts rather than by those of the proletariat, it is the latter which in the rest of Europe appears as the chief champion of the civil and personal rights of the people. The Continental bourgeoisie, in its fear for its property, has long since thrown overboard what little progressive ballast it had possessed in the first half of the present century, and the democratic ideals have been left to the care of the working classes, to whom the question of constitutional liberty is of vital importance, comprising, as it does, the rights of combination, free speech, and others, without which their position is even worse than slavery. No wonder that this has made the proletariat the object of sympathy on the part of every honest man not directly interested in its exploitation, and that Socialism, which makes the conquest and maintenance of political freedom one of the chief planks of its programme, gains adherents every day from every section of the community. One needs only carefully consider the state of things in France, where the bourgeoisie tramples under foot the elementary rights of citizenship, and is prepared to sell the country to any general possessed of a "black charger"; or in Germany, where the bulk of the middle classes, in their zeal for the favour of monarchy and its Pommeranian Junkerdom, scarcely hesitates to mortgage the budget rights of the Parliament to pass exceptional laws against different sections of the community, and even to abolish universal suffrage; or in Italy, where wanton corruption and glaring abuses of administrative power are allowed to pass without heeding for the sole reason of certain "high" personages standing at their source; or in Russia, where the Liberal sections of the middle classes have demonstrated their incapacity and cowardice over and over again, and the rest are mere slaves, ready at any time to lick the boot of their master—one needs only consider this to understand what a tremendous and attractive force Socialism must possess in these countries, being, as it is, the most, if not the only, implacable enemy of despotism, and the greatest vindicator of civil liberty human societies ever had. It is this circumstance which makes the ranks of Continental Socialists swell at every turning of history—no man can remain honest but he enters the political army of the proletariat; and it is the very absence of this which constitutes the chief barrier to the advent of Socialism in this country. The antagonism between the property-owning and the wage-earning classes may well be greater in England than elsewhere, but so long as they remain hidden under the common solidarity of interest in democratic progress, and do not appeal to the direct class sense of the proletariat by way of political opposition, the hope for the success of Socialism on these islands must remain meagre. True to its historical traditions, the English bourgeoisie still figures as a progressive element—politically speaking, of course—of the community, and, far from having spent its vital force, and being uneasy about its social position, still moves in the direction of Democracy, allowing the working classes an equal share in the civil life of the country. What wonder is it, then, that the latter do not perceive the contradictions inherent in the social system of the day, but repudiate Socialism as a phantastic conception, fit and proper, perhaps, for the Continent, but wholly unapplicable to this country?

It would be erroneous on the part of the reader to infer from the above that since Socialism on the Continent is largely dependent for its success on political causes, the Socialist movement there is, to a great extent, composed of merely Radical elements, and is bound to come to an end as soon as political freedom becomes the normal basis of national life. As regards the first, one must remember that what drives many an earnest and thinking man towards embracing Socialism is not so much the mere absence of political rights in the country—for that matter they could have formed parties of their own—as the contemptible part played by the bourgeoisie in civic life, siding, as it always does, with reaction as against the claims of Democracy. This opens the eyes of those men as to the real position of the bourgeoisie in the social world, and having thus caught a glimpse of the class antagonisms on the field of politics, they soon, when once in the Socialist ranks, find out the economic antagonisms as well, and turn from bourgeois Radicals into avowed Socialists. As regards the other of these inferences, it is easy to see that the Continental middle-classes being what they are, political liberty in Continental countries can be firmly established only when the proletariat takes possession of the political machinery of the land; but this means not only a political, but also a social revolution—that is, the realisation of those objects for the attainment of which Socialism fights. It is therefore true that the advent of a genuine and permanent Democracy in France, England and elsewhere will spell the end of the Socialist movement in this country, but not because it will be discredited, but for the reason of that Democracy being at the same time *Social*-Democracy.

Thus we see that that very circumstance—the early development of industry and of the bourgeoisie—which in the opinion of most of our Socialists ought to have been the cause of a rapid and vigorous growth of Socialism constitutes the chief reason for its failure; it is exactly because the middle classes of England entered the social and political arena at an early date that the proletariat is now unable to see the true nature of the relations which exist between them. Were it otherwise, had the middle classes attained their full growth at a later period of history, so that in their battle for political freedom they would have had to fight on two fronts, the proletariat of this country would have received their lesson in class solidarity and class-consciousness at a very early date, and Socialism would have flourished here the same as on the Continent.

Such is the proper answer to be given to the question put at the head of this article, and what may be its bearing on the future destinies of this country will be explained on some other occasion.

## 52

## *THE FIRST OF MAY: THE INTERNATIONAL LABOUR DAY* (1900) (LONDON: TWENTIETH CENTURY PRESS, 1904), 3–16.

*H.W. Lee*

[It was in Paris in 1889 that the first of May was proclaimed the day on which the workers' movement would come together internationally in a co-ordinated demonstration of solidarity. The occasion seemed inauspicious, with a unified organisation still to be achieved and two rival gatherings of socialist bodies being organised simultaneously in the city. One was organised by the so-called "Possibilists", and it was this ironically which the SDF's delegates attended along with those of the Fabians and TUC. The gathering of "Marxists", meanwhile, included delegates from the Socialist League and Keir Hardie's Scottish Labour Party, and it was this that determined the holding of an international workers' demonstration on 1 May 1890. Although initially the SDF expressed its scepticism, the differences were formally reconciled and from May Day 1890 the marking of an international day of labour came to symbolise its common aspirations across all national boundaries.

The first mobilising slogan was the eight-hour day, with which virtually every section of the movment was in full accord. If differences resurfaced, it was over whether to mark the occasion on 1 May itself, involving the possible cessation of work, or on the first Sunday in May. For some, joining the SDF meant never again working on 1 May, and the respectability of the Sunday parade was regarded with scorn (Bell 1941, 56–57). Nevertheless, as this commemorative pamphlet describes, the biggest demonstrations tended to be when the two dates coincided, and a parallel is even drawn between the workers' demonstrations of 1892 and Europe's "year of revolutions" in 1848.

The author, H.W. Lee (1865–1932), was for twenty-eight years the SDF's secretary and subsequently the editor of *Justice*. Through the London Trades Council, whose secretary James MacDonald was also an SDF stalwart, the Marxists were the moving force behind the First of May Celebration Committee whose very name made clear its commitment to demonstrating on 1 May itself. The interest of Lee's pamphlet, a revised version of one originally issued in 1900, lies partly in the international spirit in which he recounts the development of the idea of an International Labour Day. In citing the original Paris resolution, he reminds us that the date had first been adopted in the USA, where already in 1886 it provided the focal point of the eight-hours agitation and the international cause célèbre of the executed "Chicago martyrs".

This, however, features far less in Lee's treatment than does the sense of a specifically English past. There is here the same idealisation of the Middle Ages that one identifies with Morris. There is the sense of protestantism as a form of capitalist social discipline that one can trace back to earlier radicals like William Cobbett and his *History of the Protestant 'Reformation' in England and Ireland* (1824). It is easy to see how, in his much reproduced design for May Day 1891, the artist Walter Crane should have depicted "The triumph of labour" in strikingly pre-industrial terms. Lee explicitly cites the "Every-Day Book" of the radical bookseller William Hone (1780–1842) and the parallel between (white) wage and (black) chattel slavery which is here identified with Robert Owen. In years to come, the communists in London would reactivate the First of May Committee and again combine their internationalism with a reclaimed English past. For the communists, however, the essence of May Day was to be the organised stoppage of work which in Lee's pamphlet is left unmentioned.]

May-Day is universally celebrated abroad by the working classes as the International Labour Day, as the day on which fraternal greetings shall go forth to their fellow workers in all countries. Here, in the United Kingdom, the celebration of May-Day is, unfortunately, not so general. There is, it is true, a gradually increasing feeling among the British workers in favour of the recognition of the First of May as the International Labour Day. But it must be confessed that the usual English weather about the time of the First of May is rarely of a character which lends itself to outdoor parades and demonstrations, and it suggests that the May-Days of old, with all their spring-tide festivities and rejoicings, must have been held under much more favourable climatic conditions than those to which we are wearily becoming accustomed. Apart from this, however, it is certain that the real object of the International Labour demonstrations on the First of May is not nearly so well understood in this country as it is abroad, and a short statement of the real significance of these demonstrations needs, therefore, no excuse.

## The Antiquity of May-Day.

In the Middle Ages the First of May was universally kept as a day of holiday and pleasure. But May-Day was also celebrated at a much earlier period. It is, in fact, difficult to say how great is the antiquity of the May-Day Festival. The revival of vegetation which marks nature at May time, so far at any rate as Europe generally is concerned, has been the occasion for various ceremonies from even primitive times. The "Floralia" of the Romans, which in their turn are believed to have been derived from India, were no doubt the forerunners of the May-Day festivities which in this country were popular for centuries. The "Floralia," or floral games, were held in honour of Flora, the goddess of Spring, and lasted four or five days. Among the old Celtic nations of Europe, too, the Beltein festivals were akin to the Maypole dances. Gigantic fires were kindled on the hilltops to joyously proclaim the approach of summer. As the floral games of the Romans celebrated the awakening of floral life in warmer climates, so did the Beltein fires of the Celts in colder latitudes hail the appearance of the sun which, entering into its highest altitudes, meant giving fresh life and warmth to the earth after the frosts and snows of winter. Amongst the peasantry of Ireland, the Isle of Man, and the Scottish Highlands, the Beltein celebrations were in vogue, to a slight extent, even up to the seventeenth century.

There can be no doubt that the beauty of flower and leaf which nature brings forth at the end of April and the beginning of May reflected itself in the minds of men and women accustomed to a healthy life in the open-air, and it is, therefore, only natural that the joyousness thus created should find its expression in the love of that profusion of flower and blossom which called it forth, and that dance and song should hail the gathered garlands typical of nature's revival. The divorce of the vast majority of our working population of to-day from open-air life has largely killed that happy enjoyment of spring-time. How the development of the factory system has steadily crushed out this joyous spirit we shall show later.

## May-Day in the Olden Times.

In this country we have to go back some centuries to find the May-Day observances in their most complete form. In the sixteenth century it was still customary for the citizens, yeomen and peasants to go forth at an early hour of the morning of the First of May in order to gather flowers and hawthorn branches, which they brought home about sunrise. This was accompanied by singing and music, and all possible signs of joy and merriment. With these branches they would decorate every door and window in the villages. By a natural transition of ideas they gave to the hawthorn bloom the name of "May"; the ceremony was termed "the bringing home the May"; they spoke of their journey to the woods as "going amaying"; and the lads and lasses met, sang, and danced together.

The nobles were also accustomed to join in the Maying festivities. Even the King and Queen often condescended to come among the people on these occasions. In the reign of Henry VIII. the heads of the Corporation of the City of London went into the high grounds of Kent to gather the May, the King and his Queen of the moment, Catherine of Aragon, coming from Greenwich Palace and meeting the civic dignitaries on Shooter's Hill. Can we look back on these festal doings without regret—nay, sorrow—that they are no longer with us? Does it not prove that our ancestors, whatever drawbacks they may have suffered in some respects, were far freer from cramping, monotonous drudgeries than the mass of mankind are to-day? Does it not show that we are rapidly losing—in fact, most of us, perhaps, have lost—the power to receive those pleasurable impressions of nature which gave them such keen enjoyment? Happiness came more spontaneously to them than it does to us creatures of steam and electricity, whose brains and sinews are the property of the employing classes.

## The May-pole.

The central feature of the May-Day observance was the May-pole dance. This dance was revived by the First of May Celebration Committee at the celebrations held at the Crystal and Alexandra Palaces. Let us see what it was. One of the London parishes takes it name from the May-pole which in olden times overtopped the steeple of its church. The parish is that of St. Andrew Undershaft, and its May-pole is celebrated by the great English poet Chaucer, who speaks of an empty braggart:

> "Right well aloft and high ye beare your head
> As ye would beare the great shaft of Cornhill."

Stow, who is buried in this church, says that in his time the shaft was set up "every year on May-Day in the morning in the midst of the street before the south door of the said church, which shaft, when it was set on end, and fixed in the ground, was higher than the church steeple." During the rest of the year this pole was hung upon iron hooks above the doors of the neighbouring houses, and immediately beneath the projecting penthouses which kept their doors from the rain. It was destroyed in a fit of Puritanism in the third year of Edward VI.'s reign, after a sermon preached at St. Paul's Cross against May games. The inhabitants of the parish "sawed it in pieces, everie man taking for his share as much as had layne over his doore and stall, the length of his house, and they of the alley divided amongst them so much as had layne over their alley gate."

In the fifth volume of Halliwell's folio edition of Shakespeare there is a curious coloured frontispiece of a May-pole painted in continuous vertical stripes of white, red and blue, which stood in the centre of the village of Welford, in Gloucestershire, about five miles from Stratford-on-Avon. It is probably a copy of the one which succeeded that which stood there in the days when Shakespeare himself visited the village. It would appear to be of great height, and was planted in the centre of a raised mound, to which three stone steps led up.

The most renowned of the London May-poles, and the one which was in existence later than any other, was that erected in the Strand, just near the church of St. Mary-le-Strand, after the restoration of Charles II., and caused Little Drury Lane to be called May-pole Alley. This May-pole was erected to take the place of the one destroyed by the Puritans.

In some of the more remote English villages, not reached by the whirr of machinery and the shriek of the steam hooter, there existed during even last century a few of the old May-poles. But their glory had departed. They served, at best, to support local weather-cocks. No longer did the people dress them with flowers on May 1st; no longer did they form the centre of a ring of merry dancers. The factories claimed their human machines, and would not be gainsaid.

In connection with the May-Day festivities was a distinct set of sports, greatly in vogue in the fifteenth and sixteenth centuries. They were meant to represent the adventures of Robin Hood. The jacks-in-the-green, the favourite display of the sweeps on May-Day, now likewise almost a thing of the past, are doubtless the remains of these old May-Day games.

## The Economic Condition of the People in the Middle Ages.

Popular history of that period of the Middle Ages to which we have been referring lays bare the tyranny of the kings and the rapacity of the nobles; but a deeper inquiry tells us that at the period when May-Day festivities were universally celebrated throughout England, the economic condition of the wage-earners was, relatively to the general conditions of the times, far and away better and higher than it has ever since been. The political struggles between the decaying influence of the nobles—the last remaining traces of the dead feudal period—and the growing personal power of the monarchs, affected the people but little. All records go to show that the people in the main lived a healthy and vigorous life. The production of goods was carried on upon a scale which rendered the individual worker master of his own implements of labour, and the products thus manufactured were made primarily for use, only the surplus over and above that needed to satisfy local wants being brought into exchange. Such people, owning their own land and instruments of production, were of necessity free economically and socially, whatever political disabilities there may have been. Men and women then enjoyed themselves, in a rough and rude fashion perhaps, but nevertheless enjoyed themselves, because the future held few terrors for them in the way of starvation and want of employment.

These few historical facts show us clearly that the people who then lived by labour were free economically because they were in possession of the instruments which they used for the production of whatever goods they required. But they controlled their means of production because those means were such as could be handled by them individually. To-day that is impossible. The great engines of production, the enormous capitals, constantly growing greater, now required to embark on industrial enterprises, render it quite out of the question for the emancipation of the workers of our time to be achieved under the conditions which formerly gave freedom to our forefathers. Whereas the artisans and craftsmen of the Middle Ages had their economic freedom secured by their individual control of their tools of labour, so the workers of the day must possess collectively the great means of production, distribution and exchange. This, in short, is the great economic truth which underlies the Labour Celebrations throughout the world.

## May-Day Killed by Capitalism.

With the development of the industrial forces and the rise of the commercial and trading classes which commenced about the Tudor period, the great and terrible change for the workers began. Into the various stages through which the artisans and labourers passed from free craftsmen to modern wage-slaves it is impossible to enter in a pamphlet of this description. We can only deal with the main points in a brief fashion. It is a fact that, as the increase in trade and manufacture took place, so did the holidays of the people decrease. Time began to be much too precious to be wasted on enjoyment; and, moreover, when time for holiday-making means poverty, enjoyment is necessarily absent. Thus we see the May-Day festivities of old, and other festal days as well, slowly but surely falling into disuse. It is true that, under the Commonwealth, the Puritans rigorously suppressed all May-Day revels. The old May-pole in the Strand, which we have already mentioned, was destroyed by the Parliament in 1644, and May-poles generally were put down under heavy penalties. The Puritans suppressed them, of course, on the ground of their being ungodly things, but in reality their suppression succeeded because the necessities of the growing capitalist form of production for the ever-expanding markets rendered it imperative that there should be as few as possible of those stoppages in the manufacture of goods which the numerous holidays of older times would have caused. That this was the case is amply proved by the fact that the attempted revival of the May-Day festivities after the Restoration of the "Merry Monarch" lasted but for a few decades. Henceforth the May-Day celebrations were but shadows of their former splendour, and they disappeared altogether with the final development of the machine industry into the hands of the capitalist class at the end of the eighteenth and the beginning of the nineteenth centuries. The last trace we have of them is recorded in a letter sent to the editor of "Hone's Day Book," dated April 14th, 1825. This letter says:—

"There still exists among the labouring classes in Wales the custom of May dancing, wherein they still exhibit their persons to the best advantage, and distinguish their agility before the fair maidens of their own rank. . . . .

"About nine days or a week previous to the festival a collection is made of the gayest ribbons that can be procured. Each lad resorts to his favoured lass, who gives him the best she possesses, and uses her utmost interest with her friends or her mistress to obtain a loan of whatever may be necessary to supply the deficiency. Her next care is to decorate a new white shirt of fine linen. This is a principal part of her lover's dress. The bows and puffs of ribbon are disposed according to the peculiar taste of each fair girl, who is rendered happy by the pleasing task, and thus the shirts of the dancers, from the various fancies of the adorners, form a diversified and lively appearance.

"During this time the chosen garland bearer is also busily employed. Accompanied by one from among the intended dancers, who is best known among the farmers for decency of conduct and consequent responsibility, they go from house to house, throughout their parish, begging the loan of watches, silver spoons, or whatever utensils of this metal are likely to make a brilliant display; and those who are satisfied with the parties, and have a regard to the celebration of this ancient day, comply with their solicitations. When May-Day morn arrives, the group of dancers assemble at the rendezvous, the village tavern."

## Industrial Slavery of the Nineteenth Century.

The invention, introduction and development of machinery is the great economic fact which heralded in the birth of the nineteenth century. The enormous increase in the powers of production thus brought about went unchallenged into the hands of the rising capitalist class. Unchecked by trade union combination and uncontrolled by any kind of factory legislation, the manner in which the newly-developed powers of man over nature were used—or rather abused—constitutes some of the blackest pages in the history of this country. Men, women and children were literally used up to make fortunes for the factory lords. The number thrown out of employment through the rapid substitution of machinery for hand labour served but to increase the misery and degradation of the mass of the working people. Old laws concerning the relations between employer and employed which might act in favour of the latter were repealed in the interests of the former. The condition of things under the now fully-established wage-slavery, compared with that of the black slavery in the United States, was well set forth by Robert Owen. He said: "Whatever may be said to the contrary, bad or unwise as American slavery is and must continue to be, the white slavery in the manufactories of England was at this unrestricted period far worse than the slaves whom I afterwards saw in the West Indies and in the United States, and in many respects, especially as regards health, food and clothing, the latter were much better provided for than were the oppressed and degraded children and workpeople in the home manufactories of Great Britain."

But worst of all was the ruthless exploitation of the children. They were actually sold as apprentices from the London workhouses to be used as human profit-making machines by the Lancashire mill-owners. The report of the Select Committee of 1816 on children in manufactories gives clear and forcible evidence of how terrible was the treatment of the children; and manfacturers themselves declared that they saw nothing injurious in children of from seven to ten years old working in the mills for sixteen hours a day. The report also shows that children of even younger age were employed. Reports even as late as 1842 show that boys and girls were fearfully overworked in iron and coal mines, being able to get about in small veins and pits where horses and mules could not enter. The report of 1843 shows a similar state of things in the agricultural districts, save that there the air was fresher and purer. Instances of this character can be found in profusion in the reports of the time. Fortunately the best spirits in the nation began to revolt against this inhuman brutality of the capitalists in their mad rush for wealth, and the factory legislation of the last fifty years, together with the organisation of the workers themselves in trade unions, have done something to check the unrestricted exploitation which threatened to ruin the population of these islands, and which has left effects from which people in many industrial centres are still suffering.

## The Revival of May-Day.

We have now seen the significance of the old May-Day revels. What then is the meaning of its revival? May-Day in its modern sense, or Labour Day as it is now universally called, dates from 1889. At one of the two great International Socialist and Workers' Congresses held in Paris in that year—the year of one of the great French Exhibitions—the following resolution was passed:—

> "A great international demonstration shall be organised on a fixed date, in order that in all countries and in every town on the same day the workers shall demand the legal reduction of the working day to eight hours and the application of other resolutions passed by the International Congress. Further, seeing that a similar demonstration has already been decided upon for the First of May by the American Federation of Labour at its Congress of 1888 at St. Louis, this date shall be adopted for the international demonstrations. The workers of the various nations shall carry out these demonstrations under whatever conditions may be imposed by the special situation of their respective countries."

On the next May-Day, that of 1890, the effects of the decision of the International Congress held in the Rue Rochechouart, at Paris, began to be felt. In Belgium the demand for a Legal Eight Hours Working Day was vigorously taken up by the miners. May-Day Celebrations were held in the principal large towns, such as Brussels, Liège, Charleroi, Antwerp and Namur. In Denmark the workers began to organise for the First of May Celebration, but open-air processions and meetings were prohibited by the Danish Government before the day arrived. In Austria great military preparations were made to meet all emergencies. In Germany many meetings were prohibited, and the military were confined to barracks. But it was in France that the most vigorous measures were taken for putting down all manifestations on May 1st. M. Constans, then Minister of the Interior, suppressed everything in the nature of demonstrations or processions and permitted only meetings held in private halls. In short, the terror-stricken manner in which the governing class throughout Europe treated these perfectly legitimate demonstrations on the part of the workers was nothing less than a pitiful exhibition of fear at the sentiment of the international fraternity of the peoples which lay behind the May-Day Celebrations.

In London a great demonstration for the Eight Hours Working Day was held in Hyde Park on the first Sunday in May. To be quite accurate, there were two demonstrations, one by the London Trades Council, then opposed to the *Legal* Eight Hours Working Day, and one by the Central Committee for the Eight Hours Demonstration. In the following year, 1891, the London Trades Council and the Legal Eight Hours League held a conjoint demonstration on the first Sunday in May.

In the August of the same year the next International Socialist and Workers' Congress took place at Brussels. This Congress received its mandate from both International Congresses held at Paris in 1889. The question of May 1st as an International Labour Day was discussed by the Congress. Eventually the following resolution was adopted:—"That, in order to conserve to the First of May its true economic character by the demand for the Eight Hours Day and the recognition of the class struggle, there shall be held a simultaneous demonstration of the workers of all countries; that this demonstration shall take place on the First of May; and that a cessation from work be recommended wherever possible."

At the Brussels International Congress interesting reports were given in on the Socialist and Labour movements in the various countries. In these reports mention was made of the success of the First of May Demonstrations. In addition to the countries we have already given, the reports showed that international gatherings had taken place in Poland, Norway, Roumania, Hungary, and even in the Argentine Republic, where meetings had been held at Buenos Ayres, La Plata, Santa Fé, and other of the larger towns.

### Growing Popularity of Labour Day.

But 1892 was the year when the First of May manifestations reached an importance far beyond that of 1890 or 1891. The first day of May fell on a Sunday, and consequently the gatherings were everywhere immense. The day was looked forward to with anxiety throughout Europe. In most of the continental capitals the military were held in readiness to shoot or bayonet the people at a moment's notice. The authorities were everywhere pretty well scared out of their wits. It was, in fact, the nearest approach to 1848 that had occurred since that memorable year. In Belgium and Austria there was coupled with the Legal Eight Hours Working Day the demand for Universal Suffrage, a measure which, to a great extent, has been since obtained in both countries. In France, Germany, Belgium, Holland, Italy, Roumania, Spain, Switzerland, the United States of America—in fact, in every civilised and capitalist nation on the planet, the workers assembled on May 1st to declare fraternity with their fellows throughout the world. In this country meetings took place in nearly all the large provincial centres, and the most successful demonstration ever seen in Hyde Park was held conjointly by the trade unions and Socialist organisations. Deputations from that great meeting waited upon Lord Salisbury, Mr. A. J. Balfour, Mr. Gladstone, and the Metropolitan members, to place before them the views of London's workers on the Eight Hours Day.

1893 saw May-Day celebrated in all the European countries, and great meetings were held, varied with police prohibitions and disturbances at Budapest, Liège and Marseilles. The Eight Hours Demonstration in Hyde Park again took place on the first Sunday in May.

That year was also the year of the next International Socialist and Workers' Congress, held at Zurich, in Switzerland. The May-Day celebrations were again affirmed, but it was recommended, principally to meet the views of the British and German delegations, that, when impossible to demonstrate on May 1st, the meetings should be organised on the first Sunday in May.

## May 1st in London.

Early in 1894 the first steps were taken really to organise the celebrations in this country on the first day of May instead of on the first Sunday, as had been done up to that time, though there had been small meetings held in Hyde Park previously on May 1st. A delegate meeting was called by the Social-Democratic Federation to which a few trade unions sent representatives. The London Trades Council delegate expressed the sympathy of his Executive with the desire on the part of the delegates to carry out the decision of the Zurich International Congress on the First of May Celebration, but the majority of the unions affiliated to the Council had resolved to demonstrate as usual on the first Sunday in May. The May-Day Demonstration was held in Hyde Park, and was a much greater success than the most sanguine of its promoters had anticipated.

The ice having been broken, so to speak, the way was made easier for the demonstration of 1895. The first delegate meeting showed how much more popular the idea of an international celebration of May-Day had become during the previous twelve months. Whereas in 1894 but half-a-dozen trade unions took part with the Socialists in the May-Day Demonstration in Hyde Park, more than five times that number sent delegates to the first meeting in 1895, in addition to which several clubs and societies, besides the Social-Democratic Federation and Independent Labour Party, were represented. Again a demonstration was held in Hyde Park. The resolutions adopted pledged the workers to do the utmost to make Labour-Day a complete holiday; it sent fraternal greetings to the workers of all countries; it demanded the Legal Eight Hours Day and Universal Adult Suffrage; and declared that the existing class war could only be put an end to by the abolition of private property in the means and instruments of production.

## Progress of the First of May Celebrations.

The First of May Demonstrations in 1896 and 1897 found an increasing number of societies taking part in them. As the interest in the May-Day Celebrations grew, that in the Sunday Demonstration diminished. The Sunday Demonstration of 1894 showed a diminution in the number of participants to that of 1893, which still further decreased in 1895, though the number and size of provincial demonstrations increased. In 1896 the London Trades Council and most of the trade unions forming the Legal Eight Hours League threw in their lot with the First of May Celebration Committee, which now became a permanent committee whose executive carried on the business throughout the year until elected for the next celebration.

At the great International Socialist and Workers' Congress held in Queen's Hall, London, in 1896, attended by 459 British delegates and 287 foreign delegates, the following resolution was passed: "That, as far as concerns May-Day demonstrations, the Congress declares in favour of continuing to carry out the decisions of preceding Congresses, and considers that these demonstrations should have as their chief objects the obtaining of the Legal Eight Hours Day, and protests against militarism."

Again at the next International Congress, held in Paris in 1900, when even a larger number of delegates attended than in London in 1896, the reporter of the Commission on the First of May Celebration emphasised the fact that the First of May had been agreed to by successive International Congresses as the International Labour Day, and stated that the Commission recommended that in every country the recognition of the First of May as a general working class festival should be promoted by every possible means. The Commission could not accept a proposal to make this recognition obligatory on the working classes of every country, as in many cases the sacrifices and difficulties would, for the time being, be too great; but the duty of the Socialist and working-class organisations everywhere was none the less imperative to make the First of May a general holiday by every means in its power, as the most efficacious demonstration in favour of the Eight Hours Working Day.

On recent occasions the First of May Celebration Committee in London have endeavoured to add a little of the old holiday-making spirit to the purely economic and political side of May-Day, which alone had hitherto been represented by the demonstrations. Nevertheless, the political and economic character of the celebration has not been lost sight of for a single moment. Ever since its formation the First of May Celebration Committee has consistently and persistently proclaimed the socialistic principles which form the basis of the Labour Day celebrations. These principles have been set forth in the manifestoes issued by the Committee and the resolutions passed at the demonstrations. These resolutions have been two in number. The first resolution has been of a general character, sending fraternal greetings to the comrades assembled abroad, asserting with them the determination to overthrow wagedom and capitalism, and to establish that International Co-operative Commonwealth in which all the instruments of industry shall be owned and controlled by the organised communities. The second resolution has called for the enactment of such immediate measures as Free Maintenance for the Children in our public schools, the Legal Eight Hours Working Day, Universal Adult Suffrage, and such political reforms as would place, not only the vote in the hands of the workers, but, what is quite as important, the power and opportunity to use it afterwards in the interests of their class.

## The Class Solidarity of the Workers.

As important as the measures to be demanded and the principles to be set forth is the international sentiment which underlies these simultaneous demonstrations of the workers in all countries. The class that lives by the sale of its labour power to the capitalists has no interest whatever in the promotion of wars between nations. Hence a thorough understanding between the workers of all countries is the only lasting guarantee of peace. They it is who have to provide the blood and treasure for the expeditions into less civilised or barbarous countries to extend the markets for the commerce of their masters. What reward comes to them? Their portion is the misery attendant on the slackness of trade which inevitably follows a war, when factories are shut down, workshops are closed, and short time, if not actual want of employment, becomes the rule.

Warfare—the clash of arms and the crash of guns—is therefore the enemy of the whole working class. But there is another warfare—a struggle which is unceasing, and which always requires the workers to exercise the utmost vigilance. The struggle is the struggle between the employing classes and the working classes. Occasionally the struggle shows itself in an open conflict of diverse interests, but generally in this country it is so unrecognised as to cause some even of those who suffer to think that the interests of employers and employed are identical. Yet all the time the capitalist class, in the competition for world markets which grows keener with the increasing power of man over nature, strive to obtain labour power, like all other commodities, as cheaply as possible, whilst the wage-earners on their side endeavour through their trade organisations to maintain their wages at as high a level as they can under existing conditions of employment. Identity of interests, forsooth!

## Capitalist Class-Consciousness.

Here, in the United Kingdom, recent events show distinctly what the working class may have to face if they do not bestir themselves more in the future than they have done in the past. The memory of the Taff Vale case is, unfortunately, fading far too soon from their recollections. Not so with the employing classes. They do not forget to present Mr. Beasley, the General Manager of the Taff Vale Railway, with a cheque for £1,000 with some other valuable gifts, in return for the services he rendered them in his successful attack on the Amalgamated Society of Railway Servants. The classes above never fail to recognise and reward services rendered unto them; many of the workers, on the contrary, are too apt to pass by services with scarcely any recognition, and sometimes with little but adverse criticism. Let them take a lesson from the capitalists, who are as class-conscious as any class can well be.

There is also the question of the importation of cheap Chinese Labour into the Transvaal under indentured conditions which spell virtual slavery, and solely for the benefit of the set of cosmopolitan gold-grabbers and finance-mongers who practically own a large portion of South Africa, and who use their millions to corrupt politics to their own base ends. Those of the working class—and they were not a few—who were led astray at the time of the late Boer War, and who imagined that "patriotism," "equal rights," and prosperity for labour lay behind the British endeavour to subjugate the Dutch Republics, must now feel how completely they were cajoled and hoodwinked simply because they took their politics ready made, and did not take the trouble to think for themselves.

Let these International May-Day Celebrations rouse the workers of the United Kingdom to class consciousness. Let them understand that the class interests of the workers of every nation are identical, and that those class interests are and must necessarily be antagonistic to those of the landlords and capitalists. Moreover, the employing classes are finding out that that very competition which they have held up as a blessing to the workers when it provided them with cheap labour must be thrown overboard when it tends to reduce their profits. Hence the marvellous progress of the trust and ring in the United States, and its slower but no less certain introduction in this country. In fact, the number of combines which have been formed in various industries in this country during the last few years are much greater than most people have any idea of. The growth of such joint-stock enterprises as Whiteley's, Lipton's, Salmon and Gluckstein, and Spiers and Pond's is rendering the lives of small shopkeepers one continuous round of toil and care, and is gradually competing them out of existence. That is so far as the retail trade is concerned, and it benefits consumers by the cutting of prices. But not for long. The big fight between Ogdens and those tobacco manufacturers who united against the former diminished prices, and supplied the workers with nastier tobacco, until such time as the competition became too severe, when the American (Odgens) and the Imperial (Wills') Tobacco Trusts "arranged" matters for their mutual benefit. But in the big manufacturing combines the object is manifestly to control and, in many cases, augment prices, so as to increase the profits of the shareholders which would be diminished by a continuance of competition. Thus it is that competition necessarily engenders monopoly, and unless the workers make up their minds that they intend to collectively control those monopolies, they will find their position under the combine and the trust worse than even it has been under the individual employer.

With the growth of these monopolies the class struggle becomes more bitter. We have seen evidence of this fact in the strikes of the engineers and the Welsh coal miners, to take two of the more recent examples in this country; in the successful attempt of the employers to break the power of the Trade Unions by legal decisions; whilst in America the capitalist combinations never hesitate to employ the most brutal and underhanded means—the courts, the black list, and every method which their millions place at their command—to cripple working-class organisations. The progress of the trade unions has forced the employers to combine; the masters' federation have in their turn compelled the trade unions to federate also. Strikes to-day in one particular trade are no longer confined to that industry. They affect other industries to an ever-increasing extent. This sort of thing cannot possibly go on for ever.

## Workers of the World, Unite!

It remains, therefore, for the workers to bestir themselves. Let them feel that, on May-Day, they are really and truly part of the great army of the world's proletariat. Let them stretch forth their hands to their fellows abroad in international amity and concord, confident in the future, determined to henceforth take their share in the work for the emancipation of their class the world over, and resolved to hand on to the generations who come after a brighter and happier social state than that under which they now toil and suffer.

# BIBLIOGRAPHY

Adams, Matthew S. 2016. "Formulating an Anarchist Sociology: Peter Kropotkin's Reading of Herbert Spencer". *Journal of the History of Ideas* 77 (1): 49–73.

Barnes, John. 2005. "Gentleman Crusader: Henry Hyde Champion in the Early Socialist Movement". *History Workshop Journal* 60: 116–138.

Barrow, Logie, and Ian Bullock. 1996. *Democratic Ideas and the British Labour Movement 1880–1914*. Cambridge: Cambridge University Press.

Bax, E. Belfort ed. 1914. *Harry Quelch: Literary Remains*. London: Grant Richards.

Bax, E. Belfort. 1918. *Reminiscences and Reflexions of a Mid and Late Victorian*. London: Allen & Unwin.

Bell, Tom. 1941. *Pioneering Days*. London: Lawrence & Wishart.

Bernstein, Eduard. 1893. *Ferdinand Lassalle as a Social Reformer*. London: Swan Sonnenschein & Co.

Bevir, Mark. 1991. "H.M. Hyndman: A Rereading and a Reassessment". *History of Political Thought* 12 (1): 125–146.

Bevir, Mark. 1992. "The British Social Democratic Federation 1880–1885: From O'Brienism to Marxism". *International Review of Social History* 37: 207–229.

Bevir, Mark. 1993. "Ernest Belfort Bax: Marxist, Idealist, and Positivist". *Journal of the History of Ideas* 54 (1): 119–135.

Bevir, Mark. 2011. *The Making of British Socialism*. Princeton, N.J.: Princeton University Press.

Boyd, Andrew. 2001. *Jim Connell: Author of the Red Flag*. London: Socialist History Society.

Burgess, Joseph. 1911. *John Burns: The Rise and Progress of a Right Honourable*. Glasgow: Reformers' Bookstall.

Carpenter, Edward. 1916. *My Days and Dreams: Being Autobiographical Notes*. London: Allen & Unwin.

Challinor, Raymond. 1977. *The Origins of British Bolshevism*. London: Croom Helm.

Claeys, Gregory. 2010. *Imperial Sceptics: British Critics of Empire, 1850–1920*. Cambridge: Cambridge University Press.

Clayton, Joseph. 1926. *The Rise and Decline of Socalism in Great Britain 1884–1924*. London: Faber & Gwyer.

Cohen, Yves. 2013. *Le Siècle des chefs. Une histoire transnationale du commandement et de l'autorité (1890–1940)*.

Collins, Henry. 1971. "The Marxism of the Social Democratic Federation". In *Essays in Labour History 1886–1923*, edited by Asa Briggs and John Saville, 47–69. London: Macmillan.

Crick, Martin. 1988. "To Make Twelve o'clock at Eleven: The History of the Social-Democratic Federation". Huddersfield: PhD thesis.
Crick, Martin. 1994. *The History of the Social Democratic Federation*. Keele: Keele University Press.
Davis, Mike. 2001. *Late Victorian Holocausts*. London: Verso.
Duncan, Robert. 2016 edn. *James Leatham (1865–1945): Profile of a Socialist Pioneer*. Turriff: the Deveron Press.
Englander, David. 1991. "The National Union of Ex-Servicemen and the Labour Movement 1918–1920". *History* 76: 24–42.
Etherington, Norman. 1974. "Hyndman, the Social-Democratic Federation and Imperialism". *Historical Studies* 16 (62): 89–103.
Foote, Geoffrey. 1997 edn. *The Labour Party's Political Thought*. London: Routledge.
Freeden, Michael. 1979. "Eugenics and Progressive Thought: A Study in Ideological Affinity". *Historical Journal* 22 (3): 645–671.
Glasier, J. Bruce. 1921. *William Morris and the Early Days of the Socialist Movement*. London: Longmans, Green & Co.
Goodway, David. 2006. *Anarchist Seeds Beneath the Snow: Left-libertarian Thought and British Writers from William Morris to Colin Ward*. Liverpool: Liverpool University Press.
Guérin, Daniel. 1971 edn. *Anarchism: From Theory to Practice*. New York and London: Monthly Review Press.
Hannam, June, and Karen Hunt. 2002. *Socialist Women: Britain 1880s–1920s*. London: Routledge.
Hill, Jeffrey. 1981. "Manchester and Salford Politics and the Early Development of the Independent Labour Party". *International Review of Social History* 26 (2): 171–201.
Hobsbawm, Eric. 1964. "Hyndman and the SDF" in idem. *Labouring Men. Studies in the History of Labour*. London: Weidenfeld & Nicolson.
Hobsbawm, Eric. 2011. *How to Change the World: Marx and Marxism 1840–2011*. London: Little Brown.
Howell, David. 1983. *British Workers and the Independent Labour Party 1888–1906*. Manchester: Manchester University Press.
Hunt, Karen. 1996. *Equivocal Feminists: The Social Democratic Federation and the Woman Question, 1894–1911*. Cambridge: Cambridge University Press.
Hunt, Karen. 2001. "Dora Montefiore: A Different Communist". In *Party People, Communist Lives: Explorations in Biography*, edited by John McIlroy, Kevin Morgan and Alan Campbell, 29–50. London: Lawrence & Wishart.
Hunt, Karen. 2007. "Towards a Gendered and Raced Socialist Internationalism: Dora Montefiore Encounters South Africa (1912–14)". *African Studies* 66 (2–3): 321–341.
Hunt, Karen. 2011. "'Whirl'd through the World': The Role of Travel in the Making of Dora Montefiore, 1851–1933". In *Österreichische Zeitschrift für Geschichtswissenschaft*, edited by Johanna Gehmacher and Elisabeth Harvey, 41–63, 1/2011.
Hyndman, Henry Mayers. 1911. *The Record of an Adventurous Life*. London: Macmillan.
Hyndman, Henry Mayers. 1912. *Further Reminiscences*. London: Macmillan.
Johnson, Graham. 2000. "'Making Reform the Instrument of Revolution': British Social Democracy, 1881–1911". *Historical Journal* 43 (4): 977–1002.
Johnson, Graham. 2002. *Social-Democratic Politics in Britain 1881–1911*. Lampeter: Edwin Mellen Press.

Kelvin, Norman. 1987. *The Collected Letters of William Morris. Volume II, 1885–1888*. Princeton, N.J.: Princeton University Press.

Kinna, Ruth. 2000. *William Morris: The Art of Socialism*. Cardiff: University of Wales Press.

Kolakowski, Leszek. 2005. *Main Currents of Marxism. Its Rise, Growth and Dissolution*. New York: W.W. Norton & Co.

Kopkowski, Rafał. 2011. "Joseph Conrad's Essays and Letters in the Light of Postcolonial Studies". *Yearbook of Conrad Studies* 6: 23–41.

Laurent, John. 1988. *Tom Mann's Social and Economic Writings: A Pre-syndicalist Section*. Nottingham: Spokesman.

Leatham, James. 2016a. *Socialism and Character: A Contribution Towards a System of Applied Ethics*. Turriff: Deveron Press; first published 1897.

Leatham, James. 2016b. *William Morris: Master of Many Crafts*. Turriff: Deveron Press; first published 1897.

Lee, H.W., and E. Archbold. 1935. *Social Democracy in Britain. Fifty Years of the Socialist Movement*. London: Social Democratic Federation.

Macintyre, Stuart. 1980. *A Proletarian Science. Marxism in Britain 1917–1933*. Cambridge: Cambridge University Press.

Mackenzie, Norman, and Jeanne Mackenzie. 1979 edn. *The First Fabians*. London: Quartet edn.

Mann, Tom. 1923. *Tom Mann's Memoirs*. London: Labour Publishing Company.

Marx, Karl, and Friedrich Engels. 2004. *Collected Works Vol 50: Engels:1892–1895*. London: Lawrence & Wishart.

McKibbin, Ross. 1984. "Why was there no Marxism in Great Britain?". *English Historical Review* 99: 299–331.

Meisel, Joseph S. 2012. "Gladstone's Visage: Problem and Performance". In *William Gladstone: New Studies and Perspectives*, edited by Roland Quinault, Rogert Swift and Ruth Clayton Windscheffel, 73–98. Farnham: Ashgate.

Michels, Robert. 1999. *Political Parties. A Sociological Study of the Oligarchical Tendencies of Modern Democracy*. New York: Transaction Publishers.

Miller, David. 1984. *Anarchism*. London: Dent.

Morgan, Kevin. 1989. *Against Fascism and War: Ruptures and Continuities in British Communist Politics 1953–41*. Manchester: Manchester University Press.

Morgan, Kevin. 2006. *Labour Legends and Moscow Gold: Bolshevism and the British Left Part 1*. London: Lawrence & Wishart.

Morgan, Kevin. 2007. "British Guild Socialists and the Exemplar of the Panama Canal". *History of Political Thought* 28 (1): 1–38.

Morgan, Kevin. 2009. "Militarism and Anti-militarism: Socialists, Communists and Conscription in France and Britain 1900–1940". *Past and Present* 202: 207–244.

Morris, Dylan. 1982. "Labour or Socialism: Opposition and Dissent within the Independent Labour Party 1906–1914 with Special Reference to the Lancashire Division". Manchester: PhD thesis.

Owen, Nicholas. 2007a. *The British Left and India: Metropolitan Anti-Imperialism, 1885–1947*. Oxford: Oxford University Press.

Owen, Nicholas. 2007b. "MacDonald's Parties: the Labour Party and the 'Aristocratic Embrace', 1922–31". *Twentieth Century British History* 18 (1): 1–53.

Partington, John S. 2020. "A German Marxist Internationalist and the British Socialist Movement". *Socialist History* 57: 25–43.

Paul, M. Eden. 1911. *Socialism and Eugenics*. Manchester: National Labour Press.
Pierson, Stanley. 1973. *Marxism and the Origins of British Socialism. The Struggle for a New Consciousness*. Ithaca, NY: Cornell University Press.
Quail, John. 1978. *The Slow Burning Fuse: The Lost History of the British Anarchists*. London: Paladin.
Rabinovitch, Victor. 1977. "British Marxist Socialism and Trade Unionism: The Attitudes, Experiences and Activities of the Social-Democratic Federation (1884–1901)". Sussex: PhD thesis.
Rothstein, Theodore. 1929. *From Chartism to Labourism*. London: Martin Lawrence.
Rowbotham, Sheila. 1973. *Hidden From History: 300 Years of Women's Oppression and the Fight Against It*. London: Pluto Press.
Rowbotham, Sheila. 2008. *Edward Carpenter: A Life of Liberty and Love*. London: Verso.
Royle, Edward. 1980. *Radicals, Secularists and Republicans: Popular Freethought in Britain, 1866–1915*. Manchester: Manchester University Press.
Samuel, Raphael. 1980. "The British Marxist Historians, 1880–1980: Part One". *New Left Review* 120: 21–96.
Samuel, Raphael. 1988. "A Spiritual Elect? Robert Tressell and the Early Socialists". In *The Robert Tressell Lectures 1981–88*, edited by D. Alfred, 55–69. Rochester: WEA South Eastern District.
Schoyen, A.R. 1958. *The Chartist Challenge: A Portrait of George Julian Harney*. London: Heinemann.
Searle, Geoffrey. 1976. *Eugenics and Politics in Britain 1900–1914*. Leyden: Noordhoff International Publishing.
Shanker, Prabha Ravi, and Prabha Ravi Shankar. 2005–2006. "Henry Mayers Hyndman (1842–1921) and the Radicalization of the Indian National Congress". *Proceedings of the Indian History Congress*, 66: 1041–1049.
Shaw, G. Bernard. 1889. *Fabian Essays in Socialism*. London: Walter Scott.
Shaw, G. Bernard. 1892. *The Fabian Society: Its Early History*. London: Fabian Society.
Shepherd, John. 2002. *George Lansbury. At the Heart of Old Labour*. Oxford: Oxford University Press.
Snowden, Philip. 1934. *An Autobiography*. London: Ivor Nicholson & Watson, 2 vols.
Stewart, William. 1921. *Keir Hardie: A Biography*. London: Independent Labour Party.
Taylor, Antony. 1999. *"Down with the crown". British Anti-monarchism and Debates about Royalty since 1790*. London: Reaktion Books.
Thompson, E.P. 1955. *William Morris. From Romantic to Revolutionary*. London: Lawrence & Wishart.
Thompson, Paul. 1967. *Socialists, Liberals and Labour: The Struggle for London, 1885–1914*. London: Routledge & Kegan Paul.
Torr, Dona. 1956. *Tom Mann and His Times. Volume One (1856–1890)*. London: Lawrence & Wishart.
Tsuzuki, Chushichi. 1956. "The 'Impossibilist Revolt' in Britain". *International Review of Social History* 1: 377–397.
Tsuzuki, Chushichi. 1961. *H.M. Hyndman and British Socialism*. Oxford: Oxford University Press.
Tsuzuki, Chushichi. 1991. *Tom Mann 1856–1941. The Challenges of Labour*. Oxford: Oxford University Press.
Vincent, David. 1982 edn. *Bread, Knowledge and Freedom: A Study of Nineteenth-century Working Class Autobiography*. London: Methuen.

Walter, Nicholas. 2007. *The Anarchist Past and Other Essays*. Nottingham: Five Leaves.

Watmough, P.A. 1977. "The Membership of the Social Democratic Federation". *Bulletin of the Society for the Study of Labour History* 34: 35–41.

Watts, Cedric. 1977. "Conrad and Cunninghame Graham: A Discussion with Addenda to their Correspondence". *The Yearbook of English Studies* 7: 157–165.

Watts, C., and L. Davies. 1989. *Cunninghame Graham: A Critical Biography*. Cambridge: Cambridge University Press.

Webb, Beatrice. 1984. *The Diary of Beatrice Webb. Volume Three 1905–1924: The Power to Alter Things*. Edited by N. and J. Mackenzie. London: Virago.

Webb, Sidney. 1890. *Socialism in England*. London: Swan Sonnenschein edn, 1908.

Webb, Sidney, and Beatrice Webb. 1894. *The History of Trade Unionism*. London: Longmans, Green & Co.

Wright, Anthony. 1979. *G.D.H. Cole and Socialist Democracy*. Oxford: Oxford University Press.

Wright, Anthony. 1996. *Socialisms: Old and New*. London: Routledge.

Yeo, Stephen. 1977. "A New Life: The Religion of Socialism in Britain 1881–1896". *History Workshop*, 5–56.

Young, David M. 2005. "Social Democratic Federation Membership in London". *Historical Research* 78: 354–376.